TRAIL GUIDE TO LEARNING

DEBBIE STRAYER & LINDA FOWLER

Trail Guide to Learning: Paths of Settlement - Volume 1

by Debbie Strayer and Linda Fowler

Published by Geography Matters, Inc.

2 Volume Set ISBN: 978-1-931397-62-9

Library of Congress Control Number: 2010929172

Printed in the United States of America

Geography Matters, Inc.
800.426.4650
www.geomatters.com

Dedication

We dedicate this book to all those who have bravely chosen to follow the path that the Lord laid before them, in spite of the time, sacrifice and faith it took to do so. ~Debbie Strayer

This book is dedicated to all those who inspired it … and made it happen … but most especially to every mom who picks it up and breathes a sigh of relief. May it be a blessing to your family! ~Linda Fowler

Acknowledgements

Debbie~

To my dear husband Greg, who has always put the Lord's plan for our family first in his life, and by doing so, liberated all of us to be obedient to the call of God and to be blessed for doing so. Thank you so much for being such an incredible example of devotion to the Lord. You are my sweet.

My amazing children Nate, Ashley and son-in-law Alex; Each of you has inspired me by your boldness to do what you felt the Lord has given you to do, and kept me going so many times during the journey with your love and faithfulness. Each of you has been given so many gifts and talents and you freely share them with others. No mother is more blessed than I.

My dear co-author Linda; what can I say. You are a gift to me from the Lord. Your wit, intelligence, insight, devotion and determination have kept me afloat so many times. God has blessed us with an amazing friendship, and for that, I am now and will always be truly grateful.

My publishers and newly added family, Josh and Cindy Wiggers; some relationships are born out of only common wishes or dreams. Ours was born out of divine direction, and came with the blessing of common hearts and common dreams. Thank you for making this dream come true for me, and I look forward to all the future holds for us together.

My dear mentor and friend, Dr. Ruth Beechick; though I have known you for many years, I always feel as though there is so much yet to learn from you. You have freely given of your heart and knowledge to me and I am truly grateful. I pray that I may carry on your gift to me in the years to come in a way that will be a blessing to you.

Linda~

Thank you, thank you, thank you to my amazing husband, Coke, for your unfailing support of this great adventure – evidenced daily by your uncanny ability to offer just the right encouragement and, maybe more importantly, to eat take-out with a smile.

Shout-outs also to my unique and quirky kids, both those birthed and those grafted (through marriage) -- Caleb, Cathryn, Betsy, Matt, Tracy, and Travis -- for being so wonderfully individual and creative, and for giving me a measure of understanding;

to the Wiggers clan – Cindy, Josh, Alex, and Ashley -- for attaching wings to this project and allowing it to fly far beyond our hopes, for hours and hours of oiling the "engine," and for literally keeping us out of the ditch;

and to my dear friend and cohort, Debbie, one of the most genuine and gifted people I know. Thank you, Deb, for rescuing me from the aimlessness of my empty nest, for having confidence in me, and for being the creative spark-plug that you just naturally are!

May the Lord bless and protect you all as you come and go, may He give you peace, and lavish His grace on all your efforts!

Table of Contents

Preface

Why did we write the *Trail Guide to Learning* Series? xi

Why start with American history? xii

Instructions

Who can use this curriculum? xiii

How can you accommodate middle school students? xiii

Steps for Thinking xv

Answers and Appendices xv

Lesson Contents

Copywork & Dictation xvi

Reader xvii

Read-Aloud, Discussion, Narration & Reflective Writing xvii

Word Study xviii

Geography, Science & History xix

States xx

Writing, Doing & Art xxi

Independent Reading xxi

Student Notebooks xxii

Supportive Resources

Assessments xxii

Light for the Trail xxii

Lapbooks xxiii

Required Resources List xxiii

Growing Pains Unit

Lesson 1 1

Lesson 2 25

Lesson 3 41

Lesson 4 61

Lesson 5 79

Lesson 6 97

Freedom Decided Unit

Lesson 1 111
Lesson 2 131
Lesson 3 149
Lesson 4 169
Lesson 5 187
Lesson 6 207

Nation Building Unit

Lesson 1 223
Lesson 2 245
Lesson 3 267
Lesson 4 289
Lesson 5 311
Lesson 6 331

Appendix A

Lesson at a Glance

Growing Pains 351
Freedom Decided 357
Nation Building 363

Skills and Topics List

Growing Pains 369
Freedom Decided 370
Nation Building 372

Challenge Spelling Words 374

Game Answer Keys 377

Appendix B

Student pages

Reading Log 387
Native American Profile 388
Character Portrait 389

State Page 390

Regional Summary Charts 392

Word Searches 395

References

World Map 398

Perodic Table of Elements 399

3-D Map Model 400

Instructions

Making State Cards 402

Flag Folding 402

Games 403

The Newcomer Game 406

Mechanics Toolkits 411

Activities and Projects

Barometer 429

Anemometer 431

Weather Vane 434

Candle Dipping 436

Unit 1 Watercolor Activity 439

Beanbags 442

Cornhole platform 445

Weaving 448

Unit 2 Watercolor Activity 452

3-D Map 454

Pick-Up Sticks 458

Metal Punching 459

Tin Punch Lantern 461

Unit 3 Watercolor Activity 464

Resources 467

Preface

Why did we write the *Trail Guide to Learning* Series?

- We wanted to create curriculum that was easy to use, yet able to lead students to develop higher thinking skills.
- We wanted the things learned to come from real books, discussion and a variety of activities so that students would enjoy the process.
- We wanted information from different subject areas taught together in relationship to geography, as it occurs in real life.
- We wanted students to become better communicators by learning and practicing language skills along with what they were learning, instead of through separate drill and practice. That way their drawing, writing, and speaking would be a natural response to their thinking and learning.
- We wanted this book itself to be more than just a teacher's guide. We wrote it as a source of information for your student and a teacher's education course for you, giving you bite-sized and timely explanations of what we suggest you do, and why.
- Lastly, we wanted to provide a way that strengthens the worldview consistant with your family's beliefs.

It has taken years of labor and a team of workers, but we are excited to have met these goals in the second of the series, *Paths of Settlement.*

It is important for you to know who helped produce this level, because that helps explain why it is different from other curricula, and why you can have confidence when using it. The team of people who designed, wrote, read, edited, and supported this effort is impressive. It includes veteran home educators Greg and Debbie Strayer, Coke and Linda Fowler, Josh and Cindy Wiggers, as well as young adults who were home educated, Ashley (Strayer) and Alex Wiggers. Renowned home education author, Dr. Ruth Beechick, remains Debbie's mentor and continues to influence her thoughts and works through personal input. We also highly value the assistance of the families who are using the first year of the Trail Guide to Learning Series, *Paths of Exploration*, with their children and continue to give us helpful feedback.

Why does all this matter? As we say in our Steps for Thinking, "The key to understanding the actions of others is to understand their thoughts." If you know what our goals were, you will have a good starting point to use this curriculum to fit your own goals for your students. Look at the parts of the book and see how easy it is to make your goals a reality.

Why do we start with American history?

Children learn best by starting with the familiar. Studying American history helps lay a firm foundation based on your family's beliefs and shows what a good leader, government and citizen look like. It also gives your children needed time to build thinking skills. When students are older they are better able to understand the events of world history, and more importantly, the causes and results of those events. With greater maturity in place, students are then ready to compare ancient times and events to our history and lives, learning the powerful lessons that can come from such a study.

Instructions

Paths of Settlement consists of six units:

- **Growing Pains**
- **House Divided**
- **Freedom Decided**
- **Unity Restored**
- **Nation Building**
- **Sea to Shining Sea**

The first three are found in Volume 1, and the second three in Volume 2. Each unit contains six lessons with five parts that are designed to take about a week —but you retain the freedom to make the curriculum's schedule fit the needs of your students. Because of this, even though one part can take one day, this curriculum is your servant, not your master. Flexibility is built in, since every Lesson 6 completes the assignments for the unit and provides a time of review and assessment. In addition, large parts of the lessons in Unit 6, Sea to Shining Sea, are devoted to review of the other units studied throughout the year. This review is an important part of making learning permanent.

What should you know about the second level of the Trail Guide to Learning Series?

We are excited about our **expanded margin notes**. These notes provide support for you as a teaching parent and help you understand why we suggest these methods and materials. They include the expert commentary of Dr. Ruth Beechick, through excerpts from her many books, as well as excerpts from the *Ultimate Geography and Timeline Guide* by Maggie Hogan and Cindy Wiggers. Also included are encouragement and insights from the thirty-year educational experiences of author Debbie Strayer.

Support is just a click away! Our Yahoo user group gives you an opportunity to be a part of the community of those who are traveling the Trail! Post questions, share experiences and read the thoughts of others who are using our materials with their families.

http://tech.groups.yahoo.com/group/LearningSeries/

Here are some notes to make using the curriculum easier:

Because various editions of the same book often have different page numbers, the reading assignments in *Paths of Settlement* have been expanded to include the first words of each passage. You may find it helpful to mark reading assignments ahead of time so that the flow of your school is not interrupted with finding beginning and ending points.

A standard materials list is included below. Most lessons require the use of these items:

- crayons, markers or colored pencils
- scissors, glue, tape
- highlighters
- index cards

dictionary, thesaurus
extra watercolor paper
Student Notebook
Internet access or library for extra research options
CD, DVD player
2 transparencies
fine tip wet erase marker

Included at the front of each lesson is a list of books and anything else needed for that lesson that is not part of the standard materials list.

This curriculum continues to direct students to use research as an important part of gaining information. We believe parents are the best supervisors of their children's use of computers. Since online resources may be the source of information, we expect students to follow their parents' guidelines whenever they use the computer. While we have attempted to give correct Internet references in this curriculum, information locations can change, so we encourage parents to maintain supervision of all student computer use.

Grade level markings for assignments throughout the curriculum represent:

4th grade
5th grade
6th grade

Who can use this curriculum?

This curriculum targets grades 4, 5, and 6, but can be easily adapted for 3rd grade abilities by reducing reading assignments, increasing the amount the teacher reads aloud and substituting oral responses for written work. Younger students can easily fit into the activities, discussions and presentations. Lapbooks are also available that coordinate with every lesson. These are a great way to include younger students in curriculum lessons, while they have their own age appropriate activities to complete. The tactile and visual reinforcements of the graphic organizers used can increase learning and retention for many students. Older students may also take the opportunity to "be the teacher" to younger siblings, through the use of the lapbook activities. (See more about our lapbooks in the Supportive Resources section of this introduction.)

In most assignments, the recommended activity levels are noted with icons: for the lowest, for higher, and for highest. **If there is no icon present, the activity is to be completed by all levels.** Before beginning a lesson, look at the **Materials List** in Part 1 to be sure you have what you will need to complete the activities. This list will tell you what you need in addition to the list of supplies used regularly. In addition, every Part 5 contains additional resources for **Enrichment Activities**. These activities are provided for your older students (7th grade and up) who are completing the curriculum with you, or for younger students who complete the lessons quickly, or who just enjoy learning on a more in-depth level.

Enrichment Activites:

- 7th grade and up
- advanced students
- all students wanting to learn more

How can you adjust this curriculum to accommodate middle school students?

The upper level reading, thinking, presentation, and discussion activities are appropriate for this age. The Enrichment Activities provide an opportunity for more in-depth study, which is the best way to extend learning to a deeper level. Assign literature to read from the Enrichment Section, and then follow the format in the language skill section (choose a passage to write from dictation, define unknown vocabulary, identify usage and mechanics activities in the literature read, etc). In writing, extend the activities to include greater length, or greater frequency. In the science and history activities, ask your middle school students to learn more about the topic to share with you or other students. Challenge them to vary their presentation styles to include multi-media presentations, plays, games, etc. This is a perfect time to increase responsibility for learning and sharing what they know.

A Middle School Supplement is available to provide guidance for older students. It includes the same content but adds interesting and challenging activities on a higher level. You can obtain this in digital format from the publisher at geomatters.com.

Steps for Thinking

A typical lesson should begin with an introduction of the **Steps for Thinking**. These are the big ideas demonstrated through the reading, discussion, and other activities of the lesson. Explain each step to your children and talk with them about any questions or ideas they have about it. You will revisit the **Steps for Thinking** at the end of each lesson, so don't require your students to understand them thoroughly at the beginning. By the end of the lesson, they will have more experience with the concepts and be able to discuss them more thoroughly.

Answers and Appendices

Answers to the questions asked in the text and the Student Notebook are located on the last page of each lesson. Each volume has two appendices. In Volume 1, **Appendix A** contains teacher aides. This includes an At-A-Glance guide for each unit in the volume, skills and topics charts, game answer keys, and something new in this *Path*—a Challenge Spelling list. This list is comprised of words from the literature selections, and is an excellent resource when you feel your students are ready for increased difficulty in their spelling practice. **Appendix B** contains student resources, information, and games. This includes student sheets (such as the Reading Log and Regional Summary Charts); reference maps and charts; mechanic toolkits; and instructions for various games, projects, and activities assigned in the text. In Volume 2, Appendices C and D correspond to the same descriptions.

Lesson Contents

Following is an in-depth description of each section in a typical lesson, and how to use it. After you read this and begin using the curriculum, there are many margin notes in the text to remind you of the important points contained here

A. Copywork & Dictation

Copywork and dictation provides a consistent method for students to see, hear and write language correctly. It is the first step in learning language skills. Start your student with copying the passage. After copying, he should match what he has written word for word to the text, and correct anything that is not the same. This level is appropriate for many third and fourth graders throughout the year. It may also be appropriate for older students, and needs to continue for as long as your student seems sufficiently challenged. From time to time, you may want to attempt a bit of dictation by asking your child to choose a sentence himself to write from dictation. Allow him to choose a sentence or passage that he has already worked with, to build confidence. Don't worry, this isn't cheating. Your goal is to build the ability to read and write language, and *teaching* means providing the support needed to be successful. Assessment should come later.

If your student is a fifth or sixth grader, evaluate his level when he has copied the passages a few times and decide whether this activity seems too easy for him. If so, try dictating, or speaking, the first few words of the sentence slowly, and ask your student to write down what he hears. If he can write down at least a portion of the words correctly, then he is ready for dictation. The ability to write from dictation is a skill that must learned. It may be difficult at first, so give your student the help he needs. Allow him to become familiar with the sentence, or sentences, you dictate at first. You may even want to let him choose the sentence. After he is very successful at writing from dictation using this method, gradually start adding a few words of your choice. Remember that success is your goal, not quickly moving to more difficult dictation passages. Going through the process too quickly without allowing your student the time to become successful and confident may create resistance towards this type of language learning.

Another common problem, especially for younger students, is the struggle with handwriting. Before beginning the copywork and dictation process, your student needs to know how to form each letter. If handwriting is very frustrating and difficult for him, try different writing tools and surfaces. If he continues to experience difficulty, it is perfectly acceptable to allow your child to type the passages. The goal is for your student to see the words, hear the words, and write the words. Remember that it is more important for him to learn the spelling mechanics and reading skills that result from dictation and copying than it is to handwrite the passage.

B. Reader

The natural method of learning continues in this section, the **Reader** assignments. These assignments occur in real literature, and there are several reasons why this is important. Real literature is more interesting. The language used is more natural. A willingness to read builds as your student experiences the success of reading a real book.

Younger students are to read their assignments aloud. The purpose for this is to build reading fluency. Fluency, or the ability to read something effortlessly, is also an important part of comprehension. If a student can read a passage aloud with expression, correct phrasing, and attention to punctuation, it is much more likely that he will also understand the meaning of the passage. To practice fluency at all levels, use passages that your student can read without constant decoding. In other words, start with a few sentences that seem easy for the student to read. Often, you can have him choose the passages for fluency practice, and sometimes you can select them in order to gauge his growth. To do this, find a passage that is a sentence or two longer than the last one he read, or one that contains structures requiring attention to punctuation, such as dialogue. Real books are perfect for this fluency practice. Artificial fluency practice is unnecessary when literature provides such an abundant source of reading materials.

Each **Reader** is coordinated with the unit, and provides a ready-made history lesson. The lives of real people become linked to places and events. In turn, this connection brings character and convictions to light, as well as great adventures and drama. From the wellspring of literature examples of mechanics and word usage come, as well as phonics principles, spelling patterns and vocabulary.

Every student is to read or listen to **all** literature selections for the unit. Reading or hearing the various perspectives adds richness to the stories and depth to the understanding of the events and circumstances of the times. Critical thinking skills build as the related stories allow students to compare and contrast to find similarities and differences. An artist's illustrations contribute to learning about context clues, and the divisions of chapters and paragraphs help students recognize important main ideas and details that support the bigger ideas. All of these lessons come naturally from real books.

C. Read-Aloud, Discussion, Narration & Reflective Writing

Most parents agree that it is good to read aloud to young children to develop pre-reading skills. However, the benefits don't stop there. Reading aloud to children of all ages is one of the easiest, most enjoyable and effective ways to share ideas and begin thoughtful conversations. Since your child does not have to worry about decoding during read-aloud time, he can focus totally on the meaning of what he is hearing. This allows him the opportunity to think about the ideas and information being presented, and to formulate his own thoughts. It prepares your child to respond to what he has heard through discussion, retelling or reflective writing.

Read-Aloud - As you read aloud, you also model fluency, expression, and comprehension. When your voice reflects punctuation, your child can see its purpose and the way it makes the passage more understandable. As he listens and sometimes follows along with his eyes, your child sees the language and hears it read correctly, which provides an excellent example for his reading. Because of this, Read-Aloud assignments are an important part of each lesson.

Narration and Discussion - Read-Aloud assignments also provide the basis for student responses. As they listen, it is natural for them to respond by speaking, which is a good first step toward meaningful discussion. In the give-and-take of discussion, you can listen to your children's understanding of the passage, ask questions, and share your thoughts. All of these combine to expand their thinking on the topic. It also lends itself to the natural memory practice of narration, or retelling. As students become familiar with the process of retelling, their ability to recall main ideas and details develops. The last step in the process of response is that of writing.

Narration can take many forms, such as predicting outcomes, asking and answering questions, as well as retelling from the point of view of a particular character. All of these activities build the ability to narrate or retell what they have heard.

Some units may include **reflective writing**, which involves responding to a passage your children have heard by writing their thoughts about it. This is one of the most complex ways for your children to respond. It is also a very concrete way to use writing to answer questions. The answers given are correct because they come from your children's thoughts and understanding of what they heard. Discussion, narration, and reflective writing are good, natural ways for a teacher to see what her students understood from what they heard.

D. Word Study

The Word Study section exists to equip your child with strategies to gain meaning from unknown or unfamiliar words. This information must be connected to other learning in order to remain with your child on a long term basis. So the best time to teach him about phonics, word usage, mechanics, vocabulary, spelling and grammar is when he reads a word, phrase or sentence or hears it used in a story. Study of a sound or word form is natural and makes sense to your child when he sees a need to read, understand and use that word. Word Study activities occur in every lesson, taking advantage of the opportunities presented in the literature to connect meaning and structure for your student.

Vocabulary is a focus of this curriculum as students make and collect cards with words and meanings listed. The purpose of this activity is not memorization or dictionary skills, but understanding. By building an awareness of new or unusual words, you are teaching your student an important strategy for understanding what he has read or heard. New vocabulary words appear in the context of a lesson or story, which helps your child recognize that the way a word is used is closely connected to its meaning. This is an important reading strategy called using context clues. As your child completes the vocabulary activities in this curriculum, he sees the importance of learning and using new words as he reads, writes, discusses and retells.

Spelling is a skill that has several components, such as perceptual ability and memory. Some of us are naturally good at spelling, and some are not. The goal of the spelling assignments is to improve your child's ability to spell by helping him make connections to meaning, phonics and word patterns. Memorizing a list is not as valuable to your child as increasing his ability to comfortably write words that express his understanding and opinions. The goal then, is to increase your child's ability to recognize and spell more words correctly —not just to be able to spell a new word correctly for a week or two and then forget it.

E. Geography, Science & History

The studies of Geography, Science and History are connected. The knowledge of one area contributes to knowledge in the other areas. By considering the linkage of subjects in real life, connections occur naturally for the students. This helps them add to what they know when they encounter new information. It also helps students remember what they have learned. **Connections** are an important part of this curriculum.

Geography is the umbrella from which the other studies connect. Geography includes the study of places. If you learn about places, you learn about the impact those places have on people. If you learn about people, you learn about cultures and worldviews, and the impact those people have on places. So in the study of geography, you naturally learn about people, places, and all the ways they affect each other. All culture, history and science connect to concepts of geography, so we study **Science** and **History** in the light of their connection to the people and places encountered by those who built and settled America.

Science is naturally enjoyable to children through studying things, cycles, and processes that occur in nature, and connecting those things to other areas of study. We employ Charlotte Mason's approach to learning as we reinforce Earth Science concepts through observing, recording (by drawing, charting, and describing,) modeling, discussing, and evaluating — all within the context of the theme of each unit. Natural occurrences connect to one another to introduce and reinforce the order and interdependency of the earth's systems. This curriculum also uses research and reading as a means of obtaining more information, since reading about topics is often as valuable in learning science as doing activities.

Another important aspect of student confidence is to understand that he is able to use real books, not just pre-digested text. Handbooks are an integral part of this curriculum. The *Handbook of Nature Study*, as well as the *DK Pocket Books* on *Geology* and *Weather* are sources of information for thinking, discussion and activities. While these books are good sources of observations about the elements in rocks and weather patterns, the authors of this curriculum do not necessarily agree with all conclusions drawn in these guides. We hold a worldview of the earth's creation that sometimes conflicts with comments made in the introductions and assumptions written about time. If your students notice comments with which you disagree, please take advantage of the teachable moments to discuss your views as a family on these issues.

History is a daily part of the curriculum through literature readings, discussions, and activities. The study of history that focuses on dates and facts alone can be dry and hard to remember. When events in history are associated through the literature, the geography, and the relevant science concepts, it connects the learning and is much more likely to be retained. Great stories and biographies help students connect to the struggles and triumphs of the times. Literature provides a basis for discussion and evaluation of the decisions made and the results that occurred. Since some of the events covered in this volume include the violence of war and some episodes of suffering, please preview literature assignments to make sure it is appropriate for all participating students. Books read by the students, and read aloud by the teacher, provide the thread that ties the events, struggles, and decisions of the settlers and builders of America together. Learning History could not be more natural.

F. States

Since *Paths of Settlement* focuses on the establishment and growth of the United States, a study of the individual states fits naturally into its format. Lessons in the first five units provide opportunities for your students to investigate featured states, and for the information they learn to be reinforced and reviewed through mapping, State Pages, State Cards, and preparation of recipes from the specific areas. The study culminates with development of a home-state project in Unit 6, along with charting, comparing, and contrasting the various geographical regions of our country.

G. Writing, Doing & Art

Learning new things should inspire a response. Since we are not limited to conventional school-type methods, we can employ an array of effective and enjoyable ways of gaining and responding to information. **Writing** is an integrated part of this curriculum. It is not a separate subject, but rather a set of skills with which to become familiar. Writing ability improves with practice and time, both of which come in the context of literature, history, science and geography learning. Writing is best when it is a response to thinking about content learned, new ideas, or activities completed. Since writing begins with thinking, once your children engage in assigned thinking activities, the way is naturally prepared. As you use this approach, your students will begin to see themselves as writers, which is the first and most important step to becoming a writer.

Doing something is a powerful teacher and motivator, and can often provide the basis for authentic writing activities. Although activities often occur in other places throughout the lessons, this section allows active participation in skills and artistic forms that were useful and enjoyable in colonial America. This focus provides students with unique opportunities to enlarge their understanding of the times.

Making and tasting foods outside a child's normal experience, but common in other regions of the United States, reinforces the ability to follow directions as it builds confidence. Not only that, it also provides valuable glimpses into the varied preferences of fellow Americans. The included watercolor activities naturally build your children's power to observe and notice detail, which in turn equips them to communicate what they learn more effectively. Engaging students in painting regional scenes, in a medium that was accessible to colonists, helps to connect the people who settled in a region with its geography.

H. Independent Reading

This is an important part of each student's daily schedule. It provides regular practice for word study and reading skills, as well as time for practice of thinking skills. Quiet time to consider ideas and tie new information with old is essential in building new understandings. Though you may be tempted to skip this activity to save time, please don't! Completing the reading log each day also gives your student a sense of accomplishment, as well as some time to work independently. Taking on the responsibility of the reading log is also a step in developing student responsibility and independence, since this is an important part of any portfolio.

Student Notebooks

The Student Notebook is not only a vital part of the curriculum, but it also provides a **portfolio** of your student's work. Maps, charts, and other activities assigned in the textbook are included in an easy, ready-to-use format for the student.

How can you begin to transfer the responsibility for completing assignments from yourself to your student? Daily checklists are included in the Student Notebook to ease this process. The student has a ready-made task list to guide and direct his efforts, and the teacher can tell at a glance what needs to be done. This checklist system encourages your student to take responsibility for his daily work, and allows him to be easily accountable for assignments.

A portfolio is often the best possible written measure of student achievement. Completion of the Student Notebook creates an excellent, consecutive record of student work in reading, writing, geography, history, science, and art. The Student Notebook gives teacher, student and evaluator a clear picture of sequential progress in each subject area, samples of student work, and examples of creative projects. It includes dates assignments were completed, assisting with the documentation process. This helps teachers to see time spent on each unit, as well as giving your student a sense of accomplishment as he looks over the finished product.

The pages for the Student Notebook can be printed from the CD-ROM included in this curriculum. They can also be purchased in preprinted packages by volume number and grade level. Each package of notebook sheets comes three-hole punched and ready to insert in a binder.

Supportive Resources

Assessments - For those who prefer not to use the portfolio method of evaluation, or who want to supplement their child's portfolio, assessments for each level of the first five units are available on a separate CD. The assessments for this level include both objective assessments on the content presented, as well as performance assessments in writing. Guidance is included for administering the assessments, evaluating the results, conferencing with your student and planning for future improvements. These, coupled with your daily observations and interactive discussions and games, provide ample material upon which to base an accurate evaluation. There is no assessment for Unit 6, Sea to Shining Sea, since this unit is largely devoted to review of the previous five. The review activities serve as evaluation tools themselves, and can be assigned point values if you choose.

***Light for the Trail* Bible Curriculum** - This optional Bible curriculum helps your student make the most important connection of all—the one between his faith and his view of the world around him. This easy-to-use guide provides daily assignments, which include Memory Verses for the week, discussion topics, writing assignments, suggestions for in-depth study and longer-term Memory Projects. These elements blend with Prayer Times, Worship Times and Blazing the Trail (teacher sharing) to enable students to make real-life connections between the content of the curriculum and the lessons of Scripture. Compared to *Paths of Exploration* the supplement for *Paths of Settlement* includes a more in-depth level of Scripture study using the inductive method. This gives your children a chance to connect Scriptures and their application in both the past and present to the history and context of the passages themselves.

Lapbooks - Optional lapbooks are available to accompany each unit. Created by Trail Guide Series users, this is an excellent way to build and review the concepts and content taught by the curriculum with hands-on reinforcement. If you use the lapbooks, those activities are designed to **replace** any corresponding Student Notebook assignments, particularly for younger students. They may also be beneficial to many older students who prefer a more hands-on approach to learning, or for review. Assignments that have corresponding lapbooking activities are indicated by the lapbook symbol shown on this page.

Middle School Supplement - The Middle School Supplement enables older members of the family to learn together with their siblings, while tying subjects together in a meaningful way. It covers the same content with more challenging assignments. At the time of this printing the supplement is available only in CD-ROM and downloadable ebook format.

Required Resource List

The following materials are required for use with *Paths of Settlement.* For ordering information see Resources at the back of the book.

Volume 1

The Courage of Sarah Noble, by Alice Dalgliesh
Matchlock Gun, by Walter D. Edmonds
Ambush in the Wilderness, by Kris Hemphill
*Abigail Adams,*by Evelyn Witter
Munford: *The American Revolution,* by Jamie Aramini
Guns for General Washington, by Seymour Reit
George Washington, by Norma Cournow Camp
The Cabin Faced West, by Jean Fritz
Justin Morgan Had a Horse, by Marguerite Henry
Francis Scott Key, by David Collins
The Eve of Revolution, by Barbara Burt
Discovering America's Founders Drive Thru History DVD

Volume 2

Clara Barton Founder of the American Red Cross, by Augusta Stevenson
Abraham Lincoln, by David Collins
Robert E. Lee, by Lee Roddy
Laura Ingalls Wilder, Young Pioneer, by Beatrice Gormley
Janie's Freedom, by Callie Smith Grant
Samuel F. Smith, by Marguerite E. Fitch
Munford: *The Klondike Gold Rush,* by Jamie Aramini
Theodore Roosevelt An American Original, by Janet and Geoff Benge
Yankee Blue or Rebel Grey, by Kate Connell
Good Ol' Cowboy Stories, by Jack Terry

Core (used in both Volumes 1 and 2):

DK Pockets: *Weather Facts*
DK Pockets: *Rocks and Minerals*
Klutz Watercolor Book, by Thacher Hurd and John Cassidy
Wee Sing America, by Pamela Conn Beall and Susan Hagen Nipp
United States History Atlas
Children's Illustrated United States Atlas
Eat Your Way Through the USA, by Loree Pettit
Profiles from History, Volume 2, by Ashley Strayer Wiggers
Handbook of Nature Study, by Anna Comstock (print version or online)
Rock Study Kit
United States Presidents Pocket Flash Cards
United States PlaceMap
Large-Scale United States Outline Map
Mark-It Timeline of History
USA Activity CD-Rom
Student Notebook pages

Optional Supportive Resources

Assessments (CD-ROM)
Light for the Trail Bible Supplement (CD-ROM)
Lapbook Set Volume 1
Lapbook Set Volume 2
Middle School Supplement

Lesson 1, Part 1

Steps for Thinking

1. People want to be free to do what they think is right.
2. People came to America for different reasons.
3. When people have an important goal, it is easier to endure hard times.

The **Steps for Thinking** section gives you the main ideas about the topics presented. Understanding these helps you to have productive discussions with your children so they, too, understand the bigger ideas. This forms more permanent learning, contrary to just learning facts, which tends to be temporary. These steps are useful prior to instruction, and they are also useful for review at the end of the week

Materials

- *The Courage of Sarah Noble*
- *Abigail Adams*
- *Ambush in the Wilderness*
- *Atlas of the United States*
- *Eat Your Way Through the USA*
- *United States History Atlas*
- *DK Pockets: Weather Facts*
- *Profiles from History, Vol. 2*
- *Klutz Watercolor Book*
- USA Activity CD
- Paper towel
- Ingredients for recipe (Part 3)
- Outline map of U.S.
- Outdoor thermometer
- Materials for weather instrument (Part 2)
  - Wide-mouthed jar
  - Ruler
  - Masking tape
- Globe or map of the world

A. Copywork & Dictation *Language Skills, Thinking Skills*

Look carefully at your assigned passage below, and read it silently. Show your teacher any words you don't know, and practice saying them aloud. Now read the passage aloud, or ask your teacher to read it to you.

When you are finished copying or writing from dictation, compare your copy to the text and make any needed corrections.

Copy, or write as your teacher dictates, page 1, paragraph 2 ("The spring night…") in *The Courage of Sarah Noble.*

Copy, or write as your teacher dictates, page 2, paragraph 1 ("Patrick watched…") in *Ambush in the Wilderness.*

A. Copywork and dictation assignments go from an easier level (designated by the first symbol) to harder levels (designated by the second and third symbols). Take two days for the copywork if that is more comfortable for your child. Please adapt instructions to your child's individual needs. Your child should be **consistently successful** at one level before progressing to the next, **regardless of grade**.

B. Reader *Language Skills, History*

The Courage of Sarah Noble: pages 1-5 (Chapter 1)
Ambush in the Wilderness: page 1 to the bottom of page 3

Read the above assignment from *The Courage of Sarah Noble* aloud, and then follow along as someone else reads the assignment from *Ambush in the Wilderness.*

Read the above assignment from *The Courage of Sarah Noble* silently, and then read the assignment from *Ambush in the Wilderness* aloud.

Read the above assignments from *The Courage of Sarah Noble* and *Ambush in the Wilderness* silently.

C. Read-Aloud & Discussion *Language Skills, History, Thinking Skills*

Abigail Adams: page 1 through page 6, paragraph 5

Follow the directions for your level and read or listen to the assignment from *Abigail Adams.* Then ask your teacher to read the discussion questions. Think about what you know from the story, and

C. Discussion is very important in developing your child's ability to organize his thoughts. This in turn builds the ability to think and write. The goal of the discussion questions is not just to find the answer to a particular question, but also to create a situation where thoughts about the question and its answer are shared and considered in a detailed way. Do not rush this activity, but encourage your student to share his ideas relating to the topic, and any additional ideas that may come to mind. You can also share your own thoughts and questions as an example.

D. Read the list of words to your child. If he would rather spell the words aloud than write them, it is perfectly acceptable. As you dictate each word, put small dots beside any misspelled word. Then have your child copy them onto the Student Notebook page.

The small superscript numbers that appear after some of the questions in this lesson refer to answers found in the answer key, which is located immediately after Part 5.

E. Each word in bold letters is considered a vocabulary word. It is a word that may or may not be new to your child. You can write these vocabulary words on index cards and use them for occasional review, but not for memorizing. Give the child the meaning of the words if he doesn't remember. Try to use the new vocabulary words during conversation, and encourage your student to do the same.

Each time your student makes a vocabulary card for this unit, have him write *GP* (for Growing Pains) in the upper left corner. This will make it possible to review vocabulary by unit at the end of the year.

answer in your own words. Give any examples you can think of from the story that help show your answer.

Listen carefully as your teacher reads the above assignment from *Abigail Adams* aloud.

Read the above assignment from *Abigail Adams* aloud.

Discussion Questions: Tell about Abigail's birthday. Who were the special visitors and what did they bring? What made Father's gift special? Tell about your favorite birthday. What things were the same for you and Abigail? What things were different?

D. Spelling

Language Skills, Thinking Skills

Look at the list of words below. Then, in your Student Notebook underline the letters in each word that say *ow*.

town spout down loud[1]

Listen as your teacher reads the words below. Then spell each word as best you can, either aloud or by writing it in your Student Notebook.

louder	howl	house	mountain
ground	count	brown	around
Logstown	bounce	pound	scowl
gunpowder	longhouse	growling	dismount

E. History

Geography, Thinking Skills

Over 500 years ago, Christopher Columbus had a dream. More than anything else, he wanted to find a water **route**, or way to get from one place to another, to the East Indies. For a number of reasons, he had trouble convincing anyone to supply ships and money for the voyage. But he didn't give up trying, and finally his waiting paid off. At last he was able to begin his exploration!

At the time of Columbus' voyage, Europe had been settled for hundreds of years. People who lived there thought they already knew about all the land on earth. Imagine how surprised they were when Columbus brought back news of a large, beautiful piece of land that no other European had ever seen before. His discovery shook up everyone's ideas about what the earth was like, and America soon became known as the "New World." Other explorers were especially excited, and they hurried to investigate America's coastal areas. In the *United States History Atlas*, look at the map entitled "Early Voyages of Exploration." Notice how many explorers sailed to and around the New World after Columbus.

The explorers were impressed with what they saw, and sent word back to Europe that there were many opportunities in this wonderful new place. After that, it wasn't long before people who were looking for opportunity began to arrive on the shores of the New World. These **newcomers**, or people who had only recently arrived at a place, came for many different reasons. Most of them were not like Columbus and other **explorers**, who were usually the first newcomers to arrive in an area. Explorers loved the adventure of finding and investigating new places. They could hardly wait to see what was around the corner or over the next hill, and they always enjoyed the mystery of not knowing exactly what they would find. But explorers were usually not interested in building permanent homes in the places they visited.

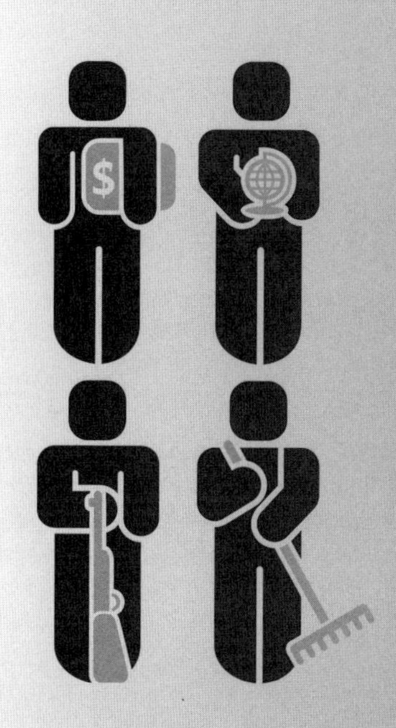

Instead of being like explorers, most of the people who traveled to America were settlers like Sarah Noble's family. A **settler** is a person who goes to a new place to make a home. The first settlers in America were brave, but in a different way from the explorers. They were brave because they chose to make homes in the New World even though they knew that there were no towns, or stores, or crops, or even roads. They knew that the land was wilderness, and that the Native Americans might not be friendly. For them, coming to America was a chance to carve out new lives for themselves and their families. It was a chance to enjoy much more freedom than they had in their homelands. These settlers looked forward to the adventure of building towns and roads, opening stores, and planting crops. Individuals, families, and groups of people with similar beliefs came to settle in America.

Other people who traveled to America were **entrepreneurs**, whose main interest was organizing and operating businesses. Entrepreneurs were a little like explorers and a little like settlers, because they often went into new areas to find out what was there, and they usually built homes. Their businesses were built around harvesting the **natural resources**, or things of value found in nature, from this rich land to sell. Sometimes European nations helped them come to America because they knew there was great wealth, and were anxious to claim as much of it as possible. In *Ambush in the Wilderness*, Patrick's father was an entrepreneur whose business was fur-trading.

Usually **soldiers** came along with the groups of settlers and entrepreneurs for protection. Sometimes these soldiers worked for the groups who hired them, and sometimes they were part of a European army.

Those who were part of an army were there to defend their country's claims in the New World. If you remember the story of the Pilgrims, Captain Myles Standish was a soldier who was hired to come along with them for protection. Also, later in *Ambush in the Wilderness,* you will read about many soldiers who were in America as part of the English army.

Think about the different types of people who came to the New World. Do you think you would have been more like an explorer, a settler, an entrepreneur, or a soldier? Talk with your teacher about why you feel as you do.

In your Student Notebook, name the group that you think you would fit into, and then write two sentences explaining why.

Write another sentence about how your group might respond to the challenges of being in the New World.

Write two more sentences about how your group might respond to the challenges of being in the New World.

The addition of Lapbook pages to regularly assigned work can be overwhelming to some students. The Lapbook activities are designed to **replace** the corresponding Student Notebook assignments, particularly for younger students. They may also be beneficial to many older students who prefer a more hands-on approach to learning, or for review.

F. States

Geography, Thinking Skills, History

This year you will take an exciting journey around the United States, and learn important things about each state you pass through. Then, in Unit 6, you will create a special project about your home state and present it to your family.

Since the characters in both *The Courage of Sarah Noble* and *Abigail Adams* came from Massachusetts, that is a good place to begin your journey. Massachusetts is located in the far northeast region of the United States, which is called New England.

In your *Atlas of the United States*, read the pages about Massachusetts. When you are finished, find the blank map of Massachusetts in your Student Notebook and complete the following assignments:

- Place a small star on the spot where Boston is located, and label it. Boston is the capital city of Massachusetts.
- Label the Atlantic Ocean, Boston Bay, and Massachusetts Bay.

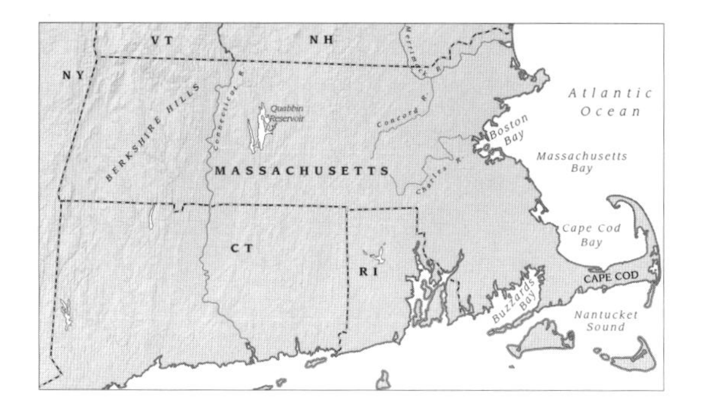

- Color the lines showing the Charles, Concord, Merrimack, and Connecticut Rivers with a blue crayon, marker, or colored pencil, and label them.
- Lightly color the area where the Berkshire Hills are located with a green crayon, marker, or colored pencil, and label them.
- Find the town of Plymouth, mark its location with a dot, and label it. Discuss anything you know about Plymouth with your teacher.[2]
- Color and label the Quabbin Reservoir. A **reservoir** is a natural or man-made pond or lake used to store water.
- Find Cape Cod, Cape Cod Bay, Buzzards Bay and Nantucket Sound, and label them.
- Label the five states that border Massachusetts.

G. Doing

Art, History

From the earliest times in American history, English explorers and mapmakers often used watercolors to show what the places they visited looked like, and to describe the wildlife they found there. Probably the most famous examples of this were done a little later by John James Audubon, who devoted his life to painting the birds of America..

At the library or, with your parent's permission, on the Internet, look at some of John James Audubon's paintings. Then find some examples of landscapes painted in watercolor by other artists. A **landscape** painting is one that shows the natural scenery in an area. This year you will learn some watercolor techniques that will help you paint landscapes from different regions in America.

Together with your teacher, read the introduction to your *Klutz Watercolor Book.* When you are finished, open the **palette**, or selection of paints, that is attached to the book. Notice that there is another plastic cover on top of the paints. There are three indentations in this cover which will come in handy later for mixing paints, so be sure to save it.

Now read the page entitled "Really Basic Watercolor Technique" and experiment with your brush and paint on the next four pages. Just relax and have fun with this activity, you do not have to complete it all today. Over the next few days, if you find you have extra time and your parents agree, play with your paints on other watercolor paper. After every painting session, rinse your brush in clear water and blot it with a paper towel. Be careful to smooth the bristles out straight with the paper towel before you put the brush away.

H. Reading fluency is developed through having frequent silent reading opportunities that continue for the length of time suggested here. Since a primary focus of this activity is to nurture your child's enjoyment of reading, help him to choose reading materials that interest him and are at a level that allows him to read with understanding by himself. You can incorporate this activity into your school day whenever it is most convenient.

If the suggested length of time is too long for your child to continue reading by himself, start with an amount of time he can accomplish successfully and make the suggested time a goal.

H. **Independent Reading** *Language Skills*

Choose something to read that you will enjoy. Then, find a quiet, comfortable place and read for the following length of time:

25 minutes 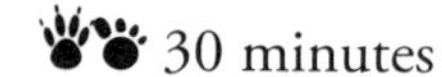 30 minutes

Over time, it's fun to see how much you have read. Be sure to write down what you read today on the Reading Log in your Student Notebook.

Lesson 1, Part 2

A. **Quotation Notebook** *Language Skills, Thinking Skills*

In the 1700s, students used behavior rules for handwriting practice. A writing book of George Washington's was found which had thirty rules in it, so people know that he copied them too. Below are some shortened and modernized samples that will still work well today.

Copy the first rule listed below into your Student Notebook, and then tell or write what it means to you.

Copy the first two rules listed below into your Student Notebook, and then tell or write what each one means to you.

Copy all three rules listed below into your Student Notebook, and then tell or write what each one means to you. Give an example of each rule from a story, someone's life, or your own life.

1. Think before you speak, and then say your words clearly and carefully.

2. It is always good manners to give a place to the last person to arrive, and try not to speak louder than ordinary.
3. Speak words that build others up, because that shows your good nature. Take time to think things through when you are upset.

B. **Reader** *Language Skills, History*

The Courage of Sarah Noble: page 6 (Chapter 2) through page 10, paragraph 4

Ambush in the Wilderness: page 3, last paragraph ("Patrick's face…") to the bottom of page 6

Read the above assignment from *The Courage of Sarah Noble* aloud, and then follow along as someone else reads the assignment from *Ambush in the Wilderness.*

Read the above assignment from *The Courage of Sarah Noble* silently, and then read the assignment from *Ambush in the Wilderness* aloud.

Read the above assignments from *The Courage of Sarah Noble* and *Ambush in the Wilderness* silently.

Teaching Tip The combination of history and language skills is a natural one. Children learn history content and the specifics of reading, writing, and speaking at the same time by studying the lives and events of the past. This is an important part of the unified approach.

C. **Read-Aloud & Narration** *Language Skills, History, Thinking Skills*

Abigail Adams: page 6, paragraph 6 ("At first…") to the bottom of page 10

Follow the directions for your level and read, or listen as your teacher reads, the above assignment from *Abigail Adams*. Then, in your own words, tell what happened in your assigned passage below. Try to remember as many details as possible. You may reread the passage or listen as your teacher rereads the part you are to retell.

Listen carefully, then retell page 8, paragraph 1 ("Tell us, Grandmother…") to paragraph 7 ("Reverend Smith thought…").

Listen carefully, then retell page 9, paragraph 5 ("Clearing the way …") to the bottom of page 10 ("Did you take me downstairs…").

Read the assignment aloud; then retell it in your own words.

C. The skill of narration is gained over time. If your child has never retold a story, start with the assignment for the lower level, no matter what grade he is in. Work up from there, being careful to allow him to stay at the level of success for a while before going to a longer section.

D. **Mechanics and Editing** *Language Skills, Thinking Skillss*

Mechanics are people who are good at fixing machines and engines and making them work better. You are going to become a writing mechanic by correcting punctuation, words, and sentences and making them work better.

Mechanics Toolkit

1A - Capitalize the first word in every sentence.

My favorite food is pizza.
The dogs are out in the yard.

D The Mechanics and Editing section in this unit begins with skills that your child may already know. It is always a good idea to begin instruction with review, so please have your child complete these activities even if he already knows the concepts presented. A great way to enjoy a review with your child is to ask him to be the teacher and present the information to you, the student!

1B - Capitalize names when they mean particular people and places.
My mother's name is Mary.
We are going to visit Florida.

2A - Use the word *a* in front of a word that starts with a consonant sound.
I am going to eat a banana.
He likes to play with a football.

2B - Use the word *an* in front of a word that starts with a vowel sound.
We got an apple for our snack.
An otter swam around the pond.

Practice these skills by correcting the sentences in your Student Notebook.[3] The number of errors in each sentence is listed after the sentence in parentheses. To show that a letter needs to be capitalized, make three lines (≡) under it. To replace an incorrect word with a correct word, draw a line through the incorrect word and write the correct word above it. Add any needed punctuation.

E. If you do not own the *Handbook of Nature Study*, you can download the parts you need from the Internet at www.archive.org. Type "Handbook of Nature Study" in the search field.

Since the language in the *Handbook of Nature Study* can be difficult to understand, you may want to discuss each paragraph with your child as you read it. In that way, you can help him understand what he is hearing.

E. **Science** *Thinking Skills, Geography*

The success of any settlement in the New World depended on how well the settlers were able to **adapt**, or change their way of living or thinking, to its location. For example, the first settlers in New England were the Pilgrims, who arrived during winter. They had a very difficult time right away because of the extreme cold. Later they found out that the soil around their settlement was not very rich. They had trouble growing food until a friendly Native American named Squanto taught them how to fertilize their crops. All in all, they had to adapt a great deal to their surroundings in order to survive.

An area's **topography**, or what it looks like on the surface, its climate, the other people and things that live there, and whether or not its soil is good for planting crops are some of the things that were very important to settlers. These important things are related to **geography**, which is the study of all the natural features of a land, and the people who live there. But many of these things are also related to another area of study called Earth Science, which explores why the natural features of the earth are the way they are. This year you will learn about **Earth Science** so that you can better understand geography, and its connection to the settlement of America.

Since the Pilgrims' first problem in New England involved weather, that is a good place to begin your study of Earth Science. Together with your teacher, read the sections near the front of your *Weather Facts* book that are entitled "How to Use This Book," "What Is Weather?" and "Weather and Climate." Then listen as your teacher reads the introductory paragraphs about climate and weather on pages 780 and 781 in the *Handbook of Nature Study*.

Talk with your teacher about the differences between weather and climate, and then write down the definition of both words in your Student Notebook.[4] Now find the word meteorologist in the Glossary at the back of your *Weather Facts* book, and write down its definition.[5] When you are finished, look up barometer, hygrometer, and anemometer in the Glossary and write down the part of weather each one measures.[6] Perhaps you know, or can guess, what rain gauges and thermometers measure, so write them in your Student Notebook along with the other tools. If you don't know, look these items up in a dictionary.

Both of the books you looked at in this section mention that weather affects many things in your life. How many things can you think of that weather affects? Discuss this with your teacher and then list as many things as you can.[7]

This year you will become a *weather watcher*, which simply involves paying attention to things that are happening in the air around you. When you think about the many things in your life that are affected by weather, becoming a weather watcher seems like a very good idea. Through the next few lessons you will make a weather station and record the things that you observe.

To help you begin observing the weather, hang an outdoor thermometer someplace where it is not in direct sunlight. This will allow your **thermometer** to get a more accurate measurement of the temperature of the air. Then use the Contents list at the front of your *Weather Facts* book to find the section entitled "Measuring Rain," and read it. When you are finished, follow the directions below to make a rain gauge. **Rain gauges** are simple tools used to measure the amount of rainfall in an area.

To make your rain gauge, use a jar that has as wide an opening as possible. It can be either glass or plastic. If you want, you can glue an inexpensive six-inch ruler to the outside of the jar, or you can use a regular ruler and a permanent marker to draw the measurements on the jar itself. If the jar is glass, stick a piece of masking tape on its side, and draw your marks on the tape. That's all there is to it! To measure rainfall at your house, be sure to place your rain gauge in an open space, a little off the ground and away from trees if possible.

On the Weather Watcher page in your Student Notebook, write down today's date and the temperature. Do the same thing tomorrow. If it rains, be sure to record how much rain falls at your house.

F. State abbreviations can be found on the back of the USA PlaceMap.

F. States
Geography, Thinking Skills, History, Drawings

Look again at the pages about Massachusetts in the *Atlas of the United States*. Then find the State Page in your Student Notebook, and fill in the information.

Make State Cards for Massachusetts by following the instructions found in Appendix B. Massachusetts is a New England state, so be sure to outline the cards in blue.

G. There is no assigned follow-up for the question your student is instructed to ask you. It is, however, intended to be an opportunity for further communication, either written or discussed.

G. Interactive Journal
Language Skills, Thinking Skills

This writing activity is for you and another person, your partner, to complete. Most of the time, your partner will be your teacher, but it could also be a parent, brother, sister, or other family member.

It is your partner's job to write first; then you will answer a question with the number of sentences assigned below. After that, write what you think about what your partner has written. Make sure to end with a question you want to ask your partner, so he or she can write back to you.

Topic for your partner: Tell your student about the time he or she was born. Include your thoughts and feelings as well as details and events.

Your question: What is the first thing you remember?

- at least four sentences
- at least five sentences
- at least one paragraph

H. Independent Reading
Language Skills

Choose something to read that you will enjoy. Then, find a quiet, comfortable place and read for the following length of time:

25 minutes 30 minutes

Be sure to write down what you read today on the Reading Log in your Student Notebook.

Lesson 1, Part 3

A. Copywork & Dictation *Language Skills, Thinking Skills*

Look carefully at your assigned passage below, and read it silently. Show your teacher any words you don't know, and practice saying them aloud. Now read the passage aloud, or ask your teacher to read it to you.

When you are finished copying or writing from dictation, compare your copy to the text and make any needed corrections.

Copy, or write as your teacher dictates from page 18, paragraph 1 ("Mistress Robinson…") in *The Courage of Sarah Noble.*

Copy, or write as your teacher dictates from page 13, paragraph 4 ("Looking at his friend…") in *Ambush in the Wilderness.*

B. Reader *Language Skills, History*

The Courage of Sarah Noble: page 10, paragraph 5 ("The children's…") through page 13

Ambush in the Wilderness: page 6, last paragraph ("Gwayo held …") to mid-page 12.

Read the above assignment from *The Courage of Sarah Noble* aloud, and then follow along as someone else reads the assignment from *Ambush in the Wilderness.*

Read the above assignment from *The Courage of Sarah Noble* silently, and then read the assignment from *Ambush in the Wilderness* aloud.

Read the above assignments from *The Courage of Sarah Noble* and *Ambush in the Wilderness* silently.

C. Read-Aloud & Discussion *Language Skills, History, Thinking Skills*

Abigail Adams: page 10, last paragraph ("Did you…") through page 15

Listen carefully as your teacher reads the above assignment from *Abigail Adams* aloud. Then make up a question about the part of the story you just heard. Write down your question and ask your teacher to answer it. After discussing your teacher's thoughts, write down the best possible answer to your question. Be sure to use complete sentences.

Follow the directions above, and make up an additional question.

Read the above assignment from *Abigail Adams* aloud. Then make up three questions about the part of the story you just read. Write down your questions and ask your teacher to answer them. After discussing her thoughts, write down the best possible answers to your questions. Be sure to use complete sentences.

A. The dictation method enables your child to hear language and correctly write down what he hears. It involves building two different skills. First, the ability to listen and understand what is heard, and second, the ability to transfer what is heard into written language. This process takes time and practice, so begin as gradually as needed to successfully reach the goal of getting the words the child hears on the paper correctly.

1. Read the whole passage, then reread one sentence at a time, giving your child time to write what he hears.
2. After he has finished, reread the passage again, allowing him to double check what he has written.
3. After steps 1 and 2, ask him to compare his writing to the model. As his skill builds, you can move more quickly through the steps, maintaining your child's level of success.

B. The readers used in this unit describe things that could have taken place. Since this time in history included violent or difficult events, you may wish to prepare your children for certain realities of the times that seem harsh, or to edit the content that you read aloud or that your children read independently.

D. One of the most important ways to develop comprehension is to build vocabulary. Becoming familiar with new words by reading, writing, speaking, and listening to them helps the new words become part of your student's functional vocabulary. Understanding the meaning and being able to use each word correctly is more important than merely memorizing the definition.

D. Vocabulary & Spelling

Language Skills, Thinking Skills

Vocabulary:

Write each vocabulary word listed below on an index card. Use a dictionary to look up the meaning of each word, and write it on the card. Then on the back of each card, draw a picture or write a clue so you can remember how the word was used in the story.

courage	**wilderness**	**musket**
settlement	**cloak**	

parchment	**transfixed**	**outsized**
permeate	**outnumbered**	

Spelling:

Look at the words below. Then, in your Student Notebook underline the letters in each word that say *ow*.

scout **brown** **powder** **bound**[8]

Look at the spelling words you wrote in Part 1. If you did not write them in that part, ask your teacher to read each word, and write it in your Student Notebook now. Check your spelling against the list and correct it if necessary. When you are finished, cover each word with your hand, and try to spell it aloud. Then uncover it and see if you were correct.

E. History

Geography, Thinking Skills

The early settlers in America came from several different European countries, but mostly France, Spain, and England. In your *United States History Atlas*, look at the map titled "French, Spanish, and English Settlements to 1776." Notice the large areas that each country claimed. Now look at the map titled, "Settlement by Ethnic Groups, c. 1755." The word **ethnic** refers to groups of people who come from the same place and have similar backgrounds. This map shows that settlers from a few other countries—Germany, the Netherlands (Dutch), Scotland (Scots-Irish), and Africa—brought their own customs, tastes, and religions to various parts of the **territory**, or area of land, controlled by England.

Different ethnic groups, with their different customs and beliefs, made the colonies that were built in English territories quite different from one another. Each group of people, even those that came from the same country, built their settlements around the ideas that were most important to them. For example, the English people who built the colony of Plymouth had very different interests from the Englishmen who built Jamestown. The Pilgrims in Plymouth, more than anything else, wanted to worship God the way they felt was right, without interference from the government. On the other hand, most of the colonists in Jamestown, who were also English, were there to make their fortunes.

Many historians say that in the early years of settlement in America, over half of the **immigrants**, or people who leave one country to settle permanently in another, came to the New World as indentured servants. An **indentured servant** was a person who signed a contract with a company or another person. The contract was an agreement to work in exchange for food, a place to live, and in this case transportation to America. These servants belonged to the people they worked for. But they were different from slaves because their agreement lasted for a specific length of time, usually around seven years. After that time, they were released and often given a small piece of land.

Although a few Africans came to America willingly as indentured servants, most were brought here against their will. They were sold as **slaves** to people who wanted inexpensive workers. Slaves had no rights and were considered the property of those who bought them. Their owners provided food, clothing, and housing in exchange for work. The practice of buying and selling slaves was not unusual at that time, even though many people believed it was wrong to own another person.

Talk with your parent about your family's ethnic background. Then look at a globe or the map of the world in Appendix B, and locate the country or countries from which your family came. Do you know why or when your relatives came to America? In your Student Notebook, write two or three sentences about the things you discussed with your teacher.

Together with your teacher, print and cut out the Newcomer Game Cards found on your Student Resources CD. Glue each one onto an index card, and then decorate the backside of the cards any way you wish (but be sure your decoration doesn't hint at what the cards say on the other side!) This may take some time, so don't worry about doing it all today. Instead, complete this project over the next couple of days. In Part 5 you will be asked to use the cards for a game.

Many settlers who arrived in America were people who could not afford to buy their own tickets on the ships that would bring them across the ocean. They were poor people who were willing to become indentured servants, and give up their freedom for a period of time, in exchange for opportunity. Discuss this practice with your teacher. Do you think it would ever be worthwhile to give up parts of your personal freedom in order to achieve your goals or dreams?[9]

From Dr. Beechick

"A technique to use often is to help children write questions they want to find answers for. Who really did reach the Mississippi first; was it the man our textbook says or the man this other book says? Who is the explorer to be admired the most? What sort of end did each cruel gold-seeker come to? Who profited from their searches? Who were the Aztecs, and where did they come from? Save the questions and write each answer as it is found or agreed upon. Some questions may be unanswerable or at least unanswerable in the time you allot for the unit. You can decide whether those are worth pursuing or whether they should be laid aside for now. Children who learn to ask questions are far ahead educationally from when they had experience only in answering questions, particularly in the fields of history and other social studies."

–*You Can Teach Your Child Successfully*, page 299

Bingo and other game cards are located on the Student Resources CD in the "Games" bookmark.

Discuss the issue of slavery with your teacher. What was different about slaves that made some people from Europe think that they were not entitled to any rights? [10]

F. States

Geography, History, Thinking Skills

Sarah Noble was helping her father make a new home for their family in Connecticut, which is another New England state.

In your *Atlas of the United States*, read the pages about Connecticut. When you are finished, find the blank map of Connecticut in your Student Notebook and complete the following assignments:

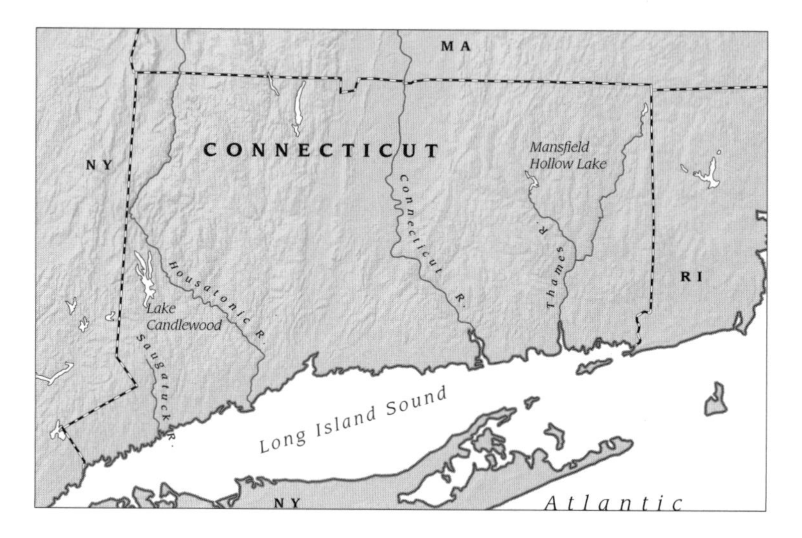

- Place a small star on the spot where Hartford is located, and label it. Hartford is the capital city of Connecticut.
- Color the lines showing the Connecticut and Thames Rivers with a blue crayon, marker, or colored pencil, and label them.
- Find the town of New London, mark its location with a dot, and label it.

Notice the name of the river that runs next to New London. Talk with your teacher about the names of these two things (the river and the city) and how you think they might have gotten their names.[11]

- Color the lines showing the Housatonic and Saugatuck Rivers with a blue crayon, marker, or colored pencil, and label them.
- Color and label the Candlewood and Mansfield Hollow Lakes.
- Label the three states that border Connecticut.
- Find and label Long Island Sound.

Use a dictionary to find the definitions of a sound and a bay, and write them in your Student Notebook. Since both of these words have many definitions, be sure to choose the ones that relate to bodies of water.

G. **Cooking** *Language Skills, Thinking Skills, Drawing*
With your parent's permission and supervision, look in *Eat Your Way Through the USA*, choose a recipe that comes from either Massachusetts or Connecticut, and prepare it for your family. After everyone has had a taste, find out who liked it, and whether anyone would like to have it again. What did you think about it?

In your Student Notebook, draw a picture of the dish you chose to make and write the following number of sentences about your family's reaction to it:

two sentences three sentences four sentences

H. **Independent Reading** *Language Skills*
Choose something to read that you will enjoy. Then, find a quiet, comfortable place and read for the following length of time:

25 minutes 30 minutes

Be sure to write down what you read today on the Reading Log in your Student Notebook.

H. Independent reading provides regular practice for word study and reading skills, as well as time for practice of thinking skills. Quiet time to consider ideas and tie new information with old is essential in building new understandings.

Lesson 1, Part 4

A. **Quotation Notebook** *Language Skills, Thinking Skills*
Copy the first rule listed below into your Student Notebook, and then tell or write what it means to you.

Copy the first two rules listed below into your Student Notebook, and then tell or write what each one means to you.

Copy all three rules listed below into your Student Notebook, and then tell or write what each one means to you. Give an example of each rule from a story, someone's life, or your own life.

1. Be not quick to believe rumors.
2. Do not compare people to one another.
3. Do not find fault with a person who tries his hardest, even if he fails.

Teaching Tip

Use the time your child spends reading aloud to encourage him to read with expression. Reading with expression shows an understanding of ideas as well as understanding of punctuation and mechanics. If your child does not read expressively, take the time to model reading with expression for him.

B. Reader *Language Skills, History*

The Courage of Sarah Noble: page 14 ("She put…") through page 18

Ambush in the Wilderness: mid-page 12 ("That night…") through page 15, paragraph 1

Read the above assignment from *The Courage of Sarah Noble* aloud, and then follow along as someone else reads the assignment from *Ambush in the Wilderness.*

Read the above assignment from *The Courage of Sarah Noble* silently, and then read the assignment from *Ambush in the Wilderness* aloud

Read the above assignments from *The Courage of Sarah Noble* and *Ambush in the Wilderness* silently.

C. Since students do not have to worry about decoding during read-aloud time, they can focus totally on the meaning of what they are hearing. This allows them the opportunity to think about the ideas and information being presented, and to formulate their own thoughts.

C. Read-Aloud & Narration *Language Skills, History, Thinking Skills*

Abigail Adams: page 16 (Chapter II) to the bottom of page 21.

Follow the directions for your level and read, or listen as your teacher reads, the above assignment from *Abigail Adams* aloud. Then, in your own words, tell what happened in your assigned passage below. Try to remember as many details as possible. You may reread the passage or listen as your teacher rereads the part you are to retell.

Listen carefully, then retell page 18 ("Mary shook her head …") to to page 19, paragraph 1 ("By this time…").

Listen carefully, then retell page 19, paragraph 1 ("By this time …") through page 20, paragraph 3 ("I was unhappy…").

Read the assignment aloud; then retell it in your own words.

D. Encourage your child to look at this activity like a scavenger hunt. The examples of each skill could be hiding, so it is his task to find them. If this activity is easily accomplished, challenge your child by asking how many examples of each skill he could find in two minutes. Get your timers ready!

D. Mechanics and Editing *Language Skills, Thinking Skills*

Reread the Mechanics Toolkit in Part 2 of this lesson. Be the teacher and tell when you are supposed to capitalize a word. Then tell when you are supposed to use *a* before a word, and when you are to use *an*.

Use your readers to find examples of each rule and either show them to your teacher or write them in your Student Notebook.

Find a sentence that starts with a capital letter.

Find a sentence with the names of particular people or places capitalized.

Find a sentence that uses *a* before a word that starts with a consonant.

Find a sentence that uses *an* before a word that starts with a vowel sound.

Find an additional sentence for each of the above categories.

E. Science

Thinking Skills

You know that weather affects your life in many ways, but do you know what causes the air around you to change from windy to calm, from hot to cold, or from dry to wet? Most settlers in the New World became very good weather watchers, because they needed to be. Sometimes their lives depended on making the right preparations when changes in the weather were coming. Also, there were no **meteorologists**, or scientists who study the weather, to help them predict the changes

Nowadays, scientists have found that several things work together to cause changes in the weather. These things all happen in the earth's **atmosphere**, which is the mixture of gases that surrounds the earth. There are three things in our atmosphere that **interact**, or affect each other, to cause different types of weather: heat energy, air pressure, and moisture. But in order to understand how those things affect each other, you first need to know a few basic things about the atmosphere. Use the Contents list in your *Weather Facts* book to find the sections entitled "What is the atmosphere?" and "Where the weather is," and read them with your teacher.

As you have read, Earth's atmosphere has five different layers. The bottom layer, called the **troposphere**, is especially important to life on Earth. This is mainly because it contains a thick, heavy mixture of gases, including the ones that humans, animals, and plants need to live. In other words, it is the air that you breathe—and in most places it contains just the right amount of oxygen for your body. As a person goes higher in the troposphere, the thinner and chillier the air is, and the less oxygen there is. That is why it is usually cooler, and often harder to catch your breath, at the top of a mountain. The troposphere is also where almost all weather happens.

The **stratosphere** is the next layer, and it is very calm. For that reason, this is where jet aircraft usually fly. The air is extremely thin, so people need to have their own supply of oxygen if they travel into this layer. But the stratosphere contains something very important to life on earth, the ozone layer. Ozone is an unusual type of oxygen molecule that forms its own layer inside the stratosphere. The ozone layer absorbs energy from the sun that could damage the Earth.

The layer above the stratosphere is called the **mesosphere**. Scientists know less about it than any other part of the Earth's atmosphere. This is because it is too high for weather balloons and planes to reach, and too low for the satellites that **orbit**, or circle, Earth. That makes it very difficult to measure and study the mesosphere. One thing scientists do know is that many meteors and other objects that enter Earth's atmosphere from space burn up in this layer. This is true even though the top of the mesosphere is the coldest part of the atmosphere. Temperatures there have been measured at more than 160 degrees colder than the freezing point of water!

The **thermosphere**, which is above the mesosphere, is the area where satellites and the International Space Station orbit. It has so little air that it is considered the beginning of outer space. It has almost no protection from the sun and is very hot, particularly during the day. The higher you go in the thermosphere, the hotter it gets—from time to time over 3,000 degrees during the daylight hours.

Finally, the outer edge of Earth's atmosphere is called the **exosphere**. It has **traces**, or barely measurable amounts, of various gases, and is the region where atoms and molecules of those gases escape into space.

Look at the Atmosphere Chart below and use it to label the layers of the atmosphere on the blank chart in your Student Notebook. If you want, use colored pencils to color the layers of the atmosphere as follows:.

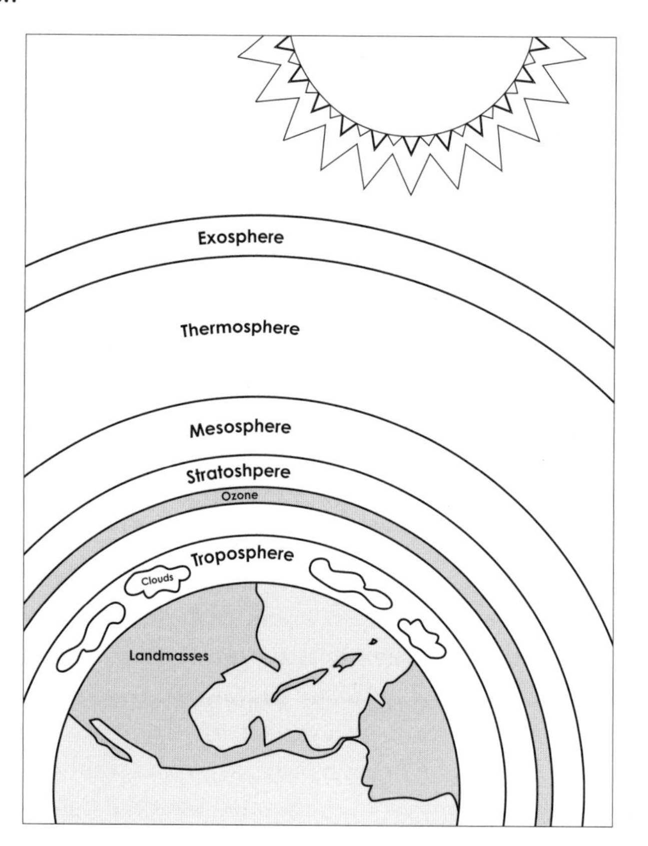

troposphere - light blue
ozone layer - red
thermosphere - darker purple
stratosphere - light purple
mesosphere - darker blue
exosphere - dark gray

When you are finished, write down one fact about each layer in the spaces provided on the next page of your Student Notebook.[12]

Be sure to record your weather observations for each of the next few days on the Weather Watcher pages in your Student Notebook.

- Write an additional fact about each layer of the atmosphere.
- Write down two additional facts about each layer of the atmosphere[12]. Then, in the portion of your *Weather Facts* book about Forecasting, read the section entitled "Traditional Methods." When you are finished, use the library or, with your parent's permission, the Internet to find two or three sayings about the weather that people made up long ago, based on their observations of the air around them. Find out what each one means, and whether or not it actually helps predict the weather. When you are finished, write the sayings in your Student Notebook, and share what you have learned with your family.

F. States *Geography, Thinking Skills, Drawing*

Look again at the pages about Connecticut in your *Atlas of the United States*. Then find the State Page in your Student Notebook, and fill in the information.

Make State Cards for Connecticut by following the instructions found in Appendix B. Connecticut is a New England state, so be sure to outline the cards in blue.

G. Writing *Language Skills, Thinking Skills*

Dialogue is a helpful addition to writing a story. **Dialogue** is the words spoken by a person or character in writing, in a movie, a play, or a book. Using dialogue every now and then gives your story variety and makes it more interesting. It is important to know how to use punctuation when you are writing the words that someone spoke, which is called a **direct quotation**.

Here is an example of telling what someone said:

> Bob said he was going to the store.

Here is how to rewrite that phrase in his words:

> Bob said, "I am going to the store."

When you write dialogue, you can tell who is speaking and then use words like said, asked, or told. Start with these, though there are many other words you could use as well.

Step 1 - After you say who is speaking (a person's name, or *he*, or *she*) and what they are doing (*said, told, asked*) you put a comma. This tells the reader that the next words will be the words of the speaker.

Step 2 - Quotation marks (") are used to let the reader know that what is inside them are the exact words the person said, so put quo-

Connect Learning to Life

Since your child has learned how to identify and write dialogue, take the opportunity to reinforce this learning naturally by pointing out dialogue in books you or he may read. Look for it in newspapers, magazines or anywhere your child encounters print. Don't pass up natural opportunities to reinforce learning.

tation marks before the place where the words that they said begin. Use a capital letter to start what the person has said.

Step 3 - When you get to the end of what the person said (which may be more than one sentence) finish it with the punctuation mark needed, like a period or question mark. The punctuation mark is part of what the person said.

Step 4 - Close up the quotation with quotation marks. This lets the reader know that the words the person spoke are now finished.

Now, look back at the Interactive Writing you and your partner did in Part 2 and follow the instructions below for your level:

Rewrite at least two sentences as dialogue. Here is an example:

My mom said, "You were the cutest baby in the world."

Rewrite at least two sentences your partner wrote, and two sentences you wrote, as dialogue. Here are some examples:

My dad said, "The day you were born was the happiest day of my life." I said, "The first thing I remember was when I got gum stuck in my hair."

Rewrite at least three sentences your partner wrote, and three sentences you wrote, as dialogue. Above are some examples.

H. **Independent Reading** *Language Skills*

Choose something to read that you will enjoy. Then, find a quiet, comfortable place and read for the following length of time:

25 minutes 30 minutes

Be sure to write down what you read today on the Reading Log in your Student Notebook.

Lesson 1, Part 5

This part is set aside for completion of any work left undone from the lesson, and review of concepts and content. It is also a time to expand the work of the lesson by doing art, mapping, or games.

- Review this lesson's Steps for Thinking, found in Part 1.
- Give your teacher your stack of vocabulary cards for the lesson. Ask her to show you each word, and then tell her the meaning of the word and how it was used in the story.

Each Step for Thinking is a concept related to the content of the unit. As you review the reading, discussions, and activities from the lesson, look for examples of the concepts and encourage your child to do the same. You may want to post the lesson's Steps for Thinking nearby for easy reference.

One of the most important ways to develop comprehension is to build vocabulary. Becoming familiar with new words by reading, writing, speaking, and listening to them helps the new words become part of your student's functional vocabulary. Understanding the meaning and being able to use each word correctly is more important than merely memorizing the definition.

- Tell your teacher what two letters go together to say *ow*. [13]

  Listen as your teacher reads the words that you studied from Part 1. Write each word in your Student Notebook as she dictates it. When you are finished, look at your word list and make any corrections needed. Show your teacher how you did.

- Use the United States map that is near the front of your *Atlas of the United States* to find Massachusetts and Connecticut. Then, on the large outline map of the U.S., draw lines around them with a blue crayon, marker, or colored pencil. Write in the names of the states, and draw small stars to show where their capital cities are located. Next to the stars, write the name of each capital city.

  In the middle, far-right side of your outline map, begin making a **legend**, or **key**, for the colors you use to outline the states. A map's legend, or key, tells what its symbols and markings mean. To start your map legend, make a short blue line and next to it write *New England*.

- Read, or listen as your teacher reads, the story about Thomas Paine in *Profiles from History, Volume 2*. Talk about the discussion question with your teacher, and then complete any other activities that she assigns.
- Use your USA Activity CD to print at least one activity for the states you studied in this lesson. Then add any that you complete to your Student Notebook.
- Complete the Newcomer Game cards that you began working on in Part 3 of this lesson. When you are finished, lay the cards out and discuss them with your teacher. Notice that four of the cards name different types of newcomers—Explorers, Settlers, Entrepreneurs, and Soldiers—and the rest of them name character traits that these newcomers often had. After you have talked about each type of newcomer, follow the instructions in Appendix B to play The Newcomer Game.

Teaching Tip

Success is encouraging. Look for gains made and improvement when evaluating your child's work. Record the number of questions or words completed successfully on student work, not the number missed. Your child understands what he missed when he looks at his paper. To encourage in a realistic manner, point to gains made as a reminder of the importance of continued effort.

Enrichment Activities

1. In your *Atlas of the United States*, look again at the states you have studied in this lesson. Scan the sections entitled "The Way It Was…" and choose a person, place, or thing from one of those sections to research. Use the library or, with your parent's permission, the Internet and try to find out more than what is written in the atlas.

   Then pretend you work for a newspaper, and you have just met the person, seen the landmark, or found out about the object. Write a

Use one or more of the Enrichment Activities if your child completes his assigned work and has the time or desire to learn more. These activities are flexible, so choose the one(s) that seem most interesting to your student. Allow him to work at a level that is appropriate for him, and remember that the learning process is more important than the product.

short article about what you have learned. Newspaper reporters always try to answer the questions *who, what, when, where,* and *how* when they write, so that readers have all the important information. Try to answer those questions in your article, and then add it to your Student Notebook.

2. In the *United States History Atlas*, look again at the map entitled "Early Voyages of Exploration." Choose two or three of the explorers named on the map to find out more about. Be sure to include the countries they came from, the areas they explored, and if possible the reasons for their explorations. Share the things you find out with your family.
3. Find out more about the ozone layer, and why it is newsworthy. Try to look at different opinions before you decide what may or may not be true. Talk with your parent about the things you learn, and then share your research with your family.

Additional Resource:

Sign of the Beaver, by Elizabeth George Speare

If you read this book, be sure to print a Book Review page from your Student Resources CD, fill it out, and place it in your Student Notebook.

Answers

1. town, spout, down, loud

2. Answers will vary, but should include a connection to Plymouth being the colony that the Pilgrims built when they first arrived in America.

3. 1. Many settlers came to America with their families. (2)
   2. Sarah went on a long trip. (2)
   3. It was a cold day when Abigail was born. (3)
   4. Patrick's mother died when he was a young boy. (2)
   5. A tribe of friends to the English were the Iriquois. (3)
   6. Grandmother Quincy brought Abigail a birthday present. (4)
   7. After a battle, many English soldiers were injured. (3)
   8. The Smith family lived in a house in New England. (5)
   9. Settlers from England and Germany came to America with a purpose. (5)

4. Weather: the condition of the air at a particular place and time, including how it moves and what it is carrying (like clouds, rain, lightning, snow, etc).
   Climate: what the weather is like in a certain place over a long period of time

5. Meteorologist: a scientist who studies the weather

6. barometer: air pressure
   thermometer: temperature
   hygrometer: humidity (moisture in the air)
   rain gauge: amount of rain
   anemometer: wind speed
   weather vane: wind direction

7. Answers will vary, but may include specifics about the type of clothes worn, the foods that are available or preferred, activities that are available or postponed, length of days, chores, and so forth.

8. scout, brown, powder, bound

9. Answers will vary but might include things like staying at a lowly job to earn advancement, devoting all one's time to study in order to earn a degree in a difficult or demanding profession, stepping away from a career or occupation for a period of time to raise children, and so forth.

10. Answers will vary, but might include thoughts like: Africans and Europeans were very different from one another in appearance and worldview; since Europeans didn't see things they recognized as "civilized" in African culture, some Europeans might have considered their way of life to be superior to that of the Africans; and so forth.

11. Make a connection between the English city of London, which is located beside the Thames River, and New London which was built beside a river the people named Thames. The people who named these things were definitely from England, perhaps from the London area, and perhaps homesick for the things they had left behind.

12. Answers will vary, but can be found in the information presented in this section.

13. ow, ou

Lesson 2, Part 1

Steps for Thinking

1. Many times, settlers came to America in families.
2. Being part of a family helped settlers endure hard times.
3. All members of a family had a role to play and were important.

Materials

- *The Courage of Sarah Noble*
- *Abigail Adams*
- *Ambush in the Wilderness*
- *Atlas of the United States*
- *Eat Your Way Through the USA*
- *DK Pockets: Weather Facts*
- *Klutz Watercolor Book*
- USA Activity CD
- Ingredients for recipe (Part 3)
- Outline map of U.S.
- Supplies for craft (Part 1)
  - 30" of rope or clothesline, Scissors
  - Masking tape
  - Yardstick, straight stick or dowel rod
- String or twine
- Supplies for weather instrument (Part 4)
  - Glass, or jar, or can with straight sides
  - Clear plastic straw
  - Small ball of modeling clay
  - Food coloring
  - Ruler
  - Tape (clear and duct)
  - Plastic wrap
  - Rubber band

A. Copywork & Dictation *Language Skills, Thinking Skills*

Look carefully at your assigned passage below, and read it silently. Show your teacher any words you don't know, and practice saying them aloud. Now read the passage aloud, or ask your teacher to read it to you.

When you are finished copying or writing from dictation, compare your copy to the text and make any needed corrections.

Copy, or write as your teacher dictates, page 24, paragraph 1 ("Then John Noble...") in *The Courage of Sarah Noble.*

Copy, or write as your teacher dictates, page 17, paragraph 3 ("When he had first arrived...") in *Ambush in the Wilderness.*

A. The dictation method enables your child to hear language and correctly write down what he hears. It involves building two different skills. First, the ability to listen and understand what is heard, and second, the ability to transfer what is heard into written language. This process takes time and practice, so begin as gradually as needed to successfully reach the goal of getting the words the child hears on the paper correctly.

1. Read the whole passage, then reread one sentence at a time, giving your child time to write what he hears.
2. After he has finished, reread the passage again, allowing him to double check what he has written.
3. After steps 1 and 2, ask him to compare his writing to the model. As his skill builds, you can move more quickly through the steps, maintaining your child's level of success.

B. Reader *Language Skills, History*

The Courage of Sarah Noble: pages 19-22 (Chapter 4)

Ambush in the Wilderness: page 15, paragraph 2 ("Patrick didn't...") through page 18

Read the above assignment from *The Courage of Sarah Noble* aloud, and then follow along as someone else reads the assignment from *Ambush in the Wilderness.*

Read the above assignment from *The Courage of Sarah Noble* silently, and then read the assignment from *Ambush in the Wilderness* aloud.

Read the above assignments from *The Courage of Sarah Noble* and *Ambush in the Wilderness* silently.

C. Read-Aloud & Discussion *Language Skills, History, Thinking Skills*

Abigail Adams: page 21, last paragraph ("When the ...") through page 27

B. The reading assignments occur in real literature, and there are several reasons why this is important. Real literature is more interesting, and the language used is more natural. A willingness to read is built as your student experiences the success of reading a real book.

Follow the directions for your level and read or listen to the above assignment from *Abigail Adams*. Then make up the assigned number of questions about the part of the story you just read or heard. Write down your questions and ask your teacher to answer them. After discussing her thoughts, write the best possible answers in your Student Notebook. Be sure to use complete sentences.

Listen carefully as your teacher reads the assigned passage.

Make up one question. Make up two questions.

Read the assigned passage aloud; then make up three questions.

D. To prepare for learning about syllables, which will be covered later, if your child says a word slowly, he can usually hear the division between the syllables. This is an easy way to learn about syllables, much easier than learning the complicated rules of syllable division.

If you or your child would like to add a greater degree of difficulty to spelling lessons, choose words from the Challenge Spelling List (in Appendix A) for the lesson you are on. The words on this list are taken from the literature being read.

Suggested words provide study that focuses on an aspect of language such as phonics, word roots or affixes. These lists include words taken from the readers. Please feel free to add up to five words each week that are particular to your child's needs.

D. Spelling

Language Skills, Thinking Skills

Look at the list of words below. Then, in your Student Notebook, underline the letter or letters in each word that say *o*. A silent *e* at the end of a word makes the vowel before it say its name, which is called its long sound.

hollow load odor wove[1]

Listen as your teacher reads the following words. Then spell each word as best you can, either aloud or by writing it in your Student Notebook.

coast	glowed	go	cloak
narrow	spoke	open	close
tomorrow	odor	petticoats	noble
Gwayo	Ohio	oaks	awoke

E. The study of history that focuses on dates and facts alone can be dry and hard to remember. When events in history are associated through the literature, the geography, and the relevant science concepts, it connects the learning and is much more likely to be retained.

E. History

Geography, Thinking Skills

No matter which European country the people came from, or why they were here, life in the early settlements centered on the family. Just about everything happened at home: school, play, worship, and work. And there was a great deal of work! Whether it was planting crops or preparing food, learning a trade or practicing a craft, making soap and candles, spinning thread or weaving cloth—everyone had to do his part. Children had **chores**, or routine jobs, and learned to help their parents almost as soon as they could walk.

In *The Courage of Sarah Noble*, which is based on a true story, Sarah was eight years old. Even though she was very young, she traveled far away with her father to cook for him while he built their new home. Talk with your teacher about what you think that was like. Is it something you would want to do? Why, or why not?

Read the following saying, and then talk with your teacher about what you think it means:

> Many hands make light work.

In your Student Notebook, write one or two sentences about what you think the saying means, and give some examples.[2]

Do you have chores? Can you think of any ways you could help with jobs done regularly in your home?

In your Student Notebook, make a list of at least four things you could or already do help with around your home. Beneath each thing on the list, write a sentence telling how or when you could or already do help with this.

In your Student Notebook, make a list of at least six things you could or already do help with around your home. Beneath each thing on the list, write a sentence telling how or when you could or already do help with this.

E. Each word in bold letters is considered a vocabulary word. It is a word that may or may not be new to your child. You can write these vocabulary words on index cards and use them for occasional review, but not for memorizing. Give the child the meaning of the words if he doesn't remember. Try to use the new vocabulary words during conversation, and encourage your student to do the same.

Each time your student makes a vocabulary card for this unit, have him write *GP* (for Growing Pains) in the upper left corner. This will make it possible to review vocabulary by unit at the end of the year.

F. States

Geography, History, Thinking Skills

In the *Atlas of the United States*, read the pages about Vermont. When you are finished, find the blank map of Vermont in your Student Notebook and complete the following assignments:

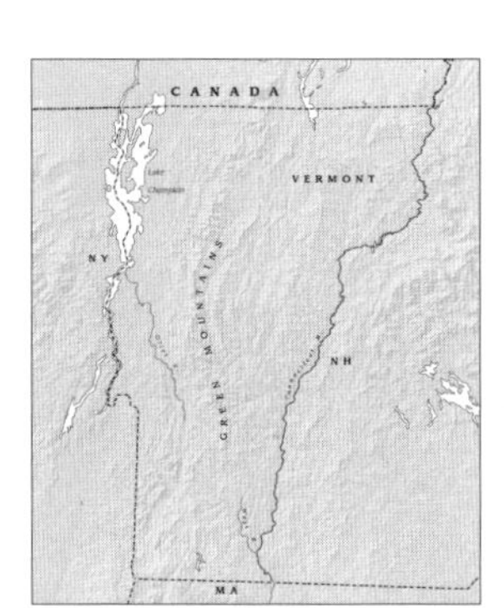

- Place a small star on the spot where Montpelier is located, and label it. Montpelier is the capital city of Vermont.
- Color the lines showing the Otter, the West, and the Connecticut Rivers with a blue crayon, marker, or colored pencil, and label them. In case you can't tell from the map, the Connecticut River runs along the eastern border of Vermont.
- Color and label Lake Champlain.
- Lightly color the area where the Green Mountains are located with a green crayon, marker, or colored pencil, and label them.

Label the three states and one country that border Vermont.

G. Doing

Thinking Skillss

Even though life in the colonies was very busy, after chores and school were done children were often allowed time to do things they enjoyed. Since most families were large, finding someone to play with was seldom difficult. Of course, games were usually homemade because there were very few, if any, stores that sold toys. One very popular game was Quoits, a ring toss game similar to one you might buy and play nowadays.

To make your own Quoits rings, you need the following things:

30 inches of rope or clothesline
Masking tape
Straight stick or dowel rod
Scissors
Yardstick

First, cut the rope or clothesline into two 15-inch lengths, and tape the ends of each length together to form a ring. Next, drive the stick or rod into the ground or, with your parent's permission wedge it between two cushions on your couch. Then toss the rings onto the stick. When you master the toss at a certain distance, try improving your skill by moving back a few steps. You can play this game alone or with others. Award a point every time someone is successful at tossing his ring on the stick.

H. **Independent Reading** *Language Skills*

Choose something to read that you will enjoy. Then, find a quiet, comfortable place and read for the following length of time:

25 minutes 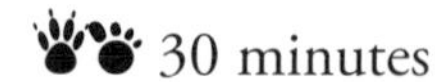 30 minutes

Over time, it's fun to see how much you have read. Be sure to write down what you read today on the Reading Log in your Student Notebook.

Lesson 2, Part 2

A. **Quotation Notebook** *Language Skills, Thinking Skills*

Copy the first rule listed below into your Student Notebook, and then tell or write what it means to you.

Copy the first two rules listed below into your Student Notebook, and then tell or write what each one means to you.

Copy all three rules listed below into your Student Notebook, and then tell or write what each one means to you. Give an example of each rule from a story, someone's life, or your own life.

1. Do not go places until you are invited. Also, do not give advice to others until they ask, and then be brief.
2. Do not try to uncover another person's secrets or be inclined to spread rumors.
3. Be courteous to others by paying attention when they speak and waiting for the right time to add your comments. Also, do not sit while they stand or walk on when they have stopped.

B. Every student should read or listen to all the literature selections for the unit. Reading or hearing the different perspectives adds depth to understanding the events and circumstances of the times.

B. **Reader** *Language Skills, History*

The Courage of Sarah Noble: page 23 (Chapter 5) through page 26
Ambush in the Wilderness: page 19 ("The twin boys…") through page 22

Read the above assignment from *The Courage of Sarah Noble* aloud, and then follow along as someone else reads the assignment from *Ambush in the Wilderness*.

Read the above assignment from *The Courage of Sarah Noble* silently, and then read the assignment from *Ambush in the Wilderness* aloud.

Read the above assignments from *The Courage of Sarah Noble* and *Ambush in the Wilderness* silently.

C. **Read-Aloud & Narration** *Language Skills, History, Thinking Skills*

Abigail Adams: page 28 ("Father looked…") through page 35, paragraph 1

Follow the directions for your level and read, or listen as your teacher reads, the above assignment from *Abigail Adams* aloud. Then, in your own words, tell what happened in your assigned passage below. Try to remember as many details as possible. You may reread the passage or listen as your teacher rereads the part you are to retell.

Listen carefully, then retell page 32, paragraph 6 ("Father was up on his feet…") to the bottom of page 33 ("Why, Nabby? …").

Listen carefully, then retell pages 32 ("Abigail has never complained,"…) through 34 ("It's a lovely…").

Read the assignment aloud; then retell it in your own words.

D. **Mechanics and Editing** *Language Skills, Thinking Skills*

Mechanics are people who are good at fixing machines and engines and making them work better. You are going to continue to become a writing mechanic by correcting punctuation, words and sentences and making them work better.

Mechanics Toolkit

1A - Capitalize particular things, and titles when used with the name of a person.

We are going to visit the *Statue of Liberty.*
I was sick, so we went to see *Dr. Smith.*

1B - Every sentence ends with a punctuation mark, such as a period for a sentence that tells you something.

We will go to the movies on Saturday.
The party starts at one o'clock.

2A - Use the word *their* to show that something belongs to a group.

Please give *their* toys back to the boys.
Our friends left *their* bikes at my house.

2B - Use the word *they're* as a contraction of the words they are.

They're going to the game with Sam.
Bill and Bob don't have a football so *they're* going to buy one.

2C - Use the word *there* to show placement.

We will put the new trees *there*.

I cannot be *there* on time.

D. The small superscript numbers that appear after some of the questions in this lesson refer to answers found in the answer key, which is located immediately after Part 5.

Practice these skills by correcting the sentences in your Student Notebook.[3] The number of errors in each sentence is listed after the sentence in parentheses. To show that a letter needs to be capitalized, make three lines (≡) under it. To replace an incorrect word with a correct word, draw a line through the incorrect word and write the correct word above it. Add any needed punctuation.

E. Science

Thinking Skills

Have you ever noticed that it is always warmer when the sun is out? This is because the sun provides most of Earth's energy in the form of heat. Heat energy is one of the things that interact with the atmosphere to help cause changes in weather.

Another name for heat energy is **radiant energy**, because it radiates from the sun in invisible waves. These **radiation** waves travel in straight lines through space. When they bump into tiny molecules in the atmosphere, however, many of them can be seen as light. Others remain invisible. Together with your teacher, read and discuss the section entitled "Absorbing Heat" in your *Weather Facts* book.

The Earth and its atmosphere interact with radiant energy in a few different ways. First, as heat waves reach the atmosphere, some of them hit water molecules and dust particles. When that happens, a few of the rays are reflected back into space, and the rest of them are scattered around in the air.

Second, some of the waves are **absorbed**, or soaked up, by the ozone layer and clouds. In fact, the ozone layer absorbs most of the invisible kind of heat waves, which are called **ultraviolet**. This is a good thing, because a little ultraviolet heat is helpful, but too much can be harmful. Ultraviolet heat waves cause sunburn.

Finally, the remaining heat waves make it all the way to the Earth's surface, where they are absorbed, or soaked up. Of course, radiant energy warms the ground when it is absorbed, but the process does not end there! Air that passes over the warmed ground is heated up. This direct transfer of heat from one substance (the ground) to another (the air) is **conduction**. In this part's reading assignment from *Ambush in the Wilderness*, Aunt Netta hung a pot over the fire to cook dinner. The fire's radiant energy heated the pot, and the pot heated the food that was in it. That is a good example of conduction.

When air close to the earth is heated it becomes less **dense**, or thick and tightly packed, and begins to rise. As the warm air travels upward, denser cool air sinks down to take its place. Then the new air heats and begins its trip upward, and so on. This process of warm air rising and cool air sinking is **convection**. Again, using the above example from *Ambush in the Wilderness*, while Aunt Netta was cooking if the liquid in her pot began to boil, it would be a good example of convection heating. This is because when something boils, bubbles push the hottest parts to the top and cooler liquid fills in the space at the bottom. This happens again and again, very quickly.

An example of heat carried by radiation waves is when Patrick, in *Ambush in the Wilderness*, stood in front of the fireplace to get warm. If you have ever done something like this, you know that the heat from the fire travels out in straight lines and warms only the part of a person that is facing the fireplace. But the other side of the person remains cold, and in order to warm it he has to turn around. When you placed your thermometer outdoors in the last lesson, the directions said to hang it where it would not be in direct sunlight. This is because a thermometer is supposed to measure the temperature of the air. If you put it in direct sunlight, it will mostly measure the sun's radiant heat energy that hits it.

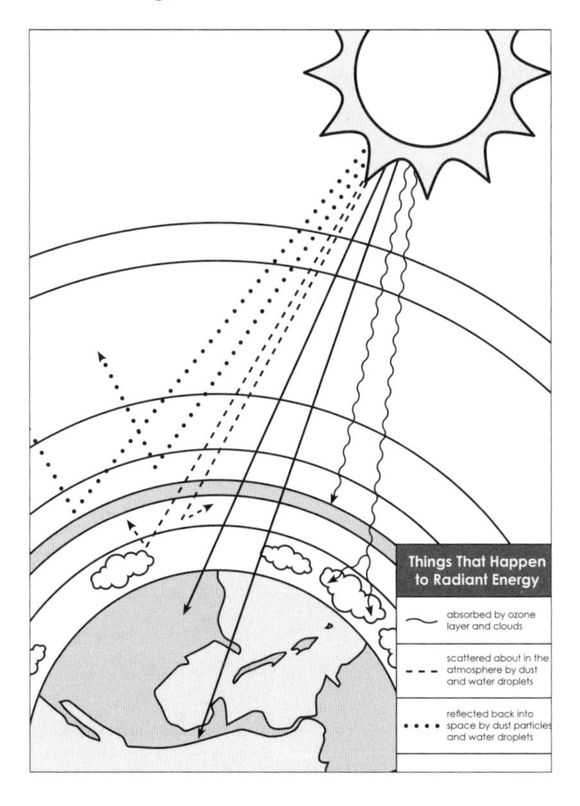

To help understand what radiation waves look like, use a piece of string that is at least 36 inches long. Ask someone to hold one end while you hold the other, and stretch it tightly against a table or another flat surface. Flick the end of the string with your finger, and notice its vibration. It doesn't stay in the place where you created it by flicking the string, but moves all the way to the other end. This is similar to what a long radiation wave looks like. Long radiation waves become the type of light you can see in the atmosphere.

Now flick the string several times very quickly, and notice how the short vibrations follow each other down the string. These vibrations are similar to the type of radiation waves that remain invisible.

Look at the chart pictured on the previous page, and notice the different things that happen to radiant energy as it approaches earth. Then, in your Student Notebook turn to the Atmosphere Chart that you labeled in Part 4 of Lesson 1. Use a ruler or straight edge to add the lines you see below to your Atmosphere Chart. Use different types of lines, like those pictured on this page, to show each type of thing that happens to the sun's radiation in our atmosphere.

At the bottom of the chart, create a key for the lines you have added. Remember, a key helps people understand the markings on a map, chart, or diagram. To make your key, draw a small line like each one you used, and then write a short explanation of what each type of line shows.

There are three different ways that heat is transferred from one place to another. They are radiation, conduction, and convection. Describe each one to your teacher. Then try to think of one or two examples of each type of heat transfer and talk about them with your teacher.[4] When you are finished, fill in the blanks on the Heat Transfer page in your Student Notebook.[5]

Be sure to record your weather observations for today and tomorrow on the Weather Watcher pages in your Student Notebook.

At the library or, with your parent's permission, on the Internet find out about the greenhouse effect. When you are finished, write at least three facts about this process in your Student Notebook. Share what you learn with your family.

From Dr. Beechick

"If you're asking about the communication level of writing, that is a longer teaching problem. I think we complicate it by using the term "creative writing," because then we think a sort of magic should happen in the brain to produce original thoughts on paper. But put something in the brain first. After your child experiences something or reads something, then you can help him develop his thoughts by conversing with him. After that preparation, he should find it easier to write it down."

– *The Homeschool Answer Book*, page 105

F. **States** *Geography, Thinking Skills, Drawing*

Look again at the pages about Vermont in your *Atlas of the United States* Then find the State Page in your Student Notebook, and fill in the information.

Make State Cards for Vermont by following the instructions found in Appendix B. Vermont is a New England state, so be sure to outline the cards in blue.

G. **Interactive Journal** *Language Skills, Thinking Skills*

Complete this writing activity with your partner.

It is your partner's job to write first; then you will answer a question with the number of sentences assigned below. After that, write several sentences telling what you think about what your partner has written. Make sure to end with a question you want to ask your partner, so he or she can write back to you.

Topic for your partner: In your read-aloud story, *Abigail Adams*, Abigail's grandmother had very particular ideas about the role, or what was expected, of women in the world at that time. Tell your student what you believe the role of women is in the world today.

Your question: Tell what you admire, or think highly of, about an important woman in your life, such as your mother.

at least four sentences

at least five sentences

at least one paragraph

H. **Independent Reading** *Language Skills*

Choose something to read that you will enjoy. Then, find a quiet, comfortable place and read for the following length of time:

25 minutes 30 minutes

Be sure to write down what you read today on the Reading Log in your Student Notebook.

Lesson 2, Part 3

A. **Copywork & Dictation** *Language Skills, Thinking Skills*

Look carefully at your assigned passage below, and read it silently. Show your teacher any words you don't know, and practice saying them aloud. Now read the passage aloud, or ask your teacher to read it to you.

When you are finished copying or writing from dictation, compare your copy to the text and make any needed corrections.

Copy, or write as your teacher dictates, page 26, paragraph 5 ("Keep up your courage…") and page 27, paragraph 1 ("The Lord did not…") in *The Courage of Sarah Noble.*

Copy, or write as your teacher dictates, page 23, paragraph 5 ("Netta, we may not…") in *Ambush in the Wilderness.*

B. **Reader** *Language Skills, History*

The Courage of Sarah Noble: page 27 ("The Lord…") through page 32
Ambush in the Wilderness: page 23 ("By late April…") through the top of page 26

Read the above assignment from *The Courage of Sarah Noble* aloud, and then follow along as someone else reads the assignment from *Ambush in the Wilderness*.

Read the above assignment from *The Courage of Sarah Noble* silently, and then read the assignment from *Ambush in the Wilderness* aloud.

Read the above assignments from *The Courage of Sarah Noble* and *Ambush in the Wilderness* silently.

C. In the give-and-take of discussion, you can listen to your student's understanding of the passage, ask questions, and share your thoughts. All of these combine to expand his thinking on the topic.

C. Read-Aloud & Discussion

Language Skills, History, Thinking Skills

Abigail Adams: page 35, paragraph 2 ("That night...") through page 40, paragraph 7

Follow the directions for your level and read or listen to the assignment from *Abigail Adams*. Then ask your teacher to read the discussion questions. Think about what you know from the story, and answer in your own words. Give any examples you can think of from the story that help show your answer.

Listen carefully as your teacher reads the above assignment from *Abigail Adams*.

Read the above assignment from *Abigail Adams* aloud.

Discussion Questions: What is going to happen at Grandmother's house that Abigail is excited about? What did Grandmother think the roles of women were in the world? Do you think Abigail agreed with Grandmother's ideas? Did she also have ideas of her own?

D. The goal of the spelling assignments is to improve your student's ability to spell by helping him make connections to meaning, phonics, and word patterns. Memorizing a list is not as valuable to students as increasing their ability to comfortably write words that express their understanding and opinions.

D. Vocabulary & Spelling

Language Skills, Thinking Skillss

Write each vocabulary word listed below on an index card. Use a dictionary to look up the meaning of each word, and write it on the card. Then on the back of each card, draw a picture or write a clue so you can remember how the word was used in the story.

johnnycake **porridge** **palisade**
impatience **namesake**

drought **poppycock** **trilling**
trencher **linsey-woolsey**

Look at the words below. Then, in your Student Notebook, underline the letter or letters in each word that say *o*.

sparrow code roast over[6]

Look at the spelling words you wrote in Part 1. If you did not write them in that part, ask your teacher to read each word, and write it in your Student Notebook now. Check your spelling against the list and correct it if necessary. When you are finished, cover each word with your hand, and try to spell it aloud. Then uncover it and see if you were correct.

E. History *Geography, Thinking Skills*

By the early 1700s, nine out of ten families in America lived on farms, which were usually small and built on the outskirts of towns and villages. Most of the farms could produce enough food for the family, with some left over to sell or trade. Boys learned the things they needed to know by working alongside their fathers, and girls learned from their mothers.

E. New vocabulary words appear in the context of a lesson or story, which helps student recognize the connection between the way a word is used and its meaning. This is an important reading strategy called using context clues.

Very often, by the time a boy was ten he knew how to plow, plant, harvest crops, and take care of the farm animals. He could clean, load, and shoot a gun to hunt for food, and chop wood for the fireplace. If he and his parents decided he should learn a skill other than farming, by this age he had become an apprentice to a tradesman. An **apprentice** is someone who works for another person in exchange for training in that person's trade. Becoming an apprentice involved signing a legal contract that agreed to the number of years of training, and often required the boy to leave home to live with the tradesman and his family.

A girl in the household, at about the same age, knew how to clean, cook, bake, and tend to the garden. She could also make soap, candles, butter, and cheese, and was learning how to weave cloth and sew clothes. Occasionally, girls became apprentices and learned skills such as making hats or wigs, but that was very rare.

If the family lived in New England, learning to read and write was more important than it was in some other areas of the country. The Puritans who had settled there believed that people needed to be able to read the Bible. Because of that, their law said that every settlement with at least 50 families had to open a school. Of course many families lived in much smaller settlements, and some lived far from other people. In those homes, if the parents thought that education was important, the mother homeschooled. Often there were no books in the house except a Bible, so children learned to read and write by copying scripture verses.

Suppose you had only one book in your school. Which book do you think it should be, and why would you choose that one? Can you

think of any reasons why getting an education nowadays might be important? If you can, what are they? Have you ever considered what you will do for a living when you are grown? If so, what? What do you think you can do to prepare for your future?[7]

After discussing these things with your teacher, write two or three sentences in your Student Notebook that tell your thoughts about these questions.

When you are finished, look at the Tradesman List on the next page of your Student Notebook. Sometimes the name of a trade describes what it is, but other times it is very difficult to know exactly what a trade is just by looking at its name. If you have never heard of one of the trades, try looking up its name in a dictionary. Then match each trade with its description.[8]

F. States *Geography, History, Thinking Skills*

In the *Atlas of the United States,* read the pages about New Hampshire. When you are finished, find the blank map of New Hampshire in your Student Notebook and complete the following assignments.

- Place a small star on the spot where Concord is located, and label it. Concord is the capital city of New Hampshire.
- Color the lines showing the Merrimack, the Pemigewasset, and the Connecticut Rivers with a blue crayon, marker, or colored pencil, and label them. In case you can't tell from the map, the Connecticut River runs along the western border of New Hampshire.
- Color and label the Umbagog and Winnipesaukee lakes.
- Lightly color the area where the White Mountains are located with a green crayon, marker, or colored pencil, and label them.
- Label the three states and one country that border New Hampshire.

G. Cooking *Language Skills, Thinking Skills, Drawing*

With your parent's permission and supervision, look in *Eat Your Way Through the USA*, choose a recipe that comes from either Vermont or New Hampshire, and prepare it for your family. After everyone has had a taste, find out who liked it, and whether anyone would like to have it again. What did you think about it?

In your Student Notebook, draw a picture of the dish you chose to make and write the following number of sentences about your family's reaction to it:

two sentences | three sentences | four sentences

H. **Independent Reading** *Language Skills*

Choose something to read that you will enjoy. Then, find a quiet, comfortable place and read for the following length of time:

25 minutes | 30 minutes

Be sure to write down what you read today on the Reading Log in your Student Notebook.

H. Completing the reading log each day gives your student a sense of accomplishment, as well as the opportunity to work independently.

Lesson 2, Part 4

A. **Quotation Notebook** *Language Skills, Thinking Skills*

Copy the first rule listed below into your Student Notebook, and then tell or write what it means to you.

Copy the first two rules listed below into your Student Notebook, and then tell or write what each one means to you.

Copy all three rules listed below into your Student Notebook, and then tell or write what each one means to you. Give an example of each rule from a story, someone's life, or your own life.

1. Read no books or papers in the presence of others, unless it is necessary. Do not look over the shoulder of someone writing a letter.
2. Speak calmly and use good judgment when you discuss a problem with someone.
3. Do not take on more than you can handle, but be careful to keep your promises.

B. **Reader** *Language Skills, History*

The Courage of Sarah Noble: pages 33-38 (Chapter 7)
Ambush in the Wilderness: page 26, paragraph 1 ("Above the steady …") through page 28

B. When your child reads, make a list of any words he has trouble with. Look for possible patterns to his mistakes, and before your next session review those words with him. You may read them aloud, or ask him to do so.

Read the above assignment from *The Courage of Sarah Noble* aloud, and then follow along as someone else reads the assignment from *Ambush in the Wilderness.*

Read the above assignment from *The Courage of Sarah Noble* silently, and then read the assignment from *Ambush in the Wilderness* aloud.

Read the above assignments from *The Courage of Sarah Noble* and *Ambush in the Wilderness* silently.

C. Since students do not have to worry about decoding during read-aloud time, they can focus totally on the meaning of what they are hearing. This allows them the opportunity to think about the ideas and information being presented, and to formulate their own thoughts.

C. Read-Aloud & Narration

Language Skills, History, Thinking Skills

Abigail Adams: page 40, paragraph 8 ("My cousin…") through page 47, paragraph 2

Follow the directions for your level and read, or listen as your teacher reads, the above assignment from *Abigail Adams*. Then, in your own words, tell what happened in your assigned passage below. Try to remember as many details as possible. You may reread the passage or listen as your teacher rereads the part you are to retell.

Listen carefully, then retell page 42, paragraph 4 ("Our new prime minister …") through page 43, paragraph 7 ("Then Grandfather went…").

Listen carefully, then retell page 40, paragraph 8 ("My cousin Dorothy …") through page 43, paragraph 7 ("Then Grandfather went…").

Read the assignment aloud; then retell it in your own words.

D. For days with several assignments that require writing, you may want to help your student do some of the assignments verbally, or have him type them. Variety in response can help keep students motivated to do a good job.

D. Mechanics and Editing

Language Skills, Thinking Skills

Reread the Mechanics Toolkit in Part 2 of this lesson. Be the teacher and tell when you are supposed to capitalize a word. Then tell when to use the words *there*, *their*, and *they're*.

Correct the sentences in your Student Notebook.[9] Do any letters need to be capitalized? Tell or write which ones, and why.

E. Science

Thinking Skills

A strong pull called **gravity**, which is the force of attraction between two objects, holds Earth's atmosphere in place. This may be hard to understand, but it is easy to observe if you drop a book onto the floor or jump up and down. The thing that keeps both you and the book from floating off into space is Earth's gravity. Of course, the farther away from Earth you go, the less effect its gravity has on you. That is why astronauts are often pictured floating around inside their space capsules or the International Space Station.

Because the air in the atmosphere is being pulled downward by gravity, it presses against the Earth's surface. The weight of the air pushing down is called **air pressure**. Along with heat energy, air pressure is another of the things that cause changes in the weather, because it is not always the same. It changes depending on the air's temperature, how much water vapor it is holding, and how high above sea level it is. *Sea level* is the level, or height, of the ocean's surface. Any measurement above sea level is called *elevation*.

All three of those things—the air's temperature, the amount of water vapor it holds, and its elevation—cause air to become less dense. When air is less dense, its push against the earth is also less. High air pressure generally means the weather is good, because there are fewer things interacting in the air. But when the pressure begins to fall it's a good guess that bad weather is on the way. Together with your teacher, read and discuss the sections in your *Weather Facts* book that are entitled "Temperature and Pressure" and "Air Masses."

When you are finished, read the section entitled "Measuring Pressure." Then follow the directions in Appendix B to make a **barometer**, which is the weather tool that measures air pressure. Making a barometer will give you three tools (a thermometer, a rain gauge, and a barometer) to use when you watch the weather. Be sure to record your weather observations for each of the next few days on the Weather Watcher pages in your Student Notebook.

Together with your parent, watch a weather report on television. If that is not possible, look at a weather map in the newspaper. Pay attention to any mention of high or low pressure areas, and what the weather forecaster says will happen because of these pressure areas. Discuss the predictions with your parent. Over the next few days, be sure to notice if the weather forecast was correct.

F. States

Geography, Thinking Skills, Drawing

Look again at the pages about New Hampshire in your *Atlas of the United States*. Then find the State Page in your Student Notebook, and fill in the information.

Make State Cards for New Hampshire by following the instructions found in Appendix B. New Hampshire is a New England state, so be sure to outline the cards in blue.

G. Writing

Language Skills, Thinking Skills

Journaling is one way to keep a record of thoughts or events. Explorers often kept journals so they could accurately share with others the events they experienced and their thoughts about those events. Journal writing can look different from writing in stories because it is often just brief thoughts. Look at the entry Abigail's father wrote in the record book he kept, on page 29, paragraph 7 ("Weymouth Meetinghouse…") of *Abigail Adams*.

G. If your child is a reluctant writer, he can dictate his answer to you and then copy the answer that you have written down. If your child gets upset about making a mistake in his writing, have him write his answer on a sheet of scratch paper. You can check to make sure it is correct and then he can copy his answer into his notebook.

Write a journal entry telling about your day yesterday according to the guidelines below. Ask someone to read your journal entry and retell what you did. Listen to see if they accurately understood what you did yesterday.

Write at least four lines that include three events, and at least one thought about those events.

Write at least five lines that include four events, and at least two thoughts about those events.

Write at least six lines that include four events, and at least three thoughts about those events.

H. **Independent Reading** *Language Skills*

Choose something to read that you will enjoy. Then, find a quiet, comfortable place and read for the following length of time:

25 minutes 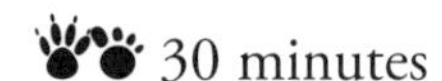 30 minutes

Be sure to write down what you read today on the Reading Log in your Student Notebook.

Lesson 2, Part 5

This part is set aside for completion of any work left undone from the lesson, and review of concepts and content. It is also a time to expand the work of the lesson by doing art, mapping, or games.

- Review this lesson's Steps for Thinking, found in Part 1.
- Give your teacher your stack of vocabulary cards for the lesson. Ask her to show you each word, and then tell her the meaning of the word and how it was used in the story.
- Tell your teacher what letter or letters go together to say *o*.[10] Listen as your teacher reads the words that you studied from Part 1. Write each word in your Student Notebook as she dictates it. When you are finished, look at your word list and make any corrections needed. Show your teacher how you did.
- Use the United States map that is near the front of your *Atlas of the United States* to find Vermont and New Hampshire. Then, on the large outline map of the U.S., draw lines around them with a blue crayon, marker, or colored pencil. Write in the names of the states, and draw small stars where their capital cities are located. Next to the stars, write the name of each capital city.

From Dr. Beechick

"I often say that the number one spelling skill is to recognize when a word may be wrong. While writing along, every so often I say, "Oops, that doesn't look right." So I ask someone, or the spell checker. That failing, I (groan) go to the dictionary.

If you agree that spelling works something like that in real life, you could try teaching that skill. For instance, you could have your daughter go over a piece of her writing and circle every word that she is not certain is spelled correctly. In this case it is not a point off to misspell a word, it is only a point off not to circle it—if you bother with points at all. The circled words will likely suggest to you a variety of useful spelling lessons. Remember that conversation—just talking about a word—is a lesson, as is rewriting the paper to get it correct before Daddy sees it."

– *The Homeschool Answer Book*, page 90

- In your *Klutz Watercolor* book, read pages 13 and 14 that begin with "The Miracle of Discovered Art." When you are finished, work on the activities those pages ask you to complete. Remember, you cannot make a mistake as long as you keep all the paint on the paper (either the watercolor paper or the newspaper that you have put around your book,) so you are free to have fun.

  Over the next few days, if you find you have extra time and your parents agree, play with your paints on other watercolor paper.
- Use your USA Activity CD to print at least one activity for the states you studied in this lesson. Then add any that you complete to your Student Notebook.
- Complete the Growing Pains Word Search located in your Student Notebook.[11]

Enrichment Activities

1. At the library or, with your parent's permission, on the Internet research a Native American tribe from either Canada or the New England region of what is now the United States. If you do not yet have a tribe in mind that you would like to find out more about, choose one from the map entitled "Native American Nations, c. 1750" in your *United States History Atlas*. Print a Native American Profile sheet from your Student Resources CD and fill it out.

   Begin a Native American Notebook by placing the completed profile sheet and picture in a special binder, or you can add them to your Student Notebook. If you started a Native American Notebook during *Paths of Exploration*, you can continue it this year.
2. Together with your teacher, explore the colonial city of Williamsburg's official website at www.history.org. There are many different areas to visit, so take your time and spend several days on this activity. As you visit each area, make notes on a piece of scrap paper about the things you find out. When you are finished, write a report about day-to-day life in colonial Williamsburg.
3. At the library or, with your parent's permission, on the Internet find out what infrared light is and how it affects the weather. How does it contribute to the greenhouse effect? Be sure to share what you learn with your family.

Additional Resources

www.history.org

Teaching Tip

Review sessions spaced out over several days or weeks are the best kind of review to help a child remember information. Reading words, writing words and discussing words all help a child connect the word and its meaning to long term memory. When they can relate it to something they already know, it is even more effective.

Use one or more of the Enrichment Activities if your child completes his assigned work and has the time or desire to learn more. These activities are flexible, so choose the one(s) that seem most interesting to your student. Allow him to work at a level that is appropriate for him, and remember that the learning process is more important than the product.

Answers

1. hollow, load, odor, wove

2. Answers will vary but should include the idea that large jobs are easier when other people help.

3. 1. John Noble went to Connecticut to build a house. (4)
   2. Do you think Sarah Noble was ever afraid? (3)
   3. General Braddock's headquarters were in Virginia. (5)
   4. Sarah missed her sisters Mary and Hannah. (4)
   5. John Noble was going to build a house in New Milford. (6)
   6. The Weymouth Meetinghouse burned to the ground. (4)
   7. Patrick's father traded furs in the Ohio Valley. (4)
   8. The French built Fort Duquesne. (5)
   9. The French and Indian War happened before the Revolutionary War. (7)

1. there	2. they're	3. their
4. they're	5. their	6. there
7. their	8. there	9. they're

4. Answers will vary, but may include the following for radiation—heat from a campfire or fireplace, heat from an electric heater, warmth on your hand in the sun; for conduction—a pan getting hot when placed on a burner, a spoon getting hot when stirring something, finger being burned when touching a hot surface; for convection—water boiling, noodles rising and falling in heated water, steam and air rising from hot soup.

5.

1. convection	2. conduction	3. radiation
4. convection	5. radiation	6. conduction
7. convection	8. radiation	9. conduction

6. sparrow, code, roast, over

7. Answers will vary.

8.

Apothecary – made medicines	Milliner – made hats
Blacksmith – made items from iron and steel	Tanner – made leather
Cobbler – made shoes and boots	Silversmith – made items with silver
Carpenter – built things out of wood	Tailor – made clothing
Weaver – made cloth	Wheelwright – made and fixed wheels
Founder – made items from brass and bronze	Wigmaker – made wigs
Gunsmith – made and repaired guns	Glassblower – made glass, and things from glass
Miller – ground corn and wheat	

9. 1. We are looking forward to visiting the White House.
   beginning of sentence — name of a particular thing

   2. General Braddock was in charge of the English troops.
   title and name of a person — name of a particular thing

   1. period 2. period

   1. there (place) 2. their (belongs to a group) 3. they're (contraction)

10. *ow, o* by itself, *o* with a silent *e*, *oa*

11. Answer key is in Appendix A.

Lesson 3, Part 1

Steps for Thinking

1. Trust is the feeling of confidence that others will do good things for you, or do what they say they will do.
2. You trust another person based on what you know of that person or what he has said or done in the past.
3. It takes courage to decide for yourself if someone is trustworthy.

Materials

- *The Courage of Sarah Noble*
- *Abigail Adams*
- *Ambush in the Wilderness*
- *The Matchlock Gun*
- *Atlas of the United States*
- *Profiles from History, Vol. 2*
- *Eat Your Way Through the USA*
- *DK Pockets: Weather Facts*
- *Klutz Watercolor Book*
- USA Activity CD
- Ingredients for recipe (Part 3)
- Outline map of U.S.
- Stop watch or watch with a second hand
- Materials for weather instruments (Parts 2 & 4))
  - Ruler
  - Scissors
  - Glue
  - Tape
  - Exacto knife
  - Paper plates
  - 2 Push-pins
  - Hole punch or awl
  - Either string, yarn, or light wire
  - Hole reinforcements (optional)
  - 2 Dowel rods or straight sticks
  - 16' Crepe paper, tissue, or ribbon streamers
- Balloon
- Permanent markers

A. Copywork & Dictation

Language Skills, Thinking Skills

Look carefully at your assigned passage below, and read it silently. Show your teacher any words you don't know, and practice saying them aloud. Now read the passage aloud, or ask your teacher to read it to you.

When you are finished copying or writing from dictation, compare your copy to the text and make any needed corrections.

Copy, or write as your teacher dictates, page 43, paragraph 4 ("Once in the night...") in *The Courage of Sarah Noble.*

Copy, or write as your teacher dictates, page 33, paragraph 4 ("Their people were...") in *Ambush in the Wilderness.*

A. Copywork and dictation assignments go from an easier level (designated by) to harder levels (designated by and). Take two days for the copywork if that is more comfortable for your child. Please adapt instructions to your child's individual needs. Your child should be **consistently successful** at one level before progressing to the next, **regardless of grade**.

B. Reader

Language Skills, History

The Courage of Sarah Noble: page 39 (Chapter 8) through page 42
Ambush in the Wilderness: page 29 ("That's nothin'... ") through the top of page 33

Read the above assignment from *The Courage of Sarah Noble* aloud, and then follow along as someone else reads the assignment from *Ambush in the Wilderness.*

Read the above assignment from *The Courage of Sarah Noble* silently, and then read the assignment from *Ambush in the Wilderness* aloud.

Read the above assignments from *The Courage of Sarah Noble* and *Ambush in the Wilderness* silently.

C. Read-Aloud & Discussion

Language Skills, History, Thinking Skills

Abigail Adams: page 47, paragraph 3 ("I was pushed...") through page 53

C. As you read aloud you model fluency, expression, and comprehension. When your voice reflects punctuation, students can see its purpose and the way it makes the passage more understandable.

Follow the directions for your level and read or listen to the assignment from *Abigail Adams*. Then ask your teacher to read the discussion questions. Think about what you know from the story, and answer in your own words. Give any examples you can think of from the story that help show your answer.

Listen carefully as your teacher reads the above assignment from *Abigail Adams*.

Read the above assignment from *Abigail Adams* aloud.

Discussion Questions: In this part of the book, Abigail says she is proud to be English. Why do you think she is proud to be English? Tell some of the reasons she says she is proud. What did she and Grandfather do on this visit that made her feel proud of her English roots?

D. The goal of the spelling assignments is to improve your student's ability to spell by helping him make connections to meaning, phonics, and word patterns. Memorizing a list is not as valuable to students as increasing their ability to comfortably write words that express their understanding and opinions.

D. Spelling

Language Skills, Thinking Skills

Reread your lists of spelling words from Lessons 1 and 2. Write each word on a separate index card. Use a yellow highlighter or crayon to underline or highlight the letters that spell the key sound focused on during that lesson. (Lesson 1, the sound of *ow*; Lesson 2, the long sound of *o*) Then sort the cards into stacks by the spelling of the key sound. Fill in the lists on your Student Notebook page.[1]

Think of at least one more word to add to each category. Make an index card for your additional word and mark the letters in the same way.

Think of at least two more words to add to each category. Make index cards for your additional words and mark the letters in the same way.

E. History

Geography, Thinking Skills

Look at the map in your *United States History Atlas*, entitled "Settlement by Ethnic Groups, c. 1755," which shows the settlement of the United States around the time your stories take place. Where do you and your family live right now? According to this map, was the area where you live settled in 1755?

Place a piece of plain white paper over the map in the History Atlas, and carefully trace it. Then color and label the areas where the different groups settled. Include as many details as you can.

In Lesson 1, Part 3 you discussed your family's background with your parent, and what country or countries your relatives came from. Look at the map you just made, and ask your teacher if she knows any of the places where your relatives first arrived in America. If she does, and the areas are shown on the map you just made, mark them with blue stars. Put your new map in your Student Notebook.

Talk with your teacher about things you have read and talked about so far in the history sections. Compare what you have learned about life in the early American colonies with your life nowadays.

With your parent's permission spend the rest of today, or all day tomorrow, without using any electricity. What do you think that will be like? What do you think you will miss if you do not have electricity? Write one or two sentences in your Student Notebook that tell what you think it will bc likc and what you will miss.

In your Student Notebook, make a list of at least four differences between life in the early colonies and your life nowadays.

After spending time without electricity, come back to this Part in your Student Notebook and write two or three sentences that tell how it went. Was it difficult? What did you have to do without? What did you miss?

Write an additional difference between life in the early colonies and your life nowadays.

Write an additional paragraph about how your time without electricity went.

F. States

Geography, History, Thinking Skills

In the *Atlas of the United States,* read the pages about Rhode Island. When you are finished, find the blank map of Rhode Island in your Student Notebook and complete the following assignments:

- Place a small star on the spot where Providence is located, and label it. Providence is the capital city of Rhode Island.
- Color the lines showing the Wood, Queen, Providence and Blackstone Rivers with a blue crayon, marker, or colored pencil, and label them.
- Find and label the Atlantic Ocean and Narragansett Bay.

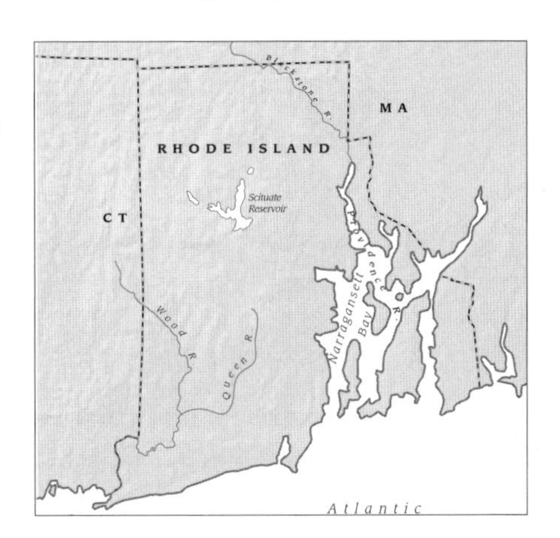

- Color and label the Scituate Reservoir. Tell your teacher what a reservoir is.
- Label the two states that border Rhode Island.

G. Doing

Art

In your *Klutz Watercolor* book, complete page 19, entitled "A Stencil and Splatter Page." Remember, you cannot make a mistake as long as you keep all the paint on the paper (either the watercolor paper or the newspaper that you have put around your book,) so have fun. Then read page 21, which is entitled "My Color Mix Pages," and complete the activity on page 20.

If you find you have extra time this week, and your parents agree, play with your paints on other watercolor paper.

H. **Independent Reading** *Language Skills*

Choose something to read that you will enjoy. Then, find a quiet, comfortable place and read for the following length of time:

25 minutes 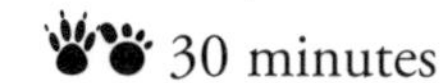 30 minutes

Over time, it's fun to see how much you have read. Be sure to write down what you read today on the Reading Log in your Student Notebook.

Lesson 3, Part 2

A. **Quotation Notebook** *Language Skills, Thinking Skills*

Copy the first rule listed below into your Student Notebook, and then tell or write what it means to you.

Copy the first two rules listed below into your Student Notebook, and then tell or write what each one means to you.

Copy all three rules listed below into your Student Notebook, and then tell or write what each one means to you. Give an example of each rule from a story, someone's life, or your own life.

1. If you value your reputation, associate with upright people. It is better to be alone than in bad company.
2. A person should be careful not to think too highly of himself.
3. Never be glad at the misfortune of another as though he were your enemy.

B. **Reader** *Language Skills, History*

The Courage of Sarah Noble: page 43 ("The pleasant...") through page 48

Ambush in the Wilderness: paragraph 1, page 33 ("At sundown...") through mid-page 36

Read the above assignment from *The Courage of Sarah Noble* aloud, and then follow along as someone else reads the assignment from *Ambush in the Wilderness.*

Read the above assignment from *The Courage of Sarah Noble* silently, and then read the assignment from *Ambush in the Wilderness* aloud.

Read the above assignments from *The Courage of Sarah Noble* and *Ambush in the Wilderness* silently.

C. Read-Aloud & Narration

Language Skills, History, Thinking Skills

Abigail Adams: page 54 (Chapter V) through page 60, paragraph 3

Follow the directions for your level and read, or listen as your teacher reads, the above assignment from *Abigail Adams*. Then, in your own words, tell what happened in your assigned passage below. Try to remember as many details as possible. You may reread the passage or listen as your teacher rereads the part you are to retell.

Listen carefully, then retell page 54 (Chapter V) through page 55 ("There were other pleasures…").

Listen carefully, then retell page 58 ("It was surprising …") through paragraph 1, page 60 ("John Adams came …").

Read the assignment aloud; then retell it in your own words.

C. The skill of narration is gained over time. If your child has never retold a story, start with the assignment for the lower level, no matter what grade he is in. Work up from there, being careful to allow him to stay at the level of success for a while before going to a longer section.

D. Mechanics and Editing

Language Skills, Thinking Skills

Today you are going to review the tools for writing that you have learned. To begin, print the Mechanics Toolkit 1 Cards from Appendix B or your Student Resources CD, and cut them out. When you are finished, place them on the table in front of you, and read all the Rule cards. Then find two Example cards that go with each rule.

You may want to mix up the Example cards to make it more of a challenge, or follow the directions in Appendix B to play Mechanics Toolkit Concentration.

Now continue your review by reading the Rule cards once again. Find two examples of each one in your reader, or any other book. Write the examples you find in your Student Notebook.[2]

Bingo and other game cards are located on the Student Resources CD in the "Games" bookmark.

E. Science

Thinking Skills

As you have learned, when air is heated by the earth it becomes less dense and begins to rise. As it rises, it no longer presses so heavily on the earth, and an area of low pressure is created. Then cooler, denser air, which has higher pressure, drops down to fill the space underneath the rising warm air. This process is convection, and the movement of the air during convection causes winds.

Together with your teacher, read and discuss the sections in your *Weather Facts* book that are entitled "Hot and Cold Air," and "Measuring Wind." When you are finished, follow the directions in

Appendix B to make an anemometer. An **anemometer** is a weather tool that measures the speed of the wind.

Although your anemometer will show that the wind is blowing, it will not show the actual speed of the wind. You can, however, take your own measurements by counting the number of turns the anemometer makes in a certain length of time. Since you decorated the backside of one sail on your anemometer differently from the others, you can clearly see when it passes the mark you made on the handle (the stick upon which it is mounted). Time yourself with a stopwatch or a watch with a second hand and count the turns for 30 seconds every time you observe the weather. That way you can tell how the wind changes from day to day.

Be sure to record your observations on the Weather Watcher pages in your Student Notebook. Don't forget to do the same thing tomorrow!

With your teacher's permission, blow up a balloon. When it is full of air, hold the end tightly. Now place the end next to your cheek and slowly let air out. Notice that the air leaving the balloon feels similar to a light wind. Do you think the air inside a balloon has higher or lower pressure than the outside air?[3] Talk with your teacher about why you think the air rushes out of the balloon.[4]

F. States *Geography, Thinking Skills, Drawing*

Look again at the pages about Rhode Island in your *Atlas of the United States*. Then find the State Page in your Student Notebook, and fill in the information.

Make State Cards for Rhode Island by following the instructions found in Appendix B. Rhode Island is a New England state, so be sure to outline the cards in blue.

G. Since writing begins with thinking, once your student engages in assigned thinking activities, the way is naturally prepared. As you use this approach, your student will begin to see himself as a writer, which is the first and most important step to becoming a writer.

There is no assigned follow-up for the question your student is instructed to ask you. It is, however, intended to be an opportunity for further communication, either written or discussed.

G. Interactive Journal *Language Skills, Thinking Skills*

Complete this writing activity with your partner.

It is your partner's job to write first; then you will answer a question with the number of sentences assigned below. After that, write several sentences telling what you think about what your partner has written. Make sure to end with a question you want to ask your partner, so he or she can write back to you.

Topic for your partner: Tell your student what your family's nation of origin is. Tell about events in your family's history that make you proud.

Your question: What has someone in your family done that has made you proud? Try to choose someone to write about other than the person you wrote about in the last lesson.

at least four sentences

at least five sentences

at least one paragraph

H. **Independent Reading** *Language Skills*

Choose something to read that you will enjoy. Then, find a quiet, comfortable place and read for the following length of time:

25 minutes   30 minutes

Be sure to write down what you read today on the Reading Log in your Student Notebook.

H. Reading fluency is developed through having frequent silent reading opportunities that continue for the length of time suggested here. Since a primary focus of this activity is to nurture your child's enjoyment of reading, help him to choose reading materials that interest him and are at a level that allows him to read with understanding by himself. You can incorporate this activity into your school day whenever it is most convenient.

If the suggested length of time is too long for your child to continue reading by himself, start with an amount of time he can accomplish successfully and make the suggested time a goal.

Lesson 3, Part 3

A. **Copywork & Dictation** *Language Skills, Thinking Skills*

Look carefully at your assigned passage below, and read it silently. Show your teacher any words you don't know, and practice saying them aloud. Now read the passage aloud, or ask your teacher to read it to you.

When you are finished copying or writing from dictation, compare your copy to the text and make any needed corrections.

Copy, or write as your teacher dictates, page 49, paragraph 3 ("Her mother had put…") in *The Courage of Sarah Noble.*

Copy, or write as your teacher dictates, page 37, paragraph 5 ("Patrick crawled out…") in *Ambush in the Wilderness.*

B. **Reader** *Language Skills, History*

The Courage of Sarah Noble: page 49 ("Tall John…") through page 54
Ambush in the Wilderness: mid-page 36 ("The air was…") through mid-page 39

Read the above assignment from *The Courage of Sarah Noble* aloud, and then follow along as someone else reads the assignment from *Ambush in the Wilderness.*

Read the above assignment from *The Courage of Sarah Noble* silently, and then read the assignment from *Ambush in the Wilderness* aloud.

Read the above assignments from *The Courage of Sarah Noble* and *Ambush in the Wilderness* silently.

C. Reading aloud to children of all ages is one of the easiest, most enjoyable, and effective ways to share ideas and begin thoughtful conversations.

C. Read-Aloud & Discussion
History, Language Skills, Thinking Skills

Abigail Adams: page 60, paragraph 4 ("On that picnic...") through page 65

Follow the directions for your level and read or listen to the above assignment from *Abigail Adams*. Then make up the assigned number of questions about the part of the story you just read or heard. Write down your questions and ask your teacher to answer them. After discussing her thoughts, write down the best possible answers in your Student Notebook. Be sure to use complete sentences.

Listen carefully as your teacher reads the assigned passage.

Make up one question. Make up two questions.

Read the assigned passage aloud; then make up three questions.

D. Vocabulary & Spelling
Language Skills, Thinking Skills

Write each vocabulary word listed below on an index card. Use a dictionary to look up the meaning of each word, and write it on the card. Then on the back of each card, draw a picture or write a clue so you can remember how the word was used in the story.

moccasins **tiresome** **outlandish** **wigwam** **outgrown**

provincials **ledger** **allegiance** **detachment** **jabbering**

Spelling:
You are the teacher. Look at the word cards you made in Part 1 of this lesson and tell others what sound the underlined or highlighted letters in each word make.

Then use the word cards that have the letter combination *ou* to write a funny story in your Student Notebook. Make it as short as possible and use all the words. Do the same thing with the words that have the letter combination *ow*. These funny stories will help you remember which words use the letters *ou* and *ow* to spell the sound *ow*.

Repeat the process with one of the ways the *o* sound is spelled.

Repeat the process with two of the ways the *o* sound is spelled

E. History
Geography, Thinking Skills

When Columbus first landed in America, he thought he had found what he was looking for–a water route from Europe to the East Indies. Because of that, it was natural for him to call the people living in America "Indians." The name stuck, even after people realized that Columbus had been a very long way from the Indies. Nowadays though, most Indians prefer to be called Native Americans, which is a much more accurate name. The word **native** means born in or originating from, and that was what these people were to America. They had lived here for many years before European explorers found them.

At first, many Native Americans were more curious about the newcomers than they were **hostile**, or warlike. But both the colonists and the Indians were cautious, and neither group fully trusted the other. They did not understand each other's **worldviews**, or beliefs and attitudes, and therefore could not understand why the other group did the things they did. It was a very uneasy situation.

Right away, some Native American tribes saw the newcomers as a **threat**, or possibly harmful, to their way of life. But others were more **optimistic**, or hopeful. They enjoyed trading with the European settlers for things that made their lives easier, like knives, axes, kettles, and even fishhooks. In turn, settlers liked to trade with Native Americans for things like furs, food, and information that helped them survive in the wilderness. But as time went on, more and more settlers arrived. People began moving away from the coastal areas and claiming land where Native Americans lived, and the threat became very real.

The challenge of history is to understand the way people thought, or their worldviews. The important things in this story are that the settlers believed that America provided God-given opportunities, and the Native Americans wanted to maintain their beliefs and way of life.

In your Student Notebook, look at the ways of thinking or doing things that are listed. Think about each one and then write it under the heading where you think it belongs.[5] When you are finished, follow the directions in your Student Notebook to play Worldview Tic-Tac-Toe with your teacher or another family member. While you play, challenge yourself by talking with your teacher about each worldview you use in the game. Discuss how that worldview might have affected relations with the other group.

F. States

Geography, History, Thinking Skills

In the *Atlas of the United States*, read the pages about Maine. When you are finished, find the blank map of Maine in your Student Notebook and complete the following assignments:

- Place a small star on the spot where Augusta is located, and label it. Augusta is the capital city of Maine.

- Color the lines showing the Kennebec, Penobscot, and St. John Rivers with a blue crayon, marker, or colored pencil, and label them. In case you can't tell from the map, the St. John River runs along part of the northern border of Maine.

- Color and label Moosehead and Chamberlain Lakes.
- Lightly color the area where the Appalachian Mountains are located with a purple crayon, marker, or colored pencil, and label them.

- Lightly color the areas where the Blue Mountains and Katahdin Mountains are located with a green crayon, marker, or colored pencil, and label them.
- Label the state and country that border Maine.

G. Cooking
Language Skills, Thinking Skills, Drawing

With your parent's permission and supervision, look in *Eat Your Way Through the USA*, choose a recipe that comes from either Rhode Island or Maine, and prepare it for your family. After everyone has had a taste, find out who liked it, and whether anyone would like to have it again. What did you think about it?

In your Student Notebook, draw a picture of the dish you chose to make and write the following number of sentences about your family's reaction to it:

two sentences three sentences four sentences

H. Independent Reading
Language Skills

Choose something to read that you will enjoy. Then, find a quiet, comfortable place and read for the following length of time:

25 minutes 30 minutes

Be sure to write down what you read today on the Reading Log in your Student Notebook.

Teaching Tip

Teach your child how to find books that he can read independently. At your bookshelf, or the library, ask your child to choose a book he has not read before. Ask him to scan through the book and choose a page to read. Ask him if there were more than five or six words that he did not know on the page. If so, tell him he may want to choose another book to read by himself. Sometimes children like looking at non-fiction books that have difficult text, but interesting pictures or illustrations. This type of book could be an occasional part of his independent reading time, but not the usual choice. The purpose of this reading time is independent practice of reading skills.

Lesson 3, Part 4

A. Quotation Notebook *Language Skills, Thinking Skills*

Copy the first rule listed below into your Student Notebook, and then tell or write what it means to you.

Copy the first two rules listed below into your Student Notebook, and then tell or write what each one means to you.

Copy all three rules listed below into your Student Notebook, and then tell or write what each one means to you. Give an example of each rule from a story, someone's life, or your own life.

1. Do not correct other people's faults. That responsibility belongs to their parents, teachers or employers.
2. Before you correct another person, remember that your own actions speak louder than your words.
3. Try very hard to keep your conscience alive, because it is a heavenly spark.

B. Reader *Language Skills, History*

The Matchlock Gun: page 1 through page 5, paragraph 2
Ambush in the Wilderness: mid-page 39 ("Patrick marched...") through the top of page 42

Read the above assignment from *The Matchlock Gun* aloud, and then follow along as someone else reads the assignment from *Ambush in the Wilderness.*

Read the above assignment from *The Matchlock Gun* silently, and then read the assignment from *Ambush in the Wilderness* aloud.

Read the above assignments from *The Matchlock Gun* and *Ambush in the Wilderness* silently.

C. Read-Aloud & Narration *Language Skills, History , Thinking Skills*

Abigail Adams: page 66 (Chapter VI) through page 71, paragraph 6

Follow the directions for your level and read, or listen as your teacher reads, the above assignment from *Abigail Adams*. Then, in your own words, tell what happened in your assigned passage below. Try to remember as many details as possible. You may reread the passage or listen as your teacher rereads the part you are to retell.

Listen carefully, then retell page 66 (Chapter VI) to ("In the fall ...").

Listen carefully, then retell pages 67 ("In the fall...") and 68 to ("John smiled...").

Read the assignment aloud; then retell it in your own words.

From Dr. Beechick

"When children can't respond to a request to tell what they just read, it's usually not because they don't know, but because they haven't learned the skills of putting all those pages of reading into a few words. Those are speech and thinking skills. So you could work on these. In the narration system that some homeschoolers use, young children learn to tell happenings in order, and older children learn to select significant items and to relate them, and so forth."

– *The Homeschool Answer Book*, page 83

D. Mechanics and Editing *Language Skills, Thinking Skills*

Today you are going to continue your review of the tools for writing that you have learned. To begin, print the Mechanics Toolkit 2 Cards from Appendix B or your Student Resources CD, and cut them out. When you are finished, place them on the table in front of you, and read all the Rule cards. Then find two Example cards that go with each rule.

You may want to mix up the Example cards to make it more of a challenge, or follow the directions in Appendix B to play Mechanics Toolkit Concentration.

Now continue your review by reading the Rule cards once again. Find two examples of each one in your Reader, or any other book. Write the examples you find in your Student Notebook.

E. Science *Thinking Skills*

If you have ever stood on the shore of an ocean or a lake, perhaps you noticed a strong breeze, or light wind. It is usually windier near a large body of water, because land heats up and cools down faster than water. The differences in temperature over the two areas cause the wind to blow. Together with your teacher, read and discuss the section in your *Weather Facts* book entitled "Seacoasts," and the small portion of the section entitled "Absorbing Heat" that tells about lakes.

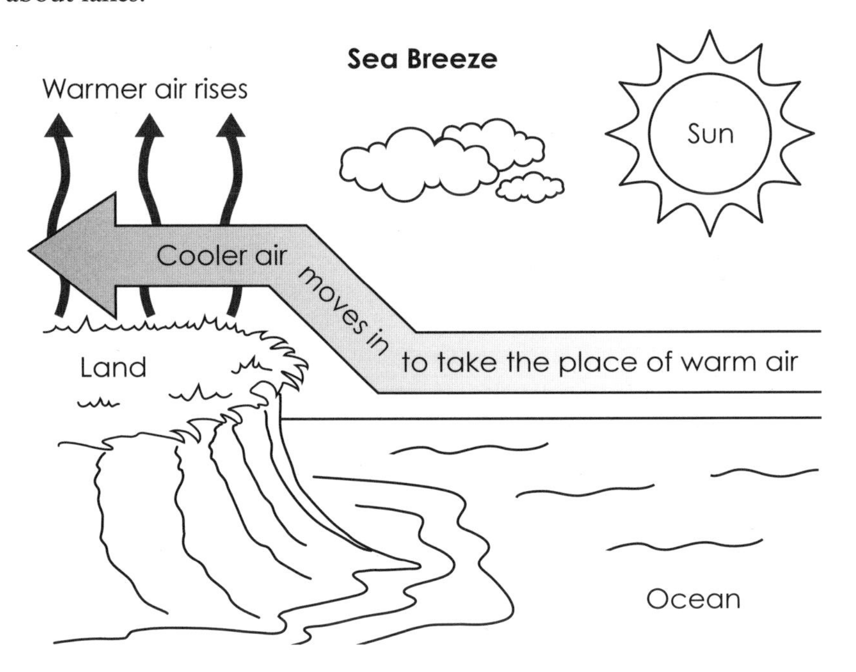

During the daytime, as air over the land is warmed and rises, much cooler air from over the water rushes in to take its place. This flow of air is called a lake or sea breeze because it is caused by the movement of air coming from a body of water. The exact opposite is true at night. The ground releases its heat much faster than water, so it quickly becomes cooler than the water when the sun goes down. As warm air rises from the water, cooler air now rushes from the land to take its place. This air flow is called a land breeze, because it is caused by the movement of air coming from the land.

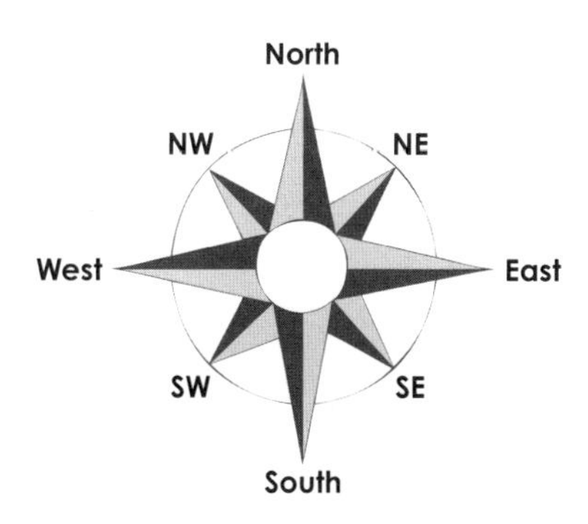

The name of a wind always tells where the wind is coming *from*. You can see this in the examples above—a sea breeze comes from the sea to the land and a land breeze flows from the land to the sea. This is also true of the winds named after directions. Perhaps you already know all about directions, but to help you remember look carefully at the picture below that shows a compass rose. A **compass rose** is a diagram of directions that you might see on the face of a compass, or on maps and charts. It shows where the different directions are located.

When the name of a wind is a direction, it means the wind is coming from that direction. For example, a west wind flows from the west to the east. Find west on the compass rose above, and put your finger on its label. Then run your finger to the east to show the flow of a west wind. Now think about a north wind, and put your finger on the north label. In what direction do you think a north wind flows?[6] In what direction does a southeast wind flow?[7]

Use the compass rose shown on this page as a model to label the one in your Student Notebook. You may want to add color with crayons, markers, or colored pencils. When you are finished, follow the directions in Appendix B to make a weather vane. A **weather vane** tells what direction the wind is blowing.

In order for your weather vane to be a useful tool in weather watching, you need to be able to tell what direction the wind is blowing. This is where the compass rose comes in! Before you can use it, however, you must know where north is located when you are at your house or school. If you aren't sure, you can find out by facing the direction in which the sun rises. That direction is generally east, but not exactly. You will learn more about this another time, but for now you can call it east.

Go to the place where you intend to use your weather vane, and stand facing east (where the sun comes up). If you now hold your left arm out to the side, it will be pointing generally north.

Hold your weather vane so that the part labeled *North* is pointing in the direction you have identified as north. Now you will be able to tell the general direction of any winds that may be blowing. Be sure to use the direction that the wind is coming from when you write your observations on the Weather Watcher pages in your Student Notebook. Don't forget to check your weather station and record your findings over the next few days.

Together with your teacher, read and discuss the section in your *Weather Facts* book that is entitled "Wind Systems." On a separate piece of paper, write a paragraph (three or four sentences) describing what you have learned, and add it to your Student Notebook.

F. States *Geography, Drawing, Thinking Skills*

Look again at the pages about Maine in your *Atlas of the United States*. Then find the State Page in your Student Notebook, and fill in the information.

Make State Cards for Maine by following the instructions found in Appendix B. Maine is a New England state, so be sure to outline the cards in blue.

G. Writing *Language Skills, Thinking Skills*

Earlier in this unit you began learning about taking the words of another person and writing them as dialogue. Today you will again practice doing this. To begin, review the steps you learned in Lesson 1, Part 4.

When you are finished, look back at the Interactive Writing you and your partner did in Part 2, and follow the directions below for your level:

Rewrite at least two sentences as dialogue. Here is an example:

> My mom said, "You were the cutest baby in the world."

Rewrite at least two sentences your partner wrote, and two sentences you wrote, as dialogue. Here are some examples:

> My dad said, "The day you were born was the happiest day of my life." I said, "The first thing I remember was when I got gum stuck in my hair."

Rewrite at least three sentences your partner wrote, and three sentences you wrote, as dialogue. Above are some examples.

H. **Independent Reading** *Language Skills*

Choose something to read that you will enjoy. Then, find a quiet, comfortable place and read for the following length of time:

25 minutes 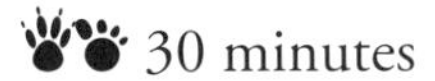

Be sure to write down what you read today on the Reading Log in your Student Notebook.

H. Independent reading provides regular practice for word study and reading skills, as well as time for practice of thinking skills. Quiet time to consider ideas and tie new information with old is essential in building new understandings.

Lesson 3, Part 5

This part is set aside for completion of any work left undone from the lesson, and review of concepts and content. It is also a time to expand the work in the lesson by doing art, timeline activities, or games.

- Review this lesson's Steps for Thinking, found in Part 1.
- Give your teacher your stack of vocabulary cards for the lesson. Ask her to show you each word, and then tell her the meaning of the word and how it was used in the story.
- Tell everyone that you have written funny stories to help remember some of the words that use the letters *ou* and *ow* to spell the sound *ow*, instead of the other sound it can make, which is *o*. Read the stories to them. Be prepared to make copies of your stories if other people want to use them to help remember which words say *ow.*

  Read one of the stories you wrote with the words that spelled the *o* sound.
- Use the United States map that is near the front of your *Atlas of the United States* to find Rhode Island and Maine. Then, on the large outline map of the U.S., draw lines around them with a blue crayon, marker, or colored pencil. Write in the names of the states, and draw small stars where their capital cities are located. Next to the stars, write the name of each capital city.
- Read, or listen as your teacher reads, the story about Samuel Adams in *Profiles from History, Vol.2*. Talk about the discussion question with your teacher, and then complete any other activities that she assigns.

Stories about famous people in history are a wonderful way to illustrate important character qualities. Children naturally enjoy the story format and more easily connect to characters and the events surrounding their lives.

- Use your USA Activity CD to print at least one activity for the states you studied in this lesson. Then add any that you complete to your Student Notebook.
- Complete the Growing Pains Word Scramble located in your Student Notebook.[8]

One of the most important skills your child can gain is the ability to do research. At the beginning levels research can include searching various locations for information such as the library and the Internet with supervision. The next step is to consider the information and decide what is useful to you or relevant to the questions you are asking.

Enrichment Activities

1. In your *Atlas of the United States*, look again at the states you have studied in this lesson. Scan the sections entitled "The Way It Was…" and choose a person, place, or thing from one of those sections to research. Use the library or, with your parent's permission, the Internet and try to find out more than what is written in the atlas.

   Then pretend you work for a newspaper, and you have just met the person, seen the landmark, or found out about the object. Write a short article about what you have learned. Newspaper reporters always try to answer the questions *who, what, when, where,* and *how* when they write, so that readers have all the important information. Try to answer those questions in your article, and then add it to your Student Notebook.

2. At the library or, with your parent's permission, on the Internet research the Coriolis force. If you can, find out what it is, what causes it, and what effect it has on Earth. When you are finished, share what you have learned with your family.

Additional Resources

Guns of Thunder by Douglas Bond
If you read this book, be sure to print a Book Review page from your Student Resources CD, fill it out, and place it in your Student Notebook.

Answers

1. *ow* that says *o*: glowed, narrow, tomorrow
   o by itself that says *o*: go, open, odor, Gwayo, Ohio
   o with a silent *e*: spoke, close, noble, awoke
   oa: coast, cloak, petticoats, oaks
   ow that says *ow*: howl, growling, brown, Logstown, scowl, gunpowder
   ou that says *ow*: louder, house, mountain, ground, count, around, bounce, around, longhouse, dismount
2. Answers will vary.
3. higher
4. The general idea here is that air rushes out because when it is forced to go inside the balloon (by blowing,) the small space it is entering causes the air molecules to become more densely, or tightly, packed together. The sides of the balloon make the air inside have a higher pressure than the air outside, so when a hole is opened the air rushes to the outside, where the pressure is lower. Cooling interacts with air in much the same way as the sides of the balloon – it packs the molecules more tightly together and creates higher pressure.
5. Answer key is in Appendix A.
6. south
7. northwest
8. Answer key is in Appendix A.

Lesson 4, Part 1

Steps for Thinking

1. Everyone has feelings of fear sometimes.
2. If you have a plan for responding to your fears, they will not seem as powerful. Then you may be able to help someone else when he is afraid.
3. People you admire can show you how to handle your fears.

The **Steps for Thinking** section gives you the main ideas about the topics presented. Understanding these helps you to have productive discussions with your children so they, too, understand the bigger ideas. This forms more permanent learning, contrary to just learning facts, which tends to be temporary. These steps are useful prior to instruction, and they are also useful for review at the end of the week.

A. Copywork & Dictation *Language Skills, Thinking Skills*

Look carefully at your assigned passage below, and read it silently. Show your teacher any words you don't know, and practice saying them aloud. Now read the passage aloud, or ask your teacher to read it to you.

When you are finished copying or writing from dictation, compare your copy to the text and make any needed corrections.

Copy, or write as your teacher dictates, page 5, paragraph 1 ("Edward felt…") in *The Matchlock Gun.*

Copy, or write as your teacher dictates, page 46, paragraph 1 ("Washington sat up…") in *Ambush in the Wilderness.*

B. Reader *Language Skills, History*

The Matchlock Gun: page 5, paragraph 3 ("Six-year-old…") through paragraph 1, page 10
Ambush in the Wilderness: page 42, paragraph 1 ("The next day…") through page 45

Read the above assignment from *The Matchlock Gun* aloud, and then follow along as someone else reads the assignment from *Ambush in the Wilderness.*

Read the above assignment from *The Matchlock Gun* silently, and then read the assignment from *Ambush in the Wilderness* aloud.

Read the above assignment from *The Matchlock Gun* and *Ambush in the Wilderness* silently,

Materials

- *The Matchlock Gun*
- *Abigail Adams*
- *Ambush in the Wilderness*
- *Atlas of the United States*
- *Handbook of Nature Study (book or download)*
- *Eat Your Way Through the USA*
- *Klutz Watercolor Book*
- *Discovering America's Founders* DVD
- USA Activity CD
- Ingredients for recipe (Part 3)
- Outline map of U.S.
- Paper cup
- Activity (Part 5)
  - 4 teabags
  - Small saucepan
  - Small, sealable container (½ cup)
- Flour
- Paper towel
- Materials for craft (Part 1)
  - 2 pounds of paraffin
  - 24 inches of candle wicking or cotton string
  - 48 oz. juice can (or similar container)
  - 3-4 quart saucepan
  - Candy thermometer
  - Wooden spoon
  - Paring knife
  - Broom or yardstick
- Weather station:
  - Rain gauge
  - Outdoor thermometer
  - Barometer
  - Anemometer
  - Stop watch or watch w/ second hand
  - Weather vane

C. In the give-and-take of discussion, you can listen to your student's understanding of the passage, ask questions, and share your thoughts. All of these combine to expand his thinking on the topic.

C. Read-Aloud & Discussion *Language Skills, Thinking Skills, History*

Abigail Adams: page 71, last paragraph (We were married...) through page 78, paragraph 8

Follow the directions for your level and read or listen to the above assignment from *Abigail Adams*. Then make up the assigned number of questions about the part of the story you just read or heard. Write down your questions and ask your teacher to answer them. After discussing her thoughts, write down the best possible answers in your Student Notebook. Be sure to use complete sentences.

Listen carefully as your teacher reads the assigned passage.

Make up one question. Make up two questions.

Read the assigned passage aloud; then make up three questions.

D. Read the list of words to your child. If he would rather spell the words aloud than write them, it is perfectly acceptable. As you dictate each word, put small dots beside any misspelled words. Then have your child copy them onto the Student Notebook page.

Suggested words provide study that focuses on an aspect of language such as phonics, word roots or affixes. These lists include words taken from the readers. Please feel free to add up to five words each week that are particular to your child's needs.

D. Spelling *Language Skills, Thinking Skills*

Look at the list of words below. Then, in your Student Notebook, underline the letter or letters in each word that say *e*.

real seem windy chief[1]

Listen as your teacher reads the following words. Then spell each word as best you can, either aloud or by writing it in your Student Notebook. Your teacher may add up to five words that are difficult for you to read or write.

seen	lean	chief	Trudy
reach	windy	knees	inky
thief	beast	Albany	screeches
meantime	agreed	Friedrich	victory

E. One of the most important ways to develop comprehension is to build vocabulary. Becoming familiar with new words by reading, writing, speaking, and listening to them helps the new words become part of your student's functional vocabulary. Understanding the meaning and being able to use each word correctly is more important than merely memorizing the definition.

E. History *Geography, Thinking Skills*

By the time the characters in your readers were born, the American colonies had changed quite a bit. Some of the settlements had grown into large cities, people with special skills had opened shops, and farmers grew enough food to feed themselves and sell to others. Even though Americans were still connected to England, they had begun to form their own customs and attitudes. America was becoming more **self-sufficient**, or able to supply its own needs.

While studying early America, you will often come across the terms Great Britain, or British. **Great Britain** is the name of the island upon which England is located, along with the countries of Wales and Scotland. All the people who come from the island of Great Britain are called **British**. So, the term British not only refers to Englishmen, but also to Welsh people from Wales, and Scots people from Scotland. The countries of Northern Ireland, England, Wales, and Scotland are also called the United Kingdom.

As English settlements continued to grow, the areas around them began to seem a little crowded. There were not as many opportunities for newcomers. The rich **frontier,** or land on the edge of settled areas, on the other side of the Appalachian Mountains began to look very appealing to English colonists who wanted to own their own land. Unfortunately, France had already claimed that land and English settlers were not welcome.

The French and English had never gotten along in Europe, and had gone to war many times. In America, the large French and English territories were right next to one another, and three wars had already been fought over who would control various lands. It began to look as though yet another war was coming.

Skirmishes, or small fights, began breaking out between the French and English, and Native American tribes in the area chose sides. This was not the first time this happened, because Native Americans had taken sides in the other wars as well. The tribes did not believe that France owned the land it claimed, but they were also unhappy about the English pushing further and further west. There was really no good choice for the Native Americans, so some tribes decided to help the English, and some sided with the French.

Use the map above to help you label the map in your Student Notebook that shows Great Britain and France, and then color it.

Notice the fairly small waterway (the English Channel) that separates France and England. In the New World, these two countries competed with one another to claim territories and add to their wealth and power. Talk with your teacher about whether you think this same attitude might have helped cause some of the many arguments and wars between those two countries over the years. Have you ever heard of someone who was very **greedy**, or always anxious to possess more and more? Think about what you might do if that person wanted to take things that belong to you.

F. States

Geography, History, Thinking Skills

Patrick, the main character in *Ambush in the Wilderness*, lived in Pennsylvania, so that is the first state you will study in the Mid-Atlantic region. There are five Mid-Atlantic states, all located beneath or slightly to the west of New England.

In the *Atlas of the United States*, read the pages about Pennsylvania. When you are finished, find the blank map of Pennsylvania in your Student Notebook and complete the following assignments:

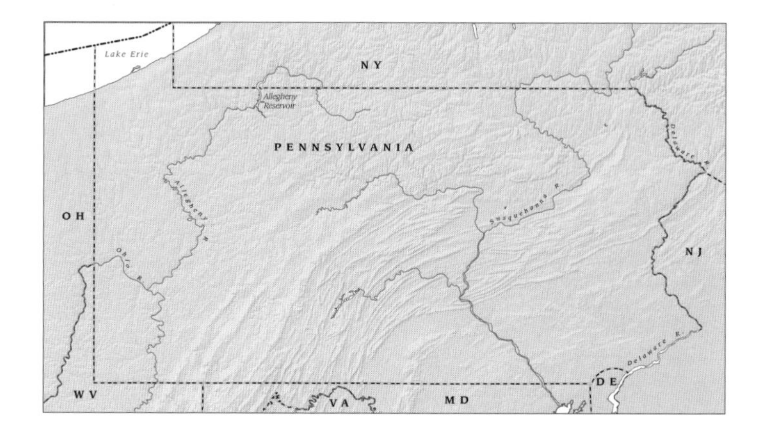

- Place a small star on the spot where Harrisburg is located, and label it. Harrisburg is the capital city of Pennsylvania.
- Color the lines showing the Ohio, Allegheny, Delaware, and Susquehanna Rivers with a blue crayon, marker, or colored pencil, and label them. In case you can't tell from the map, the Delaware River runs along the southeastern border of Pennsylvania.
- Color and label the portion of Lake Erie that touches Pennsylvania.
- Color and label the Allegheny Reservoir.
- Label the six states that border Pennsylvania.

G. Doing

History, Thinking Skills

Making candles was a chore that had to be done every year in colonial times, usually in late fall. Most of these early American candles were made from **tallow**, which is hard animal fat that had to be cooked slowly for a couple of days before it was ready to use. Tallow candles smoked a lot, and often sputtered, but they still provided welcome light.

About a hundred years after the time your stories in this unit took place, paraffin wax was introduced in the colonies, and candle-making became much simpler. Although many people still made candles with tallow, paraffin quickly became the more popular choice.

Follow the directions in Appendix B to dip your own candles. When you are finished, light them and see how they burn. With your parent's permission and supervision, try using candles to light your house for a couple of hours one night. Talk with your teacher about what it must have been like to have only the light from one or two candles and the fireplace every night.

H. **Independent Reading** *Language Skills*

Choose something to read that you will enjoy. Then, find a quiet, comfortable place and read for the following length of time:

25 minutes 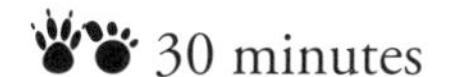 30 minutes

Over time, it's fun to see how much you have read. Be sure to write down what you read today on the Reading Log in your Student Notebook.

H. Reading fluency is developed through having frequent silent reading opportunities that continue for the length of time suggested here. Since a primary focus of this activity is to nurture your child's enjoyment of reading, help him to choose reading materials that interest him and are at a level that allows him to read with understanding by himself. You can incorporate this activity into your school day whenever it is most convenient.

If the suggested length of time is too long for your child to continue reading by himself, start with an amount of time he can accomplish successfully and make the suggested time a goal.

Lesson 4, Part 2

A. **Quotation Notebook** *Language Skills, Thinking Skills*

Copy the first rule listed below into your Student Notebook, and then tell or write what it means to you.

Copy the first two rules listed below into your Student Notebook, and then tell or write what each one means to you.

Copy all three rules listed below into your Student Notebook, and then tell or write what each one means to you. Give an example of each rule from a story, someone's life, or your own life.

1. Do not interrupt when others are speaking.
2. Pay attention when others at the table are speaking, and do not talk with food in your mouth.
3. Do not turn your back to others while they are speaking to you. Also, do not bump the table or desk while someone is reading or writing. Do not lean on others.

B. **Reader** *Language Skills, History*

The Matchlock Gun: page 10, paragraph 2 ("Teunis had...") through page 13

Ambush in the Wilderness: page 46 ("Washington sat up...") through mid-page 49

B. When your child reads, make a list of any words he has trouble with. Look for possible patterns to his mistakes, and before your next session review those words with him. You may read them aloud, or ask him to do so.

Read the above assignment from *The Matchlock Gun* aloud, and then follow along as someone else reads the assignment from *Ambush in the Wilderness.*

Read the above assignment from *The Matchlock Gun* silently, and then read the assignment from *Ambush in the Wilderness* aloud.

Read the above assignments from *The Matchlock Gun* and *Ambush in the Wilderness* silently.

C. Read-Aloud & Narration

History, Language Skills, Thinking Skills

Abigail Adams: page 78, paragraph 9 ("But in September…") to the bottom of page 84

Follow the directions for your level and read, or listen as your teacher reads, the above assignment from *Abigail Adams*. Then, in your own words, tell what happened in your assigned passage below. Try to remember as many details as possible. You may reread the passage or listen as your teacher rereads the part you are to retell.

Listen carefully, then retell page 81("The children still clinging…") through paragraph 3, page 82 ("We walked to the kitchen…").

Listen carefully, then retell page 81 ("The children still clinging…") through paragraph 4, page 84 ("After the trial…").

Read the assignment aloud; then retell it in your own words.

D. Mechanics and Editing

Language Skills, Thinking Skills

Continue your practice to become a good writing mechanic by correcting punctuation, words and sentences and making them work better.

Mechanics Toolkit

1A – Capitalize words such as mother, father, grandmother or aunt when they are used as the name of a person.

We are going to visit *Grandmother* on Saturday.
I was happy to see all my uncles and *Aunt Sally.*

1B – Every sentence ends with a punctuation mark, such as an exclamation point for a sentence or phrase that expresses strong feelings.

Don't run into the street*!*
Happy birthday*!*

2A – Use the word *was* to show that something has already happened to one person or thing.

I *was* on a baseball team.
She *was* the only person with a pet.

2B – Use the word *were* to show that something has already happened to a group of people or things.

Many animals *were* in the jungle.
Bill and Bob *were* on the winning football team.

Practice these skills by correcting the sentences in your Student Notebook.[2] The number of errors in each sentence is listed after the sentence in parentheses. To show that a letter needs to be capitalized, make three lines under it. To replace an incorrect word with a correct word, draw a line through the incorrect word and write the correct word above it. Add any needed punctuation.

E. Science

Geography, Thinking Skills

You have been learning about some of the things that cause weather, and how it affects you. But have you ever thought about how weather affects other things on the Earth? For instance, when you notice that the fabric on your lawn chair has faded, or that your bike has rust spots, you are seeing some effects of weather. Changes like these happen rather quickly to objects exposed to the atmosphere. But man-made objects are not the only things that weather helps to change. The entire Earth's surface is constantly going through a process of breaking down and changing form. This process is **weathering**.

E. The small superscript numbers that appear after some of the questions in this lesson refer to answers found in the answer key, which is located immediately after Part 5.

Weathering was very important to settlers because it is the process that forms soil. As you know, the Pilgrims almost starved during their first years in the New World because they had trouble growing enough food. A large part of that problem was the type of soil in their new home, which was not very good for farming. **Soil** is the top layer of the Earth's surface. It is formed when rocks, minerals, and other materials are continuously broken down into smaller and smaller pieces.

Together with your teacher, read and discuss pages 761 and 762 in the *Handbook of Nature Study*, beginning with the section entitled "Soil Material," and ending at the section entitled "Soil Formation." Take time to use your dictionary to look up any words you don't understand.

In the first paragraph of the section you just read, the author uses the term rock flour. What do you think she is talking about? With your teacher's permission, pour some flour onto a paper towel and examine it. Think about what you know about gravel and sand. How do you think rock flour might compare to those two items? After you have talked about this with your teacher, write what you think the term rock flour means in your Student Notebook. [3]

Now look at the caption under the picture of a rocky stream on page 760 in the *Handbook of Nature Study*. Look up the words brook and mill in a dictionary, and write their definitions in your Student Notebook. Discuss with your teacher what you think the term brook mill might mean.[4] Do you think brooks are the only type of water that does this work?[5]

Another thing that helps rock break down is freezing water. When water settles into the cracks or crevices of a rock, and then freezes, it acts like a wedge. A wedge is a tool that is thick at one end and thin at the other, that is used to pry things apart. To better understand how this works, run a little water into a paper cup. On the outside of the cup, mark the level of the water with a piece of tape or a marker. Then put the cup in the freezer for a few hours. What happens to the water when it freezes?[6] Talk with your teacher about how this would help rock break apart.[7] Don't forget to check your weather station today and tomorrow and record your findings on the Weather Watcher pages in your Student Notebook.

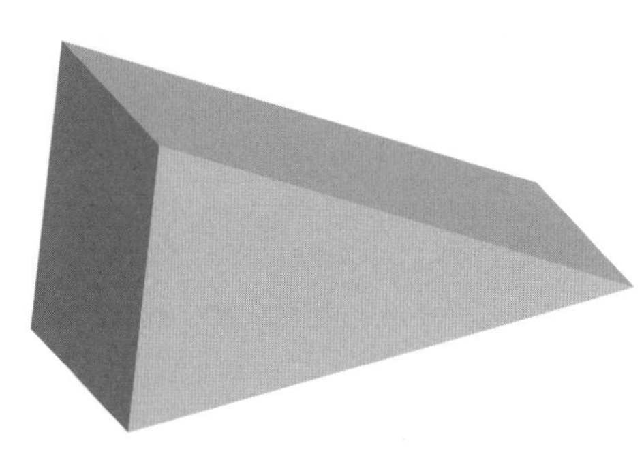

In your Student Notebook, write down three other things mentioned in the *Handbook of Nature Study* besides flowing water that help to break down and move rocks and minerals. Discuss each one with your teacher.[8]

F. State abbreviations can be found on the back of the USA PlaceMap.

F. States

Geography, Thinking Skills, Drawing

Look again at the pages about Pennsylvania in your *Atlas of the United States*. Then find the State Page in your Student Notebook, and fill in the information.

Make State Cards for Pennsylvania by following the instructions found in Appendix B. Pennsylvania is a Mid-Atlantic state, so be sure to outline the cards in green.

G. Writing is not a separate subject, but rather a set of skills with which to become familiar. Writing is best when it is a response to content learned, new ideas, or as a result of an activity or experience.

G. Interactive Journal

Language Skills, Thinking Skills

Complete this writing activity with your partner.

It is your partner's job to write first; then you will answer a question with the number of sentences assigned below. After that, write several sentences telling what you think about what your partner has written. Make sure to end with a question you want to ask your partner, so he or she can write back to you.

Topic for your partner: Tell about important events that began your family such as your wedding, how you met your husband or wife, or any other event that is special to your family's beginnings.

Your question: What do you want to be when you grow up? Remember, you can always change your mind later, so just write about what you think you would like to be right now.

- at least four sentences
- at least five sentences
- at least one paragraph

H. **Independent Reading** *Language Skills*
Choose something to read that you will enjoy. Then, find a quiet, comfortable place and read for the following length of time:

25 minutes   30 minutes

Be sure to write down what you read today on the Reading Log in your Student Notebook.

Lesson 4, Part 3

A. **Copywork & Dictation** *Language Skills, Thinking Skills*
Look carefully at your assigned passage below, and read it silently. Show your teacher any words you don't know, and practice saying them aloud. Now read the passage aloud, or ask your teacher to read it to you.

When you are finished copying or writing from dictation, compare your copy to the text and make any needed corrections.

Copy, or write as your teacher dictates, page 12, paragraph 1 ("The two children…") in *The Matchlock Gun.*

Copy, or write as your teacher dictates, page 48, paragraph 9 ("Sir," he heard…") and page 49, paragraph 1 ("Those enemy…") in *Ambush in the Wilderness.*

B. **Reader** *Language Skills, History*
The Matchlock Gun: page 14 ("She said…") through page 17
Ambush in the Wilderness: mid-page 49 ("Hurry along… ") through the top of page 52

A. The dictation method enables your child to hear language and correctly write down what he hears. It involves building two different skills. First, the ability to listen and understand what is heard, and second, the ability to transfer what is heard into written language. This process takes time and practice, so begin as gradually as needed to successfully reach the goal of getting the words the child hears on the paper correctly.

1. Read the whole passage, then reread one sentence at a time, giving your child time to write what he hears.
2. After he has finished, reread the passage again, allowing him to double check what he has written.
3. After steps 1 and 2, ask him to compare his writing to the model. As his skill builds, you can move more quickly through the steps, maintaining your child's level of success.

Read the above assignment from *The Matchlock Gun* aloud, and then follow along as someone else reads the assignment from *Ambush in the Wilderness*.

Read the above assignment from *The Matchlock Gun* silently, and then read the assignment from *Ambush in the Wilderness* aloud.

Read the above assignments from *The Matchlock Gun* and *Ambush in the Wilderness* silently.

From Dr. Beechick

"If you are thinking about leaving reading textbooks and using "real" books and other self-selected materials, it won't be long until someone says to you, "How will you teach comprehension?" This is not really a question; it's an accusation. "That's dangerous," your well-meaning friend implies. "The textbooks know how to teach comprehension, but all on your own, you don't." That thing called comprehension can intimidate you. If you can't answer your friends, you might retreat to textbooks again."

– *You Can Teach Your Child Successfully*, page 7

C. Read-Aloud & Discussion

History, Language Skills, Thinking Skills

Abigail Adams: last paragraph, page 84 ("Such enjoyment…") through page 90, paragraph 4

Follow the directions for your level and read or listen to the assignment from *Abigail Adams*. Then ask your teacher to read the discussion questions. Think about what you know from the story, and answer in your own words. Give any examples you can think of from the story that help show your answer.

Listen carefully as your teacher reads the assignment from *Abigail Adams*.

Read the assignment from *Abigail Adams* aloud.

Discussion Questions: Why did the colonists refuse to unload the tea in Boston Harbor? Tell what happened during the Boston Tea Party. What was the English governor's response to the Tea Party? Do you think that the colonists were right to refuse to pay the taxes on tea? Why do you think so?

D. The goal of the spelling assignments is to improve your student's ability to spell by helping him make connections to meaning, phonics, and word patterns. Memorizing a list is not as valuable to students as increasing their ability to comfortably write words that express their understanding and opinions.

D. Vocabulary & Spelling

Language Skills, Thinking Skills

Write each vocabulary word listed below on an index card. Use a dictionary to look up the meaning of each word, and write it on the card. Then on the back of each card, draw a picture or write a clue so you can remember how the word was used in the story.

militia **muster** **priming** **flustered** **loftily**

dehydrated **flintlock** **assault** **savages** **formidable**

Spelling:
Look at the words below. Then, in your Student Notebook, underline the letter or letters in each word that say *e*.

keen **leaf** **inky** **grief**[9]

Look at the spelling words you wrote in Part 1. If you did not write them in that part, ask your teacher to read each word, and write it in your Student Notebook now. Check your spelling against the list and correct it if necessary. When you are finished, cover each word with your hand, and try to spell it aloud. Then uncover it and see if you were correct.

E. History
Language Skills, Thinking Skills

Lapbook Activity

Benjamin Franklin was very involved in helping the colonies prepare for war with France. He recognized the threat before many others did, and helped organize settlers into **militias**, or army units made up of ordinary citizens. Even though the militiamen did not train like regular soldiers, they still practiced and drilled so that settlements could better defend themselves. Also, at the start of the war when British troops arrived in America, Benjamin organized the wagons to help them move supplies into the wilderness areas. In your book, *Ambush in the Wilderness*, Patrick and his uncle are part of one of those wagon trains.

But of course, Benjamin Franklin did many other important things in his lifetime. Together with your teacher, watch Episode 2, Chapter 3 on the *Discovering America's Founders* DVD that is about Benjamn Franklin. Before you begin, take a minute to look at the Video Profile page for this lesson in your Student Notebook, and see what kinds of questions it asks.[10]

As you watch the video lesson, keep the Video Profile page in front of you. When you notice that the **narrator**, or person telling the story, is answering one of the questions, stop the video long enough to write the answer on your Profile page. Continue doing this as often as necessary as you finish watching the video lesson.

As you watch the video lesson, use a piece of scrap paper to jot down important things that the **narrator**, or person telling the story, says about Benjamin. This is called taking notes, and is a good way to help you remember what you hear or see. You do not need to use sentences when you take notes—single words or **phrases**, which are short groups of words, will work fine as long as they help you remember the important things. If it is helpful, stop the lesson when you need to, or watch it a second time.

When you are finished, use your notes and your memory to fill in the Video Profile page.

E. As your child learns to take notes, it may be helpful to stop the video at intervals and discuss what has happened or been said. Ask questions that will help him understand the important parts of what he has seen or heard.

F. States
Geography, History, Thinking Skills

In the *Atlas of the United States*, read the pages about New York. When you are finished, find the blank map of New York in your Student Notebook and complete the following assignments.

- Place a small star on the spot where Albany is located, and label it. Albany is the capital city of New York.
- Color the lines and areas showing the Hudson, St. Lawrence, and Susquehanna Rivers with a blue crayon, marker, or colored pencil, and label them.

- Color and label Lake Champlain, Lake Ontario, Lake Erie, and the Finger Lakes.
- Lightly color the area where the Appalachian Mountains are located with a purple crayon, marker, or colored pencil, and label them.
- Find New York City, mark its location with a dot, and label it. Discuss anything you know about New York City with your teacher.
- Lightly color the areas where the Adirondack Mountains and the Catskill Mountains are located with a green crayon, marker, or colored pencil, and label them.
- Label Long Island and Long Island Sound.
- Label the five states and one country that border New York.

G. **Cooking** *Language Skills, Thinking Skills, Drawing*

With your parent's permission and supervision, look in *Eat Your Way Through the USA*, choose a recipe that comes from either Pennsylvania or New York, and prepare it for your family. After everyone has had a taste, find out who liked it, and whether anyone would like to have it again. What did you think about it?

In your Student Notebook, draw a picture of the dish you chose to make and write the following number of sentences about your family's reaction to it:

two sentences three sentences four sentences

H. **Independent Reading** *Language Skills*

Choose something to read that you will enjoy. Then, find a quiet, comfortable place and read for the following length of time:

25 minutes 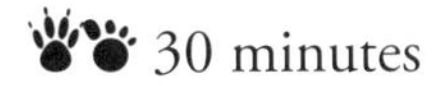 30 minutes

Be sure to write down what you read today on the Reading Log in your Student Notebook.

Lesson 4, Part 4

A. **Quotation Notebook** *Language Skills, Thinking Skills*

Copy the first rule listed below into your Student Notebook, and then tell or write what it means to you.

Copy the first two rules listed below into your Student Notebook, and then tell or write what each one means to you.

Copy all three rules listed below into your Student Notebook, and then tell or write what each one means to you. Give an example of each rule from a story, someone's life, or your own life.

1. Do not eavesdrop or try to find out about other people's affairs.
2. Keep a pleasant look on your face, but with serious matters it can be grave.
3. Receive all correction graciously when it is given. Afterwards, if you feel you do not deserve blame or disapproval, find a convenient time and place to talk about it with the person who corrected you.

B. **Reader** *Language Skills, History*

The *Matchlock Gun*: pages 18-22 (Chapter III)
Ambush in the Wilderness: page 52, paragraph 1 ("Down below…") through page 54

Read the above assignment from *The Matchlock Gun* aloud, and then follow along as someone else reads the assignment from *Ambush in the Wilderness.*

Read the above assignment from *The Matchlock Gun* silently, and then read the assignment from *Ambush in the Wilderness* aloud.

Read the above assignments from *The Matchlock Gun* and *Ambush in the Wilderness* silently.

C. Read-Aloud & Narration *History, Language Skills, Thinking Skills*

Abigail Adams: page 90, paragraph 5 ("Soon John…") through page 96, paragraph 5

Follow the directions for your level and read, or listen as your teacher reads, the above assignment from *Abigail Adams*. Then, in your own words, tell what happened in your assigned passage below. Try to remember as many details as possible. You may reread the passage or listen as your teacher rereads the part you are to retell.

Listen carefully, then retell paragraph 4, page 91 ("John had been gone…") through page 93, paragraph 3 ("You haven't run…").

Listen carefully, then retell page 91, paragraph 4 ("John had been gone…") through page 94, paragraph 6 ("The men quickly…").

Read the assignment aloud; then retell it in your own words.

D. Mechanics and Editing *Language Skills, Thinking Skills*

Reread the Mechanics Toolkit in Part 2 of this lesson. Be the teacher and tell when you are supposed to use each rule and why.

After reviewing the rules and examples, make up two sentences that show each rule being used correctly, and write them in your Student Notebook.

E. Since the language in the *Handbook of Nature Study* can be difficult to understand, you may want to discuss each paragraph with your child as you read it. In that way, you can help him understand what he is hearing.

E. Science *Thinking Skills*

Together with your teacher, read and discuss pages 762 and 763 in the *Handbook of Nature Study*, beginning with the section entitled "Soil Formation," and ending when you reach Lesson 216. Be sure to use your dictionary to look up any words you don't understand.

When you are finished, list the four soil types in your Student Notebook, and write down two characteristics of each type.[11]

Together with your teacher, read the quote from John Walton Spencer on page 760, at the beginning of the chapter about soil in the *Handbook of Nature Study*. Use your dictionary to look up the words sepulcher and resurrection. Write their definitions in your Student Notebook. Then talk with your teacher about what you think John Walton Spencer is saying in this quote.

Don't forget to check your weather station and record your findings over the next few days.

Talk with your teacher about how you would explain the formation of soil to someone who didn't know anything about it. Then, in your Student Notebook, write two or three paragraphs to that imaginary person. Tell how soil material is prepared and then changed into fertile soil.

F. States *Geography, Thinking Skills, Drawing*

Look again at the pages about New York in your *Atlas of the United States*. Then find the State Page in your Student Notebook, and fill in the information.

Make State Cards for New York by following the instructions found in Appendix B. New York is a Mid-Atlantic state, so be sure to outline the cards in green.

G. Writing *Language Skills, Thinking Skills*

Journaling is one way to keep a record of thoughts or events. Explorers often kept journals so they could accurately share with others the events they experienced and their thoughts about those events. Journal writing can look different from writing in stories because it is often just brief thoughts. Remember the entry Abigail's father wrote in the record book he kept, on page 29, paragraph 7 ("Weymouth Meetinghouse…") of *Abigail Adams*.

Write a journal entry telling about your day yesterday according to the guidelines below. Ask someone to read your journal entry and retell what you did. Listen to see if they accurately understand what you did yesterday.

Write at least four lines that include three events, and at least one thought about those events.

Write at least five lines that include four events, and at least two thoughts about those events.

Write at least six lines that include four events, and at least three thoughts about those events.

G. If your child is a reluctant writer, he can dictate his answer to you and then copy the answer that you have written down. If your child gets upset about making a mistake in his writing, have him write his answer on a sheet of scratch paper. You can check to make sure it is correct and then he can copy his answer into his notebook.

H. Independent Reading *Language Skills*

Choose something to read that you will enjoy. Then, find a quiet, comfortable place and read for the following length of time:

25 minutes 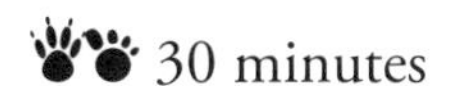 30 minutes

Be sure to write down what you read today on the Reading Log in your Student Notebook.

H. Completing the reading log each day gives your student a sense of accomplishment, as well as the opportunity to work independently.

Lesson 4, Part 5

This part is set aside for completion of any work left undone from the lesson, and review of concepts and content. It is also a time to expand the work of the lesson by doing art, mapping, or games.

- Review this lesson's Steps for Thinking, found in Part 1.

Why not just learn the meaning of a vocabulary word? Words learned individually are separate pieces of information. Words learned in the context of meaning are easier to remember and use correctly. Connecting each word to the way it was used in the story develops a more permanent link to that word in your child's mind.

- Give your teacher your stack of vocabulary cards for the lesson. Ask her to show you each word, and then tell her the meaning of the word and how it was used in the story.
- Tell your teacher what letter or letters go together to say *e*.[12]

Listen as your teacher reads the words that you studied from Part 1. Write each word in your Student Notebook as she dictates it. When you are finished, look at your word list and make any corrections needed. Show your teacher how you did.

- Use the United States map that is near the front of your *Atlas of the United States* to find Pennsylvania and New York. Then, on the large outline map of the U.S., draw lines around them with a green crayon, marker, or colored pencil. Write in the names of the states, and draw small stars where their capital cities are located. Next to the stars, write the name of each capital city.

Add to the legend you are making on your outline map by drawing a short green line under the blue one. Next to it write *Mid-Atlantic*.

When a student draws or paints a scene, there are many wonderful thinking skills taking place. The student is observing, recording, and categorizing information and then interpreting that information. All accomplished while doing something fun!

- Today you will do something a little different with your watercolors. Notice that there is no brown color in your *Klutz Watercolor* **palette**, or selection of paints. That could be a problem, since there is a lot of brown in nature.

When explorers or early colonists wanted to paint with watercolor, they often used the things around them to create their own palettes. For example, they mixed mashed berries or clay with water to make a variety of different colors. Very strong tea was a good way to make brown.

To make brown watercolor, you will need your parent's help or supervision. Place a cup of water in a small saucepan and bring it to a boil. Remove it from the heat and put four regular teabags in the water. Allow them to **steep**, or soak in the liquid, for at least an hour. Then carefully squeeze the teabags and remove them. Return the pan to the burner and bring it to a low boil for 10 minutes. Finally, pour the strong tea into a cup to cool.

Pour the cooled tea into a small, sealable container and test the color on a piece of white scrap paper. Notice that the brown color you made has a lot of red in it. To help with that, wet your brush with clear water and fill it with as much blue paint as you can. Rinse the blue paint in the container with the brown. Do this 8 – 10 times, but be sure to rinse your brush every time before you put it back in the blue paint. When you are finished you will have a nice brown paint in your palette.

You need to stir your new paint each time you use it (use the handle of your brush,) because the blue paint will tend to separate and settle on the bottom of the container. Also, since the tea mixture is already mostly water, it is important to blot your brush with a paper towel before you use the brown.

- Use your USA Activity CD to print at least one activity for the states you studied in this lesson. Then add any that you complete to your Student Notebook.
- Complete the Growing Pains Crossword Puzzle in your Student Notebook.[13]

Are games truly a valid part of school time? Absolutely! As your child revisits content, vocabulary, and concepts, an effective review of learning takes place. The game format makes review more inviting and hopefully, more frequent.

Enrichment Activities

1. At the library or, with your parent's permission, on the Internet research *Poor Richard's Almanac*. Benjamin Franklin wrote this booklet, and it became very famous. Find out who "Richard" was (in the title,) and what types of articles this booklet contained. If you can, locate two or three famous sayings that Benjamin Franklin wrote for *Poor Richard's Almanac*. Write down the things you learn, and plan to include them in your presentation at the end of Lesson 6.
2. At the library or, with your parent's permission, on the Internet research a Native American tribe from either the New England or the Mid-Atlantic regions of what is now the United States. If you do not yet have a tribe in mind that you would like to find out more about, choose one from the map entitled "Native American Nations, c. 1750" in your *United States History Atlas*. Print a Native American Profile sheet from your Student Resources CD and fill it out.

   Place the new profile sheet and picture in your Native American Notebook, or add them to your Student Notebook.

Additional Resources

Calico Captive, by Elizabeth George Speare
If you read this book, be sure to print a Book Review page from your Student Resources CD, fill it out, and place it in your Student Notebook.

Magazines

Answers

1. real, seem, windy, chief

2. 1. Great Grandfather brought the musket from far away. (3)
   2. There is trouble at King Street. (4)
   3. Grandmother Quincy taught Abigail good manners. (4)
   4. Uncle Friedrich and Aunt Netta lived on a farm. (5)
   5. The French soldiers are coming near! (3)
   6. General Braddock was the commander of the soldiers. (3)
   7. Patrick and Uncle Friedrich left before dawn with their wagon. (4)
   8. To arms! (2)
   9. The Sons of Liberty fought bad laws. (4)

1. were	2. was	3. were
4. was	5. were	6. were
7. was	8. were	9. was

3. Wording will vary, but should include the thought that rock flour has been ground up far more finely than gravel or sand.

4. Will vary, but should include the idea of a flowing stream of water that acts like a mill by breaking down rocks and gravel, and even sand into smaller and smaller particles.

5. No. Any type of water with a flow or a current can do the same thing.

6. It expands.

7. As the water in a crack expands by freezing, it pushes against the rock and makes the crack larger. If this happens over and over, eventually the rock will break.

8. glacial ice, wind, temperature changes (freezing water)

9. keen, leaf, inky, grief

10. Answer key is in Appendix A.

11. gravel- very coarse, not good for growing things
    sands- loose and open, easy to till, water drains rapidly
    loam- ideal soil for general purposes, combines good properties of sand and clay
    clay- sticky when wet, cloddy when dry, drains slowly

12. ee, ea, y, ie

13. Answer key is in Appendix A.

Lesson 5, Part 1

Steps for Thinking

1. A man, woman, or child can be a strong or brave person.
2. In times of need, people can show strength or bravery that they didn't think they had within them. They can also encourage those around them to be brave.
3. People you admire can inspire you to be brave by setting the example of acting bravely.

A. Copywork & Dictation

Language Skills, Thinking Skills

Look carefully at your assigned passage below, and read it silently. Show your teacher any words you don't know, and practice saying them aloud. Now read the passage aloud, or ask your teacher to read it to you.

When you are finished copying or writing from dictation, compare your copy to the text and make any needed corrections.

Copy, or write as your teacher dictates, the last paragraph on page 19 that continues on page 20 ("She wondered whether…") in *The Matchlock Gun.*

Copy, or write as your teacher dictates, page 57, paragraphs 6 through 8 ("I asked our tribe…") in *Ambush in the Wilderness.*

B. Reader

Language Skills, History

The Matchlock Gun: page 23 (Chapter IV) through paragraph 2, page 27

Ambush in the Wilderness: page 56 (Chapter Seven) through page 59

Read the above assignment from *The Matchlock Gun* aloud, and then follow along as someone else reads the assignment from *Ambush in the Wilderness.*

Read the above assignment from *The Matchlock Gun* silently, and then read the assignment from *Ambush in the Wilderness* aloud.

Read the above assignments from *The Matchlock Gun* and *Ambush in the Wilderness* silently.

Materials

- *The Matchlock Gun*
- *Abigail Adams*
- *Ambush in the Wilderness*
- *Atlas of the United States*
- *Handbook of Nature Study* (book or download)
- *Eat Your Way Through the USA*
- *Profiles from History, Vol. 2*
- *DK Pockets: Rocks and Minerals*
- *Klutz Watercolor Book*
- *Discovering America's Founders* DVD
- USA Activity CD
- Ingredients for recipe (Part 3)
- Rock Study Kit
- Pocket knife
- Outline map of U.S.
- Weather station:
  - Rain gauge
  - Outdoor thermometer
  - Barometer
  - Anemometer
  - Stop watch or watch w/ second hand
  - Weather vane

Additional resources for Enrichment Activities are found in Part 5.

A. Copywork and dictation assignments go from an easier level (designated by) to harder levels (designated by and). Take two days for the copywork if that is more comfortable for your child. Please adapt instructions to your child's individual needs. Your child should be **consistently successful** at one level before progressing to the next, **regardless of grade**.

C. Read-Aloud & Discussion *Language Skills, Thinking Skills, History*

Abigail Adams: page 96, paragraph 6 ("The guns…") to the bottom of page 101

Follow the directions for your level and read or listen to the assignment from *Abigail Adams*. Then ask your teacher to read the discussion questions. Think about what you know from the story, and answer in your own words. Give any examples you can think of from the story that help show your answer.

Listen carefully as your teacher reads the assignment from *Abigail Adams*.

Read the assignment from *Abigail Adams* aloud.

Discussion Questions: Abigail had to deal with many problems while John helped America become a nation. Tell about the problems she had to deal with. Where did she get the strength to keep going? When Abigail and the children heard about the Declaration of Independence that John was helping to write, they were so happy. Since you know the outcome of the work that John did to start our nation, do you think the sacrifice of his family was worth it?

D. Suggested words provide study that focuses on an aspect of language such as phonics, word roots or affixes. These lists include words taken from the readers. Please feel free to add up to five words each week that are particular to your child's needs.

D. Spelling *Language Skills, Thinking Skills*

Look at the list of words below. Then, in your Student Notebook, underline the suffix *ly* at the end of each word.[1] A **suffix** is an ending that is added to a word to change its meaning. The suffix *ly* means to do something in a certain way. For example, if you sing happily, then you sing in a happy way. This type of word is an **adverb**.

quickly slowly gratefully easily

Notice that in the words quick<u>ly</u>, slow<u>ly</u> and grateful<u>ly</u>, the suffix *ly* was added directly to the beginning word. When a word ends with *e* or *l*, you just add the suffix <u>ly</u>. Nothing has to be changed, but when a word ends with *y*, sometimes things are different. In the word easily, the suffix *ly* was added to the beginning word easy, but first the *y* had to be changed to an *i* before adding the letters *ly*.

Listen as your teacher reads the following words. Then, spell each word as best you can, either aloud or by writing it in your Student Notebook. Your teacher may add up to five words that are difficult for you to read or write.

luckily	soberly	finally	distinctly
exactly	softly	suddenly	carefully
directly	hastily	thankfully	surely
radically	happily	tightly	squarely

E. History

Thinking Skills

In your book, *Ambush in the Wilderness*, the last section is called an "Historical Postscript." A **postscript** is something added to the end of a letter or document that gives additional information. In this case, the postscript gives historical information that helps people understand the battle story in the book.

Together with your teacher, read or team read the portion of the historical postscript that begins with paragraph 2 on page 84 ("In the early part...") through the top of page 88. Be sure to start reading at paragraph 2 and stop reading at the beginning of paragraph 1 on page 88 ("By 2:00 p.m...") because you have not yet completed *Ambush in the Wilderness*, and reading more of the postscript will spoil the ending.

When you are finished, discuss what you read with your teacher. Compare the different ways that British soldiers and Indians fought. Then, in your Student Notebook list as many things as you can think of about each group's way of doing battle.[2]

Do you think either group could improve its battle plan? If so, how? When you write your answers, be sure to use complete sentences.[3]

E. To team-read, take turns reading aloud paragraph by paragraph. You should take the first turn and alternate with your child for as long as he can read with few errors. The length of each team-reading exercise depends on your child's ability to read aloud without frustration. When you decide to stop, you should finish reading whatever is left of the assignment aloud while your child looks at the words with you.

F. States

Geography, History, Thinking Skills

In the *Atlas of the United States*, read the pages about New Jersey. When you are finished, find the blank map of New Jersey in your Student Notebook and complete the following assignments:

- Place a small star on the spot where Trenton is located and label it. Trenton is the capital city of New Jersey.
- Color the lines and areas showing the Hudson and Delaware Rivers with a blue crayon, marker, or colored pencil, and label them. In case you can't tell from the map, both of these rivers form parts of New Jersey's border.
- Color and label Raritan Bay, Great Bay, and Delaware Bay.

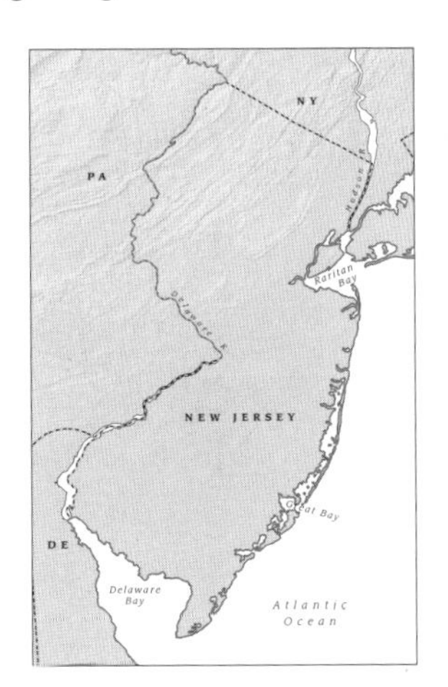

- Label the three states that border New Jersey.

G. Doing

History, Thinking Skills

There are many forests in New England, and that region is famous for its beautiful fall **foliage**, or tree leaves. If you live in an area where the foliage is changing colors, with your parent's help and supervision find a pretty tree outdoors that you would like to paint. Take your watercolors and paper outside, along with a water bottle and a cup.

Teaching Tip

If you have perfectionist children who don't want to draw or paint because it doesn't come out exactly the way they want, encourage them to think like an inventor. Many attempts create a better product!

If you do not live in such an area, or if it is not convenient go outdoors, turn to the New Hampshire page in your *Atlas of the United States*. There is a picture on that page that shows some fall foliage. Use either that picture or the tree outside as a model to complete the activity in Appendix B.

H. **Independent Reading** *Language Skills*

Choose something to read that you will enjoy. Then, find a quiet, comfortable place and read for the following length of time:

25 minutes 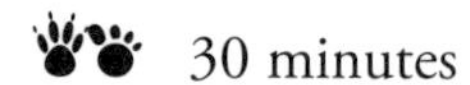 30 minutes

Over time, it's fun to see how much you have read. Be sure to write down what you read today on the Reading Log in your Student Notebook.

Lesson 5, Part 2

A. **Quotation Notebook** *Language Skills, Thinking Skills*

Copy the first rule listed below into your Student Notebook, and then tell or write what it means to you.

Copy the first two rules listed below into your Student Notebook, and then tell or write what each one means to you.

Copy all three rules listed below into your Student Notebook, and then tell or write what each one means to you. Give an example of each rule from a story, someone's life, or your own life.

1. Do not show your friend something that will frighten him.
2. Be sure that the things you do for amusement are not sinful, but rather build strength and character.
3. Even if you are inwardly pleased that someone is being justly punished, always show pity to the one receiving the punishment.

B. Every student should read or listen to all the literature selections for the unit. Reading or hearing the different perspectives adds depth to understanding the events and circumstances of the times.

B. **Reader** *Language Skills, History*

The Matchlock Gun: page 27, paragraph 3 ("He looked...") through page 31

Ambush in the Wilderness: page 60 ("The advance...") through page 62

Read the above assignment from *The Matchlock Gun* aloud, and then follow along as someone else reads the assignment from *Ambush in the Wilderness*.

- Read the above assignment from *The Matchlock Gun* silently, and then read the assignment from *Ambush in the Wilderness* aloud.
- Read the above assignments from *The Matchlock Gun* and *Ambush in the Wilderness* silently.

C. Read-Aloud & Narration *History, Language Skills, Thinking Skills*

Abigail Adams: last paragraph, page 101 ("The war…") through page 106, paragraph 5

Follow the directions for your level and read, or listen as your teacher reads, the above assignment from *Abigail Adams*. Then, in your own words, tell what happened in your assigned passage below. Try to remember as many details as possible. You may reread the passage or listen as your teacher rereads the part you are to retell.

- Listen carefully, then retell page 101, paragraph 7 ("The war went on…") through page 103, paragraph 6 ("God be praised…").
- Listen carefully, then retell page 101, paragraph 7 ("The war went on…") through page 105, paragraph 4 ("Three months later …").
- Read the assignment aloud; then retell it in your own words.

D. Mechanics and Editing *Language Skills, Thinking Skills*

Continue your practice to become a good writing mechanic by correcting punctuation, words and sentences and making them work better.

Mechanics Toolkit

1A – Capitalize names of historical events, documents and geographic names.

The Continental Congress met in *Philadelphia*.
Many great men helped create the *Declaration of Independence.*

1B – Every sentence ends with a punctuation mark, such as a question mark for a sentence that asks a question.

What happened to Patrick's friend?
Was John Adams one of the Sons of Liberty?

2A – Use the word you're as a contraction of the words *you are.*

You're my favorite coach.
If *you're* not quiet, *you're* going to wake the baby.

2B – Use the word *your* to show that something belongs to someone.

We will go to *your* house later.
What is *your* opinion of the book?

Practice these skills by correcting the sentences in your Student Notebook.[4] The number of errors in each sentence is listed after the sentence in parentheses. To show that a letter needs to be capitalized, make three lines under it. To replace an incorrect word with a correct word, draw a line through the incorrect word and write the correct word above it. Add any needed punctuation.

E. If you do not own the *Handbook of Nature Study,* you can download the parts you need from the Internet at www.archive.org. Type "Handbook of Nature Study" in the search field.

E. Science

Thinking Skills, Drawing

Rocks are just about everywhere in nature! Sometimes they are very large, sometimes they are tiny, but they are almost always there. Together with your teacher, read the sections in your *Rocks and Minerals* book that are entitled "How to Use This Book," "Rocks and Minerals," "What Are Minerals?" and "What Are Rocks?" Minerals are natural, solid substances made from combinations of chemicals, and rocks are solid objects made of one or more minerals. Then listen carefully as your teacher reads the introduction to rocks that begins at the bottom of page 744 and ends at the top of page 745 in the *Handbook of Nature Study.*

When you are finished, discuss the following questions with your teacher, and write your answers in your Student Notebook:

What is a geologist?[5]

What is the difference between a mineral and a rock?[6]

Thumb through your *Rocks and Minerals* book and find a rock or mineral that looks interesting to you. Then trace or draw and color it into your Student Notebook. Write the name of the rock or mineral you chose under its picture.

Don't forget to check your weather station today and tomorrow and record your findings on the Weather Watcher pages in your Student Notebook.

Look over the part your teacher read today from the *Handbook of Nature Study*, and list the three basic kinds of rocks in your Student Notebook. Write a short explanation of how each one is formed next to its name.[7] Be sure to use your dictionary to look up any words you are not familiar with.

Many minerals are elements. An **element** is a substance that contains only one type of atom. If you are unsure what an atom is, don't worry about that right now because it will be explained in a later lesson. Look at the Periodic Table of Elements in Appendix B. The Periodic Table is a chart that contains information about all the elements that scientists have discovered so far. Do you recognize the names of any of the elements? In your Student Notebook, make a list of all the elements that have names you recognize on the Periodic Table.

F. **States** *Geography, Thinking Skills, Drawing*

Look again at the pages about New Jersey in your *Atlas of the United States*. Then find the State Page in your Student Notebook, and fill in the information.

Make State Cards for New Jersey by following the instructions found in Appendix B. New Jersey is a Mid-Atlantic state, so be sure to outline the cards in green.

F. State abbreviations can be found on the back of the USA PlaceMap.

G. **Interactive Journal** *Language Skills, Thinking Skills*

Complete this writing activity with your partner.

It is your partner's job to write first; then you will answer a question with the number of sentences assigned below. After that, write several sentences telling what you think about what your partner has written. Make sure to end with a question you want to ask your partner, so he or she can write back to you.

Topic for your partner: Tell your student about a time in your life when you felt afraid or worried. How did you respond to those feelings? Tell how the situation turned out and if you would change anything about how you handled your fears and concerns.

Your question: What do you do when you are afraid? Does it help you? If so, tell how.

- at least four sentences
- at least five sentences
- at least one paragraph

G. Since writing begins with thinking, once your student engages in assigned thinking activities, the way is naturally prepared. As you use this approach, your student will begin to see himself as a writer, which is the first and most important step to becoming a writer.

There is no assigned follow-up for the question your student is instructed to ask you. It is, however, intended to be an opportunity for further communication, either written or discussed.

H. **Independent Reading** *Language Skills*

Choose something to read that you will enjoy. Then, find a quiet, comfortable place and read for the following length of time:

25 minutes   30 minutes

Be sure to write down what you read today on the Reading Log in your Student Notebook.

H. Independent reading provides regular practice for word study and reading skills, as well as time for practice of thinking skills. Quiet time to consider ideas and tie new information with old is essential in building new understandings.

Lesson 5, Part 3

A. **Copywork & Dictation** *Language Skills, Thinking Skills*

Look carefully at your assigned passage below, and read it silently. Show your teacher any words you don't know, and practice saying them aloud. Now read the passage aloud, or ask your teacher to read it to you.

When you are finished copying or writing from dictation, compare your copy to the text and make any needed corrections.

Copy, or write as your teacher dictates, page 40, paragraph 3 ("I am going outside...") through page 41, paragraph 4 in *The Matchlock Gun.*

Copy, or write as your teacher dictates, page 68, paragraphs 1 and 2 ("Hold your fire...") in *Ambush in the Wilderness.*

B. Reader

Language Skills, History

The Matchlock Gun: page 32 (Chapter V) through the top of page 38
Ambush in the Wilderness: page 63 (Chapter Eight) to the bottom of page 66

Read the above assignment from *The Matchlock Gun* aloud, and then follow along as someone else reads the assignment from *Ambush in the Wilderness.*

Read the above assignment from *The Matchlock Gun* silently, and then read the assignment from *Ambush in the Wilderness* aloud.

Read the above assignments from *The Matchlock Gun* and *Ambush in the Wilderness* silently.

C. Read-Aloud & Discussion

History, Language Skills, Thinking Skills

Abigail Adams: page 106, paragraph 6 ("But Charles...") through page 112, paragraph 8

Follow the directions for your level and read or listen to the above assignment from *Abigail Adams.* Then make up the assigned number of questions about the part of the story you just read or heard. Write down your questions and ask your teacher to answer them. After discussing her thoughts, write down the best possible answers in your Student Notebook. Be sure to use complete sentences.

Listen carefully as your teacher reads the assigned passage.

Make up one question. Make up two questions.

Read the assigned passage aloud; then make up three questions.

D. Vocabulary & Spelling

Language Skills, Thinking Skills

Write each vocabulary word listed below on an index card. Use a dictionary to look up the meaning of each word, and write it on the card. Then on the back of each card, draw a picture or write a clue so you can remember how the word was used in the story.

resolution	**indignant**	**flatirons**	**schnapps**	**dusky**
tourniquet	**ramrod**	**clammy**	**precision**	**acrid**

Look at the words below. Then, in your Student Notebook, underline the letters *ly* in each word. Tell what the ly suffix means, and whether it was added directly to a beginning word, the beginning word ended with an *e* or an *l*, or a *y* was changed to an *i* before the letters *ly* were added.[8]

properly scarily immediately thoughtfully

Look at the spelling words you wrote in Part 1. If you did not write them in that part, ask your teacher to read each word, and write it in your Student Notebook now. Check your spelling against the list and correct it if necessary. When you are finished, cover each word with your hand, and try to spell it aloud. Then uncover it and see if you were correct.

D. New vocabulary words appear in the context of a lesson or story, which helps student recognize the connection between the way a word is used and its meaning. This is an important reading strategy called using context clues.

To prepare for learning about syllables, which will be covered later, if your child says a word slowly, he can usually hear the division between the syllables. This is an easy way to learn about syllables, much easier than learning the complicated rules of syllable division.

E. History

Geography, Thinking Skills

Your book, *Ambush in the Wilderness*, tells about the Battle of Monongahela. This battle between the French and English took place before war was officially declared. The two countries had already fought three wars over land in America, and this would be the fourth. Altogether, these conflicts were the French and Indian Wars.

Even though France and England had argued constantly for many years, neither country could afford to pay for another war. Wars were very expensive, but both nations knew that whoever won this struggle would control North America and all its riches!

For the first few years of the last French and Indian War, France won battle after battle—largely because of its Native American **allies**, or friends with a common purpose. As time passed, however, it became more difficult for the French army to get food and **reinforcements**, or additional soldiers. The English had more than ten times as many settlers in America as the French did, and that turned out to be a great advantage. They could call on the settlers, and the militias they had organized to defend their settlements, to provide supplies and extra troops.

Even though the colonists were often unhappy about helping, after a couple of years things in the war began to change. Along with over 20,000 colonial militiamen, the British army marched into Canada, which is where most French settlers lived. After several long and very difficult battles, France finally surrendered to England.

The French left the area west of the Appalachian Mountains, called the Ohio River Valley, at the end of the French and Indian Wars. English colonists were very happy about this for two important reasons. The first was that a cruel and difficult war was finally over. The second was that they were finally free to expand westward–something that a great many people had wanted to do for a long time.

Unfortunately for the settlers, King George of England believed that the Indians were still a great threat to them. Most tribes had fought with the French during the war, and the King knew that they still feared losing all their land to the settlers. They would continue to fight in order to protect their way of life. In hopes of calming the fears of Native Americans and putting an end to fighting, the King proclaimed an imaginary line running north to south across the continent, to keep settlers from moving westward. This was the Line of Proclamation.

Many settlers were angry about the Line of Proclamation. They felt that the King had sided with the Indians, and had snatched their "prize" away from them. They also suspected that the King's real reason for the Line was to keep them living closely together, so they would be easier to govern. This may have been true, because soon after the war England began charging new taxes on everything from paper to tea. After all, England had to pay for the expensive war it had just fought! English lawmakers thought that taxing the **prosperous**, or successful, colonies was a good way to do that. They did not realize how angry the Line of Proclamation and the new taxes would make the settlers. They never thought that these things would prove to be the groundwork for revolution.

Look at the map for entitled "The First Thirteen States, 1779" in your *United States History Atlas*, which shows the Line of Proclamation and the French territory. Use the same map that you made in Lesson 3, Part 1, and add the Line of Proclamation to it. It does not have to be perfect—just do your best!

Talk with your teacher about why the colonists might have been unhappy about helping the English fight the French and Indian War. In your Student Notebook, write down two possible reasons.[9] Then, look back over the paragraphs above and write two reasons that the colonists were happy when the French finally left the Ohio River Valley.[10]

Discuss the reason King George gave for his Line of Proclamation. Do you think he had a good point? Why do you think the settler's believed he was trying to keep them close together? After you have talked about the two different points of view, write a couple of sentences in your Student Notebook telling which one you think was probably the real reason, and why.[11]

F. States *Geography, History, Thinking Skills*

In the *Atlas of the United States*, read the pages about Delaware. When you are finished, find the blank map of Delaware in your Student Notebook and complete the following assignments:

- Place a small star on the spot where Dover is located, and label it. Dover is the capital city of Delaware.
- Color the lines and areas showing the Delaware, Nanticoke, and Mispillion Rivers with a blue crayon, marker, or colored pencil, and label them.

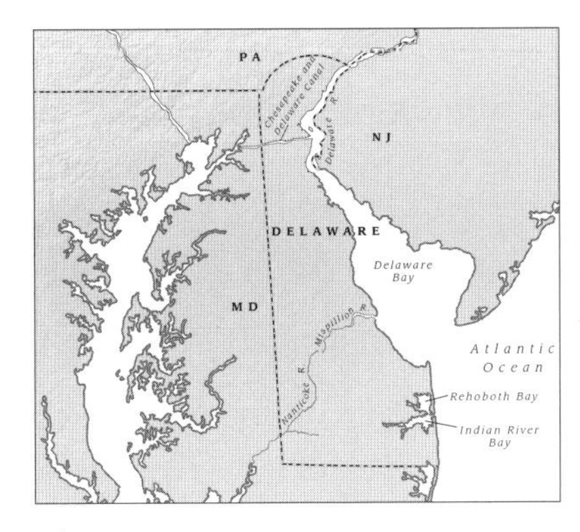

- Color and label Delaware Bay, Rehoboth Bay, and Indian River Bay.

- Label the three states that border Delaware.
- Color and label the Chesapeake and Delaware Canal. A **canal** is a man-made waterway.
- Look closely at the states of Delaware and Maryland on the map of the United States toward the front of your atlas. Show your teacher where you think the Chesapeake and Delaware Canal would be drawn if it was on this map. Talk with your teacher about some possible reasons this canal might have been built. Then do some research at the library or, with your parent's permission, on the Internet and find out why it was built. In your Student Notebook, write one or two sentences that tell about what you learned.

F. It is important for a student to be acquainted with various reference tools, such as an atlas. Since our goal is for students to be lifelong learners, use of reference tools can greatly enhance learning on any topic. Using these tools successfully requires familiarity and the opportunities to use the tool as part of learning that is connected to history, literature, science, and ultimately, life.

G. Cooking *Language Skills, Thinking Skills, Drawing*

With your parent's permission and supervision, look in *Eat Your Way Through the USA*, choose a recipe that comes from either New Jersey or Delaware, and prepare it for your family. After everyone has had a taste, find out who liked it, and whether anyone would like to have it again. What did you think about it?

In your Student Notebook, draw a picture of the dish you chose to make and write the following number of sentences about your family's reaction to it:

two sentences   three sentences   four sentences

H. Independent Reading *Language Skills*

Choose something to read that you will enjoy. Then, find a quiet, comfortable place and read for the following length of time:

25 minutes   30 minutes

Be sure to write down what you read today on the Reading Log in your Student Notebook.

Lesson 5, Part 4

A. Quotation Notebook
Language Skills, Thinking Skills

Copy the first rule listed below into your Student Notebook, and then tell or write what it means to you.

Copy the first two rules listed below into your Student Notebook, and then tell or write what each one means to you.

Copy all three rules listed below into your Student Notebook, and then tell or write what each one means to you. Give an example of each rule from a story, someone's life, or your own life.

1. Always show respect to the people that you are with.
2. Avoid overdoing compliments, but do not neglect them either.
3. Do not show anger at the table even if you feel you have a good reason, especially if there are strangers there. Remember, a good attitude can turn a simple meal into a feast.

B. Reader
Language Skills, History

The Matchlock Gun: page 38, paragraph 1 ("She had…") through page 42
Ambush in the Wilderness: last paragraph, page 66 ("I simply…") through page 69

Read the above assignment from *The Matchlock Gun* aloud, and then follow along as someone else reads the assignment from *Ambush in the Wilderness*.

Read the above assignment from *The Matchlock Gun* silently, and then read the assignment from *Ambush in the Wilderness* aloud.

Read the above assignments from *The Matchlock Gun* and *Ambush in the Wilderness* silently.

C. Read-Aloud & Narration
History, Language Skills, Thinking Skills

Abigail Adams: page 112, paragraph 9 ("Nabby and Johnny…") through page 118, paragraph 1

Follow the directions for your level and read, or listen as your teacher reads, the above assignment from *Abigail Adams*. Then, in your own words, tell what happened in your assigned passage below.

C. As you read aloud you model fluency, expression, and comprehension. When your voice reflects punctuation, students can see its purpose and the way it makes the passage more understandable.

Try to remember as many details as possible. You may reread the passage or listen as your teacher rereads the part you are to retell.

Listen carefully, then retell page 114, paragraph 1 ("The house was...") through page 115, paragraph 6 ("John gave me...").

Listen carefully, then retell page 115, paragraph 7 ("Early in 1785...") to page 117, paragraph 1 ("The day arrived...").

Read the assignment aloud; then retell it in your own words.

D. **Mechanics and Editing** *Language Skills, Thinking Skills*

Reread the Mechanics Toolkit in Part 2 of this lesson. Be the teacher and tell when you are supposed to use each rule and why.

After reviewing the rules and examples, make up two sentences that show each rule being used correctly, and write them in your Student Notebook.

D For days with several assignments that require writing, you may want to help your student do some of the assignments verbally, or have him type them. Variety in response can help keep students motivated to do a good job.

E. **Science** *Geography, Thinking Skills*

There are miles and miles of seacoast, and a great many mountains in both New England and the Mid-Atlantic regions of the United States. And that makes for a lot of rocks! One of the most common types of rock in these regions, however, is granite. In fact, New Hampshire's state motto is "The Granite State." There are large granite **quarries**, or pits from which stone is taken, in both that state and Vermont.

As you read in Part 2 of this lesson, there are three main types of rock: igneous, sedimentary, and metamorphic. Granite is a type of igneous rock. Listen carefully as your teacher reads the introduction to igneous rocks on page 746 in the *Handbook of Nature Study*, and the first two paragraphs of the section entitled "Granite."

Write a short explanation in your Student Notebook telling how igneous rocks form.[12] Then, with your teacher's supervision and help, use a piece of granite if you have one in your Rock Study Kit to complete the first activity of Lesson 209 in the *Handbook of Nature Study*. If you do not have a piece of granite, try using the pictures in your *Rocks and Minerals* book to answer some of the questions. Write your answers in your Student Notebook.[13]

Don't forget to check your weather station and record your findings over the next few days.

In your *Rocks and Minerals* book, use the index in the back to find and read about two types of quartz (crystalline and noncrystalline), feldspars, micas, and hornblende.

Thumb through your *Rocks and Minerals* book, or check the library or Internet, and find three igneous rocks, other than granite, that

E. Since the language in the *Handbook of Nature Study* can be difficult to understand, you may want to discuss each paragraph with your child as you read it. In that way, you can help him understand what he is hearing.

From Dr. Beechick

"Another science skill is observation—both under natural conditions and under experimental conditions. Louis Pasteur's close observations of fermentation led to his discoveries of bacteria and other small organisms. This led, in turn, to his development of vaccines for several diseases and to pasteurization of milk. Before Pasteur, diseases were treated with ineffective methods based on evolutionary beliefs about life, but Pasteur's work changed that forever."

– *You Can Teach Your Child Successfully*, page 324

contain quartz.[14] Then name the two types of mica you read about above. Both of these types are often found in granite.[15]

F. **States** *Geography, Thinking Skills, Drawing*
Look again at the pages about Delaware in your *Atlas of the United States*. Then find the State Page in your Student Notebook, and fill in the information.

Make State Cards for Delaware by following the instructions found in Appendix B. Delaware is a Mid-Atlantic state, so be sure to outline the cards in green.

G. **Writing** *Language Skills, Thinking Skills*
You have focused on writing dialogue several times in this unit. Now you will choose a character from your reader and have a conversation with that character. Ask the character several questions and give the answer that you think the character would have given. Remember to record your conversation with the character by using direct quotations. Remember to state your questions as direct quotations as well. For example:

I asked, "What was the hardest part about being sickly when you were growing up?" Abigail answered, "The hardest part was not being able to run and play with my sister."

- Tell which character you are having a conversation with. Ask your character at least three questions and give his or her answers.
- Tell which character you are having a conversation with. Ask your character at least four questions and give his or her answers.
- Tell which character you are having a conversation with. Ask your character at least five questions and give his or her answers.

H. **Independent Reading** *Language Skills*
Choose something to read that you will enjoy. Then, find a quiet, comfortable place and read for the following length of time:

25 minutes 30 minutes

Be sure to write down what you read today on the Reading Log in your Student Notebook.

Lesson 5, Part 5

This part is set aside for completion of any work left undone from the lesson, and review of concepts and content. It is also a time to expand the work of the lesson by doing art, mapping, or games.

- Review this lesson's Steps for Thinking, found in Part 1.
- Give your teacher your stack of vocabulary cards for the lesson. Ask her to show you each word, and then tell her the meaning of the word and how it was used in the story.
- Look at your list of spelling words for this lesson and tell your teacher how the suffix *ly* can be added to different words.[16]

  Listen as your teacher reads the words that you studied from Part 1. Write each word in your Student Notebook as she dictates it. When you are finished, look at your word list and make any corrections needed. Show your teacher how you did.
- Use the United States map that is near the front of your *Atlas of the United States* to find New Jersey and Delaware. Then, on the large outline map of the U.S., draw lines around them with a green crayon, marker, or colored pencil. Write in the names of the states, and draw small stars where their capital cities are located. Next to the stars, write the name of each capital city.
- Read, or listen as your teacher reads, the story about Paul Revere in *Profiles from History, Volume 2.* Talk about the discussion question with your teacher, and then complete any other activities that she assigns.
- Use your USA Activity CD to print at least one activity for the states you studied in this lesson. Then add any that you complete to your Student Notebook.
- Follow the directions in Appendix B and play Growing Pains Bingo.

As you discuss the Steps for Thinking with your child, feel free to share the examples that have come to your mind during the lesson. Share the steps you went through in your thinking as well as your outcomes. Modeling is a very effective type of instruction, and your child will gain insight into how to connect concepts and examples by hearing your thinking.

Teaching Tip

One way to solidify learning is to teach someone else what you know. When your child reviews what he has learned by telling someone else how to do it, the student has taken instruction and put it into his own words. This increases the likelihood that he will use the skill on his own.

Enrichment Activities

1. At the library or, with your parent's permission, on the Internet research the Iroquois Confederacy. This group was also called the Six Nations. Find out when and why it was formed, and how it was governed. Who did the Confederacy side with in the French and Indian War? Why? Write down what you learn, and make this part of your presentation at the end of this unit.
2. In your *Atlas of the United States*, look again at the states you have studied in this lesson. Scan the sections entitled "The Way It Was..." and choose a person, place, or thing from one of those sections to research. Use the library or, with your parent's permission, the Internet and try to find out more than what is written in the atlas.

   Then pretend you work for a newspaper, and you have just met the person, seen the landmark, or found out about the object. Write a short article about what you have learned. Newspaper re-

Use one or more of the Enrichment Activities if your child completes his assigned work and has the time or desire to learn more. These activities are flexible, so choose the one(s) that seem most interesting to your student. Allow him to work at a level that is appropriate for him, and remember that the learning process is more important than the product.

porters always try to answer the questions *who, what, when, where,* and *how* when they write, so that readers have all the important information. Try to answer those questions in your article, and then add it to your Student Notebook.

Additional Resources

The Last of the Mohicans (abridged) Retold from the James Fenimore Cooper original
If you read this book, be sure to print a Book Review page from your Student Resources CD, fill it out, and place it in your Student Notebook.

Answers

1. quickly (suffix added directly to beginning word,) easily (suffix added after *y* on beginning word was changed to *i*,) gratefully (suffix added to a beginning word that ended in *l*,) scarcely (suffix added to a beginning word that ended in e)

2. Answers for the English may include: carried large amounts of supplies and equipment; moved very slowly; marched on roads; marched three- or four- abreast, in straight lines; did battle from open spaces; fired guns only on command; and so forth. For Native Americans: carried supplies themselves or on pack horses; moved quickly from place to place; used the forests to hide their approach; used ambushes; fought from behind rocks and trees; often zigzagged toward the enemy; and so forth.

3. Answers will vary.

4. 1. Did Abigail stay at her home or run away? (3)
   2. Edward and his family lived in Kill Valley. (4)
   3. The English stopped ships from coming to Boston. (4)
   4. The Americans fought at Breed's Hill. (5)
   5. What happened to Patrick's friend Gwayo? (4)
   6. Did Abigail watch the Battle of Bunker Hill? (6)
   7. Congress chose George Washington to be the leader of the army. (4)
   8. John Adams helped write the Declaration of Independence. (5)
   9. General Washington crossed the Delaware River on Christmas. (6)

1. Your	2. You're	3. You're
4. your	5. You're	6. your

5. a scientist who studies rocks and minerals

6. Minerals are natural, solid substances made from combinations of chemicals; rocks are solid objects made of one or more minerals.

7. sedimentary rocks: formed from sediments, or small pieces of matter, deposited by water, wind or glaciers
   igneous rocks: formed by the solidification of molten, or melted, rock
   metamorphic rocks: formed from the other two types of rock

8. properly (added to a beginning word,) scarily (*y* changed to *i* first,) immediately (added to a word that ends with an e or *l*,) thoughtfully (added to a word that ends with an e or *l*)

9. Answers will vary, but might include the idea that the settlers were not professional soldiers—just farmers and shopkeepers or trappers; they had to leave their families, farms, and stores unprotected; they couldn't tend to their crops or work at their trades while they were gone; the English army took supplies that settlers intended to use for their families or to sell; and so forth.

10. A cruel and difficult war was finally over; they were free to move westward into the Ohio River valley.

11. Answers will vary.

12. Igneous rock forms when melted rock cools and becomes solid.

13. Answers found in the first paragraph you read today in *Handbook of Nature Study*.

14. Answers will vary.

15. mica: biotite and muscovite

16. *Ly* can be added directly to the end of a beginning word, added directly to a word that ends with e or *l*, or added to a word that ends with *y* after it has been changed to an *i*.

Lesson 6, Part 1

Materials

- *The Matchlock Gun*
- *Abigail Adams*
- *Ambush in the Wilderness*
- *Eat Your Way Through the USA*
- *Profiles from History, Vol. 2*
- *Klutz Watercolor Book*
- *Discovering America's Founders DVD*
- Ingredients for recipe (Part 3)
- Rock Study Kit
- Pocket knife
- Outline map of U.S.
- Weather station:
  - Rain gauge
  - Outdoor thermometer
  - Barometer
  - Anemometer
  - Stop watch or watch w/ second hand
  - Weather vane

Additional resources for Enrichment Activities are found in Part 5.

A. Quotation Notebook
Language Skills, Thinking Skills

Read over each quotation in your Student Notebook. Choose your favorite, and then tell or write why it is your favorite. Have you been able to apply this quotation to your life?

Think of ways you could be an example of what your favorite quotation says to others.

B. Reader
Language Skills, History

The Matchlock Gun: pages 43-47 (Chapter VII)
Ambush in the Wilderness: page 70 (Chapter Nine) through page 73, paragraph 3

Read the above assignment from *The Matchlock Gun* aloud, and then follow along as someone else reads the assignment from *Ambush in the Wilderness.*

Read the above assignment from *The Matchlock Gun* silently, and then read the assignment from *Ambush in the Wilderness* aloud.

Read the above assignments from *The Matchlock Gun* and *Ambush in the Wilderness* silently.

C. Read-Aloud & Discussion
Language Skills, Thinking Skills, History

Abigail Adams: page 118, paragraph 2 ("My lands...") through page 124, paragraph 2

Follow the directions for your level and read or listen to the above assignment from *Abigail Adams*. Then make up the assigned number of questions about the part of the story you just read or heard. Write down your questions and ask your teacher to answer them. After discussing her thoughts, write down the best possible answers in your Student Notebook. Be sure to use complete sentences.

Listen carefully as your teacher reads the assigned passage.

Make up one question. Make up two questions.

Read the assigned passage aloud; then make up three questions.

C. Discussion is very important in developing your child's ability to organize his thoughts. This in turn builds the ability to think and write. The goal of the discussion questions is not just to find the answer to a particular question, but also to create a situation where thoughts about the question and its answer are shared and considered in a detailed way. Do not rush this activity, but encourage your student to share his ideas relating to the topic, and any additional ideas that may come to mind. You can also share your own thoughts and questions as an example.

D. Spelling
Language Skills, Thinking Skills

Reread your lists of spelling words from Lessons 4 and 5. Write each word on your list on a separate index card. Use a yellow highlighter or crayon to underline, or highlight, the letters that spell the key sound focused on during that lesson:

Lesson 4 - the sounds of *e*: *ee*, *ea*, *ie* and *y*;
Lesson 5 - the suffix *ly*: added directly to the beginning word, added to a word ending with *e* or *l*, added to a word that ends with *y* changed to an *i*.

D. If you or your child would like to add a greater degree of difficulty to spelling lessons, choose words from the Challenge Spelling List (in Appendix A) for the lesson you are on. The words on this list are taken from the literature being read.

Then sort the cards into stacks by the spelling of the key sound. Fill in the lists on your Student Notebook page.[1]

E. As your child learns to take notes, it may be helpful to stop the video at intervals and discuss what has happened or been said. Ask questions that will help him understand the important parts of what he has seen or heard.

E. History

Language Skills, Thinking Skills

In this lesson, you have been reading or listening to a story about Abigail Adams. As you know, she was born in the colony of Massachusetts, and was a very typical little girl growing up in colonial times. However, today she is well-remembered largely because of the many letters she and her husband, John, wrote to one another before and during the Revolutionary War. They tell about the many challenges she faced while taking care of their farm and educating their children during this difficult time. They also speak of the loving relationship she had with her husband, and refer to him often as her "dearest friend."

Together with your teacher, watch Episode 1, Chapter 4 on the *Discovering America's Founders* DVD that is about Abigail Adams. Before you begin, take a minute to look at the Video Profile page for this lesson in your Student Notebook, and see what kinds of questions it asks.[2]

As you watch the video lesson, keep the Video Profile page in front of you. When you notice that the narrator, or person telling the story, is answering one of the questions, stop the video long enough to write the answer on your Profile page. Continue doing this as often as necessary as you finish watching the video lesson.

As you watch the video lesson, use a piece of scrap paper to jot down important things that the narrator, or person telling the story, says about Abigail. This is called *taking notes*, and is a good way to help remember what you hear or see. You do not need to use sentences when you take notes—single words or phrases, which are short groups of words, will work fine as long as they help you remember the important things. If it would be helpful, stop the lesson when you need to, or watch it a second time.

When you are finished, use your notes and your memory to fill in the Video Profile page. Be sure to answer the questions with complete sentences.

F. Personal experience helps make learning more memorable. As you do this activity with your child, recall any personal experiences you have had with each state. This could include a relative living there, a trip, friends who moved to that area, a favorite landmark or destination, etc. This connection between knowledge and experience can make information meaningful.

F. States

Geography, Thinking Skills

Look at the State Cards you have made throughout this unit. Pull out the ones that have the names of the states on them, and place the others to the side. Then, as you look at the name of each state, see if you can remember the name of its capital city, its nickname, and one interesting fact about it. It is fine to look at the other cards you made for that state if you need help remembering.

Go through the cards several times until you feel comfortable with the information about each state. When you are able to remember thc facts about a state, place its name card to the side and continue with the others.

You can make this a game with other members of your family by choosing a name card from the stack and asking another person to tell you the important information about that state. Give one point for each correct answer to the player who is answering. That way, it is possible to get three points for each state. Continue until all the name cards are eliminated.

G. Doing *Art*

Your final watercolor activity for this unit is to find a picture that shows fall foliage, and use it as a model for your own painting. Instead of using a picture, you can paint a scene outdoors if your parent agrees.

There are a couple of pictures in the *Atlas of the United States* that show pretty foliage. One of them is on the New Hampshire page mentioned in Lesson 5, Part 1, and other, smaller ones are on the Connecticut and Vermont pages. You do not need to include any buildings in your painting unless you want to.

However you choose to complete this activity is fine, as long as you have permission. It is not important to make your painting look exactly like the picture. The main points are to practice the things you have learned, and to experiment with new ideas. Above all, remember to relax and enjoy your art!

H. Independent Reading *Language Skills*

Choose something to read that you will enjoy. Then, find a quiet, comfortable place and read for the following length of time:

25 minutes 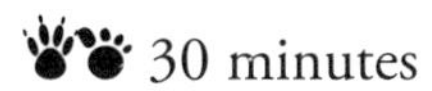 30 minutes

Over time, it's fun to see how much you have read. Be sure to write down what you read today on the Reading Log in your Student Notebook.

Lesson 6, Part 2

A. Copywork & Dictation *Language Skills, Thinking Skills*

Look carefully at your assigned passage below, and read it silently. Show your teacher any words you don't know, and practice saying them aloud. Now read the passage aloud, or ask your teacher to read it to you.

When you are finished copying or writing from dictation, compare your copy to the text and make any needed corrections.

Copy, or write as your teacher dictates, mid-paragraph that starts at the top of page 51 ("Gertrude was a good runner...") to the end of the paragraph ("Ateoord!") in *The Matchlock Gun*.

Copy, or write as your teacher dictates, page 75, paragraph 2 ("Patrick, why are you...") in *Ambush in the Wilderness*.

Write as your teacher dictates page 75, paragraphs 2 and 3 ("Patrick, why are you...") in *Ambush in the Wilderness*.

B. Reader *Language Skills, History*

The Matchlock Gun: pages 48-53 (Chapter VIII)
Ambush in the Wilderness: page 73, paragraph 4 ("When they...") through page 75

Read the above assignment from *The Matchlock Gun* aloud, and then follow along as someone else reads the assignment from *Ambush in the Wilderness*.

Read the above assignment from *The Matchlock Gun* silently, and then read the assignment from *Ambush in the Wilderness* aloud.

Read the above assignments from *The Matchlock Gun* and *Ambush in the Wilderness* silently.

C. Read-Aloud & Narration *Language Skills, Thinking Skills, History*

Abigail Adams: page 124, paragraph 3 (Back in...) through page 130, paragraph 4

Follow the directions for your level and read, or listen as your teacher reads, the above assignment from *Abigail Adams*. Then, in your own words, tell what happened in your assigned passage below. Try to remember as many details as possible. You may reread the passage or listen as your teacher rereads the part you are to retell.

Listen carefully, then retell page 128 ("That spring was cold..."). through page 129, paragraph 2 ("There was great relief...").

Read the assignment aloud; then retell it in your own words.

C. Since students do not have to worry about decoding during read-aloud time, they can focus totally on the meaning of what they are hearing. This allows them the opportunity to think about the ideas and information being presented, and to formulate their own thoughts.

D. Mechanics and Editing *Language Skills, Thinking Skills*

Today you are going to review the tools for writing that you have learned. To begin, print the Mechanics Toolkit 3 cards from Appendix B or your Student Resources CD, and cut them out. When you are finished, place them on the table in front of you, and

read all the Rule cards. Then find two Example cards that go with each rule.

You may want to mix up the Example cards to make it more of a challenge, or follow the directions in Appendix B to play Mechanics Toolkit Concentration.

Now continue your review by reading the Rule cards once again. Find two examples of each one in your reader, or any other book. Write the examples you find in your Student Notebook.

E. Science *Thinking Skills*

You have been watching the weather at your home in this unit. Now it is time to do something with the information you collected. With your teacher's help, transfer the weather observations you have recorded throughout this unit onto the Weather Chart in your Student Notebook. Since you added weather tools as you went through the unit, you will not have all the measurements for every day. Just fill in the observations you were able to make.

weather watcher

When you are finished, look over your chart with your teacher and see if you can find any connections. For example, do you think wind speed or direction ever affected changes in the weather between morning and evening? What about the air pressure moving higher or lower? Do you notice anything else? Talk with your teacher about how your weather watching abilities have or have not improved.

E. Keep your child's weather tools in a safe place, because weather watching activities will resume in the next unit.

From Dr. Beechick

"Besides asking questions and observing, what other thinking skills do scientists use? They measure, organize, classify, interpret. They make judgments based on large amounts of information. They form theories and plan experiments to check them out."

– *You Can Teach Your Child Successfully,* page 324

F. States *Geography, Thinking Skills*

Find the Regional Summary Pages in the back of your Student Notebook. Then, use your *Atlas of the United States* to fill in the information for Massachusetts, Connecticut, Vermont, New Hampshire, and Rhode Island.

When you are finished, look at the State Scramble game in your Student Notebook. Unscramble the name of each state you have studied in this unit, and write it correctly on the line provided. Then write its abbreviation on the short line. Finally, list each state under the name of the region where it is located.[3] If you need help remembering, it is fine to use your State Cards to complete this activity.

F. Frequent exposure to a word increases the likelihood that a student will read and write that word correctly, as well as remember its meaning. In this case, connecting the name of each state with its abbreviation and location in a game format gives additional exposure to several pieces of information at once and provides a memorable review. The use of State Cards should be encouraged as an additional reinforcement if needed.

G. Writing *Language Skills, Thinking Skills*

In Part 5 of this lesson you will be asked to make a Unit Presentation to your family, and tell about what you have learned in the Growing

Pains Unit. In this presentation, you will have an opportunity to share the work you've done in your Student Notebook, your Character Profiles, the crafts or special projects you have completed, and anything else you care to include.

Think about the things you would like to include in your Unit Presentation, and list them on a piece of scrap paper. Then number the items in the order that you would like to share them. Now copy your list in the correct order into your Student Notebook. You can use this list while you are giving your Unit Presentation, so that you won't forget anything you wanted to share.

H. Completing the reading log each day gives your student a sense of accomplishment, as well as the opportunity to work independently.

H. **Independent Reading** *Language Skills*

Choose something to read that you will enjoy. Then, find a quiet, comfortable place and read for the following length of time:

25 minutes 30 minutes

Be sure to write down what you read today on the Reading Log in your Student Notebook.

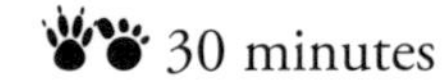

Lesson 6, Part 3

Connect Learning to Life

Your child has read and copied many quotations about wisdom in life. Now he will make up some of his own. This challenges your child to use higher level thinking skills. It is one thing to observe a pattern, and quite another to add to the pattern with your own original thinking. This also incorporates the final step of applying new information to your life.

A. **Quotation Notebook** *Language Skills, Thinking Skills*

Reread the quotations in your Student Notebook. Then make up your own quotation by writing a sentence that tells something you think is important to do. Have you been able to apply this new quotation in your own life? Tell about what happened.

Follow the directions above and make up an additional quotation.

B. When your child reads, make a list of any words he has trouble with. Look for possible patterns to his mistakes, and before your next session review those words with him. You may read them aloud, or ask him to do so.

B. **Reader** *Language Skills, History*

The Matchlock Gun: page 54 (Chapter IX) to the bottom of page 57
Ambush in the Wilderness: page 76 (Chapter Ten) through page 78

Read the above assignment from *The Matchlock Gun* aloud, and then follow along as someone else reads the assignment from *Ambush in the Wilderness.*

Read the above assignment from *The Matchlock Gun* silently, and then read the assignment from *Ambush in the Wilderness* aloud.

Read the above assignments from *The Matchlock Gun* and *Ambush in the Wilderness* silently.

C. Read-Aloud & Discussion *Language Skills, Thinking Skills, History*

Abigail Adams: page 130, paragraph 5 ("In 1793...") through page 136, paragraph 4

Follow the directions for your level and read or listen to the assignment from *Abigail Adams*. Then ask your teacher to read the discussion questions. Think about what you know from the story, and answer in your own words. Give any examples you can think of from the story that help show your answer.

Listen carefully as your teacher reads the assignment from *Abigail Adams.*

Read the assignment from *Abigail Adams* aloud.

Discussion Questions: Why do you think it was so important to John to have Abigail with him as he became President of the United States? What pressures did he have to deal with? Why do you think John wanted to avoid war with France, even though their actions could be viewed as insulting to the United States?

D. Vocabulary & Spelling *Language Skills, Thinking Skills*

Write each vocabulary word listed below on an index card. Use a dictionary to look up the meaning of each word, and write it on the card. Then on the back of each card, draw a picture or write a clue so you can remember how the word was used in the story.

barricaded **ponderous** **furrow** **treacherous** **outdistance**

desertion **retreat** **maneuvered** **copse** **surgeon**

You are the teacher. Look at the word cards you made in Part 1 of this lesson and tell others what sound the underlined or highlighted letters in each word make.

Then use the word cards that have the letter combination *ee* to write a funny story in your Student Notebook. Make it as short as possible and use all the words. Do the same thing with the word cards that have each of the other letter combinations that spell the sound e. These funny stories will help you remember which words use the letters *ee*, *ea*, *ie* and *y* to spell the sound *e*.

Repeat the process with one of the ways the suffix *ly* is added to a word.

Repeat the process with two of the ways the suffix *ly* is added to a word.

E. History *Art, Language Skills, Thinking Skills*

You are almost finished with the stories you have been reading or listening to. Follow the instructions below to create Character Portraits.

E. When your child completes the Character Portrait, he is employing important thinking skills. After learning about a character, your child will evaluate what he has learned. This evaluation takes place based upon standards of behavior, and gives you insight into how your child views the character and behavior of others. Use this activity to discuss strengths or weaknesses in real life as well.

Choose a character from either *The Courage of Sarah Noble* or *The Matchlock Gun* and complete the Character Portrait in your Student Notebook for him or her. On the following page, draw a picture of the character you chose doing something you read about in the book. If you want, instead of using your imagination you can trace one of the pictures in your book. Add color to your drawing with crayons, colored pencils, or markers.

Follow the directions above for another character of your choice from *Ambush in the Wilderness.*

Choose one character from *Ambush in the Wilderness* and another from *Abigail Adams*, and complete the Character Portraits in your Student Notebook for each of them. On the pages following each portrait, draw a picture of the character you chose. If you want, instead of drawing from your imagination, you can trace one of the pictures from each of your books. Add color to your pictures with crayons, colored pencils, or watercolors.

F. States *Geography, Thinking Skills*

Mix up your State Cards for this unit and lay them face down on the table or floor. Then Play State Card Concentration by turning up one card, and trying to find the other two cards that go with it. When you turn over three cards that don't match, return them to their face down position and try again. When you find three cards that do match, remove them from the game. Continue until you have removed all the cards that go together.

G. Cooking *Language Skills, Thinking Skills, Drawing*

G. Self-evaluation is an important part of gaining new skills and knowledge. By considering the successfulness of a lesson, you are helping your child gain needed skill for future improvement. While you will have good insights as an adult, his observations can become personal revelation about the best ways to become successful.

Talk with your teacher about your cooking experiences in this unit. Was it difficult to follow the recipes? Did you learn anything new? If so, what? Which recipe did you enjoy making the most? Which recipe did your family enjoy the most? After you discuss these questions with your teacher, in your Student Notebook write a complete sentence that summarizes your thoughts about each one.

Then, with your parent's permission and supervision choose a recipe that you enjoyed making in this unit, and prepare it again for your family. If you would prefer, you can select a different recipe from *Eat Your Way Through the USA* that comes from one of the states you have studied so far, and prepare it instead.

H. Independent Reading *Language Skills*

Choose something to read that you will enjoy. Then, find a quiet, comfortable place and read for the following length of time:

25 minutes 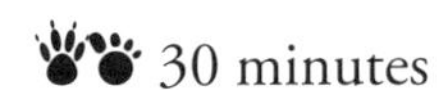 30 minutes

Be sure to write down what you read today on the Reading Log in your Student Notebook.

Lesson 6, Part 4

A. **Copywork & Dictation** *Language Skills, Thinking Skills*

Look carefully at your assigned passage below, and read it silently. Show your teacher any words you don't know, and practice saying them aloud. Now read the passage aloud, or ask your teacher to read it to you.

When you are finished copying or writing from dictation, compare your copy to the text and make any needed corrections.

Copy, or write as your teacher dictates, a portion of the paragraph at the top of page 60 ("Her head struck…") through the next two paragraphs ("… show his grandchildren, maybe.") in *The Matchlock Gun.*

Copy, or write as your teacher dictates, page 80, paragraph 4 ("Colonel Washington is alive? . .") through paragraph 6 in *Ambush in the Wilderness.*

Write as your teacher dictates page 80, paragraph 9 ("Patrick introduced …") through page 81, paragraph 2 in *Ambush in the Wilderness.*

B. **Reader** *Language Skills, History*

The Matchlock Gun: bottom of page 57 ("Edward tried…") through page 62
Ambush in the Wilderness: page 79 ("Darkness was…") through page 83

Read the above assignment from *The Matchlock Gun* aloud, and then follow along as someone else reads the assignment from *Ambush in the Wilderness.*

Read the above assignment from *The Matchlock Gun* silently, and then read the assignment from *Ambush in the Wilderness* aloud.

Read the above assignments from *The Matchlock Gun* and *Ambush in the Wilderness* silently.

C. **Read-Aloud & Narration** *Language Skills, Thinking Skills, History*

Abigail Adams: page 136, paragraph 5 ("When Congress…") through page 143

Follow the directions for your level and read, or listen as your teacher reads, the above assignment from *Abigail Adams*. Then, in your own words, retell what happened on page 143 ("It was the strength. . ."). Try to remember as many details as possible. Then tell your teacher as many ways as you can remember that John and Abigail Adams served their country. You may reread the passage or listen as your teacher rereads the part you are to retell.

Listen carefully as your teacher reads the assigned passage.

Read the assigned passage aloud.

Teaching Tip

What helps a child remember a language lesson after it is completed? The ability to identify what was learned in the pages of a real book!

D. Mechanics and Editing

Language Skills, Thinking Skills

Today you are going to continue your review of the tools for writing that you have learned. To begin, print the Mechanics Toolkit 4 cards from Appendix B or your Student Resources CD, and cut them out. When you are finished, place them on the table in front of you, and read all the Rule cards. Then find two Example cards that go with each rule.

You may want to mix up the Example cards to make it more of a challenge, or follow the directions in Appendix B to play Mechanics Toolkit Concentration.

Now continue your review by reading the Rule cards once again. Find two examples of each one in your reader, or any other book. Write the examples you find in your Student Notebook.

E. Sometimes it is helpful to take notes while your child shares his recollections of information learned. It makes what your child is saying seem important, it gives a practical example of how to use note taking, and provides a visible list for your child of all that he has accomplished.

E. Science

Thinking Skills

Complete the Earth Science Matching game in your Student Notebook.[4] When you are finished, tell your teacher what you remember about the things named in the activity. If you want help remembering, you can look back at the pages in the unit where you learned about each topic.

F. States

Geography, Thinking Skills

Find the Regional Summary Pages in the back of your Student Notebook. Then, use your *Atlas of the United States* to fill in the information for Maine, Pennsylvania, New York, New Jersey, and Delaware.

When you are finished, look at the State I.D. game in your Student Notebook, and draw a line from the map of each state to its name. On the lines at the bottom, write each state's nickname.[5] If you have trouble remembering, and your teacher agrees, it's fine to use your maps and State Pages to complete this activity.

G. Writing *Language Skills, Thinking Skills*

Now that you have completed your readers and the read-aloud book, make a book review card. The purpose of a book review card is to give a brief description of what you read or heard, and then to tell what you thought of the book. It should not include as much information as a book report. The goal is to give someone who has not read the book enough information to decide whether or not they might like to read it. In a sense, it is like an advertisement for a book. Give information about the good points without retelling the story.

G. Word banks are an excellent way to build vocabulary and encourage writing. When you provide a list for your child to use, that puts the focus on the thinking that goes into the answer, not just searching for the right word or its spelling. Vocabulary and spelling are both strengthened by reading, writing, and speaking the word correctly. It is not cheating to give your child a word bank, since the goal is to build your child's ability to give the best answer possible.

How to Create a Book Review Card:

Write your book review on a large index card or on the page provided in your Student Notebook. Include the following information:

- name of the book;
- author of the book (person who wrote the book);
- illustrator of the book (person who drew the pictures);
- name of the company that published the book;
- date the book was published.

Most of this information can be found on the title page of the book.

Rehearse, or practice telling, what you will write about the story and how you liked it. Once you have discussed your thoughts enough to know what you want to write, you can begin. If you don't know how to spell some of the words you want to use, ask your teacher to make a word bank for you.

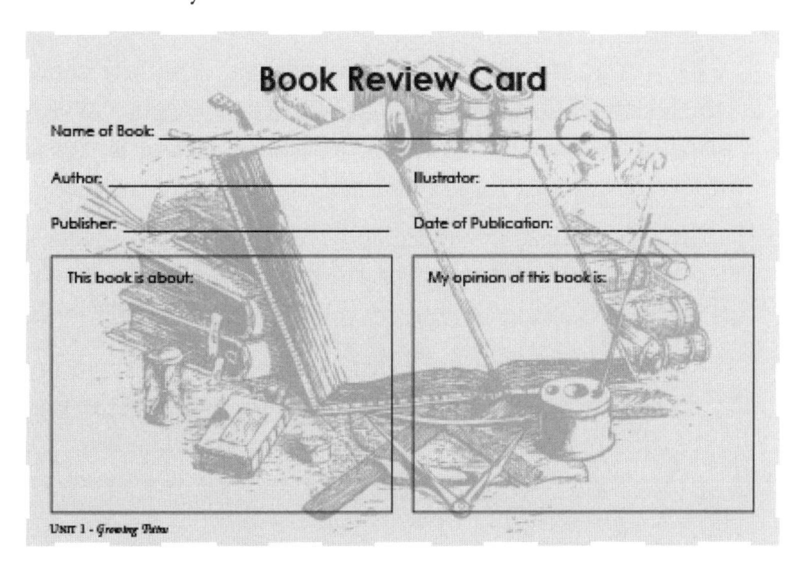

Book Review Card

Name of Book: __________

Author: __________ Illustrator: __________

Publisher: __________ Date of Publication: __________

This book is about:	My opinion of this book is:

Unit 1 - Growing Pains

Next, write a few sentences to tell what the story was about. Since you only have a few sentences, choose the most important facts to tell.

Finally, write a few sentences to tell what you thought about the story. It would be good to tell whether you liked the book and then give some examples of what you did or did not like about it. Remember to use a word bank if you need it.

- Create a book review card for either *The Courage of Sarah Noble* or *The Matchlock Gun.*
- Create a book review card for *Ambush in the Wilderness.*
- Create a book review card for *Abigail Adams.*

H. A reading log is an important part of a portfolio. It documents sequential effort and is a satisfying way for a child to see work completion. You may also want to make a list of books read for this unit, which may include bibliographical information, such as author, publisher, and copyright date. This is an easy way to build awareness of bibliographical information.

H. **Independent Reading** *Language Skills*

Choose something to read that you will enjoy. Then, find a quiet, comfortable place and read for the following length of time:

25 minutes 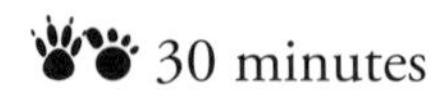 30 minutes

Congratulations on completing six weeks of independent reading! Today's entry in your Reading Log will be the last one for this unit. Make sure you have included all the information needed on your log such as book titles, authors, and dates read.

Look over all that you have accomplished during your independent reading time. If you would like, share your Reading Log with others during your Unit Presentation tomorrow.

Lesson 6, Part 5

This part is set aside for completion of any work left undone from the lesson, and review of concepts and content. It is also a time to expand the work of the lesson by doing art, mapping, or games.

As your child becomes better at connecting concepts to examples in literature and instruction, a basis is forming for doing the same thing in writing. Later units will expand this skill.

- Listen as your teacher reviews the Steps for Thinking from the Growing Pains Unit that you have just completed. Talk about how you can apply the Steps for Thinking to what you have read or discussed, and see if you can think of any examples in this unit.
- Gather your vocabulary cards together and mix them up. Randomly choose word cards. Read the word on the front and try to tell your teacher what the word means, or tell how it was used in the story. Give yourself a point for every word you can use correctly. See how many points you can get!
- Tell everyone that you have written funny stories to help remember some of the words that use the letters *ee*, *ea*, *ie* and *y* to spell the sound *e*. Read the stories to them. Be prepared to make copies of your stories if other people want to use them to help remember which letters spell the sound *e*.

Teaching Tip

Sometimes silly sayings, pictures or ideas can make information more memorable. For some children (and adults) it can be a key to making past learning more useable.

Also read one of the stories you wrote about adding the suffix *ly* to words with certain spellings.

- A timeline is another way to picture information quickly and easily. The goal is to know a few key events that help you remember the nature of the times. Cut out the timeline strips in your Student Notebook. To help you remember each event, choose a category and color for each timeline strip in your Student Notebook. Here are the categories:

  Military Action - red
  Settler/Citizen Action - green
  Government Action - blue

  Lightly write the color you have chosen on the back of each strip. Now arrange the strips in the order you think they happened.

  Check your decisions about color and order with the answer key. Once you are sure you are correct, write the date that each event happened on its strip. Then use colored pencils or crayons to lightly shade or draw a border around the strip according to its category. Now glue the strips on the timeline above the correct dates in your Student Notebook. [6]

- Make a Unit Presentation to your family that tells about what you have learned in the Growing Pains Unit. Share your Student Notebook, the character sketches, and things you made during this unit such as candles and your watercolor pictures. You might also want to invite your family to play Quoits. Don't forget to stand still and speak clearly. After your presentation, be sure to ask if anyone has questions.

- Play Growing Pains Bingo with your family.

Culminating activities are a key part of solidifying learning. By presenting information learned, opinions formed, and skills practiced, your children also connect new information to past learning. Encourage your children to be the guide to the unit, acquainting others with the key concepts, events, people, and activities. Allow students to be creative in their presentations, and to truly make them their own!

Congratulations on completing Unit 1 in *Paths of Settlement!*

Answers

1.

ee	*ea*	*ie*	*y*
seen	lean	chief	Trudy
knees	reach	Friedrich	victory
agreed	meantime	thief	windy
screeches	beast		inky
			Albany

ly added to a beginning word

soberly	distinctly	directly	exactly
softly	suddenly	tightly	

ly added to a word that ends with e or *l*:

finally	carefully	thankfully
surely	squarely	radically

ly added after a y at the end has been changed to *i*:

luckily	happily	hastily

2. Answer key is in Appendix A.

3. Answer key is in Appendix A.

4. Answer key is in Appendix A.

5. Answer key is in Appendix A.

6. (1745) Many Europeans have settled in America. (green)
(1748) More settlers move west into French territory. (green)
(1754) French and Indian War begins. (red)
(1755) George Washington survives Battle of Monongahela. (red)
(1763) Line of Proclamation established at end of French and Indian War. (blue)

Lesson 1, Part 1

Steps for Thinking

1. The connections of heritage, or where your family comes from, are strong.
2. The people in our family and community shape our first beliefs about the world. You take on their outlook because of your strong connection to them.
3. You must feel very strongly to disagree with those who are part of your heritage.

You may want to post the Steps for Thinking somewhere nearby for easy reference. Read these with your students, or have the students read them by themselves. Explain any concept or vocabulary that is not understood.

Materials

- *The American Revolution (Munford)*
- *Guns for General Washington*
- *George Washington*
- *The Eve of Revolution*
- *Atlas of the United States*
- *Profiles from History, Vol. 2*
- *Eat Your Way Through the USA*
- *Klutz Watercolor Book*
- Outline Map of the U.S.
- USA Activity CD
- Ingredients for recipe (Part 3)
- Activity (Parts 2 and 4)
  Modeling clay (3 colors)
  Toothpick
  1-pound bag of dried beans
  Clear glass or plastic bowl

A. Copywork & Dictation — *Language Skills, Thinking Skills*

Look carefully at your assigned passage below, and read it silently. Show your teacher any words you don't know, and practice saying them aloud. Now read the passage aloud, or ask your teacher to read it to you.

When you are finished copying or writing from dictation, compare your copy to the text and make any needed corrections.

Copy or write as your teacher dictates from *The American Revolution*, page 11, paragraph 1 ("It is all a little...").

Copy or write as your teacher dictates from *Guns for General Washington*, page 5, paragraph 1 ("As he hurried to join...").

Write as your teacher dictates from *Guns for General Washington*, page 4, paragraph 2 ("Behind him, Will heard...").

B. Reader — *Language Skills, History*

The American Revolution: page 7, (Chapter 1) through page 11, paragraph 1
Guns for General Washington: Chapter 1

Read the above assignment from *The American Revolution* aloud, and then follow along as someone else reads the assignment from *Guns for General Washington*.

Read the above assignment from *The American Revolution* silently, and then read the assignment from *Guns for General Washington* aloud.

Read the above assignments from *The American Revolution* and *Guns for General Washington* silently.

C. Preview, or point out, the questions your child is to answer before reading aloud. This sets the stage for active listening and better comprehension.

C. Read-Aloud & Discussion

Language Skills, Thinking Skills, History

George Washington: page 1 to the bottom of page 4

Follow the instructions below for your level. When you are finished, discuss what is happening in this section from the British point of view. Then talk about what is happening from the colonists' point of view. How are their viewpoints different? Who do you think is right? Think about what you know from the story and discuss the passage in your own words. Give any examples you can think of from the story.

Listen carefully as your teacher reads the above assignment from *George Washington* aloud.

Read the above assignment from *George Washington* aloud.

D. Suggested words provide study that focuses on an aspect of language such as phonics, word roots, or affixes. These lists include words taken from the readers. Please feel free to add up to five words each week that are particular to your child's needs.

Read the list of words to your child. If he would rather spell the words aloud than write them, it is perfectly acceptable. As you dictate each word, put small dots beside any misspelled words. Then have your child copy them onto the Student Notebook page.

D. Spelling

Language Skills, Thinking Skills

Look at the list of words below. Then in your Student Notebook, underline the prefix *un* at the beginning of each word and tell what the word means. A prefix is a group of letters added to the beginning of the word to change its meaning. The prefix *un* means not, something is missing, or the opposite. For example, if you are unhappy, that means you are not happy.

unfold unmoved uncover uncut[1]

Listen as your teacher reads each of the following words. Then spell the word as best you can either aloud or by writing it in your Student Notebook. Your teacher may add up to five words that are difficult for you to read or write.

unlikely	unloaded	unrolled	unaware
unable	uncertain	unfortunate	unkind
undecided	unbelievable	uncomfortable	unrealistic
unhappily	unpleasant	unhitched	unpredictable

E. For background information that may help during discussions, read the section entitled Background in the Reader's Guide located on the inside front cover of *The Eve of Revolution*.

E. History

Geography, Thinking Skills

Today you will begin reading *The Eve of Revolution*. Even though the main characters in this book are **fictional**, or made up, their stories can help you understand the times leading up to the Revolutionary War. The events written about by the Wilcox family in *The Eve of Revolution* begin just six years after the end of the French and Indian Wars.

Together with your teacher, read from the Introduction through page 7 in *The Eve of Revolution*. This book uses the words *Britain* and *British* a great deal. Remember that these words refer to people from the countries on the island of Great Britain—England, Wales, and Scotland.

In Lesson 5 of the last unit, you read that the French and Indian Wars were very expensive to fight, and that neither France nor England could afford to go into battle once again. Can you think of any reasons why Britain, which is another name for England, would begin to charge new taxes on things sold in the colonies?[2] Look back at the second paragraph on the Introduction page in *The Eve of Revolution*. What reason does that paragraph give for the new taxes?[3] Do you think the French and Indian Wars were really fought for that reason?[4]

Talk with your teacher about the effects of Britain's new taxes on colonial farmers. In your Student Notebook, write two or three sentences that explain how these taxes affected colonists. Be sure to include how the people felt about the taxes. Remember to use complete sentences.

Does your family pay taxes? Talk with your teacher about some of the taxes your family pays.

Pick one type of tax and research it at the library or on the Internet. When you are finished, write the tax you chose in your Student Notebook, and tell how the government uses it. Does your family benefit from this tax? Remember to use complete sentences.

E. Each word in **bold** letters is considered a vocabulary word. It is a word that may or may not be new to your child. You can write these vocabulary words on index cards and use them for occasional review, but not for memorizing. Give the child the meaning of the words if he doesn't remember. Try to use the new vocabulary words during conversation, and encourage your student to do the same.

Each time your student makes a vocabulary card for this unit, have him write *FD* (for Freedom Decided) in the upper left corner. This will make it possible to review vocabulary by unit at the end of the year.

F. States *Geography, History, Thinking Skills*

In your *Atlas of the United States*, read the pages about Maryland. When you are finished, find the blank map of Maryland in your Student Notebook and complete the following assignments:

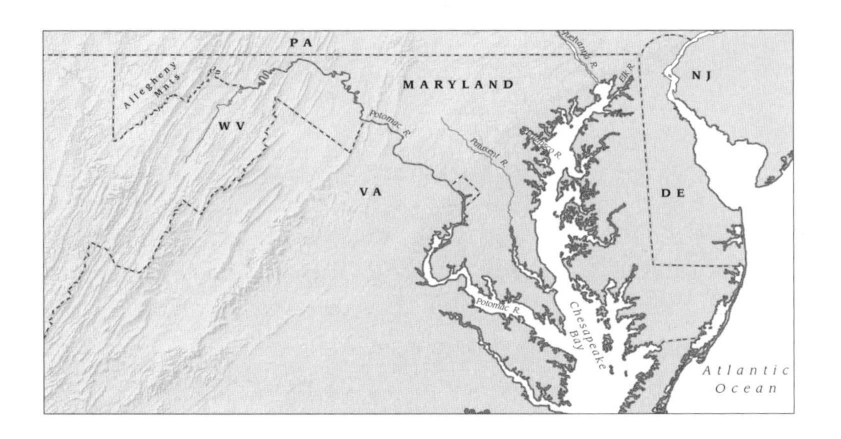

- Place a small star on the spot where Annapolis is located, and label it. Annapolis is the capital city of Maryland.
- Place a small star with a circle around it on the spot where Washington, D.C. is located, and label it. Washington, D.C. is the capital of the United States.
- Label the Atlantic Ocean and the Chesapeake Bay.

The addition of Lapbook pages to regularly assigned work can be overwhelming to some students. The Lapbook activities are designed to **replace** the corresponding Student Notebook assignments, particularly for younger students. They may also be beneficial to many older students who prefer a more hands-on approach to learning, or for review.

- Color the lines showing the Potomac, Patuxent, and Susquehanna Rivers blue, and label them.
- Lightly color the area where the Allegheny Mountains are located green, and label them.
- Color the lines showing the Patapsco and Elk Rivers blue, and label them.
- Label the four states that border Maryland.

G. **Doing** *Art*

In your *Klutz Watercolor Book*, read page 22, entitled "Colors and Color Combinations." Talk with your teacher about hot and cold colors. Then complete the activities on pages 23 and 24. Use other watercolor paper to continue playing with color combinations.

If you find you have extra time after your regular schoolwork is finished, and your parent agrees, try painting something you can see outside your window. Experiment with different color combinations.

H. **Independent Reading** *Language Skills*

Choose something to read that you will enjoy. Then, find a quiet, comfortable place and read for the following length of time:

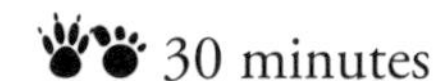

25 minutes 30 minutes

Over time, it's fun to see how much you have read. Be sure to write down what you read today on the Reading Log in your Student Notebook.

Lesson 1, Part 2

A. **Quotation Notebook** *Language Skills, History, Thinking Skills*

In this section you will copy statements from famous American documents. These documents were the result of the **principles**, or standards, of the American Revolution. Many people believed in these principles so much that they gave all that they had, including their lives, so that these standards would become the basis for their new government.

The first document quoted is the Declaration of Independence. This document told the world what the colonists believed and why they believed it. Any definitions included beneath the passage are to help you understand the meaning. Do not copy them as part of the quotation.

A. The words spoken by a person in a speech, or a copy of an original document are both considered **primary sources**. That means they did not come from a third person, but directly from the original source. Primary sources give you a unique look at history because you can judge it for yourself, rather than seeing or hearing it through the thinking of someone else.

Copy the following quotation into your Student Notebook, and then talk with your teacher about its meaning. You may want to include parts of the Declaration of Independence in your presentation at the end of this unit, so practice reading this section aloud.

> When in the Course of human events, it becomes necessary for one people to dissolve the political bands which have connected them with another,

Definition (as used in this document):
dissolve - to bring a relationship to an end

Draw or create a **symbol**, or picture, that helps you remember this part of the Declaration. Put it beneath the quotation.

A. This passage contains words that are not normally capitalized today. The author did this to emphasize the importance of these words.

B. Reader *Language Skills, History*

The American Revolution: page 11, paragraph 2 ("I wasn't sure. . .") through page 17, paragraph 2
Guns for General Washington: Chapter 2

Read the above assignment from *The American Revolution* aloud, and then follow along as someone else reads the assignment from *Guns for General Washington.*

Read the above assignment from *The American Revolution* silently, and then read the assignment from *Guns for General Washington* aloud.

Read the above assignments from *The American Revolution* and *Guns for General Washington* silently.

Teaching Tip

Point out to your child that chapter titles and headings are tools to identify main ideas. After your child reads a section or chapter, ask him to tell you how the title, or heading, relates to what he read.

C. Read-Aloud & Narration *Language Skills, Thinking Skills, History*

George Washington: page 4, last paragraph ("One afternoon…") to the bottom of page 10

Follow the instructions below for your level. Then, in your own words, tell what happened in the story from George's point of view, or pretend you are George and tell what you think happened. Try to remember as many details as possible. You may reread the passage or listen as your teacher rereads the part you are to retell.

Listen carefully as your teacher reads the above assignment from *George Washington* aloud.

Read the above assignment from *George Washington* aloud.

D. Editing *Language Skills, Thinking Skills, History*

In this section, you will read and discuss parts of a famous speech attributed to Patrick Henry. This speech took place before the delegates of the Virginia colony on March 23, 1775. These delegates were discussing whether they should join Massachusetts in declaring themselves part of the war to break free from the control of the government of England.

Not only does this speech show the beliefs of a great American patriot, it also shows how to express your thoughts well. Though some of the language used will seem old-fashioned to you, when you understand the meaning of the words he chose you will understand his thoughts and beliefs even better.

Then you will practice taking his thoughts and putting them into your own words, or paraphrasing. Here is an example:

> "No man thinks more highly than I do of the patriotism, as well as abilities, of the very worthy gentlemen who have just addressed the House."

A paraphrase:

> The fine gentlemen who just spoke to us are devoted to our country and have many abilities. No one thinks more highly of them than I do.

Read the section of the speech included in your Student Notebook. One word in the passage is underlined and in italics. Try to figure out the meaning of that word using the **context**, or words around it. Then use a dictionary to look up definitions of the words underlined in the paragraph, and any other words you do not understand. Did you get the right meaning of the word in italics by using the context?

Use a highlighter or yellow crayon to highlight or underline the appropriate sentence(s). Then paraphrase by rewriting in your own words underneath the passage.

E. **Science** *Thinking Skills*

In the first few lessons of this unit you will learn about molecules and atoms, the water cycle, and some types of clouds. Take a few minutes to discuss what you already know about these things with your teacher. When you are finished, and before reading further in this section, make a list of questions or things you would like to find out about these subjects. There is a page provided in your Student Notebook for the list. Later, you will have an opportunity to look back and see if your questions have been answered.

Munford, the main character in your book *The American Revolution*, introduced himself to you as a water molecule. You may already know about molecules, and if you do this will be a good review. If you have not yet learned about them, this is a perfect time to do so.

First of all, **molecules** are the building blocks that make up matter, and matter makes up everything around you. The chair you are sitting on, the book in front of you, and the tree outside your window are all different types of matter, containing different types of molecules. Things that describe matter, and help you to tell one type from another, are called **properties**. An object's properties include its color, shape, smell, taste, and what it feels like to the touch.

The official definition of **matter** is anything that takes up space and has mass. That is a good definition, because one property of all objects is that they take up space. For instance, you are taking up space on your chair, the book in front of you is taking up space on the table, and the tree outside your window is taking up space in the yard. Another property that all objects share is that they have **mass**. *Mass* is a measurement of how much matter an object contains, and how much the force of gravity pulls on it. When an object is close to the surface of the earth, its mass is very similar to *weight*. But it is not quite the same thing. Think about an astronaut floating in his space capsule—his mass is the same as it was on earth, but you know his weight has changed because he can now float. This is because the farther you travel upward into the atmosphere, the less pull gravity has on you.

Another important property of matter that can easily be observed is its state, or phase. Everything on earth is a solid, a liquid, or a gas—which are the three most common states, or phases, of matter. The rocks in your Rock Study kit are good examples of solid matter. Water is liquid matter, and the air you are breathing is a gas.

The molecules that make up matter are extremely small, and cannot be seen without a microscope. To get a better idea of Munford's size, look at one drop of water. Even though it is small, that single drop of water is made up of millions of water molecules just like Munford. It is hard to imagine a million of anything, so if possible compare a one-pound bag of dried beans to your drop of water. Now consider this: if each of those beans represents one water molecule, it will take more than 1,000 bags of beans like the one you are looking at to represent your tiny drop of water!

As small as molecules are, however, they are made up of even smaller pieces, called atoms. An atom is the tiniest piece of anything. So far, scientists have named over 100 different types of atoms, and they suspect there are more that have not yet been discovered. These atoms join together in different ways to make different types of matter.

For example, Munford the water molecule, like all water molecules, is made of three atoms. He has one oxygen atom and two hydrogen atoms. This particular combination of atoms gives water all its special properties. It is also why you might sometimes hear water referred to as H_2O—because it has two *H* (hydrogen) atoms and one *O* (oxygen) atom. No other combination of atoms will look, feel, taste, or act exactly like water.

From Dr. Beechick

"Asking questions is crucial to science, so children need to practice that habit. Their first questions may not be on the frontiers of science, and they may find answers to them in books or by observing nature, but they should learn the questioning habit, anyway. Before school age, most children do have a natural questioning habit, but our answer-oriented schooling system too often snuffs it out. As children grow older, questions should be more sophisticated. They should not be just the three-year-old's "Why?" but should be based on much knowledge. Questions should take into account all that a child knows and lead toward the next layer of knowledge."

– *You Can Teach Your Child Successfully*, page 328

Use modeling clay to roll a ball about the size of a ping pong ball. Choose another color and roll two balls, each about one-half the size of the first one. Use a toothpick to mark the larger ball with an *O* and each of the smaller balls with *H*. Now look at the example below and press the smaller balls into the larger one. This is a model of a water molecule like Munford.

Use the model below to label the flow chart in your Student Notebook.

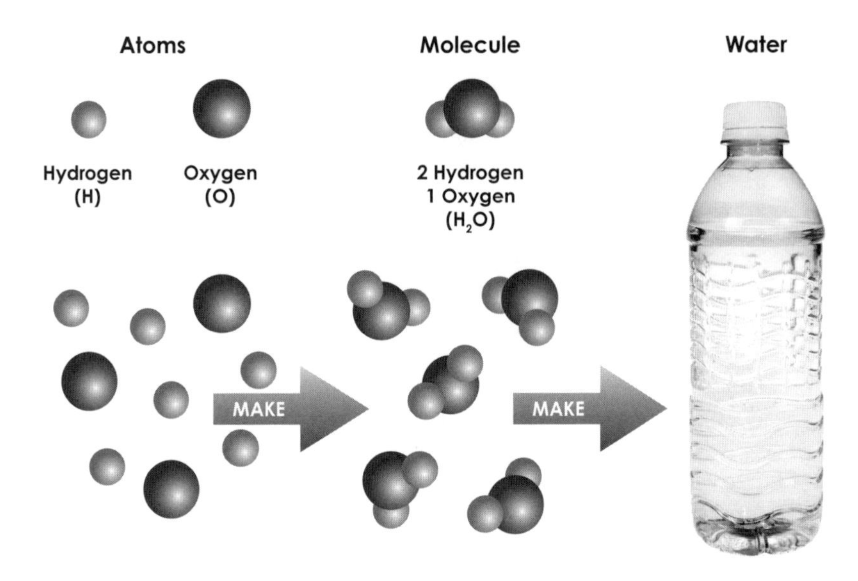

Talk with your teacher about the states of matter, and think of some examples of solids and liquids. Write three examples of each in your Student Notebook. Then list as many properties, or things that describe each one, as you can.[5]

Talk with your teacher and explain as much as you can about matter, mass, and weight. Then write at least one sentence in your Student Notebook that tells about each one.[6]

From Dr. Beechick

"Also use maps frequently in studies of history, missionaries, and current events. Maps are sometimes thought of as visual aids that help to make a Bible story or other learning "come alive," but the reverse is more probably true: the story helps to make a spot on the map come alive. In any case, map reading is complex and children need repeated practice with maps during their school years."

– You Can Teach Your Child Successfully, page 27

F. States

Geography, History, Thinking Skills, Drawing

Look again at the pages about Maryland in your *Atlas of the United States*. Then find the State Page in your Student Notebook, and fill in the information.

Make State Cards for Maryland by following the instructions found in Appendix B. Maryland is a Mid-Atlantic state, so be sure to outline the cards in green.

G. Interactive Writing

Language Skills, Thinking Skills

This writing activity is for you and another person, your partner, to complete. Most of the time, your partner is your teacher, but it could also be a parent, brother, sister, or other family member.

It is your partner's job to write first; then you will answer a question with the number of sentences assigned below. After that, write several sentences telling what you think about what your partner has written. Make sure to end with a question you want to ask your partner, so he or she can write back to you.

Topic for your partner: Has there ever been a time when you regretted, or were sorry you had committed to do something? Tell about it. How did it turn out?

Your question: Do you think it is hard to do what you promise you will do? Why do you think so?

at least four sentences

at least five sentences

at least one paragraph

Remember that a **paragraph** is a group of sentences that relate to one topic, or main idea. State the topic or main idea of a paragraph at or near its beginning. You do not want others to read for very long without knowing for sure what you are talking about!

H. **Independent Reading** *Language Skills*

Choose something to read that you will enjoy. Then, find a quiet, comfortable place and read for the following length of time:

25 minutes   30 minutes

Be sure to write down what you read today on the Reading Log in your Student Notebook.

Lesson 1, Part 3

A. **Copywork & Dictation** *Language Skills, Thinking Skills*

Look carefully at your assigned passage below, and read it silently. Show your teacher any words you don't know, and practice saying them aloud. Now read the passage aloud, or ask your teacher to read it to you.

When you are finished copying or writing from dictation, compare your copy to the text and make any needed corrections.

Copy or write as your teacher dictates from *The American Revolution*, page 19, paragraphs 5 and 6 ("Samuel nodded…").

Copy or write as your teacher dictates from *Guns for General Washington*, page 19, paragraph 1 ("Slowly the general…").

Teaching Tip

The process of copywork and dictation gives a teacher a great deal of information. Not only does it show what your child is missing, it shows what he is getting! Reading or hearing language, and then writing it down is a multi-step process that shows understanding, processing of information, and translating that information into writing. Many times over my years as an educator, just giving a student a passage to copy or write from dictation has provided great insight into the student's ability to read, write, and comprehend. Make sure to take notice of all your child does correctly when using this process, and encourage him accordingly!

Write as your teacher dictates from *Guns for General Washington*, page 18, paragraph 1 ("Both sides had…") and page 19, paragraph 1 ("Slowly the general…").

B. Reader

Language Skills, History

The American Revolution: page 18, paragraph 1 ("The sun had. . .") through page 22, paragraph 2
Guns for General Washington: Chapter 3

Read the above assignment from *The American Revolution* aloud, and then follow along as someone else reads the assignment from *Guns for General Washington*.

Read the above assignment from *The American Revolution* silently, and then read the assignment from *Guns for General Washington* aloud.

Read the above assignments from *The American Revolution* and *Guns for General Washington* silently.

C. Read-Aloud & Discussion

Language Skills, Thinking Skills, History

George Washington: bottom of page 10 ("Easter came…") through page 19, paragraph 2

Follow the directions for your level and read or listen to the above assignment from *George Washington*. Then make up the assigned number of questions about the part of the story you just read or heard. Write your questions and ask your teacher to answer them. After discussing her thoughts, write down the best possible answers in your Student Notebook. Be sure to use complete sentences.

Listen carefully as your teacher reads the assigned passage.

Make up one question. Make up two questions.

Read the assigned passage aloud; then make up three questions.

D. Vocabulary & Spelling

Language Skills, Thinking Skills

Vocabulary:
Write each vocabulary word listed below on an index card. Use a dictionary to look up the meaning of each word, and write it on the card. Then on the back of each card, draw a picture or write a clue so you can remember how the word was used in the story.

sauntered **rebellious** **glimpse** **landlocked** **precipitate**

amateur **electrify** **cobbler** **bumpkin** **treachery**

From Dr. Beechick

"How do you teach a new word to your child? First of all, you put enough context around it to make it memorable. Memorizing a definition is usually a poor way to do this. Let's say you are teaching the word compass in its meaning of "an instrument for showing direction by a swinging magnetic needle pointing north." A child who doesn't know what a compass is will still not know much about a compass after he learns the definition. Will he picture a needle like his mother sews with? Will he picture something swinging like a pendulum or like a baseball bat? He may have an inkling of the purpose of a compass, but not understanding of how or why it works or who it might be useful to. The bare, unadorned meaning he gets, whether more wrong or more right, certainly is not easy to remember, and especially so if this is just one in a list of words he is learning out of their natural context."

– *You Can Teach Your Child Successfully*, page 12

Spelling:
Look at the list of words below. Then in your Student Notebook, underline the prefix *un* at the beginning of each word and tell what the word means.

unfair unimportant uneven untrained[7]

Look at the spelling words you wrote in Part 1. If you did not write them in that part, ask your teacher to read each word, and write it in your Student Notebook now. Check your spelling against the list and correct it if necessary. When you are finished, cover each word with your hand, and try to spell it aloud. Then uncover it and see if you were correct. Review the meanings of any words that you do not remember.

Using a dictionary, look up words that begin with the prefix *un*.

In your Student Notebook, make a list of words that are new to you, according to the number of new words assigned below. Write the meaning of each new word.

four words six words eight words

E. **History** *Thinking Skills*

Together with your teacher, read page 8 ("From Benjamin's journal ...") through page 12 in *The Eve of Revolution.*

Most of the people you have read about so far in *The American Revolution* and *The Eve of Revolution* were part of groups called Sons of Liberty and Daughters of Liberty. They were **patriots**. Even though most patriots were not newcomers to the area, they had adopted a totally new attitude that set them apart from others. Many of them had been born in America, to parents who had also been born in America. Because of that, their ties to England seemed very distant and loose. As a matter of fact, most had never even visited the country that ruled them. American patriots were proud of their **self-sufficiency**, or ability to supply their own needs, and loved their independence. They felt that England did not have the right to take advantage of their hard work, and believed that those who lived in the country should be the ones to rule it.

At the library or on the Internet research the Sons and Daughters of Liberty. Find out at least three things about each group, and list them in your Student Notebook. Do you agree with the things they did? Why, or why not? Write two or three sentences in your Student Notebook telling what you agree with and why, or what you disagree with and why. Be sure to use complete sentences, and include what you learn about these groups in your presentation at the end of this unit.

E. There is a Glossary on the last page of *The Eve of Revolution* that defines all the words in bold print throughout the book.

The Internet can be a useful tool for research, but we suggest that your child use it only with your permission and supervision, and while following your family's rules.

If you lived during the colonial period in America, and the things you have been reading about were happening, how do you think you might react? Why? What would you do? Write two or three paragraphs in your Student Notebook that explain your thoughts.

F. States *Geography, History, Thinking Skills*

George Washington was born and raised in the colony of Virginia, so that is the first state you will study in the Southern region of the United States. There are 12 Southern states, all located to the south or southwest of both the New England and Mid-Atlantic regions.

In your *Atlas of the United States*, read the pages about Virginia. When you are finished, find the blank map of Virginia in your Student Notebook and complete the following assignments:

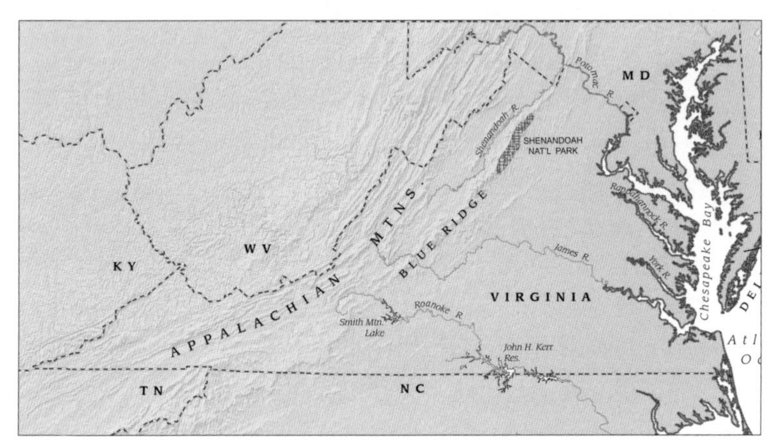

- Place a small star on the spot where Richmond is located, and label it. Richmond is the capital city of Virginia.
- Place a small star with a circle around it on the spot where Washington, D.C. is located, and label it. Washington, D.C. is the capital of the United States.
- Label the Atlantic Ocean and Chesapeake Bay.
- Label the Delmarva Peninsula, which is part of Virginia.
- Color and label the area where Shenandoah National Park is located.
- Color the lines showing the Potomac, Rappahannock, York, James, and Roanoke Rivers blue, and label them.
- Lightly color the area green where the Blue Ridge is located, and label it.

- Color and label Smith Mountain Lake and the John H. Kerr Reservoir. Explain to your teacher what a reservoir is.
- Color the line showing the Shenandoah River blue, and label it.
- Label the five states that border Virginia.

G. **Cooking** *Language Skills, Thinking Skills, Drawing*
With your parent's permission and supervision, look in *Eat Your Way Through the USA*, choose a recipe that comes from either Maryland or Virginia, and prepare it for your family. After everyone has had a taste, find out who liked it, and whether anyone would like to have it again. What did you think about it?

In your Student Notebook, draw a picture of the dish you chose to make and write the following number of sentences about your family's reaction to it:

two sentences three sentences four sentences

G. The cooking activities are a very important part of connecting meaning and context to geography learning. When a particular style of cooking or ingredient is associated with the culture or resources of a state, it makes another connection to the information learned about that state. Many aspects of geography such as culture, history, economics, and climate help students connect products with places, which relate new learning with previous learning. Plus, it's fun!

H. **Independent Reading** *Language Skills*
Choose something to read that you will enjoy. Then, find a quiet, comfortable place and read for the following length of time:

25 minutes 30 minutes

Be sure to write down what you read today on the Reading Log in your Student Notebook.

Lesson 1, Part 4

A. **Quotation Notebook** *Language Skills, History, Thinking Skills*
In this section you will continue copying statements from the Declaration of Independence. This document told the world what the colonists believed and why they believed it. Any definitions included beneath the passage are to help you understand the meaning. Do not copy them as part of the quotation.

Copy the following quotation into your Student Notebook, and then talk with your teacher about its meaning. You may want to include parts of the Declaration of Independence in your presentation at the end of this unit, so practice reading this section aloud.

> and to assume among the powers of the earth, the separate and equal station to which the Laws of Nature and of Nature's God entitle them,

Definitions (as used in this document):
assume - to take on a particular role
station - the position one holds among others like him

Draw or create a symbol that helps you remember this part of the Declaration. Put it beneath the quotation.

Teaching Tip

Since many children are reading the assignments silently, it would be good to occasionally ask your student to tell you about what he read. You may also want him to choose his favorite part of the passage and read it aloud to you. If he finds a part that is particularly dramatic or funny, ask him to read it for you expressively. If anything happens in the story that he dislikes, ask him to make sure and tell you about it, too. These are small, natural ways to do comprehension checks.

B. Reader

Language Skills, History

The American Revolution: page 22, paragraph 3 ("There was Samuel. . .") through page 28, paragraph 2
Guns for General Washington: Chapter 4

Read the above assignment from *The American Revolution* aloud, and then follow along as someone else reads the assignment from *Guns for General Washington.*

Read the above assignment from *The American Revolution* silently, and then read the assignment from *Guns for General Washington* aloud.

Read the above assignments from *The American Revolution* and *Guns for General Washington* silently.

C. Read-Aloud & Narration

Language Skills, Thinking Skills, History

George Washington: page 19, paragraph 3 ("George was …") through page 24

After reading or listening to the read-aloud assignment in *George Washington*, talk with your teacher and try to predict what will happen in the future based on what you know of the characters and events. Write down your predictions in your Student Notebook. Later you will look back and see if they were accurate. Try not to peek ahead!

Listen carefully as your teacher reads the assigned passage. Then write down something that you think will happen in the story.

Write down another thing that you think will happen in the story.

Read the assigned passage aloud. Then write down at least three things that you think will happen in the story.

D. Editing

Language Skills, Thinking Skills, History

Continue reading and discussing parts of the famous speech attributed to Patrick Henry. Read the section of the speech included in your Student Notebook. One word in the passage is underlined and in italics. Try to figure out the meaning of that word using the context, or words around it. Then use a dictionary to look up definitions of the words underlined in the paragraph, and any other words you do not understand. Did you get the right meaning of the word in italics by using the context?

Use a highlighter or yellow crayon to highlight or underline the appropriate sentence(s). Then paraphrase those sentences by rewriting them in your own words underneath the passage.

two sentences three sentences four sentences

E. Science

Thinking Skills

You know that matter is made of molecules, and molecules are made of even smaller pieces called atoms. In this part you will find out a little more about atoms and the things that make them different from one another.

To begin, look at the Periodic Table of the Elements in Appendix B. The Periodic Table is a chart showing all the **elements**, or types of atoms, that have been discovered so far. Every element has a chemical symbol, which is an abbreviation of its name. For example, you already know that the symbol for oxygen is *O*, and the symbol for hydrogen is *H*.

The center, or **nucleus**, of an atom is made of particles called protons and neutrons. In addition, other particles called electrons circle the nucleus. These three things in various combinations are what make one type of atom different from another. Look at the example at the top of your Periodic Table. The box pictured there is an enlargement of the atomic information for carbon.

Notice the arrow pointing to carbon's atomic number in the upper left corner of the box. The atomic number of an atom tells how many protons are in its nucleus, and how many electrons circle around the nucleus—which are the same. In carbon atoms, there are six protons in the nucleus and six electrons circling.

Now look at carbon's atomic weight in the upper right corner of the box. An atom's atomic weight is the number of protons plus the number of neutrons in its nucleus. The atomic weight of carbon is 12, and you already know that it has six protons. The difference between 12 and six is the number of neutrons in carbon's nucleus. Since you have all the information you need, tell your teacher how many protons, neutrons, and electrons make up one atom of carbon.[8]

Notice that the elements are arranged on the chart in order by their atomic numbers. Find the element that has an atomic number of five. Tell your teacher its name and its chemical symbol.[9] Judging by its atomic number, how many protons are in its nucleus? How many electrons circle its nucleus?[10] When you subtract boron's atomic number from its atomic weight, how many neutrons can you tell it has?[11]

Now find helium, which has an atomic number of two, and follow the directions below to make a model that shows what a helium atom looks like. To do that, you first have to decide how many protons, neutrons, and electrons are in this type of atom. Tell your teacher how many particles of each kind make up helium.[12]

E. After the lesson's end, (maybe when Dad comes home,) ask your child to use the models he has made and explain what he learned to someone not present at the lesson. Listen as he shares to find out what he has learned, and areas you may need to reinforce in the next lesson. You can encourage your child by restating what he says, just to clarify it for your understanding and his. This is an excellent way to review a lesson, and allow your child to share what he learned in his own words. Using the objects from the lesson provides additional support for memory and sharing.

Choose three colors of modeling clay. Make two marble-sized balls from the first color, and two from the second color. Press these four balls together to represent the protons and neutrons in helium's nucleus. Now make two pea-sized balls out of the third color and stick them to the inside of a clear glass or plastic bowl. Turn the bowl over on top of the nucleus you just made. The balls that are stuck to the bowl represent the electrons that circle helium's nucleus.

Talk with your teacher about each of the elements listed in your Student Notebook. Then write down the number of protons, neutrons, and electrons found in each.[13] Choose two more elements and do the same thing.

Look at the list of elements in your Student Notebook, and fill in the blanks for each one.[14]

At the library or on the Internet find out what type of electrical charges protons, neutrons, and electrons usually have. Write your answers on the lines provided in your Student Notebook.[15]

F. States

Geography, History, Thinking Skills, Drawing

Look again at the pages about Virginia in your *Atlas of the United States*. Then find the State Page in your Student Notebook, and fill in the information.

Make State Cards for Virginia by following the instructions found in Appendix B. Virginia is a Southern state, so be sure to outline the cards in purple.

Connect Learning to Life:

This activity began in the Growing Pains Unit. It is an excellent way to build writing skills in a natural way, using a conversational tone. For many students, just getting words on paper is the most difficult task. The questions asked are relevant to reading, thinking and discussion activities done, and allows the student to take previous considered ideas and apply them to real life concerns. Parent modeling is a powerful tool to show a purpose for writing skills in the real world - to tell someone how you feel, and respond to the thoughts and feelings of others!

G. Writing

Language Skills, Thinking Skills

Persuasion means to encourage someone to do something or to think a certain way. One approach you can take to **persuade**, or convince, people is by giving them **reasons**, or causes, to change what they think or do. Another way is to explain the effects their decisions or beliefs will have on others. A third way is to appeal to that person's **emotions**, or feelings, to get them to change their thoughts or actions. Writing or speaking persuasively can include one or all of these approaches.

Another part of persuasion is to consider the person giving his **opinion**, or thoughts and beliefs. If someone who is famous or well-known gives his opinion, it sometimes seems like his or her thoughts are more important than those of people who are not famous.

During this time in history, people in the colonies had strong opinions about the decisions made by the British government that concerned them. There are many examples of persuasive writing in our readers, read-aloud book, and other literature.

Look at this paragraph from the book *The American Revolution*:

> There was Samuel Adams! He was standing at the front of the room, doing his best to talk over the voices of the other men. "The new Tea Act gives the East India Company control over who can sell tea in the colonies. It is an outrage! Parliament should have no say over who can sell to the colonies. For now it is tea, but soon they will control everything we do. We must put a stop to it."

This paragraph describes Samuel Adams talking with some men. He is trying to persuade them to destroy the tea, which has arrived by ship from Britain. Reread the passage and tell about the ways he tries to persuade them.[16]

one way   two ways   three ways

One way of speaking or writing persuasively is to give someone reasons for doing something you want him to do. An example is "I think you should buy me an ice cream sundae because I have worked hard doing schoolwork and deserve a reward." Think of what you would tell your parent if you wanted to persuade him or her to buy you something expensive, or let you do something not usually allowed.

Make a list in your Student Notebook of the reasons, or explanations, you would give your parent. List at least the number of reasons as indicated below. Then talk with your parent about the effectiveness of your reasons.

two reasons   three reasons   four reasons

H. Independent Reading

Language Skills

Choose something to read that you will enjoy. Then, find a quiet, comfortable place and read for the following length of time:

25 minutes   30 minutes

Be sure to write down what you read today on the Reading Log in your Student Notebook.

Lesson 1, Part 5

This part is set aside for completion of any work left undone from the lesson, and review of concepts and content. It is also a time to expand the work in the lesson by doing art, timeline activities, or games.

Teaching Tip

Success is encouraging. Look for gains made and improvement when evaluating your child's work. Record the number of questions or words completed successfully on student work, not the number missed. Your child understands what he missed when he looks at his paper. To encourage in a realistic manner, point to gains made as a reminder of the importance of continued effort.

- Review the Steps for Thinking from the beginning of this lesson.
- Give your teacher your stack of vocabulary cards for the lesson. As she shows you each word, tell her the meaning of the word and how it was used in the story.
- Listen as your teacher reads the words that you studied from Part 1. Write each word in your Student Notebook as she dictates it. When you are finished, look at your word list and make corrections as needed. Show your teacher how you did.
- Use the United States map that is near the front of your *Atlas of the United States* to find Maryland and Virginia. Then, on the large outline map of the U.S., draw a green line around Maryland because it is a Mid-Atlantic state, and a purple line around Virginia because it is a Southern state. Write in the names of the states, and draw small stars to show where their capital cities are located. Next to the stars, write the name of each capital city.

  Add to the legend you are making on your outline map by drawing a short purple line under the green one. Next to it write *Southern.*
- Listen to or read the story about John Adams in *Profiles from History.* Talk about the discussion question with your teacher, and then complete any other activities that she assigns.

Stories help us remember the lives of real people. They help us remember the beliefs and actions that took place. It is not as important to remember details such as dates of events, as it is to place a character in a time period. With the general time period comes context for what the character did or experienced. This, in turn, reinforces the connection to the unique qualities or events of the character's life. History, literature, and thinking skills form a great partnership.

- Use your USA Activity CD to print at least one activity for the states you studied in this lesson. Then add any that you complete to your Student Notebook.
- Complete the Freedom Decided Word Search located in your Student Notebook.[17]

An activity like a word search, crossword or word scramble contributes to the seeing, hearing and understanding of a word. It provides a fun way to review learning, and gives the student another chance to encounter each word, adding to the likelihood that the child will use it again in speaking or writing. It also happens to be fun!

Enrichment Activities

1. There are differences of opinion about the role Samuel Adams played in United States' history. Research Samuel Adams at the library or on the Internet. See if you can find out what the different opinions are, and write down which one you think is probably true. Then tell why you feel as you do. When you are finished, find one or two quotes by Samuel Adams and write them down along with what you think each one means.
2. At the library or on the Internet research a Native American tribe from either the Mid-Atlantic or Southern regions of what is now the United States. If you do not have a tribe in mind that you would like to find out more about, choose one from the map entitled "Native American Nations, c. 1750" in your *United States History Atlas.* Print a Native American Profile sheet from your Student Resources CD and fill it out.

Additional Resources

The *Will Northaway* series by Susan Olasky
If you read this book, be sure to print a Book Review page from your Student Resources CD, fill it out, and place it in your Student Notebook.

Answers

1. <u>un</u>fold - not folded or opened; <u>un</u>moved - not having an emotional reaction; <u>un</u>cover - to remove the cover; <u>un</u>cut - not cut.
2. to pay for the French and Indian Wars
3. colonial defense
4. Answer might include the thought that they were fought partly for defense of the colonies, but mostly to expand Britain's territories and power in America.
5. Answers will vary.
6. Answers are contained in the second and third paragraphs of this section.
7. <u>un</u>fair – not trained; <u>un</u>important – not important; <u>un</u>even – not even; <u>un</u>trained – not trained.
8. 6 of each
9. boron, B
10. 5 of each
11. 6
12. 2 of each
13. 1. sodium, Na, 11, 11, 12, 11, 23
    2. nitrogen, N, 7, 7, 7, 7, 14
    3. aluminum, Al, 13, 13, 14, 13, 27
    4. iron, Fe, 26, 26, 30, 26, 56
    5. Answers will vary.
14. 7. calcium, Ca, 20, 20, 20, 20, 40
    8. silicon, Si, 14, 14, 14, 14, 28
    9. silver, Ag, 47, 47, 61, 47, 108
    10. gold, Au, 79, 79, 118, 79, 197
15. protons – positive charge
    neutrons – no charge
    electrons – negative charge
16. First, Samuel Adams **explained the effects** the Tea Act gave the East India Company. It meant they would have control over who could sell tea in the colonies. Then he gave his opinion—that it was an outrage, or something very insulting. This would **appeal to their emotions**. No one wants to feel like others are insulting him! He did not believe that Parliament, or the English government, should be able to decide who could sell things in the colonies. Then, he **gave a reason, or cause** for his outrage. He thought that they would not stop with controlling the sale of tea, but would soon control everything. Finally, he gave his opinion that it had to stop which may have influenced people **since he was a leader** in Boston and many people thought **his opinion was important**.
17. Answer key is in Appendix A

Lesson 2, Part 1

Steps for Thinking

1. Strong beliefs often lead to action.
2. Most people seek all other means of change based on their beliefs before going to war.
3. Good leaders help others stay true to their beliefs when life becomes difficult.

A. Copywork & Dictation

Language Skills, Thinking Skills

Look carefully at your assigned passage below, and read it silently. Show your teacher any words you don't know, and practice saying them aloud. Now read the passage aloud, or ask your teacher to read it to you.

When you are finished copying or writing from dictation, compare your copy to the text and make any needed corrections.

- Copy or write as your teacher dictates from *The American Revolution*, page 32, paragraph 4 ("I kept a lookout…").
- Copy or write as your teacher dictates from *Guns for General Washington*, page 36, paragraph 3 ("One of the ferrymen…").
- Write as your teacher dictates from *Guns for General Washington*, page 36, paragraphs 2 and 3 ("His brother laughed…").

B. Reader

Language Skills, History

The American Revolution: page 29, paragraph 1 ("I was glad. . .") through page 32, paragraph 4
Guns for General Washington: Chapter 5

- Read the above assignment from *The American Revolution* aloud, and then follow along as someone else reads the assignment from *Guns for General Washington*.
- Read the above assignment from *The American Revolution* silently, and then read the assignment from *Guns for General Washington* aloud.
- Read the above assignments from *The American Revolution* and *Guns for General Washington* silently.

Materials

- *The American Revolution (Munford)*
- *Guns for General Washington*
- *George Washington*
- *The Eve of Revolution*
- *Atlas of the United States*
- *Eat Your Way Through the USA*
- *DK Pockets: Weather Facts*
- *Klutz Watercolor Book*
- Outline Map of the U.S.
- USA Activity CD
- Ingredients for recipe (Part 3)
- Craft (Part 1)
  Fabric scraps
  Fabric glue
  1-pound bag of dry beans
  Chalk or masking tape
- Experiment (Part 2)
  Small pan
  Coffee cup
  Plastic wrap
  Paper towel
  String or a large rubber band
  Medium-sized mixing bowl
  Ice cubes
- Weather watching tools (made in Unit 1)

A. Copywork and dictation assignments go from an easier level (designated by the first symbol) to harder levels (designated by the second and third symbols). Take two days for the copywork if that is more comfortable for your child. Please adapt instructions to your child's individual needs. Your child should be **consistently successful** at one level before progressing to the next, **regardless of grade**.

C. Read-Aloud & Discussion *Language Skills, Thinking Skills, History*

George Washington: page 25 (Chapter 3) through page 33, paragraph 3

Follow the instructions below for your level. When you are finished, discuss what is happening in this section from the British point of view. Then talk about what is happening from the colonists' point of view. How are their viewpoints different? Who do you think is right? Think about what you know from the story, and discuss the passage in your own words. Give any examples you can think of from the story.

Listen carefully as your teacher reads the above assignment from *George Washington* aloud.

Read the above assignment from *George Washington* aloud.

D. These words may not seem difficult, but they are often misspelled. To increase the challenge you can use higher numbers, but make sure that the spelling of the basics is correct. Your child can also make up his own numbers to add to the spelling list.

If you or your child would like to add a greater degree of difficulty to spelling lessons, choose words from the Challenge Spelling List (in Appendix A) for the lesson you are on. The words on this list are taken from the literature being read.

D. Spelling *Language Skills, Thinking Skills*

Look at the list of words below. Then in your Student Notebook, write the numeral or ordinal number, which is a number that shows position in a sequence, for each word.

thirty-three sixteenth forty second[1]

Numbers from twenty-one (21) to ninety-nine (99) are spelled with a hyphen. If you write out a big number with words, like 135, you would write one hundred thirty-five. If you write 1,268 in words, you would write it one thousand two hundred sixty-eight. No matter where you see the numbers from 21-99, use a hyphen when you spell them. You do not need a hyphen or the word *and* between other number words.

Complete the number chart in your Student Notebook. Take numerals and ordinal numbers and turn them into words.[2] You can use a dictionary to help if needed.

E. History *Thinking Skills*

Together with your teacher, read Chapter 2 in *The Eve of Revolution*. Things were obviously getting worse in the colonies, especially in Boston. According to the last paragraph on page 12, which you read last time, what did Britain do in response to the colonists' anger?[3] Did it help?[4] How did the people in Boston react?[5] Discuss these questions with your teacher, and then use complete sentences to write your thoughts in your Student Notebook.

In your Student Notebook, make a list of things mentioned in your reading today that the people in Boston did to protest against the British government.[6] The Sons and Daughters of Liberty protested against the British, but did they approve of all these things?[7] Why?[8]

Try to put yourself in the place of a British soldier who was sent to Boston to keep order. What do you imagine you might think or feel about all that is happening?[9] After discussing this with your teacher, write two or three sentences describing what you might think or how you might feel.

F. States

Geography, History, Thinking Skills

In your *Atlas of the United States*, read the pages about North Carolina. When you are finished, find the blank map of North Carolina in your Student Notebook and complete the following assignments:

- Place a small star on the spot where Raleigh is located, and label it. Raleigh is the capital city of North Carolina.

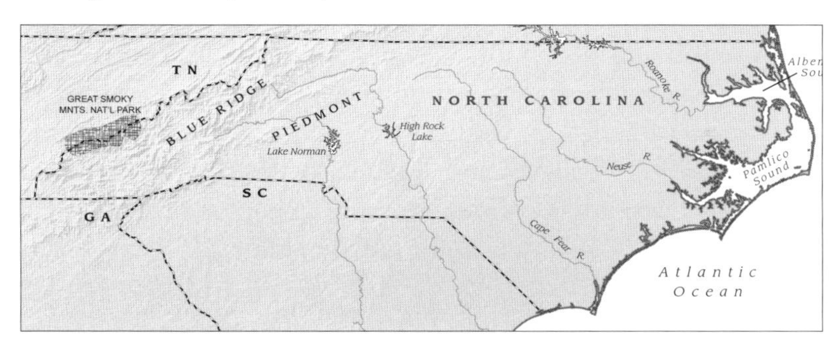

- Label the Atlantic Ocean.
- Color the lines showing the Neuse, Roanoke, and Cape Fear Rivers blue, and label them.
- Lightly color the area where the Blue Ridge and Piedmont Mountains are located green, and label them.
- Color and label the area where the Great Smoky Mountains National Park is located.

- Color and label Lake Normandy and High Rock Lake.
- Find and label Albemarle Sound and Pamlico Sound.
- Label the four states that border North Carolina.

G. Doing

History, Thinking Skills

Beanbags are simple toys that have been used by children and adults for hundreds of years, in a variety of games. They can be made from scraps of fabric and stuffed with just about anything, so it is not surprising that they were a popular toy for colonial children as well.

Follow the directions in Appendix B to make your own beanbags and play a game called hopscotch.

Connect Learning to Life:

One skill that colonial children developed was creativity during play. They often did not have many toys, so they used available things to their fullest benefit. While these beanbags are made for one specific game, think of other games you could play (or make up) with them. Like the colonial children, ask your child to create a game he can play using things he has around the house. To simulate colonial conditions, add the rule that no electricity may be used.

H. **Independent Reading** *Language Skills*

Choose something to read that you will enjoy. Then, find a quiet, comfortable place and read for the following length of time:

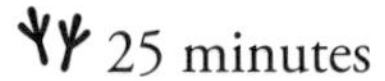 25 minutes 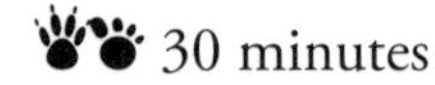 30 minutes

Over time, it's fun to see how much you have read. Be sure to write down what you read today on the Reading Log in your Student Notebook.

Lesson 2, Part 2

A. **Quotation Notebook** *Language Skills, History, Thinking Skills*

In this section you will continue copying statements from the Declaration of Independence. This document told the world what the colonists believed and why they believed it. Any definitions included beneath the passage are to help you understand the meaning. Do not copy them as part of the quotation.

Copy the following quotation into your Student Notebook, and then talk with your teacher about its meaning. You may want to include parts of the Declaration of Independence in your presentation at the end of this unit, so practice reading this section aloud.

> We hold these truths to be self-evident, that all men are created equal, that they are endowed by their Creator with certain unalienable Rights, that among these are Life, Liberty and the pursuit of Happiness.

Definitions (as used in this document):
endowed - someone is given certain desirable qualities
unalienable - not able to be transferred or given to another owner

Draw or create a symbol that helps you remember this part of the Declaration. Put it beneath the quotation.

Teaching Tip

The combination of history and language skills is a natural one. Children learn history content and the specifics of reading, writing, and speaking at the same time by studying the lives and events of the past. This is an important part of the unified approach.

B. **Reader** *Language Skills, History*

The American Revolution: page 32, paragraph 5 ("The only thing. . .") through page 38, paragraph 3
Guns for General Washington: Chapter 6

Read the above assignment from *The American Revolution* aloud, and then follow along as someone else reads the assignment from *Guns for General Washington.*

Read the above assignment from *The American Revolution* silently, and then read the assignment from *Guns for General Washington* aloud.

Read the above assignments from *The American Revolution* and *Guns for General Washington* silently.

C. **Read-Aloud & Narration** *History, Language Skills, Thinking Skills*

George Washington: page 33, paragraph 4 ("George was...") through page 40

Follow the instructions below for your level. Then, in your own words, tell what happened in the story from George's point of view, or pretend you are George and tell what you think happened. Try to remember as many details as possible. You may reread the passage or listen as your teacher rereads the part you are to retell.

Listen carefully as your teacher reads the above assignment from *George Washington* aloud.

Read the above assignment from *George Washington* aloud.

C. The skill of narration is gained over time. If your child has never retold a story, start with the assignment for the lower level, no matter what grade he is in. Work up from there, being careful to allow him to stay at the level of success for a while before going to a longer section.

D. **Editing** *Language Skills, Thinking Skills, History*

Continue reading and discussing parts of the famous speech attributed to Patrick Henry. This speech took place before the delegates of the Virginia colony, who were discussing whether they should join Massachusetts in declaring themselves part of the Revolutionary War. Not only does this speech show the beliefs of a great American patriot, it also shows how to express your thoughts well.

Read the section of the speech included in your Student Notebook. One word in the passage is underlined and in italics. Try to figure out the meaning of that word using the context, or words around it. Then use a dictionary to look up definitions of the words underlined in the paragraph, and any other words you do not understand. Did you get the right meaning of the word in italics by using the context?

Use a highlighter or yellow crayon to highlight or underline the appropriate sentence(s). Then paraphrase those sentences by rewriting them in your own words underneath the passage.

two sentences three sentences four sentences

From Dr. Beechick

"There are major big ideas in science for students to be acquainted with and to use in their thinking. Learning big ideas like these is not accomplished by simple vocabulary lessons of memorizing definitions and writing a sentence for each word. Probably the best learning activity is conversation. Talk about these ideas with your children. Then have them read more in science books, and talk again. Continue this "read and talk" plan with occasional writing assignments added. Children can write paragraphs explaining in their own words things they have read about—how the water cycle works, how it might have worked differently before the Flood, how dinosaurs came to be mostly extinct or how they might have some small-sized descendants yet today."

– *You Can Teach Your Child Successfully*, page 332-333

E. **Science** *Thinking Skills*

In *The American Revolution*, Munford refers to himself as an adventurer—yet he is simply a water molecule. How do you think those two things go together: water molecule and adventurer?

To find out, pour a glass of water and look at it very carefully. How old do you think the water in your glass is? You just got it from the

faucet or refrigerator, but how long do you think it might have been around before it arrived at your house? Possibly it fell to the earth as rain a week ago. Before that it may have floated in a cloud for a few days, but what about before that?

The truth is, the water molecules in your glass have existed since the world was created—and that is a very long time! In fact, those same water molecules have probably circled the globe many times in different forms before they got to your house. That is a strange thought, but it is exactly what Munford is talking about when he calls himself an adventurer.

Sometimes water molecules look like **vapor**, or steam; sometimes they look like clouds or rain; and sometimes they look like oceans and rivers. These are forms that water can take as it travels through the water cycle. The **water cycle** is a wonderful system that allows water to be **recycled**, or reused, constantly. Even though most of the earth is covered with water, only a small amount is useable for humans, animals and plants. This is because the world's oceans hold so much of that water, and it is too salty to be used by things that live on the land. Also, a great deal of water is frozen solid at the north and south poles.

When the sun warms oceans and rivers, the water in them heats up and begins to rise into the air as water vapor, or steam. Salt and other minerals in the ocean do not become part of the vapor. This process is called **evaporation**, and is the first step in the water cycle.

Air high above the earth is colder than the air close to land, and causes water vapor to cool as it rises. When it is cool enough, it changes into tiny droplets of water that gradually group together and form clouds. This is the second step of the water cycle, and is called **condensation**. You can see an example of condensation if you place a glass of very cold water in a warm place. Tiny droplets will form on the outside of the glass. These droplets do not come from the water inside the glass—they come from the air! When the warm air comes into contact with the cold glass, water vapor in the air changes into droplets.

Before long, the clouds become heavy and gray because they are full of water. When they can't hold any more, the water droplets fall back to earth as rain, snow, sleet or hail. This is called **precipitation**, and is the third step in the water cycle. Then when the water falls, it is either absorbed into the ground to water plants and fill up deep wells, or it ends up in lakes, rivers or oceans. This process is called **collection**. Once the water is back on earth, the cycle begins again.

Together with your teacher, read and discuss the sections in your *Weather Facts* book that are entitled "Water Cycle," "Why It Rains," and "Raindrops." When you are finished, color and label the Water Cycle Chart in your Student Notebook. Use the chart to explain each step in the water cycle to your teacher.

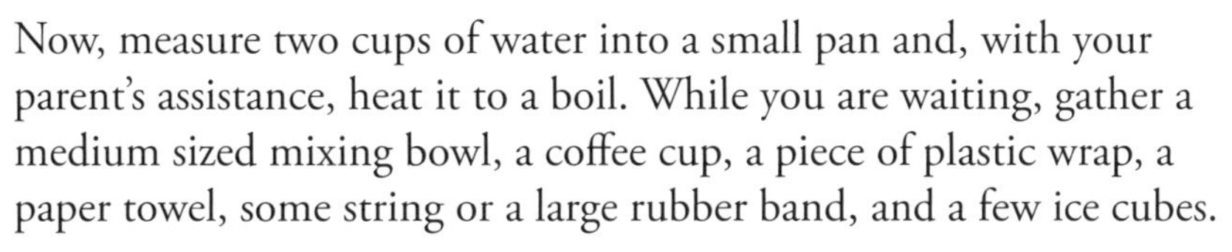

Now, measure two cups of water into a small pan and, with your parent's assistance, heat it to a boil. While you are waiting, gather a medium sized mixing bowl, a coffee cup, a piece of plastic wrap, a paper towel, some string or a large rubber band, and a few ice cubes.

Place the coffee cup inside the mixing bowl—the sides of the bowl should be higher than the cup. When the water boils, ask your parent to pour it into the bowl, being careful not to get any in the cup. Stretch the plastic wrap tightly over the bowl and secure it with a large rubber band or some string. Then place the ice cubes on top of the plastic wrap.

Pay close attention and notice what happens in the bowl over the next ten minutes. At the end of that time, remove the ice cubes and wipe the top of the plastic wrap with a paper towel. Then carefully remove the wrap, and notice how damp it is. What part of the water cycle does the moisture on the plastic wrap demonstrate?[10] What did you do in the experiment to help this process take place? [11] How does that relate to the actual water cycle?[12] Notice the water that dropped into the coffee cup, and tell your teacher which two parts of the water cycle it demonstrates.[13]

Together with your teacher, read the section entitled "Dew and Frost" in your *Weather Facts* book. Then, write three or four sentences on a piece of notebook paper that explain what you learned, and add it to your Student Notebook.

F. **States** *Geography, Thinking Skills, History, Drawing*

Look again at the pages about North Carolina in your *Atlas of the United States.* Then find the State Page in your Student Notebook, and fill in the information.

Make State Cards for North Carolina by following the instructions found in Appendix B. North Carolina is a Southern state, so be sure to outline the cards in purple.

G. **Interactive Writing** *Language Skills, Thinking Skills*

Complete this writing activity with your partner.

It is your partner's job to write first; then you will answer a question with the number of sentences assigned below. After that, write several sentences telling what you think about what your partner has written. Make sure to end with a question you want to ask your partner, so he or she can write back to you.

Topic for your partner: When you finish something that is hard to do, you feel a sense of accomplishment. Think of a time that you did something that seemed hard to you. How did you feel when you finished? Did you feel like it was worth the hard work?

Your question: Think of a goal that you would to accomplish. Tell about it. Is there anything that makes this goal hard for you?

- at least four sentences
- at least five sentences
- at least one paragraph

If you need help remembering what a paragraph is, or how to write one, look back at Lesson 1, Part 2.

H. **Independent Reading** *Language Skills*

Choose something to read that you will enjoy. Then, find a quiet, comfortable place and read for the following length of time:

25 minutes 30 minutes

Be sure to write down what you read today on the Reading Log in your Student Notebook.

Lesson 2, Part 3

A. Copywork & Dictation *Language Skills, Thinking Skills*

Look carefully at your assigned passage below, and read it silently. Show your teacher any words you don't know, and practice saying them aloud. Now read the passage aloud, or ask your teacher to read it to you.

When you are finished copying or writing from dictation, compare your copy to the text and make any needed corrections.

Copy or write as your teacher dictates from *The American Revolution*, page 39, paragraph 1 ("The kettle was removed ...").

Copy or write as your teacher dictates from *Guns for General Washington*, page 51, paragraph 1, ("One by one...").

Write as your teacher dictates from *Guns for General Washington*, page 50, paragraph 3 ("Henry squinted through...") and page 51, paragraph 1.

B. Reader *Language Skills, History*

The American Revolution: page 38, paragraph 4 ("I soon found. . .") through page 43, paragraph 3
Guns for General Washington: Chapter 7

Read the above assignment from *The American Revolution* aloud, and then follow along as someone else reads the assignment from *Guns for General Washington*.

Read the above assignment from *The American Revolution* silently, and then read the assignment from *Guns for General Washington* aloud.

Read the above assignments from *The American Revolution* and *Guns for General Washington* silently.

B. The reading assignments occur in real literature, and there are several reasons why this is important. Real literature is more interesting, and the language used is more natural. A willingness to read is built as your student experiences the success of reading a real book.

C. Read-Aloud & Discussion *Language Skills, Thinking Skills, History*

George Washington: page 41 (Chapter 4) through page 47, paragraph 5

Follow the directions below and read or listen to the above assignment from *George Washington*. Then make up the assigned number of questions about the part of the story you just read or heard. Write down your questions and ask your teacher to answer them. After discussing her thoughts, write the best possible answer in your Student Notebook. Be sure to use complete sentences.

When you are finished, look back at the prediction or predictions you made during Lesson 1, Part 4. Were you able to predict what

Teaching Tip

The skill of predicting what will happen in the story is an important one. It requires your child to remember what has already happened, consider the characters and events, and then come up with a reasonable idea of what may happen in the future. This process involves using critical thinking skills and can be a natural part of any reading your child is doing. Just ask, "What do you think will happen next?"

would happen? Be sure to mark the "Came to Pass" box for each prediction when it does happen.

Listen carefully as your teacher reads the assigned passage.

Make up one question. Make up two questions.

Read the assigned passage aloud; then make up three questions.

D. Are games truly a valid part of school time? Absolutely! As your child revisits content, vocabulary, and concepts, an effective review of learning takes place. The game format makes review more inviting and hopefully, more frequent.

D. Vocabulary & Spelling

Language Skills, Thinking Skills

Vocabulary:

Write each vocabulary word listed below on an index card. Use a dictionary to look up the meaning of each word, and write it on the card. Then on the back of each card, draw a picture or write a clue so you can remember how the word was used in the story.

spectacles **ironic** **vantage** **ragtag** **mansion**

convoy **listing** **haggard** **disgrace** **grizzled**

Spelling:

Use index cards to make a card for each numeral or ordinal on your number chart. Write only the words for that numeral or ordinal on each card.

Now find a partner and follow the directions in Appendix B to play Numeral War.

E. History

Thinking Skills

Together with your teacher, read Chapter 3 in *The Eve of Revolution*.

Even though the colonists in Philadelphia reacted to British taxes and control differently than the people of Boston, they eventually became more involved in the rebellion. In your reading today you learned that the First Continental Congress met in Philadelphia in 1774. This was a meeting of representatives from all the colonies except Georgia. Georgia did not send anyone because at that time British troops were involved in defending the colonists there from Creek Indian attacks. Because of that, Georgia did not want to anger the British.

Connect Learning to Life:

Graphs provide information at a glance. It is important for your child to be able to read a graph and interpret the information given, and it is a simple step from reading a graph to making a graph. Once you have completed this activity, be on the lookout for other graphs used in daily life and point them out to your child.

At the library or on the Internet, find out more about the First Continental Congress. In your Student Notebook, tell how many **delegates**, or representatives, attended the Congress,[14] and list at least two things that they hoped to accomplish.[15] How did King George respond?[16]

Most of the colonists in early America came from Britain, and like the British they enjoyed drinking tea. In fact, historians say that American colonists drank as much tea as the British—at least four servings a day. In your reading today, however, Margaret's letter to

Benjamin mentions that the Daughters of Liberty drank coffee, not tea. Why do you think coffee had become more popular?[17]

With your parent's permission and supervision, conduct a survey over the next few days. Politely ask your family, your family's friends, neighbors, and other people you see whether they prefer to drink coffee or tea. Try to survey at least twenty people.

Keep track of their answers and fill out the bar graph in your Student Notebook. A bar graph shows how two or more things compare to each other. It is easy to use the information you gather because a bar graph makes a picture of the results. Then write one or two sentences comparing the results and describing what you see on the bar graph. Write another sentence or two explaining whether or not you think the results are very different than they would have been during the colonial period, and why.

Convert each result in your survey to a percentage. The simplest way to do that is:

1. Make the results for each drink into a fraction. The total number of people in your survey becomes the denominator (or bottom number in the fraction,) and the number of people who prefer that drink becomes the numerator (or top number in the fraction). For example, if you survey a total of 23 people, and four of them prefer coffee, the "coffee" fraction is $4/23$.
2. Use a calculator to divide the numerator of your fraction by the denominator. For example if the fraction is $4/23$, divide 4 by 23. The result is 0.1739.
3. Since percentages are expressed in hundredths, you need to round off the answer that your calculator gives you. In the case of the above example, 39 is less than 50 so you can round down to .17, which is 17 hundredths—or 17%.

Add soda and water to your survey.

F. States *Geography, History, Thinking Skills*

In your *Atlas of the United States*, read the pages about South Carolina. When you are finished, find the blank map of South Carolina in your Student Notebook and complete the following assignments:

- Place a small star on the spot where Columbia is located, and label it. Columbia is the capital city of South Carolina.
- Label the Atlantic Ocean.

- Color the lines showing the Savannah, Great Pee Dee, Lynches, and Edisto (including its North and South Forks) Rivers blue, and label them.

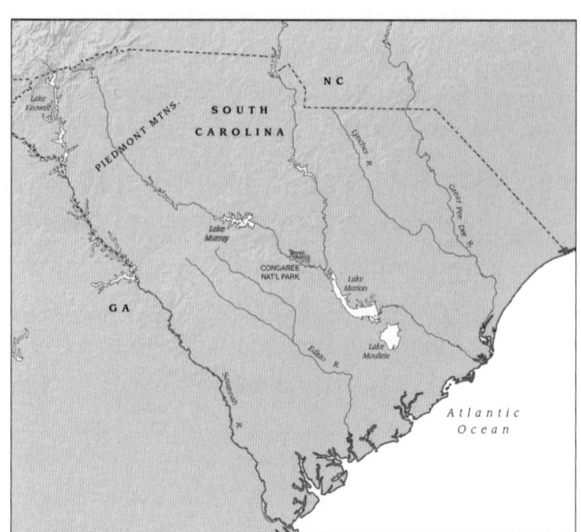

- Color and label the area where Congaree National Park is located.
- Lightly color the area where the Piedmont Mountains are located green, and label them.
- Color and label Lake Marion and Lake Moultrie.

- Color and label Lake Keowee and Lake Murray.
- Label the two states that border South Carolina.

G. Cooking *Language Skills, Thinking Skills, Drawing*

With your parent's permission and supervision, look in *Eat Your Way Through the USA*, choose a recipe that comes from either North Carolina or South Carolina, and prepare it for your family. After everyone has had a taste, find out who liked it, and whether anyone would like to have it again. What did you think about it?

In your Student Notebook, draw a picture of the dish you chose to make and write the following number of sentences about your family's reaction to it:

two sentences three sentences four sentences

H. Independent Reading *Language Skills*

Choose something to read that you will enjoy. Then, find a quiet, comfortable place and read for the following length of time:

25 minutes 30 minutes

Be sure to write down what you read today on the Reading Log in your Student Notebook.

Lesson 2, Part 4

Teaching Tip

One approach to teaching your child about a difficult task or concept is to break it down into small, manageable pieces. This keeps your child from feeling overwhelmed, yet allows him to access more difficult material that he probably would not attempt if presented all at once, or as an independent assignment without assistance.

A. Quotation Notebook

Language Skills, History, Thinking Skills

In this section you will continue copying statements from the Declaration of Independence. This document told the world what the colonists believed and why they believed it. Any definitions included beneath the passage are to help you understand the meaning. Do not copy them as part of the quotation.

Copy the following quotation into your Student Notebook, and then talk with your teacher about its meaning. You may want to include parts of the Declaration of Independence in your presentation at the end of this unit, so practice reading this section aloud.

> That to secure these rights, Governments are instituted among Men, deriving their just powers from the consent of the governed.

Definitions (as used in this document):
instituted - established
deriving - coming from a certain source
consent - agreement

Draw or create a symbol that helps you remember this part of the Declaration. Put it beneath the quotation.

B. Reader

Language Skills, History

The American Revolution: page 44, paragraph 1 ("When Parliament's . . .") through page 48, paragraph 4
Guns for General Washington: Chapter 8

Read the above assignment from *The American Revolution* aloud, and then follow along as someone else reads the assignment from *Guns for General Washington*.

Read the above assignment from *The American Revolution* silently, and then read the assignment from *Guns for General Washington* aloud.

Read the above assignments from *The American Revolution* and *Guns for General Washington* silently.

C. Read-Aloud & Narration

Language Skills, Thinking Skills, History

George Washington: page 47, paragraph 6 ("In the formal...") through page 54, paragraph 5

After reading or listening to the read-aloud assignmentin *George Washington*, talk with your teacher and try to predict what will happen in the future based on what you know of the characters and events. Write down your predictions in your Student Notebook. Later you will look back and see if they were accurate. Try not to peek ahead!

Listen carefully as your teacher reads the assigned passage. Then write down something that you think will happen in the story.

Write down another thing that you think will happen in the story.

Read the assigned passage aloud. Then write down at least three things that you think will happen in the story.

Teaching Tip

Paraphrasing is an important thinking skill that leads to a writing skill. When you take the words of another and put them into your own words, you go through several steps. First, you must understand what the words mean. You can gain meaning by discussion or looking up a definition. Then you think through that meaning and combine it with other words in the sentence to come up with the ideas spoken about. Once you do this, you restate, or put what you understood into words that are meaningful for you. Often this will come out in a shorter or simpler form.

D. **Editing** *Language Skills, History, Thinking Skills*

Continue reading and discussing parts of the famous speech attributed to Patrick Henry. Read the section of the speech included in your Student Notebook. One word in the passage is underlined and in italics. Try to figure out the meaning of that word using the context, or words around it. Then use a dictionary to look up definitions of the words underlined in the paragraph, and any other words you do not understand. Did you get the right meaning of the word in italics by using the context?

Use a highlighter or yellow crayon to highlight or underline the appropriate sentence(s). Then paraphrase those sentences by rewriting them in your own words underneath the passage.

two sentences three sentences four sentences

E. **Science** *Thinking Skills, Drawing*

Different types of clouds that appear in the sky are an important part of predicting weather. Together with your teacher, read and discuss the sections entitled "Cloud Formation," "Special Shapes," and "Fog, Mist, and Haze" in your *Weather Facts* book.

Choose four types of clouds mentioned in the sections you just read, and research them at the library or on the Internet. Then, in your Student Notebook, draw and color a picture of each type you chose and list at least three facts about it.[18]

Although you haven't watched the weather for a few lessons, start your weather station again today, and add more information about the clouds to your observations. Use the *Weather Facts* book to identify the types of clouds you see, and record your weather observations on the Weather Watcher pages in your Student Notebook.

Research and add information about two additional clouds to your Student Notebook.

Research and add information about four additional clouds to your Student Notebook.

F. States *Geography, History, Thinking Skills, Drawing*

Look again at the pages about South Carolina in your *Atlas of the United States*. Then find the State Page in your Student Notebook, and fill in the information.

Make State Cards for South Carolina by following the instructions found in Appendix B. South Carolina is a Southern state, so be sure to outline the cards in purple.

G. Writing *Language Skills, Thinking Skills*

Journaling is one way to keep a record of thoughts or events. Journal entries can look different from writing in stories because they are often just brief thoughts.

Write a journal entry telling about your day yesterday or about the Doing activity in Part 1 of this lesson. Write about three events and give your thoughts about each event as assigned below. Ask someone to read your journal entry and retell what you did. Listen to see if he or she accurately understood what you did yesterday.

at least one thought about each event

at least two thoughts about each event

at least three thoughts about each event

G. Writing is not a separate subject, but rather a set of skills with which to become familiar. Writing is best when it is a response to content learned, new ideas, or as a result of an activity or experience.

H. Independent Reading *Language Skills*

Choose something to read that you will enjoy. Then, find a quiet, comfortable place and read for the following length of time:

25 minutes 30 minutes

Be sure to write down what you read today on the Reading Log in your Student Notebook.

Connect Learning to Life:

Encouragement is a powerful thing. Be sure to recognize your child's efforts to read independently, especially if he is a reluctant reader. When I was a young person, I liked to read. I didn't realize how important it was until my father passed me one day, curled up in a chair reading, and complimented me. It was a powerful moment. I began to seek even more opportunities to read because of his encouragement. You never know the impact of just one word of recognition on your child's life and you are showing your child how to encourage others as well.

Ask your child to choose one of the Steps for Thinking and explain it to you. Ask him to share examples of the Step from the reading, activities, or discussion in the lesson. If you think your child is ready, also ask him to think of an example from the events of the day. Assist your child in thinking of examples, if needed.

Lesson 2, Part 5

This part is set aside for completion of any work left undone from the lesson, and review of concepts and content. It is also a time to expand the work in the lesson by doing art, timeline activities, or games.

- Review the Steps for Thinking from the beginning of this lesson.
- Give your teacher your stack of vocabulary cards for the lesson. As she shows you each word, tell her the meaning of the word and how it was used in the story.

Teaching Tip

Review sessions spaced out over several days or weeks are the best kind of review to help a child remember information. Reading words, writing words and discussing words all help a child connect the word and its meaning to long term memory. When he can relate it to something he already knows, it is even more effective.

Teaching Tip

If you have a perfectionist child who doesn't want to draw or paint because it doesn't come out exactly the way he wants, encourage him to think like an inventor. Many attempts create a better product!

- Read over your number chart or your index cards and practice spelling numerals or ordinals that seem difficult. Tell your teacher when you have finished practicing.

  Shuffle your deck of index cards and give it to your teacher. Listen as she calls out the numerals or ordinals written on ten of the cards. Do the best you can to correctly write each one she calls out, both as a number and in words. When you are finished, check your spelling using your number chart. Tell your teacher how you did.

  Follow the directions above with five additional numerals or ordinals.

  Follow the directions above with ten additional numerals or ordinals.

- Use the United States map that is near the front of your *Atlas of the United States* to find North Carolina and South Carolina. Then, on the large outline map of the U.S., draw lines around them with a purple crayon, marker, or colored pencil. Write in the names of the states, and draw small stars where their capital cities are located. Next to the stars, write the name of each capital city.
- In your *Klutz Watercolor Book*, read about "Playing with Your Pencil" on page 25. Then complete the activities on that page and the next. Do not worry about your drawings looking perfect–the name of this lesson tells you to play with your pencil!

  When you are finished, follow the instructions to fill up page 27. Remember to play with your watercolors whenever you have time and your parent agrees.
- Use your USA Activity CD to print at least one activity for the states you studied in this lesson. Then add any that you complete to your Student Notebook.
- Complete the Freedom Decided Word Scramble located in your Student Notebook.[19]

Enrichment Activities

1. At the library or on the Internet find out about Thomas Paine and his famous pamphlet entitled Common Sense. Why do you think this pamphlet was so popular? Do you believe it influenced people's opinions? Why, or why not. Write down the things you find out, along with your opinions, and include them in your presentation at the end of this unit.
2. In your *Atlas of the United States*, look again at the states you have studied so far in this unit. Scan the sections entitled "The Way It

Was..." and choose a person, place, or thing from one of those sections to research. Use the library or, with your parent's permission, the Internet and try to find out more than what is written in the atlas.

Then pretend you work for a newspaper, and you have just met the person, seen the landmark, or found out about the object. Write a short article about what you have learned. Newspaper reporters always try to answer the questions *who, what, when, where,* and *how* when they write, so that readers have all the important information. Try to answer those questions in your article, and then add it to your Student Notebook.

Additional Resources

George Washington by Janet and Geoff Benge
If you read this book, be sure to print a Book Review page from your Student Resources CD, fill it out, and place it in your Student Notebook.

Answers

1. 33, 16th, 40, 2nd
2. one, two, three, four, five, six, seven, eight, nine, ten

   eleven, twelve, thirteen, fourteen, fifteen, sixteen, seventeen, eighteen, nineteen, twenty

   twenty-one, twenty-two, twenty-three, twenty-four, twenty-five, twenty-six, twenty-seven, twenty-eight, twenty-nine, thirty

   thirty-one, thirty-two, thirty-three, thirty-four, thirty-five, thirty-six, thirty-seven, thirty-eight, thirty-nine, forty

   forty-one, forty-two, forty-three, forty-four, forty-five, forty-six, forty-seven, forty-eight, forty-nine, fifty

   first, second, third, fourth, fifth, sixth, seventh, eighth, ninth, tenth, eleventh, twelfth, thirteenth, fourteenth, fifteenth, sixteenth, seventeenth, eighteenth, nineteenth, twentieth
   one hundred ninety-nine, two hundred eighty-eight, three hundred seventy-seven, four hundred sixty-six, five hundred fifty-five

   one thousand nine hundred nineteen; two thousand eight hundred twenty-eight; three thousand seven hundred thirty-seven; four thousand six hundred forty-six; five thousand four hundred fifty-one

   one million two hundred ten thousand three hundred one; two million three hundred twenty-one thousand four hundred twelve; three million four hundred thirty-two thousand five hundred twenty-three; four million five hundred forty-three thousand six hundred thirty-four; five million six hundred fifty-four thousand seven hundred forty-five
3. They sent many additional soldiers to keep order.
4. Opinions may vary.
5. They resented the soldiers, threw stones at them, and called them names.
6. attacked tax collectors; boycotted, burned, or dumped British goods in the harbor; had meetings to plan protests; published newspaper articles and pamphlets; gathered on street corners to protest.
7. no
8. They did not approve of mob action.
9. Answers will vary.
10. condensation
11. put ice on the wrap
12. The colder temperatures high above the earth cause water vapor to condense and form clouds.
13. precipitation and collection
14. 56
15. Specific answers will vary, depending on how in-depth the student's research is. Answers may include: to oppose the Intolerable Acts; to compose a statement of colonial rights; to identify how the British parliament had violated those rights; to convince Britain to restore those rights; to organize a second Congress if Britain ignored them.
16. King George mostly ignored them; some documents say he punished the colonies by restricting sea fishing.
17. Tea was one of the things that people refused to buy as part of their protest against high taxes.
18. Answers will vary.
19. Answer key is in Appendix A.

Lesson 3, Part 1

Steps for Thinking

1. Most people agree that freedom is important.
2. In countries where freedom is important, there are laws and rules made to give that freedom to all people.
3. Sometimes your ideas about people and freedom have to change based on what you learn.

Read over the Steps for Thinking with your children, and ask what they think each one means. Discuss any unknown words or ideas. Remember, this is just an introduction. Do not be concerned if they do not show much connection to the ideas yet. Post the Steps, and refer to them throughout the week when examples arise in reading or discussion.

A. Copywork & Dictation

Language Skills, Thinking Skills

Look carefully at your assigned passage below, and read it silently. Show your teacher any words you don't know, and practice saying them aloud. Now read the passage aloud, or ask your teacher to read it to you.

When you are finished copying or writing from dictation, compare your copy to the text and make any needed corrections.

Copy or write as your teacher dictates from *The American Revolution*, page 49, paragraph 2 ("Mr. Adams was unmoved...").

Copy or write as your teacher dictates from *Guns for General Washington*, page 61, paragraph 8 ("Later, walking home...").

Write as your teacher dictates from *Guns for General Washington*, page 61, paragraphs 6, 7, and 8 ("Paul bridled...").

B. Reader

Language Skills, History

The American Revolution: page 48, paragraph 5 ("I liked being. . .") through page 49, paragraph 1
Guns for General Washington: Chapter 9

Read the above assignment from *The American Revolution* aloud, and then follow along as someone else reads the assignment from *Guns for General Washington*.

Read the above assignment from *The American Revolution* silently, and then read the assignment from *Guns for General Washington* aloud.

Read the above assignments from *The American Revolution* and *Guns for General Washington* silently.

Materials

- *The American Revolution (Munford)*
- *Guns for General Washington*
- *George Washington*
- *The Eve of Revolution*
- *Atlas of the United States*
- *Profiles from History, Vol. 2*
- *Eat Your Way Through the USA*
- *DK Pockets: Weather Facts*
- *Klutz Watercolor Book*
- Outline Map of the U.S.
- USA Activity CD
- Weather watching tools
- Ingredients for recipe (Part 3)
- Activity (Part 2)
  - 2 toothpicks
  - Marker
  - Lamp
  - Clock with minute marks
  - Piece of fruit (round)
- Activity (Part 4)
  - Ruler
  - Masking Tape
  - Straight pin
  - Flashlight
- Activity (Part 5)
  - Primary instructions:
    - Large box (with panels at least 18-inches x 24-inches)
    - Scissors or box cutter
    - Yardstick
    - Marker
    - Masking Tape
  - Alternate instructions:
    - Large piece of cardboard
    - (2) 1-gallon water jugs or similar supports
    - Masking Tape

C. Point of view can seem very complex, so do a simple review. Talk about a movie you have all seen. Ask your children to tell about their favorite part of the movie and then share yours. If there are any differences in what people liked, point out that the differences come from each person's way of looking at the movie and reacting to what they saw. This is a simple definition of point of view.

D. Suggested words provide study that focuses on an aspect of language such as phonics, word roots, or affixes. These lists include words taken from the readers. Please feel free to add up to five words each week that are particular to your child's needs.

E. In order to view history correctly, you have to consider the motives and understanding of the people involved. Evaluate history in the light of context, or what was happening at the time. Sometimes things done in the past are hard for us to understand. Perhaps the people would not have acted in that way if they had our perspective. Remember to evaluate people and their actions based on their knowledge and intentions.

C. Read-Aloud & Discussion

Language Skills, History, Thinking Skills

George Washington: page 54, paragraph 6 ("Winter was. . .") through page 61, paragraph 3

Follow the instructions below for your level. When you are finished, discuss what is happening in this section from the British point of view. Then talk about what is happening from the colonists' point of view. How are their viewpoints different? Who do you think is right? Think about what you know from the story, and discuss the passage in your own words. Give any examples you can think of from the story.

Listen carefully as your teacher reads the above assignment from *George Washington* aloud.

Read the above assignment from *George Washington* aloud.

D. Spelling

Language Skills, Thinking Skills

Look at the list of words below. Then, in your Student Notebook write the numeral or ordinal number, which is a number that shows position in a sequence, for each word.

fifty-eight nineteenth eighty third[1]

Remember, spell numbers from twenty-one (21) to ninety-nine (99) with a hyphen. If you write out a big number with words, like 135, you would write one hundred thirty-five. If you write 1,268 in words, you would write it one thousand two hundred sixty-eight. No matter where you see the numbers from 21-99, use a hyphen when you spell them. You do not need a hyphen or the word *and* between other number words.

Complete the number chart in your Student Notebook. Take numerals and ordinal numbers and turn them into words.[2] You can use a dictionary to help if needed.

E. History

Geography, Thinking Skill

In Lesson 2 of this unit, you read and copied some very important words from the Declaration of Independence:

> *We hold these truths to be self-evident, that all men are created equal, that they are endowed by their Creator with certain unalienable Rights, that among these are Life, Liberty and the pursuit of Happiness.*

The Declaration of Independence was a message to the world. It clearly stated the **principles**, or basic truths, for which men in America were willing to fight and even die. Yet for all this, some of the same upright men who wrote this Declaration also kept slaves. How was this possible? Although that is a difficult question, it was possible for several reasons.

First, as wrong as it might look to people nowadays, at that time it was a common, everyday practice for many. There had been slavery for thousands of years. This could happen when one nation conquered another in war. It could also happen because visitors saw different, unfamiliar beliefs in another group's way of life or religion that seemed to be **uncivilized**, or primitive when compared to their own. For one reason or another, they didn't think of those people as equals so they did not consider it wrong to enslave them.

Second, because slavery was so common at that time some people simply accepted it as a way of life, and had never taken time to examine their beliefs. Writing and signing the important papers that said they believed in liberty for all people forced them to look at their own lives, and many freed their slaves as soon as possible.

And third, slavery in America was, for some, more a business decision than a moral one. It provided a very inexpensive work force that had become necessary to their way of life. Together with your teacher, read pages 25 (Chapter 4) through 29 in *The Eve of Revolution*.

After discussing the above points about slavery, take part in a debate. Prepare by choosing one of the following statements to support:

Slavery was wrong and is not understandable in any circumstance.

Slavery was an acceptable part of life at that time and served a purpose.

Come up with at least three points to make for your side of the debate. Someone else needs to choose the other point and come up with three points for their side. It could be another student or your teacher. Take turns presenting your statement and points of support.

After you have finished, switch sides of the debate. Try to defend the opposite point of view, based on what you have learned. It is a challenge to try to support a point of view that you may not agree with, but try to give good arguments. Take turns presenting your statement and points of support.

F. **States** *Geography, History, Thinking Skills*

In the *Atlas of the United States,* read the pages about Georgia. When you are finished, find the blank map of Georgia in your Student Notebook and complete the following assignments:

- Place a small star on the spot where Atlanta is located, and label it. Atlanta is the capital city of Georgia.
- Label the Atlantic Ocean.

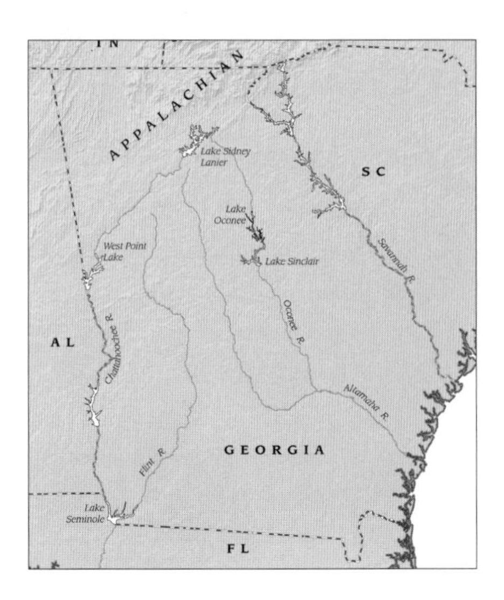

- Color the lines showing the Flint, Oconee, Altamaha, Savannah and Chattahoochee Rivers blue, and label them. In case you have trouble finding these rivers, two of them form all or part of the borders between Georgia and other states.
- Lightly color the area where the Appalachian Mountains are located purple, and label them.
- Color and label Lakes Lanier, Sinclair, and Oconee.

- Color and label Lake Seminole and West Point Lake.
- Label the five states that border Georgia.

G. **Doing** *Art*

In your *Klutz Watercolor Book*, read page 29 entitled "Washes." Then complete the activities on page 28. Washes are very important in watercolor paintings, so take your time and enjoy this activity. Over the next few days, complete all the activities through page 33. Use extra watercolor paper to continue experimenting with washes.

H. **Independent Reading** *Language Skills*

Choose something to read that you will enjoy. Then, find a quiet, comfortable place and read for the following length of time:

25 minutes 30 minutes

Over time, it's fun to see how much you have read. Be sure to write down what you read today on the Reading Log in your Student Notebook.

Lesson 3, Part 2

A. Quotation Notebook *Language Skills, History, Thinking Skills*

Copy the following quotation from the Declaration of Independence into your Student Notebook, and then talk with your teacher about its meaning. This document told the world what the colonists believed and why they believed it. You may want to include parts of the Declaration of Independence in your presentation at the end of this unit, so practice reading this section aloud.

> That whenever any Form of Government becomes destructive of these ends, it is the Right of the People to alter or to abolish it, and to institute new Government,

Definitions (as used in this document):
abolish - to put an end to something
institute - establish or set up

Draw or create a symbol that helps you remember this part of the Declaration. Put it beneath the quotation.

Teaching Tip

When at all possible, find a copy or image of a primary source document for your children to see. Reading and discussion gives meaning to the words, but an image helps your student connect the content to the actual document. In our homeschooling, we occasionally did assignments on brown or white butcher paper, rolled them up like scrolls, and singed the edges to make them look like authentic historical documents. This is a great way to remember learning by using a fun activity!

This passage contains words that that are not normally capitalized today. The author did this to emphasize the importance of these words.

B. Reader *Language Skills, Thinking Skills, History*

The American Revolution: page 51, paragraph 1 ("I was starting. . .") through page 58, paragraph 2
Guns for General Washington: Chapter 10

Read the above assignment from *The American Revolution* aloud, and then follow along as someone else reads the assignment from *Guns for General Washington*.

Read the above assignment from *The American Revolution* silently, and then read the assignment from *Guns for General Washington* aloud.

Read the above assignments from *The American Revolution* and *Guns for General Washington* silently.

C. Read-Aloud & Narration *Language Skills, History, Thinking Skills*

George Washington: page 61, paragraph 4 ("After a week...") to the bottom of page 67

Follow the instructions below for your level. Then, in your own words, tell what happened in the story from George's point of view, or pretend you are George and tell what you think happened. Try to remember as many details as possible. You may reread the passage or listen as your teacher rereads the part you are to retell.

Listen carefully as your teacher reads the above assignment from *George Washington* aloud.

Read the above assignment from *George Washington* aloud.

C. Encourage your children to get into character for this assignment. They can narrate, or retell, the passage using the pronoun I, stand up to look more impressive, use a deeper voice, etc. By encouraging this creativity, you are also encouraging critical thinking. What would the speaker sound like? What happened to him and how did he feel about it? This is a natural way to comprehend and express the thoughts of another person.

D. There are four parts to this activity Part 1 – read the speech.

Part 2 – use a dictionary to look up any unknown or underlined words. Your student does not need to copy these definitions, since the goal is just to clarify meaning.

Part 3 – have your student put the sentences in his own words, which is the challenging thinking aspect of this activity. Discussion often helps students to order their thoughts before writing.

Part 4 – have your student rewrite the sentences in his own words. These rewritings should show understanding, not just recopying. Every now and then, ask the student to explain what the sentence means to check for understanding.

Connect Learning to Life:

"Why should I learn this?" What homeschooling parent hasn't heard that question! A good answer is, "Because it will help you learn about other things." The connection between science, history, and geography is such a natural one. Each teaches important ideas that build understanding in the other. The soldiers transporting the guns in the winter, connected to the terrain, connected to the seasons. Each one informs your children about the other and their place in real life.

D. Editing

Language Skills, Thinking Skills, History

Continue reading and discussing parts of the famous speech attributed to Patrick Henry. This speech took place before the delegates of the Virginia colony, who were discussing whether they should join Massachusetts in declaring themselves part of the Revolutionary War. Not only does this speech show the beliefs of a great American patriot, it also shows how to express your thoughts well.

Read the section of the speech included in your Student Notebook. One word in the passage is underlined and in italics. Try to figure out the meaning of that word using the context, or words around it. Then use a dictionary to look up definitions of the words underlined in the paragraph, and any other words you do not understand. Did you get the right meaning of the word in italics by using the context?

Use a highlighter or yellow crayon to highlight or underline the appropriate sentence(s). Then paraphrase those sentences by rewriting them in your own words underneath the passage.

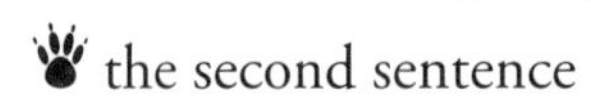
the first sentence the second sentence both sentences

E. Science

Geography, History, Thinking Skills

Take a few minutes before you begin this section to look back at the list you made in Lesson 1, Part 2, and see if your questions about molecules and atoms, the water cycle, and clouds have been answered yet. Use a highlighter to mark the ones that have not. Then over the next few days, use the library or Internet to research the questions that you highlighted, and try to find the answers. Discuss what you find out with your teacher.

In the next few lessons you will learn about seasons, the Earth's orbit, tropical storms, and how rocks form. Take a few minutes to discuss what you already know about these things with your teacher. When you are finished, and before reading further in this section, make a list of questions or things you would like to find out about these subjects. There is a page provided in your Student Notebook for the list. Later, you will have an opportunity to look back and see if your questions have been answered.

In your book, *Guns for General Washington*, Will and Henry left for Fort Ticonderoga in the winter. Many people believed they were foolish to make this trip because of the freezing cold, the ice storms, and the blizzards. True, travel would have been much easier if they had waited until spring and warmer weather, but General Washington and the Continental Army needed the guns right away. So the young men decided to do the best they could in the harsh New England winter.

Most places on earth have four seasons every year—spring, summer, fall (or autumn), and winter. You have probably noticed the changes in weather that come with different seasons, but do you know what causes the changes? In fact, a few things work together to bring about seasonal weather changes. To find out about some of these things, look at the map below. Find the North Pole and the South Pole. These are fairly easy to locate because they are at the very top and bottom.

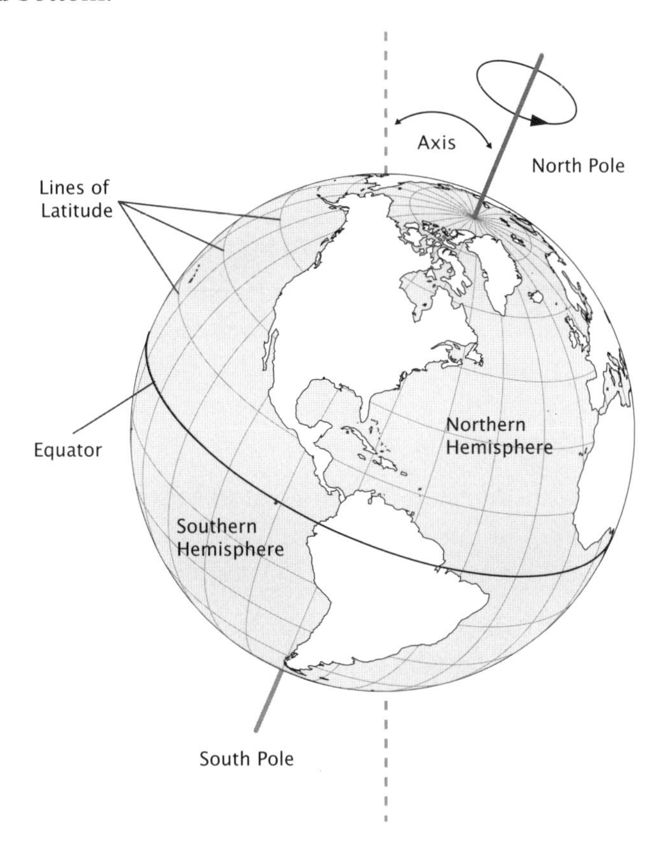

Now find the line that runs around the center of the earth. This imaginary line is the **equator**, and it divides the earth into two sections, called hemispheres. The section closest to the North Pole is the Northern Hemisphere, and the section closest to the South Pole is the Southern Hemisphere. Temperatures near the equator are usually warmer than in other places, no matter what the season. Generally, the further one moves away from the equator, the cooler the weather.

Notice the lines that circle the globe above and below the equator. These are lines of **latitude** and are used to measure how far from the equator something is.

Use a piece of fruit, round if possible, to represent the earth. With your teacher's help, draw a line around the middle of the fruit to represent the equator. Then stick toothpicks in its top and bottom to show where the North and South Poles are located. The toothpicks now represent the earth's **axis**, which is an imaginary line running through its center. The earth **rotates**, or turns, on its axis once every day, which takes about 24 hours.

Hold your right hand out so that your thumb is pointing up and your fingers are slightly curved. If your hand is the earth, and your thumb is its axis, your fingers point the direction that the earth always rotates. This direction is called **counter-clockwise**, because it is opposite the direction that the hands on a clock move.

Now hold your earth-model by its axis (toothpicks) next to a lamp. Pretend the lamp is the sun, and notice that the side of the earth facing the lamp is bright, while the backside is darker. Now slowly turn your model in a counter-clockwise direction. What do you think this activity shows?[3]

As the earth moves through space, however, its axis is not straight up and down. Place your earth-model next to a clock so that the toothpicks are even with the 12 and the six. Now keep the bottom toothpick near the six, and move the top to the four-minute mark on the clock. This position looks very much like the tilt of the earth's axis in space, and this tilt is the main thing that causes seasons. You will find out more about this later.

Put your earth-model in the refrigerator, because you will use it again in Part 4 of this lesson. Then read and discuss the section in your *Weather Facts* book entitled "Day and Night" with your teacher.

Find the earth map in your Student Notebook, and use the picture in this section as a model to label the following things:

the Equator;

the North and South Poles;

the North and South Hemispheres;

the axis;

and lines of latitude.

Talk with your teacher, and then write two or three sentences in your Student Notebook that explain what you have learned.

Be sure to record your weather observations over the next couple of days.

The Internet can be a useful tool for research, but we suggest that your child use it only with your permission and supervision, and while following your family's rules.

At the library or on the Internet find out about the North Pole. Then, list at least four facts that you learn about that area of the earth in your Student Notebook. Be sure to include this information in your presentation at the end of this unit.

Follow the instructions above for the South Pole.

F. States *Geography, Thinking Skills, History, Drawing*

Look again at the pages about Georgia in your *Atlas of the United States.* Then find the State Page in your Student Notebook, and fill in the information.

Make State Cards for Georgia by following the instructions found in Appendix B. Georgia is a Southern state, so be sure to outline the cards in purple.

G. Interactive Writing *Language Skills, Thinking Skills*

Complete this writing activity with your partner.

It is your partner's job to write first; then you will answer a question with the number of sentences assigned below. After that, write several sentences telling what you think about what your partner has written. Make sure to end with a question you want to ask your partner, so he or she can write back to you.

Topic for your partner: Think about a time when you felt discouraged. Tell about it. What encouraged you? How did you get going or keep going?

Your question: Think about someone you know of who has gone through a difficult time. How do you think he kept going? What encouraged, or strengthened him? Tell about it.

- at least four sentences
- at least five sentences
- at least one paragraph

If you need help remembering what a paragraph is, or how to write one, look back at Lesson 1, Part 2.

H. Independent Reading *Language Skills*

Choose something to read that you will enjoy. Then, find a quiet, comfortable place and read for the following length of time:

25 minutes   30 minutes

Be sure to write down what you read today on the Reading Log in your Student Notebook.

Lesson 3, Part 3

A. **Copywork & Dictation** *Language Skills, Thinking Skills*

Look carefully at your assigned passage below, and read it silently. Show your teacher any words you don't know, and practice saying them aloud. Now read the passage aloud, or ask your teacher to read it to you.

When you are finished copying or writing from dictation, compare your copy to the text and make any needed corrections.

Copy or write as your teacher dictates from *The American Revolution*, page 60, paragraph 3 ("The First Continental Congress…").

Copy or write as your teacher dictates from *Guns for General Washington*, page 71, paragraph 1 ("From the grove…").

Write as your teacher dictates from *Guns for General Washington*, page 70, paragraph 3 ("The animals were…") through page 71, paragraph 1.

B. **Reader** *Language Skills, History*

The American Revolution: page 58, paragraph 3 ("Almost as if. . .") through page 61, paragraph 1
Guns for General Washington: Chapter 11

Read the above assignment from *The American Revolution* aloud, and then follow along as someone else reads the assignment from *Guns for General Washington*.

Read the above assignment from *The American Revolution* silently, and then read the assignment from *Guns for General Washington* aloud.

Read the above assignments from *The American Revolution* and *Guns for General Washington* silently.

C. **Read-Aloud & Discussion** *Language Skills, Thinking Skills, History*

George Washington: bottom of page 67 ("Reverend…") through page 74, paragraph 7

Follow the directions below and read or listen to the above assignment from *George Washington*. Then make up the assigned number of questions about the part of the story you just read or heard. Write your questions and ask your teacher to answer them. After discussing her thoughts, write down the best possible answer in your Student Notebook. Be sure to use complete sentences.

When you are finished, look back at the prediction or predictions you made during Lesson 2, Part 4. Were you able to predict what

C. Explain to your students that the value of making predictions about the stories you are reading or listening to doesn't depend on getting it right. There is great value in taking the information you have, coming up with an idea of what will take place, and then testing that idea. If you are not correct, you may learn more than if you were correct. You have gained new information about a character or events. This is **clarification,** or making something clearer. Encourage your children not to be overly concerned about always predicting correctly. Help them to welcome the opportunity to **clarify** their understanding.

would happen? Be sure to mark the "Came to Pass" box for each prediction when it does happen.

Listen carefully as your teacher reads the assigned passage.

Make up one question. Make up two questions.

Read the assigned passage aloud; then make up three questions.

D. Vocabulary & Spelling

Language Skills, Thinking Skills

Vocabulary:
Write each vocabulary word listed below on an index card. Use a dictionary to look up the meaning of each word, and write it on the card. Then on the back of each card, draw a picture or write a clue so you can remember how the word was used in the story.

outrage **proclamation** **boycott** **reconcile** **urgency**

dreary **pier** **daft** **wharf** **burlap**

Spelling:
Use index cards to make a card for each numeral or ordinal on your number chart. Write only the words for that numeral or ordinal on each card.

Now find a partner and follow the directions in Appendix B to play Numeral War.

E. History

Geography, Art, Thinking Skills

Together with your teacher, read from page 30 ("Dear Daughter…") to the end of Chapter 4 in *The Eve of Revolution.*

Charleston was known throughout colonial America for its great beauty and **gentility**, or good manners. By the time your stories take place, it was the fourth largest city in the colonies. It **prospered**, or was successful, because it had an excellent harbor for ships, and the swampy areas around it grew huge amounts of rice and indigo.

At the library or on the Internet research Eliza Pinckney and indigo. In your Student Notebook, use complete sentences to tell at least three facts about her life, and one or two facts about indigo. Be sure

"Think about how a particular song takes you back to an experience you had. Retrieving stored knowledge is similar. When a student learns about world history he may quickly forget the facts after turning in the test. But that same student readily remembers what he learned while building a model boat, designing a chart, or when current events were associated. It's so very easy to provide association with geography! And through association, the student benefits from the "big picture" rather than separate, distinct pieces of a puzzle."

--*The Ultimate Geography and Timeline Guide*, page 8

to include what indigo was used for. Talk with your teacher about whether you think Eliza would have been an interesting person to know, and why you think as you do.

Drayton Hall, which Captain Wilcox and Benjamin visited while they were in Charleston, has been preserved as an historical site. With your parent's permission and supervision, explore the following Internet site: www.draytonhall.org. Be sure to look at the overview, research, and preservation areas on the site, and talk with your teacher about things you discover. Do you see any resemblance between the house as it is today and the picture on pages 32 and 33 in *The Eve of Revolution*?

Use your watercolors and watercolor paper to copy that picture. If you want, lightly draw in the things you want to include. Don't worry about completing the painting today, but work on it as you have time over the next few days.

F. States

Geography, History, Thinking Skills

In your *Atlas of the United States*, read the pages about Kentucky. When you are finished, find the blank map of Kentucky in your Student Notebook and complete the following assignments:

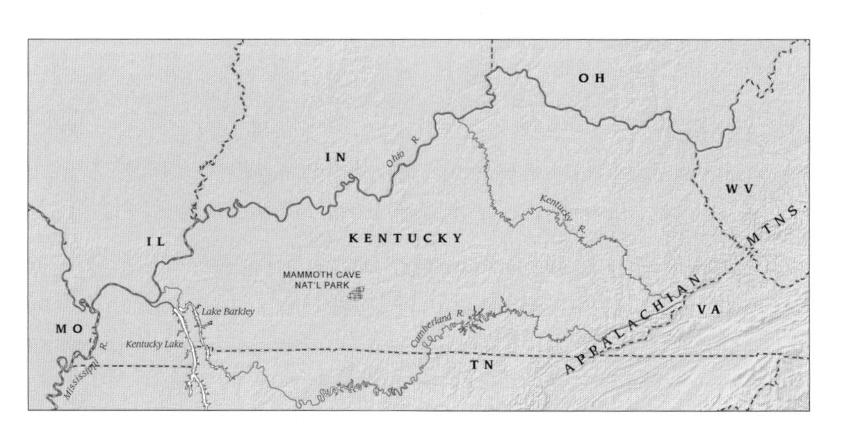

- Place a small star on the spot where Frankfort is located, and label it. Frankfort is the capital city of Kentucky.
- Color the lines showing the Kentucky, Cumberland, Mississippi, and Ohio Rivers blue, and label them. If you have trouble finding all the rivers, two of them form all or part of the borders between Kentucky and other states.
- Color the area where Mammoth Cave National Park is located, and label it.
- Lightly color the area where the Appalachian Mountains are located purple, and label them

- Color and label Lake Barkley and Kentucky Lake.
- Label the seven states that border Kentucky.

G. Cooking *Language Skills, Thinking Skills, Drawing*

With your parent's permission and supervision, look in *Eat Your Way Through the USA*, choose a recipe that comes from either Kentucky or Georgia, and prepare it for your family. After everyone has had a taste, find out who liked it, and whether anyone would like to have it again. What did you think about it?

In your Student Notebook, draw a picture of the dish you chose to make and write the following number of sentences about your family's reaction to it:

two sentences three sentences four sentences

Connect Learning to Life:

When your children make a recipe from a certain state, ask them why they think that dish is related to that state? Are the ingredients native to, or grown in that state, such as oranges in Florida or peanuts in Georgia? Is it a dish that was part of the state's culture, such as Cajun Gumbo in Louisiana? Whenever possible, connect the real things of life, such as food, to its source, history, or traditions. Looking deeper can be a natural way of teaching and life.

H. Independent Reading *Language Skills*

Choose something to read that you will enjoy. Then, find a quiet, comfortable place and read for the following length of time:

25 minutes 30 minutes

Be sure to write down what you read today on the Reading Log in your Student Notebook.

H. Ask your children to look at their reading logs and decide what type of books they read most frequently. Do they always read historical fiction? Stories about nature? Mysteries? As they analyze their own reading patterns, challenge them to stretch a bit and read something different every once in a while, at least once every unit. Tell them to mark it, and that you will be looking to see something new on their logs.

Lesson 3, Part 4

A. Quotation Notebook *Language Skills, History, Thinking Skills*

The next famous American document quoted is the Constitution of the United States. This document set up rules for our government. Any definitions included beneath the passage are to help you understand the meaning. Do not copy them as part of the quotation.

Copy the following quotation into your Student Notebook, and then talk with your teacher about its meaning. You may want to include parts of the United States Constitution in your presentation at the end of this unit, so practice reading this section aloud.

> We the People of the United States, in Order to form a more perfect Union, establish Justice, insure domestic Tranquility, provide for the common defense,

Definitions (as used in this document):
justice - fairness
domestic - relating to the events in our country
tranquility – peace

Draw or create a symbol that helps you remember this part of the Constitution. Put it beneath the quotation.

A. These are important words. Look on the Internet and try to find a copy of the document for your children to view, or an audio clip of someone reading the document in a dramatic fashion. The words used in the beginning of this document are powerful and memorable. Help your children enjoy, understand, and remember them in as many ways as possible.

B. Remember to adjust reading assignments to your children's individual needs. If they read fluently, with expression, and can retell what they have read, you may allow them to read more of the assignments silently. Occasionally ask what is happening in their story, just to get a sense of what your children are taking away from it. If your children are struggling with fluency, reading expressively, or remembering what they have read, you can increase the amount of read-aloud time.

B. Reader
Language Skills, History

The American Revolution: page 63 (Chapter 7), through page 68, paragraph 3
Guns for General Washington: Chapter 12

Read the above assignment from *The American Revolution* aloud, and then follow along as someone else reads the assignment from *Guns for General Washington*.

Read the above assignment from *The American Revolution* silently, and then read the assignment from *Guns for General Washington* aloud.

Read the above assignments from *The American Revolution* and *Guns for General Washington* silently.

C. Read-Aloud & Narration
Language Skills, Thinking Skills, History

George Washington: page 74, paragraph 8 ("George was…") through page 80, paragraph 7

After reading or listening to the read-aloud assignment in *George Washington*, talk with your teacher and try to predict what will happen in the future based on what you know of the characters and events. Write down your predictions in your Student Notebook. Later you will look back and see if they were accurate. Try not to peek ahead!

Listen carefully as your teacher reads the assigned passage. Then write down something that you think will happen in the story.

Write down another thing that you think will happen in the story.

Read the assigned passage aloud. Then write down at least three things that you think will happen in the story.

D. Editing
Language Skills, History, Thinking Skills

Continue reading and discussing parts of the famous speech attributed to Patrick Henry. Read the section of the speech included in your Student Notebook. One word in the passage is underlined and in italics. Try to figure out the meaning of that word using the context, or words around it. Then use a dictionary to look up definitions of the words underlined in the paragraph, and any other words you do not understand. Did you get the right meaning of the word in italics by using the context?

Use a highlighter or yellow crayon to highlight or underline the appropriate sentence(s). Then paraphrase those sentences by rewriting them in your own words underneath the passage.

the last two sentences

the first sentence

the entire passage

E. Science *Geography, Thinking Skills*

The earth is moving all the time! You already learned that it rotates on its axis once every day, or 24 hours. But do you know that while it is doing that, the earth is also **orbiting**, or traveling around, the sun? This is another thing that helps to cause seasons.

Sometimes people think the earth's path around the sun is like Figure 1 below—a circle, but that is not exactly true. The shape of the earth's orbit is more like Figure 2, which shows an **ellipse**. An ellipse is a stretched out circle. It takes a little more than 365 days, or one year, for the earth to complete its trip around the sun. The seasons change at about the same time each year because of the earth's position in its orbit.

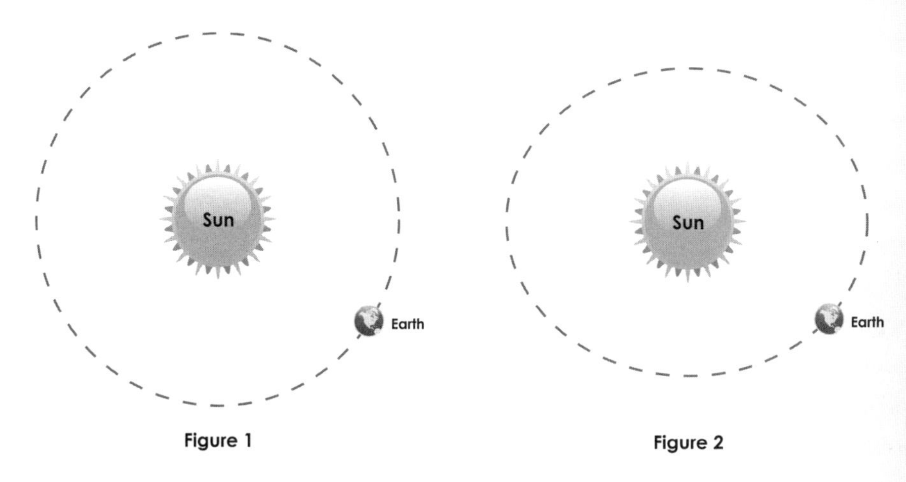

Figure 1 Figure 2

Together with your teacher, read and discuss the section in your *Weather Facts* book entitled "Weather and Seasons."

When you finish reading, look at the earth-model you used in Part 2 with its axis attached. Ask for your teacher's help, if necessary, to find a spot on the upper portion of the fruit where you think New England might be located if your model was really the earth. This is the area where the Continental Army was encamped in *Guns for General Washington*. Push a straight pin into that area so you can keep track of it. Then give a flashlight to someone, and ask that person to stand in the middle of the room with plenty of space on all sides for you to walk around. Measure about three feet out from the front and back of that person, and mark those spots on the floor with masking tape. Then measure about two feet out from the person's sides, and mark those spots with tape. If you drew a line that connected the pieces of tape, it would show an ellipse.

If you need help remembering how the tilt of the earth's axis looks, use a clock to recheck it. To do this, place the *South Pole* end of the axis beside the clock's number six, and move the *North Pole* end to four minutes past 12. Then hold your earth-model in front of you by its axis, tilted properly, and stand on the piece of tape in front of the person in the center of your ellipse. The *South Pole* end of the axis should point toward your stomach, and the *North Pole* end should be tilted toward the flashlight.

Pretend the flashlight that your center person holds is the sun. Ask her to turn it on and shine it toward your earth-model. As you stand in the first position described above, notice where New England is. Does it lean toward or away from the sun?[4] What season do you think this might represent in New England?[5] Talk with your teacher about why you think it might be that season.[6]

Now walk to the piece of tape to your right. This is the same direction that the earth moves in its orbit around the sun. Since the earth's axis does not change position, make sure that both ends are still pointing in the same directions that they were at the beginning of your orbit. Ask your sun to shine on the earth-model again. This position represents the next season. Which season do you think that might be?[7] Why?[8] Is either end of the axis tilted toward the sun?[9]

E. If you need help explaining the directions in which the axis remains pointed, use the picture in the pocket guide as an illustration. Point out that no matter where the earth is in its orbit, the axis is always in the same position.

Again, move to the next piece of tape in your orbit, and ask the sun to shine on your earth-model. Be sure that the axis continues to point in the same directions. Is New England now tilted toward the sun or away?[10] What season do you think this might represent in New England?[11] What season do you think it represents in the entire Northern Hemisphere?[12]

Complete your orbit by moving to the last piece of tape, and tell your teacher what New England season that position represents, and why.[13]

Use the picture in the "Weather and Seasons" section of your *Weather Facts* book to complete the chart in your Student Notebook.

Be sure to record your weather observations over the next few days on the Weather Watcher pages in the back of your Student Notebook.

Walk through the orbit again, but this time pay attention to the Southern Hemisphere. When you stand at the beginning point, is the Southern Hemisphere tilted toward or away from the sun?[14] Which season would it be there?[15] What about each of the other positions of the orbit?[16] How are seasons in the Southern Hemisphere different from those in the Northern Hemisphere?[17]

Once again stand at the beginning point of your orbit, and this time pay attention to the sun's light. How much light shines on the North Pole?[18] How much shines on the South Pole?[19] Go to the opposite position and answer the same questions.[20]

At the library or on the Internet find out more about what happens to the length of days as seasons change. Pay special attention to what happens at the North and South Poles. When you are finished, write one or two paragraphs in your Student Notebook that tell what you learned.

F. **States** *Geography, History, Thinking Skills, Drawing*

Look again at the pages about Kentucky in your *Atlas of the United States*. Then find the State Page in your Student Notebook, and fill in the information.

Make State Cards for Kentucky by following the instructions found in Appendix B. Kentucky is a Southern state, so be sure to outline the cards in purple.

G. **Writing** *Language Skills, Thinking Skills*

In Unit 1 you began learning about taking the words of another person and writing them as dialogue. Remember the steps you learned in Unit 1:

Step 1 - After you say who is speaking (a person's name, or *he*, or *she*) and what they are doing (*said, told, asked*) you put a comma. This tells the reader that the next words will be the words of the speaker.

Step 2 - Quotation marks (") are used to let the reader know that what is inside them are the exact words the person says, so put quotation marks before the words that they say. Use a capital letter to start what the person says.

Step 3 - When you get to the end of what the person says (which may be more than one sentence) finish it with the punctuation mark needed, like a period or question mark. The punctuation mark is part of what the person said.

Step 4 - Close up the quotation with quotation marks. This lets the reader know that the words the person spoke are now finished.

Now, look back at the Interactive Writing you and your partner did in Part 2, and follow the directions below :

- Rewrite at least two sentences as dialogue. Here is an example:

  My mom said, "You were the cutest baby in the world."

- Rewrite at least two sentences your partner wrote, and two sentences you wrote, as dialogue. Here are some examples:

  My dad said, "The day you were born was the happiest day of my life." I said, "The first thing I remember was when I got gum stuck in my hair."

- Rewrite at least three sentences your partner wrote, and three sentences you wrote, as dialogue. Above are some examples.

G. This is an example of spaced review. It has been some time since your children did the lesson about writing dialogue, so this is a reminder and review of the skills taught and their application. Sometimes if children see something they have already done, they do not think they should have to do it again. If that is the case with your children, take this opportunity to turn the tables on them! Ask them to be the teacher and review the lesson by showing you how to do it. The value is in revisiting the concepts and application, not just in the method of review.

H. **Independent Reading** *Language Skills*

Choose something to read that you will enjoy. Then, find a quiet, comfortable place and read for the following length of time:

25 minutes   30 minutes

Be sure to write down what you read today on the Reading Log in your Student Notebook.

Lesson 3, Part 5

Teaching Tip

Summary lessons and activities are very valuable. Though this may seem shorter than the other lesson parts, it is no less important. There are a variety of ways to help your children retain concepts and skills. Student presentations, review, games, and activities are all effective means of helping your children solidify and remember what they have learned. Then they can take the next big step of using it in the future, so be sure to make room for Part 5!

This part is set aside for completion of any work left undone from the lesson, and review of concepts and content. It is also a time to expand the work in the lesson by doing art, timeline activities, or games.

- Review the Steps for Thinking from the beginning of this lesson.
- Give your teacher your stack of vocabulary cards for the lesson. As she shows you each word, tell her the meaning of the word and how it was used in the story.
- Read over your number chart or your index cards and practice spelling numerals or ordinals that seem difficult. Tell your teacher when you have finished practicing.

  Shuffle your deck of index cards and give it to your teacher. Listen as she calls out the numerals or ordinals written on ten of the cards. Do the best you can to correctly write each one she calls out, both as a number and in words. When you are finished, check your spelling using your number chart. Tell your teacher how you did.

  - Follow the above directions for five additional numerals or ordinals.
  - Follow the above directions for ten additional numerals or ordinals.
- Use the United States map that is near the front of your *Atlas of the United States* to find Georgia and Kentucky. Then, on the large outline map of the U.S., draw lines around them with a purple crayon, marker, or colored pencil. Write in the names of the states, and draw small stars where their capital cities are located. Next to the stars, write the name of each capital city.
- Read, or listen as your teacher reads, the story about Nathan Hale in *Profiles from History, Volume 2.* Talk about the discussion question with your teacher, and then complete any other activities that she assigns.
- Use your USA Activity CD to print at least one activity for the states you studied in this lesson. Then add any that you complete to your Student Notebook.

What makes a person memorable? Many history books give only facts and dates, but that doesn't make historical figures seem real. Learning about their hearts—their thoughts and motives, struggles and successes, and ultimately how others remember them—makes them memorable. The purpose of learning about them is for their lives to make an impact on our lives.

- Use the beanbags you made in Lesson 2 to play cornhole. This game is similar to horseshoes, and is thought to have originated in Germany. It was brought to America by settlers, and then re-discovered in the hills of Kentucky over 100 years ago. Since then, cornhole has become quite popular in some areas of our country. Although there are official cornhole rules, platforms, and bags, you will play a more relaxed version of the game. Follow the directions in Appendix B to build a simple cardboard platform, and then enjoy the game with your family!

Enrichment Activities

1. At the library or on the Internet research the laws that American colonists called the Intolerable Acts. Make a list of them, and write a sentence or two about each one. When you are finished, share what you have learned with your family. Be sure to include this information in your presentation at the end of this unit.
2. At the library or on the Internet research a Native American tribe from either the Mid-Atlantic or Southern regions of what is now the United States. If you do not have a tribe in mind that you would like to find out more about, choose one from the map entitled "Native American Nations, c. 1750" in your *United States History Atlas*. Print a Native American Profile sheet from your Student Resources CD and fill it out.

   Place the new profile sheet and picture in your Native American Notebook, or add them to your Student Notebook.

Additional Resources

Betsy Ross, Patriot of Philadelphia by Judith St. George
If you read this book, be sure to print a Book Review page from your Student Resources CD, fill it out, and place it in your Student Notebook.

Answers

1. 58, 19th, 80, 3rd

2. fifty-one; fifty-two; fifty-three; fifty-four; fifty-five; fifty-six; fifty-seven; fifty-eight; fifty-nine; sixty
   sixty-one; sixty-two; sixty-three; sixty-four; sixty-five; sixty-six; sixty-seven; sixty-eight; sixty nine; seventy
   seventy-one; seventy-two; seventy-three; seventy-four; seventy-five; seventy-six; seventy-seven; seventy-eight; seventy-nine; eighty
   eighty-one; eighty-two; eighty-three; eighty-four; eighty-five; eighty-six; eighty-seven; eighty-eight; eighty-nine; ninety
   ninety-one; ninety-two; ninety-three; ninety-four; ninety-five; ninety-six; ninety-seven; ninety-eight; ninety-nine; one hundred
   eleventh; twelfth; thirteenth; fourteenth; fifteenth; sixteenth; seventeenth; eighteenth; nineteenth; twentieth; twenty-first; twenty-second; twenty-third; twenty-fourth; twenty-fifth; twenty-sixth; twenty-seventh; twenty-eighth; twenty-ninth; thirtieth; thirty-first; thirty-second; thirty-third; thirty-fourth; thirty-fifth; thirty-sixth; thirty-seventh; thirty-eighth; thirty-ninth; fortieth
   six hundred forty-four, seven hundred thirty-three, eight hundred twenty-two, nine hundred eleven
   six thousand three hundred sixty-two; seven thousand two hundred seventy-three; eight thousand one hundred eighty-four; nine thousand five hundred ninety-five
   six million seven hundred sixty-five thousand eight hundred fifty-six; seven million eight hundred seventy-six thousand nine hundred sixty-seven; eight million nine hundred eighty-seven thousand one hundred seventy-eight; nine million one hundred ninety-eight thousand two hundred eighty-nine

3. day and night

4. toward

5. summer

6. Answers should reflect the idea that since New England is inclined toward the sun, it is exposed to more heat.

7. fall (or autumn)

8. because fall follows summer

9. no

10. away

11. winter

12. winter

13. spring, because it follows winter

14. away

15. winter

16. spring, summer, fall

17. they are exactly opposite

18. a lot

19. very little

20. very little, a lot

Lesson 4, Part 1

Steps for Thinking

1. Sometimes it takes great sacrifices to achieve an important goal.
2. It is difficult to make sacrifices when you do not have a strong connection to the causes involved.
3. There is great strength for sacrifices when you are fighting for your home and family.

Ask your children to read over the Steps for Thinking and briefly restate each one in their own words, or give examples that they have heard or read so far. Remind them of any ideas or examples they have thought of during the past week.

A. Copywork & Dictation

Language Skills, Thinking Skills

Look carefully at your assigned passage below, and read it silently. Show your teacher any words you don't know, and practice saying them aloud. Now read the passage aloud, or ask your teacher to read it to you.

When you are finished copying or writing from dictation, compare your copy to the text and make any needed corrections.

- Copy or write as your teacher dictates from *The American Revolution*, page 69 paragraph 9 ("Revere was referring…").
- Copy or write as your teacher dictates from *Guns for General Washington*, page 78, paragraph 2 ("The General returned…").
- Write as your teacher dictates from *Guns for General Washington*, page 78, paragraph 2 ("The General returned…") through page 79, paragraph 1.

B. Reader

Language Skills, History

The American Revolution: page 68, paragraph 4 ("Finally. . .") through page 74, paragraph 1
Guns for General Washington: Chapter 13

- Read the above assignment from *The American Revolution* aloud, and then follow along as someone else reads the assignment from *Guns for General Washington*.
- Read the above assignment from *The American Revolution* silently, and then read the assignment from *Guns for General Washington* aloud.
- Read the above assignments from *The American Revolution* and *Guns for General Washington* silently.

Materials

- *The American Revolution (Munford)*
- *Guns for General Washington*
- *George Washington*
- *The Eve of Revolution*
- *Atlas of the United States*
- *Eat Your Way Through the USA*
- *DK Pockets: Weather Facts*
- *Klutz Watercolor Book*
- *Discovering America's Founders* DVD
- Outline Map of the U.S.
- USA Activity CD
- Ingredients for recipe (Part 3)
- Activity (Part 1)
  - Light cardboard (at least 4"x 6")
  - Ball of twine or hemp cord
  - Yarn needle (preferred) or twist-tie
- Weather watching tools

Teaching Tip

The process of copywork and dictation gives a teacher a great deal of information. Not only does it show what your child is missing, it shows what he is getting! Reading or hearing language, and then writing it down is a multi-step process that shows understanding, processing of information, and translating that information into writing. Many times over my years as an educator, just giving a student a passage to copy or write from dictation has provided great insight into the student's ability to read, write, and comprehend. Make sure to take notice of all your child does correctly when using this process, and encourage him accordingly!

C. Read-Aloud & Discussion *Language Skills, Thinking Skills, History*

George Washington: page 80, paragraph 8 ("George was...") through page 87, paragraph 6

Follow the instructions below for your level. When you are finished, discuss what is happening in this section from the British point of view. Then talk about what is happening from the colonists' point of view. How are their viewpoints different? Who do you think is right? Think about what you know from the story, and discuss the passage in your own words. Give any examples you can think of from the story.

Listen carefully as your teacher reads the above assignment from *George Washington* aloud.

Read the above assignment from *George Washington* aloud.

D. There are many ways to support the brain's ability to remember words. One fun way is to make associations to a funny picture, or pronounce the word so you hear its spelling, such as Ar-kansas. If your children have difficulty spelling any state names, encourage them to notice something special about the word, such as a smaller word inside the word (AlaBAMa). They can come up with a funny picture, such as an h riding on top of the word rode, to an island, to remember to include the h in Rhode Island. Unique stories and pictures are a good help to remembering individual words or names.

D. Spelling *Language Skills, Thinking Skills*

Look at the names of states below. Read them to your teacher and get help pronouncing any difficult names. Tell your teacher how many syllables you hear in each word. You can clap the syllables if that will help. Write the number of syllables in your Student Notebook.

Maine Georgia Arkansas Alabama[1]

Listen as your teacher reads each of the following words. Then spell each word as best you can either aloud or by writing it in your Student Notebook.

Alabama	Virginia	Maryland
New Hampshire	Maine	North Carolina
South Carolina	Rhode Island	Delaware
New Jersey	Arkansas	Kentucky
Georgia	New York	Vermont
Massachusetts	Connecticut	Pennsylvania
Mississippi	Tennessee	

E. History *Thinking Skills*

Together with your teacher, read Chapter 5 in *The Eve of Revolution*. Talk with your teacher about what happened in the Boston Massacre. Then, cut out the events in your Student Notebook and paste the story in its proper order. It is fine to look at the book if you need help remembering.

Why did John Adams and Josiah Quincy, Jr. defend the British soldiers who shot and killed three colonists, and wounded two others who later died?[2] Do you think they were right to do so? Why, or why not. After talking about this with your teacher, use complete sentences to write your answers in your Student Notebook.

After the Boston Massacre, Britain **repealed**, or cancelled, most of the Townshend Acts. Look back at the Introduction to *The Eve of Revolution*, and in your Student Notebook list the items that were taxed by the Townshend Acts.[3] Which tax remained when the others were cancelled?[4] Why do you think the repeal of these taxes was too late to help the situation in the colonies?[5] After talking about this with your teacher, write one or two sentences in your Student Notebook that tell what you think.

F. **States** *Geography, History, Thinking Skills*

In your *Atlas of the United States*, read the pages about Tennessee. When you are finished, find the blank map of Tennessee in your Student Notebook and complete the following assignments:

- Place a small star on the spot where Nashville is located, and label it. Nashville is the capital city of Tennessee.

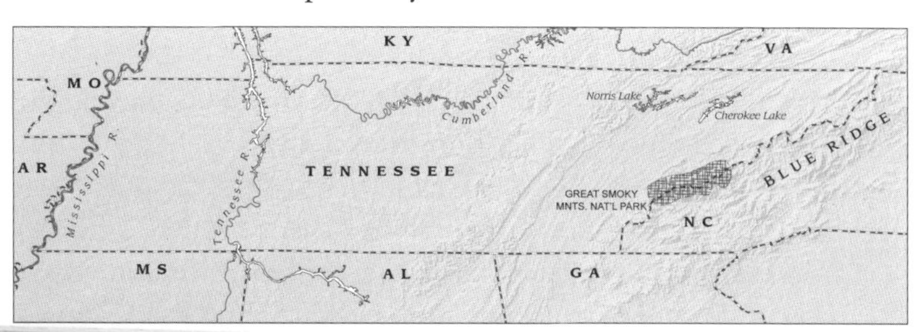

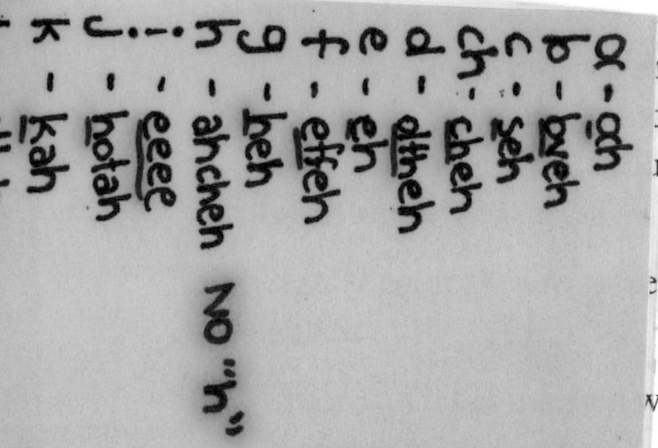

...ne Mississippi, Cumberland, and ...d label them. Notice that the Tennessee ...u have trouble finding one of the rivers, it ... Tennessee and two other states.

...ere the Blue Ridge is located green, and

...where the Great Smoky Mountains

...e Lake and Norris Lake.

...t border Tennessee.

History, Thinking Skills

...protested unfair taxes by boycotting, or ...ods. In Lesson 2 you read in *The Eve of* ...y would no longer buy the fine cloth of- ...egan to spin yarn and weave their own ...f time, and the cloth was not as pretty or soft ...ut they felt it was a worthwhile sacrifice.

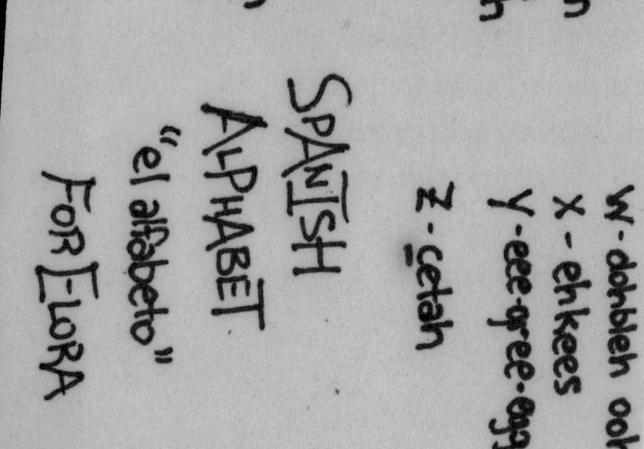

G. The word *sacrifice* has been a part of the lesson many times. Discuss this word with your children and make sure they have a working understanding of it and can put it into their own words. In our homeschooling, when we observed a special word we would challenge each other to use it as part of everyday conversation. Each time someone would use it, we would all applaud that person and be reminded of the meaning of the word. Make review and application a natural part of your days.

Follow the directions in Appendix B and weave a bag out of twine or hemp. Like many things woven during colonial times, it will not be particularly pretty—but it will be sturdy and useful! When you are finished, you can use the bag to store your vocabulary or state cards.

H. **Independent Reading** *Language Skills*

Choose something to read that you will enjoy. Then, find a quiet, comfortable place and read for the following length of time:

25 minutes 30 minutes

Over time, it's fun to see how much you have read. Be sure to write down what you read today on the Reading Log in your Student Notebook.

Lesson 4, Part 2

A. The assignment for this part is a continuation of the Constitution of the United States. Review the meaning of the word constitution with your children, to make sure they understand its meaning and the document's purpose.

A. **Quotation Notebook** *Language Skills, History, Thinking Skills*

Copy the following quotation from the United States Constitution into your Student Notebook, and then talk with your teacher about its meaning. This document set up rules for America's government. You may want to include parts of the Constitution in your presentation at the end of this unit, so practice reading this section aloud.

> promote the general Welfare, and secure the Blessings of Liberty to ourselves and our Posterity, do ordain and establish this Constitution for the United States of America.

Definitions (as used in this document):
welfare - the conditions a person lives in that are satisfactory
liberty - the rights that belong to citizens or to all people
posterity - your future generations
ordain - order something by law

Draw or create a symbol that helps you remember this part of the Constitution. Put it beneath the quotation.

B. **Reader** *Language Skills, History*

The American Revolution: page 74, paragraph 2 ("One of Paul's. . .") through page 79, paragraph 2
Guns for General Washington: Chapter 14

Read the above assignment from *The American Revolution* aloud, and then follow along as someone else reads the assignment from *Guns for General Washington.*

Read the above assignment from *The American Revolution* silently, and then read the assignment from *Guns for General Washington* aloud.

Read the above assignments from *The American Revolution* and *Guns for General Washington* silently.

C. **Read-Aloud & Narration** *Language Skills, History, Thinking Skills*
George Washington: page 87, paragraph 7 ("Before he…") through page 95

Follow the instructions below for your level. Then, in your own words, tell what happened in the story from George's point of view, or pretend you are George and tell what you think happened. Try to remember as many details as possible. You may reread the passage or listen as your teacher rereads the part you are to retell.

Listen carefully as your teacher reads the above assignment from *George Washington* aloud.

Read the above assignment from *George Washington* aloud.

D. **Editing** *Language Skills, Thinking Skills, History*
Continue reading and discussing parts of the famous speech attributed to Patrick Henry. This speech took place before the delegates of the Virginia colony, who were discussing whether they should join Massachusetts in declaring themselves part of the Revolutionary War. Not only does this speech show the beliefs of a great American patriot, it also shows how to express your thoughts well.

Use a highlighter or yellow crayon to highlight or underline the appropriate sentence(s). Then paraphrase those sentences by rewriting them in your own words underneath the passage.

the last two sentences

the first sentence

the entire passage

E. **Science** *Thinking Skills, History, Geography*
In *Guns for General Washington*, Henry Knox's men were moving huge guns through extremely cold weather. Sometimes the conditions were helpful, allowing them to move more quickly with their sleds over the snow, and to cross frozen rivers with little trouble. After leaving Saratoga, however, the group became stuck in a severe winter storm. Together with your teacher, re-read the section of that book beginning at paragraph 2, page 69 ("The next morning…") to paragraph 2 on page 70 ("In the teeth…").

Connect Learning to Life:

If your children have never lived in an area where there are snow, blizzards, and freezing temperatures, think of a close friend or relative who has. Encourage your children to talk to that person about what they experienced—both the fun things and the difficulties. While snow looks like fun to those who rarely see it, it also has problems associated with it. As often as possible, connect content learning to life experience.

Many things work together to cause different types of weather on earth. You already know that the New England region is not located close to the equator, and it is tilted away from the sun during winter. Even though there is much more involved, both of these things help to cause that area's cold winter weather.

There are several different types of winter storms. Some of the most dangerous are the ones that cover the ground with a layer of ice. You have learned that air close to the earth is usually warmer than air that is higher in the atmosphere, but ice storms are caused when those conditions are reversed. A layer of air above the earth is warm enough—above **32°F**, which is the freezing point of water—for liquid rain to begin falling. Then, as that rain drops through the colder air that is close to the surface of the earth, it begins to freeze. If the raindrops freeze completely before they hit the ground, they become sleet. If they freeze only partially on the way down, they become frozen rain. Both sleet and frozen rain make things very slippery. Of the two, however, frozen rain is probably more dangerous. This is because it is still partly liquid, so it spreads out over the things it falls on before it freezes into a solid. The result is a layer of ice on everything.

Snowflakes, on the other hand, begin as tiny ice crystals in clouds that are below the freezing point (32°F). These ice crystals bond with one another until they are heavy enough to fall. If the ground is not frozen, the snow will melt as soon as it lands. If the ground temperature is at or below the freezing point, the snowflakes will remain as they are. Many snowfalls are gentle and beautiful to watch, others can be very dangerous. Together with your teacher, read and discuss the section entitled "Snow" in your *Weather Facts* book.

The severe winter storm that *Guns for General Washington* tells about was probably a **blizzard**, which involves lots of snow combined with strong winds. Another even more dangerous winter storm is a northeaster. These storms, often called nor'easters, are winter hurricanes that usually form in the south and then move north along the eastern coast of the United States. Use the index in the back of your *Weather Facts* book to find the pages about blizzards, and read them.

Use the above model to label the Winter Precipitation chart in your Student Notebook. Then talk to your teacher about each type of winter weather. When you are finished, list three facts about each type of winter weather.[6]

Remember to record your observations on the Weather Watcher pages over the next couple of days.

At the library or on the Internet research the "Storm of the Century" that occurred in 1993. Then, in your Student Notebook list four facts about this famous storm that made it different from most northeasters.[7]

Think about preparations your family might need to make if a northeaster was predicted in your area. In your Student Notebook, write a paragraph about what you would do to prepare. Following your paragraph, make a list of supplies you would want to have on hand.

F. States

Geography, Thinking Skills, History, Drawing

Look again at the pages about Tennessee in your *Atlas of the United States.* Then find the State Page in your Student Notebook, and fill in the information.

Make State Cards for Tennessee by following the instructions found in Appendix B. Tennessee is a Southern state, so be sure to outline the cards in purple.

G. Interactive Writing

Language Skills, Thinking Skills

Complete this writing activity with your partner.

It is your partner's job to write first; then you will answer a question with the number of sentences assigned below. After that, write several sentences telling what you think about what your partner has written. Make sure to end with a question you want to ask your partner, so he or she can write back to you.

Topic for your partner: Have you ever boycotted, or refused to use a product or do something to make a point? If you haven't done that, is there anything you would boycott? Tell your student why you would do that, or why you have done it. Do you think this is the right way to make a point?

G. The interactive writing lesson today is about boycotts. Boycotting occurs when we stop using a product that we normally use to make a point. Giving up that product or service may be a *sacrifice*. Since you have discussed this word with your children, ask them to consider including it in their writing. Writing becomes clearer after thought and discussion have taken place.

Your question: Have you ever had to give up something you really liked because your parents didn't think it was good for you? Was it easy or difficult to do? What were your parents' reasons? Did you see the benefit of what they asked you to do?

at least four sentences

at least five sentences

at least one paragraph

If you need help remembering what a paragraph is, or how to write one, look back at Lesson 1, Part 2.

H. **Independent Reading** *Language Skills*
Choose something to read that you will enjoy. Then, find a quiet, comfortable place and read for the following length of time:

25 minutes 30 minutes

Be sure to write down what you read today on the Reading Log in your Student Notebook.

Lesson 4, Part 3

A. **Copywork & Dictation** *Language Skills, Thinking Skills*
Look carefully at your assigned passage below, and read it silently. Show your teacher any words you don't know, and practice saying them aloud. Now read the passage aloud, or ask your teacher to read it to you.

When you are finished copying or writing from dictation, compare your copy to the text and make any needed corrections.

Copy or write as your teacher dictates from *The American Revolution*, page 85 paragraph 2 ("Paul smiled…").

Copy or write as your teacher dictates from *Guns for General Washington*, page 90, paragraph 2 ("The weeks dragged…").

Write as your teacher dictates from *Guns for General Washington*, page 90, paragraph 2 ("The weeks dragged…") through page 91, paragraph 1.

B. When your child reads, make a list of any troublesome words. Look for possible patterns to the mistakes, and before your next session review those words. You may read them aloud, or ask your child to do so.

B. **Reader** *Language Skills, History*
The American Revolution: page 80, paragraph 1 ("I hoped. . .") through page 86, paragraph 8
Guns for General Washington: Chapter 15

Read the above assignment from *The American Revolution* aloud, and then follow along as someone else reads the assignment from *Guns for General Washington*.

Read the above assignment from *The American Revolution* silently, and then read the assignment from *Guns for General Washington* aloud.

Read the above assignments from *The American Revolution* and *Guns for General Washington* silently.

C. Read-Aloud & Discussion

Language Skills, Thinking Skills, History

George Washington: page 96 ("Martha was…") to the bottom of page 101

Follow the directions below and read or listen to the above assignment from *George Washington*. Then make up the assigned number of questions about the part of the story you just read or heard. Write your questions and ask your teacher to answer them. After discussing her thoughts, write down the best possible answer in your Student Notebook. Be sure to use complete sentences.

When you are finished, look back at the prediction or predictions you made during Lesson 3, Part 4. Were you able to predict what would happen? Be sure to mark the "Came to Pass" box for each prediction when it does happen.

Listen carefully as your teacher reads the assigned passage.

Make up one question. Make up two questions.

Read the assigned passage aloud; then make up three questions.

D. Vocabulary & Spelling

Language Skills, Thinking Skills

Vocabulary:
Write each vocabulary word listed below on an index card. Use a dictionary to look up the meaning of each word, and write it on the card. Then on the back of each card, draw a picture or write a clue so you can remember how the word was used in the story.

Godspeed **anvil** **tarnish**
transpired **correspondence**

grueling **snowbound** **peril**
privateer **anthem**

Spelling:
Look at the names of states listed below. Read them to your teacher and get help pronouncing any difficult names. Tell your teacher how many syllables you hear in each word. You can clap the syllables if that will help.

Kentucky Tennessee Pennsylvania Mississippi[8]

Look at the names of states you wrote in Part 1. If you did not write them in that part, ask your teacher to read each word, and write it in your Student Notebook now. Check your spelling against the list and correct it if necessary. When you are finished, cover each word with your hand, and try to spell it aloud. Then uncover it and see if you were correct.

E. As your child learns to take notes, it may be helpful to stop the video at intervals and discuss what has happened or been said. Ask questions that will help him understand the important parts of what he has seen or heard.

E. History

Language Skills, Thinking Skills

In both this unit and the first one, you have learned a lot about George Washington. He was a great man who did much to help establish the United States of America. That is why he is called the father of our country!

To help **summarize**, or look at the main points, of George Washington's life, watch Episode 3, Chapters 3-5 on the *Discovering America's Founders* DVD with your teacher. Before you begin though, take a minute to look at the Video Profile page for this lesson in your Student Notebook, and see what kinds of questions it asks.[9]

As you watch the video lesson, keep the Video Profile page in front of you. When you notice that the **narrator**, or person telling the story, is answering one of the questions, stop the video long enough to write the answer on your Profile page. Continue doing this as often as necessary as you finish watching the video lesson.

As you watch the video lesson, use a piece of scrap paper to jot down important things that the **narrator**, or person telling the story, says about George. This is called taking notes, and is a good way to help you remember what you hear or see. You do not need to use sentences when you take notes—single words or **phrases**, which are short groups of words, will work fine as long as they help you remember the important things. If it is helpful, stop the lesson when you need to, or watch it a second time.

When you are finished, use your notes and your memory to fill in the Video Profile page.

F. States

Geography, History, Thinking Skills

In your *Atlas of the United States*, read the pages about Mississippi. When you are finished, find the blank map of Mississippi in your Student Notebook and complete the following assignments:

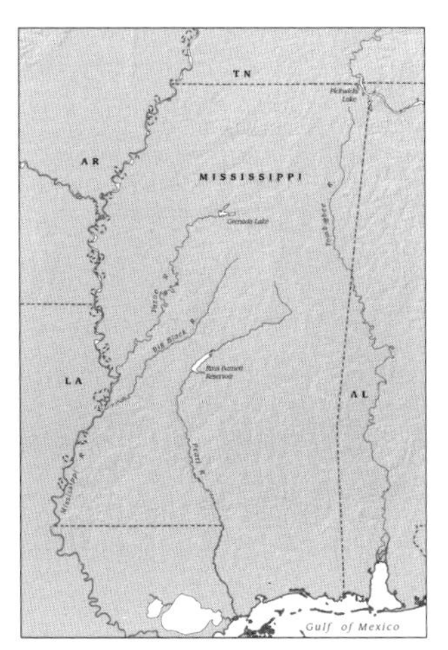

- Place a small star on the spot where Jackson is located, and label it. Jackson is the capital city of Mississippi.
- Label the Gulf of Mexico.
- Color the lines showing the Mississippi, Yazoo, Big Black, Tombigbee, and Pearl Rivers blue, and label them. If you have trouble finding one of the rivers, it forms the border between Mississippi and another state.
- Color and label Granada Lake and Pickwick Lake.
- Color and label the Ross Barnett Reservoir.
- Label the four states that border Mississippi.

Connect Learning to Life:

How do places get their names? Talk with your students about the names of the places that they are including in their mapping assignments. Where do they think the names came from? Talk about the names of places where you live. Discuss the origins of the names. Even street names can be of interest. Ask your children to be on the lookout for interesting names of places near where you live. Use the resources available to you such as the library, Internet or local residents to find out the source of the names. Research can arise out of every-day questions!

G. Cooking

Language Skills, Thinking Skills, Drawing

With your parent's permission and supervision, look in *Eat Your Way Through the USA*, choose a recipe that comes from either Mississippi or Tennessee, and prepare it for your family. After everyone has had a taste, find out who liked it, and whether anyone would like to have it again. What did you think about it?

In your Student Notebook, draw a picture of the dish you chose to make and write the following number of sentences about your family's reaction to it:

two sentences — three sentences — four sentences

H. Independent Reading

Language Skills

Choose something to read that you will enjoy. Then, find a quiet, comfortable place and read for the following length of time:

25 minutes — 30 minutes

Be sure to write down what you read today on the Reading Log in your Student Notebook.

Connect Learning to Life:

The Legislative Branch of the national government is still at work today. Each state also has a legislative branch. Encourage or assist your children in finding out who represents your family in the United States House and Senate. For further study, you can help them determine who represents your family in the state legislature. This information is located in many places such as the library, the Internet, and in your community. Phone books often give the listings for these individuals as well.

B. A short passage in today's assignment in *Guns for General Washington* may be offensive to some. Pending your review, omit reading from paragraph 4, page 93 ("On this very spot...") through paragraph 1 on page 94.

Teaching Tip

The skill of predicting what will happen in the story is an important one. It requires your child to remember what has already happened, consider the characters and events, and then come up with a reasonable idea of what may happen in the future. This process involves using critical thinking skills and can be a natural part of any reading your child is doing. Just ask, "What do you think will happen next?"

Lesson 4, Part 4

A. Quotation Notebook

Language Skills, History, Thinking Skills

In this section you will continue copying statements from the United States Constitution. This document set up rules for our government.

Find a copy of the Constitution at the library or on the Internet. Together with your teacher, read Article 1 of the Constitution. This Article established the Legislative Branch of the government. **Legislative** means involved with creating and passing laws. Choose a quotation from this Article and copy it into your Student Notebook.

Draw or create a symbol that helps you remember this part of the Constitution. Put it beneath the quotation.

B. Reader

Language Skills, History

The American Revolution: page 87, paragraph 1 ("We rode. . .") through page 91, paragraph 2
Guns for General Washington: page 92 (Chapter 16) through page 93, paragraph 3. Continue reading from page 94, paragraph 2 ("J.P. held...") through page 96

Read the above assignment from *The American Revolution* aloud, and then follow along as someone else reads the assignment from *Guns for General Washington*.

Read the above assignment from *The American Revolution* silently, and then read the assignment from *Guns for General Washington* aloud.

Read the above assignments from *The American Revolution* and *Guns for General Washington* silently.

C. Read-Aloud & Narration

Language Skills, Thinking Skills, History

George Washington: bottom of page 101 ("In Williamsburg...") through page 109

After reading or listening to the read-aloud assignment in *George Washington*, talk with your teacher and try to predict what will happen in the future based on what you know of the characters and events. Write down your predictions in your Student Notebook. Later you will look back and see if your predictions they were accurate. Try not to peek ahead!

Listen carefully as your teacher reads the assigned passage. Then write down something that you think will happen in the story.

Write down another thing that you think will happen in the story.

Read the assigned passage aloud. Then write down at least three things that you think will happen in the story.

D. Editing *Language Skills, Thinking Skills, History*

Continue reading and discussing parts of the famous speech attributed to Patrick Henry. Read the section of the speech included in your Student Notebook. One word in the passage is underlined and in italics. Try to figure out the meaning of that word using the context, or words around it. Then use a dictionary to look up definitions of the words underlined in the paragraph, and any other words you do not understand. Did you get the right meaning of the word in italics by using the context?

Use a highlighter or yellow crayon to highlight or underline the appropriate sentence(s). Then paraphrase those sentences by rewriting them in your own words underneath the passage.

two sentences three sentences four sentences

D. New vocabulary words appear in the context of a lesson or story, which helps students recognize the connection between the way a word is used and its meaning. This is an important reading strategy called using context clues.

E. Science *History, Thinking Skills*

Earlier in this lesson, you read in *Guns for General Washington* that General Howe was expecting reinforcements any day. But the group of ships, or **convoy**, bringing those supplies and troops was blown off course by a hurricane. Of course, this was bad news for General Howe, but wonderful news for General Washington.

To understand hurricanes, it is important to know that air pressure systems spin—high air pressure spins outward, and low air pressure spins inward. This inward spin of a low pressure system causes air to pileup in the center with nowhere to go except up. So it rises, cools, condenses, and forms clouds. This is why low pressure moving into an area almost always means bad weather, and sometimes strong storms.

If several of those storms cluster together over warm ocean water and begin to rotate, they are called a tropical depression. If the tropical depression forms large cumulonimbus clouds and its winds strengthen to 40 miles per hour, it becomes a tropical storm. Then finally, if the winds reach at least 74 miles per hour, the tropical storm is classified as a hurricane. The hurricane season, or period of time when most of these storms form, is through the summer and fall.

Together with your teacher, read and discuss the sections entitled "Hurricanes" and "Tracking the Damage" in your *Weather Facts* book. After reading those pages, with your parent's permission continue your research on the Internet at:
http://skydiary.com/kids/hurricanes.html.

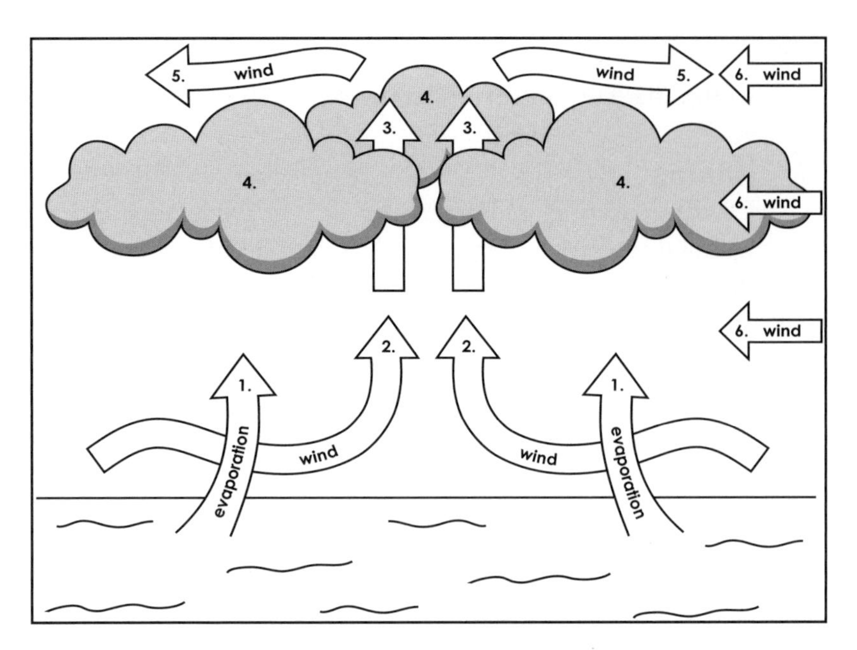

Now talk with your teacher about the diagram pictured above that describes how a low pressure system turns into a hurricane. When you are finished, cut out the weather conditions printed in your Student Notebook, and paste them in the order necessary for a hurricane to form.[10] Then use the things you have learned in this section to complete the Hurricane Matching game.[11]

F. States
Geography, History, Thinking Skills, Drawing

Look again at the pages about Mississippi in your *Atlas of the United States*. Then find the State Page in your Student Notebook, and fill in the information.

Make State Cards for Mississippi by following the instructions found in Appendix B. Mississippi is a Southern state, so be sure to outline the cards in purple.

G. Writing
Language Skills, Thinking Skills

Advertising is a very common way that businesses and other organizations try to **persuade**, or convince, people to do a certain thing, like buy a product, or to believe a certain way, like voting for a candidate. When you advertise something, you share with others the good qualities of your product, and maybe the bad qualities of someone else's product.

Together with your teacher, look at advertisements that appear in magazines, newspapers, or on television or radio. Talk with your teacher about the way those advertisements try to convince you to buy a product, visit their location, vote for a candidate, or agree with certain beliefs. Notice the describing words, or **adjectives** that the advertisements use to make their products or beliefs sound good.

Follow the directions below for your level and evaluate the advertisements you looked at or heard. When you are finished, make a poster encouraging others to join the boycott of tea. Remember the wording used in the advertisements you considered. Also, remember the passionate beliefs of the colonists. Think about your poster displayed in an area where colonists have not yet decided what to do about the boycott on tea, and help them come to a decision!

Think of at least one advertisement that you considered. Make a list of two ways that the advertisement tried to influence you. Did you agree with the statements included in the ad? Would you buy the product or support the cause?

Think of at least two advertisements that you considered. Make a list of three ways that each advertisement tried to influence you. Did you agree with the statements included in the ads? Would you buy the products or support the causes?

Follow the instructions above with one more advertisement that you considered.

H. **Independent Reading** *Language Skills*

Choose something to read that you will enjoy. Then, find a quiet, comfortable place and read for the following length of time:

25 minutes 30 minutes

Be sure to write down what you read today on the Reading Log in your Student Notebook.

From Dr. Beechick

"Sometimes the back-to-basics movements ignore this need to build understandings. In their desire to get on with the solid stuff they just teach everything as facts. Principles, generalizations, conclusions, and so forth are simply facts to be learned and tested and scored. Some students may reach higher level thinking anyway. But not all."

– *Heart and Mind*, page 91

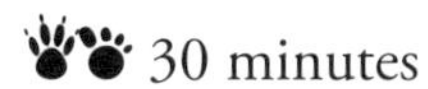

Lesson 4, Part 5

This part is set aside for completion of any work left undone from the lesson, and review of concepts and content. It is also a time to expand the work of the lesson with art, mapping, or games.

- Review the Steps for Thinking from the beginning of this lesson.
- Give your teacher your stack of vocabulary cards for the lesson. As she shows you each word, tell her the meaning of the word and how it was used in the story.
- Listen as your teacher reads the names of states that you studied from Part 1. Write each name in your Student Notebook as she dictates it. When you are finished, look back to your word list and make any corrections needed. Show your teacher how you did.
- Use the United States map that is near the front of your *Atlas of the United States* to find Tennessee and Mississippi. Then, on the large

Teaching Tip

Success is encouraging. Look for gains made and improvement when evaluating your child's work. Record the number of questions or words completed successfully on student work, not the number missed. Your child understands what he missed when he looks at his paper. To encourage in a realistic manner, point to gains made as a reminder of the importance of continued effort.

When a student draws or paints a scene, there are many wonderful thinking skills taking place. The student is observing, recording, and categorizing information and then interpreting that information. All accomplished while doing something fun!

outline map of the U.S., draw lines around them with a purple crayon, marker, or colored pencil. Write in the names of the states, and draw small stars where their capital cities are located. Next to the stars, write the name of each capital city.

- It is always interesting to observe things in nature. With your parent's permission, take your watercolors and some paper outside. You will need to carry a water bottle, and the cup you usually use to practice painting. If there is not a good place to observe nature in your yard, perhaps you and your family could spend some time at a park.

  When you find a place that you like, sit and observe the scenery around you for a short time. Pretend you are an explorer who found this area, and you would like to show others what it looks like. Use your watercolors to paint a picture of the things around you. Remember to relax – there is no wrong way to do this activity as long as you keep the paint on the paper. This is practice, so have fun with it When you are finished, follow the instructions to fill up page 27. Remember to play with your watercolors whenever you have time and your parent agrees.

- Use your USA Activity CD to print at least one activity for the states you studied in this lesson. Then add any that you complete to your Student Notebook.

- Complete the Freedom Decided Crossword Puzzle located in your Student Notebook.[12]

Enrichment Activities

1. Watch Episode 2, Chapter 4 on the *Discovering America's Founders* DVD, about Dr. Benjamin Rush. You may take notes while you watch, or stop the video from time to time to write things down. When you are finished, make a list of at least ten interesting facts about Dr. Rush, and add them to your Student Notebook.

2. In your *Atlas of the United States*, look again at the states you have studied so far in this unit. Scan the sections entitled "The Way It Was..." and choose a person, place, or thing from one of those sections to research. Use the library or, with your parent's permission, the Internet and try to find out more than what is written in the atlas.

   Then pretend you work for a newspaper, and you have just met the person, seen the landmark, or found out about the object. Write a short article about what you have learned. Newspaper reporters always try to answer the questions *who*, *what*, *when*, *where*, and *how* when they write, so that readers have all the important information. Try to answer those questions in your article, and then add it to your Student Notebook.

3. Research Hurricane Andrew, a large hurricane that hit the United States in 1992. Prepare a short report to include in your Unit End Presentation. Include information about the storm and pictures, if possible. Explain the category system by which hurricanes are classified. Tell about how much preparation time people had as the storm approached, the course that it followed, and its impact on all areas that it struck.

Additional Resources

Mr. Revere and I: Being an Account of certain Episodes in the Career of Paul Revere,Esq. as Revealed by his Horse by Robert Lawson

If you read this book, be sure to print a Book Review page from your Student Resources CD, fill it out, and place it in your Student Notebook.

Answers

1. 1, 2, 3, 4

2. They defended the British soldiers to prove to the world that the colonists were fair-minded and obeyed the law.

3. paint, tea, paper, glass, and lead

4. tea

5. Answers will vary.

6. Answers in text and field guide.

7. Answers will vary.

8. 3, 3, 4, 4

9. Answer key is in Appendix A.

10. 1. Lots of evaporation from warm ocean water makes the air humid.
    2. Air in the low pressure system spins inward, causing a pileup in the center.
    3. As air collides in the center it is forced upward.
    4. Water vapor in rising humid air forms storm clouds.
    5. Winds flow outward above the clouds, allowing more humid air to rise from the center
    6. Winds from outside steer the low pressure system, and help it to grow.

11. Answer key is in Appendix A.

12. Answer key is in Appendix A.

Lesson 5, Part 1

Steps for Thinking

1. People are valuable and deserve the freedom to pursue life, liberty and happiness in the ways they think are best.
2. Since people have value, they should have a voice in making laws and rules that affect them.
3. When people's beliefs are in conflict with their government, it is their right to make their disagreements known to the government.

The Steps for Thinking section gives you the main ideas about the topics presented. Understanding these helps you to have productive discussions with your children so they, too, understand the bigger ideas. This forms more permanent learning, contrary to just learning facts, which tends to be temporary. These steps are useful prior to instruction, and they are also useful for review at the end of the week.

Materials

- *The American Revolution (Munford)*
- *Guns for General Washington*
- *George Washington*
- *The Eve of Revolution*
- *Profiles from History, Vol. 2*
- *DK Pockets: Rocks and Minerals*
- *Atlas of the United States*
- *Eat Your Way Through the USA*
- *Wee Sing America* CD and songbook
- *Klutz Watercolor Book*
- Outline Map of the U.S.
- USA Activity CD
- USA PlaceMap
- 2 overhead transparency sheets
- Water based transparency markers
- Ingredients for recipe (Part 3)
- Permanent markers
- Rock Study Kit
- Weather watching tools

Additional resources for Enrichment Activities are found in Part 5.

A. Copywork & Dictation *Language Skills, Thinking Skills*

Look carefully at your assigned passage below, and read it silently. Show your teacher any words you don't know, and practice saying them aloud. Now read the passage aloud, or ask your teacher to read it to you.

When you are finished copying or writing from dictation, compare your copy to the text and make any needed corrections.

- Copy or write as your teacher dictates from *The American Revolution*, page 96, paragraph 2 ("I was now in an…").
- Copy or write as your teacher dictates from *Guns for General Washington*, page 101, paragraph 1 ("As they pushed…").
- Write as your teacher dictates from *Guns for General Washington*, page 100, paragraph 4 ("Leaving Claverack and the…") through page 101, paragraph 1.

B. Reader *Language Skills, History*

The American Revolution: page 92, paragraph 2 ("All that stopping…") through page 96, paragraph 2
Guns for General Washington: Chapter 17

- Read the above assignment from *The American Revolution* aloud, and then follow along as someone else reads the assignment from *Guns for General Washington*.
- Read the above assignment from *The American Revolution* silently, and then read the assignment from *Guns for General Washington* aloud.
- Read the above assignments from *The American Revolution* and *Guns for General Washington* silently.

Teaching Tip

Take the opportunities that occur in daily life to illustrate and help your children understand point of view. For example, watch or listen to a newscast together or read a newspaper or Internet article that presents an opinion about a current event. Ask your children what their point of view is on the subject, and perhaps share yours. Include as many family members as you think appropriate in the discussion. Are your points of view the same as or different from the authors of the articles or newscasts?

D. Read the list of words to your child. If he would rather spell the words aloud than write them, it is perfectly acceptable. As you dictate each word, put small dots beside any misspelled words. Then have your child copy them onto the Student Notebook page.

C. Read-Aloud & Discussion *Language Skills, Thinking Skills, History*

George Washington: page 110 ("The sweet… ") through page 116

Follow the instructions below for your level. When you are finished, discuss what is happening in this section from the British point of view. Then talk about what is happening from the colonists' point of view. How are their viewpoints different? Who do you think is right? Think about what you know from the story, and discuss the passage in your own words. Give any examples you can think of from the story.

Listen carefully as your teacher reads the above assignment from *George Washington* aloud.

Read the above assignment from *George Washington* aloud.

D. Spelling *Language Skills, Thinking Skills*

Look at the list of words below. *Agree* is the base word for each one. A base word is a word that other words connect to by their meaning. If you know the meaning of the base word, then you have a start to figure out the meaning and spelling of every word that uses the base word. Tell how the base word *agree* was changed to make each new word. Then tell your teacher what you think each word means.

agreement disagree agreeable agreed[1]

Listen as your teacher reads each of the following words. Then spell the word as best you can either aloud or by writing it in your Student Notebook. Your teacher may add up to five words that are difficult for you to read or write.

move	remove	moveable	movement
careful	carefree	caretaker	carelessness
direct	misdirect	direction	indirectly
continue	continuous	discontinue	continuation

E. History *Thinking Skills, Music*

Together with your teacher, read the Epilogue at the end of *The Eve of Revolution.*

After the Boston Massacre, many people, though not all, became more and more convinced that America needed to break its ties with Britain. For years, colonists had been taking sides in this heated argument between the two countries. People who wanted America to remain under England's control were loyalists, and those who wanted to break away were patriots. The two groups disagreed on just about every issue, they spied on one another, and sometimes violence broke out. There was no easy solution, so although everyone hoped to avoid war they also knew that it was a strong possibility.

Militias, or army units made up of ordinary citizens, had been formed for protection during the French and Indian Wars, and they had never been disbanded. To prepare for the conflict that might be coming, patriot militias secretly began **stockpiling**, or collecting and storing, guns and ammunition. They organized relay systems and signals to quickly communicate important information throughout the countryside, in case there was a need.

It was one of those stockpiles of weapons and ammunition that finally started the Revolutionary War. The British army found out about the storehouse at Concord, Massachusetts, and immediately marched to destroy it. Thanks to Paul Revere and several other messengers, however, news of their plans traveled ahead of the army.

The small town of Lexington, Massachusetts, was on the road to Concord. When Lexington's militia heard about the approaching attack, about 70 men and boys bravely lined up to face over 700 British troops. No one knows who fired first, but that shot was later called the shot heard around the world. The patriots managed to save their storehouse of weapons, and attacked the British soldiers from behind rocks and trees all the way back to Boston.

With your teacher's permission and supervision, visit http://www.earlyamerica.com/series.html on the Internet. You may wish to return later and watch all the videos on that site, but for now watch the two that are entitled *Paul Revere, Messenger of the Revolution*, and *The Shot Heard Around the World.* When you are finished, talk with your teacher about anything you learned or found interesting in these videos.

E. The Internet can be a useful tool for research, but we suggest that your child use it only with your permission and supervision, and while following your family's rules.

Perhaps you have heard the song "Yankee Doodle". When it was written during the French and Indian Wars, it was intended as an insult to Americans. The word doodle was a British slang word that meant half-wit, or stupid. Americans never really took it as an insult, however, and during the Revolutionary War this little song became a great inspiration to the colonial army. Everyone could make up verses, and they sang them proudly in camp and while they were marching. Look at "Yankee Doodle" in your *Wee Sing America* songbook, and listen to it on the CD. Try to become familiar with the words and music so that you can sing along, or learn to play it on an instrument of your choice. You may want to recite, sing, or play this song during your presentation at the end of this unit.

F. States

Geography, History, Thinking Skills

In your *Atlas of the United States*, read the pages about Alabama. When you are finished, find the blank map of Alabama in your Student Notebook and complete the following assignments:

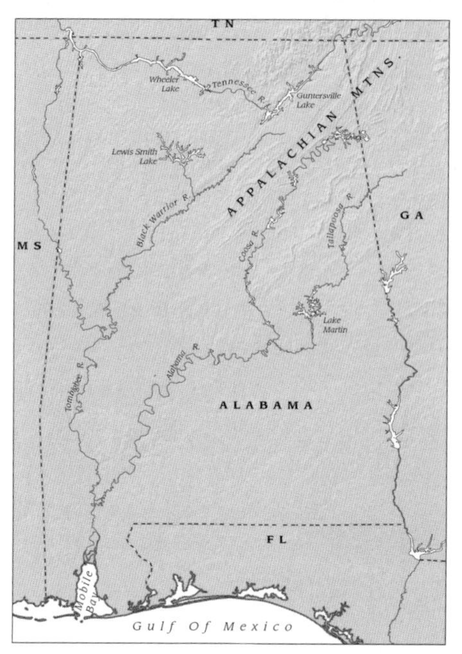

- Place a small star on the spot where Montgomery is located, and label it. Montgomery is the capital city of Alabama.
- Label the Gulf of Mexico.
- Color the lines showing the Tombigbee, Alabama, Coosa, Tallapoosa, Black, Warrior, and Tennessee Rivers blue, and label them.
- Lightly color the area where the Appalachian Mountains are located purple, and label them.
- Color and label Wheeler Lake, Guntersville Lake, Lewis Smith Lake, and Lake Martin.

- Label Mobile Bay.
- Label the four states that border Alabama.

G. Doing

Art

In this unit you began studying the Southern region of the United States, and you experimented with watercolor washes. Look again at the pages about Tennessee in your Atlas of the United States. The picture of mountains in that section will be your watercolor project in the next lesson, and is perfect for practicing washes!

Today you will mainly experiment, so don't try to make a finished painting. This will give you an opportunity to find out exactly what your paints will do in this type of situation. Follow the directions for Unit 2 Watercolor Activity in Appendix B, and then experiment on your own if you want. Have fun!

H. **Independent Reading** *Language Skills*

Choose something to read that you will enjoy. Then, find a quiet, comfortable place and read for the following length of time:

25 minutes   30 minutes

Over time, it's fun to see how much you have read. Be sure to write down what you read today on the Reading Log in your Student Notebook.

Lesson 5, Part 2

A. **Quotation Notebook** *Language Skills, History, Thinking Skills*

In this section you will continue copying statements from the United States Constitution. This document set up rules for our government.

Find a copy of the Constitution at the library or on the Internet. Together with your teacher, read Article 2 of the Constitution. This Article established the **Executive** Branch of the government. The Executive Branch carries out laws made by the Legislative Branch. Choose a quotation from this Article and copy it into your Student Notebook.

Draw or create a symbol that helps you remember this part of the Constitution. Put it beneath the quotation.

B. **Reader** *Language Skills, History*

The American Revolution: page 96, paragraph 3 ("He had been. . .") through page 101, paragraph 2

Guns for General Washington: Chapter 18

Read the above assignment from *The American Revolution* aloud, and then follow along as someone else reads the assignment from *Guns for General Washington.*

Read the above assignment from *The American Revolution* silently, and then read the assignment from *Guns for General Washington* aloud.

Read the above assignments from *The American Revolution* and *Guns for General Washington* silently.

C. **Read-Aloud & Narration** *Language Skills, History, Thinking Skills*

George Washington: page 117 (Chapter 10) to the bottom of page 122

Connect Learning to Life:

The Executive Branch of the national government is still at work today. Talk with your children about the person holding the office of President of the United States. Was this person someone you voted for? Why or why not? For further study, you can help them determine who is the Governor, or head of the Executive Branch of government, in your state. Again, is this person someone you wanted to see elected? Also tell your children about any experiences you have had with supporting a candidate by volunteering or donating to their campaign. Was it a worthwhile sacrifice for you?

Follow the instructions below for your level. Then, in your own words, tell what happened in the story from George's point of view, or pretend you are George and tell what you think happened. Try to remember as many details as possible. You may reread the passage or listen as your teacher rereads the part you are to retell.

Listen carefully as your teacher reads the above assignment from *George Washington* aloud.

Read the above assignment from *George Washington* aloud.

D. There are four parts to this activity Part 1 – read the speech.

Part 2 – use a dictionary to look up any unknown or underlined words. Your student does not need to copy these definitions, since the goal is just to clarify meaning.

Part 3 – have your student put the sentences in his own words, which is the challenging thinking aspect of this activity. Discussion often helps students to order their thoughts before writing.

Part 4 – have your student rewrite the sentences in his own words. These rewritings should show understanding, not just recopying. Every now and then, ask the student to explain what the sentence means to check for understanding.

D. Editing

Language Skills, Thinking Skills, History

Continue reading and discussing parts of the famous speech attributed to Patrick Henry. This speech took place before the delegates of the Virginia colony, who were discussing whether they should join Massachusetts in declaring themselves part of the Revolutionary War. Not only does this speech show the beliefs of a great American patriot, it also shows how to express your thoughts well.

Use a highlighter or yellow crayon to highlight or underline the appropriate sentence(s). Then paraphrase those sentences by rewriting them in your own words underneath the passage.

two sentences three sentences four sentences

E. Science

Thinking Skills

You already learned that there are three classes of rocks: igneous, sedimentary, and metamorphic. These three classes of rocks form, change, and relate to one another in specific ways. Together with your teacher, read and discuss the pages entitled "The Rock Cycle" in your *Rocks and Minerals* book. Then look carefully at the Rock

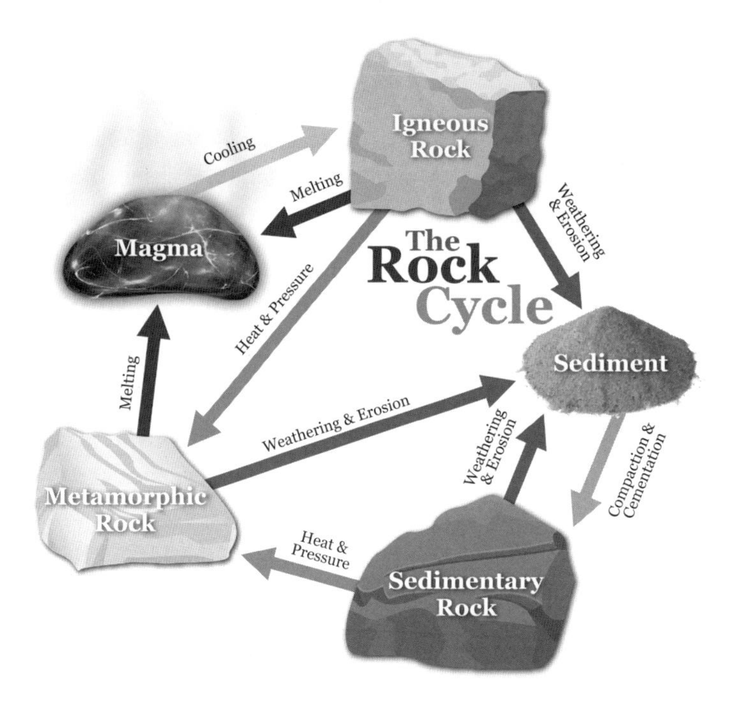

Cycle chart on this page. It is a little simpler, and helps to describe some of the basic relationships between the three types of rocks. These changes can happen over a number of years or very quickly, depending on things like volcanic activity, weather conditions, how much water is present, and so forth. Talk with your teacher about the changes and relationships described by each arrow on the chart. Use it as a model to cut out and paste the items on the similar Rock Cycle chart in your Student Notebook. Add color if you want. Then answer the questions found in your Student Notebook.[2]

Be sure to record your observations on the Weather Watcher pages in your Student Notebook.

E. Have your child use a dictionary to look up any words used on the Rock Cycle Chart that he does not understand.

F. **States** *Geography, Thinking Skills, History, Drawing*

Look again at the pages about Alabama in your *Atlas of the United States.* Then, find the State Page in your Student Notebook, and fill in the information.

Make State Cards for Alabama by following the instructions found in Appendix B. Alabama is a Southern state, so be sure to outline the cards in purple.

G. **Interactive Writing** *Language Skills, Thinking Skills*

Complete this writing activity with your partner.

It is your partner's job to write first; then you will answer a question with the number of sentences assigned below. After that, write several sentences telling what you think about what your partner has written. Make sure to end with a question you want to ask your partner, so he or she can write back to you.

Topic for your partner: Are you proud to be a citizen? Tell your student what you like most about being a citizen of this country.

Your question: Think about the leaders of the American Revolution that you have learned about. Tell which leader you are most proud of and why.

- at least four sentences
- at least five sentences
- at least one paragraph

If you need help remembering what a paragraph is, or how to write one, look back at Lesson 1, Part 2.

G. Writing is not a separate subject, but rather a set of skills with which to become familiar. Writing is best when it is a response to content learned, new ideas, or as a result of an activity or experience.

H. **Independent Reading** *Language Skills*

Choose something to read that you will enjoy. Then, find a quiet, comfortable place and read for the following length of time:

25 minutes   30 minutes

Be sure to write down what you read today on the Reading Log in your Student Notebook.

Lesson 5, Part 3

A. Copywork & Dictation *Language Skills, Thinking Skills*

Look carefully at your assigned passage below, and read it silently. Show your teacher any words you don't know, and practice saying them aloud. Now read the passage aloud, or ask your teacher to read it to you.

When you are finished copying or writing from dictation, compare your copy to the text and make any needed corrections.

- Copy or write as your teacher dictates from *The American Revolution*, page 103, paragraph 3 ("This new army…").
- Copy or write as your teacher dictates from *Guns for General Washington*, page 109, paragraph 3 ("The men came running…").
- Write as your teacher dictates from *Guns for General Washington*, page 109, paragraphs 3 and 4 ("The men came running…").

B. Reader *Language Skills, History*

The American Revolution: page 102, paragraph 1("We arrived. . .") through page 105, paragraph 4
Guns for General Washington: Chapter 19

- Read the above assignment from *The American Revolution* aloud, and then follow along as someone else reads the assignment from *Guns for General Washington*.
- Read the above assignment from *The American Revolution* silently, and then read the assignment from *Guns for General Washington* aloud.
- Read the above assignments from *The American Revolution* and *Guns for General Washington* silently.

C. Read-Aloud & Discussion *Language Skills, Thinking Skills, History*

George Washington: bottom of page 122 ("The game…") through page 128

Follow the directions for your level and read or listen to the above assignment from *George Washington*. Then make up the assigned number of questions about the part of the story you just read or heard. Write your questions and ask your teacher to answer them.

From Dr. Beechick

" Others thinking about this problem have come to see that the most important factor in reading comprehension is what the reader brings to the book or passage. What's in the reader's head? Does he know enough about this subject and its vocabulary to understand what the passage is saying? If he does, then all the so-called skills fall into place. If he doesn't, then they don't."

– *You Can Teach Your Child Successfully*, page 7

Teaching Tip

When you know a subject well enough to teach it to someone else, you know it well. Asking questions for others to answer is an activity that requires students to know the subject well enough to guide others into learning about it. Not only is this a great way to enable students to consider the information as a whole and then choose what to ask about, it also requires them to evaluate the answers given to see if they meet the criteria for correctness. In addition, it emphasizes that we are all both teachers and learners!

After discussing her thoughts, write down the best possible answer in your Student Notebook. Be sure to use complete sentences.

When you are finished, look back at the prediction or predictions you made during Lesson 4, Part 4. Were you able to predict what would happen? Be sure to mark the "Came to Pass" box for each prediction when it does happen.

Listen carefully as your teacher reads the assigned passage.

Make up one question. Make up two questions.

Read the assigned passage aloud; then make up three questions.

D. Vocabulary & Spelling *Language Skills, Thinking Skills*

Vocabulary:
Write each vocabulary word listed below on an index card. Use a dictionary to look up the meaning of each word, and write it on the card. Then on the back of each card, draw a picture or write a clue so you can remember how the word was used in the story.

orchard **duty** **treason** **delegate**
frantically

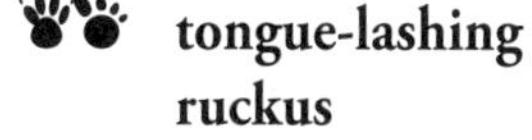

tongue-lashing **rations** **ice floe** **mortar**
ruckus

Spelling:
Look at the list of words below. Tell what the base word is for this group of words and how it changed to make each new word. Then tell your teacher what you think each word means.

worker rework unworkable workbook[3]

Look at the spelling words you wrote in Part 1. If you did not write them in that part, ask your teacher to read each word, and write it in your Student Notebook now. Check your spelling against the list and correct it if necessary. When you are finished, cover each word with your hand, and try to spell it aloud. Then uncover it and see if you were correct. Review the meanings of any words that you do not remember.

E. History *Thinking Skills*

Shortly after the fighting at Lexington and Concord, the siege of Boston that you are reading about in *Guns for General Washington* began. A **siege** is a military action that is meant to prevent people or goods from entering or leaving a place, and this one lasted for over a year. The large guns brought from Fort Ticonderoga helped greatly to encourage the volunteers who made up the Continental Army.

In the meantime, the Second Continental Congress began meeting in Philadelphia. At first the Congress wanted to make peace with King George III of England and avoid a war, but the King refused to even read their letter. After that, their main job was coming into agreement and writing the Declaration of Independence. It was finally approved and sent out to the colonies on July 4, 1776. July 4th is the United State's official birthday.

Declaring independence, however, did not automatically free the colonies. They still had to fight a long and difficult war that lasted more than eight years. At first, the Continental Army lost far more battles than it won. But finally, 15 months after the Declaration of Independence was signed, Americans won their first major victory at the Battle of Saratoga. Almost 6,000 British troops surrendered. When the French heard this news, they entered the war on the side of the American patriots.

A few months after the Battle of Saratoga, General Washington chose Valley Forge, Pennsylvania, for his army's winter quarters. By this time, his men were tired and hungry, their clothes were tattered, and many had no shoes. After reaching the valley, General Washington wrote, "… you might have tracked the army from White Marsh to Valley Forge by the blood on their feet." In spite of these problems, the Baron von Steuben (a volunteer from Germany) kept the men busy every day with a training program that improved the army's skill and discipline. His training prepared them to fight more efficiently when they returned to battle, and

increased their confidence. As a result, by the end of spring the Continental Army was stronger than it had ever been, and Valley Forge came to symbolize the heroism of American troops.

Fighting continued for three more years, and then an important battle was fought at Yorktown, Virginia. American and French soldiers greatly outnumbered British troops, and attacked them day and night for almost a month. Eventually, British General Cornwallis surrendered to General Washington at Yorktown, and that event signaled that the end of the war was near. A year later the two countries signed a peace treaty in Paris, which was eventually approved by both governments. The war was over, and the United States of America was now an independent nation!

The 13 colonies that fought in the Revolutionary War became the first 13 United States. Today you will attach clear overlay pages to your PlaceMap and trace the boundaries of the original 13 colonies on one of the overlays. To do so you will need two overhead transparency sheets, clear tape (wide packing tape is best) and the USA PlaceMap. Put the PlaceMap with the map side up on a table. Lay one transparency lengthwise alongside the left side. The transparency and PlaceMap should line up exactly from top to bottom. Tape the two together along the seam, hinge style. Put an additional long piece of tape along the seam on the back side as well. Using the other transparency sheet, follow the same instructions for the right side of the PlaceMap. Fold both transparency sheets at the hinge and lay over the map. If you have lined up everything just right, they should meet in the middle. You are now ready to make your first overlay map.

Find the outline map in your Student Notebook that shows the original 13 states and the Line of Proclamation. Slip the map under the right transparency and line it up carefully with the top, right, and bottom of the PlaceMap. Trace the boundaries of the 13 colonies on the transparency sheet using a Vis a Vis overhead projector pen or other water-based marker. If you make a mistake you can erase with a damp paper towel or sponge and try again. When you are finished, remove the template. Look at the maps carefully, and compare your new transparency with the United States map pictured on the PlaceMap. Discuss their differences with your teacher. Do you notice anything interesting about the colony of Massachusetts on the new transparency?[4] Do you see any other differences?[5]

Look carefully at the picture of the first American flag below. Notice how many stars and stripes are on the flag. Why do you think there were that many?[6] The colors of the flag are also symbolic. Red stands for hardiness and valor, white means purity and innocence, and blue represents vigilance, perseverance, and justice. Use a dictionary to look up definitions for each of the above words, and write them in your Student Notebook. Then color the flag on that page.

F. States *Geography, History, Thinking Skills*

In your *Atlas of the United States*, read the pages about Arkansas. When you are finished, find the blank map of Arkansas in your Student Notebook and complete the following assignments:

- Place a small star on the spot where Little Rock is located, and label it. Little Rock is the capital city of Arkansas.
- Color the lines showing the Mississippi, Arkansas, Buffalo, White, St. Francis, and Red Rivers blue, and label them.
- Lightly color the areas where the Ozark, Boston, and Ouachita Mountains are located green, and label them.
- Color and label Millwood Lake, Lake Ouachita, Bull Shoals Lake, and Norfolk Lake.
-  Label the six states that border Arkansas.

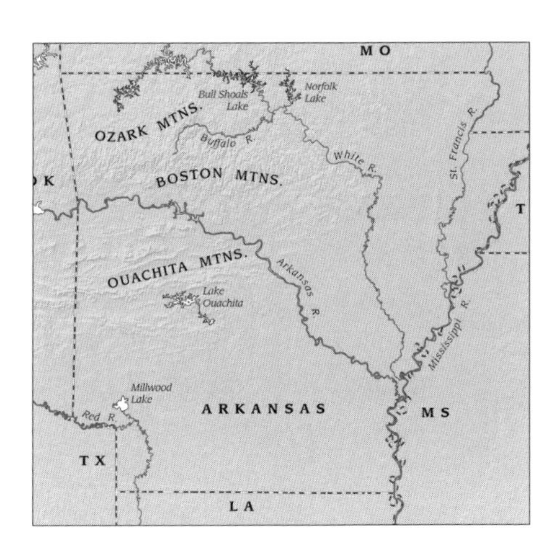

G. Cooking *Language Skills, Thinking Skills, Drawing*

With your parent's permission and supervision, look in *Eat Your Way Through the USA*, choose a recipe that comes from either Alabama or Arkansas, and prepare it for your family. After everyone has had a taste, find out who liked it, and whether anyone would like to have it again. What did you think about it?

In your Student Notebook, draw a picture of the dish you chose to make and write the following number of sentences about your family's reaction to it:

two sentences three sentences four sentences

H. Independent Reading *Language Skills*

Choose something to read that you will enjoy. Then, find a quiet, comfortable place and read for the following length of time:

25 minutes 30 minutes

Be sure to write down what you read today on the Reading Log in your Student Notebook.

H. Independent reading provides regular practice for word study and reading skills, as well as time for practice of thinking skills. Quiet time to consider ideas and tie new information with old is essential in building new understandings.

Lesson 5, Part 4

A. Quotation Notebook *Language Skills, History, Thinking Skills*

In this section you will continue copying statements from the United States Constitution. This document set up rules for our government.

Find a copy of the Constitution at the library or on the Internet. Together with your teacher, read Article 3 of the Constitution. This Article established the **Judicial** Branch of the government. The **Judicial** Branch makes decisions that keep our system of government just, or fair. Choose a quotation from this Article and copy it into your Student Notebook.

Draw or create a **symbol** that helps you remember this part of the Constitution. Put it beneath the quotation.

Connect Learning to Life:

The Judicial Branch of the national government is still at work today. Talk with your children about the people who are judges in the highest court in America, the Supreme Court. How is someone chosen for the Supreme Court? Tell your children about any famous decisions made by the Supreme Court and how you felt about those decisions. For further study, you can help them determine who is on the Supreme Court of your state. There are also many other state, local, and federal judges to investigate. If possible, determine what court has jurisdiction, or rules on cases, in your area.

B. Reader *Language Skills, History*

The American Revolution: page 105, paragraph 5 ("Thomas ran. . .") through page 113, paragraph 1

Guns for General Washington: Chapter 20 (See margin note.)

Read the above assignment from *The American Revolution* aloud, and then follow along as someone else reads the assignment from *Guns for General Washington*.

Read the above assignment from *The American Revolution* silently, and then read the assignment from *Guns for General Washington* aloud.

Read the above assignments from *The American Revolution* and *Guns for General Washington* silently.

"The notebook approach is proactive. It stimulates the student's reasoning and response abilities. Ideally, the notebook requires the student to write in complete sentences, most often stimulates original and independent thought processes, and provides a means for the expression of true learning. The notebook provides an opportunity for the student to record through essays, drawing, diagrams, and any other way that expresses the individuality of the student what the student reasoned for himself from the material he learned."

--*The Ultimate Geography and Timeline Guide*, page 14

C. **Read-Aloud & Narration** *Language Skills, Thinking Skills, History*

George Washington: page 129 (And snow…) through page 134

After reading or listening to the read-aloud assignment in *George Washington*, talk with your teacher and try to predict what will happen in the future based on what you know of the characters and events. Write down your predictions in your Student Notebook. Later you will look back and see if they were accurate. Try not to peek ahead!

Listen carefully as your teacher reads the assigned passage. Then write down something that you think will happen in the story.

Write down another thing that you think will happen in the story.

Read the assigned passage aloud. Then write down at least three things that you think will happen in the story.

D. **Editing** *Language Skills, Thinking Skills, History*

Continue reading and discussing parts of the famous speech attributed to Patrick Henry. Read the section of the speech included in your Student Notebook. One word in the passage is underlined and in italics. Try to figure out the meaning of that word using the context, or words around it. Then use a dictionary to look up definitions of the words underlined in the paragraph, and any other words you do not understand. Did you get the right meaning of the word in italics by using the context?

Use a highlighter or yellow crayon to highlight or underline the appropriate sentence(s). Then paraphrase those sentences by rewriting them in your own words underneath the passage.

two sentences three sentences four sentences

E. Because of variations in Rock Study Kits, it is possible that yours may contain one or two specimens that are minerals, and cannot technically be classified as igneous, sedimentary, or metamorphic. If so, these will be useful in Unit 5 when minerals and crystals are investigated.

E. **Science** *Thinking Skills, Art*

In this part, you will continue to learn about igneous rocks. Together with your teacher, use the Contents list in the front, or the index in the back of your *Rocks and Minerals* book to find the section entitled "Igneous Rocks," and read it. Then read and discuss the introduction to the section entitled "Identifying Rocks," and the small portion that is specifically about igneous rocks. This section is part of the chapter that tells about rocks located toward the front of the book.

In your Student Notebook, write one or two sentences that explain the ways intrusive and extrusive igneous rocks are formed.[7] Then write at least one sentence telling the difference between lava and magma.[8]

In your Rock Study Kit, you may have some of the rocks mentioned in the above sections. Choose one of your igneous **specimens**, or samples, and examine it with a magnifying glass. Then check the index in the back of the *Rocks and Minerals* book to see if it mentions the rock you chose. If it does, read about it. If it does not, use the library or Internet to find out more about the specimen you are investigating. When you are finished, write three facts about the rock in your Student Notebook. Then trace or draw and color a picture of it in the space provided.

Follow the directions above for two other igneous specimens from your Rock Study Kit.

Be sure to record your observations for the next few days on the Weather Watcher pages in your Student Notebook.

Find out about another igneous sample in your Rock Study Kit by looking in the *Rocks and Minerals* book, at the library, or on the Internet. Write three facts about this rock in your Student Notebook. Then use the sample or a picture as a model to draw and color it.

F. States *Geography, History, Thinking Skills, Drawing*

Look again at the pages about Arkansas in your *Atlas of the United States*. Then find the State Page in your Student Notebook, and fill in the information.

Make State Cards for Arkansas by following the instructions found in Appendix B. Arkansas is a Southern state, so be sure to outline the cards in purple.

F. It is important for students to be acquainted with various reference tools, such as an atlas. Since your goal is for students to be lifelong learners, use of reference tools can greatly enhance learning on any topic. Using these tools successfully requires familiarity and the opportunities to use the tools as part of learning that is connected to history, literature, science, and ultimately, life.

G. Writing *Language Skills, Thinking Skills*

Poems often are made of stanzas, or verses. A **stanza** is a group of lines of verse that have a rhyming pattern. There can be different numbers of lines in each stanza. Today you will look at a poem that has six lines in each stanza. There is an order to the lines, based on the last word in the line.

Here is an example:

These units tell of gallant men,
Of courageous women too.
They speak of those named George and Ben,
And many brave and true.
The Sons and Daughters of Liberty
Stood up in the face of tyranny.

Now mark the rhyme pattern of this poem in your Student Notebook. Assign a letter to each line, starting with *a* assigned to the first line. Every line that ends with a word that rhymes with *men* (the last word in the first line) will also be assigned the letter *a* (so lines 1 and 3 are both assigned the letter *a*).

Line 2 ends with the word *too*, so give it the letter *b*. Every line that ends with a word that rhymes with *too* is also given the letter *b*. The words do not have to be spelled the same way, they just have to rhyme. So the fourth line will also be given the letter *b* because *true* rhymes with *too*.

The fifth line has a new ending sound so give this line a new letter, the letter *c*. (Assign new letters in the order of the alphabet.) The last line ends with a word that rhymes with *liberty*, so it will also get the letter *c*. Here is the poem again with the rhyming pattern marked:

These units tell of gallant men,	a
Of courageous women, too.	b
It tells of those named George and Ben,	a
And many both brave and true.	b
The Sons and Daughters of Liberty,	c
Stood up in the face of tyranny.	c

The pattern of this poem is then *ababcc*.

Read the poem "Washington" by Nancy Byrd Turner. With your parent's permission, you can find it online by typing the name of the poem and the author into a search engine. Once you find the poem, print it out or make a hand-written copy. Read the poem silently several times, and then read it aloud. Tell your teacher about the picture you think this poem paints of George Washington. What does this poem describe George Washington doing?[9]

In the last two sentences, the poem draws a conclusion about George Washington. What is it?[10]

Write down the rhyme pattern of the first stanza of this poem in your Student Notebook by assigning letters to the lines.[11]

Write down the rhyme pattern for the second stanza as well. Remember to keep going in the alphabet with a new letter for each new rhyming word.[12]

Write down the rhyme pattern for the third stanza. Be careful because the rhyme pattern is not the same as the previous two verses.[13]

Now try your hand at writing a poem that follows this rhyming pattern. You can write the poem about anything you want, or you can try to use ideas, places, or names from your readers, read-aloud books, history, science, or geography.

Write a poem that has one stanza with six lines that follow the *ababcc* pattern.

Write a poem with two stanzas, each with six lines that follow the *ababcc* and *dedeff* patterns.

Write a poem with three stanzas, each with six lines that follow the *ababcc*, *dedeff*, and *ghghii* patterns.

H. **Independent Reading** *Language Skills*

Choose something to read that you will enjoy. Then, find a quiet, comfortable place and read for the following length of time:

25 minutes 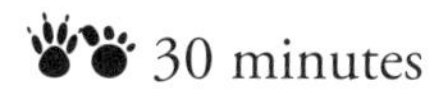 30 minutes

Be sure to write down what you read today on the Reading Log in your Student Notebook.

Lesson 5, Part 5

This part is set aside for completion of any work left undone from the lesson, and review of concepts and content. It is also a time to expand the work of the lesson with art, mapping, or games.

- Review the Steps for Thinking from the beginning of this lesson.
- Give your teacher your stack of vocabulary cards for the lesson. As she shows you each word, tell her the meaning of the word and how it was used in the story.
- Look at the list of spelling words from Part 1. Tell your teacher the base word for each one, and how it was changed. Cover each word with your hand, and try to spell it aloud. Then uncover it and see if you were correct. Review the meanings of any words that you do not remember.

  Listen as your teacher dictates the words, and write each one in your Student Notebook. When you are finished, look back to your word list and make corrections as needed. Show your teacher how you did.

As you discuss the Steps for Thinking with your child, feel free to share the examples that have come to your mind during the lesson. Share the steps you went through in your thinking as well as your outcomes. Modeling is a very effective type of instruction, and your child will gain insight into connecting concepts and examples by hearing your thinking.

- Use the United States map that is near the front of your *Atlas of the United States* to find Alabama and Arkansas. Then, on the large outline map of the U.S., draw lines around them with a purple crayon, marker, or colored pencil. Write in the names of the states, and draw small stars where their capital cities are located. Next to the stars, write the name of each capital city.

Are games truly a valid part of school time? Absolutely! As your child revisits content, vocabulary, and concepts, an effective review of learning takes place. The game format makes review more inviting and hopefully, more frequent.

- Read, or listen as your teacher reads, the story about Molly Pitcher in *Profiles from History., Volume 2.* Talk about the discussion question with your teacher, and then complete any other activities that she assigns.
- Use your USA Activity CD to print at least one activity for the states you studied in this lesson. Then add any that you complete to your Student Notebook.
- Follow the directions in Appendix B, and play Freedom Decided Bingo.

Use one or more of the Enrichment Activities if your child completes assigned work and has the time or desire to learn more. These activities are flexible, so choose the one(s) that seem most interesting to your student. Allow work to be at an appropriate level, and remember that the learning process is more important than the product.

Enrichment Activities

1. Research King George, III, of England. Try to find out what he thought about American independence, and why he thought as he did. How did he respond to the First Continental Congress's efforts for a peaceful solution to the problems between Britain and America? Do you think his attitudes helped bring about the Revolutionary War? What do you think he could have done differently that might have helped to avoid war?

Stories help us remember the lives of real people. They help us remember the beliefs and actions that took place. It is not as important to remember details such as dates of events, as it is to place a character in a time period. With the general time period comes context for what the character did or experienced. This, in turn, reinforces the connection to the unique qualities or events of the character's life. History, literature and thinking skills form a great partnership.

2. At the library or on the Internet research a Native American tribe from the Southern region of what is now the United States. If you do not have a tribe in mind that you would like to find out more about, choose one from the map entitled "Native American Nations, c. 1750" in your *United States History Atlas.* Print a Native American Profile sheet from your Student Resources CD and fill it out.

   Place the new profile sheet and picture in your Native American Notebook, or add them to your Student Notebook.

Additional Resources

http://www.earlyamerica.com/series.html

The American Revolution by Bruce Bliven, Jr.
If you read this book, be sure to print a Book Review page from your Student Resources CD, fill it out, and place it in your Student Notebook.

Answers

1. Suffix (letters added to the end of a word that change its meaning)
   -ment was added, means two or more people sharing the same opinion;
   prefix *dis-* was added, means to not agree;
   suffix *-able* was added, means something is pleasing;
   last e was removed, suffix *-ed* was added, means that the agreeing has already taken place.

2. 1, 2, 3 (any order) magma – melting;
   metamorphic rock – heat and pressure;
   sediment – weathering and erosion

   4, 5 (either order) sediment – weathering and erosion;
   metamorphic rock – heat and pressure

   6, 7 (either order) sediment – weathering and erosion;
   magma – melting

   8. igneous rock – cooling
   9. sedimentary rock – compaction and cementation

3. Base word is work; suffix -er was added, means someone who works; prefix re- was added, means to work on something again; prefix un-and suffix -able was added, means something is not able to work; word book was added to make a compound word, means a book where work is done or answers are recorded.

4. It includes the area that is now the state of Maine.

5. Answers will vary, but might include mention that the colonies of Georgia, North Carolina, Virginia, and Pennsylvania, were smaller than they are now; New York includes the area that is now Vermont, and does not stretch as far north and west as it does now.

6. 13 stars and 13 stripes, one to symbolize each of the original states

7. Extrusive igneous rocks form when lava cools and hardens on top of the earth's surface. Intrusive igneous rocks are formed when magma cools and hardens underground.

8. Magma is melted rock that is still underground, but it is called lava when it erupts from a volcano.

9. He answers the call to serve his country as a soldier.

10. No matter what the circumstances, George Washington always loved America.

11. ababcc

12. dedeff, the same pattern as the first stanza.

13. ghhgii

Lesson 6, Part 1

A. **Copywork & Dictation** *Language Skills, Thinking Skills*

Look carefully at your assigned passage below, and read it silently. Show your teacher any words you don't know, and practice saying them aloud. Now read the passage aloud, or ask your teacher to read it to you.

When you are finished copying or writing from dictation, compare your copy to the text and make any needed corrections.

- Copy or write as your teacher dictates from *The American Revolution*, page 118, paragraph 3 ("They finally decided...").
- Copy or write as your teacher dictates from *Guns for General Washington*, page 119, paragraph 2, ("As a climax to the festivities...").
- Write as your teacher dictates from *Guns for General Washington*, page 119, paragraphs 2 and 3 ("As a climax to the festivities...").

B. **Reader** *Language Skills, History*

The American Revolution: page 113, paragraph 2 ("Thomas Jefferson. . .") through page 119, paragraph 1
Guns for General Washington: Chapter 21

- Read the above assignment from *The American Revolution* aloud, and then follow along as someone else reads the assignment from *Guns for General Washington*.
- Read the above assignment from *The American Revolution* silently, and then read the assignment from *Guns for General Washington* aloud.
- Read the above assignments from *The American Revolution* and *Guns for General Washington* silently.

C. **Read-Aloud & Discussion** *Language Skills, Thinking Skills, History*

George Washington: page 135 ("Autumn leaves...") through page 140

Follow the instructions below for your level. When you are finished, discuss what is happening in this section from the British point of view. Then talk about what is happening from the colonists' point of view. How are their viewpoints different? Who do you think is right? Think about what you know from the story, and discuss the passage in your own words. Give any examples you can think of from the story.

- Listen carefully as your teacher reads the above assignment from *George Washington* aloud.
- Read the above assignment from *George Washington* aloud.

Materials

- *The American Revolution (Munford)*
- *Guns for General Washington*
- *George Washington*
- *Profiles from History, Vol. 2*
- *Atlas of the United States*
- *Eat Your Way Through the USA*
- *Wee Sing America* CD and songbook
- *Klutz Watercolor Book*
- Outline Map of the U.S.
- USA Activity CD
- *Discovering America's Founders* DVD
- Ingredients for recipe (Part 3)

Additional resources for Enrichment Activities are found in Part 5.

A. To help your children make the transition from copying to dictation, begin gradually. Once copying is finished, ask your children to choose a sentence and write it after you read it to them. Allow them to write this sentence on a non-permanent surface, like a chalkboard, dry erase board or scrap of paper. The point you are trying to make by doing this is that it is truly practice, not something you will keep and score. They can take what they write and check it using their copywork passage. You can build confidence for gaining a new skill this way. Over time, they will see that they are getting better at it, and many will then be willing to make the switch to dictation.

Teaching Tip

Children have different feelings about a competitive setting such as a spelling bee. Some children welcome the opportunity to compete, even against themselves, and are very confident. Other children are greatly distressed if they make a mistake in a public setting like this, and will avoid it. Work within your child's comfort zone to make this type of activity a positive experience. Continue the bee until a certain number of words have been missed, not just one. With each practice, you can decrease the acceptable number missed by one to make it a realistic challenge. Remember, progress is taking your child from where he is right now and moving forward, not making it all the way in one single leap.

E. As your child learns to take notes, it may be helpful to stop the video at intervals and discuss what has happened or been said. Ask questions that will help him understand the important parts of what he has seen or heard.

D. Spelling

Language Skills, Thinking Skills

Review the spelling words from Unit 1 to prepare for a personal Spelling Bee. To begin, cut out the Word Slips in your Student Notebook. Then turn each slip over, spell the word to yourself, and check the slip to see if you were correct. Set aside any words that you spelled incorrectly and review them again at the end of your practice session.

When you finish, put your Unit 1 Word Slips in a safe place so they can be used again at the end of this lesson.

E. History

Thinking Skills, Music

Haym Salomon was a Jewish immigrant who arrived in America in 1772, only four years before the Revolutionary War began. He longed for the **liberty**, or freedom, to live and worship according to his conscience. In his homeland of Poland he had seen and experienced **persecution**, or unfair treatment, because of religion. In that way he was much like the Pilgrims, even though his religion was different from theirs. Because he believed freedom was important, Haym gave a lot of his own money to help finance, or pay for, the revolution. He also raised much more from other people, acted as a spy for the colonists, and convinced France to send troops to help with the war.

Together with your teacher, watch Episode 3, Chapters 6 and 7 on the *Discovering America's Founders* DVD that is about Haym Salomon. Before you begin though, take a minute to look at the Video Profile page for this lesson in your Student Notebook, and see what kinds of questions it asks.[1] Then follow the directions below to answer them.

After you have watched the video and answered the questions, create five true statements about Haym Saloman, but make each one a "fill in the blank" question by leaving out an important word. Give your statements to someone else who has watched the video, and ask that person to fill in the correct word. Be sure to make an answer key for your statements.

As you watch the video lesson, keep the Video Profile page in front of you. When you notice that the narrator, or person telling the story, is answering one of the questions, stop the video long enough to write the answer on your Profile page. Continue doing this as often as necessary as you finish watching the video lesson.

As you watch the video lesson, use a piece of scrap paper to jot down important things that the narrator, or person telling the story, says about Haym. This is called taking notes, and is a good way to help you remember what you hear or see. You do not need to use sentences when you take notes—single words or phrases, which are short groups of words, will work fine as long as they help you remember the important things. If it is helpful, stop the lesson when you need to, or watch it a second time.

When you are finished, use your notes and your memory to fill in the Video Profile page.

F. **States** *Geography, Thinking Skills*

Look at the State Cards you have made throughout this unit. Pull out the ones that have only the names of the states on them, and place the others to the side. Then, as you look at the name of each state, see if you can remember the name of its capital city, its nickname, and one interesting fact about it. It is fine to look at the other cards you made for that state if you need help remembering.

Go through the cards several times until you feel comfortable with the information about each state. When you are able to remember the facts about a state, place its name card to the side and continue with the others.

You can make this a game with other members of your family by choosing a name card from the stack and asking another person to tell you the important information about that state. Give one point for each correct answer to the player who is answering. That way, it is possible to get three points for each state. Continue until all the name cards are eliminated.

G. **Doing** *Art, Music*

Look at the song entitled "America, America" in your *Wee Sing America* songbook, and read the historical notes that are above it in the book. Now listen to it on the *Wee Sing America* CD. Try to become familiar with the words and music so that you can sing along, or learn to play it on an instrument of your choice. You may want to recite, sing, or play this song during your presentation at the end of this unit.

Your final watercolor activity for this unit is to look at the mountain picture on the pages about Tennessee in your *Atlas of the United States*, and use it as a model for your own painting. Instead of using a picture, you can paint a scene outdoors if you would prefer and your parent agrees.

However you choose to complete this activity is fine, as long as you have permission. It is not important to make your painting look exactly like the picture. The main points are to practice the things you have learned, and to experiment with new ideas. Above all, remember to relax and enjoy your art!

H. Remind your children that their reading logs for this unit will conclude during Part 4 of this lesson. They may want to check over their log for completeness of titles, authors, and pages read. Since this is an important record of work accomplished, remind them that neatness counts!

H. **Independent Reading** *Language Skills*

Choose something to read that you will enjoy. Then, find a quiet, comfortable place and read for the following length of time:

25 minutes 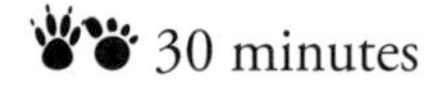 30 minutes

Over time, it's fun to see how much you have read. Be sure to write down what you read today on the Reading Log in your Student Notebook.

Lesson 6, Part 2

A. **Quotation Notebook** *Language Skills, History, Thinking Skills*

The next famous American document quoted is the Bill of Rights, which consists of the first ten **amendments**, or additions, to the Constitution. This document set up protections for the citizens of the United States. Any definitions included beneath the passage are to help you understand the meaning. Do not copy them as part of the quotation.

Copy the following quotation into your Student Notebook, and then talk with your teacher about its meaning. You may want to include parts of the Bill of Rights in your presentation at the end of this unit, so practice reading this section aloud.

> Amendment 1
>
> Congress shall make no law respecting an establishment of religion, or prohibiting the free exercise thereof; or abridging the freedom of speech, or of the press;

Definitions (as used in this document):
establishment - to set up something meant to be permanent
exercise - to carry out a choice or right
abridge - to take something away from someone
press - those who gather and report on the news, particularly journalists who work on newspapers

Draw or create a symbol that helps you remember this part of the Constitution. Put it beneath the quotation.

B. **Reader** *Language Skills, History*

The American Revolution: page 119, paragraph 2 ("I knew. . .") through page 123, paragraph 1
Guns for General Washington: Chapter 22

Read the above assignment from *The American Revolution* aloud, and then follow along as someone else reads the assignment from *Guns for General Washington*.

Read the above assignment from *The American Revolution* silently, and then read the assignment from *Guns for General Washington* aloud.

Read the above assignments from *The American Revolution* and *Guns for General Washington* silently.

C. Read-Aloud & Narration

Language Skills, History, Thinking Skills

George Washington: page 141 ("The sight. . .") through page 149

Follow the instructions below for your level. Then, in your own words, tell what happened in the story from George's point of view, or pretend you are George and tell what you think happened. Try to remember as many details as possible. You may reread the passage or listen as your teacher rereads the part you are to retell.

Listen carefully as your teacher reads the above assignment from *George Washington* aloud.

Read the above assignment from *George Washington* aloud.

C. Talk with your children about any improvement they have made during this unit in their ability to narrate what they have read. Just like spaced review, occasional review of performance can give needed encouragement. Point out any specifics that have improved, like the ability to retell more details or the overall picture of the story. Help them see evaluation as a natural part of making progress.

D. Editing

Language Skills, Thinking Skills, History

Continue reading and discussing parts of the famous speech attributed to Patrick Henry. This speech took place before the delegates of the Virginia colony, who were discussing whether they should join Massachusetts in declaring themselves part of the Revolutionary War. Not only does this speech show the beliefs of a great American patriot, it also shows how to express your thoughts well.

Use a highlighter or yellow crayon to highlight or underline the appropriate sentence(s). Then paraphrase those sentences by rewriting them in your own words underneath the passage.

two sentences three sentences four sentences

E. Science

Thinking Skills

Take a few minutes before you begin this section to look back at the list you made in Lesson 3, Part 2, and see if your questions about seasons, the Earth's orbit, severe storms, and how rocks form have been answered yet. Use a highlighter to mark the ones that have not. Then over the next few days, research the questions that you highlighted at the library or on the Internet, and try to find the answers. Discuss what you find out with your teacher.

You have been watching the weather at your home in this unit. Now it is time to do something with the information you collected. With your teacher's help, transfer the weather observations you have recorded throughout this unit onto the Weather Chart in your Student Notebook.

When you are finished, look over your chart with your teacher and see how accurate your predictions were. Do you notice any connections between the various weather conditions? For example, do you think wind speed or direction ever affected changes in the weather between morning and evening? What about the air pressure moving higher or lower, or the types of clouds you could see? Do you notice anything else? Talk with your teacher about how your weather watching and predicting abilities have or have not improved.

F. **States** *Geography, Thinking Skills*

Find the Regional Summary Pages in your Student Notebook. Then, use your *Atlas of the United States* to fill in the information for Maryland, Virginia, North Carolina, South Carolina, and Georgia.

When you are finished, look at the State Scramble game in your Student Notebook. Unscramble the name of each state you have studied in this unit, and write it correctly on the line provided. Then write its abbreviation on the short line. Finally, list each state under the name of the region where it is located.[2] If you need help remembering, it is fine to use your State Cards to complete this activity.

G. Encourage your children to use their Student Notebooks to consider all that they have done in this unit and come up with the things they would like to share in their Unit Presentation. If your children have difficulty deciding, encourage them to share the things that were the most fun, the most interesting, and new information they learned. If there was an area of particular skill for them, be sure to include that as well. Book review cards, Steps for Thinking and their State Cards also give a good overview of the unit's focus. They may want to make their Student Notebooks available for others to view, so now is the time to check them for neatness.

G. **Writing** *Language Skills, Thinking Skills*

In Part 5 of this lesson you will be asked to make a Unit Presentation to your family, and tell about what you have learned in the Freedom Decided Unit. In this presentation, you will have an opportunity to share the work you have done in your Student Notebook, your book review, the crafts or special projects you have completed, and anything else you care to include.

Think about the things you would like to include in your Unit Presentation, and list them on a piece of scrap paper. Then number the items in the order that you would like to share them. Now copy your list in the correct order into your Student Notebook. You can use this list while you are giving your Unit Presentation, so that you won't forget anything you wanted to share.

H. **Independent Reading** *Language Skills*

Choose something to read that you will enjoy. Then, find a quiet, comfortable place and read for the following length of time:

25 minutes 30 minutes

Be sure to write down what you read today on the Reading Log in your Student Notebook.

Lesson 6, Part 3

A. Copywork & Dictation

Language Skills, Thinking Skills

Look carefully at your assigned passage below, and read it silently. Show your teacher any words you don't know, and practice saying them aloud. Now read the passage aloud, or ask your teacher to read it to you.

When you are finished copying or writing from dictation, compare your copy to the text and make any needed corrections.

- Copy or write as your teacher dictates from *The American Revolution*, page 127, paragraph 1 ("I arrived at…").
- Copy or write as your teacher dictates from *Guns for General Washington*, page 130, paragraph 2 ("Washington, anxious about…").
- Write as your teacher dictates from *Guns for General Washington*, page 130, paragraphs 2 and 3 ("Washington, anxious about…").

B. Reader

Language Skills, History

The American Revolution: page 124, paragraph 1 ("What were. . .") through page 127, paragraph 4
Guns for General Washington: Chapter 23

- Read the above assignment from *The American Revolution* aloud, and then follow along as someone else reads the assignment from *Guns for General Washington*.
- Read the above assignment from *The American Revolution* silently, and then read the assignment from *Guns for General Washington* aloud.
- Read the above assignments from *The American Revolution* and *Guns for General Washington* silently.

From Dr. Beechick

"In any one project children will not use all thinking skills but maybe only one or two, or more. Reading books can be active learning too, and can exercise the thinking skills. It all depends on what happens in the brain. If interest is high, if children are finding out answers to their questions, their brains are just as active while reading as while working on a fish pond."

– *You Can Teach Your Child Successfully*, page 330

C. Read-Aloud & Discussion

Language Skills, Thinking Skills, History

George Washington: page 150 ("Bells chimed…") through page 156

Follow the directions below and read or listen to the above assignment from *George Washington*. Then make up the assigned number of questions about the part of the story you just read or heard. Write your questions and ask your teacher to answer them. After discussing her thoughts, write down the best possible answer in your Student Notebook. Be sure to use complete sentences.

When you are finished, look back at the prediction or predictions you made during Lesson 5, Part 4. Were you able to predict what would happen? Be sure to mark the "Came to Pass" box for each prediction when it does happen.

Listen carefully as your teacher reads the assigned passage.

Make up one question. Make up two questions.

Read the assigned passage aloud; then make up three questions.

Connect Learning to Life:

Together with your children, look through the stack of vocabulary cards they made during this unit. Ask them to find their favorite words, words they have started using in conversation, and words that were the most challenging to learn. Remind them that they can use this approach to learn new words any time, and with any book or topic. As they look through the cards, they are doing a natural review and categorizing the words according to the way that they worked with them. Take these natural opportunities to show your children that they have used great thinking skills that are useful in many areas of life.

D. Vocabulary & Spelling

Language Skills, Thinking Skills

Vocabulary:

Write each vocabulary word listed below on an index card. Use a dictionary to look up the meaning of each word, and write it on the card. Then on the back of each card, draw a picture or write a clue so you can remember how the word was used in the story.

default **convened** **portable** **anonymously** **petition**

parapet **brig** **skiff** **elated** **quadrille**

Spelling:

Review the spelling words from this unit to prepare for a personal Spelling Bee. To begin, cut out the Word Slips in your Student Notebook. Then turn each slip over, spell the word to yourself, and check the slip to see if you were correct. Set aside any words that you spelled incorrectly and review them again at the end of your practice session.

When you finish, put your Unit 2 Word Slips in a safe place so they can be used again at the end of this lesson.

E. History

Thinking Skills

In this unit you have had an opportunity to learn about people and events related to the Revolutionary War. Find the history review in your Student Notebook and follow the directions below.[3]

Use the Word Bank on that page to answer the Who or What Am I questions.

Use the information you have learned in this unit to answer the Who or What Am I questions.

Teaching Tip

Throughout this curriculum you will find games. Their purpose is to practice skills and review content in a fun and effective manner. Once your children become familiar with the games, they can become part of game days, family game nights, and any other time that this format fits into life. Since your children are most familiar with them, they can be leaders by helping others learn the games, rules, and the ideas behind them!

F. States

Geography, History, Thinking Skills

Mix up your State Cards and lay them face down on the table or floor. Then Play State Card Concentration by turning up one card, and trying to find the other two cards that go with it. When you turn over three cards that don't match, return them to their face down position and try again. When you find three cards that do match, remove them from the game. Continue until you have removed all the cards that go together.

G. **Cooking** *Language Skills, Thinking Skills*

Talk with your teacher about your cooking experiences in this unit. Was it difficult to follow the recipes? Did you learn anything new? If so, what? Which recipe did you enjoy making the most? Which recipe did your family enjoy the most? After you discuss these questions with your teacher, in your Student Notebook write a complete sentence that summarizes your thoughts about each one.

Then, with your parent's permission and supervision choose a recipe that you enjoyed making in this unit, and prepare it again for your family. If you would prefer, you can select a different recipe from *Eat Your Way Through the USA* that comes from one of the states you have studied so far, and prepare it instead.

H. **Independent Reading** *Language Skills*

Choose something to read that you will enjoy. Then, find a quiet, comfortable place and read for the following length of time:

25 minutes 30 minutes

Be sure to write down what you read today on the Reading Log in your Student Notebook.

Lesson 6, Part 4

A. **Quotation Notebook** *Language Skills, History, Thinking Skills*

Copy the following quotation from the Bill of Rights into your Student Notebook, and then talk with your teacher about its meaning. This document set up protections for the citizens of the United States. You may want to include parts of the Bill of Rights in your presentation at the end of this unit, so practice reading this section aloud.

> or the right of the people to peaceably assemble, and to petition the Government for a redress of grievances.

Definitions (as used in this document):
assemble - to bring people together in one place
petition - to make an appeal to a higher authority
redress - to change a situation to make things fair
grievance - a formal complaint about something that is unfair

Draw or create a symbol that helps you remember this part of the Constitution. Put it beneath the quotation.

B. Reader
Language Skills, History

The American Revolution: page 128, paragraph 1 ("The weather. . .") through page 135
Guns for General Washington: Chapters 24 and 25

Read the above assignment from *The American Revolution* aloud, and then follow along as someone else reads the assignment from *Guns for General Washington*.

Read the above assignment from *The American Revolution* silently, and then read the assignment from *Guns for General Washington* aloud.

Read the above assignments from *The American Revolution* and *Guns for General Washington* silently.

Teaching Tip

Speaking comfortably and confidently in front of others is a skill your children can gain. As with other skills discussed in this curriculum, progress is your goal. If possible, a very effective tool to use for self-evaluation is to videotape them while practicing.As they view the recording, ask them to decide what they liked about the way they spoke. Do they notice anything they did that might distract their audience? Help them to view their performance with an eye to find both strengths and areas needing adjustment.

C. Read-Aloud & Speech
Language Skills, Thinking Skills, History

George Washington: page 157 ("Washington worked. . .") through page 164

Follow the instructions below for your level, and then tell what you think others thought about George Washington. Since he just passed away in your story, give a speech about him to others. Remember to tell about the things he did to help America, the kind of man he was, and what you think most people will remember about him. You can practice your speech and write it down on index cards to help remember what you want to say. A good length for your speech is about two to three minutes. Use visual aids (such as pictures) to help others visualize the man about whom you are talking.

Listen carefully as your teacher reads the above assignment from *George Washington*.

Read the above assignment from *George Washington* aloud.

D. Editing
Language Skills, Thinking Skills

Read, or listen as your teacher reads, the story about Patrick Henry in *Profiles from History, Volume 2*. Talk about the discussion question with your teacher, and then complete any other activities that she assigns.

Today you will present the last paragraph of the speech attributed to Patrick Henry to your family or class. Introduce the paragraph by telling your audience the purpose for this speech, the audience, and the date spoken.

> "It is in vain, sir, to extenuate the matter. Gentlemen may cry, "Peace! Peace!" — but there is no peace. The war is actually begun! The next gale that sweeps from the north will bring to our ears the clash of resounding arms! Our brethren are already

> in the field! Why stand we here idle? What is it that gentlemen wish? What would they have? Is life so dear, or peace so sweet, as to be purchased at the price of chains and slavery? Forbid it, Almighty God! I know not what course others may take; but as for me, give me liberty, or give me death!"

You may read this part of the speech, or recite it from memory. Since you are presenting words that held much emotion for Mr. Henry, pretend to be him as you read or recite his speech. Act as though you want to win over your audience. After you are finished reading or reciting, ask your audience if they think he persuaded, or convinced, the delegates to vote for his resolutions.[4]

Before you speak or recite, give a summary of the rest of the speech. Take approximately one minute to tell about the arguments Patrick Henry used in this speech to encourage Virginia to join the American Revolution alongside the colony of Massachusetts.

Choose and present a second paragraph from the speech before presenting the last paragraph. Make sure the paragraph you choose represents Patrick Henry's thoughts and feelings about this situation well.

E. Science *Thinking Skills*

Complete the Earth Science Matching game in your Student Notebook.[5] When you are finished, tell your teacher what you remember about the things named in the activity. If you want help remembering, you can look back at the pages in the unit where you learned about each thing.

E. Sometimes it is helpful to take notes while your child shares his recollections of information learned. It makes what your child is saying seem important, it gives a practical example of how to use note taking, and provides a visible list for your child of all that he has accomplished.

F. States *Geography, History, Thinking Skill*

Find the Regional Summary Pages in your Student Notebook. Then, use your *Atlas of the United States* to fill in the information for Kentucky, Tennessee, Mississippi, Alabama, and Arkansas.

When you are finished, look at the State I.D. game in your Student Notebook, and draw a line from the map of each state to its name. On the lines at the bottom, write each state's nickname.[6] If you have trouble remembering, and your teacher agrees, it's fine to use your maps and State Pages to complete this activity.

G. Writing *Language Skills, Thinking Skills*

Now that you have completed your readers and the read-aloud book, make a book review card. The purpose of a book review card is to give a brief description of what you read or heard, and then to tell what you thought of the book. It should not include as much information as a book report. The goal is to give someone who has not read the book enough information to decide whether or not they might like to read it. In a sense, it is like an advertisement for a book. Give information about the good points without retelling the story.

G. Word banks are an excellent way to build vocabulary and encourage writing. When you provide a list for your child to use, that puts the focus on the thinking that goes into the answer, not just searching for the right word or its spelling. Vocabulary and spelling are both strengthened by reading, writing, and speaking the word correctly. It is not cheating to give your child a word bank, since the goal is to build your child's ability to give the best answer possible.

How to Create a Book Review Card:

Your book review can be written on a large index card or on the page provided in your Student Notebook. Include the following information on your card:

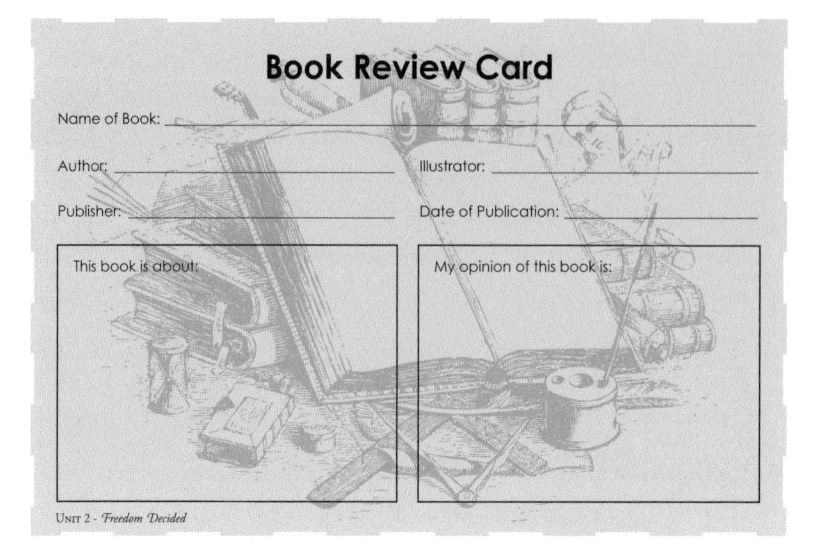

Book Review Card

Name of Book:

Author: Illustrator:

Publisher: Date of Publication:

This book is about:

My opinion of this book is:

UNIT 2 - *Freedom Decided*

- name of the book
- author of the book (person who wrote the book)
- illustrator of the book (person who drew the pictures)
- name of the company who published the book
- date the book was published

Most of this information can be found on the title page of the book.

Rehearse, or practice telling, what you will say about the story and how you liked it. Once you have discussed your thoughts enough to know what you want to write, you can begin. If you don't know how to spell some of the words you want to use, ask your teacher to make a word bank for you.

Next, write a few sentences to tell what the story was about. Since you only have a few sentences, choose the most important facts to tell.

Finally, write a few sentences to tell what you thought about the story. It would be good to tell whether you liked the book and then give some of examples of what you did or did not like about it. Remember to use a word bank if you need it.

Create a book review card for *The American Revolution.*

Create a book review card for *Guns for General Washington.*

Create a book review card for the read-aloud book, *George Washington.*

H. **Independent Reading** *Language Skills*

Choose something to read that you will enjoy. Then, find a quiet, comfortable place and read for the following length of time:

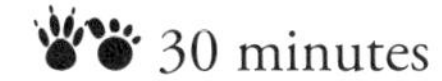

25 minutes 30 minutes

Congratulations on completing six weeks of independent reading! Today's entry in your Reading Log will be the last one for this unit. Make sure you have included all the information needed on your log such as book titles, authors, and dates read.

Look over all that you have accomplished during your independent reading time. If you would like, share your Reading Log with others during your Unit Presentation tomorrow.

H. A reading log is an important part of a portfolio. It documents sequential effort and is a satisfying way for a child to see work completion. You may also want to make a list of books read for this unit, which may include bibliographical information, such as author, publisher and copyright date. This is an easy way to build awareness of bibliographical information.

Lesson 6, Part 5

This part is set aside for completion of any work left undone from the lesson, and review of concepts and content. It is also a time to expand the work of the lesson with art, mapping, or games.

- Listen as your teacher reviews the Steps for Thinking from the Freedom Decided Unit that you have just completed. Talk about how you can apply the Steps for Thinking to what you have read or discussed, and see if you can think of any examples in this unit.
- Gather your vocabulary cards together and mix them up. Randomly choose word cards. Read the word on the front and try to tell your teacher what the word means, or tell how it was used in the story. Give yourself a point for every word you can use correctly. See how many points you can get!
- Have your own Spelling Bee. You can be the only participant, or you can ask others to join you. Use the Spelling Slips for Unit 1 and Unit 2 words that you reviewed earlier in this lesson. Mix them up in a basket or other container, and give them to your teacher. As she draws out a slip and reads the word, spell it the best you can.

  There are several ways to accomplish your Spelling Bee. Try to spell every word and then count the number of words you spelled correctly. Write down the results and try to improve at the end of the next unit! If you compete against someone else, you may want to use the "three strikes and you're out system," rather than being eliminated after only one mistake. If you are able to spell all the words correctly, try adding three to five Challenge words during

If you have chosen to use the assessments, remember to set aside time for that purpose when you have completed this unit. You can use the results of the assessment in various ways: to determine if there is any area that needs additional study, to assign grades, or just to familiarize your child with taking assessments. Lesson 6 of each unit provides review that should help prepare your child for each assessment.

Culminating activities are a key part of solidifying learning. By presenting information learned, opinions formed, and skills practiced, your child also connects new information to past learning. Encourage your child to be the guide to the unit, acquainting others with the key concepts, events, people, and activities. Allow your children to be creative in their presentations, and to truly make them their own!

each lesson of the next unit. Challenge words for your level can be found in Appendix A.

- A timeline is another way to picture information quickly and easily. The goal is to know a few key events that help you remember the nature of the times. Cut out the timeline strips in your Student Notebook. To help you remember each event, choose a category and color for each timeline strip in your Student Notebook. Here are the categories:

    Military Action - red
    Settler/Citizen Action - green
    Government Action - blue

  Lightly write the color you have chosen on the back of each strip. Now arrange the strips in the order you think they happened.

  Check your decisions about color and order with the answer key. Once you are sure you are correct, write the date that each event happened on its strip. Then use colored pencils or crayons to lightly shade or draw a border around the strip according to its category. Now glue the strips on the timeline above the correct dates in your Student Notebook.[7]

- Make a Unit Presentation to your family that tells about what you have learned in the Freedom Decided Unit. Share your Student Notebook, and things you made during this unit such as your weaving and your watercolor picture. Remember to include the portions of important American documents that you copied into your Quotation Notebook! You might also want to invite your family to play cornhole or hopscotch. Don't forget to stand still and speak clearly. After your presentation, be sure to ask if anyone has questions.

- Play Freedom Decided Bingo with your family.

Congratulations on completing Unit Two in *Paths of Settlement!*

Answers

1. Answer key is in Appendix A.
2. Answer key is in Appendix A.
3. Answer key is in Appendix A.
4. His resolutions passed by a close vote and Virginia joined the Revolution!
5. Answer key is in Appendix A.
6. Answer key is in Appendix A.
7. (1765) Sons and Daughters of Liberty formed to protest taxes. (green)
   (1770) Boston Massacre occurs. (red)
   (1773) Boston Tea Party occurs. (green)
   (1775) George Washington named Commander-in-Chief. (blue)
   (1776) Declaration of Independence begins Revolutionary War. (blue)
   (1777) Washington's troops camp at Valley Forge. (red)
   (1783) Treaty of Paris ends Revolutionary War. (blue)

Lesson 1, Part 1

You may want to post the Steps for Thinking somewhere nearby for easy reference. Read these with your students, or have the students read them by themselves. Explain any concept or vocabulary that is not understood.

Steps for Thinking

1. Building a new nation required leaders who were committed to sacrifice and hard work.
2. Members of the community had to join in the commitment, sacrifice and hard work.
3. Success also depended on the children accepting the need for sacrifice and hard work.

Materials

- *The Cabin Faced West*
- *Justin Morgan Had a Horse*
- *Francis Scott Key*
- *Eat Your Way Through the USA*
- *Klutz Watercolor Book*
- *United States History Atlas*
- *Children's Illustrated United States Atlas*
- *Profiles from History, Vol. 2*
- *Wee Sing America* CD and songbook
- USA PlaceMap with overlays
- Water based transparency markers
- U.S. Presidents Pocket Flash Cards
- Outline Map of the U.S.
- USA Activity CD
- Globe (optional)
- Activity (Part 2)
  Newspaper, newsmagazine, or online news source
- Activity (Parts 2 and 4)
  All purpose flour
  Salt
  Mixing bowl
  Cookie sheet (at least 12" x 16")
  Heavy-duty aluminum foil
  Yardstick
  Ruler
  Fine-line permanent marker
- Ingredients for recipe (Part 3)

A. Copywork & Dictation *Language Skills, Thinking Skills*

Look carefully at your assigned passage below, and read it silently. Show your teacher any words you don't know, and practice saying them aloud. Now read the passage aloud, or ask your teacher to read it to you.

When you are finished copying or writing from dictation, compare your copy to the text and make any needed corrections.

Copy or write as your teacher dictates from *The Cabin Faced West*, page 10, paragraphs 1 and 2 ("We've cast our lot…").

Copy or write as your teacher dictates from *Justin Morgan Had a Horse*, the Foreword, paragraph 1 ("This is the story…").

Choose one additional paragraph from today's assignment in *Justin Morgan Had a Horse* to write from dictation.

B. Reader *Language Skills, History*

The Cabin Faced West: page 9 (Chapter 1) through the top of page 14
Justin Morgan Had a Horse: page 11 (Chapter 1) through page 18, paragraph 3

Read the above assignment from *The Cabin Faced West* aloud, and then follow along as someone else reads the assignment from *Justin Morgan Had a Horse.*

Read the above assignment from *The Cabin Faced West* silently, and then read the assignment from *Justin Morgan Had a Horse* aloud.

Read the above assignments from *The Cabin Faced West* and *Justin Morgan Had a Horse* silently.

B. Every student should read or listen to all the literature selections for the unit. Reading or hearing the different perspectives adds depth to understanding the events and circumstances of the times.

C. Read-Aloud & Discussion
Language Skills, History, Thinking Skills

Francis Scott Key: page 1 through page 5, paragraph 3

Read over the following questions that you will discuss later. Then read, or listen carefully as your teacher reads, the above assignment from *Francis Scott Key* aloud. You may want to take notes to help answer the questions after you listen. If needed, you can look back at the story to find specific details.

Pretend you are a news reporter and choose an event that you heard or read about today. Think about what you know from the story, and in your own words answer the following questions about that event:

- What took place?
- When did it take place?
- Where did it take place?
- Who were the main people involved?
- How does this event affect Francis Scott Key's life?
- Why do you think it took place?

Choose a second event to report on using the questions listed above.

Tell how the two events you reported on are related. For example, were they both things that happened to family members? Did the events relate to the war? Did they both occur on the farm? Did both events have something to do with "The Star Spangled Banner?" Decide what factors are common between the two events you reported.

D. Read the list of words to your child. If your student would rather spell the words aloud than write them, it is perfectly acceptable. As you dictate each word, put small dots beside any misspelled words. Then have your child copy them onto the Student Notebook page.

D. Spelling
Language Skills, Thinking Skills

Look at the list of words below, and copy each one onto an index card. Organize the words by prefixes and suffixes, similar vowel or letter sounds, similar meaning, word length or by any other similarities that you see. Try to see if there is anything about each word that can help you remember its spelling, like unusual spelling patterns (for example, where *ch* makes the /k/ sound,) or a small word in a big word (like Ala-BAM-a). Show your teacher how you organized the words.

Turn your cards face down and listen as your teacher dictates the words on your spelling list. Spell each word the best that you can, either aloud or by writing it in your Student Notebook. Your teacher may add up to five words that are difficult for you to read or write.

diary	precious	vegetable	disappeared
impishness	particular	expression	exasperation
obliged	porridge	fledgling	Ebenezer
imagination	investigated	discouragement	scholars

E. History

Geography, Thinking Skills

Nation building, or growth in the size of a nation, happens in many ways. One of the ways of building America was by the signing of treaties. A **treaty**, or formal agreement between more than one country or group, sometimes comes through discussion and agreements, and sometimes it comes after a long fight. When two or more groups sign a treaty, usually all receive something they want. Fighting may stop or each group may give money or land to the other group.

E. In order to view history correctly, you have to consider the motives and understanding of the people involved. Evaluate history in the light of context, or what was happening at the time. Sometimes things done in the past are hard for us to understand. Perhaps the people would not have acted in that way if they had our perspective. Remember to evaluate people and their actions based on their knowledge and intentions.

The Treaty of Paris, signed in 1783, is an example of nation building by treaty. After several years of struggle with the English, and then the Revolutionary War, talks began between the English and the Americans. Benjamin Franklin led the commission that **negotiated**, or came to agreement through discussion and compromise, a treaty that brought about peace for the United States. It was named the Treaty of Paris because it took place in Paris, France. In it, the King of England said that the thirteen colonies, now considered states, were free of English rule, making them a new and independent country.

The Treaty of Paris also set boundaries for the new country. The United States of America, its new name, now included all the land between the Appalachian Mountains and the Mississippi River. The boundary on the north was Canada and the southern boundary was Florida. Canada still belonged to the English and Florida belonged to Spain.

After the treaty was signed, the British army sailed home to England. The American troops, led by General George Washington, marched into New York the winners of a long and difficult struggle for freedom. This was the beginning of the new nation and government of the United States of America.

The frontier, or furthest edge of settlement by pioneers before a greater number of settlers move in, is usually the most difficult place to live. This was certainly true of the land the United States acquired because of this treaty. There were still many Native American Indians living in the newly acquired land, and they did not necessarily recognize the right of the Americans to move in.

The Native Americans wanted to continue the traditions of their culture. Most of the settlers moving west towards the frontier came from traditions that encouraged people to find a place and build a permanent home. This home would be a place to raise a family and grow crops, and raise farm animals. Soon towns were built where others lived to help support the development of the area such as doctors, bankers, and store owners. While both groups made attempts to work together, these often failed and ended in violence. The government tried to make the process peaceful by negotiating treaties with the Indians. In return, the Indians gave over control of large sections of land to the government. For many reasons, these treaties were often broken. The government later made decisions to settle the disputes between Native Americans and settlers. In the end, not everyone was happy and the process of making sure fair dealings occurred still continues to this day.

With the beginning of the new nation of America, even more people wanted to come here to live. Many of the people who already lived here wanted to own their own land, so many pioneers moved to the new lands given to the United States through the Treaty of Paris. Fighting between some of the pioneers and the Native Americans seemed bound to happen.

Think of the literature you have read so far. Tell about an example that you can think of where the Native Americans and the pioneer settlers got along. Now think of an example where the Native Americans and the pioneer settlers did not get along. Tell your teacher why you think they got along, and why they fought.

Today you will draw another map on the PlaceMap overlays. First, find the map in your *United States History Atlas* entitled "Growth of the United States to 1853." Notice the area that was added by the Treaty of Paris. Now carefully draw the western boundary of that area directly onto the transparency that is folded over the PlaceMap. Use the water based pen you used for the 13 colonies map. The eastern boundary runs mostly along the Line of Proclamation, and the western boundary follows the Mississippi River almost all the way to the top, where it is slightly different. You may cross over a bit on the left transparency sheet if needed. Remember, your boundaries do not have to be perfect—just do your best! When you are finished, color and label the Treaty of Paris on the map overlay.

Compare your new transparency to the one you made in Lesson 2, and notice how the size of America changed because of the Treaty of Paris. You can see by looking at the maps, that this was a great leap forward in the size of our nation.

On this map, you can see the names of the states and their borders shown by dotted lines. These dotted lines show the borders of each state as it is today. In your Student Notebook, make a list of the states that **expanded**, or grew larger, because of the Treaty of Paris.[1]

Look at the map in your history atlas again. Now make a list of current states that were established on land that was added to the United States by the Treaty of Paris.[2]

 Look again at the map transparencies you have made. How much of an increase to the size of America did the Treaty of Paris bring about? You can answer this by estimating or by finding an exact amount.[3]

Imagine that you are the negotiator of a treaty between the Native Americans and the pioneer settlers. Based on what you have learned through the literature, make a list in your Student Notebook of what you think each group would want. Talk with your teacher about what you would propose to each group. Tell whether you think that your treaty would stop the conflict between the two groups.

Choose one of the following treaties signed by Native Americans with the United States. Learn more about it and then choose a statement you agree with for number one and number two. Tell your teacher why you agree with the statement you chose.

The Treaty of New Echota (1835)
Treaty with the Florida Tribes of Indians (1823)
Treaty with the Chickasaw (1832)

1) The treaty was a good deal for the Native Americans because:
   The treaty was a bad deal for the Native Americans because:

2) The treaty was a good deal for the settlers because:
   The treaty was a bad deal for the settlers because:

F. States

Geography, History, Thinking Skills

In your *United States Atlas*, read the pages about Louisiana. When you are finished, find the blank map of Louisiana in your Student Notebook and complete the following assignments:

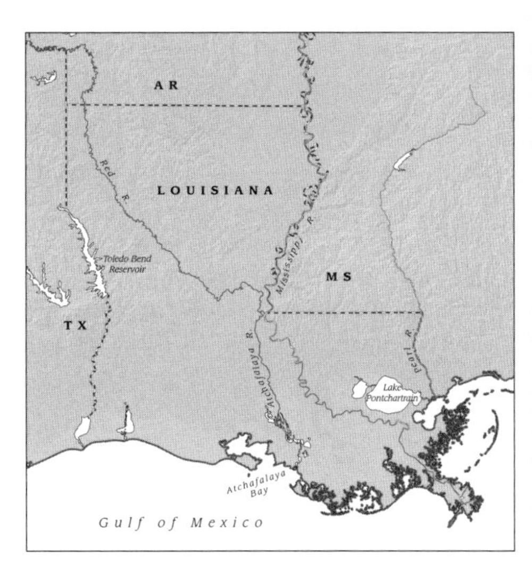

- Place a small red star on the spot where Baton Rouge is located, and label it. Baton Rouge is the capital city of Louisiana.
- Label the Gulf of Mexico.
- Color the lines showing the Mississippi, Red, Atchafalaya, and Pearl Rivers blue, and label them.
- Color and label Lake Pontchartrain.

- Place a dot on the spot where New Orleans is located, and label it. Then discuss anything you know about New Orleans with your teacher.[4]
- Label Toledo Bend Reservoir and Atchafalaya Bay.
- Label the three states that border Louisiana.

G. When a student draws or paints a scene, there are many wonderful thinking skills taking place. The student is observing, recording and categorizing information and then interpreting that information—all accomplished while doing something fun!

G. Doing *Art, Music*

Look at the song entitled "Blow the Man Down" in your *Wee Sing America* songbook, and read the historical note about it in the book. This type of song was sung by sailors when they were working, and its rhythm helped them do things in **unison**, or at the same time. Now listen to it on the *Wee Sing America* CD. Try to become familiar with the words and music so that you can sing along, or learn to play it on an instrument of your choice. You may want to recite, sing, or play this song during your presentation at the end of this unit.

Look at page 34 in your *Klutz Watercolor Book*, which begins a short section about experimenting with landscapes. That is exactly what you should do on the next few pages! You can get ideas of what to paint by looking at pictures, going out in your yard (only with your parent's permission,) or thinking of things in nature you have noticed. Then complete pages 34, 35, and 36. This is a good chance to combine the things you have learned with new ideas. Remember, it is impossible to make a mistake as long as you keep the paint on the paper!

If you find you have extra time after your regular schoolwork is finished, and your parent agrees, continue to experiment with painting small parts of landscapes over the next few days.

H. Independent Reading *Language Skills*

Choose something to read that you will enjoy. Then, find a quiet, comfortable place and read for the following length of time:

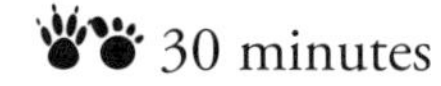

25 minutes 30 minutes

Be sure to write down what you read today on the Reading Log in your Student Notebook.

Lesson 1, Part 2

A. Imagery is a picture in your mind, often created by using words. It is very individual, since it depends on your understanding of the words and your experiences. This activity builds imagery. Poetry often uses imagery as an important part of enjoying and understanding the words of others.

A. Quotation Notebook *History, Language Skills, Music*

In this section you will copy verses from the American National Anthem, "The Star Spangled Banner." This song sprang from the experiences of Francis Scott Key during the War of 1812. The events at that time sparked the words he wrote, but they came from the heart of a man who served his country and was deeply patriotic. The words of the song found widespread acceptance and reflected the patriotic feelings of many who heard it. Every American should be familiar with the words and meaning of "The Star Spangled Banner," though its love of country and freedom will connect with citizens of free and democratic nations everywhere. As you examine the song, consider the imagery created by the words. Since it is also a poem, consider its rhyme pattern as well (introduced in Unit 2, Lesson 5, Part 4).

> O say, can you see, by the dawn's early light,
> What so proudly we hailed at the twilight's last gleaming?

Copy the above passage into your Student Notebook. Talk with your teacher about the meaning of the verse and any unknown words. You may want to present the "Star Spangled Banner" to your family at the end of this unit, so listen to it on the *Wee Sing America* CD and follow along with the words in the songbook. Practice reading or singing each section of the song aloud.

In your Student Notebook there are phrases from this part of the verse that produce an image in your mind. Draw a picture or write a description of each image created in your Student Notebook.

Choose two words from the verse and write at least one synonym for each one. Make sure you find a meaning that goes with its **context**, or use in the verse.

B. Reader *Language Skills, History*

The Cabin Faced West: page 14, paragraph 1 ("Ann moved…") through the top of page 19
Justin Morgan Had a Horse: page 18, paragraph 4 ("The smaller colt…") through the top of page 27

Read the above assignment from *The Cabin Faced West* aloud, and then follow along as someone else reads the assignment from *Justin Morgan Had a Horse.*

Read the above assignment from *The Cabin Faced West* silently, and then read the assignment from *Justin Morgan Had a Horse* aloud.

Read the above assignments from *The Cabin Faced West* and *Justin Morgan Had a Horse* silently.

C. Read-Aloud & Narration *Language Skills, History, Thinking Skills*

Francis Scott Key: page 5, paragraph 4 ("It was sunset…") through page 8

Follow the instructions below for your level. Then, in your own words, tell what happened in the story from Francis' point of view, or pretend you are Francis and tell what you think happened. Try to remember as many details as possible. You may reread the passage or listen as your teacher rereads the part you are to retell.

C. Encourage your children to get into character for this assignment. They can narrate, or retell, the passage using the pronoun *I*, stand up to look more impressive, use a deeper voice, etc. By encouraging this creativity, you are also encouraging critical thinking. What would the speaker sound like? What happened to him and how did he feel about it? This is a natural way to comprehend and express the thoughts of another person.

Listen carefully as your teacher reads the above assignment from *Francis Scott Key* aloud.

Read the above assignment from *Francis Scott Key* aloud.

D. The Mechanics and Editing section in this unit begins with skills that your child may already know. It is always a good idea to begin instruction with review, so please have your child complete these activities even if he already knows the concepts presented. A great way to enjoy a review with your child is to ask him to be the teacher and present the information to you, the student!

D. Editing

Language Skills, Thinking Skills

Mechanics are people who are good at fixing machines and engines and making them work better. You are going to become a writing mechanic by correcting punctuation, words and sentences and making them correct. Not every rule is included about hyphens, apostrophes and pronouns, but this is a good start to thinking about how to use them correctly. Check a grammar handbook if you would like to learn more, or you can use a dictionary or the spell check function on your computer (with your teacher's permission) to check if you are not sure when writing.

Mechanics Toolkit

1A - A pronoun for one person or thing can be the subject of a sentence.

> I like ice cream. You will be my friend.
> He loves to play football. She likes to read.
> It was my favorite present.

1B - A name and a pronoun for one person can be used together as the subject of a sentence. (Remember the Golden Rule - put yourself last!)

> Sam and I will go for a bike ride.
> He and Bob play ball together.

2A - Use an apostrophe (') to show the missing letters in a contraction.

> I don't (*o* is missing from *not*) want to fall and get hurt.
> They're (*a* is missing from *are*) going to come with us.

Practice these skills by correcting the sentences in your Student Notebook.[5] The number of errors in each sentence is listed after the sentence in parentheses. To show that a letter needs to be capitalized, make three lines (≡) underneath the letter that should be capitalized. To replace an incorrect word with a correct word, draw a line through the incorrect word and write the correct word above it. Add any needed punctuation.

E. Science

Geography, Thinking Skills, Art

In the first few lessons of this unit you will learn about the oceans and their water, erosion, the continental shelf, and the continental slope. Take a few minutes to discuss what you already know about these things with your teacher. When you are finished, and before

reading further in this section, make a list of questions or things you would like to find out about these subjects. There is a page provided in your Student Notebook for the list. Later, you will have an opportunity to look back and see if your questions have been answered.

Even though most of the states you have studied so far this year are located close to the Atlantic Ocean, you have not yet learned much about that large body of water. So, in this section you will begin a study of oceans and their properties.

Look at a globe or the map of the world in Appendix B, and notice how much space water takes up. In fact, the earth has more than two times as much water as it does land, and most of it is contained in the oceans and seas. See if you can find and point to the five main oceans, and then write their names in your Student Notebook.[6] How many seas can you find? Write the names of three or four seas in your Student Notebook.[7]

Notice on your globe or map that all the oceans are connected to one another. So even though different areas have different names, they are really just one continuous body of water. It is surprising that only a small part (about ten percent) of this huge underwater territory has ever been explored. But **oceanographers**, or scientists who study the ocean, have still learned many things about it. For example, they have used things like sound waves to get an idea of what the ocean floor looks like.

Today you will begin making a 3-D map of a small part of the ocean floor. A 3-D map shows the various heights of the land in an area. Even though your map will not be exact, it will help you **visualize**, or picture in your mind, what the ocean floor looks like. To get started, look at the map-model in Appendix B, or print it from the Student Resource CD, and notice the lines that divide it into small squares. These squares form a **grid**, or framework of parallel lines, that will help you transfer this map onto a larger surface. To get started, follow the directions for this section in Appendix B.

E. Each word in bold letters is considered a vocabulary word. It is a word that may or may not be new to your children. You can write these vocabulary words on index cards and use them for occasional review, but not for memorizing. Give your children the meaning of the words if they don't remember. Try to use the new vocabulary words during conversation, and encourage your students to do the same.

Each time your students make a vocabulary card for this unit, have them write *NB* (for Nation Building) in the upper left corner. This will make it possible to review vocabulary by unit at the end of the year.

F. States

Geography, Thinking Skills, History, Drawing

Look again at the pages about Louisiana in your *United States Atlas*. Then find the State Page in your Student Notebook, and fill in the information.

Make State Cards for Louisiana by following the instructions found in Appendix B. Louisiana is a Southern state, so be sure to outline the cards in purple.

G. Interactive Writing

Language Skills, Thinking Skills

This writing activity is for you and another person, your partner, to complete. Most of the time, your partner is your teacher, but it could also be a parent, brother, sister, or other family member.

Choose an article from a newspaper, news magazine, or online source of news that is acceptable to your parents that relates to a current event in local, state or national government. Topics can include an action taken by the President, Congress, or Supreme Court, or a decision made by your Governor, Mayor, or Town Council, and so forth. Ask your partner to read the article and then answer the following questions in your Student Notebook:

Do you agree with the article; why or why not?
What do you think should happen in the future regarding this issue?

Tell about the news story using the number sentences indicated below. Then tell what you think about what your partner wrote. Write several sentences in reply, including whether or not you agree with your partner, and why. End with a question for your partner.

- at least four sentences
- at least five sentences
- Tell about the news story with at least one paragraph. Then tell what you think about what your partner wrote with a second paragraph.

Remember that a paragraph is a group of sentences that relate to one topic, or main idea. State the topic or main idea of the paragraph at or near the beginning of the paragraph. You do not want the reader to read your paragraph for very long without knowing for sure what you think!

H. Reading fluency is developed through having frequent silent reading opportunities that continue for the length of time suggested here. Since a primary focus of this activity is to nurture your child's enjoyment of reading, help him to choose reading materials that interest him and at a level that allows him to read with understanding by himself. You can incorporate this activity into your school day whenever it is most convenient.

H. Independent Reading

Language Skills

Choose something to read that you will enjoy. Then, find a quiet, comfortable place and read for the following length of time:

25 minutes   30 minutes

Be sure to write down what you read today on the Reading Log in your Student Notebook.

Lesson 1, Part 3

A. Copywork & Dictation *Language Skills, Thinking Skills*

Look carefully at your assigned passage below, and read it silently. Show your teacher any words you don't know, and practice saying them aloud. Now read the passage aloud, or ask your teacher to read it to you.

When you are finished copying or writing from dictation, compare your copy to the text and make any needed corrections.

Copy or write as your teacher dictates from *The Cabin Faced West*, page 20, paragraph 6 ("She read what…").

Copy or write as your teacher dictates from *Justin Morgan Had a Horse*, page 37, paragraph 2 ("Joel and Bub…").

Choose one additional paragraph from today's assignment in *Justin Morgan Had a Horse* to write from dictation.

B. Reader *Language Skills, History*

The Cabin Faced West: page 19, paragraph 1 ("She scuffed…") through the top of page 24
Justin Morgan Had a Horse: page 27, paragraph 1 ("Joel's hands…") through page 33, paragraph 2

Read the above assignment from *The Cabin Faced West* aloud, and then follow along as someone else reads the assignment from *Justin Morgan Had a Horse*.

Read the above assignment from *The Cabin Faced West* silently, and then read the assignment from *Justin Morgan Had a Horse* aloud.

Read the above assignments from *The Cabin Faced West* and *Justin Morgan Had a Horse* silently.

Teaching Tip

If your child needs to practice reading aloud to gain fluency, but feels that it is babyish for him to have to do so, suggest that he read into a tape recorder by himself. That way, he can read, listen, and practice rereading parts that don't sound smooth. You can listen to the passage without him present to identify areas that need further practice. When you keep the tapes and your child listens to them later, they can be a proof of improvement!

C. Read-Aloud & Discussion *Language Skills, History, Thinking Skills*

Francis Scott Key: page 10 (Chapter 2) through page 14, paragraph 5

Follow the directions below to read or listen to the above assignment from *Francis Scott Key*. Then make up the assigned number of questions about the part of the story you just read or heard. Write down your questions and ask your teacher to answer them. After discussing her thoughts, write down the best possible answer in your Student Notebook. Be sure to use complete sentences.

Listen carefully as your teacher reads the above assignment from *Francis Scott Key* aloud.

Make up one question. Make up two questions.

Read the above assignment from *Francis Scott Key* aloud; then make up three questions.

D. Vocabulary & Spelling

Language Skills, Thinking Skills

Vocabulary:

Write each vocabulary word on an index card. Then use a thesaurus to find a **synonym**, or word that means almost the same thing for each word. To find a word in a thesaurus or dictionary, you may need to remove any endings that have been added, such as an *s* or *ed*. If you cannot find a synonym, use a dictionary to look up the meaning of the word. On the back of each card, draw a picture or write a clue so you can remember how each word was used in the story. Write a *D* or *S* by your clue to tell whether you wrote a definition or synonym.

squatters **makeshift** **scolded** **prowling** **mockery**

descendant **fledgling** **perchance** **gangly** **awl**

Spelling:

Look at the list of words on your Student Notebook page. Divide each word into syllables by drawing a slash line (/) between the syllables, like this: um/brel/la. After you have marked each word, use a dictionary to check your work.[8] If you don't know what the word means, read the definition while you are checking your syllable markings. Then place a check next to each word to show that you know what the word means.

Look at the spelling word cards you made in Part 1. Read each word, and then cover it with your hand and try to spell it aloud. Then uncover it and see if you were correct. Review the meanings of any words that you do not remember.

E. History

Geography, Thinking Skills

Presidential Focus: As you learn about nation building, you will hear the names of many different American presidents. Since this unit begins with the end of the Revolutionary War, you will begin with the first president, George Washington. Read the U.S. Presidents Flash Cards about George Washington and John Adams. Use the things you learn to fill out the Presidential Focus page in your Student Notebook.

As you have learned, people whose families came from other countries **founded**, or set up, the United States. From the beginning, the United States was very unusual in the world. That is because its Constitution allowed **citizens**, or legal residents, to participate in electing the people and making the laws that would govern them.

At first, the laws that explained who was actually a citizen were not perfect, and many people who lived in the United States were not included. But over the years the laws gradually changed, and nowadays everyone born in the United States is automatically a *natural* citizen. In addition, all people who come to America legally and settle here have the opportunity to become *naturalized* citizens.

To do that, people first have to live in this country for at least five years and be at least 18 years old. They must have good moral character, and be willing to promise their loyalty to the United States. If they meet those requirements, they can fill out applications for citizenship. Then, after a short wait, applicants meet with a government representative for an interview. There, they show that they can understand, speak, and write in English, and they take a test about this nation's history and government. After a successful interview, the final step is to appear before a judge and take the **oath of allegiance**, or promise of loyalty, to the United States.

In your Student Notebook, make a list of the six requirements for naturalization.[9]

Natural and naturalized citizens are alike, except for one thing. In order to serve as President or Vice President of the United States, a person must be born in this country. Other than that, all citizens have the same rights and the same responsibilities. Following are some important rights that make United States citizenship desirable to many people all over the world:

Freedom of religion;
Freedom of assembly;
Freedom to keep and bear arms;
Freedom of speech;
Freedom of the press;
Protection for those accused of crimes; and
Opportunity to vote on people and issues.

But citizenship is more than just enjoying rights—it also involves taking responsibility so that people can keep their rights. For example, if citizens do not take the responsibility to vote, there is a better chance for laws to be passed that go against their values. Or if they do not take the responsibility to serve on a jury when asked, someone might not receive a fair trial. Following are some of the responsibilities that help protect the freedoms of United States citizens:

Vote;
Support and defend the Constitution;
Serve the country when necessary;
Pay taxes honestly;
Respect and obey laws;
Respect the rights, beliefs, and opinions of others; and
Participate on juries or as a witness when asked.

Read and discuss the rights and responsibilities listed above with your teacher. Then, choose two from each category that interest you. In your Student Notebook, tell which ones you chose. Then write two or three sentences about each one that explain why that right or responsibility is important.

E. The Internet can be a useful tool for research, but we suggest that your child use it only with your permission and supervision, and while following your family's rules.

Use the library or the Internet to find out about the 15th Amendment to the United States Constitution. Then talk to your teacher about what you learn. Be sure to tell her when the amendment was approved and what it was about. Include any problems that surrounded it.

Find out about the 19th Amendment to the United States Constitution. Then talk to your teacher about what you learn. Be sure to tell her when the amendment was approved and what it was about. Include any problems that surrounded it.

F. It is important for students to be acquainted with various reference tools, such as an atlas. Since your goal is for students to be lifelong learners, use of reference tools can greatly enhance learning on any topic. Using these tools successfully requires familiarity and the opportunities to use the tools as part of learning that is connected to history, literature, science, and ultimately, life.

F. States

Geography, History, Thinking Skills

In your *United States Atlas*, read the pages about Florida. When you are finished, find the blank map of Florida in your Student Notebook and complete the following assignments:

- Place a small red star on the spot where Tallahassee is located, and label it. Tallahassee is the capital city of Florida.
- Label the Atlantic Ocean, the Gulf of Mexico, and Tampa Bay.
- Color the lines showing the St. John's, Suwannee, Peace, and Apalachicola Rivers blue, and label them.
- Color and label Lake Okeechobee, Lake George, and Lake Kissimmee.

- Color and label the area where the Everglades National Park is located.

- Label the Florida Keys, and the city of Key West with a dot. Key West is the southernmost city in the United States.

- Place a dot on the spot where Cape Canaveral is located, and label it. Then discuss anything you know about Cape Canaveral with your teacher.[10]
- Label the two states that border Florida.

G. **Cooking** *Language Skills, Thinking Skills, Drawing*

With your parent's permission and supervision, look in *Eat Your Way Through the USA*, choose a recipe that comes from either Florida or Louisiana, and prepare it for your family. After everyone has had a taste, find out who liked it, and whether anyone would like to have it again. What did you think about it?

In your Student Notebook, draw a picture of the dish you chose to make and write the following number of sentences about your family's reaction to it:

two sentences three sentences four sentences

Connect Learning to Life:

Food is a powerful connection between events and memories. When you make a dish that connects the knowledge and understanding gained about a place, event, or literature to an experience, learning becomes more lasting. My children will probably never forget the "Swiss Family Robinson" dinner we made after reading the book. We sat on the floor, ate nothing but island food and used candles! They loved it, and can still tell about it years later.

H. **Independent Reading** *Language Skills*

Choose something to read that you will enjoy. Then, find a quiet, comfortable place and read for the following length of time:

25 minutes 30 minutes

Be sure to write down what you read today on the Reading Log in your Student Notebook.

Lesson 1, Part 4

A. **Quotation Notebook** *History, Language Skills, Music*

Continue copying verses from the American National Anthem, "The Star Spangled Banner." As you examine this song, consider the imagery created by the words. Since it is also a poem, consider its rhyme pattern as well (introduced in Unit 2, Lesson 5, Part 4).

> Whose broad stripes and bright stars, through the perilous fight,
> O'er the ramparts we watched were so gallantly streaming!

Copy the above passage into your Student Notebook, and talk with your teacher about its meaning and any unknown words. Then listen to it on the *Wee Sing America* CD and follow along with the words in the songbook. Practice reading or singing each section of the song aloud.

A. If your child seems uncomfortable with the idea of drawing images, go to the library and look for books about the National Anthem that may include artwork. Encourage your child to understand that people create different pictures, or images in their mind, so there is no one correct answer.

Under each phrase printed in your Student Notebook, draw a picture or write an explanation that describes the image it creates in your mind.

Choose two words from the verse and write at least one synonym for each one. Make sure you find a meaning that goes with its context, or use in the verse.

B. Reader *Language Skills, History*

The Cabin Faced West: page 24, paragraph 1 ("As he stepped...") through page 28

Justin Morgan Had a Horse: page 33, paragraph 3 ("This was...") through page 38

Read the above assignment from *The Cabin Faced West* aloud, and then follow along as someone else reads the assignment from *Justin Morgan Had a Horse*.

Read the above assignment from *The Cabin Faced West* silently, and then read the assignment from *Justin Morgan Had a Horse* aloud.

Read the above assignments from *The Cabin Faced West* and *Justin Morgan Had a Horse* silently.

Teaching Tip

The skill of predicting what will happen in the story is an important one. It requires your child to remember what has already happened, consider the characters and events, and then come up with a reasonable idea of what may happen in the future. This process involves using critical thinking skills and can be a natural part of any reading your child is doing. Just ask, "What do you think will happen next?"

C. Read-Aloud & Narration *Language Skills, History, Thinking Skills*

Francis Scott Key: page 5, paragraph 4 ("It was sunset...") through page 8

After reading or listening to the read-aloud assignment, talk with your teacher and try to predict what will happen in the future based on what you know of the characters and events. Write down your predictions in your Student Notebook. Later you will look back and see if they were accurate. Try not to peek ahead!

Listen carefully as your teacher reads the above assignment from *Francis Scott Key* aloud. Then write down something that you think will happen in the story.

Write down another thing that you think will happen in the story.

Read the above assignment from *Francis Scott Key* aloud. Then write down three things that you think will happen in the story.

D. For days with several assignments that require writing, you may want to do some of the assignments verbally or have your student complete some of them by typing. Variety in response can help keep students motivated to do a good job.

D. Editing *Language Skills, Thinking Skills*

Reread the Mechanics Toolkit from Part 2 of this lesson. Be the teacher and tell what each skill means and how it is used.

Use your readers to find two examples of each rule, and either show them to your teacher or write them in your Student Notebook.

Use your readers to find four examples of each rule, and either show them to your teacher or write them in your Student Notebook.

E. Science
Geography, Thinking Skills, Art

Today you will continue working on your 3-D map. If you have not finished drawing the land areas, the continental shelf, and the continental slope, do so now. Then follow the "3-D Map, con't" directions for this section in Appendix B to make salt dough. When you are finished, set it aside for the time being.

Look again at a globe or the map of the world in Appendix B. Notice that there are several large land areas on the earth, as well as many smaller ones. The large areas are continents, and there are seven of them. See if you can find and point to the seven continents, and then write their names in your Student Notebook.[11] How many islands can you find? Write the names of four or five of thc larger islands in your Student Notebook.[12]

The first feature you will build on your 3-D map is the continent of North America, which is the outline you drew on the west side of your map-base. Use a small spatula, dinner knife, or your hands to pile and smooth salt dough on this area until it is at least ¾-inch high and covers the whole outline. Push or trim the edges with a dinner knife or popsicle stick so that your salt-dough continent remains inside its outline. Now do the same with the islands that you outlined.

When you are finished, and with your parent's supervision, heat the oven to 150°. Put your map in the oven for one hour, and then remove it carefully. If Cuba and Puerto Rico are not sticking well, wait until your map is cool, and put a little glue on their bottoms. Then store your map in a safe place for the next few days.

The salt dough you put on the 3-D map today is only the first layer of the land masses. You will add another layer in the next lesson, so that the continent and islands are about 1½-inches high. Of course, all land is not the same height, but on your 3-D map, 1½-inches represent sea level, or the height at which the ocean and land meet.

F. States
Geography, Thinking Skills, History, Drawing

Look again at the pages about Florida in your *United States Atlas*. Then find the State Page in your Student Notebook, and fill in the information.

Make State Cards for Florida by following the instructions found in Appendix B. Florida is a Southern state, so be sure to outline the cards in purple.

G. Writing
Language Skills, Thinking Skills

News stories are important to the citizens of a nation. Since no one can be everywhere, people rely on others to tell them what is happening in other places. They want the person who is telling what happened, or the **reporter**, to tell the truth, as free as possible from bias. **Bias** means to be unfairly for or against something.

Teaching Tip

Rather than look for a new source of articles for each interactive writing assignment, you may want to choose a publication or website and use articles from it regularly.

When reporters are biased, it means that you cannot depend on their reporting to provide the **facts** fairly. Bias is similar to point of view. However, the goal of reporting in general is to clearly state the facts, or what can be shown to have taken place. Then people can decide for themselves what they believe about something that happened, and what is best to do about it. If reporters are biased, they may present the news in such a way that the reader or listener does not get all the facts clearly. It is best to tell your audience if you are stating an **opinion**, or what you think about something.

Here are some examples:

Fact - The sun shines during the daytime.
Opinion - Daytime is better than nighttime because the sun is shining.

Unbiased statement - The Tigers won the football game.
Biased statement - The Tigers only won the football game because they were lucky.

News stories tell facts and have many parts. They also tend to be shorter than other stories because they usually have to fit into a smaller space. The first part of a news story is the *headline*, which is a title printed at the top that gives the main idea, or a summary of the story. The *byline* comes right below the headline and tells who wrote the story. Next, the first paragraph of the news story begins with the *lead*, which tells the main idea again and gives the most important facts. After this comes the *body* of the story which answers the questions who, what, when, where, why and how the story took place. The *ending* gives a final thought about the story, and is a conclusion. Since this is the last part of the story, try to make it something your reader will remember. It makes a story more interesting to add quotes from those who were present, making them primary sources.

Here is a sample news story:

Billy Smith Cleans His Room

by Anna Smith

Yesterday Billy was the talk of the Smith household because he cleaned his room. He picked up his toys, made his bed, straightened his shelves, and cleaned under his bed.

"I'm really glad I cleaned my room," Billy said. "Not only do I feel better, but I found many toys under my bed that I had completely forgotten about. Now I am excited about playing with them again," he stated.

The room cleaning did not take long, with Billy starting at about 9 A.M. and finishing by noon. His mom felt that the help he got organizing made a big difference in his success. "The new bins for his toys gave him a place to put everything and really got him going," she said.

Are you wondering why he cleaned his room now? Grama and Grampa are coming for a visit, and Mom said everyone had to clean up. Billy took this direction to heart and got the job done. Does he plan to keep his room clean in the future?

Billy smiled while he shared, "I'm excited about being able to find things and sit on my bed when I want to. I hope to keep my room this way all the time!"

Think of an event that has happened at your home. It could be a normal, everyday event such as cooking dinner or giving the dog a bath. Collect information about the event as a reporter would. Talk directly to those who were involved. Get the facts straight and then write a news story about the event you chose. Make sure you have included all the parts listed for a news story. When you are finished ask the family member, or people involved, to read it. Consider using their input to make any **revisions**, or changes, that correct the facts or make your story better. You may also want to include photographs, since they are a common part of news stories.

Choose a less frequent event such as someone's birthday celebration or a sick family member. Then follow the directions above to write another news story about the event you chose.

Think about what might happen if a news story reported facts that were not true. What could the effects be? Talk with your teacher about ways that an incorrect news story can be corrected, such as by printing a *retraction*. Look up this word and tell what it means. News stories are often printed or reported quickly in an attempt to get information to people as soon as possible. How can that make mistakes more frequent? If someone printed a story about you that you did not think was true, what should you do? How would you feel?

H. Independent Reading

Language Skills

Choose something to read that you will enjoy. Then, find a quiet, comfortable place and read for the following length of time:

25 minutes   30 minutes

Be sure to write down what you read today on the Reading Log in your Student Notebook.

Lesson 1, Part 5

This part is set aside for completion of any work left undone from the lesson, and review of concepts and content. It is also a time to expand the work of the lesson with art, mapping, or games.

- Review the Steps for Thinking found in Part 1.
- Give your teacher your stack of vocabulary cards for the lesson. As she shows you each word, tell her the meaning of the word and how it was used in the story.
- Listen as your teacher reads the words that you studied from Part 1. Write each word in your Student Notebook as she dictates it. When you are finished, look back at your spelling word cards and make corrections as needed. Show your teacher how you did.
- Use the United States map that is near the front of your *Atlas of the United States* to find Louisiana and Florida. Then, on the large outline map of the U.S., draw purple lines around them because they are Southern states. Write in the names of the states, and draw small stars where their capital cities are located. Next to the stars, write the name of each capital city.
- Read, or listen as your teacher reads, the story about Daniel Webster in *Profiles from History, Volume 2*. Talk about the discussion question with your teacher, and then complete any other activities that she assigns.
- Use your USA Activity CD to print at least one activity for the states you studied in this lesson. Then add any that you complete to your Student Notebook.
- Complete the Nation Building Word Search located in your Student Notebook.[13]

Educators have many different feelings about grading. For a child who struggles, grading can be very discouraging. For a child who is competitive, grading may seem like a good idea, but not if the child is overly focused on competing with others. Better to focus on personal improvement than competition with peers. Keep grading in perspective.

History is easier to understand when you learn about the lives of real people; not just the events that took place, but what was important to the person. Those who do great things, do so because of their strong beliefs and passion. The passion of others can inspire us to do great things as well!

Enrichment Activities

1. Use the library or the Internet to answer these questions: When did Native Americans begin to vote? Why do you think it took so long? Why couldn't these people become American citizens? Does the United States still consider Indian reservations to be separate nations? Write at least four paragraphs that answer these questions and include any other information that you find interesting. When you are finished, add your report to your Student Notebook.
2. In your *United States Atlas*, look again at the states you have studied in this lesson. Scan the sections entitled "The Way It Was..." and choose a person, place, or thing from one of those sections

to research. Use the library or, with your parent's permission, the Internet and try to find out more than what is written in the atlas.

Then pretend you work for a newspaper, and you have just met the person, seen the landmark, or found out about the object. Write a short article about what you have learned. Newspaper reporters always try to answer the questions who, what, when, where, and how when they write, so that readers have all the important information. Try to answer those questions in your article, and then add it to your Student Notebook.

Additional Resources

Martha Washington: America's First Lady (Childhood of Famous Americans), by Jean Brown Wagoner

Servant to Abigail Adams: The Early American Adventures of Hannah Cooper, by Kate Connell

Information and activities related to the branches of government: http://library.thinkquest.org/5873/

If you read any of the above books, be sure to print a Book Review page from your Student Resources CD, fill it out, and place it in your Student Notebook.

Answers

1. New York, Pennsylvania, West Virginia, Virginia, North Carolina, and Georgia.

2. Ohio, Kentucky, Tennessee, Alabama, Mississippi, Illinois, Indiana, Wisconsin and Michigan.

3. The land mass of the United States more than doubled.

4. Answers will vary, but may open the door to discuss the area's low sea level and the difficulties New Orleans faces as a result.

5. 1. George Washington didn't support the British.
   2. He wasn't afraid of great responsibility.
   3. Were she and Margaret still best friends?
   4. There weren't many soldiers left from the days of Valley Forge.
   5. He and Joel went on a trip to Massachusetts.
   6. Wasn't John Key the master of Terra Rubra?
   7. He and Little Bub weren't the property of Farmer Beane anymore.
   8. Did Mrs. Key speak to Mr. Key about the abused slave?
   9. The Hamilton family didn't plan to go back to Pennsylvania.

6. Atlantic, Pacific, Indian, Arctic, Southern

7. Answers will vary.

8. di/a/ry, pre/cious, veg/e/ta/ble, dis/ap/peared, imp/ish/ness, par/tic/u/lar, ex/pres/sion, ex/as/per/a/tion
   o/bliged, por/ridge, fledg/ling, Eb/e/ne/zer
   i/mag/i/na/tion, in/ves/ti/ga/ted, dis/cour/age/ment, schol/ars

9. Must have lived in U.S. for at least 5 years; be at least 18; have good moral character; be willing to promise loyalty; understand, speak, and write English; and have knowledge of U.S. history and government .

10. Answers may vary, but should include mention of NASA and the space program which is based there.

11. Africa, Asia, Australia, Antarctica, North America, South America, Europe

12. Answers will vary.

13. Answers are in Appendix A.

Lesson 2, Part 1

Steps for Thinking

1. Learning was an important part of building the new nation. The people learned how to defend their nation, make and follow laws, and gain basic skills such as reading and writing.
2. Many kinds of practical knowledge were important in areas such as cooking, farming, hunting, building, doctoring, and understanding the weather and seasons.
3. There were many ways for knowledge to pass on: from parent to child, teachers to students, masters to apprentices, or friend to friend.

Materials

- *The Cabin Faced West*
- *Justin Morgan Had a Horse*
- *Francis Scott Key*
- *Eat Your Way Through the USA*
- *Klutz Watercolor Book*
- *United States History Atlas*
- *Children's Illustrated United States Atlas*
- *Discovering America's Founders* DVD
- *Wee Sing America* CD and songbook
- USA PlaceMap with overlays
- Water based transparency markers
- United States Presidents Flash Cards
- Outline Map of the U.S.
- USA Activity CD
- Globe (optional)
- Activity (Part 1)
  30 bamboo skewers
  Red, blue, green, black, and yellow (optional) paint or markers
  Fine- to medium-grain sandpaper
  Wire cutters or shears
- Activity (Part 2)
  Newspaper, newsmagazine, or online news source
- Activity (Parts 2 and 4)
  All purpose flour
  Salt
  Mixing bowl
  Ruler
  Fine-line permanent marker
- Ingredients for recipe (Part 3)

A. Copywork & Dictation *Language Skills, Thinking Skills*

Look carefully at your assigned passage below, and read it silently. Show your teacher any words you don't know, and practice saying them aloud. Now read the passage aloud, or ask your teacher to read it to you.

When you are finished copying or writing from dictation, compare your copy to the text and make any needed corrections.

Copy or write as your teacher dictates from *The Cabin Faced West*, page 30, paragraphs 4 and 5 ("Doesn't believe in planting...").

Copy or write as your teacher dictates from *Justin Morgan Had a Horse*, page 39, paragraphs 1 and 2 ("Man and boy...").

Choose one additional paragraph from today's assignment in *Justin Morgan Had a Horse* to write from dictation.

B. Reader *Language Skills, History*

The Cabin Faced West: page 29 (Chapter 3) through the top of page 34
Justin Morgan Had a Horse: page 39 (Chapter 4) through page 45, paragraph 4

Read the above assignment from *The Cabin Faced West* aloud, and then follow along as someone else reads the assignment from *Justin Morgan Had a Horse*.

Read the above assignment from *The Cabin Faced West* silently, and then read the assignment from *Justin Morgan Had a Horse* aloud.

Read the above assignments from *The Cabin Faced West* and *Justin Morgan Had a Horse* silently.

Teaching Tip

If your child needs help remembering specific information from the reading, take a piece of blank paper and fold it in half, and then fold it in thirds. This will create a paper with six boxes. Before reading, have your child write a word in each box, such as who, what, when, where, why, and how. After listening and choosing the event to describe, have your child fill in the boxes with brief descriptions to support retelling. You can use this tool for many types of note taking.

C. Read-Aloud & Discussion

Language Skills, History, Thinking Skills

Francis Scott Key: page 18, paragraph 2 ("Whenever...") through the top of page 23

Read over the following questions that you will discuss later. Then read, or listen carefully as your teacher reads, the above assignment from *Francis Scott Key* aloud. You may want to take notes to help answer the questions after you listen. If needed, you can look back at the story to find specific details.

Pretend you are a news reporter and choose an event that you heard or read about today. Think about what you know from the story, and in your own words answer the following questions about that event:

- What took place?
- When did it take place?
- Where did it take place?
- Who were the main people involved?
- How does this event affect Francis Scott Key's life?
- Why do you think it took place?

Choose a second event to report on using the questions listed above.

Tell how the two events you reported on are related.

D. If you or your child would like to add a greater degree of difficulty to spelling lessons, choose words from the Challenge Spelling List (in Appendix A) for the lesson you are on. The words on this list are taken from the literature being read.

D. Spelling

Language Skills, Thinking Skills

Look at the list of words below, and copy each one onto an index card. Then look back at Lesson 1, Part 1 for ideas about how to organize the words, and ways to remember their spelling. Show your teacher how you organized them.

Turn your cards face down and listen as your teacher dictates the words on your spelling list. Spell each word the best that you can, either aloud or by writing it in your Student Notebook. Your teacher may add up to five words that are difficult for you to read or write.

neighbor	medicine	emergency	impatient
important	loneliness	potatoes	stomach
fatigues	interfere	sufficient	junction
cautiously	desperately	nervously	vigorously

E. History

Geography, Thinking Skills

The second method of nation building, or growing in size, was to purchase land. Since America was a young country, and certainly not wealthy yet, the idea of purchasing large amounts of land was not an obvious way for the country to grow. Circumstances had to be just

right for this to happen, and it turns out that in this case they were. Events in history connect, which means that what one group of people does affects the other people around them. This was true for the United States and France, and the Louisiana Territory.

Was this agreement the beginning of America's relationship with the people of France? No, the people of France had come to North America many years before. Look at the map entitled "European Exploration of North America" in your *United States History Atlas.* Trace the voyages of the French explorers who came to the New World. They were the first explorers from Europe to travel down the Mississippi River from the area of the Great Lakes to the Gulf of Mexico.

E. After the lesson's end (maybe when Dad comes home) ask your child to use the models he has made and explain what he learned to someone not present at the lesson. Listen as he shares to find out what he has learned, and areas you may need to reinforce in the next lesson. You can encourage your child by restating what he says, just to clarify it for your understanding and his. This is an excellent way to review a lesson, and allow your child to share what he learned in his own words. Using the objects from the lesson provides additional support for memory and sharing.

This exploration led to the establishment of many French military bases and **outposts**, or settlements on the frontier, in what came to be the United States and Canada. As you learned in Unit 1, the French and many tribes of Indians fought against the English in the French and Indian War. They fought to protect their rights to hunt, trap, and take lumber and other natural resources from the land in this territory to sell. After that long war, the boundaries were changed and the English took over much of the land that the French had controlled. This territory was part of the land the United States received from England in the Treaty of Paris.

The people of France had been at war with England for many years, so when Americans began to fight the English for independence, the French became their **allies**, or friends, in that fight. American ambassadors signed the Treaty of Paris, ending the Revolutionary War, in the capital city of France because of their friendship with the French people. Even so, it made President Thomas Jefferson uncomfortable to have France control large sections of land along the United States' border. There was also the question of who controlled the port city of New Orleans. This was an important port because it was the ending place of the Mississippi River. Whoever controlled that port also controlled access to the border of the United States. Look at the map entitled "Louisiana Purchase and Western Exploration, 1804-1807" in your *United States History Atlas.* The area shaded in green belonged to France.

President Jefferson wanted the port and the Mississippi River available for Americans to use, so he sent **envoys**, or diplomats acting for the government of the United States, to meet with Napoleon, who was the leader of France. He wanted these envoys to try to purchase the port city of New Orleans from France, so that travel on the Mississippi River would be safe for Americans. During this time, Napoleon was fighting his own war with England and needed money to buy supplies for his troops, so he offered the American envoys a surprising deal. He offered to sell them all of the territory held by France in the United States. What an opportunity! Even though it was more than President Jefferson wanted to spend, the envoys felt the offer was too good to pass up, so they said yes. The two governments agreed to a treaty, or agreement for the sale of the land. Even though this deal did not make everyone happy in the United States Senate, after much discussion the senators approved the sale. In one day, the size of the United States increased by 828,000 square miles through the Louisiana Purchase, which cost America fifteen million dollars.

As the United States grew, even more people wanted to come here to live. Many of the people who already lived here still wanted to own their own land, so settlers moved to the new lands added by the Louisiana Purchase. Think of the literature you have read so far. Now think of some of the struggles faced by settlers. In your Student Notebook, make a list of some difficulties faced by settlers in your literature. Then answer this question with a complete sentence: Did they think the results were worth the struggles? Remember to begin your answer with "Yes, they thought it was worth it because…", or "No, they did not think it was worth it because…". Then tell why you gave that answer.

Today you will continue working on the map overlay you began in Lesson 1. To get started, look again at the map in your *United States History Atlas* entitled "Growth of the United States to 1853," and find the area that shows the Louisiana Purchase. Now use a wet erase marker to draw the western boundary of that area directly onto the left overlay. You may cross over on the right transparency sheet if needed. Use the state borders to decide where your lines should go and remember, it doesn't have to be perfect—just do your best! Remember, if you make a mistake you can erase with a damp paper towel or sponge and try again. When you are finished, color and label the Louisiana Purchase on the map overlay.

On the PlaceMap, you can see the names of the states and their borders as they are today. In your Student Notebook, name the current state that expanded, or grew larger, by the Louisiana Purchase.[1]

Look at the map again. Now make a list of current states that were established on land that was added to the United States by the Louisiana Purchase.[2]

Look at the map. How much of an increase in the size of America did the Louisiana Purchase bring about? Do this by estimating.[3]

This was a very bold decision by President Jefferson. Once the United States had acquired so much new land through the Louisiana Purchase, there was much to do. President Jefferson wanted information about the new territory, partly to help settlers as they moved westward. To get this information, he sent Meriwether Lewis and William Clark to explore this huge wilderness and beyond. If you used *Paths of Exploration*, look back at the unit about Lewis and Clark's journey, as well as the Student Notebook pages you completed. If you did not use *Paths of Exploration*, you might want to find out more about this famous expedition at the library or on the Internet. You can see the route of this expedition on the "Louisiana Purchase and Western Exploration 1804-1807" map in the *United States History Atlas.*

Pretend you are a settler, and think of at least four reasons to move into the Louisiana territory immediately, and four reasons to wait before you move. Fill in the chart in your Student Notebook with the pros (or reasons to do something) and the cons (the reasons not to do something). At the bottom of the chart, tell which list you think is more convincing to you. Be sure to use a complete sentence.

Choose one of the following statements to support. Then write at least one paragraph that makes a case for your decision. Use the statement as your main idea, or topic sentence. Give at least four examples that support your topic sentence. They can be the same reasons you gave on the chart in your Student Notebook. When you write the reasons in this paragraph, make it more like a conversation than a list by adding how you feel about some of the statements. Here is an example:

I would not want to move to the new lands immediately because there were many Indians that still thought the land belonged to them. It would be terrible to worry every day about angry Indians attacking us!

1) I would want to move to the new lands that were part of the Louisiana Purchase immediately because:

2) I would not want to move to the new lands that were part of the Louisiana Purchase immediately because:

F. States

Geography, History, Thinking Skills

In your *United States Atlas*, read the pages about West Virginia. When you are finished, find the blank map of West Virginia in your Student Notebook and complete the following assignments:

- Place a small red star on the spot where Charleston is located, and label it. Charleston is the capital city of West Virginia.

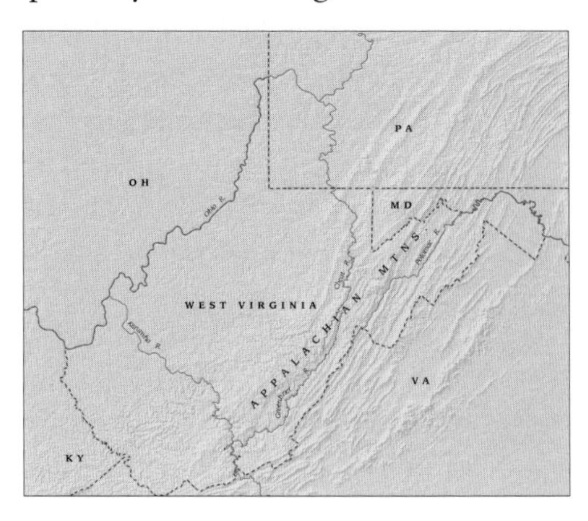

- Color the lines showing the Ohio, Potomac, Cheat, and Greenbrier Rivers blue, and label them.
- Lightly color the area where the Appalachian Mountains are located with a purple crayon, marker, or colored pencil, and label them.

- Color the line showing the Kanawha River blue, and label it.
- Label the five states that border West Virginia.

Connect Learning to Life

Games are a great way to learn about a culture. Often they are a reflection of the time and natural resources available, as well as what was interesting or popular at the time. Like food, the things enjoyed by a group of people helps connect us to the events and people of history.

G. Doing

Music, Thinking Skills

Look at the song entitled "Erie Canal" in your *Wee Sing America* songbook, and read any historical notes about it that may be in the book. Like "Blow the Man Down," this song was also sung by men as they were working. Now listen to it on the *Wee Sing America* CD. Try to become familiar with the words and music so that you can sing along, or learn to play it on an instrument of your choice. You may want to recite, sing, or play this song during your presentation at the end of this unit.

The game of pick-up sticks, sometimes called Jackstraws, has been played in America from the earliest days of settlement. There are several stories about where this game came from—some say it began with the Native Americans, and some say it was brought from Europe. But the games always involve thin sticks (made of wood, straw, or other materials) that are painted or marked for scoring.

Follow the directions in Appendix B to make your own set of pick-up sticks. Then read the rules of the game and play it with your family.

H. Independent Reading

Language Skills

Choose something to read that you will enjoy. Then, find a quiet, comfortable place and read for the following length of time:

25 minutes 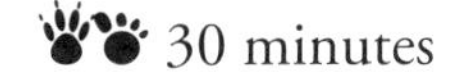 30 minutes

Be sure to write down what you read today on the Reading Log in your Student Notebook.

Lesson 2, Part 2

A. Quotation Notebook *History, Language Skills, Music*

Continue copying verses from the American National Anthem, "The Star Spangled Banner." As you examine this song, consider the imagery created by the words. Since it is also a poem, consider its rhyme pattern as well.

> And the rockets' red glare, the bombs bursting in air,
> Gave proof through the night that our flag was still there.

Copy the above passage into your Student Notebook, and talk with your teacher about its meaning and any unknown words. Then listen to it on the *Wee Sing America* CD and follow along with the words in the songbook. Practice reading or singing each section of the song aloud.

Under each phrase printed in your Student Notebook, draw a picture or write an explanation that describes the image it creates in your mind.

Choose two words from the verse and write at least one synonym for each one. Make sure you find a meaning that goes with its context, or use in the verse.

A. The words spoken by a person in a speech, or a copy of an original document, are both considered **primary sources.** That means they did not come from a third person, but directly from the original source. Primary sources give you a unique look at history because you can judge it for yourself, rather than seeing or hearing it through the thinking of someone else.

B. Reader *Language Skills, History*

The Cabin Faced West: page 34, paragraph 1 ("Her apron…") through page 38

Justin Morgan Had a Horse: page 45, paragraph 5 ("Master Morgan bent…") through page 51, paragraph 3

Read the above assignment from *The Cabin Faced West* aloud, and then follow along as someone else reads the assignment from *Justin Morgan Had a Horse.*

Read the above assignment from *The Cabin Faced West* silently, and then read the assignment from *Justin Morgan Had a Horse* aloud.

Read the above assignments from *The Cabin Faced West* and *Justin Morgan Had a Horse* silently.

C. **Read-Aloud & Narration** *Language Skills, History, Thinking Skills*

Francis Scott Key: page 23, paragraph 1 ("Maybe it was…") through page 27, paragraph 3

Follow the instructions below for your level. Then, in your own words, tell what happened in the story from Francis' point of view, or pretend you are Francis and tell what you think happened. Try to remember as many details as possible. You may reread the passage or listen as your teacher rereads the part you are to retell.

Listen carefully as your teacher reads the above assignment from *Francis Scott Key* aloud.

Read the above assignment from *Francis Scott Key* aloud.

D. **Editing** *Language Skills, Thinking Skills*

Continue your practice to become a good writing mechanic by looking at the rules about hyphens, apostrophes, and pronouns in the toolkit below. Not every rule is included, but this is a good start. Check a grammar handbook, a dictionary, or spell check on the computer if you are not sure how to use the rules when writing.

Mechanics Toolkit

1A - A pronoun for more than one person or thing can be the subject of a sentence.

We like ice cream. You will be my friends.
They are my favorite presents.

2A - Use an apostrophe (') to show that something belongs to someone.

That is Ann's book.
Bob's game is on the table

3A - Use a hyphen (-) to make a describing word, or adjective, that comes before a naming word, or noun.

Sue really likes her new tie-dyed shirt.
Her mother is a big-hearted person.

Practice these skills by correcting the sentences in your Student Notebook.[4] The number of errors in each sentence is listed after the sentence in parentheses. To show that a letter needs to be capitalized, make three lines (≡) underneath the letter that should be capitalized. To replace an incorrect word with a correct word, draw a line through the incorrect word and write the correct word above it. Add any needed punctuation.

E. Science *Geography, Thinking Skills, Art*

The most noticeable feature of the oceans is their water, which covers about ⅔ of the earth.

Ocean water is very different from most water found on land, because it is made up of many gases and solids dissolved in pure water. Of course, you probably already know that the main thing dissolved in ocean water is salt. But in addition to salt, it also contains tiny amounts of over 80 of the elements you looked at on the Periodic Table of Elements in Unit 2.

Scientists don't fully understand why the oceans are so salty, but they do know three things that help. The first is underwater volcanoes, which you will learn more about in another lesson. However, when this type of volcano erupts, gases and melted rock spill out. Both of these things contain salts and minerals that dissolve in the surrounding ocean water.

The second thing that deposits salt in the ocean is land erosion. **Erosion** is similar to weathering, which you learned about in Unit 1, but it is a separate process. Weathering breaks down the rocks and minerals, and erosion moves them from one place to another. Five things cause erosion to happen—gravity, wind, running water, ice, and waves—and all of them help move **sediment**, or weathered materials, into the ocean. This sediment contains salts and other elements that dissolve in the water.

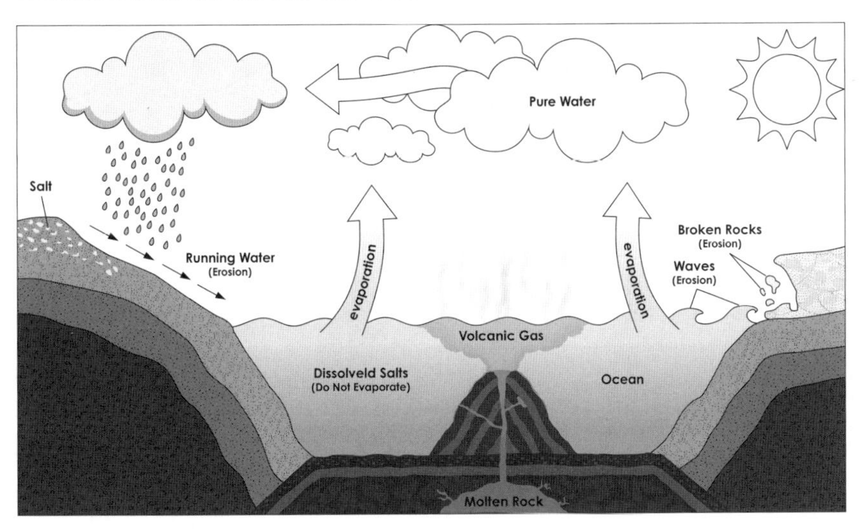

The third process that helps make the ocean salty does not deposit more salt like the other two. Instead, it removes water, and makes the remaining salt more concentrated. This process is the water cycle, which you learned about in Unit 2. Even though you can't drink salty water, the ocean is still a very important part of the water cycle. This is because most of the evaporation in the water cycle occurs over the oceans. Since dissolved salt and other elements do not evaporate,

From Dr. Beechick

"There are major big ideas in science for students to be acquainted with and to use in their thinking. Learning big ideas like these is not accomplished by simple vocabulary lessons of memorizing definitions and writing a sentence for each word. Probably the best learning activity is conversation. Talk about these ideas with your children. Then have them read more in science books, and talk again. Continue this "read and talk" plan with occasional writing assignments added. Children can write paragraphs explaining in their own words things they have read about—how the water cycle works, how it might have worked differently before the Flood, how dinosaurs came to be mostly extinct or how they might have some small-sized descendants yet today."

– *You Can Teach Your Child Successfully,* pages 332-333

only pure water rises into the air, forms clouds, and eventually falls back to earth as rain. As you learned from the experiment in Unit 2, Lesson2, the salt and minerals are left behind in the ocean.

Discuss the above chart with your teacher. See if you can identify and explain each of the three things that scientists know help make ocean water salty. Then use this chart as a model to label the one in your Student Notebook. When you are finished, write two or three sentences that explain each process on the following page.

Discuss weathering and erosion with your teacher, and then write one or two sentences in your Student Notebook that describe the difference between the two processes.

Continue working on your 3-D map by adding salt dough to the land areas you started in the last lesson, until they are 1½ inches high. Blend the outside edges downward so that the new layer of dough will stick well. Remember—it doesn't have to be perfect! Whenever necessary, use the salt dough recipe to make more dough.

When you are finished, with your parent's permission, put your 3-D map in an oven that is heated to 150°. Then, with your parent's help, remove it carefully after an hour and store it in a safe place for the next couple of days.

F. States *Geography, Thinking Skills, History, Drawing*

Look again at the pages about West Virginia in your *United States Atlas*. Then find the State Page in your Student Notebook, and fill in the information.

Make State Cards for West Virginia by following the instructions found in Appendix B. West Virginia is a Southern state, so be sure to outline the cards in purple.

G. Interactive Writing *Language Skills, Thinking Skills*

Complete this writing activity with your partner.

Choose an article from a newspaper, news magazine, or online news source that relates to a current event in local, state or national government. Then ask your partner to read the article and answer the following questions in your Student Notebook:

Do you agree with the article; why or why not?
What do you think should happen in the future regarding this issue?

Tell about the news story using the number sentences indicated below. Then tell what you think about what your partner wrote. Write several sentences in reply, including whether or not you agree with your partner, and why. End with a question for your partner.

G. After completing the interactive writing assignment, you may want to continue the conversation. Since your child has had a chance to think about the topic, he may feel more equipped to carry on a conversation that includes other friends or family. If your child is shy, you may want to get his permission before bringing the topic up in front of others.

at least four sentences

at least five sentences

Tell about the news story with at least one paragraph. Then tell what you think about what your partner wrote with a second paragraph.

Remember that a paragraph is a group of sentences that relate to one topic, or main idea. State the topic or main idea of the paragraph at or near the beginning of the paragraph. You do not want the reader to read your paragraph for very long without knowing for sure what you think!

H. **Independent Reading** *Language Skills*

Choose something to read that you will enjoy. Then, find a quiet, comfortable place and read for the following length of time:

25 minutes 30 minutes

Be sure to write down what you read today on the Reading Log in your Student Notebook.

Connect Learning to Life

The most powerful influence on your children is your behavior. If you want your children to value reading, make sure they see you reading! If you read for fun, read to find information, or read as part of your spiritual life, you help make reading a natural part of your children's future.

Lesson 2, Part 3

A. **Copywork & Dictation** *Language Skills, Thinking Skills*

Look carefully at your assigned passage below, and read it silently. Show your teacher any words you don't know, and practice saying them aloud. Now read the passage aloud, or ask your teacher to read it to you.

When you are finished copying or writing from dictation, compare your copy to the text and make any needed corrections.

Copy or write as your teacher dictates from *The Cabin Faced West*, page 39, paragraphs 3 and 4 ("But you don't want to…").

Copy or write as your teacher dictates from *Justin Morgan Had a Horse*, page 53, paragraphs 4 and 6 ("Thank you, Joel…").

Choose one additional paragraph from today's assignment in *Justin Morgan Had a Horse* to write from dictation.

A. The dictation method enables your child to hear language and correctly write down what he hears. It involves building two different skills. First, the ability to listen and understand what is heard, and second, the ability to transfer what is heard into written language. This process takes time and practice, so begin as gradually as needed for successfully reaching the goal of getting the words the child hears on the paper correctly.

1. Read the whole passage, then reread one sentence at a time, giving your child time to write what he hears.

2. After he has finished, reread the passage again, allowing him to double check what he has written.

3. After steps 1 and 2, ask him to compare his writing to the model. As his skill builds, you can move more quickly through the steps, maintaining your child's level of success.

B. **Reader** *Language Skills, History*

The Cabin Faced West: page 39 ("Andy dropped…") through the top of page 44

Justin Morgan Had a Horse: page 51, paragraph 4 ("The schoolmaster…") through page 56

Read the above assignment from *The Cabin Faced West* aloud, and then follow along as someone else reads the assignment from *Justin Morgan Had a Horse.*

Read the above assignment from *The Cabin Faced West* silently, and then read the assignment from *Justin Morgan Had a Horse* aloud.

Read the above assignments from *The Cabin Faced West* and *Justin Morgan Had a Horse* silently.

C. Explain to your students that the value of making predictions about the stories you are reading or listening to doesn't depend on getting it right. There is great value in taking the information you have, coming up with an idea of what will take place, and then testing that idea. If you are not correct, you may learn more than if you were correct. You have gained new information about a character or events. This is clarification, or making something clearer. Encourage your children not to be overly concerned about always predicting correctly. Help them to welcome the opportunity to clarify their understanding.

C. Read-Aloud & Discussion

Language Skills, History, Thinking Skills

Francis Scott Key: page 27, paragraph 4 ("As the general…") through the top of page 32

Follow the directions below to read or listen to the above assignment from *Francis Scott Key.* Then make up the assigned number of questions about the part of the story you just read or heard. Write down your questions and ask your teacher to answer them. After discussing her thoughts, write down the best possible answer in your Student Notebook. Be sure to use complete sentences.

When you are finished, look back at the prediction or predictions you made during Lesson 1, Part 4. Were you able to predict what would happen? Be sure to mark the "Came to Pass" box for each prediction when it does happen.

Listen carefully as your teacher reads the above assignment from *Francis Scott Key.*

Make up one question. Make up two questions.

Read the above assignment from *Francis Scott Key* aloud; then make up three questions.

D. Dividing a word into syllables is another way for a child to connect to spelling and meaning. Remind your child that a syllable usually has a vowel sound. When you divide a word into syllables, make sure each syllable has a vowel sound.

D. Vocabulary & Spelling

Language Skills, Thinking Skills

Vocabulary:
Write each vocabulary word on an index card, and use a thesaurus to find a synonym for it. If you cannot find a synonym, use a dictionary to look up the meaning of the word. Then, on the back of each card, draw a picture or write a clue so you can remember how each word was used in the story. Write a *D* or *S* by your clue to tell whether you wrote a definition or synonym.

quirked **swagger** **jutted** **hardship**
conspirators

grudging **tomfoolery** **apprentice** **doleful**
gentle (having to do with animals)

Spelling:
Look at the list of words on your Student Notebook page, and divide each one into syllables by drawing a slash line (/) between

the syllables. After you have marked each word, use a dictionary to check your work.[5] If you don't know what the word means, read the definition while you are checking your syllable markings. Then place a check next to each word to show that you know what the word means.

Look at the spelling word cards you made in Part 1. Read each word, and then cover it with your hand and try to spell it aloud. Then uncover it and see if you were correct. Review the meanings of any words that you do not remember.

E. **History** *Language Skills, Thinking Skills*

Presidential Focus: Continue your study of American presidents by reading the U.S. Presidents Flash Cards about Thomas Jefferson and James Madison. Use the things you learn to fill out the Presidential Focus page in your Student Notebook.

E. As your child learns to take notes, it may be helpful to stop the video at intervals and discuss what has happened or been said. Ask questions that will help him understand the important parts of what he has seen or heard.

Together with your teacher, watch Episode 3, Chapter 8 on the *Discovering America's Founders* DVD that is about Noah Webster. Noah wrote the first American dictionary. Before you begin though, take a minute to look at the Video Profile page for this lesson in your Student Notebook, and see what kinds of questions it asks.[6]

As you watch the video lesson, keep the Video Profile page in front of you. When you notice that the narrator, or person telling the story, is answering one of the questions, stop the video long enough to write the answer on your Profile page. Continue doing this as often as necessary as you finish watching the video lesson.

As you watch the video lesson, use a piece of scrap paper to jot down important things that the narrator, or person telling the story, says about Noah. This is called taking notes, and is a good way to help you remember what you hear or see. You do not need to use sentences when you take notes—single words or phrases, which are short groups of words, will work fine as long as they help you remember the important things. If it is helpful, stop the lesson when you need to, or watch it a second time.

When you are finished, use your notes and your memory to fill in the Video Profile page.

From Dr. Beechick

"Also use maps frequently in studies of history, missionaries, and current events. maps are sometimes thought of as visual aids that help to make a Bible story or other learning "come alive," but the reverse is more probably true: the story helps to make a spot on the map come alive. In any case, map reading is complex and children need repeated practice with maps during their school years."

– *You Can Teach Your Child Successfully*, page 27

F. States
Geography, History, Thinking Skills

In your book, *The Cabin Faced West*, the Hamilton family had recently moved from a well-established town in Pennsylvania to the wilderness of Ohio. Ohio is the first state you will learn about in the Midwest Region of the United States.

In your *United States Atlas*, read the pages about Ohio. When you are finished, find the blank map of Ohio in your Student Notebook and complete the following assignments:

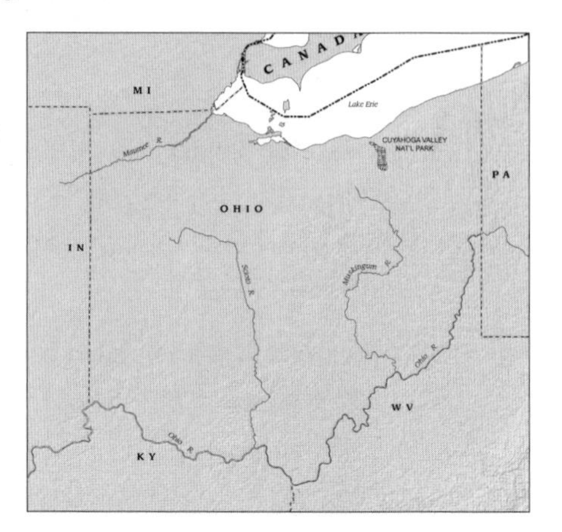

- Place a small red star on the spot where Columbus is located, and label it. Columbus is the capital city of Ohio.
- Color the lines showing the Ohio, Scioto, Muskingum, and Maumee Rivers blue, and label them.
- Color and label the portion of Lake Erie that borders Ohio.
- Color and label the area where Cuyahoga Valley National Park is located.
- Label the five states that border Ohio.

G. Cooking
Language Skills, Thinking Skills, Drawing

With your parent's permission and supervision, look in *Eat Your Way Through the USA*, choose a recipe that comes from either West Virginia or Ohio, and prepare it for your family. After everyone has had a taste, find out who liked it, and whether anyone would like to have it again. What did you think about it?

In your Student Notebook, draw a picture of the dish you chose to make and write the following number of sentences about your family's reaction to it:

2 sentences   3 sentences   4 sentences

H. Independent Reading
Language Skills

Choose something to read that you will enjoy. Then, find a quiet, comfortable place and read for the following length of time:

25 minutes   30 minutes

Be sure to write down what you read today on the Reading Log in your Student Notebook.

Lesson 2, Part 4

A. Quotation Notebook *History, Language Skills, Music*

Continue copying verses from the American National Anthem, "The Star Spangled Banner." As you examine this song, consider the imagery created by the words. Since it is also a poem, consider its rhyme pattern as well.

O say, does that Star Spangled Banner yet wave
O'er the land of the free and the home of the brave?

Copy the above passage into your Student Notebook, and talk with your teacher about its meaning and any unknown words. Then listen to it on the *Wee Sing America* CD and follow along with the words in the songbook. Practice reading or singing each section of the song aloud.

Under each phrase printed in your Student Notebook, draw a picture or write an explanation that describes the image it creates in your mind.

Choose two words from the verse and write at least one synonym for each one. Make sure you find a meaning that goes with its context, or use in the verse.

"Have you noticed that when you look up a word in the dictionary or find a place in an atlas, that you found something else of interest? Maybe while locating the Bering Sea in the classroom atlas you've noticed Alaska is farther west than Hawaii. Not only that, but a part of Alaska's Aleutian Islands actually cross the International Date Line. You found what you were looking for—the Bering Sea—but like osmosis, other bits of information absorbed into your brain without any effort on your part!"

--*The Ultimate Geography and Timeline Guide*, page 3

B. Reader *Language Skills, History*

The Cabin Faced West: page 44, paragraph 1 ("Ann started…") through mid-page 49
Justin Morgan Had a Horse: page 57 ("Hmmmm! . .") through page 62

Read the above assignment from *The Cabin Faced West* aloud, and then follow along as someone else reads the assignment from *Justin Morgan Had a Horse*.

Read the above assignment from *The Cabin Faced West* silently, and then read the assignment from *Justin Morgan Had a Horse* aloud.

Read the above assignments from *The Cabin Faced West* and *Justin Morgan Had a Horse* silently.

Teaching Tip

Since many children are reading the assignments silently, it would be good to occasionally ask your student to tell you about what he read. You may also want him to choose his favorite part of the passage and read it aloud to you. If he finds a part that is particularly dramatic or funny, ask him to read it for you expressively. If anything happens in the story that he dislikes, ask him to make sure and tell you about it, too. These are small, natural ways to do comprehension checks.

C. Read-Aloud & Narration *Language Skills, History, Thinking Skills*

Francis Scott Key: page 32, paragraph 1 ("Growing boys…") through page 35

After reading or listening to the read-aloud assignment, talk with your teacher and try to predict what will happen in the future based on what you know of the characters and events. Write down your predictions in your Student Notebook. Later you will look back and see if they were accurate. Try not to peek ahead!

Listen carefully as your teacher reads the above assignment from *Francis Scott Key* aloud. Then write down something that you think will happen in the story.

Write down another thing that you think will happen in the story.

Read the above assignment from *Francis Scott Key* aloud. Then write down three things that you think will happen in the story.

D. **Editing** *Language Skills, Thinking Skills*

Reread the Mechanics Toolkit from Part 2 of this lesson. Be the teacher and tell what each skill means and how it is used.

Use your readers to find two examples of each rule, and either show them to your teacher or write them in your Student Notebook.

Use your readers to find four examples of each rule, and either show them to your teacher or write them in your Student Notebook.

E. **Science** *Geography, Thinking Skills, Art*

The edge of a body of water, where it meets the land, is its **shoreline**. Look again at your globe or a map of the world and notice all the ocean shorelines. It looks as though the continents simply end—are cut off—at their ocean shorelines. But that isn't the case at all. In fact, continents extend into the water for many miles in some places beyond their shorelines. This part of a continent that continues outward under the water is called the **continental shelf**.

Teaching Tip

The unified approach to learning takes every opportunity to connect topics like science, history, and geography using activities and discussion. In this way, children come to view learning as an activity without subject boundaries. Doesn't that seem more like real life?

Not only are continental shelves excellent fishing areas, but in many places they are also rich in oil and gas. One of the United States that has large oil deposits off its coast is Louisiana, which you studied in the last lesson. Valuable minerals like cobalt, gold, and diamonds can also be found on some parts of the continental shelf and beyond, but they are very difficult and expensive to mine.

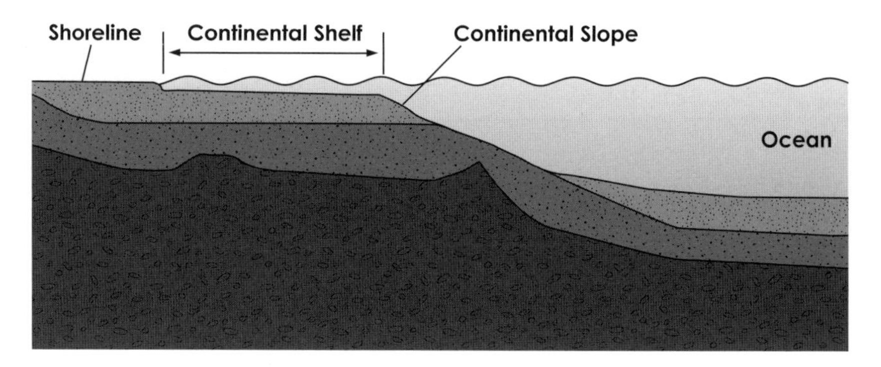

A continental shelf slants downward slightly to its edge, and then it drops steeply to the ocean floor. This drop is the **continental slope**, and marks the actual boundary of the continent. Continental slopes look a lot like cliffs, and in the deepest parts of the ocean they may drop more than six miles. The next time you are traveling someplace in your family's car, ask your parent to help you see how far six miles is. On your map, the drop of the continental slope represents about three miles. In the actual ocean, sometimes it is less than that, and sometimes it is more.

Discuss the continental shelf and continental slope with your teacher. Then, in your Student Notebook list three things you have learned about each one. When you are finished, begin building these features on your 3-D map.

To do that, use a spatula or your hands to place salt dough in the areas you outlined around North America and Cuba to show the continental shelf. The area around Puerto Rico shown on your map only has a small portion of continental shelf. That is because it is right next to the Puerto Rico Trench, which is one of the deepest parts of the ocean.

Notice that the continental shelf is very narrow in some places, and wide in others. Build this new feature on your map the same way you did the land masses. Make sure the salt dough you add is about ¾ inch high and that it touches the sides of the land masses. Push or trim the edges with a dinner knife or popsicle stick so that your salt-dough continental shelf does not spill over its outline.

On the map-model in Appendix B, notice where the Appalachian Mountains are located. Use a pencil to lightly mark that area on your continent. Then roll a "snake" out of salt dough that is about ½-inch thick and 6-inches long, and place it in the middle of the area you marked. Push and blend the bottom edges into the continent and pinch the dough along the top to make peaks. Add one or two smaller salt-dough snakes to the edges to fill up the whole area occupied by the Appalachian Mountains. Be sure to blend their bottoms and peak their tops. Most of your mountains should be a little over ¼-inch high, but the highest ones might be as tall as ½-inch.

With your parent's permission, put your 3-D map in an oven that is heated to 150°. Then, with your parent's help, remove it carefully after an hour and store it in a safe place for the next couple of days. Remember—every time you add salt dough to your map, it will become heavier. If you need help putting it in or taking it out of the oven, be sure to ask. You don't want to accidentally drop your hard work!

F. States *Geography, Thinking Skills, History, Drawing*

Look again at the pages about Ohio in your *United States Atlas*. Then find the State Page in your Student Notebook, and fill in the information.

Make State Cards for Ohio by following the instructions found in Appendix B. Ohio is a Midwestern state, so be sure to outline the cards in red.

Connect Learning to Life

Many families create newsletters to share with family and friends. You may want to take this opportunity to encourage your children to use their writing skills to help create the family newsletter. Family members who live far away treasure journal entries and news stories written about family events. It is a great way to give purpose to a school time activity!

G. **Writing** *Language Skills, Thinking Skills*

Journaling is one way to keep a record of thoughts or events. Leaders often kept journals so they could accurately share with others the events they experienced and their thoughts about those events. Journal writing is often just brief thoughts, so it can look different from writing in stories. Today's journal activity will focus on facts or events, and opinions about them. Review Lesson 1, Part 4 and tell your teacher the difference between a fact and an opinion.

Write a journal entry telling about your day yesterday or about the Doing activity you did in Lesson 2, Part 1. Follow the guidelines below. Ask someone to read your journal entry and retell what you did. Listen to see if he or she accurately understood what you did and how you felt about it.

- Write about three facts or events, and give at least one opinion about each fact.
- Write about three facts or events, and give at least two opinions about each fact.
- Write about four facts or events, and give at least two opinions about each fact.

H. **Independent Reading** *Language Skills*

Choose something to read that you will enjoy. Then, find a quiet, comfortable place and read for the following length of time:

25 minutes 30 minutes

Be sure to write down what you read today on the Reading Log in your Student Notebook.

Lesson 2, Part 5

This part is set aside for completion of any work left undone from the lesson, and review of concepts and content. It is also a time to expand the work of the lesson with art, mapping, or games.

- Review the Steps for Thinking found in Part 1.
- Give your teacher your stack of vocabulary cards for the lesson. As she shows you each word, tell her the meaning of the word and how it was used in the story.

The best way to learn vocabulary is in the context of meaning. It is easier to remember words as they relate to a story than it is to remember them in isolation. From time to time, ask your children to take out a stack of vocabulary cards from a past unit, play teacher, and review the words for you!

- Listen as your teacher reads the words that you studied from Part 1. Write each word in your Student Notebook as she dictates it. When you are finished, look back at your spelling word cards and make corrections as needed. Show your teacher how you did.
- Use the United States map that is near the front of your *Atlas of the United States* to find West Virginia and Ohio. Then, on the large outline map of the U.S., draw a purple line around West Virginia because it is a Southern state, and a red line around Ohio because it is a Midwestern state. Write in the names of the states, and draw small stars where their capital cities are located. Next to the stars, write the name of each capital city.

  Add to the legend you are making on your outline map by drawing a short red line under the purple one. Next to it write *Midwestern.*

Color-coding State Cards gives children another way to retain information. The visual reminder of the states with that color border helps them remember the group to which they belong. As they develop the legend, they are reinforcing the categorization of the states in each group.

- In your *Klutz Watercolor Book,* look at page 37 which is entitled "Black and White Oddscapes." This page gives you a chance to see how interesting painting with only black can be. Experiment with some of the techniques you have learned, like washes, smears, and splatters.

  When you are finished, complete the activities on pages 38 and 39. Remember to have fun as you populate your zoo!
- Use your USA Activity CD to print at least one activity for the states you studied in this lesson. Then add any that you complete to your Student Notebook.
- Complete the Nation Building Word Scramble located in your Student Notebook.[7]

Teaching Tip

Word Scrambles are a fun way to reinforce the recognition and spelling of words that are important to learn. After your children complete this Word Scramble, encourage them to make their own. Ask them to share these with each other, with friends, or with you. Remember, these activities are models for you and your children to make your own as well!

Enrichment Activities

1. Learn about Napoleon's role in France's history. Read about him on the Internet or at the library. Tell your teacher what his role was in the Louisiana Purchase. Then give him a thumbs-up or thumbs-down as a leader, and tell your teacher why you voted that way.
2. At the library or on the Internet research a Native American tribe from the Southern or Midwestern regions of the United States. If you do not yet have a tribe in mind that you would like to find out more about, choose one from the map entitled "Native American Nations, c. 1750" in your *United States History Atlas.* Print a Native American Profile sheet from your Student Resources CD and fill it out.

   Place the new profile sheet and picture in your Native American Notebook, or add them to your Student Notebook.

3. Although some First Ladies are more well-known than others, each was an important part of her husband's presidency. At the library or on the Internet, find out at least three facts about the First Ladies who shared the White House with the U.S. Presidents you studied in this lesson. Add your research to your Student Notebook.

Additional Resources

Lewis and Clark Hands On Activities, by Sharon Jeffus

Sacagawea: American Pathfinder (Childhood of Famous Americans), by Flora Warren Seymour

Meriwether Lewis: Off the Edge of the Map (Heroes of History), by Janet and Geoff Benge

If you read any of the above books, be sure to print a Book Review page from your Student Resources CD, fill it out, and place it in your Student Notebook.

Answers

1. Minnesota

2. Iowa, Missouri, Arkansas, Louisiana, Oklahoma, Kansas, Colorado, Nebraska, South Dakota, North Dakota, Montana, and Wyoming

3. It looks like the United States doubled in size due to the Louisiana Purchase.

4. 1. Did Ann's family work hard on Hamilton Hill?
   2. Joel could hear the far-off sound of Little Bub's high whinny.
   3. They brought Ebenezer and Little Bub back to Vermont.
   4. Ann's new-smelling baby brother was named Johnny.
   5. We were happy to arrive at the house of Master Morgan's sister, Eunice.
   6. Did Frank enjoy spending time at Uncle Philip's house in Annapolis?
   7. Did Horse-Trader Hawkes eye Little Bub for Master Morgan?
   8. Squire Key was a well-respected man at St. John's School.
   9. They were Ann's dearest possessions brought from Gettysburg.

5. neigh/bor, med/i/cine, e/mer/gen/cy, im/pa/tient, im/por/tant, lone/li/ness, po/ta/toes, stom/ach
   fa/tigues, in/ter/fere, suf/fi/cient, junc/tion
   cau/tious/ly, des/per/ate/ly, nerv/ous/ly, vig/or/ous/ly

6. Answers are in Appendix A.

7. Answers are in Appendix A.

Lesson 3, Part 1

Steps for Thinking

1. Wisdom, or knowledge and experience, was an equally important part of building the nation.
2. Wisdom passed from parent to child, from elders within communities or families, from teacher to students, or ministers to congregations.
3. Demonstrating wisdom was an important part of building strong families, which helped build the nation.

Materials

- *The Cabin Faced West*
- *Justin Morgan Had a Horse*
- *Francis Scott Key*
- *Eat Your Way Through the USA*
- *Klutz Watercolor Book*
- *United States History Atlas*
- *Children's Illustrated United States Atlas*
- *Profiles from History, Vol. 2*
- *Wee Sing America* CD and songbook
- 5 marbles
- USA PlaceMap with overlays
- Water based transparency markers
- United States Presidents Flash Cards
- Outline Map of the U.S.
- USA Activity CD
- Globe (optional)
- Activity (Part 2)
  Newspaper, newsmagazine, or online news source
- Activity (Parts 2 and 4)
  - All purpose flour
  - Salt
  - Mixing bowl
  - Ruler
  - Fine-line permanent marker
  - Toothpick
- Ingredients for recipe (Part 3)

If you have chosen to use the assessments, remember to set aside time for that purpose when you have completed this unit. You can use the results of the assessment in various ways: to determine if there is any area that needs additional study, to assign grades, or just to familiarize your child with taking assessments. Lesson 6 of each unit provides review that should help prepare your child for each assessment.

A. Copywork & Dictation
Language Skills, **Thinking Skills**

Look carefully at your assigned passage below, and read it silently. Show your teacher any words you don't know, and practice saying them aloud. Now read the passage aloud, or ask your teacher to read it to you.

When you are finished copying or writing from dictation, compare your copy to the text and make any needed corrections.

Copy or write as your teacher dictates from *The Cabin Faced West*, page 50, paragraph 1 ("Oh, Mother...").

Copy or write as your teacher dictates from *Justin Morgan Had a Horse*, page 64, paragraphs 2-4 ("Suddenly all the tiredness...").

Choose one additional paragraph from today's assignment in *Justin Morgan Had a Horse* to write from dictation.

B. Reader
Language Skills, History

The Cabin Faced West: page 49, paragraph 1 ("Maybe they...") through page 53, paragraph 2
Justin Morgan Had a Horse: page 63 (Chapter 7) through page 69, paragraph 4

Read the above assignment from *The Cabin Faced West* aloud, and then follow along as someone else reads the assignment from *Justin Morgan Had a Horse*.

Read the above assignment from *The Cabin Faced West* silently, and then read the assignment from *Justin Morgan Had a Horse* aloud.

Read the above assignments from *The Cabin Faced West* and *Justin Morgan Had a Horse* silently.

C. Preview, or point out, the questions your child is to answer before reading aloud. This sets the stage for active listening, and better comprehension.

C. Read-Aloud & Discussion *Language Skills, History, Thinking Skills*

Francis Scott Key: page 36 ("Another boy…") through page 41, paragraph 2

Read over the following questions that you will discuss later. Then read, or listen carefully as your teacher reads, the above assignment from *Francis Scott Key* aloud. You may want to take notes to help answer the questions after you listen. If needed, you can look back at the story to find specific details.

Pretend you are a news reporter and choose an event that you heard or read about today. Think about what you know from the story, and in your own words answer the following questions about that event:

- What took place?
- When did it take place?
- Where did it take place?
- Who were the main people involved?
- How does this event affect Francis Scott Key's life?
- Why do you think it took place?

Choose a second event to report on using the questions listed above.

Tell how the two events you reported on are related.

D. Allowing children to organize words in their own way encourages them to see patterns or other associations, like meaning. You are encouraging them to look for connections between words that help them remember how to read, spell, and use a word correctly.

D. Spelling *Language Skills, Thinking Skills*

Look at the list of words below, and copy each one onto an index card. Then look back at Lesson 1, Part 1 for ideas about how to organize the words, and ways to remember their spelling. Show your teacher how you organized them.

Turn your cards face down and listen as your teacher dictates the words on your spelling list. Spell each word the best that you can, either aloud or by writing it in your Student Notebook. Your teacher may add up to five words that are difficult for you to read or write.

frontier	patiently	ammunition	interrupting
thunderous	innocently	defiance	disappointment
ache	accepted	spectacles	muscles
apprentice	actually	fierceness	announced

E. History *Geography, Thinking Skills*

The third main way the land size of the United States of America grew was by the **ceding**, or giving up, of land from another country to us. This giving up of land may follow fighting or a treaty, but in the end the land is given, not purchased, from another country. This was the case with the land known as Florida.

Many different governments ruled Florida before it became a part of the United States. The first country to claim the land of Florida was Spain. They came here in the early days of the exploration in the New World. Explorers like Christopher Columbus, Ponce de Leon and others claimed land and islands near Florida for the country of Spain, and began settlements. Some of these did not last long. Others, like St. Augustine, still exist to this day. The French also tried to colonize the area, and the French and Spanish fought over who controlled the territory. In Florida, the Spanish won. The Indians who lived in the area were sometimes friendly and sometimes warlike, depending on how they were treated. They did not want to give up their customs and homes, so they battled with many newcomers for a long time.

The French settled in the Louisiana area, so they were nearby. Before the Revolutionary War, the Seven Years War took place in Europe. It was between the English and the French, but after a while the Spanish joined the French side. That turned out badly, because the English won the war and forced the Spanish to give them Florida as part of a treaty. Then the English divided Florida into two parts—East Florida, which was everything east of the Apalachicola River, and West Florida, everything west of the Apalachicola River.

After the start of the Revolutionary War, the Spanish once again took sides against the English. This time they helped the Americans fight the English in West Florida. They made all the English colonists and leaders leave. They also really wanted to get East Florida back, so when the English lost the war with the Americans, part of the Treaty of Paris gave Florida back to the Spanish.

As time went on, there was still fighting between the settlers, Indians, free blacks, and Spanish. Florida was a hard place for the Spanish to rule, as it had been for the English. In 1819, the Spanish and the Americans signed a treaty ceding, or giving, the territory of Florida to the United States. Though the United States had tried to buy Florida from the Spanish many times, no money ever changed hands for that purpose.

Today you will add to the map overlay you've been working on in this unit. To get started, look again at the map in your *United States History Atlas* entitled "Growth of the United States to 1853," and find the area that shows the territory added by the Florida Cession. Notice that the northern border of this territory is exactly the same as the current border of Florida. Trace over this boundary on the transparency, then color and label it.

On the PlaceMap, you can see the names of the states and their borders as they are today. In your Student Notebook, list the current states that expanded, or grew larger, by the Florida Cession.[1]

Look at the map in your history atlas again. Now name the current state that was established on land that was added to the United States by the Florida Cession.[2]

Conflicts, or disagreements, played a role in the way the United States grew. This nation began as a colony, or settlement, started by England. Through disagreement, the colonists struggled against England and finally fought for and won their **independence**, or freedom. Since Americans won the war, the land that had belonged to England now belonged to America. This became final when America and England signed the Treaty of Paris.

About twenty years later, Napoleon, the leader of France, was at war with Spain and needed money to buy supplies for his troops. He decided that selling France's land in America was a good way to raise money, so he did. This was the Louisiana Purchase and greatly increased the size of our country. President Thomas Jefferson and Congress approved the purchase of over eight hundred thousand acres of land, for fifteen million dollars.

By this time in America's history, three different nations had already ruled Florida—Spain, France and England. There had been many struggles for the people who lived there: people from the ruling country, settlers, Indians, and blacks who had been slaves. It was not easy for any ruling country to keep peace in Florida, so after many problems, Spain ceded, or gave, Florida to the United States. The Florida Cession was the result of many struggles over several hundred years. Once Florida became a possession of America's, it wasn't long before it was an official part of the United States.

Look at the chart in your Student Notebook. Summarize, or tell the main points, about how each nation building took place. List at least two main points.

- Follow the directions above, and list one additional main point.
- Follow the directions above, and list two additional main points.

F. States *Geography, History, Thinking Skills*

In your *United States Atlas*, read the pages about Indiana. When you are finished, find the blank map of Indiana in your Student Notebook and complete the following assignments:

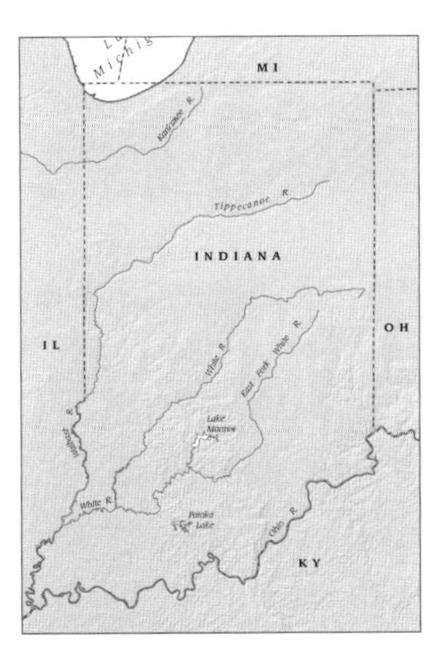

- Place a small red star on the spot where Indianapolis is located, and label it. Indianapolis is the capital city of Indiana.
- Color the lines showing the Ohio, Kankakee, Tippecanoe, and Wabash Rivers, and both forks of the White River blue, and label them.
- Color and label Lake Monroe, Patoka Lake, and the portion of Lake Michigan that borders Indiana.

- Label the four states that border Indiana.

G. Doing *Art, Music*

Look at the song entitled "I've Been Workin' on the Railroad" in your *Wee Sing America* songbook, and read the historical note about it in the book. This song was written and became popular during the period of history that you are studying, as railroad systems were being built. Now listen to it on the *Wee Sing America* CD. Try to become familiar with the words and music so that you can sing along, or learn to play it on an instrument of your choice. You may want to recite, sing, or play this song during your presentation at the end of this unit.

Complete the activities on pages 40 and 41 in your *Klutz Watercolor Book*. Learning how to be creative with letters and numbers can be very useful, so relax and let your imagination go! Don't get stuck on one style, but keep trying different things as you go through the alphabet. Remember that there is no way to make a mistake in this activity.

Teaching Tip

If you have a perfectionist child who doesn't want to draw or paint because it doesn't come out exactly the way he wants, encourage him to think like an inventor. Many attempts create a better product.

H. Independent Reading *Language Skills*

Choose something to read that you will enjoy. Then, find a quiet, comfortable place and read for the following length of time:

25 minutes 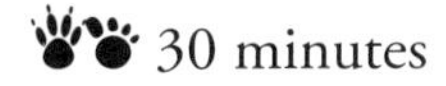 30 minutes

Over time, it's fun to see how much you have read. Be sure to write down what you read today on the Reading Log in your Student Notebook.

Lesson 3, Part 2

A. Imagery is a picture in your mind, often created by using words. It is very individual, since it depends on your understanding of the words and your experiences. This activity builds imagery. Poetry often uses imagery as an important part of enjoying and understanding the words of others.

A. Quotation Notebook
History, Language Skills, Music

Continue copying verses from the American National Anthem, "The Star Spangled Banner." As you examine this song, consider the imagery created by the words. Since it is also a poem, consider its rhyme pattern as well.

> On the shore, dimly seen through the mists of the deep,
> Where the foe's haughty host in dread silence reposes.

Copy the above passage into your Student Notebook, and talk with your teacher about its meaning and any unknown words. Then listen to it on the *Wee Sing America* CD and follow along with the words in the songbook. Practice reading or singing each section of the song aloud.

Under each phrase printed in your Student Notebook, draw a picture or write an explanation that describes the image it creates in your mind.

Choose two words from the verse and write at least one synonym for each one. Make sure you find a meaning that goes with its context, or use in the verse.

B. Reader
Language Skills, History

The Cabin Faced West: page 53, paragraph 3 ("Ann stole…") through page 57, paragraph 2
Justin Morgan Had a Horse: page 69, paragraph 5 ("The next afternoon…") through page 76, paragraph 3

Read the above assignment from *The Cabin Faced West* aloud, and then follow along as someone else reads the assignment from *Justin Morgan Had a Horse.*

Read the above assignment from *The Cabin Faced West* silently, and then read the assignment from *Justin Morgan Had a Horse* aloud.

Read the above assignments from *The Cabin Faced West* and *Justin Morgan Had a Horse* silently.

From Dr. Beechick

"Review has a broader use than just a quick review after one reading selection. If the material is something a student must remember for a test or for studying future topics, then more reviews spaced out over time are needed to set the learning more permanently. One of the most effective ways for the students to reinforce their learning is to discuss things with you, or with other older people. Older students and adults think on higher levels; thus, such conversations stretch younger students' thinking."

– *You Can Teach Your Child Successfully*, page 18

C. Read-Aloud & Narration
Language Skills, History, Thinking Skills

Francis Scott Key: page 41, paragraph 3 ("So, it was to be…") through page 45, paragraph 4

Follow the instructions below for your level. Then, in your own words tell what happened in the story from Francis' point of view, or pretend you are Francis and tell what you think happened. Try to remember as many details as possible. You may reread the passage or listen as your teacher rereads the part you are to retell.

Listen carefully as your teacher reads the above assignment from *Francis Scott Key* aloud.

Read the above assignment from *Francis Scott Key* aloud.

D. **Editing** *Language Skills, Thinking Skills*

Today you are going to review the tools for writing that you have learned. To begin, print the Mechanics Toolkit 5 Cards from Appendix B or your Student Resources CD, and cut them out. When you are finished, place them on the table in front of you, and read all the Rule cards. Then find two Example cards that go with each rule.

You may want to mix up the Example cards to make it more of a challenge, or follow the directions in Appendix B to play Mechanics Toolkit Concentration.

Now continue your review by reading the Rule cards once again. When you are finished, make up the appropriate number of sentences that show each rule used correctly and write them in your Student Notebook.

two sentences three sentences four sentences

E. **Science** *Geography, Thinking Skills, Art*

Take a few minutes before you begin this section to look back at the list you made in Lesson 1, Part 2, and see if your questions about the oceans and their water, erosion, the continental shelf, and the continental slope have been answered yet. Use a highlighter to mark the ones that have not. Then over the next few days, research the questions that you highlighted at the library or on the Internet, and try to find the answers. Discuss what you find out with your teacher.

E. The Internet can be a useful tool for research, but we suggest that your child use it only with your permission and supervision, and while following your family's rules.

In the next few lessons you will learn about waves, tides, an underwater mountain range, and sedimentary rocks. Take a few minutes to discuss what you already know about these things with your teacher. When you are finished, and before reading further in this section, make a list of questions or things you would like to find out about these subjects. There is a page provided in your Student Notebook for the list. Later, you will have an opportunity to look back and see if your questions have been answered.

Ocean water is always moving. Some of its movements are easy to observe, like waves and the regular rise and fall of the tides. Today you will learn a little about waves.

Just like radiant waves that come from the sun, which you learned about in Unit 1, waves in the water are also pulses of energy. They can be set in motion by earthquakes or the moon's gravity, but most of the time ocean waves are started by wind blowing across the surface of the water.

As wind continues to blow it transfers more and more energy to the water, and small ripples build into larger swells. **Swells** are waves that have rounded tops, and they usually occur in deeper water. They can travel through the ocean for hundreds of miles in a very regular, up-and-down pattern that is a perfect picture of all energy waves. The highest part of an energy wave is its **crest**, and the lowest part is the **trough**. The distance between crests is the **wavelength**, and the measurement from the trough to the crest is the wave height.

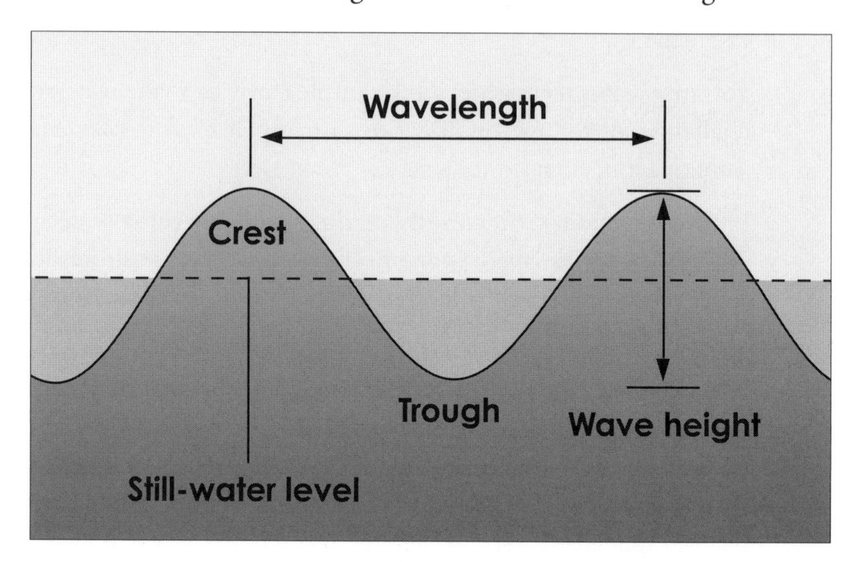

When you observe a wave, it seems as though a large mass of water is surging forward. But in reality only a small amount is actually moving. What you are observing is energy moving through the water—so it is possible for something floating on the water to barely move when a swell, or energy pulse, passes under it. To see how this works, open any book to one of the center pages. Line up four marbles, touching one another, in the crease of the book. Then roll a fifth marble forcefully so that it hits one of the ends. What happens? Talk with your teacher about how this experiment illustrates wave movement.[3] If you have Internet access, visit the following site to experiment with waves:

http://www.nationalgeographic.com/volvooceanrace/interactives/waves/index.html

Wave energy does not only move forward in whatever direction the wind is blowing, it also moves downward. The distance downward that it travels depends on the strength of the wave, but in deep water it seldom reaches the ocean floor. It is this downward energy that causes ocean swells to change as they move into shallower water. As the downward energy hits the floor of the continental shelf, it is pushed back upwards and makes the waves higher. The slant of the ocean floor also slows the waves down as they near the shore, and they get closer and closer together. Finally, the waves crash forward as breakers. Water that breaks onto the shore is called **surf**.

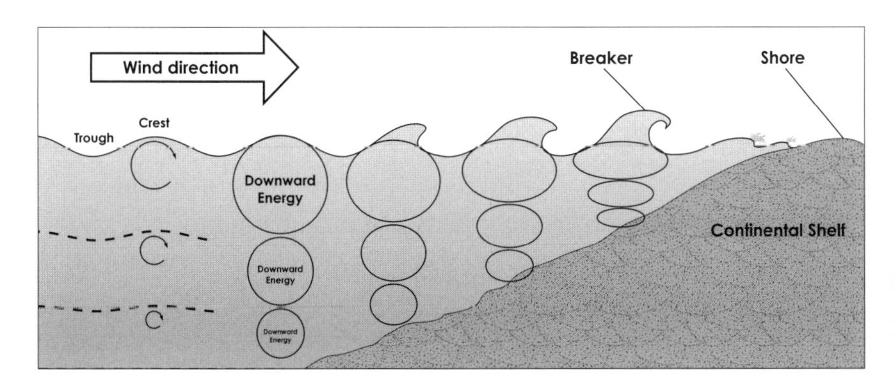

Discuss the different parts of the chart above with your teacher, and then use it as a model to label the one in your Student Notebook.

Continue working on your 3-D map by adding salt dough to the continental shelf that you began in the last lesson. Build it up to a height that is almost even with the land mass it is next to, and blend it into the shoreline. Then press down lightly on your new continental shelf to create a small slant. The inside edge should remain almost even with the land, and the outside edge should measure about ⅛-inch less. Make sure the outside edge of your shelf shows a steep drop-off.

Use the map-model in Appendix B to draw the outline of the continental slope. Be sure to go over your pencil lines with a permanent marker. Now build the continental slope by rolling salt dough snakes about ½ -inch thick and placing them next to the continental shelf. Blend each snake upwards so that it forms a slant about half-way up the side of the continental shelf. It does not need to be smooth, because there are ridges and canyons in real continental slopes. Then press the dough down at a slant until it fills the outline. Add more dough to the larger areas, and pinch it away from the narrower places.

By now your map is quite heavy, so when you are finished ask for your parent's help to put your 3-D map in an oven that is heated to 150°. After an hour, remove it carefully with your parent's help, and store it in a safe place for the next couple of days.

F. States *Geography, Thinking Skills, History, Drawing*

Look again at the pages about Indiana in your *United States Atlas*. Then find the State Page in your Student Notebook, and fill in the information.

Make State Cards for Indiana by following the instructions found in Appendix B. Indiana is a Midwestern state, so be sure to outline the cards in red.

Teaching Tip

If you are using the curriculum with more than one child, you do not have to do your part of the interactive writing differently for each child. Actually, it is interesting to see how your children respond differently to the same response from you. If you need to save time, type out your response and make copies for each child.

G. **Interactive Writing** *Language Skills, Thinking Skills*

Complete this writing activity with your partner.

Choose an article from a newspaper, news magazine, or online news source that relates to a current event in local, state or national government. Then ask your partner to read the article and answer the following questions in your Student Notebook:

Do you agree with the article; why or why not?
What do you think should happen in the future regarding this issue?

Tell about the news story using the number sentences indicated below. Then tell what you think about what your partner wrote. Write several sentences in reply, including whether or not you agree with your partner, and why. End with a question for your partner.

at least four sentences

at least five sentences

Tell about the news story with at least one paragraph. Then tell what you think about what your partner wrote with a second paragraph.

Remember that a paragraph is a group of sentences that relate to one topic, or main idea. State the topic or main idea of the paragraph at or near the beginning of the paragraph. You do not want the reader to read your paragraph for very long without knowing for sure what you think!

H. Ask your children to look at their reading logs and decide what type of books they read most frequently. Do they always read historical fiction? Stories about nature? Mysteries? As they analyze their own reading patterns, challenge them to stretch a bit and read something different every once in a while, at least once every unit. Tell them to mark it, and that you will be looking to see something new on their logs.

H. **Independent Reading** *Language Skills*

Choose something to read that you will enjoy. Then, find a quiet, comfortable place and read for the following length of time:

25 minutes   30 minutes

Be sure to write down what you read today on the Reading Log in your Student Notebook.

Lesson 3, Part 3

A. **Copywork & Dictation** *Language Skills, Thinking Skills*

Look carefully at your assigned passage below, and read it silently. Show your teacher any words you don't know, and practice saying them aloud. Now read the passage aloud, or ask your teacher to read it to you.

When you are finished copying or writing from dictation, compare your copy to the text and make any needed corrections.

Copy or write as your teacher dictates from *The Cabin Faced West*, page 60, paragraphs 2 and 3 ("Mr. Scott…") through page 62, paragraph 1 ("Land…").

Copy or write as your teacher dictates from *Justin Morgan Had a Horse*, page 82, paragraphs 2 and 3 ("Then as if a dike…").

Choose one additional paragraph from today's assignment in *Justin Morgan Had a Horse* to write from dictation.

B. Reader

Language Skills, History

The Cabin Faced West: page 57, paragraph 3 ("Daniel started…") to the bottom of page 63
Justin Morgan Had a Horse: page 76, paragraph 4 ("Joel heard…") through page 82

Read the above assignment from *The Cabin Faced West* aloud, and then follow along as someone else reads the assignment from *Justin Morgan Had a Horse*.

Read the above assignment from *The Cabin Faced West* silently, and then read the assignment from *Justin Morgan Had a Horse* aloud.

Read the above assignments from *The Cabin Faced West* and *Justin Morgan Had a Horse* silently.

C. Read-Aloud & Discussion

Language Skills, History, Thinking Skills

Francis Scott Key: page 45, paragraph 5 ("I soon discovered…") through page 48

Follow the directions below to read or listen to the above assignment from *Francis Scott Key*. Then make up the assigned number of questions about the part of the story you just read or heard. Write your questions and ask your teacher to answer them. After discussing her thoughts, write down the best possible answer to your questions. Be sure to use complete sentences.

When you are finished, look back at the prediction or predictions you made during Lesson 2, Part 4. Were you able to predict what would happen? Be sure to mark the "Came to Pass" box for each prediction when it does happen.

Listen carefully as your teacher reads the above assignment from *Francis Scott Key*.

Make up one question.   Make up two questions

Teaching Tip

The process of copywork and dictation gives a teacher a great deal of information. Not only does it show what your child is missing, it shows what he is getting! Reading or hearing language, and then writing it down is a multi-step process that shows understanding, processing of information, and translating that information into writing. Many times over my years as an educator, just giving a student a passage to copy or write from dictation has provided great insight into the student's ability to read, write, and comprehend. Make sure to take notice of all your child does correctly when using this process, and encourage him accordingly!

Read the above assignment from *Francis Scott Key* aloud; then make up three questions.

D. Dividing a word into syllables is another way for a child to connect to spelling and meaning. Remind your child that a syllable usually has a vowel sound. When you divide a word into syllables, make sure each syllable has a vowel sound.

D. Vocabulary & Spelling

Language Skills, Thinking Skills

Vocabulary:
Write each vocabulary word on an index card, and use a thesaurus to find a synonym for it. If you cannot find a synonym, use a dictionary to look up the meaning of the word. Then, on the back of each card, draw a picture or write a clue so you can remember how each word was used in the story. Write a *D* or *S* by your clue to tell whether you wrote a definition or synonym.

scowl **cringed** **bounding** **proposition** **exasperation**

scorn **galvanize** **ominous** **exertion** **cagey**

Spelling:
Look at the list of words on your Student Notebook page, and divide each word into syllables by drawing a slash line (/) between the syllables. After you have marked each word, use a dictionary to check your work.[8] If you don't know what the word means, read the definition while you are checking your syllable markings. Then place a check next to each word to show that you know what the word means.

Look at the spelling word cards you made in Part 1. Read each word, and then cover it with your hand and try to spell it aloud. Then uncover it and see if you were correct. Review the meanings of any words that you do not remember.

E. The Presidential Focus is part of the unified approach used in this curriculum. As your child learns about nation building, it is important to be familiar with those elected to positions of leadership as well. Your child will gather information on the presidents mentioned in the literature selections. Later your children will use this information to draw conclusions and make comparisons.

E. History

Geography, Thinking Skills

Presidential Focus: Continue your study of American presidents by reading the U.S. Presidents Flash Cards about James Monroe and John Quincy Adams. Use the things you learn to fill out the Presidential Focus page in your Student Notebook.

In this part you will review the things you have learned so far about nation building. Use the cards and clues located on the Student Resources CD to play Building Blocks Bingo with your family.

F. States *Geography, History, Thinking Skills*

In your *United States Atlas*, read the pages about Illinois. When you are finished, find the blank map of Illinois in your Student Notebook and complete the following assignments:

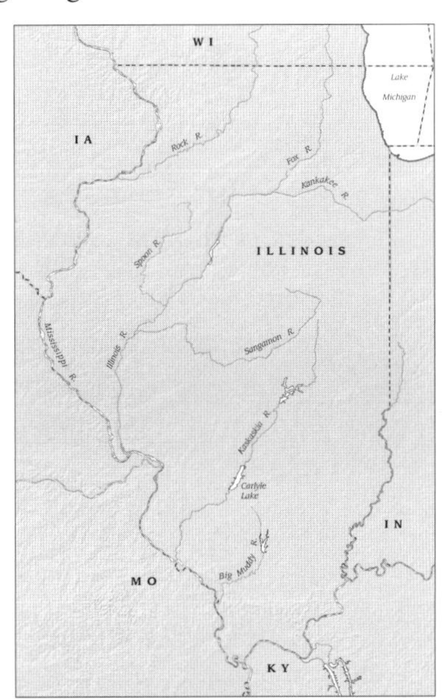

- Place a small red star on the spot where Springfield is located, and label it. Springfield is the capital city of Illinois.
- Color the lines that show the Mississippi, Illinois, Kaskaskia, Sangamon, and Spoon Rivers blue, and label them.
- Color and label Carlyle Lake and the portion of Lake Michigan that borders Illinois.
-  Color the lines that show the Rock, Fox, Kankakee, and Big Muddy Rivers blue, and label them.
- Label the five states that border Illinois.

G. Cooking *Language Skills, Thinking Skills, Drawing*

With your parent's permission and supervision, look in *Eat Your Way Through the USA*, choose a recipe that comes from either Indiana or Illinois, and prepare it for your family. After everyone has had a taste, find out who liked it, and whether anyone would like to have it again. What did you think about it?

In your Student Notebook, draw a picture of the dish you chose to make and write the following number of sentences about your family's reaction to it:

2 sentences 3 sentences 4 sentences

G. The cooking activities are a very important part of connecting meaning and context to geography learning. When a particular style of cooking or ingredient is associated with the culture or resources of a state, it makes another connection to the information learned about that state. Many aspects of geography such as culture, history, economics, and climate help students connect products with places, which relate new learning with previous learning. Plus, it's fun!

H. Independent Reading *Language Skills*

Choose something to read that you will enjoy. Then, find a quiet, comfortable place and read for the following length of time:

25 minutes 30 minutes

Be sure to write down what you read today on the Reading Log in your Student Notebook.

Lesson 3, Part 4

A. Quotation Notebook

History, Language Skills, Music

Continue copying verses from the American National Anthem, "The Star Spangled Banner." As you examine this song, consider the imagery created by the words. Since it is also a poem, consider its rhyme pattern as well.

> What is that which the breeze, o'er the towering steep,
> As it fitfully blows, half conceals, half discloses?

Copy the above passage into your Student Notebook, and talk with your teacher about its meaning and any unknown words. Then listen to it on the *Wee Sing America* CD and follow along with the words in the songbook. Practice reading or singing each section of the song aloud.

Under each phrase printed in your Student Notebook, draw a picture or write an explanation that describes the image it creates in your mind.

Choose two words from the verse and write at least one synonym for each one. Make sure you find a meaning that goes with its context, or use in the verse.

Teaching Tip

Point out to your child that chapter titles and headings are tools to identify main ideas. After your child reads a section or chapter, ask him to tell you how the title, or heading, relates to what he read.

B. Reader

Language Skills, History

The Cabin Faced West: page 63, the last paragraph ("That evening...") through the top of page 68
Justin Morgan Had a Horse: pages 83-89 (Chapter 9)

Read the above assignment from *The Cabin Faced West* aloud, and then follow along as someone else reads the assignment from *Justin Morgan Had a Horse*.

Read the above assignment from *The Cabin Faced West* silently, and then read the assignment from *Justin Morgan Had a Horse* aloud.

Read the above assignments from *The Cabin Faced West* and *Justin Morgan Had a Horse* silently.

C. Since students do not have to worry about decoding during read-aloud time, they can focus totally on the meaning of what they are hearing. This allows them the opportunity to think about the ideas and information being presented, and to formulate their own thoughts.

C. Read-Aloud & Narration

Language Skills, History, Thinking Skills

Francis Scott Key: pages 49-53 (Chapter 6)

After reading or listening to the read-aloud assignment, talk with your teacher and try to predict what will happen in the future based on what you know of the characters and events. Write down your predictions in your Student Notebook. Later you will look back and see if they were accurate. Try not to peek ahead!

Listen carefully as your teacher reads the above assignment from *Francis Scott Key* aloud. Then write down something that you think will happen in the story.

Write down another thing that you think will happen in the story.

Read the above assignment from *Francis Scott Key* aloud. Then write down three things that you think will happen in the story.

D. Editing

Language Skills, Thinking Skills

Today you are going to review the tools for writing that you have learned. To begin, print the Mechanics Toolkit 6 Cards from Appendix B or your Student Resources CD, and cut them out. When you are finished, place them on the table in front of you, and read all the Rule cards. Then find two Example cards that go with each rule.

You may want to mix up the Example cards to make it more of a challenge, or follow the directions in Appendix B to play Mechanics Toolkit Concentration.

Now continue your review by reading the Rule cards once again. When you are finished, make up sentences that show each rule used correctly, and write them in your Student Notebook.

two sentences three sentences four sentences

E. Science

Geography, Thinking Skills, Art

One of the most interesting features of the Atlantic Ocean is an underwater mountain range called the Mid-Atlantic Ridge. This ridge runs from the Arctic Ocean almost all the way to Antarctica—about 8,000 miles. That makes it by far the longest mountain range in the world. It is positioned right where its name says, in the middle of the Atlantic Ocean. Look at your globe or the map of the world in Appendix A and place your finger slightly northeast of Greenland, at the top of the Atlantic Ocean. Now run your finger down the map, keeping it almost perfectly in the center of the continents, all the way to the bottom of South America. That is the length of the Mid-Atlantic Ridge!

Most of the earth's volcanoes are in the oceans, and there are quite a few along the Mid-Atlantic Ridge. When an underwater volcano **erupts**, or explodes, melted rock and gases from deep inside the earth are forced upward and spill into the surrounding water. Many underwater volcanoes are so deep in the oceans that it is difficult to tell when they erupt; others are close to the surface and spew smoke and rock into the air. Hardened rock substances that come from volcanoes help make the mountains larger and form the ocean floor, while gases and minerals, including salts, are dissolved in the water.

On your map or globe look at the island of Iceland, which is located just east of Greenland. This island is actually part of the Mid-Atlantic Ridge. It was formed when underwater volcanoes that were very close together erupted over and over again. With each eruption more **lava**, or melted rock, hardened on the sides of the volcanoes. Eventually they were high enough to stick up out of the ocean water, and broad enough to form a large island. In fact, many of the earth's islands were formed by underwater volcanoes.

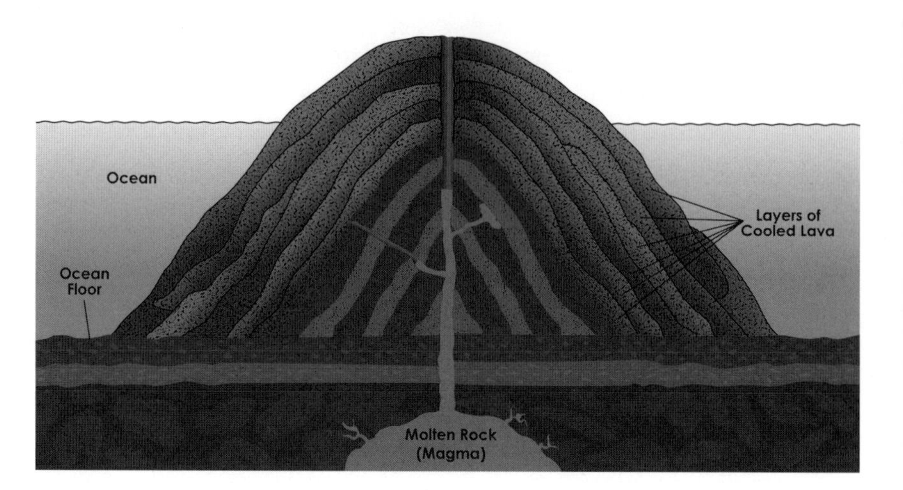

Another interesting feature of the Mid-Atlantic Ridge is a **rift**, or split, that runs along the middle of the mountains almost their entire length. This rift is a deep, wide valley that contains many **vents**, or places where hot magma is allowed to **ooze**, or leak out slowly, into the ocean waters. Magma is melted rock under the earth's surface, and the type of opening that allows it to come out this way is called a fissure volcano. **Fissure** is another word for split, or crack.

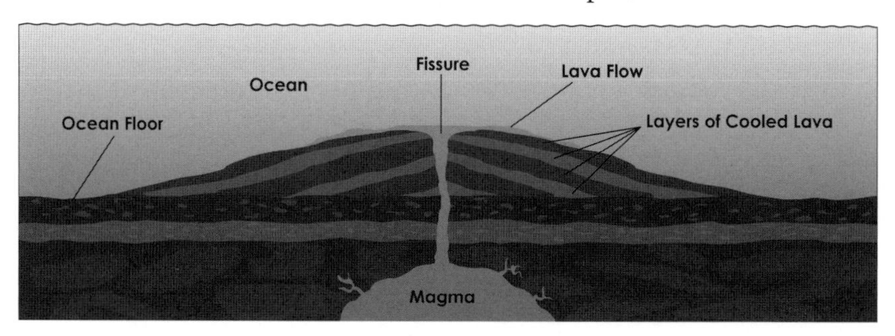

Discuss the different parts of the fissure volcano pictured above with your teacher, and talk about what makes this type of volcano different from other types.[5] Then use this chart as a model to label the one in your Student Notebook. When you are finished, list three facts about the Mid-Atlantic Ridge.

To continue building your 3-D map, use the map-model in Appendix B to draw the outline of the Mid-Atlantic Ridge on your base. Then roll a snake of salt dough that is about 1½ -inches thick.

Make it long enough to stretch the whole length of the ridge. Place this large snake in the middle of the area you outlined. Blend its bottom onto the base and pinch the top to make peaks. Add smaller salt-dough snakes to the edges to fill up the whole area occupied by the Mid-Atlantic Ridge. Be sure to blend their bottoms and peak their tops. The highest parts of your ridge should be from ¾- to 1-inch high. Compare the height and size of this mountain range to the Appalachian Mountains you made on North America.

Finally, use a toothpick to make a rift along the highest part of the ridge, from one end to the other.

By now your map is quite heavy, so when you are finished ask for your parent's help to put your 3-D map in an oven that is heated to 150°. After an hour, remove it carefully with your parent's help, and store it in a safe place for the next couple of days.

F. States

Geography, History, Drawing, Thinking Skills

Look again at the pages about Illinois in your *United States Atlas*. Then find the State Page in your Student Notebook, and fill in the information.

Make State Cards for Illinois by following the instructions found in Appendix B. Illinois is a Midwestern state, so be sure to outline the cards in red.

G. Writing

Language Skills, Thinking Skills

In Unit 1, you began learning about writing dialogue. Today you will continue to practice taking the words of another person and writing them as dialogue. Read over the steps you learned in Unit 1, and notice that a new step has been added:

Step 1 - After you say who is speaking (a person's name, or he, or she) and what they are doing (said, told, asked) you put a comma. This tells the reader that the next words will be the words of the speaker.

Step 2 - Quotation marks (") are used to let the reader know that what is inside them are the exact words the person said, so put quotation marks before the words that they said begin. Use a capital letter to start what the person has said.

Step 3 - When you get to the end of what the person said (which may be more than one sentence) finish it with the punctuation mark needed, like a period or question mark. The punctuation mark is part of what the person said.

Step 4 - Close up the quotation with quotation marks. This lets the reader know that the words the person spoke are now finished.

G. Brief, spaced review is the best kind. It keeps learning fresh and it helps your child continue to connect new learning to previous knowledge. It also builds memory skills naturally.

Step 5 - If you are quoting more than one sentence by a person, you do not need to put quotation marks before and after each sentence. Only put a quotation mark before the first sentence the person says, and close the quote after the last sentence the person says. For example:

> My dad said, "It's time to go to baseball practice. Make sure and get all your equipment. Meet me at the car as soon as you are ready."

Look back at the Interactive Writing you and your partner did in Lesson 3, Part 2. Rewrite at least two sentences as dialogue. Here is an example:

> My mom said, "You were the cutest baby in the world."

Look back at the Interactive Writing you and your partner did in Lesson 3, Part 2. Rewrite at least two sentences your partner wrote, and two sentences you wrote, as dialogue. Here are some examples:

> My dad said, "The day you were born was the happiest day of my life." I said, "The first thing I remember was when I got gum stuck in my hair."

Look back at the Interactive Writing you and your partner did in Lesson 3, Part 2. Rewrite at least three sentences your partner wrote, and three sentences you wrote, as dialogue. Above are some examples.

H. **Independent Reading** *Language Skills*

Choose something to read that you will enjoy. Then, find a quiet, comfortable place and read for the following length of time:

25 minutes 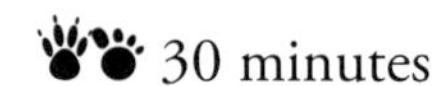 30 minutes

Be sure to write down what you read today on the Reading Log in your Student Notebook.

Lesson 3, Part 5

This part is set aside for completion of any work left undone from the lesson, and review of concepts and content. It is also a time to expand the work of the lesson with art, mapping, or games.

- Review the Steps for Thinking found in Part 1.
- Give your teacher your stack of vocabulary cards for the lesson. As she shows you each word, tell her the meaning of the word and how it was used in the story.

Each Step for Thinking is a concept related to the content of the unit. As you review the reading, discussions, and activities from the lesson, look for examples of the concepts and encourage your child to do the same. You may want to post the week's Steps for Thinking nearby for easy reference.

- Listen as your teacher reads the spelling words that you studied from Part 1. Write each word in your Student Notebook as she dictates it. When you are finished, look back at your spelling word cards and make corrections as needed. Show your teacher how you did.
- Use the United States map that is near the front of your *Atlas of the United States* to find Indiana and Illinois. Then, on the large outline map of the U.S., draw red lines around them because they are Midwestern states. Write in the names of the states, and draw small stars where their capital cities are located. Next to the stars, write the name of each capital city.
- Read, or listen as your teacher reads, the story about Dolley Madison in *Profiles from History, Volume 2*. Talk about the discussion question with your teacher, and then complete any other activities that she assigns.
- Use your USA Activity CD to print at least one activity for the states you studied in this lesson. Then add any that you complete to your Student Notebook.
- Choose a game that you have enjoyed playing in *Paths of Settlement*, and play it again with your family.

What makes a person memorable? Many history books give only facts and dates, but that doesn't make historical figures seem real. Learning about their hearts—their thoughts and motives, struggles and successes, and ultimately how others remember them—makes them memorable. The purpose of learning about them is for their lives to make an impact on our lives.

Enrichment Activities

1. Watch Episode 1, Chapter 3 on the *Discovering America's Founders* DVD, about John Adams. You may take notes while you watch, or stop the video from time to time to write things down. When you are finished, make a list of at least ten interesting facts about John Adams, and add them to your Student Notebook.
2. Learn about Andrew Jackson's role in Florida's history by reading about him on the Internet or at the library. Tell your teacher what his role was in Florida becoming a part of the United States. Then give him a thumbs-up or thumbs-down as a leader and tell your teacher why you voted that way.
3. Listen to Tchaikovsky's "1812 Overture," and find out why it was written. Then write two or three paragraphs that tell what you learned about this famous composition. Be sure to include your opinion of the music, and whether or not you think it fulfilled the purpose for which it was written. Add your report to your Student Notebook.
4. In your *United States Atlas*, look again at the states you have studied in this lesson. Scan the sections entitled "The Way It Was..." and choose a person, place, or thing from one of those sections to research. Use the library or, with your parent's permission, the

Enrichment activities are suggestions for ways your child can learn more about a topic of interest, dig deeper into a subject, or gain research skills. Please feel free to use these activities as guides for your child to do as stated, or amended to better fit his particular abilities, needs, or interests.

Internet and try to find out more than what is written in the atlas.

Then pretend you work for a newspaper, and you have just met the person, seen the landmark, or found out about the object. Write a short article about what you have learned. Newspaper reporters always try to answer the questions *who, what, when, where,* and *how* when they write, so that readers have all the important information. Try to answer those questions in your article, and then add it to your Student Notebook.

5. Although some First Ladies are more well-known than others, each was an important part of her husband's presidency. At the library or on the Internet, find out at least three facts about the First Ladies who shared the White House with the U.S. Presidents you studied in this lesson. Add your research to your Student Notebook.

Additional Resources

http://www.whitehousemuseum.org/overview.htm

Little Women, by Louisa May Alcott

The Great Little Madison, by Jean Fritz

If you read any of the above books, be sure to print a Book Review page from your Student Resources CD, fill it out, and place it in your Student Notebook.

Answers

1. Louisiana, Mississippi and Alabama
2. Florida
3. The marble you roll represents wind energy, and the row of marbles represents water molecules. When the marble hits the row, energy is transferred and travels to the other end, barely disturbing the row.
4. fron/tier, pa/tient/ly, am/mu/ni/tion, in/ter/tupt/ing, thun/der/ous, in/no/cent/ly, de/fi/ance, dis/ap/point/ment
   ache, ac/cept/ed, spec/ta/cles, mus/cles
   ap/pren/tice, ac/tu/al/ly, fierce/ness, an/nounced
5. Other volcanoes explode lava, rocks, and steam up into the air when they erupt. Fissure volcanoes don't explode, but allow lava to ooze out.

Lesson 4, Part 1

Steps for Thinking

1. The things done for fun in a community were often a part of things done for work.
2. The opportunity for work in a community also became an opportunity for getting to know neighbors and build the bonds of friendship.
3. In a community, respect is the reward for skill and hard work, no matter your age.

Read over the Steps for Thinking with your children, and ask what they think each one means. Discuss any unknown words or ideas. Remember, this is just an introduction. Do not be concerned if they do not show much connection to the ideas yet. Post the Steps, and refer to them throughout the week when examples arise in reading or discussion.

A. Copywork & Dictation

Language Skills, Thinking Skills

Look carefully at your assigned passage below, and read it silently. Show your teacher any words you don't know, and practice saying them aloud. Now read the passage aloud, or ask your teacher to read it to you.

When you are finished copying or writing from dictation, compare your copy to the text and make any needed corrections.

Copy or write as your teacher dictates from *The Cabin Faced West*, page 68, paragraph 4 ("There was such…").

Copy or write as your teacher dictates from *Justin Morgan Had a Horse*, page 90, paragraphs 1 and 2 ("On pleasant evenings…").

Choose one additional paragraph from today's assignment in *Justin Morgan Had a Horse* to write from dictation.

B. Reader

Language Skills, History

The Cabin Faced West: page 68, paragraph 1 ("As Mr. Scott…") through page 72

Justin Morgan Had a Horse: page 90 (Chapter 10) through the top of page 97

Read the above assignment from *The Cabin Faced West* aloud, and then follow along as someone else reads the assignment from *Justin Morgan Had a Horse.*

Read the above assignment from *The Cabin Faced West* silently, and then read the assignment from *Justin Morgan Had a Horse* aloud.

Read the above assignments from *The Cabin Faced West* and *Justin Morgan Had a Horse* silently.

Materials

- *The Cabin Faced West*
- *Justin Morgan Had a Horse*
- *Francis Scott Key*
- *Eat Your Way Through the USA*
- *Klutz Watercolor Book*
- *United States History Atlas*
- *Children's Illustrated United States Atlas*
- *Discovering America's Founders* DVD
- *Wee Sing America* CD and songbook
- USA PlaceMap with overlays
- Water based transparency markers
- United States Presidents Flash Cards
- Outline Map of the U.S.
- USA Activity CD
- Activity (Part 1)
  Nail with a head
  Hammer
  Yarn or string
  Wooden board or block
  9-inch disposable, foil type pie pan
- Optional Activity (Part 1)
  Tea light candle
  Towel
  Needle nose pliers
  Duct tape
  Empty, medium-sized can
  12 inches of medium gauge wire
- Activity (Part 2)
  Newspaper, newsmagazine, or online news source
- Activity (Parts 2 and 4)
  All purpose flour
  Salt
  Mixing bowl
  Ruler
  Fine-line permanent marker
- Ingredients for recipe (Part 3)

From Dr. Beechick

"This technique of focusing on content has the double effect of helping children learn the subject matter at hand and also helping them grow in reading ability. When children have good understanding of what a passage is saying, they can figure out the main idea, the supporting details, whether it is fact or fiction, and so on. Skills in these grow together, not separately."

– *You Can Teach Your Child Successfully*, page 9

C. Read-Aloud & Discussion

Language Skills, History, Thinking Skills

Francis Scott Key: page 54 (Chapter 7) through page 57

Read over the following questions that you will discuss later. Then read, or listen carefully as your teacher reads, the above assignment from *Francis Scott Key* aloud. You may want to take notes to help answer the questions after you listen. If needed, you can look back at the story to find specific details.

Pretend you are a news reporter and choose an event that you heard or read about today. Think about what you know from the story, and in your own words answer the following questions about that event:

- What took place?
- When did it take place?
- Where did it take place?
- Who were the main people involved?
- How does this event affect Francis Scott Key's life?
- Why do you think it took place?

Choose a second event to report on using the questions listed above.

Tell how the two events you reported on are related.

D. Read the list of words to your child. If your student would rather spell the words aloud than write them, it is perfectly acceptable. As you dictate each word, put small dots beside any misspelled words. Then have your child copy them onto the Student Notebook page.

D. Spelling

Language Skills, Thinking Skills

Look at the list of words below, and copy each one onto an index card. Then look back at Lesson 1, Part 1 for ideas about how to organize the words, and ways to remember their spelling. Show your teacher how you organized them.

Turn your cards face down and listen as your teacher dictates the words on your spelling list. Spell each word the best that you can, either aloud or by writing it in your Student Notebook. Your teacher may add up to five words that are difficult for you to read or write.

surrounded	interference	lonesome	cinnamon
critically	decisively	material	wickedness
community	breathlessly	swiveled	continued
instruction	fashionable	contentedly	generosity

E. History

Geography, Thinking Skills

America continued its growth as a nation. You will look at three main areas of expansion in this lesson and how they added greatly to the size of America, though they did not come without some conflict. Many people wanted to see America's borders extend from the Atlantic Ocean to the Pacific Ocean and from Canada to Mexico. Look at the map entitled "Growth of the United States to 1853" in your *United States History Atlas* to see the additions made during this time of growth:

Texas Annexation of 1845: Settlers had lived for many years in the area of the country known at that time as Texas. It was part of Mexico at first, but later became an independent republic in 1836. The people who lived in the Republic of Texas wanted to become a part of the United States, and voted to approve an annexation ordinance. In this case, **annexation** means the addition of a territory into an existing country. There had been some conflict in the United States over adding Texas as a state. Those who opposed slavery believed that Texas would support slavery, and so they opposed the annexation. However, President Tyler signed the Annexation Ordinance, approved by Congress before he left office in 1845. This move did not sit well with Mexico, and war with Mexico was not far behind this action.

Oregon Country gained by treaty with Great Britain in 1846: In 1818, both America and Great Britain claimed the Oregon Country and agreed that citizens of both countries could live there. In the coming years, many Americans settled in the area. The British settlers were primarily there for the fur trade, which had grown smaller. As the American population grew larger, the time came to reconsider the agreement between America and Great Britain. The British wanted to keep a good trading relationship with America, so in 1846 the two countries signed a treaty giving the Oregon Country to America.

Mexican Cession of 1848: This describes lands ceded, or given up, to the United States at the end of the Mexican War. The Treaty of Guadalupe Hidalgo was signed at the end of the war and accomplished several things, including giving all the land sought to America. The Mexicans received fifteen million dollars for those lands, and the border between America and Mexico was set at the Rio Grande River.

Today you will finish the map overlay you've been working on in this unit. To get started, look again at the map in your *United States History Atlas* entitled "Growth of the United States to 1853," and notice the territories added by the above actions. Use a wet erase marker to draw the boundaries of these areas directly onto the transparency. Remember to pay attention to the state borders when you decide where your lines should go. Now, trace the Texas Annexation in the middle and the others on the left transparency. Color and label the new territories on the map overlay.

Several types of nation building appear in this lesson: cession, treaties and annexation. More than one element of nation building was seen in the Mexican Cession, since land was ceded, a treaty was signed, and money was paid for the lands received. Often expansion had more than one element of nation building as part of the process to gain new lands.

Use your PlaceMap to fill in the chart in your Student Notebook with the states, or parts of states, added to the U.S. by each event.[1]

Choose from the three events in this part, as indicated below, and learn more about it or them. Tell what country each territory belonged to before America, how it became a part of America and future states added by this action. Make a list of three events it took to bring this about, and then tell why the addition was good for America.

one of the three events

two of the three events

all three events

F. States *Geography, History, Thinking Skills*

In your *United States Atlas*, read the pages about Michigan. When you are finished, find the blank map of Michigan in your Student Notebook and complete the following assignments:

- Place a small red star on the spot where Lansing is located, and label it. Lansing is the capital city of Michigan.

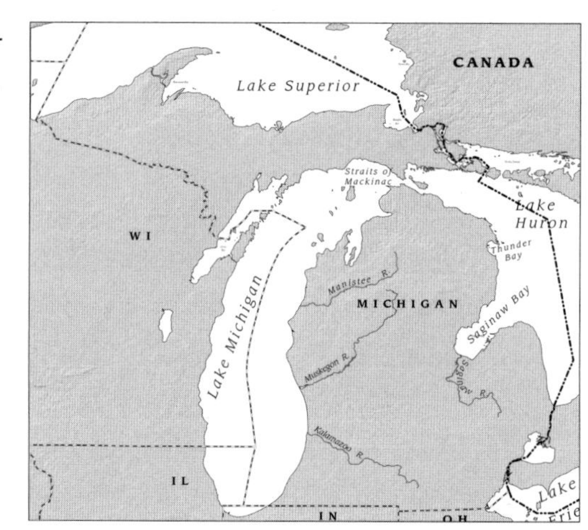

- Color and label the portions of Lake Michigan, Lake Erie, Lake Huron, and Lake Superior that border Michigan.
- Color the lines showing the Muskegon, Kalamazoo, and Manistee Rivers blue, and label them.
- Label Saginaw Bay.

- Label Thunder Bay and the Straits of Mackinac. Look up the word *strait* in your dictionary, and tell your teacher what it is.
- Color the line that shows the Saginaw River blue, and label it. This river is not labeled in your atlas, but it is the line that runs down from the Saginaw Bay.
- Label the three states and one country that border Michigan.

Teaching Tip

Experience is a great teacher, and a great way to develop memory skills. Once your children participate in an activity that illustrates a period in history, they are more likely to remember what they have learned. It is also one more way to connect to the events of the time. Doing something done in the past also helps your children get a taste of life then, which is fun and thought provoking.

G. Doing *Art, Music*

Look at the song entitled "Sweet Betsy from Pike" in your *Wee Sing America* songbook. This is a folk song that became popular as Americans were moving westward. Now listen to it on the *Wee Sing America* CD. Try to become familiar with the words and music so that you can sing along, or learn to play it on an instrument of your choice. You may want to recite, sing, or play this song during your presentation at the end of this unit.

Another skill that was popular and useful during the colonial period is tin-punching. Like its name hints, this art involves punching holes to make designs in metal. Punched metal was fairly easy to do, and made everyday things like foot and bed warmers, food coverings, and lanterns work better and look nicer.

Follow the directions in Appendix B to make a wall decoration out of punched metal. If you enjoy this craft and your parent agrees, you may also want to use the second page of instructions and make a simple lantern as well.

H. **Independent Reading** *Language Skills*

Choose something to read that you will enjoy. Then, find a quiet, comfortable place and read for the following length of time:

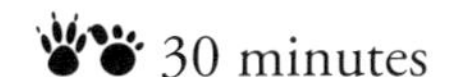

25 minutes 30 minutes

Over time, it's fun to see how much you have read. Be sure to write down what you read today on the Reading Log in your Student Notebook.

Lesson 4, Part 2

A. **Quotation Notebook** *History, Language Skills, Music*

Continue copying verses from the American National Anthem, "The Star Spangled Banner." As you examine this song, consider the imagery created by the words. Since it is also a poem, consider its rhyme pattern as well.

> Now it catches the gleam of the morning's first beam,
> In full glory reflected now shines on the stream.

Copy the above passage into your Student Notebook, and talk with your teacher about its meaning and any unknown words. Then listen to it on the *Wee Sing America* CD and follow along with the words in the songbook. Practice reading or singing each section of the song aloud.

Under each phrase printed in your Student Notebook, draw a picture or write an explanation that describes the image it creates in your mind.

A. You may want to begin previewing ideas for the unit-end presentation with your children. This will help everyone focus on similar goals for the presentation, as well as give them time to practice and get feedback for improvement.

C. As you read aloud, you model fluency, expression, and comprehension. When your voice reflects punctuation, students can see its purpose and the way it makes the passage more understandable.

- Choose two words from the verse and write at least one synonym for each one. Make sure you find a meaning that goes with its context, or use in the verse.

B. Reader *Language Skills, History*

The Cabin Faced West: page 73 ("She didn't...") through page 77, paragraph 1
Justin Morgan Had a Horse: page 97, paragraph 1 ("Ezra Fisk...") through page 103, paragraph 3

- Read the above assignment from *The Cabin Faced West* aloud, and then follow along as someone else reads the assignment from *Justin Morgan Had a Horse*.
- Read the above assignment from *The Cabin Faced West* silently, and then read the assignment from *Justin Morgan Had a Horse* aloud.
- Read the above assignments from *The Cabin Faced West* and *Justin Morgan Had a Horse* silently.

C. Read-Aloud & Narration *Language Skills, History, Thinking Skills*

Francis Scott Key: page 58 ("It was an...") through page 61

Follow the instructions below for your level. Then, in your own words, tell what happened in the story from Francis' point of view, or pretend you are Francis and tell what you think happened. Try to remember as many details as possible. You may reread the passage or listen as your teacher rereads the part you are to retell.

- Listen carefully as your teacher reads the above assignment from *Francis Scott Key* aloud.
- Read the above assignment from *Francis Scott Key* aloud.

D. Editing *Language Skills, Thinking Skills*

Continue your practice to become a good writing mechanic by looking at the rules about hyphens, apostrophes, and pronouns in the toolkit below. Not every rule is included, but this is a good start. Check a grammar handbook, a dictionary, or spell check on the computer if you are not sure how to use the rules when writing.

Mechanics Toolkit

1A - A pronoun for one person or thing can be the focus, or object, of a preposition (word that shows relationships between words such as *for, to, with,* or *in*).

Dad makes ice cream for <u>me</u>.
Mom will play a game with <u>you</u>.
Give the football to <u>him</u>.

The book belongs to her.
Put the toys in it.

1B - These pronouns can be used together as the focus, or object of a preposition (word that shows relationships between words such as *for, to, with,* or *in*). (Remember the Golden Rule - put yourself last!)

Dad will go for a bike ride with you and me.
Mom plays ball with him and her.

1C - A name and a pronoun for one person can be used together as the focus, or object, of a preposition (word that shows relationships between words such as *for, to, with,* or *in*). (Remember the Golden Rule - put yourself last!)

Dad will go for a bike ride with Billy and me.
Mom plays ball with her and Jenny.

2A - Use a hyphen to divide a word when you run out of room at the end of a line. Divide words between syllables. Use your dictionary to check for syllables if needed. Don't leave one or two letters by themselves, either.

Some famous people in American history are George Washington and Ben Franklin.
Some very big battles took place in the state of Massachusetts.

Practice these skills by correcting the sentences in your Student Notebook.[2] The number of errors in each sentence is listed after the sentence in parentheses. To show that a letter needs to be capitalized, make three lines (≡) underneath the letter that should be capitalized. To replace an incorrect word with a correct word, draw a line through the incorrect word and write the correct word above it. Add any needed punctuation.

E. Science *Geography, Thinking Skills, Art*

Look again at a globe or map of the world, and place your finger slightly northeast of Greenland, in the Arctic Ocean. Now, once again, trace the length of the Mid-Atlantic Ridge. Run your finger down the map, keeping it almost perfectly in the center of the continents, all the way to the bottom of South America. As you know, that line represents the longest mountain range in the world.

But there are several other underwater mountain ranges besides the Mid-Atlantic Ridge. Look at the chart above that shows where the underwater ranges are located, and discuss it with your teacher. Notice how they connect, and almost encircle the entire earth. The mountains in all these ranges are much like those in the Mid-Atlantic Ridge, and were formed mostly by fissure volcanoes that ooze lava onto the ocean floor when they erupt. That makes them very different from most mountains on the continents. Although there are quite a few volcanoes on land, most of the continental mountain ranges were formed in other ways. Use the above chart as a model to draw and label the chart in your Student Notebook.

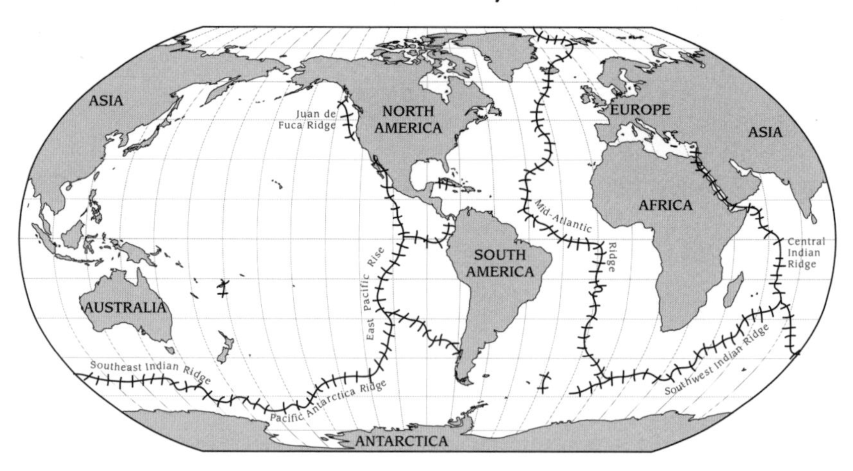

In addition to mountain ranges, there are thousands of volcanic mountains, called **seamounts**, scattered about the ocean floor. Seamounts rise at least 3,000 feet high, and some of them are tall enough to form islands on the surface of the water. The islands of Bermuda on your 3-D map were formed on top of very high seamounts. The Bermuda Rise is a large area that is elevated off the ocean floor. It probably was once a group of seamounts that were worn down over many years.

Large, mostly flat areas of the ocean floor are **abyssal plains**, and are covered with thick layers of sediment. On the other hand, there are also steep **trenches**, or cracks, in the ocean floor that can be more than six miles deep. The Puerto Rico Trench on your 3-D map is about five miles deep, which makes it the deepest part of the Atlantic Ocean.

Continue building your 3-D map by using the map-model in Appendix B to draw the outline of the Bermuda Rise. Be sure to trace over your pencil lines with a marker. Every time you add a new feature to your map it becomes a little harder to use the letters and numbers on the outer edges—but don't worry. It doesn't have to be perfect, so just do your best.

Since the Bermuda Islands are located on top of the Bermuda Rise you will have to build up the area toward the center of the rise so that one or two seamounts reach sea level, or 1½ -inches high. There are also several smaller seamounts on the rise, so add a few wherever you want.

Now add the Bahama Islands. Notice that they are located on part of the continental slope off the coast of Florida. There are several islands in the Bahamas, but for your map just build up that area so that three or four seamounts reach sea level. Remember that both Bermuda and the Bahamas are tiny compared to the continent of North America, so these islands will just be the very tops of the mountains.

Cover the rest of your map with the very thinnest layer of salt dough you can manage. It only has to be thick enough to cover the foil, and it represents the plains, or flat areas, in this part of the ocean. When that is done, look at your map-model and add a few other mountains and any other features you want to the ocean floor.

By now your map is quite heavy, so when you are satisfied with the salt dough you have added, ask for your parent's help to put your 3-D map in an oven that is heated to 150°. After an hour, remove it carefully with your parent's help, and store it in a safe place for the next couple of days.

F. States *Geography, Thinking Skills, History, Drawing*

Look again at the pages about Michigan in your *United States Atlas*. Then find the State Page in your Student Notebook, and fill in the information.

Make State Cards for Michigan by following the instructions found in Appendix B. Michigan is a Midwestern state, so be sure to outline the cards in red.

G. Interactive Writing *Language Skills, Thinking Skills*

Complete this writing activity with your partner.

Choose an article from a newspaper, news magazine, or online news source that relates to a current event in local, state or national government. Then ask your partner to read the article and answer the following questions in your Student Notebook:

Do you agree with the article; why or why not?
What do you think should happen in the future regarding this issue?

Tell about the news story using the number sentences indicated below. Then tell what you think about what your partner wrote. Write several sentences in reply, including whether or not you agree with your partner, and why. End with a question for your partner.

- at least four sentences
- at least five sentences
- Tell about the news story with at least one paragraph. Then tell what you think about what your partner wrote with a second paragraph.

Remember that a paragraph is a group of sentences that relate to one topic, or main idea. State the topic or main idea of the paragraph at

From Dr. Beechick

"If you're asking about the communication level of writing, that is a longer teaching problem. I think we complicate it by using the term "creative writing," because then we think a sort of magic should happen in the brain to produce original thoughts on paper. But put something in the brain first. After your child experiences something or reads something, then you can help him develop his thoughts by conversing with him. After that preparation, he should find it easier to write it down."

– *You Can Teach Your Child Successfully*, page 299

or near the beginning of the paragraph. You do not want the reader to read your paragraph for very long without knowing for sure what you think!

H. **Independent Reading** *Language Skills*

Choose something to read that you will enjoy. Then, find a quiet, comfortable place and read for the following length of time:

25 minutes — 30 minutes

Be sure to write down what you read today on the Reading Log in your Student Notebook.

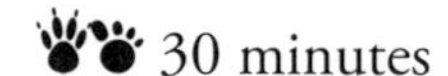

Lesson 4, Part 3

A. Copywork and dictation assignments go from an easier level (designated by) to harder levels (designated by and) Take two days for the copywork if that is more comfortable for your child. Please adapt instructions to your child's individual needs. Your child should be **consistently successful** at one level before progressing to the next, **regardless of grade.**

A. **Copywork & Dictation** *Language Skills, Thinking Skills*

Look carefully at your assigned passage below, and read it silently. Show your teacher any words you don't know, and practice saying them aloud. Now read the passage aloud, or ask your teacher to read it to you.

When you are finished copying or writing from dictation, compare your copy to the text and make any needed corrections.

- Copy or write as your teacher dictates from *The Cabin Faced West*, page 79, paragraph 4 ("Ann waited…").
- Copy or write as your teacher dictates from *Justin Morgan Had a Horse*, page 105, paragraph 5 ("Nor did the New Yorkers…") through page 106, paragraph 1.
- Choose one additional paragraph from today's assignment in *Justin Morgan Had a Horse* to write from dictation.

B. The reading assignments occur in real literature, and there are several reasons why this is important. Real literature is more interesting, and the language used is more natural. A willingness to read is built as your student experiences the success of reading a real book.

B. **Reader** *Language Skills, History*

The Cabin Faced West: page 77, paragraph 2 ("Carrying…") through page 82, paragraph 2

Justin Morgan Had a Horse: page 103, paragraph 4 ("At last the crowd…") to the bottom of page 111

- Read the above assignment from *The Cabin Faced West* aloud, and then follow along as someone else reads the assignment from *Justin Morgan Had a Horse.*
- Read the above assignment from *The Cabin Faced West* silently, and then read the assignment from *Justin Morgan Had a Horse* aloud.

Read the above assignments from *The Cabin Faced West* and *Justin Morgan Had a Horse* silently.

C. Read-Aloud & Discussion *Language Skills, History, Thinking Skills*

Francis Scott Key: page 62 (Chapter 8) through page 68, paragraph 8

Follow the directions below to read or listen to the above assignment from *Francis Scott Key*. Then make up assigned number of questions about the part of the story you just heard. Write your question and ask your teacher to answer it. After discussing her thoughts, write down the best possible answer to your question. Be sure to use complete sentences.

When you are finished, look back at the prediction or predictions you made during Lesson 3, Part 4. Were you able to predict what would happen? Be sure to mark the "Came to Pass" box for each prediction when it does happen.

Listen carefully as your teacher reads the above assignment from *Francis Scott Key*.

Make up one question. Make up two questions.

Read the above assignment from *Francis Scott Key* aloud; then make up three questions.

D. Vocabulary & Spelling *Language Skills, Thinking Skills*

Vocabulary:
Write each vocabulary word on an index card, and use a thesaurus to find a synonym for it. If you cannot find a synonym, use a dictionary to look up the meaning of the word. Then on the back of each card, draw a picture or write a clue so you can remember how each word was used in the story. Write a *D* or *S* by your clue to tell whether you wrote a definition or synonym.

full-fledged	**politics**	**foothold**	**gaped**	**glowering**
hullabaloo	**vehemence**	**skylarking**	**despicable**	**dandy**

Spelling:
Look at the list of words on your Student Notebook page, and divide each word into syllables by drawing a slash line (/) between the syllables. After you have marked each word, use a dictionary to check your work.[3] If you don't know what the word means, read the definition while you are checking your syllable markings. Then place a check next to each word to show that you know what the word means.

Look at the spelling word cards you made in Part 1. Read each word, and then cover it with your hand and try to spell it aloud. Then uncover it and see if you were correct. Review the meanings of any words that you do not remember.

E. As your child learns to take notes, it may be helpful to stop the video at intervals and discuss what has happened or been said. Ask questions that will help him understand the important parts of what he has seen or heard.

E. **History** *Thinking Skills*

Presidential Focus: Continue your study of American presidents by reading the U.S. Presidents Flash Cards about Andrew Jackson and Martin Van Buren. Use the things you learn to fill out the Presidential Focus page in your Student Notebook.

Together with your teacher, watch Episode 1, Chapter 5 on the *Discovering America's Founders* DVD about John Quincy Adams, who was the sixth president of the United States.

Before you begin though, take a minute to look at the Video Profile page for this lesson in your Student Notebook, and see what kinds of questions it asks.[4]

As you watch the video lesson, keep the Video Profile page in front of you. When you notice that the narrator, or person telling the story, is answering one of the questions, stop the video long enough to write the answer on your Profile page. Continue doing this as often as necessary as you finish watching the video lesson.

As you watch the video lesson, use a piece of scrap paper to jot down important things that the **narrator**, or person telling the story, says about John Quincy Adams. This is called taking notes, and is a good way to help you remember what you hear or see. You do not need to use sentences when you take notes—single words or **phrases**, which are short groups of words, will work fine as long as they help you remember the important things. If it is helpful, stop the lesson when you need to, or watch it a second time.

When you are finished, use your notes and your memory to fill in the Video Profile page.

F. **States** *Geography, History, Thinking Skills*

In your *United States Atlas*, read the pages about Iowa. When you are finished, find the blank map of Iowa in your Student Notebook and complete the following assignments:

- Place a small red star on the spot where Des Moines is located, and label it. Des Moines is the capital city of Iowa.
- Color the lines showing the Des Moines, Missouri, Mississippi, and Cedar Rivers blue, and label them. If you have trouble finding them, two of these rivers lie along the east and west borders of Iowa.

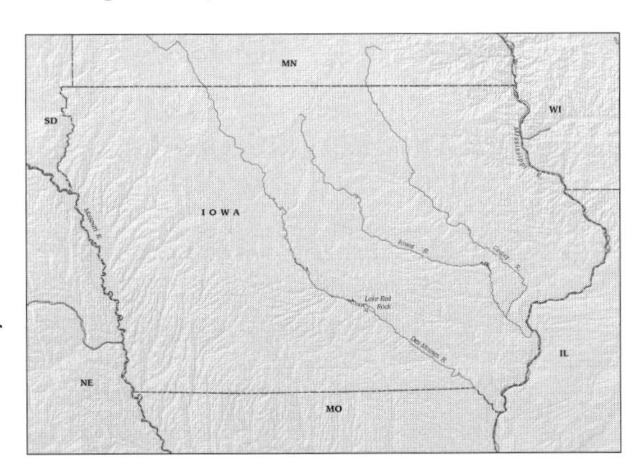

- Color and label Lake Red Rock.

- Color the line showing the Iowa River blue, and label it. This river is not labeled in your atlas, but it runs through Iowa City.
- Label the six states that border Iowa.

G. Cooking *Language Skills, Thinking Skills, Drawing*

With your parent's permission and supervision, look in *Eat Your Way Through the USA*, choose a recipe that comes from either Michigan or Iowa, and prepare it for your family. After everyone has had a taste, find out who liked it, and whether anyone would like to have it again. What did you think about it?

In your Student Notebook, draw a picture of the dish you chose to make and write the following number of sentences about your family's reaction to it:

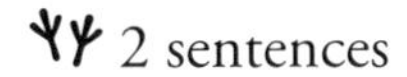 2 sentences  3 sentences  4 sentences

H. Independent Reading *Language Skills*

Choose something to read that you will enjoy. Then, find a quiet, comfortable place and read for the following length of time:

25 minutes 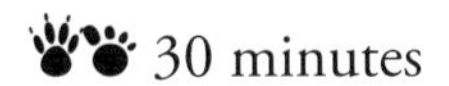 30 minutes

Be sure to write down what you read today on the Reading Log in your Student Notebook.

Lesson 4, Part 4

A. Quotation Notebook *History, Language Skills, Music*

Continue copying verses from the American National Anthem, "The Star Spangled Banner." As you examine this song, consider the imagery created by the words. Since it is also a poem, consider its rhyme pattern as well.

> 'Tis the Star Spangled Banner! O long may it wave
> O'er the land of the free and the home of the brave!

Copy the above passage into your Student Notebook, and talk with your teacher about its meaning and any unknown words. Then listen to it on the *Wee Sing America* CD and follow along with the words in the songbook. Practice reading or singing each section of the song aloud.

Under each phrase printed in your Student Notebook, draw a picture or write an explanation that describes the image it creates in your mind.

Choose two words from the verse and write at least one synonym for each one. Make sure you find a meaning that goes with its context, or use in the verse.

B. Reader *Language Skills, History*

The Cabin Faced West: page 82, paragraph 3 ("The sun had…") through page 87, paragraph 6
Justin Morgan Had a Horse: page 111, the last paragraph ("The roar of…") through page 116

Read the above assignment from *The Cabin Faced West* aloud, and then follow along as someone else reads the assignment from *Justin Morgan Had a Horse*.

Read the above assignment from *The Cabin Faced West* silently, and then read the assignment from *Justin Morgan Had a Horse* aloud.

Read the above assignments from *The Cabin Faced West* and *Justin Morgan Had a Horse* silently.

C. In the give-and-take of discussion, you can listen to your student's understanding of the passage, ask questions, and share your thoughts. All of these combine to expand his thinking on the topic.

C. Read-Aloud & Narration *Language Skills, History, Thinking Skills*

Francis Scott Key: pagc 68, paragraph 9 ("I took my…") through page 73, paragraph 1

After reading or listening to the read-aloud assignment, talk with your teacher and try to predict what will happen in the future based on what you know of the characters and events. Write down your predictions in your Student Notebook. Later you will look back and see if they were accurate. Try not to peek ahead!

Listen carefully as your teacher reads the above assignment from *Francis Scott Key* aloud. Then write down something that you think will happen in the story.

Write down another thing that you think will happen in the story.

Read the above assignment from *Francis Scott Key* aloud. Then write down three things that you think will happen in the story.

D. Editing
Language Skills, Thinking Skills

Reread the Mechanics Toolkit from Lesson 4, Part 2. Be the teacher and tell what each skill means and how it is used.

Use your readers to find two examples of each rule, and either show them to your teacher or write them in your Student Notebook.

Use your readers to find four examples of each rule, and either show them to your teacher or write them in your Student Notebook.

E. Science
Geography, Thinking Skills, Art

In Lesson 2 you learned about waves, which are one way that ocean water is always moving. In this part you will learn about another type of movement in the ocean waters—the tides. These movements are not always as easy to observe as waves are, but if you live near an ocean and pay attention, you can see them or their effects.

Ocean tides are the regular rise and fall of the water level over a period of time. A high tide, also called **flood tide**, causes the water in an area to become deeper and go further up on the beaches. Low tide, also known as **ebb tide**, causes exactly the opposite—water becomes shallower and withdraws from the shoreline. It usually takes about 12 hours for tides to change from high to low, or from low to high.

Although many things can affect tides, these changes in water level are basically caused by gravity—gravity from the moon, the sun, and the earth. As you know, the moon circles the earth, and earth's gravity holds it in orbit. In turn, as the moon's gravity pulls back on the earth, it causes two large bulges in the oceans. One of these bulges occurs on the side of the earth facing the moon, and the other happens on the exact opposite side of the earth. Both bulges cause a high tide on nearby beaches. At the same time these high tides occur, it is low tide in the places between.

Some high tides are higher than others, and happen when the sun and the moon are in line with earth. This adds the sun's gravitational pull to the moon's, and the larger bulges they produce together are called **spring tides**. Spring tides have nothing to do with the season, and happen when the moon is either in its full- or new-moon phase. A full moon is when the entire side facing the earth is visible, and a new moon is when it can't be seen at all. There are two spring tides each month.

From Dr. Beechick

"So as teacher, you do not have to be an "answer giver." That should take pressure off practically all of us, since only a few science professionals probably feel qualified to take that role. A more useful role is "interest partner." If you are interested in children's science pursuits, you will have opportunities to help them think through problems, decide what to read next, or what to observe or experiment on next. You can raise questions about children's science topics that they may not think of. Your adult thinking skills are more advanced than theirs, so they advance by interacting with you."

– *You Can Teach Your Child Successfully*, page 328

When high tides are lower than usual, it is because the sun's gravitational pull cancels out the moon's, and lessens its effect. These are called **neap tides**, and occur during the first and last quarter-moon phases. A quarter-moon is when only half of the side facing the earth is visible. There are two neap tides each month.

Discuss the chart below with your teacher, and then use it as a model to complete the one in your Student Notebook. When you are finished, write one or two sentences that explain what tides are and what causes them. Then write a short explanation of spring tides, and neap tides.

You have finished building all the features on your 3-D map, so today you will paint it with your watercolors. If you don't have time to finish, with your parent's permission you can complete it over the next couple of days.

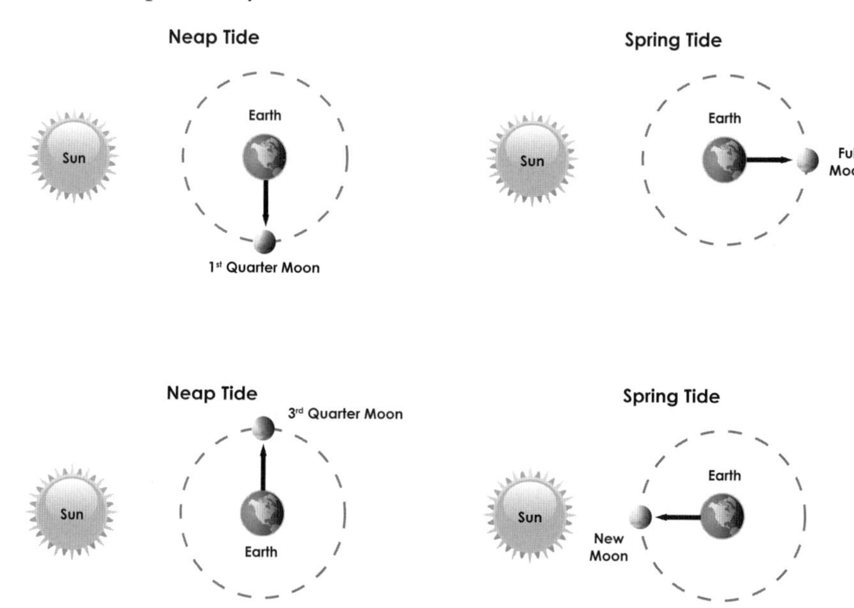

Begin by coloring all the land areas green. Try not to let green paint get on the continental shelf, which is very close to the land. Don't forget the islands—Cuba, Puerto Rico, Bermuda, and the Bahamas. Since you are using watercolor, you may want to let the first coat dry and then add another to get a brighter color. Add a little brown to the Appalachian Mountains.

Next, paint parts of the rift in the Mid-Atlantic Ridge red, and allow the red to spill over the sides and run down the mountains in some places. Then finish it by painting all the mountains in the ridge dark grey. Add black to the inside of the rift that you didn't color red, and paint the Puerto Rico Trench black. Paint the rest of the seamounts dark grey, including the ones that hold the islands of Bermuda and the Bahamas. Don't paint the Bermuda Rise grey, just the seamounts on it.

Make the ocean floor dark blue, the continental slope and Bermuda Rise medium blue, and the continental shelf light blue. Making the colors darker may require a couple of coats of paint. When you are finished, admire your hard work! Be sure to show off your 3-D map in your Unit End Presentation.

F. States *Geography, Thinking Skills, History, Drawing*

Look again at the pages about Iowa in your *United States Atlas*. Then find the State Page in your Student Notebook, and fill in the information.

Make State Cards for Iowa by following the instructions found in Appendix B. Iowa is a Midwestern state, so be sure to outline the cards in red.

G. Writing *Language Skills, Thinking Skills*

In Unit 2, you learned about the Bill of Rights. The first amendment of the Constitution **guarantees**, or promises citizens of the United States the right to freedom of expression and freedom of the press. This means that citizens have the right to share their thoughts and opinions in a newspaper or other way of reporting news, like television, radio or an online news program.

For many years, the best way to tell others your opinion has been writing a letter to the editor of a newspaper. A letter to the editor usually gives your position on a current event or problem that you think exists in your community. It is also usually about something that is of interest to others. You want to give your opinion and let readers know how you feel about the problem, but you should also support your point of view with facts and examples.

A letter to the editor is a type of business letter, and is more formal than a friendly letter you might write to a friend or your grandmother. Because of this, there are certain things that should be included. The first is the *return address*, which tells where the letter has come from. Write the date beneath the return address without using any abbreviations. The next part is the *inside address*. This is the name and address of the person or organization where you are sending the letter. The next part is the *salutation*, or greeting. If you know the name of the editor, address it to that person. If not, you can use several greetings such as "Dear Sir", "Dear Madam", or "Dear Editor". Follow each salutation with a colon.

The *body* is the next part of the letter. This is where you tell the purpose of your letter and then give the facts that support your purpose. If you have more than one fact, or reason that supports your purpose, give each one of those reasons its own paragraph, but remem-

Connect Learning to Life

Writing skills are preparation for real life, not just a school time activity. Whenever you do an activity that equips your children for life, such as learning how to write a letter to the editor, point it out to them. Take time to think about the connections you see between what you are teaching your children and the way they might actually use the knowledge or skills in their daily life. Doing this regularly will help you answer that age-old question, "Will I ever use what I'm learning?"

ber to be brief. Do not indent your paragraphs—just skip a line between them. Even if you feel strongly about your opinion, always be respectful to the readers. The *closing* is next. The most common closings are "Yours Truly" or "Sincerely", followed by a comma. The last part of the letter is your signature. If you are typing the letter, go down four lines after your closing and type your name. Whatever way you type your name is the same way you should sign the letter.

When published, these letters are in a special section in many newspapers called "Letters to the Editor". Below is a sample letter to an editor. (The addresses and names used are not real.) Look at this letter for examples of spacing and placement of the parts of the letter.

123 Apple Road
Happy Beach, Florida 91919
June 5, 2009

Mr. Bob Smith, Editor
Happy Beach News
456 Orange Street
Happy Beach, Florida 91919

Dear Mr. Smith:

I think the speed limit needs to be lower on Apple Road, which is a part of the town of Happy Beach. My family lives on this road and so I have many concerns.

I have younger brothers and sisters. Even though we have a fence around our yard, it would be terrible if they were to accidentally get out and run in the street. I think the cars on this road go very fast (the speed limit is 45 miles per hour,) and so it would be difficult for them to stop if someone ran out in the road. That would be awful!

We also have many pets. Some of our pets are older, and do not hear or see very well. Since we lived here before this road was built, they might not know to stay out of the road. Again, it would be hard for a car going 45 mph to stop for them. I read that it takes a car going that fast a long time to stop. That would not give a driver enough time to miss our sweet kitty Puffy, or our great old dog, Bucky.

This situation does not just affect us. There have been many accidents on this road. The Happy Beach Transportation Department says that there have been more accidents on this road than any other road in town. I think there would be fewer accidents with a lower speed limit.

Thank you for reading my letter. I hope others will agree and encourage Happy Beach to make the speed limit lower on Apple Road.

Yours truly,

Sally Jones

Think of an issue in your family that you feel strongly about. Discuss this topic with your teacher to organize your thoughts about it. Then write a **rough draft**, or first copy, of a letter to the editor of a pretend newspaper about your issue. Once you are finished, check to make sure that you included all the parts of a business letter in your letter, and give it to another person to read. Consider any input given, and then revise your letter to reflect the changes needed. As a final step, type or rewrite your letter to make it look more business-like.

Think of an issue in your neighborhood that you feel strongly about. Then follow all the directions above and write a letter to the editor.

Think of an issue in your community that you feel strongly about. Then follow the instructions above for writing another letter to the editor.

H. **Independent Reading** *Language Skills*

Choose something to read that you will enjoy. Then, find a quiet, comfortable place and read for the following length of time:

25 minutes 30 minutes

Be sure to write down what you read today on the Reading Log in your Student Notebook.

H. Independent reading provides regular practice for word study and reading skills, as well as time for practice of thinking skills. Quiet time to consider ideas and tie new information with old is essential in building new understandings.

Lesson 4, Part 5

This part is set aside for completion of any work left undone from the lesson, and review of concepts and content. It is also a time to expand the work of the lesson with art, mapping, or games.

- Review the Steps for Thinking found in Part 1.
- Give your teacher your stack of vocabulary cards for the lesson. As she shows you each word, tell her the meaning of the word and how it was used in the story.

One of the most important ways to develop comprehension is to build vocabulary. Becoming familiar with new words by reading, writing, speaking, and listening to them helps the new words become part of your student's functional vocabulary. Understanding the meaning and being able to use each word correctly is more important than merely memorizing the definition.

Sometimes children have difficulty remembering the difference between cities, counties, states, and countries. Mapping helps children distinguish between these geographic areas and terms. Placing the information on state cards also helps reinforce these categories.

Teaching Tip

Crossword puzzles, word scrambles, and other word games are great ways to increase recognition of important terms and the spelling of those words. The more frequently a child reads a word and thinks about its meaning, the more likely that child is to remember the word and use it in the future.

- Listen as your teacher reads the spelling words that you studied from Part 1. Write each word in your Student Notebook as she dictates it. When you are finished, look back at your spelling word cards and make corrections as needed. Show your teacher how you did.
- Use the United States map that is near the front of your *Atlas of the United States* to find Michigan and Iowa. Then, on the large outline map of the U.S., draw red lines around them because they are Midwestern states. Write in the names of the states, and draw small stars to show where their capital cities are located. Next to the stars, write the name of each capital city.
- It is always interesting to observe things in nature. With your parent's permission, take your watercolors and some paper outside. You will need to carry a water bottle, and the cup you usually use to practice painting. If there is not a good place to observe nature in your yard, perhaps you and your family could spend some time at a park.

  When you find a place that you like, sit and observe the scenery around you for a short time. Pretend you are an explorer who found this area, and you would like to show others what it looks like. Use your watercolors to paint a picture of the things around you. Remember to relax—there is no wrong way to do this activity as long as you keep the paint on the paper. This is practice, so have fun with it.
- Use your USA Activity CD to print at least one activity for the states you studied in this lesson. Then add any that you complete to your Student Notebook.
- Complete the Nation Building Crossword Puzzle in your Student Notebook.[5]

Enrichment Activities

1. Watch Episode 2, Chapter 5 on the *Discovering America's Founders* DVD about Benjamin Banneker. You may take notes while you watch, or stop the video from time to time to write things down. When you are finished, make a list of at least ten interesting facts about Benjamin, and add them to your Student Notebook.
2. At the library or on the Internet research a Native American tribe from the Midwestern region of the United States. If you do not yet have a tribe in mind that you would like to find out more about, choose one from the map entitled "Native American Nations, c. 1750" in your *United States History Atlas*. Print a Native American Profile sheet from your Student Resources CD and fill it out.

Place the new profile sheet and picture in your Native American Notebook, or add them to your Student Notebook.

3. Although some First Ladies are more well-known than others, each was an important part of her husband's presidency. At the library or on the Internet, find out at least three facts about the First Ladies who shared the White House with the U.S. Presidents you studied in this lesson. Add your research to your Student Notebook.

Additional Resources

Davy Crocket: Young Rifleman (Childhood of Famous Americans), by Aileen Wells Park

Daniel Webster: Defender of the Union (Sower series), by Robert Allen

If you read any of the above books, be sure to print a Book Review page from your Student Resources CD, fill it out, and place it in your Student Notebook.

Answers

1. Texas Annexation (1845) - Texas, New Mexico, Oklahoma, Kansas and Colorado
   Oregon Country (1846) - Washington, Oregon, Idaho, Montana, Wyoming
   Mexican Cession (1848) - California, Nevada, Arizona, Utah, Colorado, Wyoming, New Mexico.

2. 1. Andy McPhale's family were neighbors of the Hamiltons.
   2. After the log-pulling contest, Little Bub was a leg-weary horse.
   3. Polly and Francis answered Uncle Philip's invitation to come to Washington.
   4. Daniel Scott was part of George Washington's force at Valley Forge.
   5. Some high-duck dandies challenged Morgan's horse to a race in Brookfield.
   6. Did Francis enjoy his work at St. John's as a Sunday school teacher?
   7. Much to Joel's delight, Morgan's horse beat Silvertail to the finish line.
   8. Little Bub beat both the high-duck horses and won the fifty-dollar purse for Justin Morgan.
   9. Did Master Morgan sell Little Bub to Horse-Trader Hawkes?

3. sur/round/ed, in/ter/fer/ence, lone/some, cin/na/mon, crit/i/cal/ly, de/ci/sive/ly, ma/te/ri/al, wick/ed/ness
   com/mu/ni/ty, breath/less/ly, swiv/eled, con/tin/ued
   in/struc/tion, fash/ion/a/ble, con/tent/ed/ly, gen/er/os/i/ty

4. Answers are in Appendix A.

5. Answers are in Appendix A.

Lesson 5, Part 1

Steps for Thinking

1. Success during difficult times depends on the ability of the people to follow a leader or purpose and work together.
2. There are many different ways for citizens to serve with determination during difficult times, all of which are important.
3. A nation grows stronger by recognizing and remembering the sacrifices made by those who served others during difficult times.

The **Steps for Thinking** section gives you the main ideas about the topics presented. Understanding these helps you to have productive discussions with your children so they, too, understand the bigger ideas. This forms more permanent learning, contrary to just learning facts, which tends to be temporary. These steps are useful prior to instruction, and they are also useful for review at the end of the week.

Materials

- *The Cabin Faced West*
- *Justin Morgan Had a Horse*
- *Francis Scott Key*
- *Eat Your Way Through the USA*
- *Klutz Watercolor Book*
- *United States History Atlas*
- *Children's Illustrated United States Atlas*
- *Profiles from History, Vol. 2*
- *Wee Sing America* CD and songbook
- *Handbook of Nature Study* (book or download)
- *DK Pockets: Rocks and Minerals*
- Rock Study Kit
- United States Presidents Flash Cards
- Outline Map of the U.S.
- USA Activity CD
- Activity (Part 2)
  Newspaper, newsmagazine, or online news source
- Ingredients for recipe (Part 3)

A. Copywork & Dictation *Language Skills, Thinking Skills*

Look carefully at your assigned passage below, and read it silently. Show your teacher any words you don't know, and practice saying them aloud. Now read the passage aloud, or ask your teacher to read it to you.

When you are finished copying or writing from dictation, compare your copy to the text and make any needed corrections.

Copy or write as your teacher dictates from *The Cabin Faced West*, page 88, paragraph 2 ("After breakfast...").

Copy or write as your teacher dictates from *Justin Morgan Had a Horse*, page 122, paragraphs 3 and 4 ("Our Bub is in fine...").

Choose one additional paragraph from today's assignment in *Justin Morgan Had a Horse* to write from dictation.

B. Reader *Language Skills, History*

The Cabin Faced West: page 87, paragraph 7 ("But all the way...") through page 92, paragraph 3
Justin Morgan Had a Horse: pages 117-123 (Chapter 13)

Read the above assignment from *The Cabin Faced West* aloud, and then follow along as someone else reads the assignment from *Justin Morgan Had a Horse*.

Read the above assignment from *The Cabin Faced West* silently, and then read the assignment from *Justin Morgan Had a Horse* aloud.

Read the above assignments from *The Cabin Faced West* and *Justin Morgan Had a Horse* silently.

D. Read the list of words to your child. If your student would rather spell the words aloud than write them, it is perfectly acceptable. As you dictate each word, put small dots beside any misspelled words. Then have your child copy them onto the Student Notebook page.

C. Read-Aloud & Discussion

Language Skills, History, Thinking Skills

Francis Scott Key: page 73, paragraph 2 ("Slowly the doctor…") through the top of page 77

Read over the following questions that you will discuss later. Then read, or listen carefully as your teacher reads, the above assignment from *Francis Scott Key* aloud. You may want to take notes to help answer the questions after you listen. If needed, you can look back at the story to find specific details.

Pretend you are a news reporter and choose an event that you heard or read about today. Think about what you know from the story, and in your own words answer the following questions about that event:

- What took place?
- When did it take place?
- Where did it take place?
- Who were the main people involved?
- How does this event affect Francis Scott Key's life?
- Why do you think it took place?

Choose a second event to report on using the questions listed above.

Tell how the two events you reported on are related.

D. Spelling

Language Skills, Thinking Skills

Look at the list of words below, and copy each one onto an index card. Then look back at Lesson 1, Part 1 for ideas about how to organize the words, and ways to remember their spelling. Show your teacher how you organized them.

Turn your cards face down and listen as your teacher dictates the words on your spelling list. Spell each word the best that you can, either aloud or by writing it in your Student Notebook. Your teacher may add up to five words that are difficult for you to read or write.

comparison	possessions	urgings	motioned
whinnying	shoulder	psalm	smudged
dandelion	clamored	pilgrimage	shimmering
auction	apprehending	permission	astonishment

E. History

Thinking Skills

A country's flag is very important, because it is the outward symbol of the land, the people, and the government of that country. It stands for the values and attitudes of a nation. In Unit 2, you learned what the colors on the first American flag meant, and why there were a certain number of stars and stripes. Talk with your teacher about what you remember from that lesson, and then review by looking back at the Student Notebook pages for Lesson 5, Part 3 of Unit 2.

Now look at the flag on this page, and compare it to the flag that is pictured in Unit 2. What has changed?[1] Write your observations in your Student Notebook.

The design of the flag changed often—over 20 times—in the early years of the United States. But stars and stripes were always included in the variations, sometimes with other symbols. Finally, in 1912 the design became official and ended up being very similar to the first flag. If the United States adds a new state, then its flag changes by the addition of another star. From the earliest days, Americans referred to their flag as the Stars and Stripes and Old Glory. Then when Francis Scott Key's poem became popular, so did a new nickname for the American flag—the Star Spangled Banner. These three names are still in use today.

Because the American flag represents our nation and its values, many people believe it deserves honor and respect. In fact, shortly after the flag's design was finalized a Flag Code that describes how the flag is to be carried, hung, folded, raised, lowered, and even disposed of was published. Later the Flag Code became a federal law, but there are no penalties for people who choose not to follow it, and the law is seldom enforced. Even so, most Americans try to show their **patriotism**, or love of country, by respecting their flag.

According to the Flag Code, no other flag should fly above the Stars and Stripes, and it should never be allowed to touch the ground. When it passes by in a parade or other occasion, military people in uniform should stand and salute in the regular way. Other people should stand, remove their hats, and place their right hands over their hearts to show respect and loyalty. People should turn to face the flag and salute in the ways described above when they hear "The Star Spangled Banner", which is the National Anthem for the United States.

Connect Learning to Life

Learning about the flag that represents your country is a very important activity. It is a national symbol, but it is also a personal connection to the other citizens of your nation. Encourage your children to practice flag etiquette as proud citizens.

The American flag flies at **half-staff**, or only half way up its pole, as a sign that the nation is **mourning**, or grieving for, a national tragedy or someone in the government who has died. The president or a governor of a state must order this to happen. It is also against the Flag Code to carry the Stars and Stripes horizontally, or flat, at any time.

Today you will learn how to fold the American flag properly. If you have a flag at home, with your parent's permission you can use it for this activity. If you don't, use a towel and pretend. It takes two people to fold the flag, one at each end, so find a partner to work with you. Follow the Flag Folding instructions found in Appendix B.

In your Student Notebook, read the questions about flag **etiquette**, or manners, with your teacher. Consider what you have learned in this lesson, and then answer each one with a *T* for true or an *F* for false.[2]

Design a flag for your family in your Student Notebook. If you want, use the library or the Internet to find out about the character qualities various colors and symbols stand for. Then, for your design, choose some that represent values and attitudes that are important to your family. Use construction paper, stickers, crayons, markers, colored pencils, or anything else you want to create your flag. Then, on the next page list each color and symbol you chose, and tell why it was included.

Lapbook Activity

F. States　　*Geography, History, Thinking Skills*

In your *United States Atlas*, read the pages about Wisconsin. When you are finished, find the blank map of Wisconsin in your Student Notebook and complete the following assignments:

- Place a small red star on the spot where Madison is located, and label it. Madison is the capital city of Wisconsin.
- Color the lines that show the Mississippi, St. Croix, Chippewa, Black, and Wisconsin Rivers blue, and label them.
- Color and label Lake Winnebago, and the portions of Lake Michigan and Lake Superior that border Wisconsin.
- Label Green Bay.

- Label the four states that border Wisconsin.

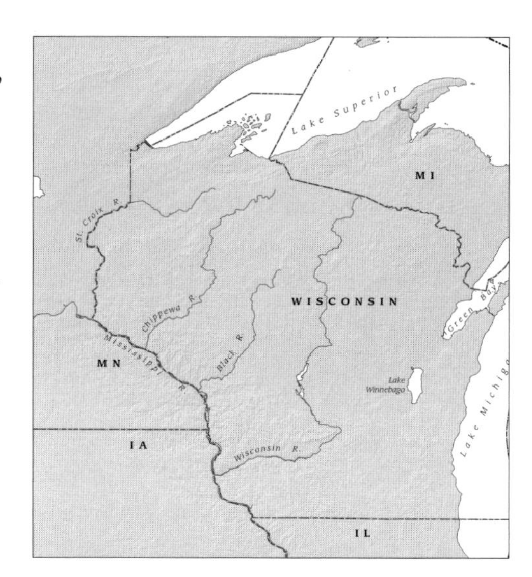

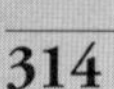

G. **Doing** *Art, Music*

Look at the song entitled "There Are Many Flags" in your *Wee Sing America* songbook. This is a folk song that has been sung through the years to express respect for the American flag. Now listen to it on the *Wee Sing America* CD. Try to become familiar with the words and music so that you can sing along, or learn to play it on an instrument of your choice. You may want to recite, sing, or play this song during your presentation at the end of this unit.

In this unit you spent a lot of time learning about oceans, so today you will practice painting shorelines and sea grasses. This will involve using colored pencils and watercolors together to get some interesting effects—and you may come up with a few ideas of your own that you'd like to try out. Remember, your artwork does not have to look like anyone else's!

Follow the directions for Unit 3 Watercolor Activity in Appendix B to get started. and then use pictures or your own ideas to experiment further.

G. Encourage your children to see their artwork as part of a process. After completing a piece of artwork, ask them to tell you what they like about it, as well as things they might like to improve. Share with them aspects of their artwork that you enjoy. To model this process, you may want to try the activity with them and ask them to share their opinions with you!

H. **Independent Reading** *Language Skills*

Choose something to read that you will enjoy. Then, find a quiet, comfortable place and read for the following length of time:

25 minutes 30 minutes

Over time, it's fun to see how much you have read. Be sure to write down what you read today on the Reading Log in your Student Notebook.

Lesson 5, Part 2

A. **Quotation Notebook** *History, Language Skills, Music*

Continue copying verses from the American National Anthem, "The Star Spangled Banner." As you examine this song, consider the imagery created by the words. Since it is also a poem, consider its rhyme pattern as well.

> O thus be it ever, when freemen shall stand
> Between their loved homes and the war's desolation!

Copy the above passage into your Student Notebook, and talk with your teacher about its meaning and any unknown words. Then listen to it on the *Wee Sing America* CD and follow along with the words in the songbook. Practice reading or singing each section of the song aloud.

Under each phrase printed in your Student Notebook, draw a picture or write an explanation that describes the image it creates in your mind.

Choose two words from the verse and write at least one synonym for each one. Make sure you find a meaning that goes with its context, or use in the verse.

B. Reader

Language Skills, History

The Cabin Faced West: page 92, paragraph 4 ("Some of the...") through page 96, paragraph 2

Justin Morgan Had a Horse: pages 124-129 (Chapter 14)

Read the above assignment from *The Cabin Faced West* aloud, and then follow along as someone else reads the assignment from *Justin Morgan Had a Horse.*

Read the above assignment from *The Cabin Faced West* silently, and then read the assignment from *Justin Morgan Had a Horse* aloud.

Read the above assignments from *The Cabin Faced West* and *Justin Morgan Had a Horse* silently.

C. Read-Aloud & Narration

Language Skills, History, Thinking Skills

C. Since students do not have to worry about decoding during read-aloud time, they can focus totally on the meaning of what they are hearing. This allows them the opportunity to think about the ideas and information being presented, and to formulate their own thoughts.

Francis Scott Key: page 77, paragraph 1 ("But when news...") to the bottom of page 80

Follow the instructions below for your level. Then, in your own words, tell what happened in the story from Francis' point of view, or pretend you are Francis and tell what you think happened. Try to remember as many details as possible. You may reread the passage or listen as your teacher rereads the part you are to retell.

Listen carefully as your teacher reads the above assignment from *Francis Scott Key* aloud.

Read the above assignment from *Francis Scott Key* aloud.

D. Editing

Language Skills, Spelling Skills

Continue your practice to become a good writing mechanic by looking at the rules about hyphens, apostrophes, and pronouns in the toolkit below. Not every rule is included, but this is a good start. Check a grammar handbook, a dictionary, or spell check on the computer if you are not sure how to use the rules when writing.

Mechanics Toolkit

1A - A pronoun for more than one person or thing can be the focus, or object of a preposition (word that shows relationships between words such as *for, to, with* or *in*).

Dad makes ice cream for us.
Give the football to them.
Bill will get chairs for you.

1B - These pronouns can be used together as the focus, or object of a preposition (word that shows relationships between words such *for, to, with* or *in*). (Remember the Golden Rule - put yourself last!)

Dad will bring bikes for you and us.
Coach has new bats for them and us.

2A - Use a hyphen to to write two-word numbers under one hundred, and fractions.

There are twenty-five people at the show.
One-half of the people in the show are girls.

3A - Add an apostrophe at the end of a word ending in *s* to show that something belongs to more than one.

The students' books were on their desks.
The boys' cars are their favorite toys.

Practice these skills by correcting the sentences in your Student Notebook.[3] The number of errors in each sentence is shown in parentheses after the sentence. Put three lines underneath a letter that needs to be capitalized. To replace an incorrect word with a correct word, draw a line through the incorrect word and write the correct word above it. Add any needed punctuation.

E. Science

Thinking Skills

There is more sedimentary rock on the earth's surface than any other type, and most of it is formed underwater—in quiet areas of oceans, rivers, and lakes.

Together with your teacher, read the section in your *Rocks and Minerals* book that is entitled "Sedimentary Rocks," and the small portion about this type of rock in the section entitled "Identifying Rocks." This section is part of the chapter that tells about rocks located toward the front of the book. Then listen carefully as your teacher reads about this type of rock on page 745 in the *Handbook of Nature Study*. When she is finished, discuss the things that you have read and heard.

Sedimentary rock can be formed from weathered rocks and minerals, or from the remains of plants and animals. Either way, as sediments build up over time, the upper layers get heavier and heavier until their weight begins to press and **compact**, or crush, the lower layers. This pressure eventually squeezes all the liquid and spaces out of the sediment, and minerals cement the particles together to form rock.

E. If you do not own the *Handbook of Nature Study*, you can download the parts you need from the Internet at www.archive.org. Type "Handbook of Nature Study" in the search field.

Using the information that you have heard and read, write a short explanation in your Student Notebook telling how sedimentary rocks form. Be sure to include at least four steps in your explanation.

Examine a sedimentary rock specimen from your Rock Study kit, and check the index in the back of the *Rocks and Minerals* book to see if it mentions the one you chose. If it does, read about it. If it does not, use the library or Internet to find out more about the specimen you are investigating. When you are finished, write three facts about the rock in your Student Notebook. Then trace or draw and color a picture of it in the space provided.

Can you think of a good reason, not specifically mentioned in this lesson, why underwater is such a good place for sedimentary rocks to form?[4] Discuss this question with your teacher, and then record your answer in your Student Notebook.

F. States
Geography, Thinking Skills, History, Drawing

Look again at the pages about Wisconsin in your *United States Atlas*. Then find the State Page in your Student Notebook, and fill in the information.

Make State Cards for Wisconsin by following the instructions found in Appendix B. Minnesota is a Midwestern state, so be sure to outline the cards in red.

G. Interactive Writing
Language Skills, Thinking Skills

Complete this writing activity with your partner.

Choose an article from a newspaper, news magazine, or online news source that relates to a current event in local, state or national government. Then ask your partner to read the article and answer the following questions in your Student Notebook:

Do you agree with the article; why or why not?
What do you think should happen in the future regarding this issue?

Tell about the news story using the number sentences indicated below. Then tell what you think about what your partner wrote. Write several sentences in reply, including whether or not you agree with your partner, and why. End with a question for your partner.

at least four sentences

at least five sentences

Tell about the news story with at least one paragraph. Then tell what you think about what your partner wrote with a second paragraph.

Remember that a paragraph is a group of sentences that relate to one topic, or main idea. State the topic or main idea of the paragraph at or near the beginning of the paragraph. You do not want the reader to read your paragraph for very long without knowing for sure what you think!

H. **Independent Reading** *Language Skills*
Choose something to read that you will enjoy. Then, find a quiet, comfortable place and read for the following length of time:

25 minutes 30 minutes

Be sure to write down what you read today on the Reading Log in your Student Notebook.

H. Completing the reading log each day gives your student a sense of accomplishment, as well as the opportunity to work independently.

Lesson 5, Part 3

A. **Copywork & Dictation** *Language Skills, Thinking Skills*
Look carefully at your assigned passage below, and read it silently. Show your teacher any words you don't know, and practice saying them aloud. Now read the passage aloud, or ask your teacher to read it to you.

When you are finished copying or writing from dictation, compare your copy to the text and make any needed corrections.

Copy or write as your teacher dictates from *The Cabin Faced West*, page100, paragraph 1 ("We have much…").

Copy or write as your teacher dictates from *Justin Morgan Had a Horse*, page 133, paragraph 2 ("Days stretched. . . ").

Choose one additional paragraph from today's assignment in *Justin Morgan Had a Horse* to write from dictation.

A. The goal of copywork and dictation is for your children to become familiar with the language they hear and write. As your children become more familiar with the process, you can use a more natural delivery of dictation with fewer repetitions. Be careful to continue providing what your children need to be successful; but you can let them know when they are successful, you will add a little challenge by speaking at a more natural rate.

B. **Reader** *Language Skills, History*
The Cabin Faced West: page 96, paragraph 3 ("Ann stood…") through page 101, paragraph 2
Justin Morgan Had a Horse: pages 130-136 (Chapter 15)

Read the above assignment from *The Cabin Faced West* aloud, and then follow along as someone else reads the assignment from *Justin Morgan Had a Horse*.

Read the above assignment from *The Cabin Faced West* silently, and then read the assignment from *Justin Morgan Had a Horse* aloud.

Read the above assignments from *The Cabin Faced West* and *Justin Morgan Had a Horse* silently.

C. **Read-Aloud & Discussion** *Language Skills, History, Thinking Skills*

Francis Scott Key: page 80, the last paragraph ("The British...") through page 86, paragraph 1

Follow the directions below to read or listen to the above assignment from *Francis Scott Key*. Then make up the assigned number of questions about the part of the story you just read or heard. Write your questions and ask your teacher to answer them. After discussing her thoughts, write down the best possible answer to your questions. Be sure to use complete sentences.

When you are finished, look back at the prediction or predictions you made during Lesson 4, Part 4. Were you able to predict what would happen? Be sure to mark the "Came to Pass" box for each prediction when it does happen.

Listen carefully as your teacher reads the above assignment from *Francis Scott Key*.

Make up one question. Make up two questions.

Read the above assignment from *Francis Scott Key* aloud; then make up three questions.

By modeling the habit of looking up information, you have profited the student in four ways:

1. You're showing that words are a very significant part of life. Understanding the words to which we are personally exposed improves our discernment of the world around us.
2. Having the "look it up" attitude yourself shows your students that it doesn't take long to look up a word in the dictionary or a place in an atlas.
3. Osmosis learning is taking place.
4. You're promoting the value of being a "lifelong independent learner" yourself!

--*The Ultimate Geography and Timeline Guide*, page 13

D. **Vocabulary & Spelling** *Language Skills, Thinking Skills*

Vocabulary:

Write each vocabulary word on an index card, and use a thesaurus to find a synonym for it. If you cannot find a synonym, use a dictionary to look up the meaning of the word. Then on the back of each card, draw a picture or write a clue so you can remember how each word was used in the story. Write a *D* or *S* by your clue to tell whether you wrote a definition or synonym.

puny **deserter** **peculiar** **flimsy** **mercy**

miscreants **gruel** **conscience** **jovial** **frigate**

Spelling:

Look at the list of words on your Student Notebook page, and divide each word into syllables by drawing a slash line (/) between the syllables. After you have marked each word, use a dictionary to check your work.[5] If you don't know what the word means, read the definition while you are checking your syllable markings. Then place a check next to each word to show that you know what the word means.

Look at the spelling word cards you made in Part 1. Read each word, and then cover it with your hand and try to spell it aloud. Then uncover it and see if you were correct. Review the meanings of any words that you do not remember.

E. **History** *Geography, Thinking Skills*

Presidential Focus: Continue your study of American presidents by reading the U.S. Presidents Flash Cards about William Henry Harrison and John Tyler. Use the things you learn to fill out the Presidential Focus page in your Student Notebook.

You have been learning about nation building. One of the responsibilities of a nation is to defend its citizens. By successfully taking care of its people, the nation is stronger. Even though the United States was a young nation, many people felt that between the years of 1807 and 1812, Great Britain was doing things to American citizens that they should not be doing. One of these things was capturing sailors at sea and forcing them to work on British ships. Also, the British and French were still fighting and didn't want America to trade with or help out the other nation. Though Napoleon, the leader of France, said they would stop interfering with American trade, his navies continued to attack American ships. This problem was hurting the economy in America.

Another area of conflict existed on American soil. Since many settlers moved west, they had conflicts with the Native Americans who had lived there for many years. The British gave weapons to the Native Americans to attack the settlers, so that people would be discouraged from moving west. Also, there were many battles along the border of what is now Canada. At that time, Canada belonged to Great Britain. Because the United States had broken free from Great Britain during the Revolutionary War, they still were not friends. Some struggles started over land and resources along the border of Canada and this increased the feelings of many people that the United States must fight Great Britain once again. All these things led to the War of 1812.

One of the worst parts of the war was the British attack on the capital city of Washington. President Madison was with the troops when the British headed for Washington. Dolley Madison, his wife, had remained at the **White House**, the presidential home, to save whatever important articles she could. She piled a wagon high with silver, books, and papers while British cannon fire could be heard in the distance. She also managed to save an important national treasure:

From Dr. Beechick

"The children are right. What is the point of knowing that a war was fought in 1812 and that a treaty was signed? Is this education? Does this help children understand man's problems and follies in this world? Does it help them think? Does it make them better citizens and decision makers today?"

– *You Can Teach Your Child Successfully*, page 296

the painting of George Washington done by Gilbert Stuart. When the British arrived, they burned the **Capitol**, where the House of Representatives and the Senate meet, and the White House. This was a hard blow for the young nation.

After several years of fighting, the issues causing the conflict seemed to be falling by the wayside, and neither side seemed to have the will to continue. Fighting the war spread soldiers out into many different parts of the United States. It was difficult for either country to continue fighting on so many fronts. Both countries sent negotiators to Belgium to try to come up with a treaty that would end the war. The United States did not consider the first terms demanded by the British fair, so they kept trying. A decisive battle took place around that time, stopping British plans to invade the United States from Canada. After this, the British were more willing to talk about peace. On December 24, 1814, representatives signed the **Treaty of Ghent**, ending the war. There were not many permanent changes because of the war. Things returned to the way they were before all the problems started, except a boundary between Canada and the United States was established. This would be very helpful in avoiding future problems.

Use the above information, or what you learned from your readers or read-aloud book in this unit, and answer the following questions about the War of 1812. Tell your teacher if you think each statement is true or false.[6] If the statement is false, correct it so that it is true:

1. The War of 1812 was a fight mainly between the United States and Great Britain.
2. The new nation of America had a large army and navy.
3. People had to help supply the army with horses and wagons because the government did not always have money for such things.
4. Many people felt that the United States caused this fight.
5. The United States fought to defend its citizens, lands and resources.
6. Many of the American soldiers who fought in the War of 1812 were only part-time soldiers and did other work most of the time.
7. The British soldiers did not harm the buildings or people in the capitol city of Washington.
8. James Madison saved many important articles such as books and paintings from the White House before the British destroyed it.

- Add a true statement and a false statement about the War of 1812 to the list. Give the correction for the false statement.
- Add two true statements and two false statements about the War of 1812 to the list. Give the corrections for the false statements.

F. States *Geography, History, Thinking Skills*

In your *United States Atlas*, read the pages about Minnesota. When you are finished, find the blank map of Minnesota in your Student Notebook and complete the following assignments:

- Place a small red star on the spot where St. Paul is located, and label it. St. Paul is the capital city of Minnesota.
- Color the lines showing the Mississippi, Minnesota, St. Croix, Red, and Rainy Rivers blue, and label them. Several of these rivers help form the borders of Minnesota.

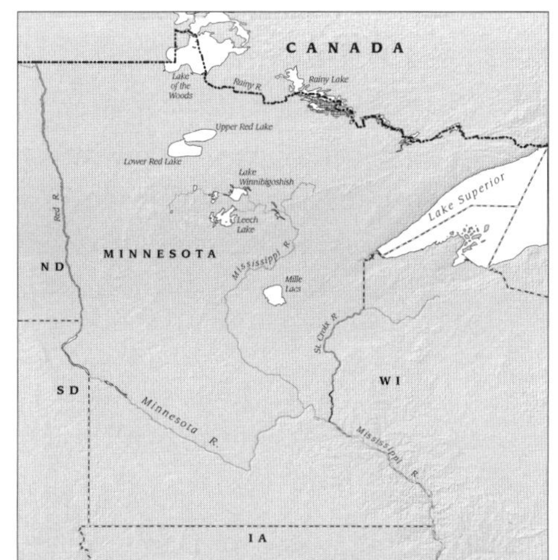

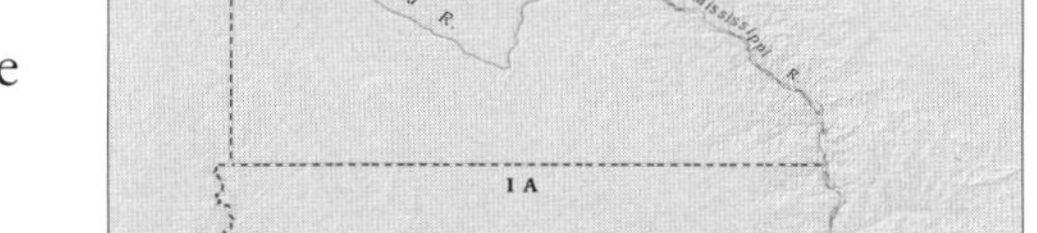

- Color and label Red Lake, Lake Winnibigoshish, Leech Lake, and Mille Lacs.
- Label the portion of Lake Superior that borders Minnesota.
- Color and label the area where Voyageurs National Park is located.
- Label the portions of Lake of the Woods and Rainy Lake that border Minnesota.
- Label the four states and one country that border Minnesota

F. Personal experience helps make learning more memorable. As you do this activity with your child, recall any personal experiences you have had with each state. This could include a relative living there, a trip, friends who moved to that area, a favorite landmark or destination, etc. This connection between knowledge and experience can make information meaningful.

G. Cooking *Language Skills, Thinking Skills, Drawing*

With your parent's permission and supervision, look in *Eat Your Way Through the USA*, choose a recipe that comes from either Wisconsin or Minnesota, and prepare it for your family. After everyone has had a taste, find out who liked it, and whether anyone would like to have it again. What did you think about it?

In your Student Notebook, draw a picture of the dish you chose to make and write the following number of sentences about your family's reaction to it:

2 sentences 3 sentences 4 sentences

H. Independent Reading *Language Skills*

Choose something to read that you will enjoy. Then, find a quiet, comfortable place and read for the following length of time:

25 minutes 30 minutes

Be sure to write down what you read today on the Reading Log in your Student Notebook.

Lesson 5, Part 4

A. Quotation Notebook *History, Language Skills, Music*

Continue copying verses from the American National Anthem, "The Star Spangled Banner." As you examine this song, consider the imagery created by the words. Since it is also a poem, consider its rhyme pattern as well.

> Blest with victory and peace, may the heaven-rescued land
> Praise the Power that hath made and preserved us a nation.

Copy the above passage into your Student Notebook, and talk with your teacher about its meaning and any unknown words. Then listen to it on the *Wee Sing America* CD and follow along with the words in the songbook. Practice reading or singing each section of the song aloud.

Under each phrase printed in your Student Notebook, draw a picture or write an explanation that describes the image it creates in your mind.

Choose two words from the verse and write at least one synonym for each one. Make sure you find a meaning that goes with its context, or use in the verse.

B. Reader *Language Skills, History*

The Cabin Faced West: page 101, paragraph 3 ("It came...") through page 106, paragraph 1
Justin Morgan Had a Horse: page 137 (Chapter 16) through page 143, paragraph 2

Read the above assignment from *The Cabin Faced West* aloud, and then follow along as someone else reads the assignment from *Justin Morgan Had a Horse.*

Read the above assignment from *The Cabin Faced West* silently, and then read the assignment from *Justin Morgan Had a Horse* aloud.

Read the above assignments from *The Cabin Faced West* and *Justin Morgan Had a Horse* silently.

Teaching Tip

Use the time your child spends reading aloud to encourage him to read with expression. Reading with expression shows an understanding of ideas as well as understanding of punctuation and mechanics. If your child does not read expressively, take the time to model reading with expression for him.

C. Read-Aloud & Narration *Language Skills, History, Thinking Skills*

Francis Scott Key: page 86, paragraph 2 ("Our ship...") to the bottom of page 89

After reading or listening to the read-aloud assignment, talk with your teacher and try to predict what will happen in the future based on what you know of the characters and events. Write down your predictions in your Student Notebook. Later you will look back and see if they were accurate. Try not to peek ahead!

Listen carefully as your teacher reads the above assignment from *Francis Scott Key* aloud. Then write down something that you think will happen in the story.

Write down another thing that you think will happen in the story.

Read the above assignment from *Francis Scott Key* aloud. Then write down at least three things that you think will happen in the story.

D. Editing

Language Skills, Thinking Skills

Reread the Mechanics Toolkit from Lesson 5, Part 2. Be the teacher and tell what each skill means and how it is used.

Use your readers to find two examples of each rule, and either show them to your teacher or write them in your Student Notebook.

Use your readers to find four examples of each rule, and either show them to your teacher or write them in your Student Notebook.

D. For days with several assignments that require writing, you may want to do some of the assignments verbally or have your student complete some of them by typing. Variety in response can help keep students motivated to do a good job.

E. Science

Thinking Skills

When sediment is deposited in an ocean or a lake, often the remains of dead animals or plants are included in the mix of weathered rocks and minerals. Then, as pressure is applied to these layers of sediment, the remains can be preserved in the rock formation as fossils. In fact, most fossils are found in sedimentary rocks because, unlike other types of rocks, they form at temperatures and pressures that do not destroy fossil remains. Listen carefully as your teacher reads about fossils on page 756 in the *Handbook of Nature Study*, then look at and discuss the pictures on page 757.

Examine three specimens of sedimentary rock from your Rock Study Kit. Then check the index in the back of the *Rocks and Minerals* book to see if it mentions any of the rocks you chose. If it does, read about them. If it does not, use the library or Internet to find out more about the specimens you are investigating. Compare your samples to the pictures you find in your book or other places. Are they similar?[7] In your Student Notebook, trace or draw and color the rocks you have examined, and list three facts about each one.

Find out about another sedimentary rock sample in your Rock Study Kit by looking in the *Rocks and Minerals* book, at the library, or on the Internet. Then write three facts about it in your Student Notebook, and use the sample or a picture as a model to draw and color it.

E. Since the language in the *Handbook of Nature Study* can be difficult to understand, you may want to discuss each paragraph with your child as you read it. In that way, you can help him understand what he is hearing.

F. States

Geography, History, Drawing, Thinking Skills

Look again at the pages about Minnesota in your *United States Atlas*. Then find the State Page in your Student Notebook, and fill in the information.

Make State Cards for Minnesota by following the instructions found in Appendix B. Minnesota is a Midwestern state, so be sure to outline the cards in red.

G. **Writing** *Language Skills, Thinking Skills*

Poems are often made of **stanzas**, or verses. A stanza is a group of lines in the poem that have a rhyming pattern. There can be different numbers of lines in each stanza. Today you will look at "The Star Spangled Banner", which has eight lines in each stanza. There is an order to the stanza, based on the last word in each line. Here is an example:

O say, can you see, by the dawn's early light,
What so proudly we hailed at the twilight's last gleaming?
Whose broad stripes and bright stars, through the perilous fight,
O'er the ramparts we watched, were so gallantly streaming?
And the rockets' red glare, the bombs bursting in air,
Gave proof through the night that our flag was still there.
O say, does that Star Spangled Banner yet wave
O'er the land of the free and the home of the brave?

Now you can make the rhyme pattern of this poem. Assign a letter to each line, starting with an *a* for the first line. Every line that ends with a word that rhymes with *light* will also be assigned the letter *a*, so lines 1 and 3 are both assigned an *a*. Line 2 ends with the word *gleaming* and is given the letter *b*. Every other line that ends with a word that rhymes with *gleaming* is also given the letter *b*. The words do not need to have the same spelling. They just have to rhyme. The fifth line has a new ending sound, so you need to give this line a new letter, the letter *c*. (Assign new letters in the order of the alphabet.) The last two lines end with words that rhyme with *wave*, so they get the letter *d*. Here is the poem again with the rhyming pattern marked:

O say, can you see, by the dawn's early light,	a
What so proudly we hailed at the twilight's last gleaming?	b
Whose broad stripes and bright stars, through the perilous fight,	a
O'er the ramparts we watched, were so gallantly streaming?	b
And the rockets' red glare, the bombs bursting in air,	c
Gave proof through the night that our flag was still there.	c
O say, does that Star Spangled Banner yet wave	d
O'er the land of the free and the home of the brave?	d

The pattern of this stanza is *ababccdd*.

Talk with your teacher about how the rockets' red glare and the bombs bursting in air gave proof that the flag was still there.[8]

Look at the second stanza of this poem in your Student Notebook and write down the rhyme pattern by assigning letters to the lines. The letters *a—d* were used in the first stanza, so begin with the letter *e*. Also, since the last two rhyming words are the same as those in the first stanza, assign them the same letter, *d*. Underline the rhyming word connected to each letter.[9]

Look at the fourth stanza of this poem in your Student Notebook and write down the rhyme pattern by assigning letters to the lines. Since the letters *a—g* have been assigned to the first and second stanzas, begin with the letter *h*. Again, since the last two rhyming words are the same as those in the first stanza, assign them the same letter, *d*. Underline the rhyming word connected to each letter.[10]

Now you are going to try your hand at writing a poem about our flag. Make a list of words in your Student Notebook that relate to the flag such as red, white, blue and any other word that you think describes the flag or what it stands for. After you finish your list, think of words that rhyme with each word you wrote and that also might relate to your topic. Remember, the words don't have to be spelled the same. They just have to rhyme.

Write a poem that has one stanza with six lines that follow the pattern *ababcc*. When finished, you may want to illustrate your poem with a picture of a flag.

Write a poem with two stanzas, each with six lines that follow the patterns *ababcc* and *dedeff*. When finished, you may want to illustrate your poem with a picture of a flag.

Write a poem with three stanzas, each with six lines that follow the pattern *ababcc*, *dedeff*, and *ghghii*. Or, you may want to attempt a poem with eight lines and a rhyme pattern of ababccdd. When finished, you may want to illustrate your poem with a picture of a flag.

H. Independent Reading *Language Skills*

Choose something to read that you will enjoy. Then, find a quiet, comfortable place and read for the following length of time:

25 minutes 30 minutes

Be sure to write down what you read today on the Reading Log in your Student Notebook.

Lesson 5, Part 5

This part is set aside for completion of any work left undone from the lesson, and review of concepts and content. It is also a time to expand the work of the lesson with art, mapping, or games.

Ask your children to read over the Steps for Thinking and briefly restate each one in their own words, or give examples that they have heard or read so far. Remind them of any ideas or examples they have thought of during the past week.

- Review the Steps for Thinking found in Part 1.
- Give your teacher your stack of vocabulary cards for the lesson. As she shows you each word, tell her the meaning of the word and how it was used in the story.
- Listen as your teacher reads the spelling words that you studied from Part 1. Write each word in your Student Notebook as she dictates it. When you are finished, look back at your spelling word cards and make corrections as needed. Show your teacher how you did.

Stories help us remember the lives of real people. They help us remember the beliefs and actions that took place. It is not as important to remember details such as dates of events, as it is to place a character in a time period. With the general time period comes context for what the character did or experienced. This, in turn, reinforces the connection to the unique qualities or events of the character's life. History, literature, and thinking skills form a great partnership.

- Use the United States map that is near the front of your *Atlas of the United States* to find Wisconsin and Minnesota. Then, on the large outline map of the U.S., draw red lines around them because they are Midwestern states. Write in the names of the states, and draw small stars where their capital cities are located. Next to the stars, write the name of each capital city.
- Read, or listen as your teacher reads, the story about Tecumseh in *Profiles from History, Volume 2*. Talk about the discussion question with your teacher, and then complete any other activities that she assigns.
- Use your USA Activity CD to print at least one activity for the states you studied in this lesson. Then add any that you complete to your Student Notebook.
- Follow the directions in Appendix B, and play Nation Building Bingo.

Are games truly a valid part of school time? Absolutely! As your child revisits content, vocabulary, and concepts, an effective review of learning takes place. The game format makes review more inviting and hopefully, more frequent.

Enrichment Activities

1. You have read that the design of the American flag changed many times in the early years of the United States. Find information about some of these designs at the library or on the Internet. Pick at least two, and draw and color a picture of each. Then write several sentences telling why each design you chose was proposed, and why it was eventually rejected. Be sure to include whether you like the old design better, or not as much, as the American flag's current design.

2. In your *United States Atlas*, look again at the states you have studied in this lesson. Scan the sections entitled "The Way It Was..." and choose a person, place, or thing from one of those sections to research. Use the library or, with your parent's permission, the Internet and try to find out more than what is written in the atlas.

   Then pretend you work for a newspaper, and you have just met the person, seen the landmark, or found out about the object. Write a short article about what you have learned. Newspaper reporters always try to answer the questions *who, what, when, where,* and *how* when they write, so that readers have all the important information. Try to answer those questions in your article, and then add it to your Student Notebook.

4. Although some First Ladies are more well-known than others, each was an important part of her husband's presidency. At the library or on the Internet, find out at least three facts about the First Ladies who shared the White House with the U.S. Presidents you studied in this lesson. Add your research to your Student Notebook.

Additional Resources

Louisa May Alcott: Young Novelist (Childhood of Famous Americans), by Beatrice Gormley and Meryl Henderson

Gold Fever! Tales from the California Gold Rush, by Rosalyn Schanzer

If you read any of the above books, be sure to print a Book Review page from your Student Resources CD, fill it out, and place it in your Student Notebook.

Answers

1. Only the number and arrangement of the stars.

2. 1. F
   2. F
   3. T
   4. F
   5. T
   6. T
   7. F
   8. F
   9. T
   10. T

3. 1. Ann and the McPhales tried to save as much food as possible for them and us.
   2. The boys' bags filled with corn as they hurried to save at least one- half of the crop grown at Hamilton Hill.
   3. The House of Representatives declared war on England by a vote of seventy-nine to forty-nine.
   4. Did Andy's idea about leaving the farm to go visit Cousin Margaret back in Gettysburg make Ann feel like a deserter?
   5. When not working for Miller Chase or Mistress Chase, Joel always found comfort in the horses' stalls.
   6. Many Americans who would fight the English again in the War of 1812 still remembered the War of Independence.
   7. When Joel tried to buy Little Bub at the auction in Randolph, he hoped his bid of three and one-half dollars would be enough.
   8. President Madison quickly approved the efforts of Francis to free Dr. Beanes from the British warship.
   9. Did Justin Morgan send his last letter to Joel while he was staying with Sheriff Rice and his family in Randolph?

4. Water is very heavy, adding to the pressure that compacts layers of sediment, and helping in the formation of rock.

5. com/par/i/son, pos/ses/sions, ur/gings, mo/tioned, whin/ny/ing, shoul/der, psalm, smudged
   dan/de/li/on, clam/ored, pil/grim/age, shim/mer/ing
   auc/tion, ap/pre/hend/ing, per/mis/sion, a/ston/ish/ment

6. 1. T
   2. F
   3. T
   4. F
   5. T
   6. T
   7. F
   8. T

7. Answers will vary because samples in the kits are not exactly the same.

8. Since it was night, the light produced by the bombs and rockets enabled him to see that the American flag was still flying over Fort McHenry.

9. rhyme pattern: *efefggdd*; rhyming words for each line:
   e - deep, f - reposes, e - steep, f - discloses, g - beam, g - stream, d - wave, d - brave.

10. The rhyme pattern for the fourth stanza is *hihijjdd*. Rhyming words for each line:
    h - stand, i - desolation, h - land, i - nation, j - just, j - trust, d - wave, d - brave.

Lesson 6, Part 1

A. Copywork & Dictation *Language Skills, Thinking Skills*

Look carefully at your assigned passage below, and read it silently. Show your teacher any words you don't know, and practice saying them aloud. Now read the passage aloud, or ask your teacher to read it to you.

When you are finished copying or writing from dictation, compare your copy to the text and make any needed corrections.

Copy or write as your teacher dictates from *The Cabin Faced West*, page 112, paragraph 4 ("Ann fell silent…").

Copy or write as your teacher dictates from *Justin Morgan Had a Horse*, page 155, paragraphs 2 and 3 ("Now Ezra seemed…").

Choose one additional paragraph from today's assignment in *Justin Morgan Had a Horse* to write from dictation.

B. Reader *Language Skills, History*

The Cabin Faced West: page 106, paragraph 2 ("It certainly…") through page 110, paragraph 2
Justin Morgan Had a Horse: page 143, paragraph 3 ("But on the sixth…") through page 150, paragraph 2

Read the above assignment from *The Cabin Faced West* aloud, and then follow along as someone else reads the assignment from *Justin Morgan Had a Horse.*

Read the above assignment from *The Cabin Faced West* silently, and then read the assignment from *Justin Morgan Had a Horse* aloud.

Read the above assignments from *The Cabin Faced West* and *Justin Morgan Had a Horse* silently.

C. Read-Aloud & Discussion *Language Skills, History, Thinking Skills*

Francis Scott Key: page 89, the last paragraph ("My head pounded…") through page 94

Read over the following questions that you will discuss later. Then read, or listen carefully as your teacher reads, the above assignment from *Francis Scott Key* aloud. You may want to take notes to help answer the questions after you listen. If needed, you can look back at the story to find specific details.

Pretend you are a news reporter and choose an event that you heard or read about today. Think about what you know from the story, and in your own words answer the following questions about that event:

Materials

- *The Cabin Faced West*
- *Justin Morgan Had a Horse*
- *Francis Scott Key*
- *Eat Your Way Through the USA*
- *Klutz Watercolor Book*
- *Children's Illustrated United States Atlas*
- Wee Sing America CD and songbook
- Klutz Watercolor Book
- Mark-It Timeline of History
- Outline Map of the U.S.
- Ingredients for recipe (Part 3)

From Dr. Beechick

"In summary, we have shown that the content of phonics and other curriculum can be organized in ways that encourage a higher level of thinking. The curriculum itself does not always do this. Minds are bigger than our theories, and many students will see patterns and relationships no matter how poorly the curriculum may be organized. But our efforts in this direction will help many more children to achieve this kind of thinking."

– *Heart and Mind*, page 105

- What took place?
- When did it take place?
- Where did it take place?
- Who were the main people involved?
- How does this event affect Francis Scott Key's life?
- Why do you think it took place?

Choose a second event to report on using the questions listed above.

Tell how the two events you reported on are related.

D. Spelling *Language Skills, Thinking Skills*

Look at the list of words below, and copy each one onto an index card. Then look back at Lesson 1, Part 1 for ideas about how to organize the words, and ways to remember their spelling. Show your teacher how you organized them.

Turn your cards face down and listen as your teacher dictates the words on your spelling list. Spell each word the best that you can, either aloud or by writing it in your Student Notebook. Your teacher may add up to five words that are difficult for you to read or write.

difference	gloriously	dreadful	familiar
attention	introduced	persuaded	helplessness
flotilla	recruits	angrily	intelligent
delicious	obediently	naturally	appetite

E. History *Thinking Skills*

A timeline is another way to picture information quickly and easily. The goal is to know a few key events that help you remember the nature of the times. Cut out the timeline strips in your Student Notebook. To help you remember each event, choose a category and color for each timeline strip in your Student Notebook. Here are the categories:

Military Action - red
Settler/Citizen Action - green
Government Action - blue

Lightly write the color you have chosen on the back of each strip. Then arrange the strips in the order you think they happened. Check your decisions about color and order with the answer key. Once you are sure you are correct, write the date that each event happened on its strip. Then use colored pencils or crayons to lightly shade or draw a border around the strip according to its category. Now glue the strips on the timeline above the correct dates in your Student Notebook.[1]

Teaching Tip

If you are utilizing the assessment, remember to include time in your schedule for comfortable administration. You can give a few sections or all at once. Remember, this is an opportunity to familiarize your child with ways to be successful during assessments, so don't try to squeeze it in as an afterthought, increasing everyone's stress!

From Dr. Beechick

"While timelines will not magically mature your children's minds into adult minds, there are ways to profitably use them. First, you must reverse the thinking implied in the preceding paragraphs. For children, timelines are not for pulling together the scattered pieces of knowledge, as they do so well for adults; children haven't yet collected enough pieces to pull together. What timelines can do for children is to provide a framework into which they can put pieces of knowledge as they learn them. For this framework purpose, timelines should be very simple—so simple that children can memorize them."

– *You Can Teach Your Child Successfully,* page 303

Print and cut out the cards from the Student Resources CD, and play *Who or What Am I* Concentration. Shuffle all the cards and then place them face down. Try to match each question to the correct answer.[2]

- Use the blank cards in the Student Resources CD to make up two more *Who or What Am I* questions and answers.
- Use the blank cards in the Student Resources CD to make up four more *Who or What Am I* questions and answers.

F. States

Geography, History, Thinking Skills

Look at the State Cards you have made throughout this unit. Pull out the ones that have only the names of the states on them, and place the others to the side. Then, as you look at the name of each state, see if you can remember the name of its capital city, its nick-name, and one interesting fact about it. It is fine to look at the other cards you made for that state if you need help remembering.

Go through the cards several times until you feel comfortable with the information about each state. When you are able to remember the facts about a state, place its name card to the side and continue with the others.

You can make this a game with other members of your family by choosing a name card from the stack and asking another person to tell you the important information about that state. Give one point for each correct answer to the player who is answering. That way, it is possible to get three points for each state. Continue until all the name cards are eliminated.

G. Doing

Art, Music

Look at the song entitled "Pick a Bale o' Cotton" in your *Wee Sing America* songbook, and read the historical note about it in the book. In this unit you have listened to and sung several different types of work songs, and this is another. Music often seems to make hard work a little easier, and songs like this were sung by slaves as they labored in the fields. Now listen to it on the *Wee Sing America* CD. Try to become familiar with the words and music so that you can sing along, or learn to play it on an instrument of your choice. You may want to recite, sing, or play this song during your presentation at the end of this unit.

Your final watercolor activity for this unit is to look at the small lakeshore picture on the pages about Indiana, or the seashore picture on the pages about New Jersey, in your *Atlas of the United States*. Use whichever one you choose, or a combination of both, as a model for your own painting. Instead of using a picture, you can paint a scene outdoors if you would prefer and your parent agrees.

G. Encourage your children to see their artwork as part of a process. After completing a piece of artwork, ask them to tell you what they like about it, as well as things they might like to improve. Share with them aspects of their artwork that you enjoy. To model this process, you may want to try the activity with them and ask them to share their opinions with you!

However you choose to complete this activity is fine, as long as you have permission. It is not important to make your painting look exactly like someone else's picture. The main points are to practice the things you have learned, and to experiment with new ideas. Above all, remember to relax and enjoy your art!

H. **Independent Reading** *Language Skills*
Choose something to read that you will enjoy. Then, find a quiet, comfortable place and read for the following length of time:

25 minutes 30 minutes

Over time, it's fun to see how much you have read. Be sure to write down what you read today on the Reading Log in your Student Notebook.

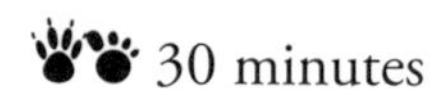

Lesson 6, Part 2

A. Imagery is a picture in your mind, often created by using words. It is very individual, since it depends on your understanding of the words and your experiences. This activity builds imagery. Poetry often uses imagery as an important part of enjoying and understanding the words of others.

A. **Quotation Notebook** *History, Language Skills, Music*
Continue copying verses from the American National Anthem, "The Star Spangled Banner." As you examine this song, consider the imagery created by the words. Since it is also a poem, consider its rhyme pattern as well.

> Then conquer we must, when our cause it is just,
> And this be our motto: "In God is our trust,"

Copy the above passage into your Student Notebook, and talk with your teacher about its meaning and any unknown words. Then listen to it on the *Wee Sing America* CD and follow along with the words in the songbook. Practice reading or singing each section of the song aloud.

Under each phrase printed in your Student Notebook, draw a picture or write an explanation that describes the image it creates in your mind.

Choose two words from the verse and write at least one synonym for each one. Make sure you find a meaning that goes with its context, or use in the verse.

From Dr. Beechick

"When children can't respond to a request to tell what they just read, it's usually not because they don't know, but because they haven't learned the skills of putting all those pages of reading into a few words. Those are speech and thinking skills. So you could work on these. In the narration system that some homeschoolers use, young children learn to tell happenings in order, and older children learn to select significant items and to relate them, and so forth."

–*The Homeschool Answer Book*, page 83

B. **Reader** *Language Skills, History*
The Cabin Faced West: page 110, paragraph 3 ("For a moment…") through page 114, paragraph 3
Justin Morgan Had a Horse: page 150, paragraph 3 ("The bewildered…") through page 156

Read the above assignment from *The Cabin Faced West* aloud, and then follow along as someone else reads the assignment from *Justin Morgan Had a Horse.*

Read the above assignment from *The Cabin Faced West* silently, and then read the assignment from *Justin Morgan Had a Horse* aloud.

Read the above assignments from *The Cabin Faced West* and *Justin Morgan Had a Horse* silently.

C. Read-Aloud & Narration

Language Skills, History, Thinking Skills

Francis Scott Key: page 95 (Chapter 12) through page 100, paragraph 2

Follow the instructions below for your level. Then, in your own words, tell what happened in the story from Francis' point of view, or pretend you are Francis and tell what you think happened. Try to remember as many details as possible. You may reread the passage or listen as your teacher rereads the part you are to retell.

Listen carefully as your teacher reads the above assignment from *Francis Scott Key* aloud.

Read the above assignment from *Francis Scott Key* aloud.

D. Editing

Language Skills, Thinking Skills

Today you are going to review the tools for writing that you have learned. To begin, print the Mechanics Toolkit 7 Cards from Appendix B or your Student Resources CD, and cut them out. When you are finished, place them on the table in front of you, and read all the Rule cards. Then find two Example cards that go with each rule.

You may want to mix up the Example cards to make it more of a challenge, or follow the directions in Appendix B to play Mechanics Toolkit Concentration.

Now continue your review by reading the Rule cards once again. When you are finished:

Make up two sentences that show each rule used correctly, and write them in your Student Notebook.

Make up three sentences that show each rule used correctly, and write them in your Student Notebook.

Make up four sentences that show each rule used correctly, and write them in your Student Notebook.

E. Science

Thinking Skills

Take a few minutes before you begin this section to look back at the list you made in Lesson 3, Part 2, and see if your questions about waves, tides, an underwater mountain range, things that live in the oceans, and sedimentary rocks have been answered yet. Use a highlighter to mark the ones that have not. Then over the next few days, research the questions that you highlighted at the library or on the Internet, and try to find the answers. Discuss what you find out with your teacher.

Next, look at the chart in your Student Notebook that shows much of what you have learned about the ocean in this unit. Use the Word Bank provided with the chart to label it.

F. States

Geography, Thinking Skills

Find the Regional Summary Pages in the back of your Student Notebook. Then, use your *United States Atlas* to fill in the information for Louisiana, Florida, West Virginia, Ohio, and Indiana.

When you are finished, look at the State Scramble game in your Student Notebook. Unscramble the name of each state you have studied in this unit, and write it correctly on the line provided. Then write its abbreviation on the short line. Finally, list each state under the name of the region where it is located.[3] If you need help remembering, it is fine to use your State Cards to complete this activity.

G. Writing

Language Skills, Thinking Skills

In Part 5 of this lesson you will be asked to make a Unit Presentation to your family, and tell about what you have learned in the Nation Building Unit. In this presentation, you will have an opportunity to share the work you have done in your Student Notebook, your book review, the crafts or special projects you have completed, and anything else you care to include.

Think about the things you would like to include in your Unit Presentation, and list them on a piece of scrap paper. Then number the items in the order that you would like to share them. Now copy your list in the correct order into your Student Notebook. You can use this list while you are giving your Unit Presentation, so that you won't forget anything you wanted to share.

H. Independent Reading

Language Skills

Choose something to read that you will enjoy. Then, find a quiet, comfortable place and read for the following length of time:

25 minutes 30 minutes

Be sure to write down what you read today on the Reading Log in your Student Notebook.

From Dr. Beechick

"A technique to use often is to help children write questions they want to find answers for. Who really did reach the Mississippi first; was it the man our textbook says or the man this other book says? Who is the explorer to be admired the most? What sort of end did each cruel gold-seeker come to? Who profited from their searches? Who were the Aztecs, and where did they come from? Save the questions and write each answer as it is found or agreed upon. Some questions may be unanswerable or at least unanswerable in the time you allot for the unit. You can decide whether those are worth pursuing or whether they should be laid aside for now. Children who learn to ask questions are far ahead educationally from when they had experience only in answering questions, particularly in the fields of history and other social studies."

– *You Can Teach Your Child Successfully*, page 299

G. Talk with your children about their presentations, and ask if they need any help preparing. If possible, you may want to offer to video tape them practicing their presentations this week. Ask them to review the video with you, telling what they like and would like to improve. Ask them if they would like you to choose one or two items to point out for improvement. Make sure to highlight one or two things done well. Keep your feedback balanced.

Lesson 6, Part 3

A. Copywork & Dictation
Language Skills, Thinking Skills

Look carefully at your assigned passage below, and read it silently. Show your teacher any words you don't know, and practice saying them aloud. Now read the passage aloud, or ask your teacher to read it to you.

When you are finished copying or writing from dictation, compare your copy to the text and make any needed corrections.

Copy or write as your teacher dictates from *The Cabin Faced West*, page 116, paragraphs 3 and 4 ("The future is traveling…").

Copy or write as your teacher dictates from *Justin Morgan Had a Horse*, page 159, paragraphs 3 and 4 ("In every move…").

Choose one additional paragraph from today's assignment in *Justin Morgan Had a Horse* to write from dictation.

Teaching Tip

As your children prepare for their presentations, it is good for them to select materials ahead of time and become familiar with the order that they will present them. Help younger children understand that they are not to share everything they have completed, just samples of work. Encourage your children to continually share how the activities, projects, notebooks, and artwork relate to the Steps for Thinking.

B. Reader
Language Skills, History

The Cabin Faced West: page 114, paragraph 4 ("Later…") to the bottom of page 119
Justin Morgan Had a Horse: page 157 ("Miller Chase…") through page 162

Read the above assignment from *The Cabin Faced West* aloud, and then follow along as someone else reads the assignment from *Justin Morgan Had a Horse.*

Read the above assignment from *The Cabin Faced West* silently, and then read the assignment from *Justin Morgan Had a Horse* aloud.

Read the above assignments from *The Cabin Faced West* and *Justin Morgan Had a Horse* silently.

C. Read-Aloud & Discussion
Language Skills, History, Thinking Skills

Francis Scott Key: page 100, paragraph 3 ("One night…") to the bottom of page 103

Follow the directions below to read or listen to the above assignment from *Francis Scott Key*. Then make up the assigned number of questions about the part of the story you just read or heard. Write your questions and ask your teacher to answer them. After discussing her thoughts, write down the best possible answer in your Student Notebook. Be sure to use complete sentences.

When you are finished, look back at the prediction or predictions you made during Lesson 5, Part 4. Were you able to predict what would happen? Be sure to mark the "Came to Pass" box for each prediction when it does happen.

C. Encourage your children to look through their Student Notebooks at the predictions they have made about their reading. Have they improved over the course of the unit? Ask them if the process of making predictions has become easier for them and give them your observations about their progress with this skill.

Listen carefully as your teacher reads the above assignment from *Francis Scott Key*.

Make up one question. Make up two questions.

Read the above assignment from *Francis Scott Key* aloud; then make up three questions.

D. Vocabulary & Spelling

Language Skills, Thinking Skills

Vocabulary:

Write each vocabulary word on an index card, and use a thesaurus to find a synonym for it. If you cannot find a synonym, use a dictionary to look up the meaning of the word. Then on the back of each card, draw a picture or write a clue so you can remember how each word was used in the story. Write a *D* or *S* by your clue to tell whether you wrote a definition or synonym.

peter **dignified** **daze** **envy** **despair**

barrage **cavalry** **pedigree** **animate** **helter-skelter**

Spelling:

Look at the list of words on your Student Notebook page, and divide each word into syllables by drawing a slash line (/) between the syllables. After you have marked each word, use a dictionary to check your work.[4] If you don't know what the word means, read the definition while you are checking your syllable markings. Then place a check next to each word to show that you know what the word means.

Look at the spelling word cards you made in Part 1. Read each word, and then cover it with your hand and try to spell it aloud. Then uncover it and see if you were correct. Review the meanings of any words that you do not remember.

E. History

Thinking Skills

The **population**, or number of citizens, of America has grown tremendously since our country's founding. The growth in our population shows how much people wanted to come and be a part of our **republic**, or system of government where people elect representatives to govern. In the House of Representatives, each state elects a number of representatives based on the state's population. Larger states have larger numbers of representatives to serve so that all people are able to contact their representatives if they have a need or want to share their opinions.

Sometimes looking at the way the population has grown in the past gives us a clue as to how it will grow in the future. Local, state and national governments make plans based on the number of citizens who live in an area. Things such as number and size of roads, size of the police force, libraries, and other public services are decided based on population. Every ten years, our country takes a **census**, or official count of the population. In America, the census began in 1790 and has continued every ten years since then. Other people who may use the census information are businesses, universities, or anyone who depends on customers to keep making income. When a certain area is growing, businesses that want to expand may look at that area to open a new store.

A **line graph** shows change over time. Remember that a graph is a picture that helps you get information quickly and easily. Take the information given below and follow the directions to fill in the line graph in your Student Notebook. Then answer the questions about what you see.

Data for charts: Years and US Population

1790 - 3,929,214
1800 - 5,308,483
1810 - 7,239,881
1820 - 9,638,453
1830 - 12, 860,702
1840 - 17,063,353
1850 - 23,191,876
Data from U.S. Census Bureau, Website: www.census.gov

There are two axes to label. The first one is the *x* axis, which goes from left to right, or horizontally. Write in the dates you are graphing, beginning with the first census in 1790. Then write in the dates for each ten-year **interval**, or period, from one census to the next until the last date, which is 1850.

Next label the *y* axis, which goes from bottom to top, or vertically. On this axis, write in the numbers that show how many people were in the population, in millions. Start with four million and end with twenty-four million. This shows the **range**, or beginning and ending numbers, possible for the population at that time. You will only write a number like 5 to show five million, 20 to show twenty million, and so forth. Round off the populations you are given to the nearest million.

After you have rounded the populations off to the nearest million, put your finger on the year and draw it up the line for that year until you come to the line that crosses it with the correct number of millions of people. Put a dark dot at the point where the two lines **intersect**, or cross. Repeat this process for each census year. When you are finished, you should have seven dark dots, or one for each census year, showing the population for that year in millions.

"Geography is so all encompassing that it's easy to incorporate within the context of most any other subject matter. Your students will remember their geography better if it's associated with something else. As you gain a fuller understanding of geography's five themes, you'll awaken to opportunities to connect a current subject of study with a geography activity. Successfully incorporate geography throughout the curriculum and it won't be necessary to teach a separate geography class until high school, when a geography course is recommended for well-rounded global cognitive awareness."

--*The Ultimate Geography and Timeline Guide*, page 3

Next, get a ruler or something with a firm, straight edge. You will use this to help you draw straight lines to connect the dots, starting with the dot for the year 1790, since this was the year of the first census. Connect this dot with the dot for the next year, which was 1800. Then connect the dot for 1800 to the dot for 1810, and so on, until you reach the dot for 1850. Stop your line at the dot for the population in 1850.

Answer the questions in your Student Notebook about the line graph.

Find the population of your state in your *United States Atlas*. Look at the timeline included for your state. Now predict the years when you think the population of your state made large gains. Tell your teacher why you chose those times. Find information on population growth in your state either on the Internet or at the library. Were your predictions correct?

F. States
Geography, History, Thinking Skills

Mix up your State Cards and lay them face down on the table or floor. Then Play State Card Concentration by turning up one card, and trying to find the other two cards that go with it. When you turn over three cards that don't match, return them to their face down position and try again. When you find three cards that do match, remove them from the game. Continue until you have removed all the cards that go together.

G. Cooking
Language Skills, Thinking Skills

Talk with your teacher about your cooking experiences in this unit. Was it difficult to follow the recipes? Did you learn anything new? If so, what? Which recipe did you enjoy making the most? Which recipe did your family enjoy the most? After you discuss these questions with your teacher, in your Student Notebook write a complete sentence that summarizes your thoughts about each one.

Then, with your parent's permission and supervision choose a recipe that you enjoyed making in this unit, and prepare it again for your family. If you would prefer, you can select a different recipe from *Eat Your Way Through the USA* that comes from one of the states you have studied so far, and prepare it instead.

H. Independent Reading
Language Skills

Choose something to read that you will enjoy. Then, find a quiet, comfortable place and read for the following length of time:

25 minutes 30 minutes

Be sure to write down what you read today on the Reading Log in your Student Notebook.

Lesson 6, Part 4

A. Quotation Notebook *History, Language Skills, Music*

Continue copying verses from the American National Anthem, "The Star Spangled Banner." As you examine this song, consider the imagery created by the words. Since it is also a poem, consider its rhyme pattern as well.

> And the Star Spangled Banner in triumph shall wave
> O'er the land of the free and the home of the brave!

Copy the above passage into your Student Notebook, and talk with your teacher about its meaning and any unknown words. Then listen to it on the *Wee Sing America* CD and follow along with the words in the songbook. Practice reading or singing each section of the song aloud.

Under each phrase printed in your Student Notebook, draw a picture or write an explanation that describes the image it creates in your mind.

Choose two words from the verse and write at least one synonym for each one. Make sure you find a meaning that goes with its context, or use in the verse.

B. Reader *Language Skills, History*

The Cabin Faced West: page 119, the last paragraph ("All the excitement…") through page 124
Justin Morgan Had a Horse: page 163 ("Now they were…") through page 170

Read the above assignment from *The Cabin Faced West* aloud, and then follow along as someone else reads the assignment from *Justin Morgan Had a Horse*.

Read the above assignment from *The Cabin Faced West* silently, and then read the assignment from *Justin Morgan Had a Horse* aloud.

Read the above assignments from *The Cabin Faced West* and *Justin Morgan Had a Horse* silently.

B. Your children are about to finish the readers assigned for this unit. They will complete a Book Review Card later in this part of Lesson 6. Have your children bring out the Book Review Cards they have made for the past units. Ask them to choose their favorite reader so far and put a star on the Book Review Card for their favorite.

C. Read-Aloud & Speech *Language Skills, History, Thinking Skills*

Francis Scott Key: page 103, the last paragraph ("Day after day…") through page 110

After reading or listening to the above assignment, tell what you think others thought about *Francis Scott Key*. Since he just passed away in your story, give a speech about him to others. Remember to tell about the things he did to help America, the kind of man he was, and what you think most people will remember about him. You can practice your speech and write it down on index cards to help remember what you want to say. A good length for your speech is about two to three minutes. Use visual aids (such as pictures) to help others visualize the man about whom you are talking.

Listen carefully as your teacher reads the above assignment from *Francis Scott Key*.

Read the above assignment from *Francis Scott Key* aloud.

D. Editing

Language Skills, Thinking Skills

Today you are going to review the tools for writing that you have learned. To begin, print the Mechanics Toolkit 8 Cards from Appendix B or your Student Resources CD, and cut them out. When you are finished, place them on the table in front of you, and read all the Rule cards. Then find two Example cards that go with each rule.

You may want to mix up the Example cards to make it more of a challenge, or follow the directions in Appendix B to play Mechanics Toolkit Concentration.

Now continue your review by reading the Rule cards once again. When you are finished:

Make up two sentences that show each rule used correctly, and write them in your Student Notebook.

Make up three sentences that show each rule used correctly, and write them in your Student Notebook.

Make up four sentences that show each rule used correctly, and write them in your Student Notebook.

E. Science

Thinking Skills

Complete the Earth Science Matching game in your Student Notebook by drawing a line from each term to its correct definition.[5] When you are finished, tell your teacher what you remember about the things named in the activity. If you want help remembering, you can look back at the pages in the unit where you learned about each thing.

F. States

Geography, Thinking Skills

Find the Regional Summary Pages in the back of your Student Notebook. Then, use your *United States Atlas* to fill in the information for Illinois, Michigan, Iowa, Wisconsin, and Minnesota.

When you are finished, look at the State I.D. game in your Student Notebook, and draw a line from the map of each state to its name. On the lines at the bottom, write each state's nickname.[6] If you have trouble remembering, and your teacher agrees, it's fine to use your maps and State Pages to complete this activity.

G. Writing

Language Skills, Thinking Skills

Now that you have completed your readers and the read-aloud book, make a book review card. The purpose of a book review card is to give a brief description of what you read or heard, and then to tell what you thought of the book. It should not include as much information as a book report. The goal is to give someone who has not read the book enough information to decide whether or not they might like to read it. In a sense, it is like an advertisement for a book. Give information about the good points without retelling the story.

G. Word banks are an excellent way to build vocabulary and encourage writing. When you provide a list for your child to use, that puts the focus on the thinking that goes into the answer, not just searching for the right word or its spelling. Vocabulary and spelling are both strengthened by reading, writing, and speaking the word correctly. It is not cheating to give your child a word bank, since the goal is to build your child's ability to give the best answer possible.

How to Create a Book Review Card:

Write your book review on a large index card or on the page provided in your Student Notebook. Include the following information:

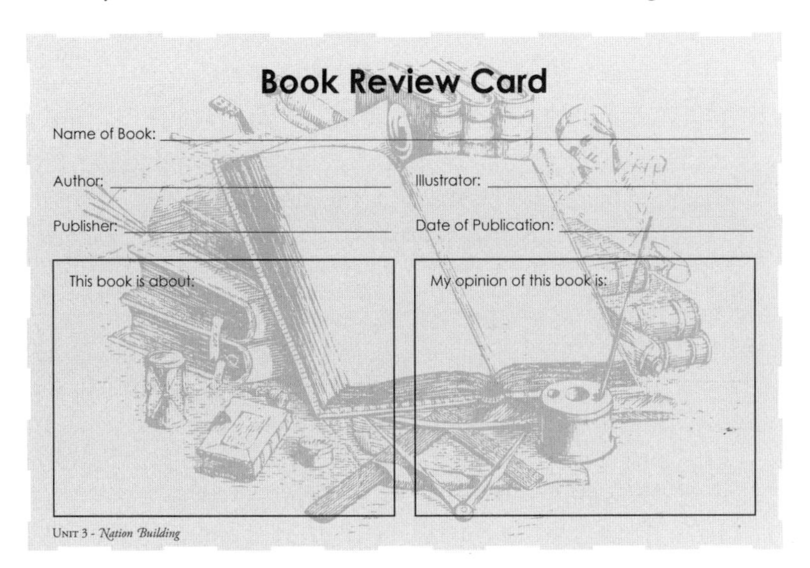
Book Review Card

Name of Book:

Author: Illustrator:

Publisher: Date of Publication:

This book is about:

My opinion of this book is:

Unit 3 - Nation Building

- name of the book
- author of the book (person who wrote the book)
- illustrator of the book (person who drew the pictures)
- name of the company who published the book
- date the book was published

Most of this information can be found on the title page of the book.

Rehearse, or practice telling, what you will write about the story and how you liked it. Once you have discussed your thoughts enough to know what you want to write, you can begin. If you don't know how to spell some of the words you want to use, ask your teacher to make a word bank for you.

Next, write a few sentences to tell what the story was about. Since you only have a few sentences, choose the most important facts to tell.

Finally, write a few sentences to tell what you thought about the story. It would be good to tell whether you liked the book and then give some of examples of what you did or did not like about it. Remember to use a word bank if you need it.

Create a book review card for *The Cabin Faced West.*

Create a book review card for *Justin Morgan Had a Horse.*

Create a book review card for the read-aloud book, *Francis Scott Key.*

H. **Independent Reading** *Language Skills*

Choose something to read that you will enjoy. Then, find a quiet, comfortable place and read for the following length of time:

25 minutes 30 minutes

Congratulations on completing six weeks of independent reading! Today's entry in your reading log will be the last one for this unit. Make sure you have included all the information needed on your log such as book titles, authors, and dates read.

Look over all that you have accomplished during your independent reading time. If you would like, share your reading log with others during your Unit Presentation tomorrow.

H. A reading log is an important part of a portfolio. It documents sequential effort and is a satisfying way for a child to see work completion. You may also want to make a list of books read for this unit, which may include bibliographical information, such as author, publisher and copyright date. This is an easy way to build awareness of bibliographical information.

Lesson 6, Part 5

This part is set aside for completion of any work left undone from the lesson, and review of concepts and content. It is also a time to expand the work of the lesson with art, mapping, or games.

- Listen as your teacher reviews the Steps for Thinking from the Nation Building Unit that you have just completed. Talk about how you can apply the Steps for Thinking to what you have read or discussed, and see if you can think of any examples in this unit.
- Gather your vocabulary cards together and mix them up. Randomly choose word cards. Read the word on the front and try to tell your teacher what the word means, or tell how it was used in the story. Give yourself a point for every word you can use correctly. See how many points you can get!
- Listen as your teacher reads the spelling words that you studied from Part 1. Write each word in your Student Notebook as she dictates it. When you are finished, look back at your spelling word cards and make corrections as needed. Show your teacher how you did.

Teaching Tip

Summary lessons and activities are very valuable. Though this may seem shorter than the other lesson parts, it is no less important. There are a variety of ways to help your children retain concepts and skills. Student presentations, review, games and activities are all effective means of helping your children solidify and remember what they have learned. Then they can take the next big step of using it in the future, so be sure to make room for Part 5!

- To review the actions taken in this volume, look at the events on your Student Notebook timelines and write them on the Mark-It Timeline of History. Each unit will use **two lines** on the undated side of the Mark-It Timeline.

  Unit 1 Directions: This section of your timeline begins in 1745 and ends in 1765. Each notch on the timeline adds one year. Write in the dates underneath the notched lines. Next, add the Unit 1 events using a wet erase marker in the color of the event's category.

  Unit 2 Directions: This section of your timeline begins in 1765 and continues until 1785. Again, each notch on the timeline adds one year. Write in the dates underneath the notched lines. Next, add the Unit 2 events using a wet erase marker in the color of the event's category.

  Unit 3 Directions: This section of your timeline begins in 1800 and continues until 1860. Each notch on the timeline adds three years. Write in the dates underneath the notched lines. Start with 1800, then 1803, 1806, 1809, 1812, 1815, and so forth. Next, add the Unit 3 events using a wet erase marker in the color of the event's category.

- Make a Unit Presentation to your family that tells about what you have learned in the Nation Building Unit. Share your Student Notebook, and things you made during this unit such as your 3-D map, your metal-punching, and your watercolor picture. Remember to include the portions of important American documents that you copied into your Quotation Notebook! You might also want to invite your family to play pick-up sticks. Don't forget to stand still and speak clearly. After your presentation, be sure to ask if anyone has questions.
- Play Nation Building Bingo with your family.

Congratulations on completing Unit 3 of *Paths of Settlement!*

"This timeline may be designed in strips with dates every fifty or one hundred years, or it may be done in poster form, a card file, or notebook. The student should place important information on the timeline in the form of figures or pictures, or simply by writing in the proper place. An activity timeline will provide students with the hands-on learning experience that most often increases memory retention. This visual representation will aid the student's memory as well."

--*The Ultimate Geography and Timeline Guide*, page 288

From Dr. Beechick

"Many teachers and parents know intuitively about teaching to the heart. This is probably a major reason that homeschoolers do so well. In academic tests, the homeschool children on average score well above the national average, and it doesn't matter whether their parents are trained teachers, college graduates, high school graduates only, or anything in between. Some schoolteachers-turned-homeschoolers say they have to unlearn most of what they learned about teaching. Homeschooling is largely heart to heart. The methods and even the curriculum do not matter nearly as much as the relationship between child and parent."

– *Heart and Mind*, page 126

Answers

1. 1803) Louisiana Purchase completed. (blue)
   (1814) War of 1812 ends. (red)
   (1819) Spain cedes Florida to U.S. (blue)
   (1845) Texas annexed by U.S. (blue)
   (1846) Treaty with Britain adds Oregon Country. (blue)
   (1848) Mexican Cession adds western territories. (blue)
2. Answers are in Appendix A.
3. Answers are in Appendix A.
4. dif/fer/ence, glo/ri/ous/ly, dread/ful, fa/mil/iar, at/ten/tion, in/tro/duced, per/suad/ed, help/less/ness
   flo/til/la, re/cruits, an/gri/ly, in/tel/li/gent
   de/li/cious, o/be/di/ent/ly, nat/u/ral/ly, ap/pe/tite
5. Answers are in Appendix A.
6. Answers are in Appendix A.

Paths of Settlement
- Appendix -

Appendix A

Lesson at a Glance

Growing Pains 351

Freedom Decided 357

Nation Building 363

Skills and Topics List

Growing Pains 369

Freedom Decided 370

Nation Building 372

Challenge Spelling Words 374

Answer Keys 377

Growing Pains Unit – Lesson 1 At A Glance

A. Copywork & Dictation & Quotation Notebook		The Courage of Sarah Noble	Ambush in the Wilderness	
	Part 1	❑ Page 1, paragraph 2	❑ Page 2, paragraph 1	
	Part 2	❑ Copy first rule	❑ Copy first two rules	❑ Copy all three rules
	Part 3	❑ Page 18, paragraph 1	❑ Page 13, paragraph 4	
	Part 4	❑ Copy first rule	❑ Copy first two rules	❑ Copy all three rules
B. Reader		The Courage of Sarah Noble	Ambush in the Wilderness	Abigail Adams
	Part 1	❑ Pages 1 - 5 (Chapter 1)	❑ Page 1 - bottom of page 3	❑ Page 1 - page 6, paragraph 5
	Part 2	❑ Page 6 (Chapter 2) - page 10, paragraph 4	❑ Page 3, last paragraph - bottom page 6	❑ Page 6, paragraph 6 - bottom page 10
	Part 3	❑ Page 10, paragraph 5 - page 13	❑ Page 6, last paragraph - middle of page 12	❑ Page 10 last paragraph - page 15
	Part 4	❑ Pages 14 - 18	❑ Mid-page 12 - page 15, paragraph 1	❑ Page 16 (Chapter II) - bottom of page 21
C. Read Aloud		Abigail Adams		
	Part 1	❑ Page 1 - page 6. paragraph 5	❑ Discussion	
	Part 2	❑ Page 6, paragraph 6 - bottom page 10	❑ Narration	
	Part 3	❑ Page 10, last paragraph - page 15	❑ Discussion	
	Part 4	❑ Page 16 (Chapter II) - bottom of page 21	❑ Narration	
D. Language Skills	Part 1	❑ *ow* words ❑ Spelling list	❑ Additional words	❑ Additional words
	Part 2	❑ Mechanics Toolkit ❑ Edit sentences	❑ Edit additional sentences	❑ Edit additional sentences
	Part 3	❑ Vocabulary cards ❑ *ow* words ❑ Spelling practice	❑ Additional vocabulary cards	
	Part 4	❑ Find examples	❑ Find additional examples	
E. History/Science	Part 1	❑ Early Settlement ❑ Which group? ❑ Why	❑ Response to challenges	
	Part 2	❑ Definitions ❑ Tools ❑ Rain Gauge ❑ Observe weather		
	Part 3	❑ Ethnicity ❑ Discuss & record ❑ Observe weather	❑ Indentured servants ❑ Discuss	❑ Slavery ❑ Discuss
	Part 4	❑ Atmosphere, 1 fact for each layer ❑ Observe weather	❑ Additional fact	❑ Additional fact ❑ Weather sayings
F. States	Part 1	❑ Massachusetts	❑ Research ❑ Mapping	
	Part 2		❑ State Page ❑ State Cards	
	Part 3	❑ Connecticut	❑ Research ❑ Mapping	
	Part 4		❑ State Page ❑ State Cards	
G. Doing	Part 1	❑ Introduction to watercolor		
	Part 2	❑ Interactive Journaling		
	Part 3	❑ MA or CT recipe ❑ Drawing ❑ Record reactions		
	Part 4	❑ Quotation rules ❑ Rewrite 2 sentences	❑ Rewrite 4 sentences	❑ Rewrite 6 sentences
H. Independent Reading		25minutes daily ❑❑❑❑	30 minutes daily ❑❑❑❑	30 minutes daily ❑❑❑❑
Review	Part 5	❑ Steps for Thinking review ❑ Map activity ❑ Vocabulary & Spelling review ❑ Thomas Paine Profile ❑ The Newcomer Game		
Materials		*The Courage of Sarah Noble*, *Ambush in the Wilderness*, *Eat Your Way Through the USA*, *United States History Atlas*, *Atlas of the United States*, *Handbook of Nature Study* (book or download), *Abigail Adams*, *DK Pockets: Weather Facts*, *Klutz Watercolor Book*, *Profiles from History, Vol. 2*, *USA Activities CD*	Watercolor paper, Faper towel, Dictionary, Ingredients for recipe (Part 3), Outline map of U.S., Markers, crayons, or colored pencils, Index cards, Outdoor thermometer, Globe or map of the world, Materials for weather instrument (Part 2):wide-mouthed jar, ruler, masking tape	

Growing Pains Unit – Lesson 2 At A Glance

A. Copywork or Dictation/Quotation Notebook		*The Courage of Sarah Noble*	*Ambush in the Wilderness*	
	Part 1	❑ Page 24, paragraph 1	❑ Page 17, paragraph 3	
	Part 2	❑ Copy first rule	❑ Copy first two rules	❑ Copy all three rules
	Part 3	❑ Page 26, paragraph 5 - page 27, paragraph 1	❑ Page 23, paragraph 5	
	Part 4	❑ Copy first rule	❑ Copy first two rules	❑ Copy all three rules
B. Reader		*The Courage of Sarah Noble*	*Ambush in the Wilderness*	*Abigail Adams*
	Part 1	❑ Pages 19 - 22 (Chapter 4)	❑ Page 15, paragraph 2 - page 18	❑ Page 21, last paragraph - page 27
	Part 2	❑ Pages 23 (Chapter 5) - 26	❑ Pages 19 - 22	❑ Pages 28 - 35, paragraph 1
	Part 3	❑ Pages 27 - 32	❑ Page 23 - top of page 26	❑ Page 35, paragraph 2 - page 40, paragraph 7
	Part 4	❑ Pages 33 - 38 (Chapter 7)	❑ Page 26, paragraph 1 - page 28	❑ Page 40, paragraph 8 - page 47, paragraph 2
C. Read Aloud		*Abigail Adams*		
	Part 1	❑ Page 21, last paragraph - page 27	❑ Discussion	
	Part 2	❑ Pages 28 - 35, paragraph 1	❑ Narration	
	Part 3	❑ Page 35, paragraph 2 - page 40, paragraph 7	❑ Discussion	
	Part 4	❑ Page 40, paragraph 8 - page 47, paragraph 2	❑ Narration	
D. Language Skills				
	Part 1	❑ *o* words ❑ Spelling list	❑ Additional words	❑ Additional words
	Part 2	❑ Mechanics Toolkit ❑ Edit sentences	❑ Edit additional sentences	❑ Edit additional sentences
	Part 3	❑ Vocabulary cards ❑ *o* words ❑ Spelling practice	❑ Additional vocabulary cards	
	Part 4	❑ Mechanics Toolkit ❑ Edit sentences	❑ Edit additional sentences	❑ Edit additional sentences
E. History/Science				
	Part 1	❑ Colonial family ❑ 4 chores ❑ Explain ❑ Observe weather		❑ Additional chores ❑ Explain
	Part 2	❑ Heat energy ❑ Chart ❑ Exp. ❑ Heat transfer ❑ Observe weather		❑ Research greenhouse effect. ❑ 3 facts
	Part 3	❑ Family life discussion ❑ Tradesman Match ❑ Observe weather		
	Part 4	❑ Air pressure, barometer ❑ Observe weather	❑ Weather report	
F. States				
	Part 1	❑ Vermont	❑ Research ❑ Mapping	
	Part 2		❑ State Page ❑ State Cards	
	Part 3	❑ New Hampshire	❑ Research ❑ Mapping	
	Part 4		❑ State Page ❑ State Cards	
G. Doing				
	Part 1	❑ Make Quoits		
	Part 2	❑ Interactive Journaling		
	Part 3	❑ VT or NH recipe ❑ Drawing ❑ Record reactions		
	Part 4	❑ Journaling		
H. Independent Reading		25minutes daily ❑❑❑❑	30 minutes daily ❑❑❑❑	30 minutes daily ❑❑❑❑
Review	Part 5	❑ Steps for Thinking review ❑ Map activity ❑ Vocabulary & Spelling review ❑ Watercolor ❑ Growing Pains Word Search		
Materials		*The Courage of Sarah Noble* *Ambush in the Wilderness* *Eat Your Way Through the USA* *United States History Atlas* *Atlas of the United States* *Abigail Adams* *DK Pockets: Weather Facts* *Klutz Watercolor Book* *USA Activities CD*	Watercolor paper, Ingredients for recipe (Part 3), Outline map of U.S., Markers, crayons, or colored pencils, Index cards, Supplies for craft (Part 1): 30" of rope or clothesline, Scissors, Masking tape, Yardstick, Straight stick or dowel rod. String or twine, Ruler, Supplies for weather instrument (Part 4): balloon, glass jar, rubber band, plastic straw, toothpick, glue, unsharpened pencil, thread spool.	

GROWING PAINS UNIT – *Lesson 3 At A Glance*

A. COPYWORK & DICTATION & QUOTATION NOTEBOOK		*The Courage of Sarah Noble*	*Ambush in the Wilderness*	
	Part 1	❑ Page 43, paragraph 4	❑ Page 33, paragraph 4	
	Part 2	❑ Copy first rule	❑ Copy first two rules	❑ Copy all three rules
	Part 3	❑ Page 49, paragraph 3	❑ Page 37, paragraph 5	
	Part 4	❑ Copy first rule	❑ Copy first two rules	❑ Copy all three rules
B. READER		*The Courage of Sarah Noble*	*Ambush in the Wilderness*	*Abigail Adams*
	Part 1	❑ Pages 39 (Chapter 8) - 42	❑ Page 29 - top of page 33	❑ Page 47, paragraph 3 - page 53
	Part 2	❑ Pages 43 - 48	❑ Page 33, paragraph 1 - mid-page 36	❑ Pages 54 - 60, paragraph 3
	Part 3	❑ Pages 49 - 54	❑ Mid-page 36 - mid-page 39	❑ Page 60, paragraph 4 - page 65
	Part 4	❑ *The Matchlock Gun,* Pages 1 - 5, paragraph 2	❑ Mid-page 39 - top of page 42	❑ Pages 66 - 71, paragraph 6
C. READ ALOUD		*Abigail Adams*		
	Part 1	❑ Page 47, paragraph 3 - page 53	❑ Discussion	
	Part 2	❑ Pages 54 (Chapter V) - 60, paragraph 3	❑ Narration	
	Part 3	❑ Page 60, paragraph 4 - page 65	❑ Discussion	
	Part 4	❑ Pages 66 (Chapter VI) - 71, paragraph 6	❑ Narration	
D. LANGUAGE SKILLS				
	Part 1	❑ Review ❑ Categorize	❑ Add 1 word	❑ Add 2 words
	Part 2	❑ Mechanics Toolkit Cards ❑ Examples ❑ Game		
	Part 3	❑ Cards ❑ Spelling review		
	Part 4	❑ Mechanics Toolkit Cards ❑ Examples ❑ Game		
E. HISTORY/SCIENCE				
	Part 1	❑ Map overlays ❑ Observe weather		
	Part 2	❑ Winds ❑ Anenometer ❑ Observe weather	❑ Experiment ❑ Discuss	
	Part 3	❑ Worldviews ❑ Worldview Tic-Tac-Toe ❑ Observe weather		
	Part 4	❑ Winds ❑ Comp. Rose ❑ Weather Vein ❑ Observe weather	❑ Wind Systems	
F. STATES				
	Part 1	❑ Rhode Island	❑ Research ❑ Mapping	
	Part 2		❑ State Page ❑ State Cards	
	Part 3	❑ Maine	❑ Research ❑ Mapping	
	Part 4		❑ State Page ❑ State Cards	
G. DOING				
	Part 1	❑ Watercolor activity		
	Part 2	❑ Interactive Journaling		
	Part 3	❑ RI or ME recipe ❑ Drawing ❑ Record reactions		
	Part 4	❑ Writing dialogue ❑ Rewrite 2 sentences	❑ Additional 2 sentences (total of 4)	❑ Additional 4 sentences (total of 6)
H. INDEPENDENT READING				
		25minutes daily ❑❑❑❑	30 minutes daily ❑❑❑❑	30 minutes daily ❑❑❑❑
REVIEW	Part 5	❑ Steps for Thinking review ❑ Map activity ❑ Vocabulary & Spelling review ❑ Samuel Adams Profile		
MATERIALS		*he Courage of Sarah Noble* *Ambush in the Wilderness* *Eat Your Way Through the USA* *Profiles from History, Vol. 2* *Atlas of the United States* *Abigail Adams* *The Matchlock Gun* *Klutz Watercolor Book* *DK Pockets: Weather Facts* *USA Activities CD*	Watercolor paper, Student Notebook, Dictionary, Ingredients for recipe (Part 3), Outline map of U.S., Markers, crayons, or colored pencils, Index cards, Stop watch or watch with a second hand, Balloon, Transparency paper, Permanent markers, Materials for weather instruments (Parts 2 & 4): ruler, scissors, glue, tape, exacto knife, either string, yarn, or light wire, paper plates, hole punch or awl, hole reinforcements (optional), push-pins (2), dowel rods or straight sticks (2), crepe paper, tissue, or ribbon streamers (16')	

Growing Pains Unit – *Lesson 4 At A Glance*

Section	Part			
A. Copywork & Dictation & Quotation Notebook		*The Matchlock Gun*	*Ambush in the Wilderness*	
	Part 1	❑ Page 5, paragraph 1	❑ Page 46, paragraph 1	
	Part 2	❑ Copy first rule	❑ Copy first two rules	❑ Copy all three rules
	Part 3	❑ Page 12, paragraph 1	❑ Page 48, paragraph 9 and page 49, paragraph 1	
	Part 4	❑ Copy first rule	❑ Copy first two rules	❑ Copy all three rules
B. Reader		*The Matchlock Gun*	*Ambush in the Wilderness*	*Abigail Adams*
	Part 1	❑ Page 5, paragraph 3 - page10, paragraph 1	❑ Page 42, paragraph 1 - page 45	❑ Page 71, last paragraph - page 78, paragraph 8
	Part 2	❑ Page 10, paragraph 2 - page 13	❑ Page 46-mid - page 49	❑ Page 78, paragraph 9 - bottom page 84
	Part 3	❑ Pages 14 - 17	❑ Mid-page 49 - top of page 52	❑ Page 84, last paragraph - page 90, paragraph 4
	Part 4	❑ Pages 18 (Chapter III) - 22	❑ Page 52, paragraph 1 - page 54	❑ Page 90, paragraph 5 - page 96, paragraph 5
C. Read Aloud		*Abigail Adams*		
	Part 1	❑ Page 71, last paragraph - page 78, paragraph 8	❑ Discussion	
	Part 2	❑ Page 78, paragraph 9 - bottom page 84	❑ Narration	
	Part 3	❑ Page 84, last paragraph - page 90, paragraph 4	❑ Discussion	
	Part 4	❑ Page 90, paragraph 5 - page 96, paragraph 5	❑ Narration	
D. Language Skills				
	Part 1	❑ *e* words, ❑ Spelling list	❑ Additional words	❑ Additional words
	Part 2	❑ Mechanics Toolkit ❑ Edit sentences	❑ Edit additional sentences	❑ Edit additional sentences
	Part 3	❑ Vocabulary cards ❑ Spelling practice		
	Part 4	❑ Mechanics Toolkit ❑ Make up examples		
E. History/Science				
	Part 1	❑ Label map ❑ Discussion ❑ Observe weather		
	Part 2	❑ Weathering ❑ Terms ❑ Water Wedge ❑ Observe weather	❑ Add'l weathering agents	
	Part 3	❑ Drive Thru - Ben Franklin ❑ J25 ❑ Observe weather		
	Part 4	❑ Soil ❑ Types ❑ Quote ❑ Observe weather		❑ Soil formation
F. States				
	Part 1	❑ Pennsylvania	❑ Research ❑ Mapping	
	Part 2		❑ State Page ❑ State Cards	
	Part 3	❑ New York	❑ Research ❑ Mapping	
	Part 4		❑ State Page ❑ State Cards	
G. Doing				
	Part 1	❑ Dipping candles		
	Part 2	❑ Interactive Journaling		
	Part 3	❑ PA or NY recipe ❑ Drawing ❑ Record reactions		
	Part 4	❑ Journaling		
H. Independent Reading		25minutes daily ❑❑❑❑	30 minutes daily ❑❑❑❑	30 minutes daily ❑❑❑❑
Review	Part 5	❑ Steps for Thinking review ❑ Map activity ❑ Growing Pains Crossword ❑ Watercolor activity ❑ Newcomer game		
Materials		*The Matchlock Gun*, *Ambush in the Wilderness*, *Eat Your Way Through the USA*, *Discovering America's Founders* Drive Thru History DVD, *Atlas of the United States*, *Handbook of Nature Study* (book or download), *Abigail Adams*, *Klutz Watercolor Book*, *USA Acitivties CD*	Watercolor paper, DVD player, Dictionary, Ingredients for recipe (Part 3), Outline map of U.S., Markers, crayons, or colored pencils, Index cards, Paper cup, Activity (Part 5): 4 teabags, small, sealable container (½ cup), small saucepan, Tape, Flour, Paper towel, Materials for craft (Part 1): 2 pounds of paraffin, 24 inches of candle wicking or cotton string, 48 oz. juice can (or similar container), 3-4 quart saucepan, candy thermometer, wooden spoon, paring knife, broom or yardstick Weather station: rain gauge, outdoor thermometer, barometer, anemometer, stop watch or watch with a second hand,weather vane.	

GROWING PAINS UNIT – *Lesson 5 At A Glance*

A. COPYWORK & DICTATION & QUOTATION NOTEBOOK		*The Matchlock Gun*	*Ambush in the Wilderness*	
	Part 1	☐ Bottom, page 19 - page 20 rest of paragraph	☐ Page 57, paragraphs 6 - 8	
	Part 2	☐ Copy first rule	☐ Copy first two rules	☐ Copy all three rules
	Part 3	☐ Page 40, paragraph 3 - page 41, paragraph 4	☐ Page 68, paragraphs 1 - 2	
	Part 4	☐ Copy first rule	☐ Copy first two rules	☐ Copy all three rules
B. READER		*The Matchlock Gun*	*Ambush in the Wilderness*	*Abigail Adams*
	Part 1	☐ Pages 23 (Chapter IV) - 27, paragraph 2	☐ Pages 56 (Chapter Seven) - 59	☐ Page 96, paragraph 6 - bottom page 101
	Part 2	☐ Page 27, paragraph 3 - page 31	☐ Pages 60 - 62	☐ Page 101, last paragraph - page 106, paragraph 5
	Part 3	☐ Pages 32 (Chapter V) - 38, top of page	☐ Page 63 - bottom page 66	☐ Page 106, paragraph 6 - page 112, paragraph 8
	Part 4	☐ Page 38, paragraph 1 - page 42	☐ Page 66, last paragraph - page 69	☐ Page 112, paragraph 9 - page 118, paragraph 1
C. READ ALOUD		*Abigail Adams*		
	Part 1	☐ Page 96, paragraph 6 - bottom page 101	☐ Discussion	
	Part 2	☐ Page 101, last paragraph - page 106, paragraph 5	☐ Narration	
	Part 3	☐ Page 106, paragraph 6 - page 112, paragraph 8	☐ Discussion	
	Part 4	☐ Page 112, paragraph 9 - page 118, paragraph 1	☐ Narration	
D. LANGUAGE SKILLS				
	Part 1	☐ *ly* words, ☐ Spelling list	☐ Additional words	☐ Additional words
	Part 2	☐ Mechanics Toolkit ☐ Edit sentences	☐ Edit additional sentences	☐ Edit additional sentences
	Part 3	☐ Vocabulary cards ☐ Spelling practice		
	Part 4	☐ Mechanics Toolkit ☐ Make up examples		
E. HISTORY/SCIENCE				
	Part 1	☐ Historical postscript ☐ Discuss ☐ List ☐ Observe weather		
	Part 2	☐ Rocks ☐ Definitions ☐ Drawing ☐ Observe weather	☐ 3 kinds of rocks	☐ Minerals that are elements
	Part 3	☐ Map overlay ☐ Reactions to Fr & In War ☐ Observe weather	☐ Reaction to Line of Proclamation	
	Part 4	☐ Igneous rock ☐ Granite activity ☐ Observe weather	☐ Additional activity	
F. STATES				
	Part 1	☐ New Jersey	☐ Research ☐ Mapping	
	Part 2		☐ State Page ☐ State Cards	
	Part 3	☐ Delaware	☐ Research ☐ Mapping	
	Part 4		☐ State Page ☐ State Cards	
G. DOING				
	Part 1	☐ Watercolor activity		
	Part 2	☐ Interactive Journaling		
	Part 3	☐ NJ or DE recipe ☐ Drawing ☐ Record reactions		
	Part 4	☐ Dialogue ☐ 3 questions	☐ Additional questions (total of 4)	☐ Additional questions (total of 6)
H. INDEPENDENT READING		25minutes daily ☐☐☐☐	30 minutes daily ☐☐☐☐	30 minutes daily ☐☐☐☐
REVIEW	Part 5	☐ Steps for Thinking review ☐ Map activity ☐ Vocabulary & Spelling review ☐ Paul Revere Profile ☐ Growing Pains Bingo ☐ Vocabulary Charades		
MATERIALS		*The Matchlock Gun*, *Ambush in the Wilderness*, *Eat Your Way Through the USA*, *United States History Atlas*, *Atlas of the United States*, *Discovering America's Founders DVD*, *Abigail Adams*, *Klutz Watercolor Book*, *Profiles from History, Vol. 2*, *Handbook of Nature Study*, *DK Pockets: Rocks & Minerals*, *USA Activities CD*	Watercolor paper, Dictionary, Ingredients for recipe (Part 3), Rock Study Kit, Pocket knife, Outline map of U.S., Markers, crayons, or colored pencils, Index cards, Weather station: rain gauge, outdoor thermometer, barometer, anemometer, stop watch or watch with a second hand,weather vane.	

Growing Pains Unit – *Lesson 6 At A Glance*

A. Copywork & Dictation & Quotation Notebook		*The Matchlock Gun*	*Ambush in the Wilderness*	*Ambush in the Wilderness*
	Part 1	❑ Favorite quotation, Why?		❑ Example
	Part 2	❑ Page 51, mid-paragraph - end	❑ Page 75, paragraph 2	❑ Page 75, paragraphs 2 & 3
	Part 3	❑ Make up quotation ❑ Discussion		❑ Make up quotation ❑ Application
	Part 4	❑ Top page 60 - next 2 paragraphs	❑ Page 80, paragraph 4 - 6	❑ Page 80, paragraph 9 - page 81, paragraph 2
B. Reader		*The Matchlock Gun*	*Ambush in the Wilderness*	*Abigail Adams*
	Part 1	❑ Pages 43 - 47 (Chapter VII)	❑ Page 70 (Chapter Nine) - paragraph 3, page 73	❑ Page 118, paragraph 2 - page 124, paragraph 2
	Part 2	❑ Pages 48 - 53 (Chapter VIII)	❑ Page 73, paragraph 4 - page 75	❑ Page 124, paragraph 3 - page 130, paragraph 4
	Part 3	❑ Page 54 - bottom page 57 (Chapter IX)	❑ Pages 76 (Chapter Ten) - 78	❑ Page 130, paragraph 5 - page 136, paragraph 4
	Part 4	❑ Page 57, last paragraph - page 62	❑ Pages 79 - 83	❑ Page 136, paragraph 5 - page 143
C. Read Aloud		*Abigail Adams*		
	Part 1	❑ Page 118, paragraph 2 - page 124, prgph 2	❑ Discussion	
	Part 2	❑ Page 124, paragraph 3 - page 130, prgph 4	❑ Narration	
	Part 3	❑ Page 130, paragraph 5 - page 136, prgph 4	❑ Discussion	
	Part 4	❑ Page 136, paragraph 5 - page 143	❑ Narration	
D. Language Skills				
	Part 1	❑ Spelling review cards ❑ Categorize		
	Part 2	❑ Mechanics Toolkit Cards ❑ Examples ❑ Game		
	Part 3	❑ Vocabulary cards ❑ Spelling Review		
	Part 4	❑ Mechanics Toolkit Cards ❑ Examples ❑ Game		
E. History/Science				
	Part 1	❑ Drive Thru - Abigail Adams ❑ Video Profile ❑ Obs. weather		
	Part 2	❑ Weather chart ❑ Connections		
	Part 3	❑ Character Portrait	❑ Additional Character Portrait	
	Part 4	❑ Weather & Soil Matching		
F. States				
	Part 1	❑ Review with State Cards		
	Part 2	❑ State scramble		
	Part 3	❑ State Card Concentration		
	Part 4	❑ Map Matching ❑ State I.D. game		
G. Doing				
	Part 1	❑ Watercolor activity		
	Part 2	❑ Unit Presentation		
	Part 3	❑ Questions ❑ Choose a recipe		
	Part 4	❑ Book review		
H. Independent Reading		25minutes daily ❑❑❑❑	30 minutes daily ❑❑❑❑	30 minutes daily ❑❑❑❑
Review	Part 5	❑ Steps for Thinking review ❑ Timeline Activity ❑ Unit Presentation ❑ Growing Pains Bingo ❑ Vocabulary Charades		
Materials		*The Matchlock Gun*, *Ambush in the Wilderness*, *Eat Your Way Through the USA*, *Discovering America's Founders* Drive Thru History DVD, *Abigail Adams*, *Klutz Watercolor Book*, *Profiles from History Vol. 2*	DVD player, Watercolor paper, Ingredients for recipe (Part 3), Markers, crayons, or colored pencils, Index cards, Weather station: rain gauge, outdoor thermometer, barometer, anemometer, stop watch or watch with a second hand,weather vane.	

Freedom Decided Unit – Lesson 1 At A Glance

A. Copywork & Dictation & Quotation Notebook		*The American Revolution (Munford)*	*Guns for General Washington*	*Guns for General Washington*
	Part 1	❑ Page 11, paragraph 1	❑ Page 5, paragraph 1	❑ Page 4, paragraph 2
	Part 2	❑ Declaration of Independence	❑ Declaration of Independence	❑ Declaration of Independence ❑ Symbol
	Part 3	❑ Page 19, paragraphs 5 and 6	❑ Page 19, paragraph 1	❑ Page 18, paragraph 1 and page 19, paragraph 1
	Part 4	❑ Declaration of Independence	❑ Declaration of Independence	❑ Declaration of Independence ❑ Symbol
B. Reader		*The American Revolution (Munford)*	*Guns for General Washington*	*General Washington*
	Part 1	❑ Page 7, (Chapter 1) - page 11, paragraph 1	❑ Chapter 1	❑ Page 1 - bottom of page 4
	Part 2	❑ Page 11, paragraph 2 - page 17, paragraph 2	❑ Chapter 2	❑ Bottom page 4 - bottom page 10
	Part 3	❑ Page 18, paragraph 1 - page 22, paragraph 2	❑ Chapter 3	❑ Bottom page 10 - page 19, paragraph 2
	Part 4	❑ Page 22, paragraph 3 - page 28, paragraph 2	❑ Chapter 4	❑ Page 19, paragraph 4 - page 24
C. Read Aloud		*George Washington*		
	Part 1	❑ Page 1 - bottom of page 4	❑ Discussion	
	Part 2	❑ Bottom page 4 - bottom page 10	❑ Narration	
	Part 3	❑ Bottom page 10 - page 19, paragraph 2	❑ Discussion ❑ Make up question	❑ Make up additional questions
	Part 4	❑ Page 19, paragraph 3 - page 24	❑ Prediction	❑ Additional predictions
D. Language Skills				
	Part 1	❑ *un* words	❑ Additional spelling words	❑ Additional spelling words
	Part 2	❑ Patrick Henry speech ❑ Paraphrase first sentence	❑ Paraphrase the second sentence	❑ Paraphrase both sentences
	Part 3	❑ Vocabulary ❑ Spelling practice ❑ 4 add'l *un* words	❑ Additional vocabulary words ❑ 6 add'l *un* words	❑ Additional vocabulary words ❑ 8 add'l *un* words
	Part 4	❑ Patrick Henry speech ❑ Paraphrase 2 sentences	❑ Paraphrase 3 sentences	❑ Paraphrase 4 sentences
E. History/Science		*Eve of Revolution* (History)		
	Part 1	❑ Introduction-page 7 ❑ Taxes	❑ Additional discussion	❑ Research
	Part 2	❑ Molecules ❑ Model ❑ Properties of matter	❑ Record explanations of matter, mass, weight	
	Part 3	❑ Pages 8-12 ❑ Research Sons & Daughters of Liberty		❑ Reflective writing
	Part 4	❑ Atoms ❑ Model ❑ Periodic Table activities	❑ Additional Periodic Table activities	❑ Research particle charges
F. States				
	Part 1	❑ Maryland	❑ Research ❑ Mapping	
	Part 2		❑ State Page ❑ State Cards	
	Part 3	❑ Virginia	❑ Research ❑ Mapping	
	Part 4		❑ State Page ❑ State Cards	
G. Doing				
	Part 1	❑ Watercolor activity		
	Part 2	❑ Interactive Journaling ❑ 4 sentences and reaction	❑ 5 sentences and reaction	❑ Paragraph and reaction
	Part 3	❑ MD or VA recipe ❑ Drawing ❑ Record reactions		
	Part 4	❑ Identify methods of persuasion ❑ Methods you would use	❑ Additional identification ❑ Add'l personal methods	❑ Additional identification ❑ Add'l personal methods
H. Independent Reading		25minutes daily ❑❑❑❑	30 minutes daily ❑❑❑❑	30 minutes daily ❑❑❑❑
Review	Part 5	❑ Steps for Thinking review ❑ Vocabulary & Spelling review	❑ Map activity ❑ John Adams Profile ❑ Freedom Decided Word Search	
Materials		*The American Revolution (Munford)*, *Guns for General Washington*, *George Washington*, *Klutz Watercolor Book*, *Atlas of the United States*, *The Eve of Revolution*, *Profiles from History, Vol. 2*, *Eat Your Way Through the USA*, *USA Activities CD*	Extra watercolor paper, Outline map of the U.S., Crayons, markers, or colored pencils, Index cards, Dictionary, Ingredients for recipe (Part 3), Highlighter or yellow crayon, Activity (Parts 2 and 4): Modeling clay (3 colors), Toothpick, 1-pound bag of dried beans, clear glass or plastic bowl	

Freedom Decided Unit – *Lesson 2 At A Glance*

Subject	Part	Level 1	Level 2	Level 3
A. Copywork & Dictation & Quotation Notebook		*The American Revolution (Munford)*	*Guns for General Washington*	*Guns for General Washington*
	Part 1	❑ Page 32, paragraph 4	❑ Page 36, paragraph 3	❑ Page 36, paragraphs 2-3
	Part 2	❑ Declaration of Independence	❑ Declaration of Independence	❑ Declaration of Independence ❑ Symbol
	Part 3	❑ Page 39, paragraph 1	❑ Page 51, paragraph 1	❑ Page 50, paragraph 3 - page 51, paragraph 1
	Part 4	❑ Declaration of Independence	❑ Declaration of Independence	❑ Declaration of Independence ❑ Symbol
B. Reader		*The American Revolution (Munford)*	*Guns for General Washington*	*General Washington*
	Part 1	❑ Page 29, paragraph 1 - page 32, paragraph 4	❑ Chapter 5	❑ Page 25 - page 33, paragraph 3
	Part 2	❑ Page 32, paragraph 5 - page 38, paragraph 3	❑ Chapter 6	❑ Page 33, paragraph 4 - page 40
	Part 3	❑ Page 38, paragraph 4 - page 43, paragraph 3	❑ Chapter 7	❑ Page 41 - page 47, paragraph 5
	Part 4	❑ Page 44, paragraph 1 - page 48, paragraph 4	❑ Chapter 8	❑ Page 47, paragraph 6 - page 54, paragraph 5
C. Read Aloud		*George Washington*		
	Part 1	❑ Page 25 (Chapter 3) - page 33, paragraph 3	❑ Discussion	
	Part 2	❑ Page 33, paragraph 4 - page 40	❑ Narration	
	Part 3	❑ Page 41 (Chapter 4) - page 47, paragraph 5	❑ Discussion ❑ Make up question	❑ Make up additional questions
	Part 4	❑ Page 47, paragraph 6 - page 54, paragraph 5	❑ Prediction	❑ Additional predictions
D. Language Skills				
	Part 1	❑ Numeral and ordinal number words	❑ Additional words	❑ Additional words
	Part 2	❑ Patrick Henry speech ❑ Paraphrase 2 sentences	❑ Paraphrase 3 sentences	❑ Paraphrase 4 sentences
	Part 3	❑ Vocabulary ❑ Number word cards ❑ Game	❑ Additional vocabulary words	❑ Additional vocabulary words
	Part 4	❑ Patrick Henry speech ❑ Paraphrase 2 sentences	❑ Paraphrase 3 sentences	❑ Paraphrase 4 sentences
E. History/Science		*Eve of Revolution* (History)		
	Part 1	❑ Chapter 2 ❑ British response	❑ Other perspective	
	Part 2	❑ Water cycle ❑ Label & explain ❑ Experiment ❑ How it relates		❑ Dew point
	Part 3	❑ Chapter 3 ❑ 1st Cont.Congress ❑ Survey ❑ Graph	❑ Convert to percentage	❑ Enlarged survey ❑ Graph
	Part 4	❑ Clouds ❑ Drawing ❑ Observe weather	❑ Additional clouds ❑ Drawing	❑ Additional clouds ❑ Drawing
F. States				
	Part 1	❑ North Carolina	❑ Research ❑ Mapping	
	Part 2		❑ State Page ❑ State Cards	
	Part 3	❑ South Carolina	❑ Research ❑ Mapping	
	Part 4		❑ State Page ❑ State Cards	
G. Doing				
	Part 1	❑ Beanbags ❑ Game		
	Part 2	❑ Interactive Journaling ❑ 4 sentences and reaction	❑ 5 sentences and reaction	❑ Paragraph and reaction
	Part 3	❑ NC or SC recipe ❑ Drawing ❑ Record reactions		
	Part 4	❑ Journal entry		
H. Independent Reading		25minutes daily ❑❑❑❑	30 minutes daily ❑❑❑❑	30 minutes daily ❑❑❑❑
Review	Part 5	❑ Steps for Thinking review ❑ Vocabulary & Spelling review	❑ Map activity ❑ Watercolor Activity ❑ Freedom Decided Word Scramble	
Materials		*The American Revolution (Munford)* *The Eve of Revolution* *Guns for General Washington* *Profiles from History, Vol. 2* *George Washington* *Eat Your Way Through the USA* *Klutz Watercolor Book* *DK Pockets: Weather Facts* *Atlas of the United States*	Extra watercolor paper, Outline map of the U.S., Crayons, markers, or colored pencils, Index cards, Dictionary, Highlighter or yellow crayon, Ingredients for recipe (Part 3), Craft (Part 1): 1-pound bag of dry beans, Fabric scraps, Fabric glue, Chalk or masking tape, Scissors. Experiment (Part 2): One-fourth cup salt, 1 tablespoon sand or dirt, Small pan, Weather watching tools (made in Unit 1)	

Freedom Decided Unit – Lesson 3 At A Glance

Section	Part			
A. Copywork & Dictation & Quotation Notebook		*The American Revolution (Munford)*	*Guns for General Washington*	*Guns for General Washington*
	Part 1	❑ Page 49, paragraph 2	❑ Page 61, paragraph 8	❑ Page 61, paragraphs 6-8
	Part 2	❑ Declaration of Independence	❑ Declaration of Independence	❑ Declaration of Independence ❑ Symbol
	Part 3	❑ Page 60, paragraph 3	❑ Page 71, paragraph 1	❑ Page 70, paragraph 3 - page 71, paragraph 1
	Part 4	❑ U.S. Constitution	❑ U.S. Constitution	❑ U.S. Constitution ❑ Symbol
B. Reader		*The American Revolution (Munford)*	*Guns for General Washington*	*General Washington*
	Part 1	❑ Page 48, paragraph 5 - page 49, paragraph 1	❑ Chapter 9	❑ Page 54, paragraph 6 - page 61, paragraph 3
	Part 2	❑ Page 51, paragraph 1 - page 58, paragraph 2	❑ Chapter 10	❑ Page 61, paragraph 4 - page 67
	Part 3	❑ Page 58, paragraph 3 - page 61, paragraph 1	❑ Chapter 11	❑ Bottom of page 67 - page 74, paragraph 7
	Part 4	❑ Page 63 (Chapter 7) - page 68, paragraph 3	❑ Chapter 12	❑ Page 74, paragraph 7 - page 80, paragraph 7
C. Read Aloud		*George Washington*		
	Part 1	❑ Page 54, paragraph 6 - page 61, paragraph 3	❑ Discussion	
	Part 2	❑ Page 61, paragraph 4 - bottom of page 67	❑ Narration	
	Part 3	❑ Bottom of page 67 - page 74, paragraph 7	❑ Discussion ❑ Make up question	❑ Make up additional questions
	Part 4	❑ Page 74, paragraph 8 - page 80, paragraph 7	❑ Prediction	❑ Additional predictions
D. Language Skills				
	Part 1	❑ Numeral and ordinal number words	❑ Additional words	❑ Additional words
	Part 2	❑ Patrick Henry speech ❑ Paraphrase 1 sentence	❑ Paraphrase 2 sentences	❑ Paraphrase both sentences
	Part 3	❑ Vocabulary ❑ Number word cards ❑ Game	❑ Additional vocabulary words	❑ Additional vocabulary words
	Part 4	❑ Patrick Henry speech ❑ Paraphrase	❑ Additional paraphrase	❑ Additional paraphrase
E. History/Science		*Eve of Revolution* (History)		
	Part 1	❑ Pages 25 - 29 ❑ Slavery disc. ❑ Debate ❑ Observe weather		❑ Switch sides in debate
	Part 2	❑ Seasons ❑ Activity ❑ Labeling ❑ Observe weather	❑ Research North Pole	❑ Research South Pole
	Part 3	❑ Pages 30 - 34 ❑ Watercolor ❑ Observe weather	❑ I-net tour	
	Part 4	❑ Earth's orbit ❑ Activity ❑ Labeling ❑ Observe weather	❑ Southern Hemisphere	❑ Length of days
F. States				
	Part 1	❑ Georgia	❑ Research ❑ Mapping	
	Part 2		❑ State Page ❑ State Cards	
	Part 3	❑ Kentucky	❑ Research ❑ Mapping	
	Part 4		❑ State Page ❑ State Cards	
G. Doing				
	Part 1	❑ Watercolor activity		
	Part 2	❑ Interactive Journaling ❑ 4 sentences and reaction	❑ 5 sentences and reaction	❑ Paragraph and reaction
	Part 3	❑ Recipe ❑ Drawing ❑ Record reactions		
	Part 4	❑ Dialogue rules ❑ Rewrite 2 sentences	❑ Rewrite 4 sentences	❑ Rewrite 6 sentences
H. Independent Reading		25minutes daily ❑❑❑❑	30 minutes daily ❑❑❑❑	30 minutes daily ❑❑❑❑
Review	Part 5	❑ Steps for Thinking review ❑ Vocabulary & Spelling review	❑ Map activity ❑ Nathan Hale Profile ❑ Cornhole game	
Materials		*The American Revolution (Munford)*, *Guns for General Washington*, *George Washington*, *Klutz Watercolor Book*, *Atlas of the United States*, *The Eve of Revolution*, *Profiles from History, Vol. 2*, *Eat Your Way Through the USA*, *DK Pockets: Weather Facts*, *USA Activities CD*	Extra watercolor paper, Crayons, markers, or colored pencils, Index cards, Outline map of the U.S., Highlighter or yellow crayon, Ingredients for recipe (Part 3), Activity (Part 2): Piece of fruit (round if possible), 2 toothpicks, Marker, Lamp, Clock with minute marks; Activity (Part 4): Ruler, Masking tape, Straight pin, Flashlight; Scissors, Glue, Weather watching tools, Activity (Part 5): Primary instructions: Large box (with panels at least 18-inches x 24-inches), Scissors or box cutter, Yardstick, Marker, Masking tape, Alternate instructions: Large piece of cardboard, (2) 1-gallon water jugs or similar supports, Masking tape.	

Freedom Decided Unit – Lesson 4 At A Glance

Subject	Part			
A. Copywork & Dictation & Quotation Notebook		*The American Revolution (Munford)*	*Guns for General Washington*	*Guns for General Washington*
	Part 1	❑ Page 69, paragraph 9	❑ Page 78, paragraph 2	❑ Page 78, paragraph 2 - page 79, paragraph 1
	Part 2	❑ U.S. Constitution	❑ U.S. Constitution	❑ U.S. Constitution ❑ Symbol
	Part 3	❑ Page 85, paragraph 2	❑ Page 90, paragraph 2	❑ Page 90, paragraph 2 - page 91, paragraph 1
	Part 4	❑ U.S. Constitution	❑ U.S. Constitution	❑ U.S. Constitution ❑ Symbol
B. Reader		*The American Revolution (Munford)*	*Guns for General Washington*	*General Washington*
	Part 1	❑ Page 68, paragraph 4 - page 74, paragraph 1	❑ Chapter 13	❑ Page 80, paragraph 8 - page 87, paragraph 6
	Part 2	❑ Page 74, paragraph 2 - page 79, paragraph 2	❑ Chapter 14	❑ Page 87, paragraph 7 - page 95
	Part 3	❑ Page 80, paragraph 1 - page 86, paragraph 8	❑ Chapter 15	❑ Page 96 - bottom of page 101
	Part 4	❑ Pge 87, paragraph 1 - page 91, paragraph 2	❑ Chapter 16	❑ Bottom page 101 - page 109
C. Read Aloud		*George Washington*		
	Part 1	❑ Page 80, paragraph 8 - page 87, paragraph 6	❑ Discussion	
	Part 2	❑ Page 87, paragraph 7 - page 95	❑ Narration	
	Part 3	❑ Page 96 - bottom of page 101	❑ Discussion ❑ Make up question	❑ Make up additional question
	Part 4	❑ Bottom page 101 - page 109	❑ Prediction	❑ Additional predictions
D. Language Skills				
	Part 1	❑ State names	❑ Additional state names	❑ Additional state names
	Part 2	❑ Patrick Henry speech ❑ Paraphrase last 2 sentences	❑ Paraphrase first sentence	❑ Paraphrase entire passage
	Part 3	❑ Vocabulary ❑ Spelling practice	❑ Additional vocabulary words	❑ Additional vocabulary words
	Part 4	❑ Patrick Henry speech ❑ Paraphrase 2 sentences	❑ Paraphrase 3 sentences	❑ Paraphrase 4 sentences
E. History/Science		*Eve of Revolution* (History)		
	Part 1	❑ Chapter 5 ❑ Boston Massacre ❑ Events ❑ Observe weather	❑ Townshend Acts ❑ Discuss ❑ List ❑ Opinion	
	Part 2	❑ Winter storms ❑ Precip. chart ❑ Facts ❑ Observe weather	❑ Storm of the Century (1993)	❑ Preparations for severe weather
	Part 3	❑ Drive-Thru - George Washington ❑ Observe weather		
	Part 4	❑ Hurricanes ❑ Formation ❑ Matching ❑ Observe weather		
F. States				
	Part 1	❑ Tennessee	❑ Research ❑ Mapping	
	Part 2		❑ State Page ❑ State Cards	
	Part 3	❑ Mississippi	❑ Research ❑ Mapping	
	Part 4		❑ State Page ❑ State Cards	
G. Doing				
	Part 1	❑ Weaving activity		
	Part 2	❑ Interactive Journaling ❑ 4 sentences and reaction	❑ 5 sentences and reaction	❑ Paragraph and reaction
	Part 3	❑ TN or MS recipe ❑ Drawing ❑ Record reactions		
	Part 4	❑ Ads ❑ Evaluation ❑ Agree? ❑ Persuaded?	❑ Additional evaluation	❑ Additional evaluation
H. Independent Reading		25minutes daily ❑❑❑❑	30 minutes daily ❑❑❑❑	30 minutes daily ❑❑❑❑
Review	Part 5	❑ Steps for Thinking review ❑ Vocabulary & Spelling review	❑ Map activity ❑ Watercolor Activity ❑ Freedom Decided Crossword	
Materials		*The American Revolution (Munford)* *The Eve of Revolution* *Guns for General Washington* *George Washington* *Eat Your Way Through the USA* *Klutz Watercolor Book* *DK Pockets: Weather Facts* *Atlas of the United States* *Discovering America's Founders* Drive Thru History DVD	Extra watercolor paper, Crayons, markers, or colored pencils, Index cards, Outline map of the U.S., Highlighter or yellow crayon, Ingredients for recipe (Part 3, Activity (Part 1): Light cardboard (at least 4"x 6"), Ball of twine or hemp cord, Yarn needle (preferred) or twist-tie, Weather watching tools	

FREEDOM DECIDED UNIT – *Lesson 5 At A Glance*

		The American Revolution (Munford)	*Guns for General Washington*	*Guns for General Washington*
A. COPYWORK & DICTATION & QUOTATION NOTEBOOK	Part 1	❑ Page 96, paragraph 2	❑ Page 101, paragraph 1	❑ Page 100, paragraph 4 - page 101, paragraph 1
	Part 2	❑ U.S. Constitution	❑ U.S. Constitution	❑ U.S. Constitution ❑ Symbol
	Part 3	❑ Page 103, paragraph 3	❑ Page 109, paragraph 3	❑ Page 109, paragraphs 3 - 4
	Part 4	❑ U.S. Constitution	❑ U.S. Constitution	❑ U.S. Constitution ❑ Symbol
B. READER		*The American Revolution (Munford)*	*Guns for General Washington*	*General Washington*
	Part 1	❑ Page 92, paragraph 2 - page 96, paragraph 2	❑ Chapter 17	❑ Pages 110 - 116
	Part 2	❑ Page 96, paragraph 3 - page 101, paragraph 2	❑ Chapter 18	❑ Page 117 - bottom of page 128
	Part 3	❑ Page 102, paragraph 1 - page 105, paragraph 4	❑ Chapter 19	❑ Bottom of page 122 - page 128
	Part 4	❑ Page 105, paragraph 5 - page 113, paragraph 1	❑ Chapter 20	❑ Pages 129 - 134
C. READ ALOUD		*George Washington*		
	Part 1	❑ Pages 110 - 116	❑ Discussion	
	Part 2	❑ Page 117 - bottom of page 122	❑ Narration	
	Part 3	❑ Bottom of page 122 - page 128	❑ Discussion ❑ Make up question	❑ Make up additional questions
	Part 4	❑ Pages 129 - 134	❑ Predictions	
D. LANGUAGE SKILLS				
	Part 1	❑ Base words ❑ Spelling words	❑ Additional spelling words	❑ Additional spelling words
	Part 2	❑ Patrick Henry speech ❑ Paraphrase 2 sentences	❑ Paraphrase 3 sentences	❑ Paraphrase 4 sentences
	Part 3	❑ Vocabulary ❑ Spelling practice	❑ Additional vocabulary words	❑ Additional vocabulary words
	Part 4	❑ Patrick Henry speech ❑ Paraphrase 2 sentences	❑ Paraphrase 3 sentences	❑ Paraphrase 4 sentences
E. HISTORY/SCIENCE		*Eve of Revolution* (History)		
	Part 1	❑ Epilogue ❑ I-net videos ❑ We Sing ❑ Observe weather		
	Part 2	❑ Rock cycle ❑ Labeling ❑ Observe weather		
	Part 3	❑ War overview ❑ Map overlay ❑ 1st flag ❑ Observe weather		
	Part 4	❑ Rock examination ❑ Facts ❑ Drawing ❑ Observe weather		❑ Additional rock examination ❑ Facts ❑ Drawing
F. STATES				
	Part 1	❑ Alabama	❑ Research ❑ Mapping	
	Part 2		❑ State Page ❑ State Cards	
	Part 3	❑ Arkansas	❑ Research ❑ Mapping	
	Part 4		❑ State Page ❑ State Cards	
G. DOING				
	Part 1	❑ Watercolor activity		
	Part 2	❑ Interactive Journaling ❑ 4 sentences and reaction	❑ 5 sentences and reaction	❑ Paragraph and reaction
	Part 3	❑ AL or AR recipe ❑ Drawing ❑ Record reactions		
	Part 4	❑ Rhyming pat. ❑ Copy poem ❑ Discuss ❑ Write stanza	❑ Additional stanza	❑ Additional stanza
H. INDEPENDENT READING		25minutes daily ❑❑❑❑	30 minutes daily ❑❑❑❑	30 minutes daily ❑❑❑❑
REVIEW	Part 5	❑ Steps for Thinking review ❑ Vocabulary & Spelling review	❑ Map activity ❑ Molly Pitcher Profile	❑ Freedom Decided Bingo
MATERIALS		*The American Revolution (Munford)* *The Eve of Revolution* *Guns for General Washington* *Profiles from History, Vol. 2* *George Washington* *Eat Your Way Through the USA* *Klutz Watercolor Book* *We Sing America* CD *DK Pockets: Rocks & Minerals* *Atlas of the United States* *Discovering America's Founders* Drive Thru History DVD	Extra watercolor paper, Crayons, markers, or colored pencils, Index cards, Outline map of the U.S., Highlighter or yellow crayon, Rock study kit, Ingredients for recipe (Part 3), Scissors, Glue, Transparency paper , Permanent markers, Weather watcher tools	

Freedom Decided Unit – Lesson 6 At A Glance

A. Copywork & Dictation & Quotation Notebook		*The American Revolution (Munford)*	*Guns for General Washington*	*Guns for General Washington*
	Part 1	❑ Page 118, paragraph 3	❑ Page 119, paragraph 2	❑ Page 119, paragraphs 2 and 3
	Part 2	❑ Bill of Rights	❑ Bill of Rights	❑ Bill of Rights ❑ Symbol
	Part 3	❑ Page 127, paragraph 1	❑ Page 130, paragraph 2	❑ Page 130, paragraphs 2 and 3
	Part 4	❑ Bill of Rights	❑ Bill of Rights	❑ Bill of Rights ❑ Symbol
B. Reader		*The American Revolution (Munford)*	*Guns for General Washington*	*General Washington*
	Part 1	❑ Page 113, paragraph 2 - page 119, paragraph 1	❑ Chapter 21	❑ Pages 135 - 140
	Part 2	❑ Page 119, paragraph 2 - page 123, paragraph 1	❑ Chapter 22	❑ Pages141 - 149
	Part 3	❑ Page 124, paragraph 1 - page 127, paragraph 4	❑ Chapter 23	❑ Pages 150 - 156
	Part 4	❑ Page 128, paragraph 1 - page 135	❑ Chapter 24 - 25	❑ Pages 157 - 164
C. Read Aloud		*George Washington*		
	Part 1	❑ Pages 135 - 140	❑ Discussion	
	Part 2	❑ Pages141 - 149	❑ Narration	
	Part 3	❑ Pages 150 - 156	❑ Discussion ❑ Make up question	❑ Make up additional questions
	Part 4	❑ Pages 157 - 164		
D. Language Skills				
	Part 1	❑ Review Unit 1 spelling words	❑ Additional Unit 1 words	❑ Additional Unit 1 words
	Part 2	❑ Patrick Henry speech ❑ Paraphrase 2 sentences	❑ Paraphrase 3 sentences	❑ Paraphrase 4 sentences
	Part 3	❑ Vocabulary ❑ Spelling practice	❑ Additional vocabulary words	
	Part 4	❑ Speech presentation ❑ Patrick Henry profile	❑ Summary of speech	❑ Additional presentation
E. History/Science				
	Part 1	❑ Drive Thru - Haym Salomon ❑ Weather observation	❑ List important things	
	Part 2	❑ Compile Weather Chart		
	Part 3	❑ Who or What Am I?		
	Part 4	❑ Earth Science Matching		
F. States				
	Part 1	❑ Review State Cards, Game		
	Part 2	❑ State Scramble ❑ Regional summary		
	Part 3	❑ State Card Concentration		
	Part 4	❑ State I.D. ❑ Regional summary		
G. Doing				
	Part 1	❑ Watercolor activity		
	Part 2	❑ Unit Presentation		
	Part 3	❑ Questions ❑ Choose a recipe		
	Part 4	❑ Book Review	❑ Additional evaluation	❑ Additional evaluation
H. Independent Reading		25minutes daily ❑❑❑❑	30 minutes daily ❑❑❑❑	30 minutes daily ❑❑❑❑
Review	Part 5	❑ Steps for Thinking review ❑ Vocabulary & Spelling review	❑ Timeline Activity ❑ Unit Presentation	❑ Freedom Decided Bingo
Materials		*The American Revolution (Munford)* *The Eve of Revolution* *Guns for General Washington* *Profiles from History, Vol. 2* *George Washington* *Eat Your Way Through the USA* *Klutz Watercolor Book* *Atlas of the United States* *DK Pockets: Rocks & Minerals* *USA Activities CD* *Discovering America's Founders* Drive Thru History DVD	Extra watercolor paper, Crayons, markers, or colored pencils, Index cards, Outline map of the U.S., Highlighter or yellow crayon, Ingredients for recipe (Part 3), Weather watcher tools	

NATION BUILDING UNIT – *Lesson 1 At A Glance*

A. COPYWORK & DICTATION & QUOTATION NOTEBOOK		*The Cabin Faced West*	*Justin Morgan Had a Horse*	*Justin Morgan Had a Horse*
	Part 1	❑ Page 10, paragraphs 1 and 2	❑ Foreword, paragraph 1	❑ Additional paragraph
	Part 2	❑ Star Spangled Banner ❑ Description	❑ Star Spangled Banner ❑ Description	❑ Synonyms
	Part 3	❑ Page 20, paragraph 6	❑ Page 37, paragraph 2	❑ Additional paragraph
	Part 4	❑ Star Spangled Banner ❑ Description	❑ Star Spangled Banner ❑ Description	❑ Synonyms
B. READER		*The Cabin Faced West*	*Justin Morgan Had a Horse*	*Francis Scott Key*
	Part 1	❑ Page 9 (Chapter 1) - top of page 14	❑ Page 11 (Chapter 1) - page 18, paragraph 3	❑ Page 1 - page 5, paragraph 3
	Part 2	❑ Page 14, paragraph 1 - top of page 19	❑ Page 18, paragraph 4 - top of page 27	❑ Page 5, paragraph 4 - page 8
	Part 3	❑ Page 19, paragraph 1 - top of page 24	❑ Page 27, paragraph 1 - page 33, paragraph 2	❑ Page 10 - page 14, paragraph 5
	Part 4	❑ Page 24, paragraph 1 - page 28	❑ Page 33, paragraph 3 - page 38	❑ Page 14, paragraph 6 - page 18, paragraph 1
C. READ ALOUD		*Francis Scott Key*		
	Part 1	❑ Page 1 - page 5, paragraph 3	❑ Report events	❑ Report additional events ❑ Show relationships
	Part 2	❑ Page 5, paragraph 4 - page 8	❑ Narration ❑ Point of view	
	Part 3	❑ Page 10 (Chapter 2) - page 14, paragraph 5	❑ Discussion ❑ Make up question	❑ Make up additional questions
	Part 4	❑ Page 14, paragraph 6 - page 18, paragraph 1	❑ Prediction	❑ Additional predictions
D. LANGUAGE SKILLS				
	Part 1	❑ Spelling cards ❑ Organize ❑ Practice	❑ Additional words	❑ Additional words
	Part 2	❑ Mechanics Toolkit ❑ Correct sentences	❑ Additional sentences	❑ Additional sentences
	Part 3	❑ Vocabulary cards ❑ Synonyms ❑ Syllables ❑ Spelling practice	❑ Additional vocabulary	
	Part 4	❑ Mechanics Toolkit ❑ Examples of rules	❑ Additional examples	
E. HISTORY/SCIENCE				
	Part 1	❑ Treaty of Paris ❑ Map Overlay ❑ Expansion	❑ Negotiate a treaty	❑ Discuss treaties
	Part 2	❑ Write questions ❑ Identify oceans ❑ Seas ❑ 3-D Map		
	Part 3	❑ Presidential focus ❑ Citizenship ❑ Rights/Responsibilities	❑ 15th Amendment	❑ 19th Amendment
	Part 4	❑ Continents ❑ Islands ❑ 3-D Map		
F. STATES				
	Part 1	❑ Louisiana	❑ Research ❑ Mapping	
	Part 2		❑ State Page ❑ State Cards	
	Part 3	❑ Florida	❑ Research ❑ Mapping	
	Part 4		❑ State Page ❑ State Cards	
G. DOING				
	Part 1	❑ Watercolor activity		
	Part 2	❑ Interactive writing ❑ 4 Sentences ❑ Reaction	❑ 5 sentences ❑ Reaction	❑ Paragraph ❑ Reaction
	Part 3	❑ LA or FL recipe ❑ Drawing ❑ Record reactions		
	Part 4	❑ News article ❑ Revision	❑ Additional news article ❑ Revision	❑ Additional news article ❑ Revision
H. INDEPENDENT READING				
		25minutes daily ❑❑❑❑	30 minutes daily ❑❑❑❑	30 minutes daily ❑❑❑❑
REVIEW	Part 5	❑ Steps for Thinking review ❑ Vocabulary & Spelling review	❑ Map activity ❑ Daniel Webster Profile	❑ Nation Building Word Search
MATERIALS		*The Cabin Faced West* *Francis Scott Key* *Klutz Watercolor Book* *Profiles from History, Vol. 2* *Atlas of the United States* *Justin Morgan Had a Horse* *Eat Your Way Through the USA* *United States History Atlas*	United States Presidents Pocket Flash Cards, Extra watercolor paper, Crayons, markers, or colored pencils, Index cards, Outline map of the U.S., Highlighter, Transparency paper, Scissors, Thesaurus, Globe (optional), Activity (Part 2): Newspaper, newsmagazine, or online news source; Activity (Parts 2 and 4): All purpose flour, Salt, Mixing bowl, Cookie sheet (at least 12" x 16"), Heavy-duty aluminum foil, Yardstick, Ruler, Fine-line permanent marker; Ingredients for recipe (Part 3)	

Nation Building Unit – *Lesson 2 At A Glance*

A. Copywork & Dictation & Quotation Notebook		*The Cabin Faced West*	*Justin Morgan Had a Horse*	*Justin Morgan Had a Horse*
	Part 1	☐ Page 30, paragraphs 4 and 5	☐ Page 39, paragraphs 1 and 2	☐ Additional paragraph
	Part 2	☐ Star Spangled Banner ☐ Description	☐ Star Spangled Banner ☐ Description	☐ Synonyms
	Part 3	☐ Page 39, paragraphs 3 and 4	☐ Page 53, paragraphs 4 and 6	☐ Additional paragraph
	Part 4	☐ Star Spangled Banner ☐ Description	☐ Star Spangled Banner ☐ Description	☐ Synonyms
B. Reader		*The Cabin Faced West*	*Justin Morgan Had a Horse*	*Francis Scott Key*
	Part 1	☐ Page 29 (Chapter 3) - top of page 34	☐ Page 39 (Chapter 4) - page 45, paragraph 4	☐ Page 18, paragraph 2 - top of page 23
	Part 2	☐ Page 34, paragraph 1 - page 38	☐ Page 45, paragraph 5 - Page 51, paragraph 3	☐ Page 23, paragraph 1 - Page 27, paragraph 3
	Part 3	☐ Page 39 - top of page 44	☐ Page 51, paragraph 4 - page 56	☐ Page 27, paragraph 4 - top of page 32
	Part 4	☐ Page 44, paragraph 1 - mid-page 49	☐ Pages 57 - 62	☐ Page 32, paragraph 1 - page 35
C. Read Aloud		*Francis Scott Key*		
	Part 1	☐ Page 18, paragraph 2 - top of page 23	☐ Report events	☐ Report additional events ☐ Show relationships
	Part 2	☐ Page 23, paragraph 1 - Page 27, paragraph 3	☐ Narration ☐ Point of view	
	Part 3	☐ Page 27, paragraph 4 - top of page 32	☐ Discussion ☐ Make up question	☐ Make up additional questions
	Part 4	☐ Page 32, paragraph 1 - page 35	☐ Prediction	☐ Additional predictions
D. Language Skills				
	Part 1	☐ Spelling cards ☐ Organize ☐ Practice	☐ Additional words	☐ Additional words
	Part 2	☐ Mechanics Toolkit ☐ Correct sentences	☐ Additional sentences	☐ Additional sentences
	Part 3	☐ Vocabulary cards ☐ Synonyms ☐ Syllables ☐ Spelling practice	☐ Additional vocabulary	
	Part 4	☐ Mechanics Toolkit ☐ Examples of rules	☐ Additional examples	
E. History/Science				
	Part 1	☐ LA Purchase ☐ Struggles faced ☐ Map overlay	☐ Lewis & Clark ☐ Pros & cons of moving	☐ Paragraph to support opinion
	Part 2	☐ Ocean water ☐ Label chart ☐ 3-D map		
	Part 3	☐ Presidential focus ☐ Drive Thru - Noah Webster		
	Part 4	☐ Cont. shelf ☐ Cont. slope ☐ List facts ☐ 3-D map		
F. States				
	Part 1	☐ West Virginia	☐ Research ☐ Mapping	
	Part 2		☐ State Page ☐ State Cards	
	Part 3	☐ Ohio	☐ Research ☐ Mapping	
	Part 4		☐ State Page ☐ State Cards	
G. Doing				
	Part 1	☐ Make pick-up sticks ☐ Play game		
	Part 2	☐ Interactive writing ☐ 4 Sentences ☐ Reaction	☐ 5 sentences ☐ Reaction	☐ Paragraph ☐ Reaction
	Part 3	☐ WV or OH recipe ☐ Drawing ☐ Record reactions		
	Part 4	☐ Journal entry ☐ 3 facts ☐ 3 opinions	☐ 3 facts ☐ 6 opinions	☐ 4 facts ☐ 8 opinions
H. Independent Reading		25minutes daily ☐☐☐☐	30 minutes daily ☐☐☐☐	30 minutes daily ☐☐☐☐
Review	Part 5	☐ Steps for Thinking review ☐ Vocabulary & Spelling review	☐ Map activity ☐ Watercolor Activity	☐ Nation Building Word Scramble
Materials		*The Cabin Faced West*, *Justin Morgan Had a Horse*, *Francis Scott Key*, *Eat Your Way Through the USA*, *Klutz Watercolor Book*, *United States History Atlas*, *Children's Illustrted Atlas of the United States*, *Discovering America's Founders* Drive Thru History DVD	United States Presidents Pocket Flash Cards, Extra watercolor paper, Crayons, markers, or colored pencils, Index cards, Outline map of the U.S., Scissors, Thesaurus, Globe (optional), Activity (Part 1): 30 bamboo skewers, Red, blue, green, black, and yellow (optional) paint or markers, Fine-to medium-grain sandpaper, Wire cutters or shears; Activity (Part 2): Newspaper, newsmagazine, or online news source; Activity (Parts 2 and 4): All purpose flour, Salt, Mixing bowl, Ruler, Fine-line permanent marker; Ingredients for recipe (Part 3)	

Nation Building Unit – *Lesson 3 At A Glance*

A. Copywork & Dictation & Quotation Notebook		*The Cabin Faced West*	*Justin Morgan Had a Horse*	*Justin Morgan Had a Horse*
	Part 1	❑ Page 50, paragraph 1	❑ Page 64, paragraphs 2 - 4	❑ Additional paragraph
	Part 2	❑ Star Spangled Banner ❑ Description	❑ Star Spangled Banner ❑ Description	❑ Synonyms
	Part 3	❑ Page 60, paragraphs 2 and 3 - page 62, paragraph 1	❑ Page 82, paragraphs 2 and 3	❑ Additional paragraph
	Part 4	❑ Star Spangled Banner ❑ Description	❑ Star Spangled Banner ❑ Description	❑ Synonyms
B. Reader		*The Cabin Faced West*	*Justin Morgan Had a Horse*	*Francis Scott Key*
	Part 1	❑ Page 49, paragraph 1 - pg. 53, paragraph 2	❑ Page 63 (Chapter 7) - page 69, paragraph 4	❑ Page 36 - page 41, paragraph 2
	Part 2	❑ Page 53, paragraph 3 - pg. 57, paragraph 2	❑ Page 69, paragraph 5 - page 76, paragraph 3	❑ Page 41, paragraph 3 - page 45, paragraph 4
	Part 3	❑ Page 57, paragraph 3 - bottom page 63	❑ Page 76, paragraph 4 - page 82	❑ Page 45, paragraph 5 - page 48
	Part 4	❑ Page 63, last paragraph - top of page 68	❑ Pages 83 - 89 (Chapter 9)	❑ Pages 49 - 53
C. Read Aloud		*Francis Scott Key*		
	Part 1	❑ Page 36 - page 41, paragraph 2	❑ Report events	❑ Report additional events ❑ Show relationships
	Part 2	❑ Page 41, paragraph 3 - page 45, paragraph 4	❑ Narration ❑ Point of view	
	Part 3	❑ Page 45, paragraph 5 - page 48	❑ Discussion ❑ Make up question	❑ Make up additional questions
	Part 4	❑ Pages 49 - 53 (Chapter 6)	❑ Prediction	❑ Additional predictions
D. Language Skills				
	Part 1	❑ Spelling cards ❑ Organize ❑ Practice	❑ Additional words	❑ Additional words
	Part 2	❑ Mechanics Toolkit game ❑ Make up examples	❑ Additional examples	❑ Additional examples
	Part 3	❑ Vocabulary cards ❑ Synonyms ❑ Syllables ❑ Spelling practice	❑ Additional words	
	Part 4	❑ Mechanics Toolkit game ❑ Make up examples	❑ Additional examples	❑ Additional examples
E. History/Science				
	Part 1	❑ FL cession ❑ Map overlay ❑ Expansion ❑ Summary points	❑ Additional point	❑ Additional points
	Part 2	❑ Questions ❑ Waves ❑ Chart ❑ 3-D map		
	Part 3	❑ Presidential focus ❑ Building Blocks bingo		
	Part 4	❑ Mid-Atlantic Ridge ❑ Fissure volcanoes ❑ 3-D map		
F. States				
	Part 1	❑ Indiana	❑ Research ❑ Mapping	
	Part 2		❑ State Page ❑ State Cards	
	Part 3	❑ Illinois	❑ Research ❑ Mapping	
	Part 4		❑ State Page ❑ State Cards	
G. Doing				
	Part 1	❑ Watercolor activity		
	Part 2	❑ Interactive writing ❑ 4 Sentences ❑ Reaction	❑ 5 sentences ❑ Response	❑ Paragraph ❑ Response
	Part 3	❑ IN or IL recipe ❑ Drawing ❑ Record reactions		
	Part 4	❑ Writing dialogue ❑ Rewrite 2 sentences	❑ Rewrite 4 sentences	❑ Rewrite 6 sentences
H. Independent Reading		25minutes daily ❑❑❑❑	30 minutes daily ❑❑❑❑	30 minutes daily ❑❑❑❑
Review	Part 5	❑ Steps for Thinking review ❑ Vocabulary & Spelling review	❑ Map activity ❑ Dolley Madison Profile	❑ Game of choice
Materials		*The Cabin Faced West* *Francis Scott Key* *Klutz Watercolor Book* *Profiles from History, Vol. 2* *Atlas of the United States* *Justin Morgan Had a Horse* *Eat Your Way Through the USA* *United States History Atlas*	United States Presidents Pocket Flash Cards, Extra watercolor paper, Crayons, markers, or colored pencils, Index cards, Outline map of the U.S., Globe (optional), Thesaurus, Highlighter, Scissors, Activity (Part 2): Newspaper, newsmagazine, or online news source; Activity (Parts 2 and 4): All purpose flour, Salt, Mixing bowl, Ruler, Fine-line permanent marker; Ingredients for recipe (Part 3)	

NATION BUILDING UNIT – *Lesson 4 At A Glance*

A. COPYWORK & DICTATION & QUOTATION NOTEBOOK		*The Cabin Faced West*	*Justin Morgan Had a Horse*	*Justin Morgan Had a Horse*
	Part 1	❑ Page 68, paragraph 4	❑ Page 90, paragraphs 1 and 2	❑ Additional paragraph
	Part 2	❑ Star Spangled Banner ❑ Description	❑ Star Spangled Banner ❑ Description	❑ Synonyms
	Part 3	❑ Page 79, paragraph 4	❑ Page 105, paragraph 5 - page 106, paragraph 1	❑ Additional paragraph
	Part 4	❑ Star Spangled Banner ❑ Description	❑ Star Spangled Banner ❑ Description	❑ Synonyms
B. READER		*The Cabin Faced West*	*Justin Morgan Had a Horse*	*Francis Scott Key*
	Part 1	❑ Page 68, paragraph 1 - page 72	❑ Page 90 (Chapter 10) -top of page 97	❑ Pages 54 - 57
	Part 2	❑ Page 73 - page 77, paragraph 1	❑ Page 97, paragraph 1 - page 103, paragraph 3	❑ Pages 58 - 61
	Part 3	❑ Page 77, paragraph 2 - page 82, paragraph 2	❑ Page 103, paragraph 4 - bottom page 111	❑ Page 62 - page 68, paragraph 8
	Part 4	❑ Page 82, paragraph 3 - page 87, paragraph 6	❑ Page 111, last paragraph - page 116	❑ Page 68, paragraph 9 - page 73, paragraph 1
C. READ ALOUD		*Francis Scott Key*		
	Part 1	❑ Pages 54 - 57 (Chapter 7)	❑ Report events	❑ Report additional events ❑ Show relationships
	Part 2	❑ Pages 58 - 61	❑ Narration ❑ Point of view	
	Part 3	❑ Page 62 (Chapter 8) - page 68, paragraph 8	❑ Discussion ❑ Make up question	❑ Make up additional questions
	Part 4	❑ Page 68, paragraph 9 - page 73, paragraph 1	❑ Prediction	❑ Additional predictions
D. LANGUAGE SKILLS	Part 1	❑ Spelling cards ❑ Organize ❑ Practice	❑ Additional words	❑ Additional words
	Part 2	❑ Mechanics Toolkit ❑ Correct sentences	❑ Additional sentences	❑ Additional sentences
	Part 3	❑ Vocabulary cards ❑ Synonyms ❑ Syllables ❑ Spelling practice	❑ Additional words	
	Part 4	❑ Mechanics Toolkit ❑ Examples of rules	❑ Additional examples	❑ Additional examples
E. HISTORY/SCIENCE	Part 1	❑ 3 land additions ❑ Map overlay ❑ Expansion ❑ Research	❑ Additional research	❑ Additional research
	Part 2	❑ Mid-ocean ranges ❑ Chart ❑ Add'l features ❑ 3-D map		
	Part 3	❑ Presidential focus ❑ Drive Thru - John Quincy Adams		
	Part 4	❑ Tides ❑ Chart ❑ Explanations ❑ Paint 3-D map		
F. STATES	Part 1	❑ Michigan	❑ Research ❑ Mapping	
	Part 2		❑ State Page ❑ State Cards	
	Part 3	❑ Iowa	❑ Research ❑ Mapping	
	Part 4		❑ State Page ❑ State Cards	
G. DOING	Part 1	❑ Tin-punching		
	Part 2	❑ Interactive writing ❑ 4 Sentences ❑ Response	❑ 5 sentences ❑ Response	❑ Paragraph ❑ Reaction
	Part 3	❑ MI or IA recipe ❑ Drawing ❑ Record reactions		
	Part 4	❑ Letter to the editor	❑ Additional letter	❑ Additional letters
H. INDEPENDENT READING		25minutes daily ❑❑❑❑	30 minutes daily ❑❑❑❑	30 minutes daily ❑❑❑❑
REVIEW	Part 5	❑ Steps for Thinking review ❑ Vocabulary & Spelling review	❑ Map activity ❑ Watercolor activity ❑ Nation Building Crossword	
MATERIALS		*The Cabin Faced West* *Francis Scott Key* *Klutz Watercolor Book* *Profiles from History, Vol. 2* *Atlas of the United States* *Discovering America's Founders* Drive Thru History DVD *Justin Morgan Had a Horse* *Eat Your Way Through the USA* *United States History Atlas*	United States Presidents Pocket Flash Cards, Extra watercolor paper, Crayons, markers, or colored pencils, Index cards, Outline map of the U.S., Thesaurus, Activity (Part 1): 9-inch aluminum pie pan (disposable foil type), Nail with a head, Hammer, Wooden board or block, Yarn or string; Optional Activity (Part 1): Empty, medium-sized can, 12 inches of medium gauge wire, Tea light candle, Towel, Needle nose pliers, Duct tape, Scissors; Activity (Part 2): Newspaper, newsmagazine, or online news source; Activity (Parts 2 and 4): All purpose flour, Salt, Mixing bowl, Ruler, Fine-line permanent marker; Ingredients for recipe (Part 3)	

Nation Building Unit – *Lesson 5 At A Glance*

Subject	Part			
A. Copywork & Dictation & Quotation Notebook		*The Cabin Faced West*	*Justin Morgan Had a Horse*	*Justin Morgan Had a Horse*
	Part 1	☐ Page 88, paragraph 2	☐ Page 122, paragraphs 3 and 4	☐ Additional paragraph
	Part 2	☐ Star Spangled Banner ☐ Description	☐ Star Spangled Banner ☐ Description	☐ Synonyms
	Part 3	☐ Page 100, paragraph 1	☐ Page 133, paragraph 2	☐ Additional paragraph
	Part 4	☐ Star Spangled Banner ☐ Description	☐ Star Spangled Banner ☐ Description	☐ Synonyms
B. Reader		*The Cabin Faced West*	*Justin Morgan Had a Horse*	*Francis Scott Key*
	Part 1	☐ Page 87, paragraph 7 - page 92, paragraph 3	☐ Pages 117 - 123 (Chapter 13)	☐ Page 73, paragraph 2 - top of page 77
	Part 2	☐ Page 92, paragraph 4 - page 96, paragraph 2	☐ Pages 124 - 129 (Chapter 14)	☐ Page 77, paragraph 1 - bottom page 80
	Part 3	☐ Page 96, paragraph 3 - page 101, paragraph 2	☐ Pages 130 - 136 (Chapter 15)	☐ Page 80, bottom - page 86, paragraph 1
	Part 4	☐ Page 101, paragraph 3 - page 106, paragraph 1	☐ Page 137 (Chapter 16) - page 143, paragraph 2	☐ Page 86, paragraph 2 - bottom page 89
C. Read Aloud		*Francis Scott Key*		
	Part 1	☐ Page 73, paragraph 2 - top of page 77	☐ Report events	☐ Report additional events ☐ Show relationships
	Part 2	☐ Page 77, paragraph 1 - bottom page 80	☐ Narration ☐ Point of view	
	Part 3	☐ Page 80, last paragraph - page 86, paragraph 1	☐ Discussion ☐ Make up question	☐ Make up additional questions
	Part 4	☐ Page 86, paragraph 2 - bottom page 89	☐ Prediction	☐ Additional predictions
D. Language Skills				
	Part 1	☐ Spelling cards ☐ Organize ☐ Practice	☐ Additional words	☐ Additional words
	Part 2	☐ Mechanics Toolkit ☐ Correct sentences	☐ Additional sentences	☐ Additional sentences
	Part 3	☐ Vocabulary cards ☐ Synonyms ☐ Syllables ☐ Spelling practice	☐ Additional words	
	Part 4	☐ Mechanics Toolkit ☐ Examples of rules	☐ Additional examples	
E. History/Science				
	Part 1	☐ Flag etiquette ☐ Folding	☐ Research symbols ☐ Design flag	
	Part 2	☐ Sedimentary rock formation ☐ Shale		☐ Additional discussion
	Part 3	☐ Presidential focus ☐ War of 1812 ☐ T/F statements	☐ Additional statements	☐ Additional statements
	Part 4	☐ Sedimentary rock identification ☐ Fossils		☐ Research additional rock
F. States				
	Part 1	☐ Wisconsin	☐ Research ☐ Mapping	
	Part 2		☐ State Page ☐ State Cards	
	Part 3	☐ Minnesota	☐ Research ☐ Mapping	
	Part 4		☐ State Page ☐ State Cards	
G. Doing				
	Part 1	☐ Watercolor activity		
	Part 2	☐ Interactive writing ☐ 4 Sentences ☐ Response	☐ 5 sentences ☐ Response	☐ Paragraph ☐ Response
	Part 3	☐ WI or MN recipe ☐ Drawing ☐ Record reactions		
	Part 4	☐ Rhyme pattern ☐ Rhyming words ☐ Write 1 stanza	☐ Write 2 stanzas	☐ Write 3 stanzas
H. Independent Reading		25minutes daily ☐☐☐☐	30 minutes daily ☐☐☐☐	30 minutes daily ☐☐☐☐
Review	Part 5	☐ Steps for Thinking review ☐ Vocabulary & Spelling review	☐ Map activity ☐ Tecumseh Profile ☐ Nation Building Bingo	
Materials		*The Cabin Faced West*, *Francis Scott Key*, *Klutz Watercolor Book*, *Profiles from History, Vol. 2*, *Handbook of Nature Study* (book or download), *DK Pockets: Rocks and Minerals*, *Justin Morgan Had a Horse*, *Eat Your Way Through the USA*, *United States History Atlas*, *Atlas of the United States*	United States Presidents Pocket Flash Cards, Rock Study Kit, Extra watercolor paper, Crayons, markers, or colored pencils, Index cards, Outline map of the U.S., Scissors, Thesaurus, Activity (Part 2): Newspaper, newsmagazine, or online news source; Ingredients for recipe (Part 3)	

Nation Building Unit – *Lesson 6 At A Glance*

Subject	Part			
A. Copywork & Dictation & Quotation Notebook		*The Cabin Faced West*	*Justin Morgan Had a Horse*	*Justin Morgan Had a Horse*
	Part 1	❑ Page 112, paragraph 4	❑ Page 155, paragraphs 2 and 3	❑ Additional paragraph
	Part 2	❑ Star Spangled Banner ❑ Description	❑ Star Spangled Banner ❑ Description	❑ Synonyms
	Part 3	❑ Page 116, paragraphs 3 and 4	❑ Page 159, paragraphs 3 and 4	❑ Additional paragraph
	Part 4	❑ Star Spangled Banner ❑ Description	❑ Star Spangled Banner ❑ Description	❑ Synonyms
B. Reader		*The Cabin Faced West*	*Justin Morgan Had a Horse*	*Francis Scott Key*
	Part 1	❑ Page 106, paragraph 2 - page 110, paragraph 2	❑ Page 143, paragraph 3 - page 150, paragraph 2	❑ Page 89, bottom - page 94
	Part 2	❑ Page 110, paragraph 3 - page 114, paragraph 3	❑ Page 150, paragraph 3 - page 156	❑ Page 95 - page 100, paragraph 2
	Part 3	❑ Page 114, paragraph 4 - bottom page 119	❑ Pages 157 - 162	❑ Page 100, paragraph 3 - bottom page 103
	Part 4	❑ Page 119, last paragraph - page 124	❑ Pages 163 - 170	❑ Page 103, bottom - page 110
C. Read Aloud		*Francis Scott Key*		
	Part 1	❑ Page 89, last paragraph - page 94	❑ Report events	❑ Report additional events ❑ Show relationships
	Part 2	❑ Page 95 (Chapter 12) - page 100, paragraph 2	❑ Narration ❑ Point of view	
	Part 3	❑ Page 100, paragraph 3 - bottom page 103	❑ Discussion ❑ Make up question	❑ Make up additional questions
	Part 4	❑ Page 103, last paragraph - page 110	❑ Prediction	❑ Additional predictions
D. Language Skills				
	Part 1	❑ Spelling cards ❑ Organize ❑ Practice	❑ Additional words	❑ Additional words
	Part 2	❑ Mechanics Toolkit game ❑ Make up examples	❑ Additional examples	❑ Additional examples
	Part 3	❑ Vocabulary cards ❑ Synonyms ❑ Syllables ❑ Spelling practice	❑ Additional words	
	Part 4	❑ Mechanics Toolkit game ❑ Make up examples	❑ Additional examples	❑ Additional examples
E. History/Science				
	Part 1	❑ Timeline activity ❑ Who or What Am I?	❑ Additional questions	❑ Additional questions
	Part 2	❑ Check questions ❑ Review chart		
	Part 3	❑ Population line graph ❑ Questions		❑ Research ❑ Predict
	Part 4	❑ Earth science matching		
F. States				
	Part 1	❑ Review State Cards ❑ Game		
	Part 2	❑ State Scramble ❑ Regional summary		
	Part 3	❑ State Card Concentration		
	Part 4	❑ State I.D. ❑ Regional summary		
G. Doing				
	Part 1	❑ Watercolor activity		
	Part 2	❑ Unit presentation preparation		
	Part 3	❑ Questions, ❑ Choose a recipe		
	Part 4	❑ Book review		
H. Independent Reading		25minutes daily ❑❑❑❑	30 minutes daily ❑❑❑❑	30 minutes daily ❑❑❑❑
Review	Part 5	❑ Steps for Thinking review ❑ Vocabulary & Spelling review	❑ Timeline Review ❑ Unit Presentation ❑ Nation Building Bingo	
Materials		*The Cabin Faced West*, *Francis Scott Key*, *Klutz Watercolor Book*, *Atlas of the United States*, *Justin Morgan Had a Horse*, *Eat Your Way Through the USA*	Mark-It Timeline of History, Extra watercolor paper, Crayons, markers, or colored pencils, Index cards, Outline map of the U.S., Highlighter, Scissors, Thesaurus, Ingredients for recipe (Part 3)	

Appendix A

Unit 1 - Growing Pains

	Skills & Topics			
Thinking Skills	Analyzing information	•	•	•
	Categorizing	•	•	•
	Compare and contrast	•	•	•
	Comprehension	•	•	•
	Deductive reasoning	•	•	•
	Discussion	•	•	•
	Drawing conclusions	•	•	•
	Evaluating information	•	•	•
	Fact and opinion	•	•	•
	Following directions	•	•	•
	Identifying examples	•	•	•
	Inductive reasoning	•	•	•
	Listening skills	•	•	•
	Main idea	•	•	•
	Making inferences	•	•	•
	Narration	•	•	•
	Observation skills	•	•	•
	Organizational skills	•	•	•
	Point of view	•	•	•
	Sequencing	•	•	•
	Summarizing	•	•	•
	Symbolism	•	•	•
	Synthesizing information	•	•	•
	Using context	•	•	•
	Questioning skills	•	•	•
	Review/evaluation	•	•	•
Language Skills	Adverbs	•	•	•
	Base words	•	•	•
	Decoding	•	•	•
	Dictionary/Thesaurus skills	•	•	•
	Editing	•	•	•
	Presentation skills	•	•	•
	Proofreading	•	•	•
	Proper nouns	•	•	•
	Punctuation:			
	Articles	•	•	•
	Capitalization	•	•	•
	Commas	•	•	•
	Ending punctuation	•	•	•
	Quotation marks	•	•	•
	Reading for enjoyment	•	•	•
	Reading with understanding	•	•	•
	Research/reference skills	•	•	•
	Sentence skills	•	•	•
	Spelling strategies	•	•	•
	Suffix	•	•	•
	Syllabication	•	•	•
	Vocabulary	•	•	•
	Word usage	•	•	•

	Skills & Topics			
Writing	Book reviews	•	•	•
	Character portraits	•	•	•
	Composition	•	•	•
	Dialogue	•	•	•
	Direct quotations	•	•	•
	Interactive writing	•	•	•
	Journaling	•	•	•
	List making	•	•	•
	Maintaining a log	•	•	•
	Note taking	•	•	•
	Paragraph writing	•	•	•
	Recording observations	•	•	•
	Revision	•	•	•
	Sentence skills	•	•	•
	Word banks	•	•	•
Earth Science:	Air pressure	•	•	•
	Atmosphere	•	•	•
	Charts/graphs	•	•	•
	Elements			•
	Experimenting	•	•	•
	Gravity	•	•	•
	Greenhouse effect			•
	Heat transfer	•	•	•
	Minerals/rocks	•	•	•
	Periodic Table	•	•	•
	Radiant energy	•	•	•
	Soil formation	•	•	•
	Types of soil	•	•	•
	Weather observations/measurements:			
	Anemometer	•	•	•
	Barometer	•	•	•
	Rain gauge	•	•	•
	Thermometer	•	•	•
	Windsock	•	•	•
	Weathering	•	•	•
	Weather sayings			•
	Wind	•	•	•
	Wind systems		•	•
Art, Doing & Music:	Candle-making	•	•	•
	Cooking	•	•	•
	Drawing	•	•	•
	Early American games: Quoits	•	•	•
	Illustration	•	•	•
	Making paint	•	•	•
	Watercolor painting:			
	Basic technique	•	•	•
	Color mixing	•	•	•

Growing Pains, con't

Geography, Social Studies & History:

Skills & Topics			
Boston Tea Party	•	•	•
British Isles	•	•	•
Ethnicity	•	•	•
French and Indian War	•	•	•
Historical maps	•	•	•
Historical figures:			
Abigail Adams	•	•	•
Samuel Adams	•	•	•
John Audubon	•	•	•
Benjamin Franklin	•	•	•
Thomas Paine	•	•	•
Paul Revere	•	•	•
Historical postscripts	•	•	•
Line of Proclamation	•	•	•
Map skills:			
Compass Rose	•	•	•
Legends, keys	•	•	•
Mapmaking	•	•	•
Map reading	•	•	•
Native Americans	•	•	•
Physical maps	•	•	•
Political maps	•	•	•
State information:			
Abbreviation	•	•	•
Bodies of water	•	•	•
Capitals	•	•	•
Highest point	•	•	•
Land Area	•	•	•
National parks	•	•	•
Physical features	•	•	•
Population	•	•	•
Regions	•	•	•
Year of statehood	•	•	•
States:			
Connecticut	•	•	•
Delaware	•	•	•
Maine	•	•	•
Massachusetts	•	•	•
New Hampshire	•	•	•
New Jersey	•	•	•
New York	•	•	•
Pennsylvania	•	•	•
Rhode Island	•	•	•
Vermont	•	•	•
Timeline	•	•	•
Trades	•	•	•
Types of settlers	•	•	•
Worldview	•	•	•

Unit 2 - Freedom Decided

Thinking Skills

Skills & Topics			
Categorizing	•	•	•
Cause and effect	•	•	•
Compare and contrast	•	•	•
Deductive reasoning	•	•	•
Discussion	•	•	•
Drawing conclusions	•	•	•
Fact and opinion	•	•	•
Following directions	•	•	•
Identifying a position	•	•	•
Defending a position	•	•	•
Identifying details	•	•	•
Identifying examples	•	•	•
Imagery	•	•	•
Inductive reasoning	•	•	•
Making inferences	•	•	•
Narration	•	•	•
Observation skills	•	•	•
Paraphrasing	•	•	•
Point of view	•	•	•
Predicting	•	•	•
Questioning skills	•	•	•
Sequencing	•	•	•
Summarizing	•	•	•
Symbolism			•
Using context	•	•	•
Analyzing information	•	•	•
Comprehension	•	•	•
Review and Evaluation	•	•	•
Listening skills	•	•	•

Language Skills

Skills & Topics			
Adjectives	•	•	•
Base words	•	•	•
Debate skills	•	•	•
Decoding	•	•	•
Dictionary/Thesaurus skills	•	•	•
Editing	•	•	•
Fiction/non-fiction	•	•	•
Imagery	•	•	•
Prefixes	•	•	•
Presentation skills	•	•	•
Proofreading	•	•	•
Proper nouns	•	•	•
Punctuation: Quotation marks	•	•	•
Reading for enjoyment	•	•	•
Reading with understanding	•	•	•
Research/reference skills	•	•	•
Rhyme patterns	•	•	•
Sentence skills	•	•	•
Spelling strategies	•	•	•
Syllabication	•	•	•
Vocabulary	•	•	•

FREEDOM DECIDED, CON'T

	Skills & Topics			
WRITING:	Book reviews	•	•	•
	Descriptive writing	•	•	•
	Dialogue	•	•	•
	Graph and chart making	•	•	•
	Interactive writing	•	•	•
	Journaling	•	•	•
	List making	•	•	•
	Maintaining a log	•	•	•
	Note taking	•	•	•
	Numerals and ordinal numbers	•	•	•
	Paragraph writing	•	•	•
	Paraphrasing	•	•	•
	Persuasive writing	•	•	•
	Poetry writing	•	•	•
	Record keeping	•	•	•
	Sequencing	•	•	•
	Summary writing	•	•	•
	Word Banks	•	•	•
EARTH SCIENCE:	Atoms	•	•	•
	Clouds	•	•	•
	Dew and frost			•
	Earth's axis	•	•	•
	Earth's orbit	•	•	•
	Elements	•	•	•
	Experimenting	•	•	•
	Igneous rock formation	•	•	•
	Length of days			•
	Matter	•	•	•
	Model-making	•	•	•
	Molecules	•	•	•
	North Pole		•	•
	Observation	•	•	•
	Recording observations	•	•	•
	Rock Cycle	•	•	•
	Seasons	•	•	•
	South Pole			•
	Storm of the Century		•	•
	Storm preparations			•
	Types of rock:			
	Igneous	•	•	•
	Sedimentary	•	•	•
	Metamorphic	•	•	•
	Water Cycle	•	•	•
	Weather:			
	Winter weather	•	•	•
	Hurricanes	•	•	•
ART, DOING & MUSIC:	"America, America"	•	•	•
	Cooking	•	•	•
	Drawing	•	•	•
	Early American games:			
	Beanbags	•	•	•
	Cornhole	•	•	•
	Illustration	•	•	•
	Watercolor painting:			
	Color combining	•	•	•
	Using the pencil	•	•	•
	Washes	•	•	•
	Weaving	•	•	•
	"Yankee Doodle"		•	•
GEOGRAPHY, SOCIAL STUDIES & HISTORY:	Boston Tea Party	•	•	•
	Boston Massacre	•	•	•
	Branches of Government:	•	•	•
	Drayton Hall		•	•
	French and Indian War	•	•	•
	Graphs/Charts:			
	Bar graph	•	•	•
	Diagrams	•	•	•
	Flow chart	•	•	•
	Historical maps	•	•	•
	Making and reading maps	•	•	•
	Physical maps	•	•	•
	Political maps	•	•	•
	Primary Source Documents:			
	Declaration of Independence	•	•	•
	U. S. Constitution	•	•	•
	Bill of Rights	•	•	•
	Revolutionary War:			
	Battles	•	•	•
	Causes	•	•	•
	First American flag	•	•	•
	Valley Forge	•	•	•
	Sons and Daughters of Liberty	•	•	•
	Speech:Patrick Henry	•	•	•
	Historical figures:			
	John Adams	•	•	•
	Nathan Hale	•	•	•
	Patrick Henry	•	•	•
	Molly Pitcher	•	•	•
	Haym Salomon	•	•	•
	State information:			
	Abbreviation	•	•	•
	Bodies of water	•	•	•
	Capitals	•	•	•
	Highest point	•	•	•
	Land Area	•	•	•
	National parks	•	•	•
	Physical features	•	•	•
	Population	•	•	•
	Regions	•	•	•
	Year of statehood	•	•	•
	States:			
	Alabama	•	•	•
	Arkansas	•	•	•
	Georgia	•	•	•
	Kentucky	•	•	•
	Maryland	•	•	•
	Mississippi	•	•	•
	North Carolina	•	•	•
	South Carolina	•	•	•
	Tennessee	•	•	•
	Virginia	•	•	•
	Taxation	•	•	•
	Timeline	•	•	•

Unit 3 - Nation Building

	Skills & Topics			
Thinking Skills	Analyzing information	•	•	•
	Categorizing	•	•	•
	Cause and effect	•	•	•
	Compare and Contrast	•	•	•
	Comprehension	•	•	•
	Deductive reasoning	•	•	•
	Discussion	•	•	•
	Drawing conclusions	•	•	•
	Evaluating information	•	•	•
	Fact and opinion	•	•	•
	Following directions	•	•	•
	Identifying bias	•	•	•
	Identifying examples	•	•	•
	Inductive Reasoning	•	•	•
	Identifying relationships			•
	Listening skills	•	•	•
	Main idea	•	•	•
	Making inferences	•	•	•
	Narration	•	•	•
	Negotiation		•	•
	Observation skills	•	•	•
	Organizational skills	•	•	•
	Point of view	•	•	•
	Predicting & questioning skills	•	•	•
	Review/evaluation	•	•	•
	Summarizing	•	•	•
	Symbolism	•	•	•
	Using context	•	•	•
Language Skills	5 W's (who, what, where, when, why)	•	•	•
	Contractions	•	•	•
	Decoding	•	•	•
	Dictionary/Thesaurus skills	•	•	•
	Editing	•	•	•
	Imagery	•	•	•
	Object pronouns	•	•	•
	Possessives	•	•	•
	Prefixes	•	•	•
	Presentation skills	•	•	•
	Pronouns	•	•	•
	Proofreading	•	•	•
	Punctuation:			
	Apostrophes	•	•	•
	Hyphens	•	•	•
	Reading for enjoyment	•	•	•
	Reading with understanding	•	•	•
	Research/Reference skills	•	•	•
	Rhyme patterns	•	•	•
	Sentence skills	•	•	•
	Spelling strategies	•	•	•
	Subject pronouns	•	•	•
	Suffixes	•	•	•
	Syllabication	•	•	•
	Synonyms	•	•	•
	Vocabulary	•	•	•

	Skills & Topics			
Writing:	Book reviews	•	•	•
	Composition	•	•	•
	Descriptive writing	•	•	•
	Interactive writing	•	•	•
	Letter writing	•	•	•
	Maintaining a log	•	•	•
	News reporting	•	•	•
	Note taking	•	•	•
	Paragraph writing	•	•	•
	Poetry writing	•	•	•
	Revising/editing	•	•	•
	Rough draft	•	•	•
	Speech writing	•	•	•
Earth Science:	Continental shelf	•	•	•
	Continental slope	•	•	•
	Erosion	•	•	•
	Fissure volcanoes	•	•	•
	Mid-Atlantic Ridge	•	•	•
	Mid-ocean ranges	•	•	•
	Natural resources	•	•	•
	Observation	•	•	•
	Oceans	•	•	•
	Salt water	•	•	•
	Sedimentary rocks	•	•	•
	Tides	•	•	•
	Waves	•	•	•
Art/Doing/Music:	3-D map: Sculpting	•	•	•
	"Blow the Man Down"	•	•	•
	Cooking	•	•	•
	Design		•	•
	Drawing	•	•	•
	Early American games: Jackstraws	•	•	•
	"Erie Canal"	•	•	•
	Illustration	•	•	•
	"I've Been Workin' on the Railroad"	•	•	•
	"Pick a Bale o' Cotton"	•	•	•
	"Sweet Betsy from Pike"	•	•	•
	"There Are Many Flags"	•	•	•
	"The Star-Spangled Banner"	•	•	•
	Watercolor painting:			
	Black and white	•	•	•
	Landscapes	•	•	•

Nation Building, con't

Geography/Social Studies/History/Science:

Skills & Topics			
Citizenship:			
Census	•	•	•
Flag etiquette	•	•	•
National anthem	•	•	•
Natural citizens	•	•	•
Naturalized citizens	•	•	•
Rights and responsibilities	•	•	•
White House	•	•	•
Current events/government	•	•	•
Florida Cession	•	•	•
Globe Skills	•	•	•
Graphs/Charts:			
Pie Chart	•	•	•
Periodic Table	•	•	•
Line Graph	•	•	•
Historical maps	•	•	•
Historical figures:			
John Adams	•	•	•
John Quincy Adams	•	•	•
William Henry Harrison	•	•	•
Andrew Jackson	•	•	•
Thomas Jefferson	•	•	•
Francis Scott Key	•	•	•
James Madison	•	•	•
James Monroe	•	•	•
Napoleon	•	•	•
Tecumseh	•	•	•
John Tyler	•	•	•
Martin Van Buren	•	•	•
George Washington	•	•	•
Daniel Webster	•	•	•
Noah Webster	•	•	•
Louisiana Purchase	•	•	•
Map Skills:			
Map Grid	•	•	•
Mapmaking	•	•	•
Map reading	•	•	•

Geography/Social Studies/History/Science:

Skills & Topics			
Mexican Cession	•	•	•
Oregon Country Treaty	•	•	•
Physical map	•	•	•
Poetry reading	•	•	•
Political map	•	•	•
Revolutionary War	•	•	•
State information:			
Abbreviation	•	•	•
Bodies of water	•	•	•
Capitals	•	•	•
Highest point	•	•	•
Land Area	•	•	•
National parks	•	•	•
Physical features	•	•	•
Population	•	•	•
Regions	•	•	•
Year of statehood	•	•	•
States:			
Florida	•	•	•
Illinois	•	•	•
Indiana	•	•	•
Iowa	•	•	•
Louisiana	•	•	•
Michigan	•	•	•
Minnesota	•	•	•
Ohio	•	•	•
West Virginia	•	•	•
Wisconsin	•	•	•
Texas Annexation	•	•	•
Timeline	•	•	•
Treaty of Paris	•	•	•
War of 1812	•	•	•
15th Amendment		•	•
19th Amendment			•

Challenge Spelling List

If your child masters the majority of the words presented on the pretest, given during each Part 1, you may want to choose some words from the next higher level in the lesson or from the Challenge Spelling List for that lesson. You may choose as many or as few words as you would like to add to the current list. The words on this list come from the literature assigned in each lesson. Use the same procedures described in lessons to teach and study the words. Remember that success and use of the words in discussion and writing are the goal, not just memorizing spelling.

Unit 1 Lesson 1

colonial	encroaching	sensible	burial	nauseous
bracelets	unmistakable	examine	honorably	permeate
hurriedly	abruptly	dissipated	wretched	negotiate

Unit 1 Lesson 2

immediately	occupied	livelihood	courageous	monstrous
descending	regiment	provision	official	militia
strategic	expedition	assortment	drought	campaign

Unit 1 Lesson 3

breeches	cartridge	incessant	perspiration	immediately
audience	inherit	experience	bulk	bloodshot
colonel	schedule	several	accommodate	appeared

Unit 1 Lesson 4

recommend	formidable	preserve	recollection	approach
messenger	endeavor	condition	proceed	incident
division	victorious	continental	column	charcoal

Unit 1 Lesson 5

concentrate	reins	explosion	identical	passageway
probably	reinforce	tourniquet	advance	regular
sword	pivot	terrible	soldier	engulf

Unit 2 Lesson 1

sentinel	dangerous	telescope	disease	delegate
officer	incredible	traitor	staunch	bombard
causeway	puny	skirmish	headquarters	morale

Unit 2 Lesson 2

precious	solemn	currency	confidence	brawny
carriage	anxious	marvelous	authority	miniature
contempt	ominous	rebellion	instrument	dismantle

Unit 2 Lesson 3

neutral	council	relief	substitute	fierce
entitled	worrisome	optimistic	peril	civilization
schooner	terrain	conference	weary	blockade

Unit 2 Lesson 4

commander	organize	overruled	hurricane	approval
privateer	vehicle	question	frightened	caravan
menacing	ceremony	outburst	reinforcement	gratefully

Unit 2 Lesson 5

courier	wreckage	hurtling	argument	vigorous
community	treacherous	juggernaut	meanwhile	challenge
mishap	wistfully	chasm	underbrush	gorge

Unit 3 Lesson 1

reluctantly	hoist	catamounts	eminence	righteousness
persuasively	caperings	obbligato	mischief	plantation
miraculously	christening	terrestrial	varmint	disagreement

Unit 3 Lesson 2

squirrels	disrespectful	considerable	hesitantly	highwaymen
sauntered	heartening	aforesaid	scrumptious	ordinary
sumac	remembrance	completion	companion	judgment

Unit 3 Lesson 3

loathe	hysterically	disqualified	twinges	unavoidable
tongue	lunged	ciphered	knowledge	necessary
wielding	quizzical	congregation	answered	distinguished

Unit 3 Lesson 4

edification	scheming	elaborate	prominent	contributions
thoroughbred	handkerchiefs	stamina	attorney	ingeniously
trickster	dignitaries	violently	temperatures	representatives

Unit 3 Lesson 5

tumult	unashamedly	volunteers	peninsula	lieutenant
cantankerous	whereabouts	sergeant	physician	nightmare
harpsichord	convenient	occasional	strength	symbolized

Unit 3 Lesson 6

ricocheted	committee	quavering	professors	periodicals
responsibilities	bloodshed	procession	masterpiece	auditorium
dejectedly	Methuselah	picturesque	recognition	inauguration

Answer Keys

Tradesman Matching - Lesson 2, Part 3

Apothecary – made medicines
Milliner – made hats
Blacksmith – made items from iron and steel
Tanner – made leather
Cobbler – made shoes and boots
Silversmith – made items out of silver
Carpenter – built things out of wood
Tailor – made clothing
Weaver – made cloth
Wheelwright – made and fixed wheels
Founder – made items from brass and bronze
Wigmaker – made wigs
Gunsmith – made and repaired guns
Glassblower – made glass, and things from glass
Miller – ground corn and wheat

GP - Word Search - Lesson 2, Part 5

G R A N I T E N T R E P R E N E U R S F F T W
S Q R K E X H H I F I F B F Q D D F O O C V I
D P X D P S C Q B V J R E M O D M R P O Q I N
T U Q F C Q G T G R S E X I G N E O U S X Z D
U W Z M X G L O W N B N P L E G T N Y E Z J E
P P H E G K B I Q Y M C L I O I E T R T N I N
N E W C O M E R V V N H O T L K O I D T R P T
E H W D F W D K M B Q A R I O Z R E A L A Y U
W A P P R E N T I C E N E A G S O R Y E D M R
E Q L K A V Z I N S T D R S I N L Q Y R I J E
N D E N N O W M E K Y I S C S I O O B S A V D
G E L T C A O P R B T N O I T N G J X T N I S
L C C H E B A D A F P D L Q R D I J G W T E E
A J R P O V P U L R T I D W Z I S I K Z M L R
N M G K T H A E S H F A I J J A T Q Z V D P V
D N H K T Y G R W S A N E F N N S B Q F F U A
T F D W O R L D V I E W R J E S O W Z E Z Y N
D G K K P K H F W B E A S L A V E B P B X W T
T O M K L I N E O F P R O C L A M A T I O N H
F I J V N D N V E I A A A F H X T F F M H A Z

Worldview Tic-Tac-Toe - Lesson 3, Part 3

Europeans:

Settlements were permanent.
Important things were written down.
Wanted to own property.
Nature not part of religion.
Used money and trading.

Native Americans:

Nature was an important part of religion.
Did not own property.
Important things passed along by word of mouth.
Did not use money.
Whole villages could move.

GP - Word Scramble - Lesson 3, Part 5

1. apprentice
2. settlers
3. explorers
4. entrepreneurs
5. soldiers
6. indentured servant
7. slave
8. Indians
9. newcomer
10. worldview
11. france
12. frontier
13. militias
14. watercolor
15. Mid-Atlantic
16. meteorologist
17. geologist
18. minerals
19. Line of Proclamation
20. granite
21. French and Indian war
22. New England
23. igneous
24. radiant

Video Profile: - Lesson 4, Part 3

Benjamin Franklin

1. scientist, businessman, revolutionary, librarian, writer, printer, inventor, statesman, diplomat, musician, governor, Founding Father, abolitionist, philanthropist
2. Boston, Massachusetts
3. F
4. T
5. lightning rod, stove, bifocals, odometer, daylight savings time, an experiment to show the conduction of electricity
6. weather predictions, moon cycles, eclipses, short stories, news items, opinions, witty sayings
7. bed, rise, healthy, wealthy, wise
8. F
9. T
10. T
11. Congress, Fathers
12. F

GP - Crossword - Lesson 4, Part 5

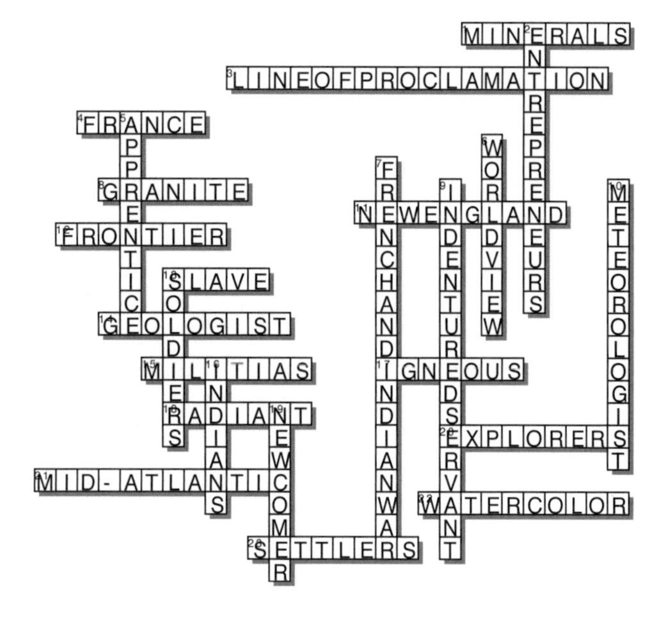

Video Profile: - Lesson 6, Part 1

Abigail Adams

1. John Adams
2. John Quincy Adams
3. woman
4. Massachusetts
5. minister
6. T
7. F
8. writing, woman
9. went to camps to help the army, boycotted English goods, served as spies, took care of sick and wounded, defended homes, some even served as soldiers
10. family, farm, business
11. T
12. F
13. T
14. slavery
15. educated

State Scramble - Lesson 6, Part 2

1. Pennsylvania (PA, Mid-Atlantic)
2. Connecticut (CT, New England)
3. Rhode Island (RI, New England)
4. New Jersey (NJ, Mid-Atlantic)
5. Massachusetts (MA, New England)
6. Vermont (VT, New England)
7. Delaware (DE, Mid-Atlantic)
8. Maine (ME, New England)
9. New Hampshire (NH, New England)
10. New York (NY, Mid-Atlantic)

Earth Science Matching - Lesson 6, Part 4

1. science that explores why the earth is the way it is
2. a scientist who studies the weather
3. measures rainfall
4. measures temperature
5. the mixture of gases that surrounds the earth
6. energy that radiates from the sun
7. strong force that holds the atmosphere in place
8. height of the ocean's surface
9. a type of igneous rock
10. type of soil that is very sticky when wet
11. scientist who studies rocks and minerals
12. solid substances that rocks are made of

13. measures air pressure
14. process of breaking down and changing the earth
15. layer of the atmosphere that contains the air you breathe
16. heat transfer caused by warm air rising and cool air sinking
17. direct transfer of heat from one object to another

18. layer of the atmosphere where the space station orbits
19. measures the speed of the wind
20. layer of the atmosphere where jets usually fly
21. contains only one type of atom
22. type of soil that's ideal for general purposes

State I.D. - Lesson 6, Part 4

Massachusetts: Bay State
Connecticut: Constitution State
Vermont: Green Mountain State
New Hampshire: Granite State
Rhode Island: Ocean State
Maine: Pine Tree State
Pennsylvania: Keystone State
New York: Empire State
New Jersey: Garden State
Delaware: First State

FD - Word Search - Lesson 1, Part 5

```
O W C A J C X B O S T O N T E A P A R T Y I Q
R R Y L T A R X M P T P B L I Z Z A R D A C R
Y O R I W F K I V A L L E Y F O R G E G N O V
F C O N T I N E N T A L C O N G R E S S K N F
O K D C A P A U L R E V E R E G T U X O E T W
B C T S X H S G O I R Y M H G R S K O A E I V
W Y W U I X V X Y O X L Q T R Y V K Y C D N D
Q C M M S K M U A T H I R T E E N G G D O E D
X L T S O I S L L S Z X F T E R K Z P E O N R
D E C L A R A T I O N G C A C Z K N X B D T P
M I L I T I A N S Q D M L F V D C Y E Z L A K
M B R E V O L U T I O N A R Y W A R Y P E L K
T G L A M B H D S M J W K W D K B L V M X A V
K F G E O R G E W A S H I N G T O N P E I R H
D T U P H I L A D E L P H I A N Y L P P N M X
H M B O S T O N M A S S A C R E C J E N G Y L
T B Y A S I Y R S J G Z C N C A O W J O T A L
V G F R K S T F C N A N B J C L T H D Q O C H
J J V E V H U R R I C A N E U A T I M S N P T
N F Z U Y U A X A L I N D E P E N D E N C E G
```

FD - Word Scramble - Lesson 2, Part 5

1. British
2. patriots
3. George Washington
4. tax
5. loyalists
6. Boston
7. Philadelphia
8. Continental Congress
9. Declaration of Independence
10. Revolutionary War
11. Boston Massacre
12. Lexington
13. Paul Revere
14. militia
15. boycott
16. Yankee Doodle
17. Continental Army
18. Valley Forge
19. rock cycle
20. thirteen
21. Boston Tea Party
22. blizzard
23. hurricane
24. axis

Video Profile: - Lesson 4, Part 3

George Washington

1. T
2. F; (George was schooled in America.)
3. T
4. F; (George's first battles were against the French and their allies.)
5. T
6. Indian
7. defeated
8. two, four
9. Providence (God)
10. Heaven
11. T
12. F; (Washington's army was trapped in Long Island, New York.)
13. F; (He crossed the Delaware River.)
14. T
15. F; (He was chosen to be the first President of America.)

16-18. Answers will vary.

19. future presidents
20. greatest

Hurricane Matching game - Lesson 4, Part 4

1. area in which the air spins inward
2. calm area in the center of a hurricane
3. area of highest winds in a hurricane
4. weather tool that measures air pressure
5. rotating thundcrstorms with winds at least 40 miles per hour
6. rotating thunderstorms with winds at least 74 miles per hour
7. time of year when most tropical storms form
8. thunderstorms that begin to rotate
9. cluster of big thunderstorms
10. area in which the air spins outward
11. rise in sea level during hurricanes
12. type of clouds in a tropical storm or hurricane

FD - Crossword - Lesson 4, Part 5

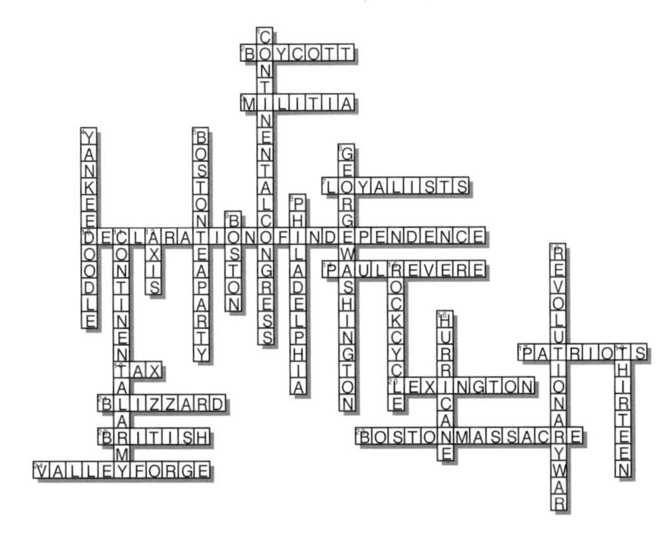

Video Profile: - Lesson 6, Part 1

Haym Salomon

1. genius

2, 3. 200,000; 3.5 million

4. Yorktown
5. Polish
6. F; (He was persecuted because he was Jewish.)
7. T
8. F; (He acted as a spy.)
9. T
10. F; (He did translate for the Hessian soldiers.)

11 - 15 (Make your own answer key.)

16. T
17. T
18. F; (He was a part of a large Jewish community in Philadelphia, Pennsylvania.)
19. T
20. F; (He made great profits which he gave to assist the American cause.)

21, 22, 23. time, ability, finances

24, 25. Robert Morris, George Washington

State Scramble - Lesson 6, Part 2

1. Tennessee (TN, Southern)
2. Georgia (GA, Southern)
3. Kentucky (KY, Southern)
4. South Carolina (SC, Southern)
5. Maryland (MD, Mid-Atlantic)
6. Arkansas (AR, Southern)
7. Virginia (VA, Southern)
8. North Carolina (NC, Southern)
9. Alabama (AL, Southern)
10. Mississippi (MS, Southern)

Who or What Am I? - Lesson 6, Part 3

1. George Washington
2. Samuel Adams
3. Fort Ticonderoga
4. Boston Tea Party
5. slave
6. Boston Massacre
7. Charleston
8. Paul Revere
9. Thomas Jefferson
10. patriot
11. Patrick Henry
12. Declaration of Independence
13. Continental Congress
14. Valley Forge
15. July 4, 1776
16. Stamp Act
17. Townshend Acts
18. Lexington, Massachusetts
19. loyalist
20. Haym Salomon

Earth Science Matching - Lesson 6, Part 4

1. two H atoms and one O atom
2. anything that has mass and takes up space
3. solid, liquid, gas
4. season that follows winter
5. things that describe matter
6. one of the particles that make up atoms
7. earth's system of recycling water
8. the first step in the water cycle
9. a class of rock
10. strong rainstorm with winds higher than 74 miles per hour
11. imaginary line through the center of the earth
12. shape of the earth's orbit around the sun
13. chart showing all atoms that have been discovered
14. lines that measure the distance north or south from the equator
15. partially frozen rain
16. a winter hurricane
17. one of the main types of clouds
18. a chart that describes relationships between rocks
19. igneous rocks that are formed underground
20. usually brings bad weather

State I.D. - Lesson 6, Part 4

Maryland: Old Line State
Virginia: Old Dominion State
North Carolina: Tar Heel State
South Carolina: Palmetto State
Georgia: Peach State
Kentucky: Bluegrass State
Tennessee: Volunteer State
Mississippi: Magnolia State
Alabama: Heart of Dixie State
Arkansas: Natural State

NB - Word Search - Lesson 1, Part 5

```
J V B N F G R D O D N A T U R A L M S T C H T
C Z N I O N A T U R A L I Z E D E D M H O J G
R A M D Q I N S I E U M T N A P O L E O N C K
W I I A P J C E S S I O N I V G D U Z M S O O
B U D T B T I D I Y Z F M C I S R B F A T N E
L F A S U S S I A N N E X A T I O N O S I T V
Z V T V L N S M N M Z K D W R T J P S J T I U
T M L I I A C E A W E A T H E R I N G E U N Q
Z W A Y H G O N T E R U Q I P N W O N F T E J
E E N M P N T T E F Q R A T U L A L T F I N X
H V T F Z T T A R L H P C E B D R D J E O T N
W U I P P K K R R A S Z X H L M O G P R N A B
N C C N M Q E Y I G Z N G O I E F L M S O L W
J M R K U U Y P T C E D H U C U 1 O Y O N S N
Z T A N U O R O O O T O Z S D Q 8 R B N S H A
B N N B H V Q A R D B O E E O I 1 Y H S G E U
O R G T J N G V Y E R O S I O N 2 O C J U L C
C C E N S U S E Z J X M F P P T Q C R G T F I
X T H E S T A R S P A N G L E D B A N N E R S
```

Video Profile: - Lesson 2, Part 3

Noah Webster

1. - 4. Answers could include dictionary author, textbook author, writer, editor, soldier, educator, legislator, or judge.
5. 1806
6. Textbook on medicine and disease.
7. Answers will vary.
8. federal
9. Yes
10. F
11. T
12. T
13. F
14. T
15. Answers will vary.

NB - Word Scramble - Lesson 2, Part 5

1. treaty
2. cession
3. The Star Spangled Banner
4. Old Glory
5. Francis Scott Key
6. Louisiana Territory
7. Napoleon
8. flag
9. Thomas Jefferson
10. Treaty of Paris
11. flag code
12. naturalized
13. natural
14. constitution
15. annexation
16. White House
17. republic
18. census
19. War of 1812
20. weathering
21. sedimentary
22. continental shelf
23. Mid-Atlantic Range
24. erosion

Video Profile: - Lesson 4, Part 3

John Quincy Adams

1. John Adams
2. Abigail Adams
3. He watched the first major battle of the Revolutionary War with his mother.
4. He went with his father, John Adams, to France.
5. The voyage began during winter, which was very unsafe. It was also wartime and his father was a famous man and a target of the enemy.
6. Youngest appointed diplomat, serving as official secretary to his father, John Adams, Ambassador to France.
7. He thought difficult times built character more than easy times.
8. T
9. F
10. T
11. F
12. T
13. President, Congressmen
14. Answers will vary.

NB - Crossword - Lesson 1, Part 5

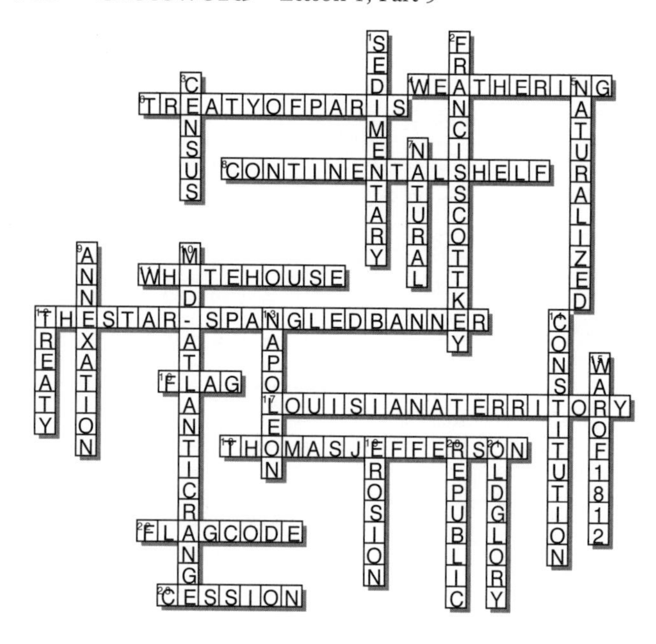

Who or What Am I? - Lesson 6, Part 1

1. Treaty of Paris
2. Louisiana Purchase
3. Florida
4. Thomas Jefferson
5. Napoleon
6. Noah Webster
7. Natural citizen
8. Naturalized citizen
9. War of 1812
10. American flag
11. Native Americans
12. Dolley Madison

State Scramble - Lesson 6, Part 2

1. Iowa (IA, Midwestern)
2. West Virginia (WV, Southern)
3. Illinois (IL, Midwestern)
4. Minnesota (MN, Midwestern)
5. Florida (FL, Southern)
6. Indiana (IN, Midwestern)
7. Louisiana (LA, Southern)
8. Wisconsin (WI, Midwestern)
9. Ohio (OH, Midwestern)
10. Michigan (MI, Midwestern)

Earth Science Matching - Lesson 6, Part 4

1. scientist who studies the ocean
2. waves that have rounded tops
3. process that moves weathered materials from one place to another
4. process that breaks down rocks and minerals
5. weathered materials
6. part of the water cycle that occurs mostly over the oceans
7. type of rock formed from layers of sediment
8. part of a continent that continues outward, underwater
9. steep drop-off to the ocean floor
10. pulses of energy that run through the water
11. underwater volcanic mountain
12. the lowest part of a wave
13. the highest part of a wave
14. deep valley at the top of the Mid-Atlantic Ridge
15. the remains of dead plants or animals preserved in rocks
16. type of high tide that is higher than normal
17. the distance between the crests of waves
18. type of volcano that oozes lava instead of exploding
19. type of high tide that is lower than normal
20. very deep crack in the ocean floor

State I.D. - Lesson 6, Part 4

Louisiana: Pelican State
Florida: Sunshine State
West Virginia: Mountain State
Ohio: Buckeye State
Indiana: Hoosier State
Illinois: Land of Lincoln
Michigan: Wolverine State
Iowa: Hawkeye State
Wisconsin: Badger State
Minnesota: North Star State

Appendix B

Student pages

Reading Log 387

Native American Profile 388

Character Portrait 389

State Page 390

Regional Summary Charts 392

Word Searches 395

References

World Map 398

Periodic Table of Elements 399

3-D Map Model 400

Instructions

Making State Cards 402

Flag Folding 402

Games 403

The Newcomer Game 406

Mechanics Toolkit Cards 411

Activities and Projects

Barometer 429

Anemometer 431

Weather Vane 434

Candle Dipping 436

Unit 1 Watercolor Activity 439

Beanbags 442

Cornhole platform 445

Weaving 448

Unit 2 Watercolor Activity 452

3-D Map 454

Pick-Up Sticks 458

Metal Punching 459

Tin Punch Lantern 461

Unit 3 Watercolor Activity 464

_______________ **Reading Log**
unit

____
student name

PAGES	TITLE	AUTHOR	DATE

Native American Profile

Name of Tribe: ______________________________

Where did they live? ____________________

Their main source of food was

____

In what kind of dwellings did they live?

____

Use a colored pencil to shade areas where this tribe lived

Were they warlike ___ or

peaceful ___ toward settlers?

Did they stay in one place or move around?

____

Draw a picture of one of their dwellings

Does this tribe still exist today? ____________

If so, where does the tribe live now? ____________________

If not, what happened to them? ____________________

Are there any members of this tribe who are famous in history? If so, who and why?

____

____

What is the most interesting thing you learned about this tribe? ____________

____

List two more facts about this tribe:

1. ____________________

____

2 ____________________

____

On another sheet of paper, draw and color a picture that describes some part of this tribe's life.
You may use markers, crayons, colored pencils, or watercolors on watercolor paper.

Character Portrait

____
(name)

____
(book title)

What this person looks like: ______________________________

____

____

____

What kind of person he or she is: ______________________________

____

____

____

____

Two things this person did in the story

1. ______________________________

____

2. ______________________________

____

Do you like this character? yes _______ no_______

Why or why not? ______________________________

____

____

____

____

State Page

for

____

______________________ Capital City
______________________ Region
__________ Abbreviation

Meaning of state name: ______________________________

____

Nickname: ______________________________

____

State Bird

State Flower

State Facts:

1. ______________________________

____

2. ______________________________

____

An interesting event from the Timeline in my U.S. Atlas:

____

____

Interesting facts from "The Way It Was. . ." in my U.S. Atlas:

1. ______________________________

____

2. ______________________________

____

STATE PAGE

for

____

How This State Was Settled

Use the timeline in your atlas to write a short paragraph that tells how this state was settled.

New England Region

Name of State	Land Area (square miles)	Population	Highest Point	Year of Statehood
Massachusetts				
Connecticut				
Vermont				
New Hampshire				
Rhode Island				
Maine				

Mid-Atlantic Region

Name of State	Land Area (square miles)	Population	Highest Point	Year of Statehood
Pennsylvania				
New York				
New Jersey				
Delaware				
Maryland				

Southwestern Region

Name of State	Land Area (square miles)	Population	Highest Point	Year of Statehood
Texas				
Oklahoma				
New Mexico				
Arizona				

Southern Region

Name of State	Land Area (square miles)	Population	Highest Point	Year of Statehood
Virginia				
North Carolina				
South Carolina				
Georgia				
Kentucky				
Tennessee				
Mississippi				
Alabama				
Arkansas				
Louisiana				
Florida				
West Virginia				

Pacific Coast Region

Name of State	Land Area (square miles)	Population	Highest Point	Year of Statehood
California				
Washington				
Oregon				
Alaska				
Hawaii				

Midwestern Region

Name of State	Land Area (square miles)	Population	Highest Point	Year of Statehood
Ohio				
Indiana				
Illinois				
Michigan				
Iowa				
Wisconsin				
Minnesota				
Missouri				
Kansas				
Nebraska				
North Dakota				
South Dakota				

Rocky Mountain Region

Name of State	Land Area (square miles)	Population	Highest Point	Year of Statehood
Colorado				
Montana				
Idaho				
Wyoming				
Utah				
Nevada				

Growing Pains Word Search

G R A N I T E N T R E P R E N E U R S F F T W
S Q R K E X H H I F I F B F Q D D F O O C V I
D P X D P S C Q B V J R E M O D M R P O Q I N
T U Q F C Q G T G R S E X I G N E O U S X Z D
U W Z M X G L O W N B N P L E G T N Y E Z J E
P P H E G K B I Q Y M C L I O I E T R T N I N
N E W C O M E R V V N H O T L K O I D T R P T
E H W D F W D K M B Q A R I O Z R E A L A Y U
W A P P R E N T I C E N E A G S O R Y E D M R
E Q L K A V Z I N S T D R S I N L Q Y R I J E
N D E N N O W M E K Y I S C S I O O B S A V D
G E L T C A O P R B T N O I T N G J X T N I S
L C C H E B A D A F P D L Q R D I J G W T E E
A J R P O V P U L R T I D W Z I S I K Z M L R
N M G K T H A E S H F A I J J A T Q Z V D P V
D N H K T Y G R W S A N E F N N S B Q F F U A
T F D W O R L D V I E W R J E S O W Z E Z Y N
D G K K P K H F W B E A S L A V E B P B X W T
T O M K L I N E O F P R O C L A M A T I O N H
F I J V N D N V E I A A A F H X T F F M H A Z

apprentice
entrepreneurs
explorers
France
French and Indian War
frontier
geologist
granite

igneous
indentured servant
Indians
Line of Proclamation
meteorologist
Mid-Atlantic
militias
minerals

New England
newcomer
radiant
settlers
slave
soldiers
worldview

Freedom Decided Word Search

O W C A J C X B O S T O N T E A P A R T Y I Q
R R Y L T A R X M P T P B L I Z Z A R D A C R
Y O R I W F K I V A L L E Y F O R G E G N O V
F C O N T I N E N T A L C O N G R E S S K N F
O K D C A P A U L R E V E R E G T U X O E T W
B C T S X H S G O I R Y M H G R S K O A E I V
W Y W U I X V X Y O X L Q T R Y V K Y C D N D
Q C M M S K M U A T H I R T E E N G G D O E D
X L T S O I S L L S Z X F T E R K Z P E O N R
D E C L A R A T I O N G C A C Z K N X B D T P
M I L I T I A N S Q D M L F V D C Y E Z L A K
M B R E V O L U T I O N A R Y W A R Y P E L K
T G L A M B H D S M J W K W D K B L V M X A V
K F G E O R G E W A S H I N G T O N P E I R H
D T U P H I L A D E L P H I A N Y L P P N M X
H M B O S T O N M A S S A C R E C J E N G Y L
T B Y A S I Y R S J G Z C N C A O W J O T A L
V G F R K S T F C N A N B J C L T H D Q O C H
J J V E V H U R R I C A N E U A T I M S N P T
N F Z U Y U A X A L I N D E P E N D E N C E G

axis
blizzard
Boston
Boston Massacre
Boston Tea Party
boycott
British
Continental Army
Continental Congress
Declaration
Independence
George Washington
hurricane
Lexington
loyalists
militia
patriots
Paul Revere
Philadelphia
Revolutionary War
rock cycle
tax
thirteen
Valley Forge
Yankee Doodle

Nation Building Word Search

Y S H U G X F E L Y T R E A T Y T U R U U K V
J V B N F G R D O D N A T U R A L M S T C H T
C Z N I O N A T U R A L I Z E D E D M H O J G
R A M D Q I N S I E U M T N A P O L E O N C K
W I I A P J C E S S I O N I V G D U Z M S O O
B U D T B T I D I Y Z F M C I S R B F A T N E
L F A S U S S I A N N E X A T I O N O S I T V
Z V T V L N S M N M Z K D W R T J P S J T I U
T M L I I A C E A W E A T H E R I N G E U N Q
Z W A Y H G O N T E R U Q I P N W O N F T E J
E E N M P N T T E F Q R A T U L A L T F I N X
H V T F Z T T A R L H P C E B D R D J E O T N
W U I P P K K R R A S Z X H L M O G P R N A B
N C C N M Q E Y I G Z N G O I E F L M S O L W
J M R K U U Y P T C E D H U C U 1 O Y O N S N
Z T A N U O R O O O T O Z S D Q 8 R B N S H A
B N N B H V Q A R D B O E E O I 1 Y H S G E U
O R G T J N G V Y E R O S I O N 2 O C J U L C
C C E N S U S E Z J X M F P P T Q C R G T F I
X T H E S T A R S P A N G L E D B A N N E R S

treaty
annexation
census
cession
Constitution
Continental shelf
erosion
flag

Flag Code
Francis Scott Key
Louisiana Territory
Mid-Atlantic Range
Napoleon
natural
naturalized
Old Glory

republic
sedimentary
The Star-Spangled Banner
Thomas Jefferson
Treaty of Paris
War of 1812
weathering
White House

World Map

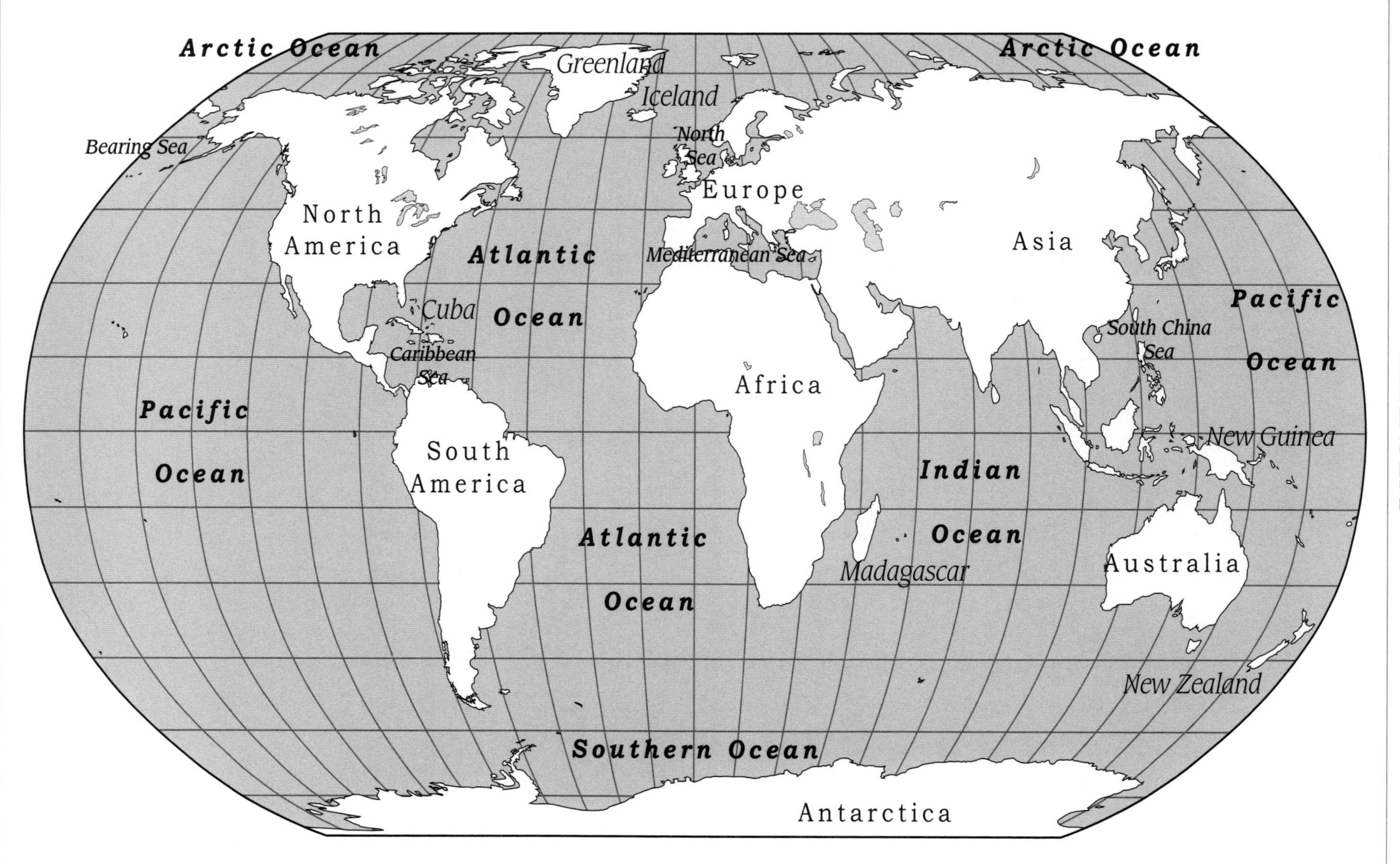
Arctic Ocean
Arctic Ocean
Bearing Sea
Greenland
Iceland
North Sea
Europe
North America
Atlantic Ocean
Mediterranean Sea
Asia
Pacific Ocean
Cuba
Caribbean Sea
South China Sea
Africa
Pacific Ocean
New Guinea
South America
Indian Ocean
Atlantic Ocean
Madagascar
Australia
New Zealand
Southern Ocean
Antarctica

Periodic Table of Elements

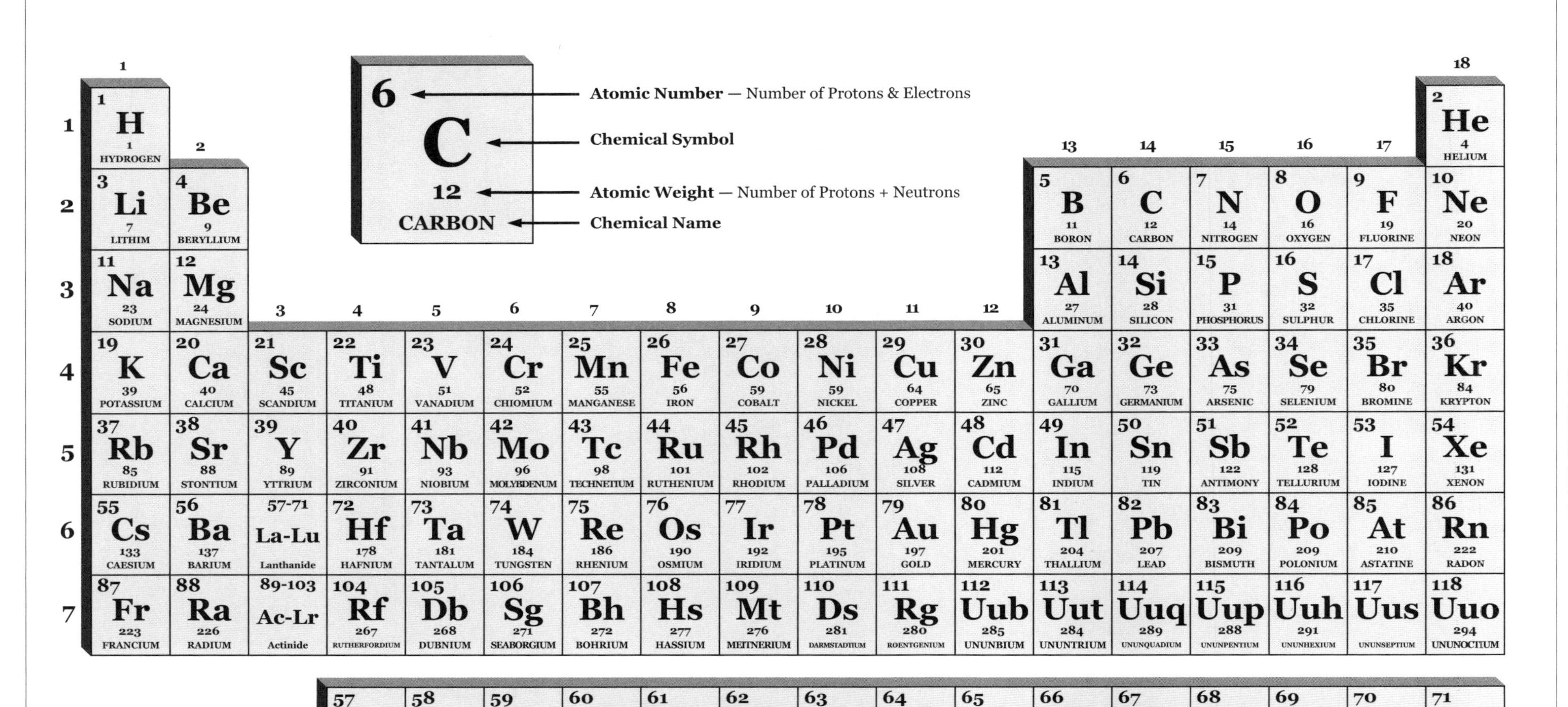

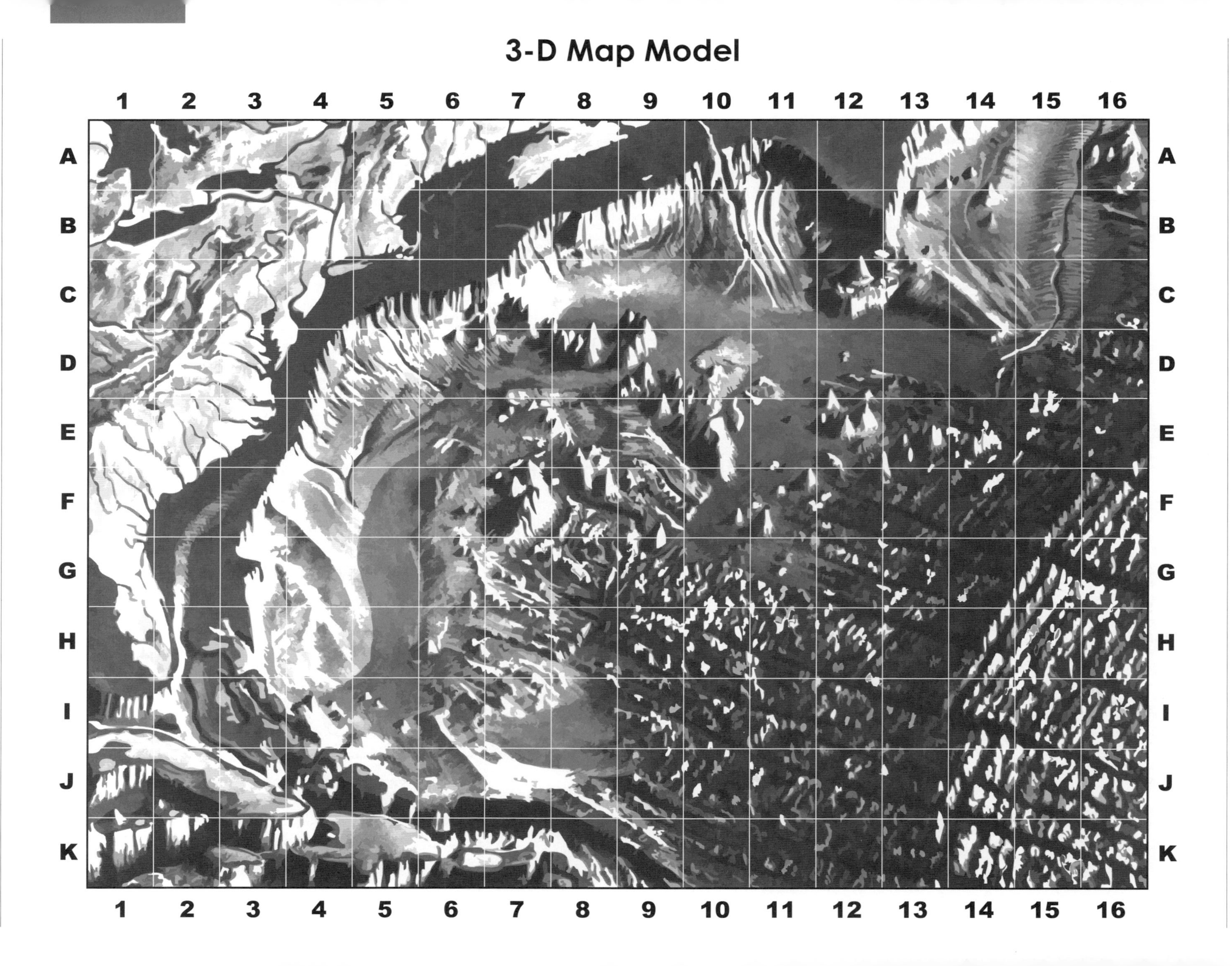
3-D Map Model
1
2
3
4
5
6
7
8
9
10
11
12
13
14
15
16
A
B
C
D
E
F
G
H
I
J
K

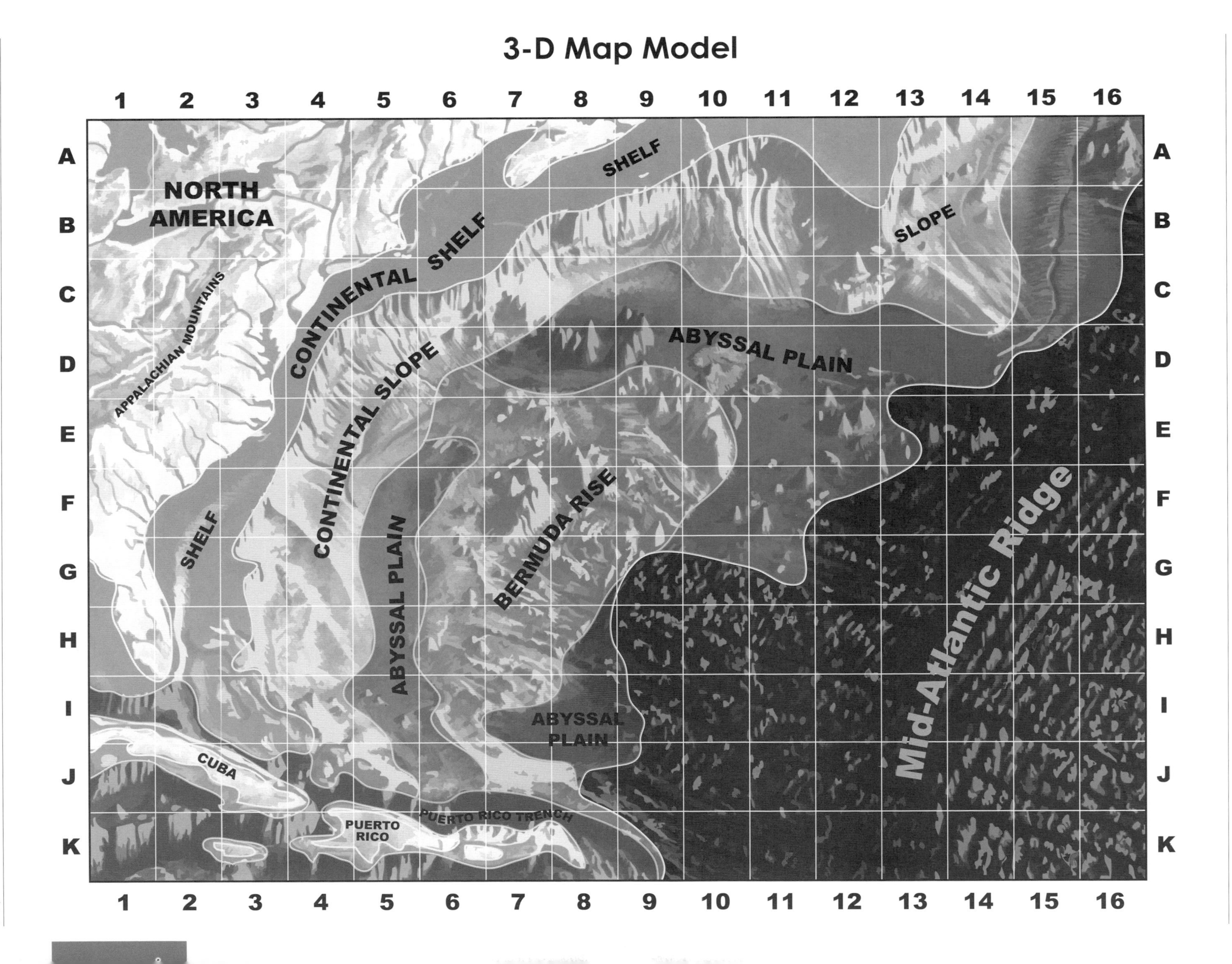
3-D Map Model
NORTH AMERICA
SHELF
CONTINENTAL SHELF
SLOPE
APPALACHIAN MOUNTAINS
CONTINENTAL SLOPE
ABYSSAL PLAIN
SHELF
CONTINENTAL
ABYSSAL PLAIN
BERMUDA RISE
Mid-Atlantic Ridge
ABYSSAL PLAIN
CUBA
PUERTO RICO
PUERTO RICO TRENCH

Instructions

State Cards

Outline three index cards with crayon, marker, or colored pencil as indicated below. Each color will remind you of the region where the state is located. On the first card write the name of the state and its abbreviation, and on the second write the name of its capital. Then, on the third card write its nickname and one other interesting fact you found out about it. Write the state's abbreviation in the upper left corner of the second and third cards. Later in each unit you will use these cards to play a game.

Use blue for **New England** states

Use green for **Mid-Atlantic** states

Use red for **Midwestern** states

Use purple for **Southern** states

Flag Folding (Nation Building Lesson 5, Part 1)

1. When folding the flag, it is all right to hold it horizontally between you and your partner. Hold it lengthwise by its corners, with the blue field in the upper left (as you're looking at it) corner. Then carefully bring the striped bottom half up over the blue field.
2. Fold it in half again, lengthwise.

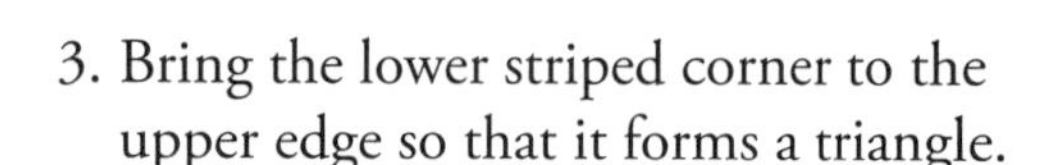

3. Bring the lower striped corner to the upper edge so that it forms a triangle.

4. Fold that triangle inward, to form another triangle. Then fold it down to the lower edge. Repeat this rocess until you are almost to the end, and only the blue field is showing.

5. Bring the remaining end around and tuck it into the fold on the opposite side.

Word Search

Circle or highlight the words from the list provided. Mark off each word as you find it.

Word Scramble

Unscramble the words and write them on the lines provided.

Crosswords

Use the clues provided and write the answers in the correct places across or down.

Bingo

Give each player at least one Bingo game board and a number of tokens such as buttons, pennies, or dried beans. Listen as someone reads the Bingo clues. Place tokens in the squares that provide the correct answers to the clues. The first player to place tokens on all boxes in a row that runs across, down, or diagonally says, "Bingo!" and wins that round. Play as many rounds as you wish.

The Newcomer Game (Growing Pains, Lesson 1, Part 5)

The object of The Newcomer Game is to put at least two Trait cards with the name of a Newcomer, and lay them down on the table, face up. Once a set is started other players can lay down their trait cards that belong with that set. In other words, if Player #1 has the 3 cards that say "Explorers," "loved adventure and mystery," and "were usually the first to arrive in an area" in his hand, he can lay them down as a set when it is his turn. When it is Player #2's turn, if he has "investigated new places" in his hand he can lay it down also, and it counts in his favor. A player must have the name of a Newcomer before he can begin a set. When all the cards are played, the game is over. Players get one point for each card they have played.

To Play: Mix up The Newcomer Cards, and give each player four cards. Leave the rest of the cards in a stack to draw from. This is a Go Fish type game, so Player #1 begins by asking another player if he has either a Newcomer (name) card, or a Trait card for a specific type of newcomer. (For instance, if Player #1 wants to collect Explorers cards, he would simply ask for an Explorer Trait card. He does not need to specify which trait he wants.) If the other player has what Player #1 asked for, the player hands it over and the next person takes a turn. If the player does not have the requested card, Player #1 draws from the stack on the table before play passes to the next person.

CHALLENGE: Once students become familiar with the traits for each group, they can ask for specific traits from the other players.

Worldview Tic-Tac-Toe (Growing Pains, Lesson 3, Part 3)

Cut out the Worldview Tic-Tac-Toe markers in your Student Notebook. Color the markers that name European worldviews one color, and the ones that name Native American worldviews another. Use the markers to play Tic-Tac-Toe with a family member or a friend. While you play, challenge yourself by telling about each worldview you use in the game. Discuss how that worldview might have affected relations with the other group.

Mechanics Toolkit Concentration (Growing Pains & Nation Building Lesson 3, Parts 2 and 4)

Mix up the cards and place them on the table in rows, face down. Turn over one card, and then try to turn over two more that match the first one. If the three cards you turn over on the first round match, remove them from the table and take another turn. If they don't, play passes to the next person.

Hopscotch (Freedom Decided Lessons 2, Part 1 & 6, Part 5)

Hopscotch is a hopping game that can be played just about anywhere – indoors, or outdoors on a driveway, a sidewalk, or a bare patch of ground. All you have to do is draw (with chalk or a stick) or tape out (with masking tape) a diagram of squares large enough to hop into. Of course, the chalk or stick is used to make the diagram outdoors, and the tape is used for inside floors or carpets. There is a sample diagram in this section, but you can make yours any way you want as long as there are eight to ten squares, connected and numbered in order.

Rules vary, so you and your family can adapt them so that everyone has fun. Many people play according to the following:

1. Player 1 stands behind the starting line and tosses his or her beanbag into the first square.
2. Then Player 1 hops on one foot over that square to the second one, and continues hopping through the diagram. When two squares are next to one another, the player can put both feet down. Also, sometimes people put a half-circle (see sample) at the end of their diagram so players can rest for a moment with both feet down before hopping back. Other than that, players must use only one foot.
3. When turning around to come back, even in the rest-area, you must hop – not walk.
4. After Player 1 turns around, he or she hops back through the diagram until reaching square 2. The player stops there, stands on one foot and reaches down to pick up his or her beanbag. Then that player can hop in square #1 and out of the diagram.
5. Play continues as Player 1 again stands behind the starting line and tosses the beanbag into square 2.
6. At no time can players hop into a square where there is a beanbag – either their own or another player's. They must hop over squares that hold other player's beanbags, and bend down to pick up their own on the trip back.
7. Play moves to the next person if Player 1's beanbag does not land in the proper square; the hopper steps on a line; the hopper loses balance when bending over to pick up the beanbag and puts a second hand or foot down; the hopper goes into a square where a marker is; or the hopper puts two feet down in a single box. The player's beanbag remains in the square where it was last tossed (or can be moved to the next position if the players agree.)

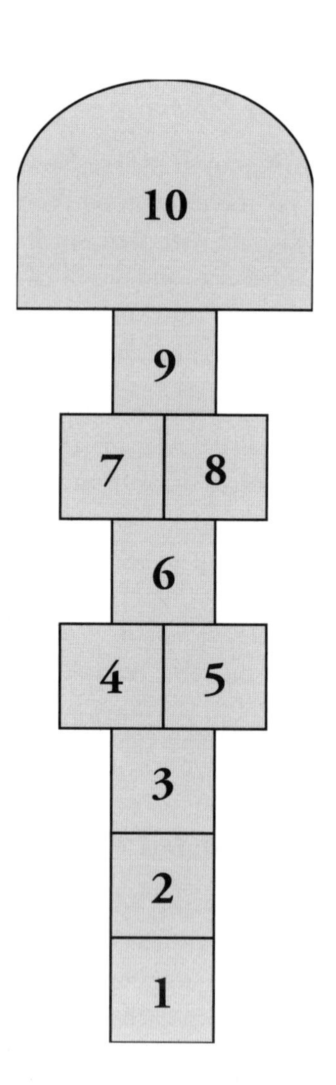

Cornhole (Freedom Decided Lessons 3, Part 5 & 6 Part 5)

The idea of this game is to toss beanbags, or similar objects, through the hole in the cornhole platform. You can find the official rules at the library or, with your parent's permission on the Internet at the official American Cornhole Association website: www.playcornhole.org. Although there are official rules for the game, and even tournaments, informal play can be adjusted for age and ability. Above all, have fun!

First, mark the "pitcher's line" with masking tape. This can be any distance you want from the cornhole platform, but officially it is 21 feet for junior players.

Players take turns standing behind the Pitcher's Line and tossing a beanbag underhand toward the cornhole platform.

If the beanbag goes completely through the hole it is called a "hole-in," and counts three points. If it does not go in the hole, but any part of it lands on the platform it is called "in-the-court," and counts one point.

If a player steps over the pitcher's line while making a toss, he or she loses a turn.

Pick-Up Sticks (Nation Building Lesson 2, Part 1)

This game can be played by one person, but is usually more fun if others participate. The object is to remove the sticks, one at a time, from a pile without causing any of the other sticks to move.

1. Gather the sticks into a bundle and hold them upright in one hand, so that their ends touch the table.
2. Gently loosen your grip and let the sticks fall. Be sure to move your hand away quickly when you let go, so the sticks can fall in all directions.
3. The first player tries to remove, by lifting or sliding, a single stick from the pile without letting any other sticks move. If successful, his turn continues until he causes another stick to move. Then the stick he was trying to pick up stays where it is, and play passes to the next person.

OR, players take turns removing one stick at a time from the pile without moving other sticks.

4. The black stick is special for two reasons. First, it counts more points than any of the others; and second, the player who removes it can, if he wants, use it as a tool for the rest of the game to help get other sticks out of the pile.
5. The game is over when all the sticks have been picked up. Players count up the points they have earned, and the highest score wins. The point value of each stick is:

Black - 25 points   Red - 10 points   Blue - 5 points
Green - 2 points; and   Yellow - 1 point.

Numeral War (Freedom Decided Lessons 2, Part 3 & 3, Part 3)

Shuffle the spelling cards and then deal them out face down so that each player gets the same number of cards. A turn consists of each player turning over a card at the same time and reading his card aloud. The card with the highest number wins and that player gets to keep both cards. Play until all the cards are gone. To see who wins, each player counts the cards he has collected. You may want to play more than one hand and see how many games you can win. If a numeral comes up against an ordinal, the higher number value wins. For example, if the cards for eight and fourteenth are turned over, fourteenth wins because it is a higher number.

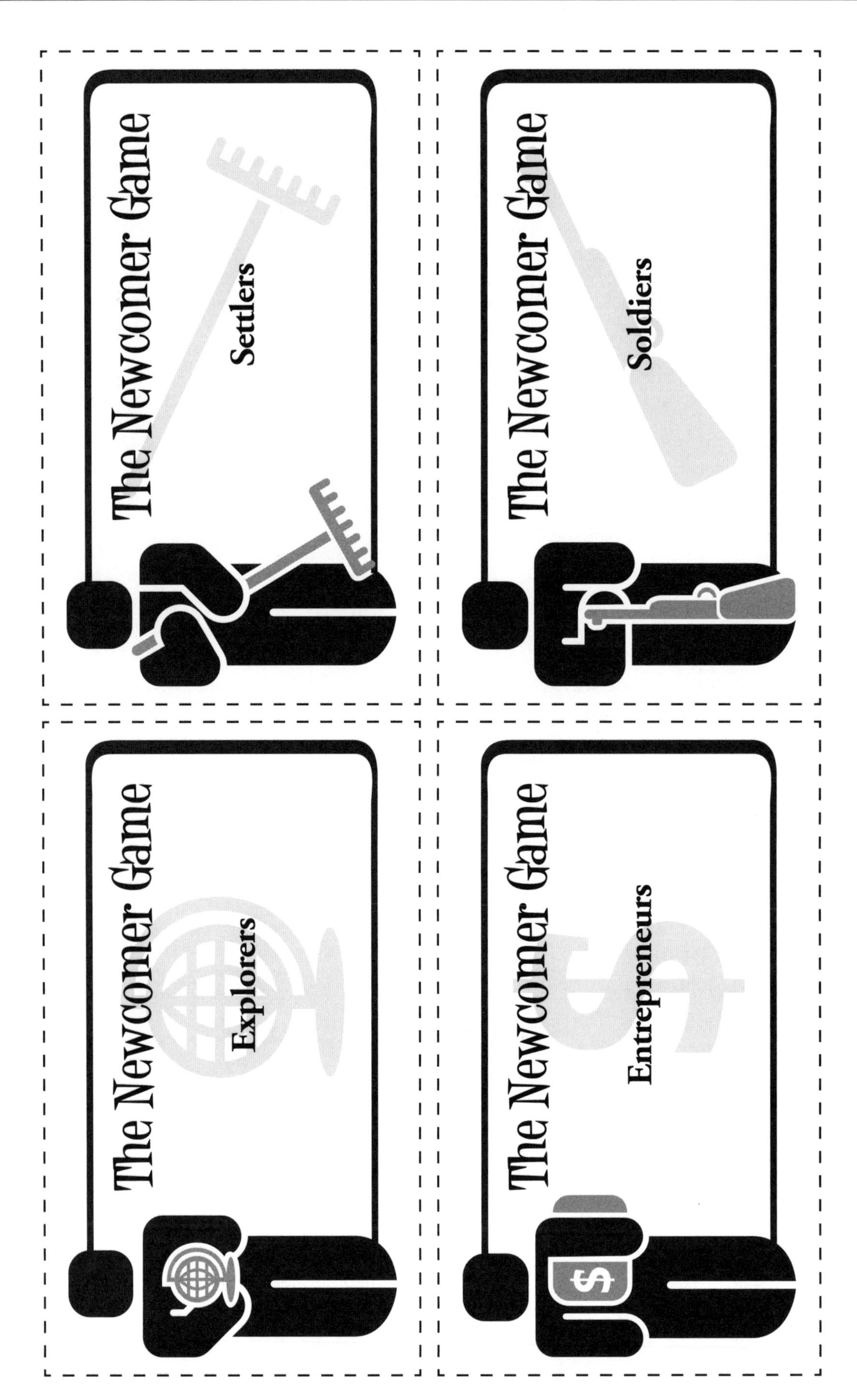

Instructions for playing this game are found on page 405.

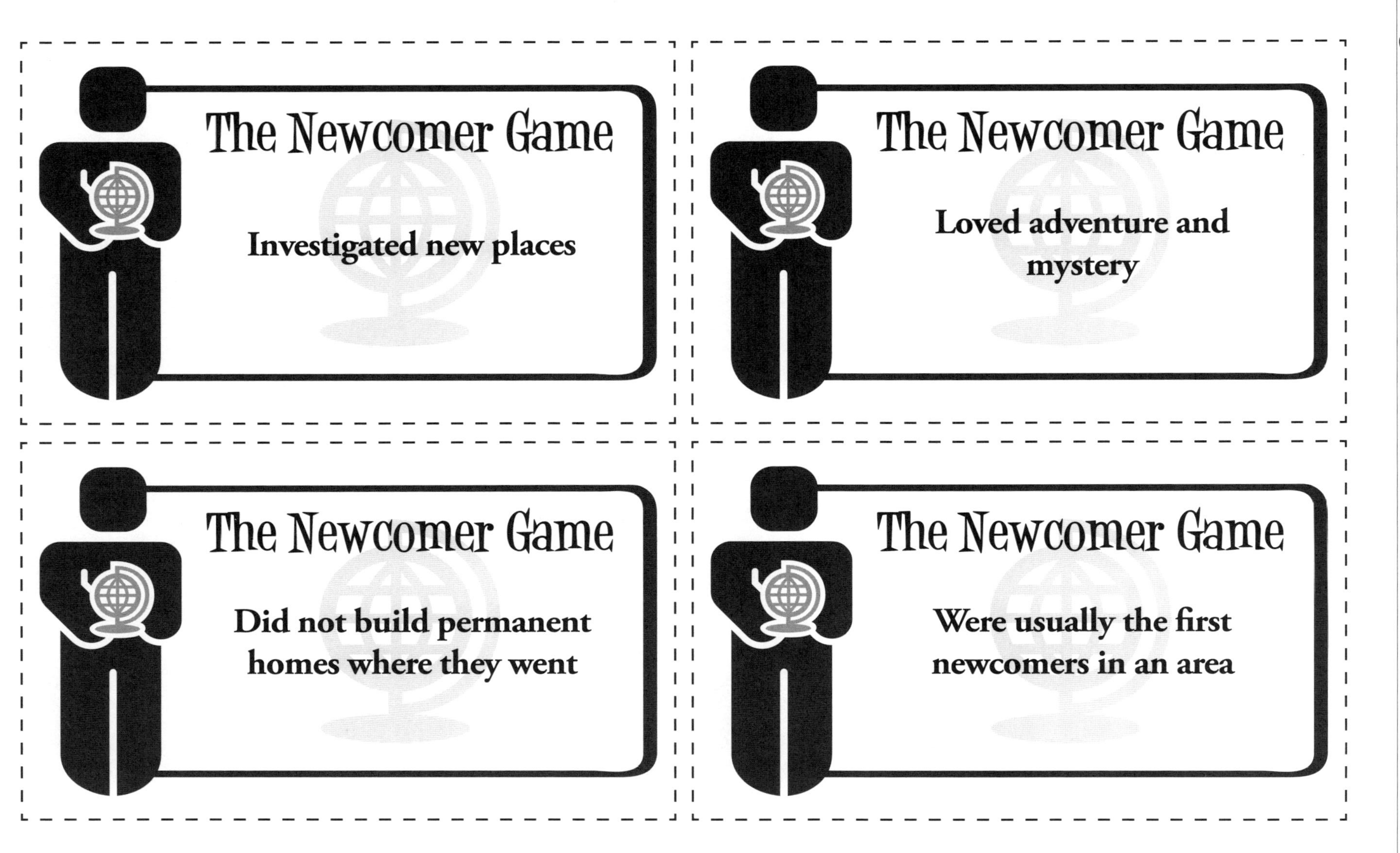

The Newcomer Game
Investigated new places
The Newcomer Game
Loved adventure and mystery
The Newcomer Game
Did not build permanent homes where they went
The Newcomer Game
Were usually the first newcomers in an area

Instructions for playing this game are found on page 405.

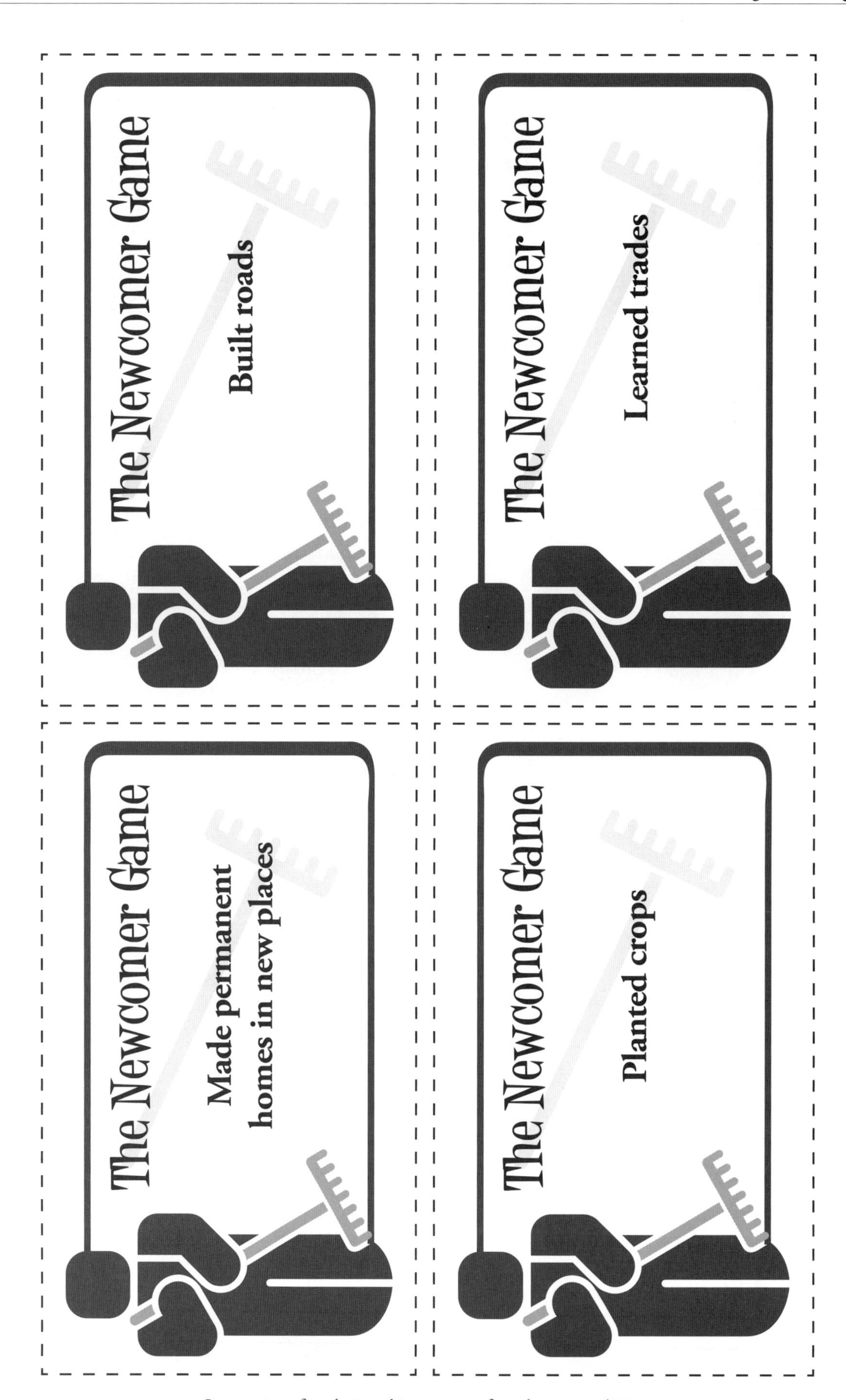

The Newcomer Game
Built roads
The Newcomer Game
Learned trades
The Newcomer Game
Made permanent homes in new places
The Newcomer Game
Planted crops

Instructions for playing this game are found on page 405.

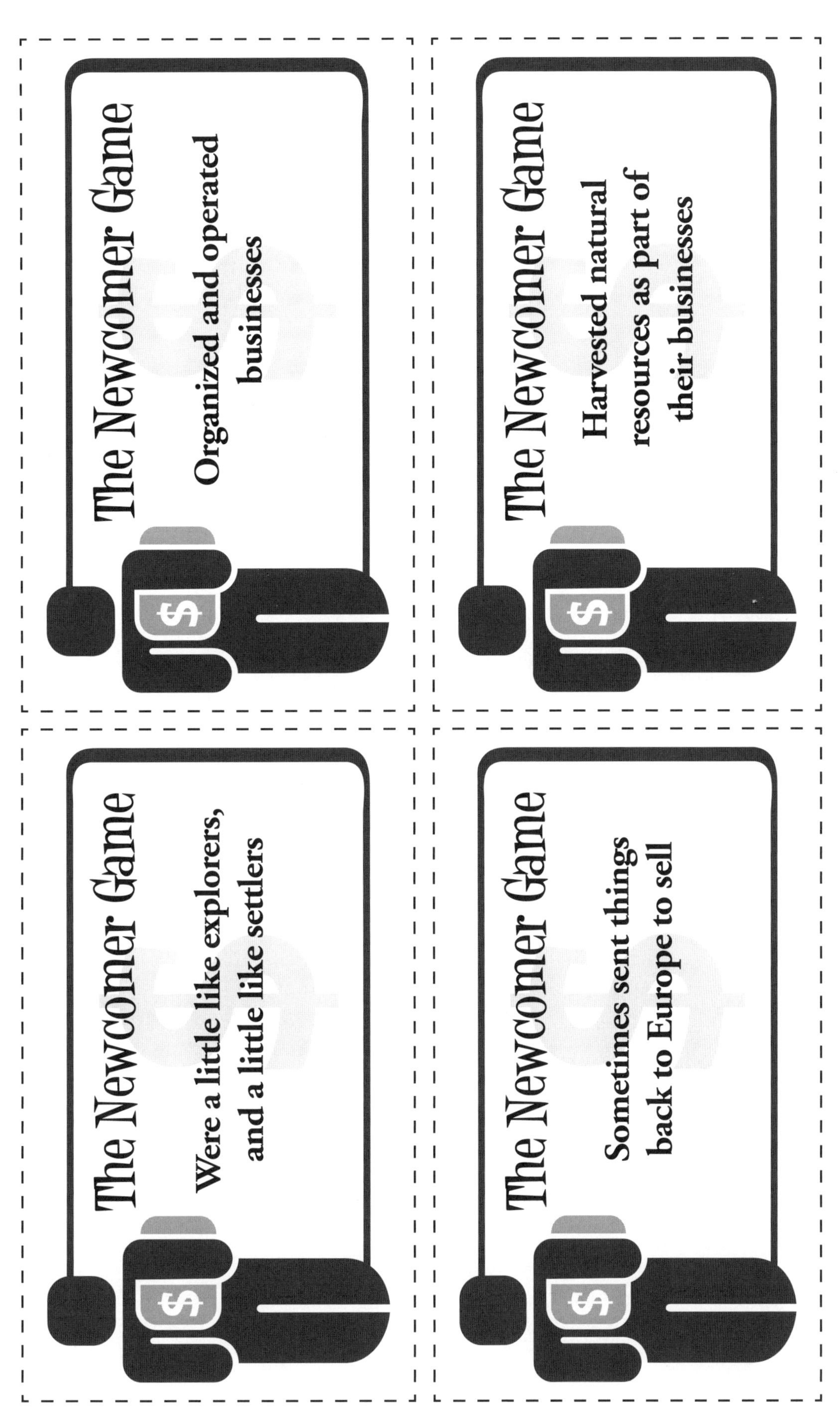

The Newcomer Game
Organized and operated businesses
The Newcomer Game
Harvested natural resources as part of their businesses
The Newcomer Game
Were a little like explorers, and a little like settlers
The Newcomer Game
Sometimes sent things back to Europe to sell

Instructions for playing this game are found on page 405.

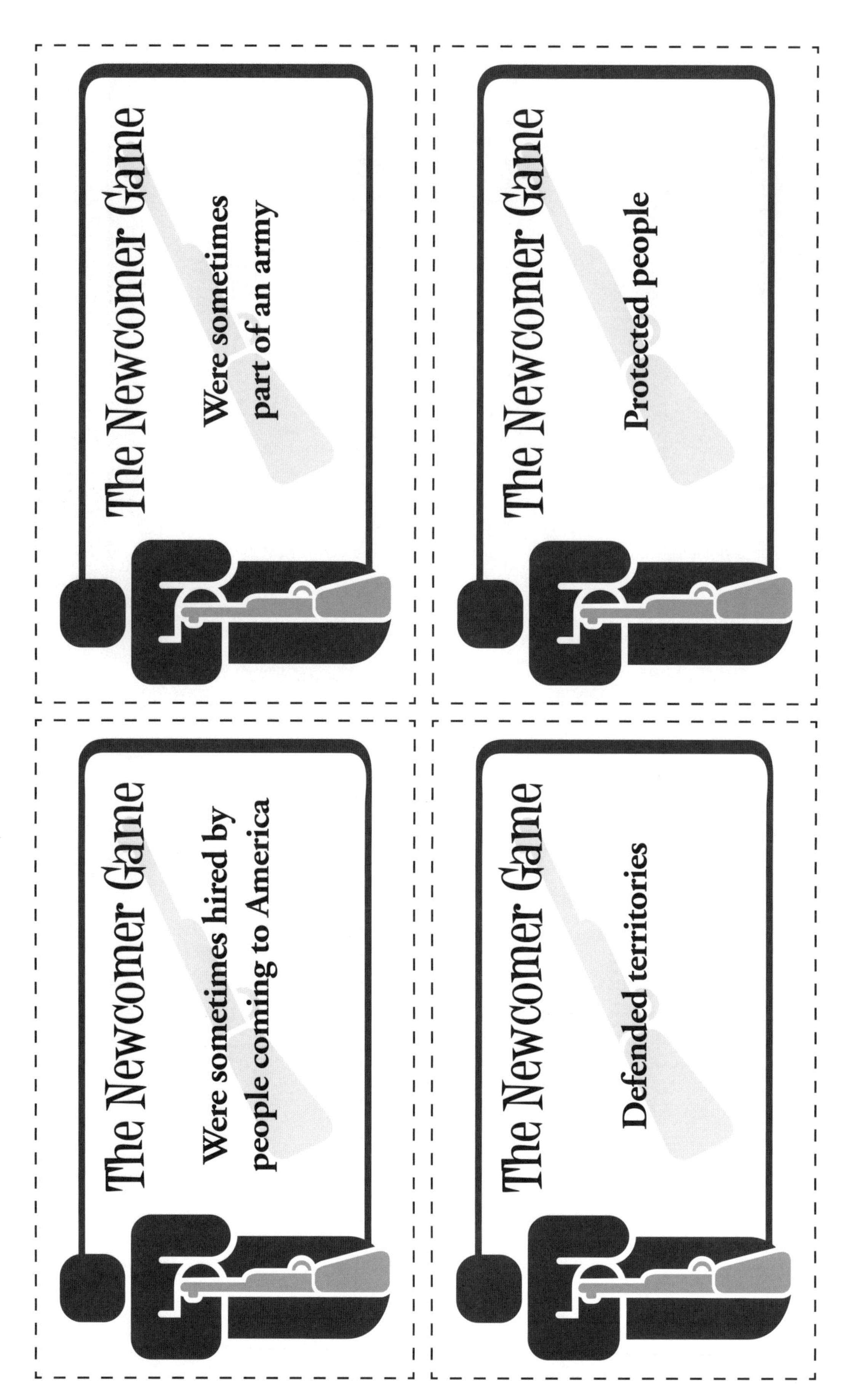

The Newcomer Game
Were sometimes part of an army
The Newcomer Game
Protected people
The Newcomer Game
Were sometimes hired by people coming to America
The Newcomer Game
Defended territories

Instructions for playing this game are found on page 405.

Mechanics
1
Toolkit
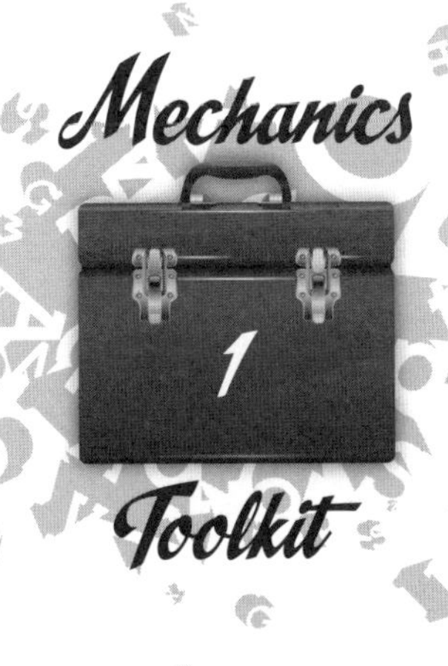
Mechanics
1
Toolkit

Mechanics
1
Toolkit

Mechanics
1
Toolkit
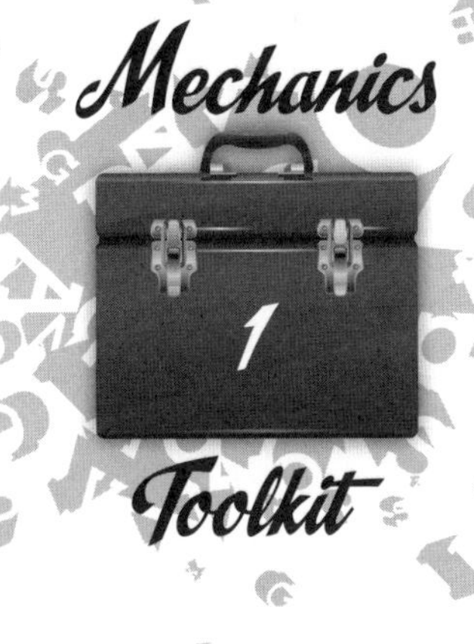
Mechanics
1
Toolkit

Mechanics
1
Toolkit

Mechanics
1
Toolkit
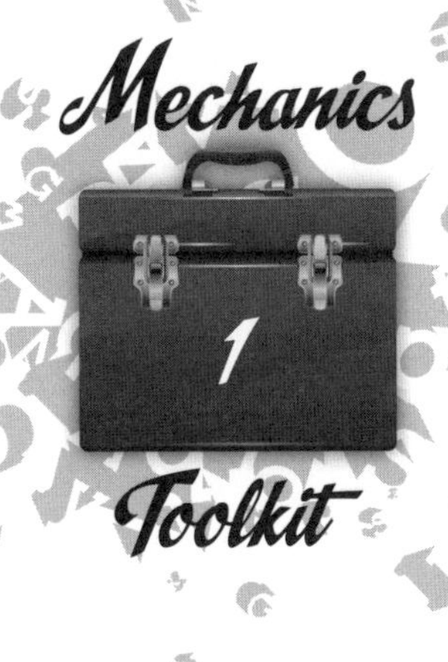
Mechanics
1
Toolkit

Mechanics
1
Toolkit

Mechanics
1
Toolkit

Mechanics
1
Toolkit

Mechanics
1
Toolkit

RULE	EXAMPLE	EXAMPLE
Capitalize the first word in every sentence.	My favorite food is pizza.	The dogs are out in the yard.
RULE	**EXAMPLE**	**EXAMPLE**
Capitalize names when they mean particular people and places.	My mother's name is Mary.	We are going to visit Florida.
RULE	**EXAMPLE**	**EXAMPLE**
Use the word *a* in front of a word that starts with a consonant sound.	I am going to eat a banana.	He likes to play with a football.
RULE	**EXAMPLE**	**EXAMPLE**
Use the word *an* in front of a word that starts with a vowel sound.	We got an apple for our snack.	An otter swam around the pond.

Instructions for playing this game are found on page 406.

Mechanics
2
Toolkit

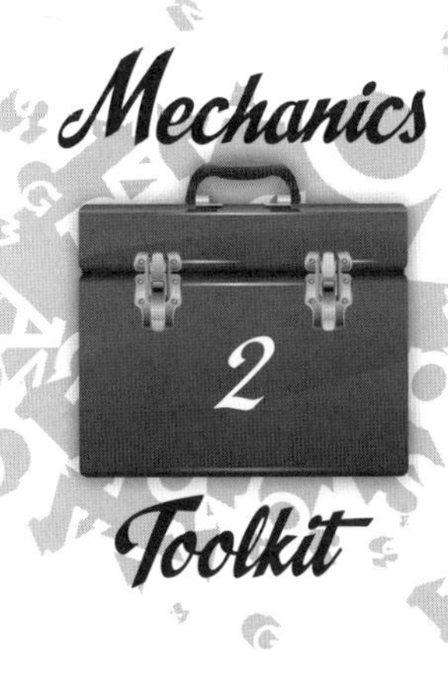
Mechanics
2
Toolkit

Mechanics
2
Toolkit

Mechanics
2
Toolkit
Mechanics
2
Toolkit

Mechanics
2
Toolkit

Mechanics
2
Toolkit

Mechanics
2
Toolkit

Mechanics
2
Toolkit

Mechanics
2
Toolkit

Mechanics
2
Toolkit

Mechanics
2
Toolkit

RULE	EXAMPLE	EXAMPLE
Capitalize particular things, and titles when used with the name of a person.	We are going to visit the Statue of Liberty.	I was sick so we went to see Dr. Smith.
RULE	**EXAMPLE**	**EXAMPLE**
Every sentence ends with a punctuation mark such as a period for a sentence that tells you something.	We will go to the movies on Saturday.	The party starts at one o'clock.
RULE	**EXAMPLE**	**EXAMPLE**
Use the word *their* to show that something belongs to a group.	Please give their toys back to the boys.	Our friends left their bikes at my house.
RULE	**EXAMPLE**	**EXAMPLE**
Use the word *they're* as a contraction of the words they are.	They're going to the game with Sam.	Bill and Bob don't have a football so they're going to buy one.

Instructions for playing this game are found on page 406.

Mechanics
2
Toolkit

Mechanics
2
Toolkit

Mechanics
2
Toolkit

Mechanics
2
Toolkit

Mechanics
2
Toolkit

Mechanics
2
Toolkit

Mechanics
2
Toolkit

Mechanics
2
Toolkit

Mechanics
2
Toolkit

Mechanics
2
Toolkit

Mechanics
2
Toolkit

RULE	EXAMPLE	EXAMPLE
Use the word *there* to show placement.	We will put the new trees <u>there</u>.	I cannot be <u>there</u> on time.

RULE	EXAMPLE	EXAMPLE

RULE	EXAMPLE	EXAMPLE

RULE	EXAMPLE	EXAMPLE

Instructions for playing this game are found on page 406.

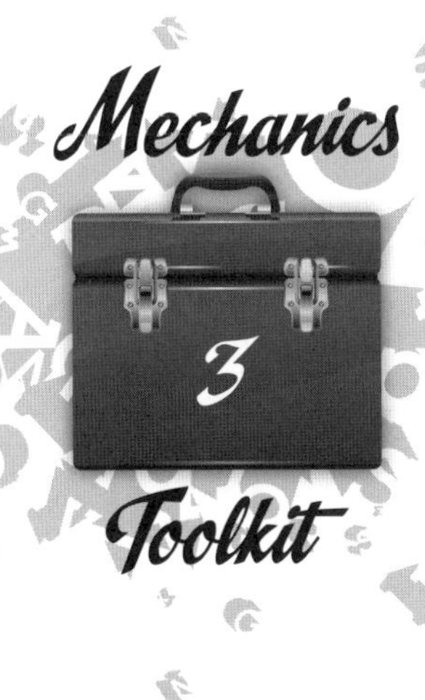
Mechanics
3
Toolkit

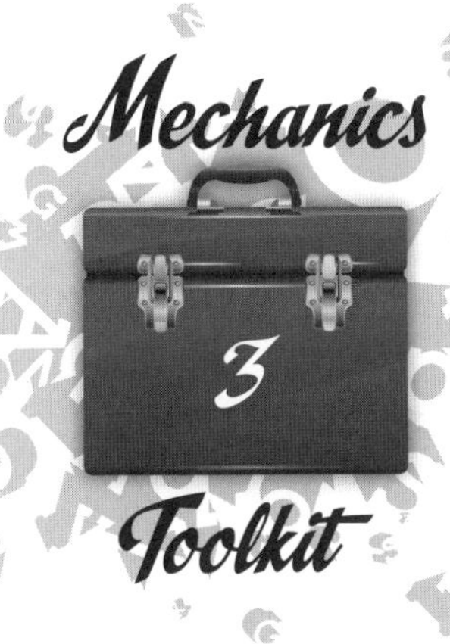
Mechanics
3
Toolkit

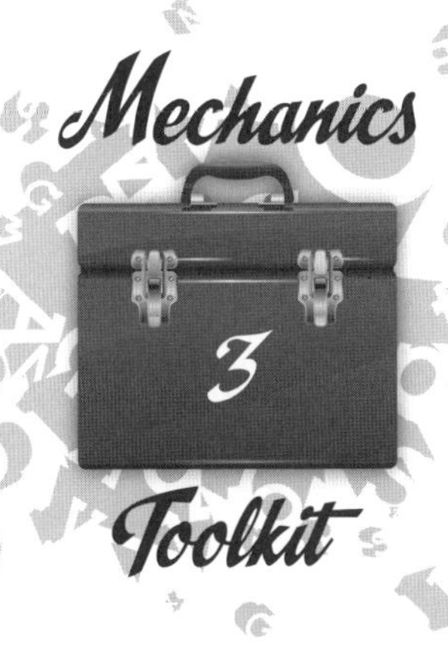
Mechanics
3
Toolkit

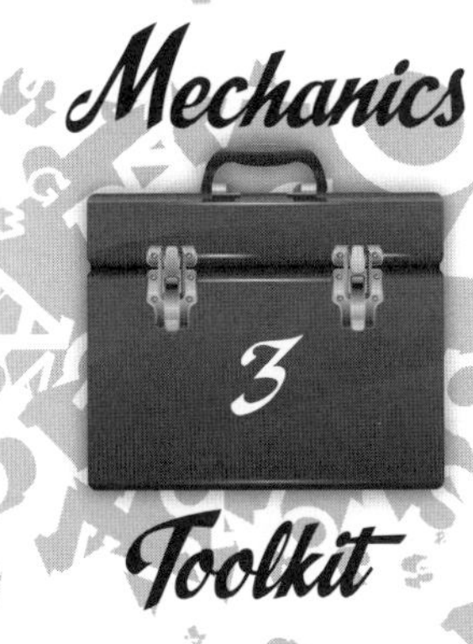
Mechanics
3
Toolkit

Mechanics
3
Toolkit

Mechanics
3
Toolkit

Mechanics
3
Toolkit

Mechanics
3
Toolkit

Mechanics
3
Toolkit

Mechanics
3
Toolkit

Mechanics
3
Toolkit

Mechanics
3
Toolkit

RULE	EXAMPLE	EXAMPLE
Capitalize words such as *mother, father, grandmother* or *aunt* when they are used as the name of a person.	We are going to visit Grandmother on Saturday.	I was happy to see all my uncles and Aunt Sally.

RULE	EXAMPLE	EXAMPLE
Every sentence ends with a punctuation mark, such as an exclamation point for a sentence or phrase that expresses strong feelings.	Don't run into the street!	Happy birthday!

RULE	EXAMPLE	EXAMPLE
Use the word *was* to show that something has already happened to one person or thing.	I was on a baseball team.	She was the only person with a pet.

RULE	EXAMPLE	EXAMPLE
Use the word *were* to show that something has already happened to a group of people or things.	Many animals were in the jungle.	Bill and Bob were on the winning football team.

Instructions for playing this game are found on page 406.

Mechanics
4
Toolkit

Mechanics
4
Toolkit

Mechanics
4
Toolkit

Mechanics
4
Toolkit

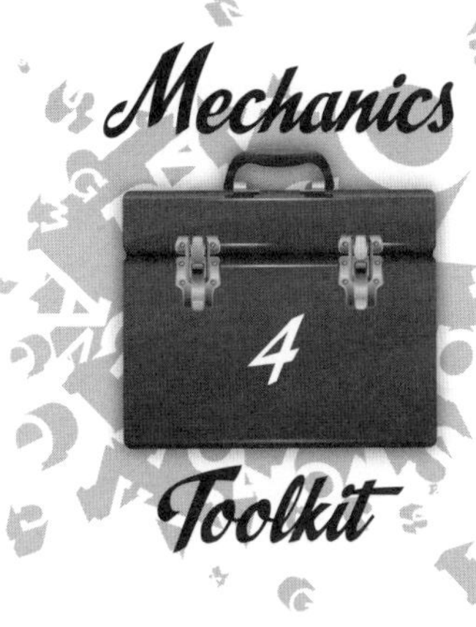
Mechanics
4
Toolkit

Mechanics
4
Toolkit

Mechanics
4
Toolkit

Mechanics
4
Toolkit

Mechanics
4
Toolkit

Mechanics
4
Toolkit

Mechanics
4
Toolkit

Mechanics
4
Toolkit

RULE	EXAMPLE	EXAMPLE
Capitalize names of historical events, documents and geographic names.	The Continental Congress met in <u>Philadelphia</u>.	Many great men helped create the <u>Declaration of Independence</u>.
RULE	**EXAMPLE**	**EXAMPLE**
Every sentence ends with a punctuation mark, such as a question mark for a sentence that asks a question.	What happened to Patrick's friend<u>?</u>	Was John Adams one of the Sons of Liberty<u>?</u>
RULE	**EXAMPLE**	**EXAMPLE**
Use the word *you're* as a contraction of the words you are.	<u>You're</u> my favorite coach.	If <u>you're</u> not quiet, <u>you're</u> going to wake the baby.
RULE	**EXAMPLE**	**EXAMPLE**
Use the word *your* to show that something belongs to someone.	We will go to <u>your</u> house later.	What is <u>your</u> opinion of the book?

Instructions for playing this game are found on page 406.

Mechanics

5
Toolkit

Mechanics
5
Toolkit

Mechanics
5
Toolkit

Mechanics
5
Toolkit

Mechanics
5
Toolkit

Mechanics
5
Toolkit

Mechanics
5
Toolkit

Mechanics
5
Toolkit

Mechanics
5
Toolkit

Mechanics
5
Toolkit

Mechanics
5
Toolkit

Mechanics
5
Toolkit

RULE	EXAMPLE	EXAMPLE
A pronoun for one person or thing can be the subject of a sentence.	Sam and I will go for a bike ride.	He and Bob play ball together.
A name and a pronoun for one person can be used together as the subject of a sentence.	He loves to play football.	She likes to read.
Use an apostrophe (') to show the missing letters in a contraction.	I don't want to fall and get hurt.	They're going to come with us.

Instructions for playing this game are found on page 406.

Mechanics

6
Toolkit

Mechanics
6
Toolkit

Mechanics
6
Toolkit

Mechanics
6
Toolkit

Mechanics
6
Toolkit

Mechanics
6
Toolkit

Mechanics
6
Toolkit

Mechanics
6
Toolkit

Mechanics
6
Toolkit

Mechanics
6
Toolkit

Mechanics
6
Toolkit

Mechanics
6
Toolkit

RULE	EXAMPLE	EXAMPLE
A pronoun for more than one person or thing can be the subject of a sentence.	We like ice cream.	They are my favorite presents.

RULE	EXAMPLE	EXAMPLE
Use an apostrophe to show that something belongs to someone.	That is Ann's book.	Bob's game is on the table.

RULE	EXAMPLE	EXAMPLE
Use a hyphen (-) to make a describing word, or adjective, that comes before a naming word, or noun.	Sue really likes her new tie-dyed shirt.	Her mother is a big-hearted person.

RULE	EXAMPLE	EXAMPLE

Instructions for playing this game are found on page 406.

Mechanics

7
Toolkit

Mechanics

7
Toolkit

Mechanics
7
Toolkit

Mechanics
7
Toolkit

Mechanics
7
Toolkit

Mechanics
7
Toolkit

Mechanics
7
Toolkit

Mechanics
7
Toolkit

Mechanics
7
Toolkit

Mechanics
7
Toolkit

Mechanics
7
Toolkit

Mechanics
7
Toolkit

RULE

A pronoun for one person or thing can be the focus, or object, of a preposition (word that shows relationships between words such as *for, to, with,* or *in*.)

EXAMPLE

Give the football to him.

EXAMPLE

The book belongs to her.

RULE

These pronouns can be used together as the focus, or object of a preposition (word that shows relationships between words such as *for, to, with,* or *in*.)

EXAMPLE

Dad will go for a bike ride with you and me.

EXAMPLE

Mom plays ball with him and her.

RULE

A name and a pronoun for one person can be used together as the focus, or object, of a preposition (word that shows relationships between words such as *for, to, with,* or *in*.)

EXAMPLE

Dad will go for a bike ride with Billy and me.

EXAMPLE

Mom plays ball with her and Jenny.

RULE

Use a hyphen to divide a word when you run out of room at the end of a line.

EXAMPLE

Some famous people in American history are George Washington and Ben Franklin.

EXAMPLE

Some very big battles took place in the state of Massachusetts.

Instructions for playing this game are found on page 406.

Mechanics
8
Toolkit

Mechanics
8
Toolkit

Mechanics
8
Toolkit

Mechanics
8
Toolkit

Mechanics
8
Toolkit

Mechanics
8
Toolkit

Mechanics
8
Toolkit

Mechanics
8
Toolkit

Mechanics
8
Toolkit

Mechanics
8
Toolkit

Mechanics
8
Toolkit

RULE

A pronoun for more than one person or thing can be the focus, or object, of a preposition (word that shows relationships between words such as *for, to, with,* or *in*.)

EXAMPLE

Dad makes ice cream for <u>us</u>.

EXAMPLE

Give the footballs to <u>them</u>.

RULE

These pronouns can be used together as the focus, or object of a preposition (word that shows relationships between words such as *for, to, with,* or *in*.)

EXAMPLE

Dad will bring bikes for <u>you and us</u>.

EXAMPLE

Coach has new bats for <u>them and us</u>.

RULE

Use a hyphen to write two-word numbers under one hundred, and fractions.

EXAMPLE

There are <u>twenty-five</u> people at the show.

EXAMPLE

<u>One-half</u> of the people in the show are girls.

RULE

Add an apostrophe at the end of a word ending in *s* to show that something belongs to more than one.

EXAMPLE

The <u>students'</u> books were on their desks.

EXAMPLE

The <u>boys'</u> cars are their favorite toys.

Instructions for playing this game are found on page 406.

Barometer

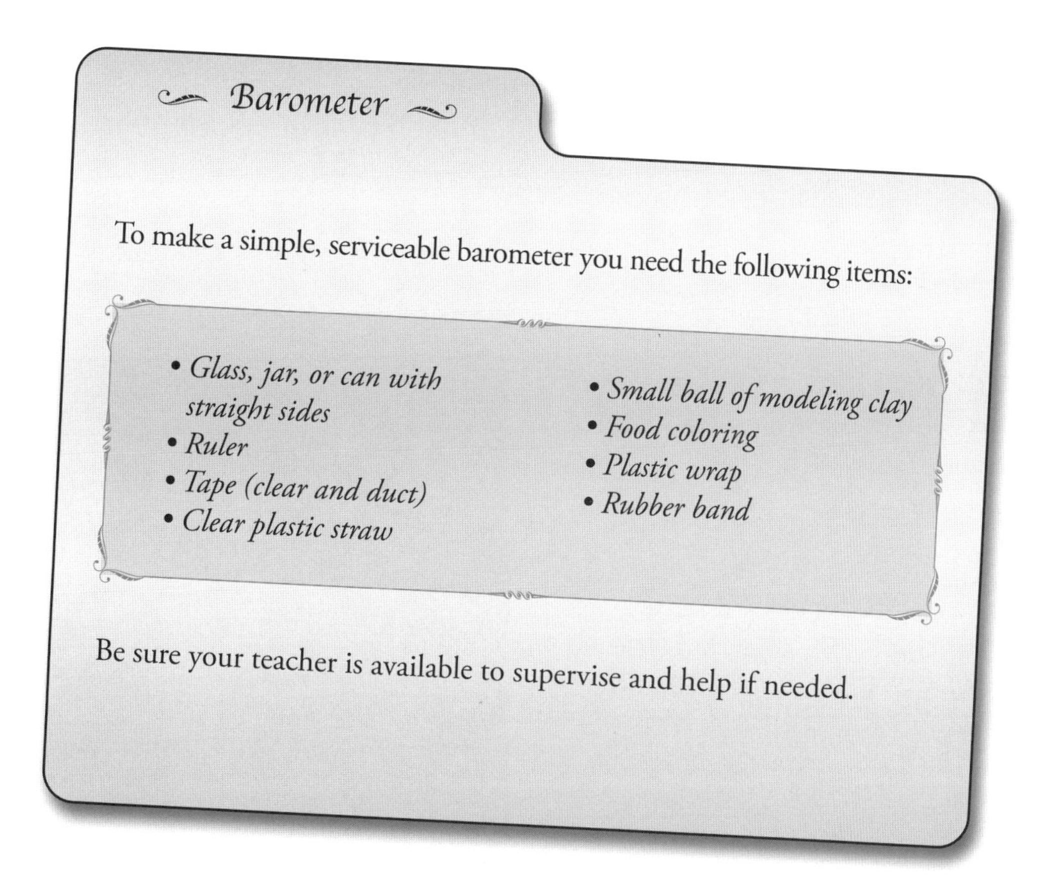

Barometer
To make a simple, serviceable barometer you need the following items:
• Glass, jar, or can with straight sides
• Ruler
• Tape (clear and duct)
• Clear plastic straw
• Small ball of modeling clay
• Food coloring
• Plastic wrap
• Rubber band
Be sure your teacher is available to supervise and help if needed.

Instructions

1. Fill the glass about half-full of water, and add two drops of food coloring.

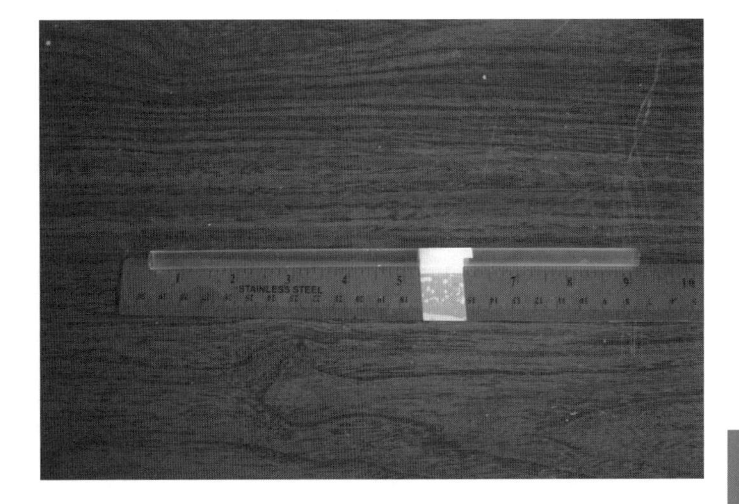

2. Carefully tape the straw to the ruler, positioning it about ½-inch from the end. Make sure you can see the measurements on the ruler clearly. Place the ruler and straw in the glass of colored water.

3. Bend the straw slightly so you can suck gently on the end and draw water almost all the way up. Use your tongue to trap the water, and quickly slide the ball of modeling clay onto the end to seal it.

   This can be tricky, and you may have to try a couple of times before you are able to contain about half a straw-full of water.

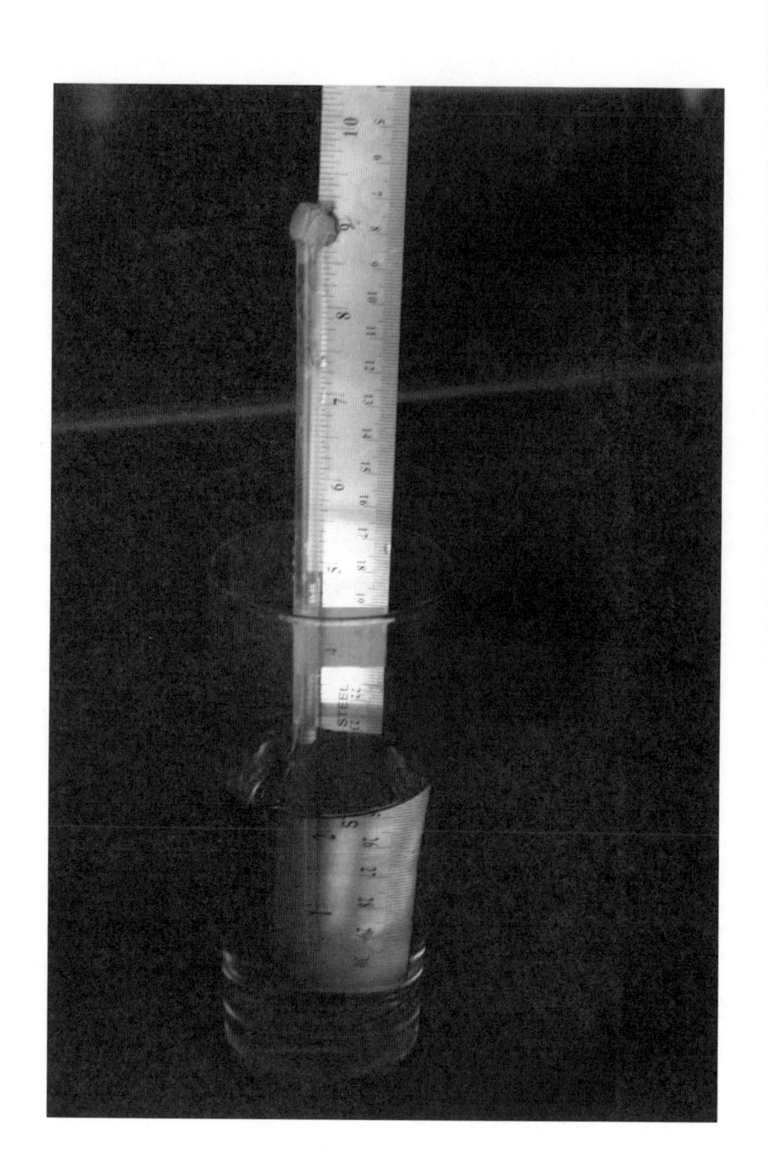

4. Roll a piece of duct tape, and use it to stick the back of the ruler to the inside of the glass.

5. Write down the starting measurement of the water so you can tell if it has changed when you next check it. The water in the tube will rise or fall depending on how heavily the air presses on the water in the glass. If the air pressure increases, it will push more water into the tube, causing the level to rise. When the air pressure decreases, some of the water will move down out of the tube, causing the level to fall.

   Changes in air pressure can help you forecast the weather. If the measurement goes down, it usually means that a low pressure area is approaching, and there will be clouds and precipitation. If the measurement goes up, it usually means that a high pressure area is approaching, and there will be clear weather.

6. Cover the container with plastic wrap held on with a rubber band, but make sure you can see the water levels clearly. Then place your barometer in a safe place outdoors.

Anemometer

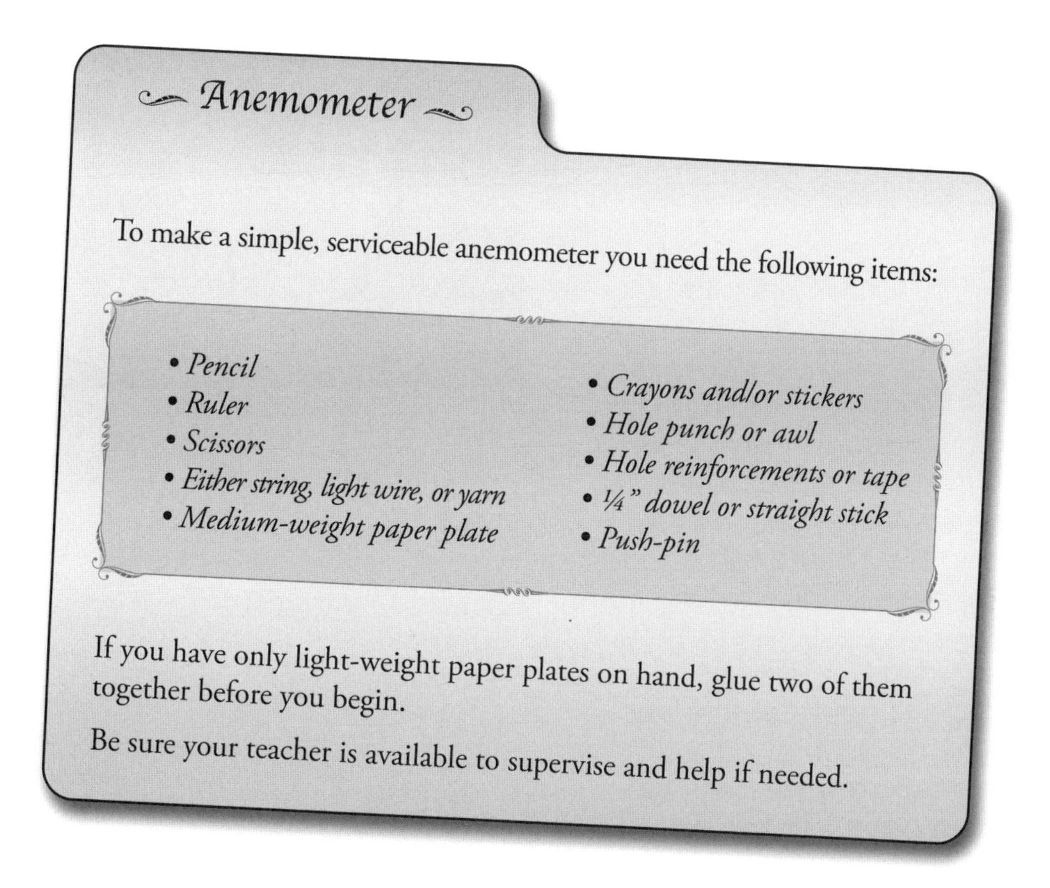

Anemometer
To make a simple, serviceable anemometer you need the following items:
• Pencil
• Ruler
• Scissors
• Either string, light wire, or yarn
• Medium-weight paper plate
• Crayons and/or stickers
• Hole punch or awl
• Hole reinforcements or tape
• ¼" dowel or straight stick
• Push-pin
If you have only light-weight paper plates on hand, glue two of them together before you begin.
Be sure your teacher is available to supervise and help if needed.

Instructions

1. Divide the paper plate you are using for the "anemometer base" into quarters. A simple way to do this is to use your plate as a model to trace a circle onto a piece of paper and cut it out; or use another paper plate that is the same size. Fold the paper circle or plate in half one way, then match the crease lines from the first fold together and fold it the other way. When you open it up, the crease lines show the center of the circle or plate (where the lines cross), as well as the four quarters. Place this model on top of your anemometer base plate. On the outer edge of the base plate, mark the places where the crease lines of the model touch. Then stick a push-pin through the middle (where the crease lines cross).

2. Remove the push-pin and the model, and make a dot at the center of the plate, where the push-pin hole is. Then use a ruler to draw lines connecting the marks you made that show the quarters.

3. On each line you just drew, mark a dot ¾ inch from the center dot. Now cut along each line from the outside edge to the dot that is ¾ inch from the center.

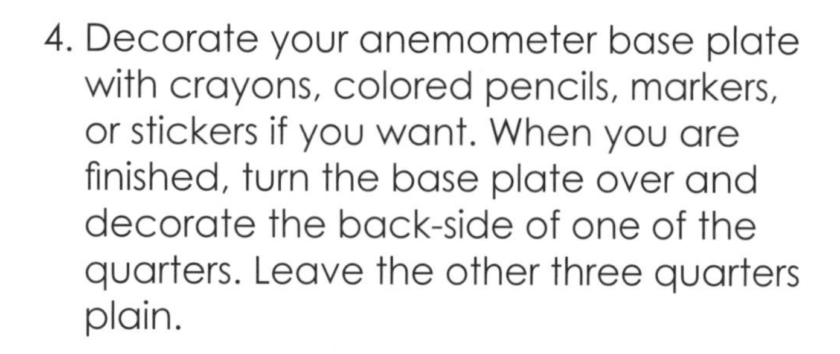

4. Decorate your anemometer base plate with crayons, colored pencils, markers, or stickers if you want. When you are finished, turn the base plate over and decorate the back-side of one of the quarters. Leave the other three quarters plain.

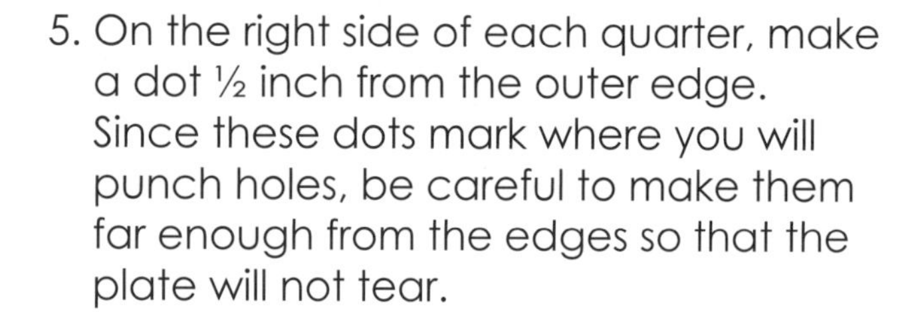

5. On the right side of each quarter, make a dot ½ inch from the outer edge. Since these dots mark where you will punch holes, be careful to make them far enough from the edges so that the plate will not tear.

6. On the left side of each quarter, make a dot 2 ½ inches from the outer edge. If you want, put hole reinforcements around each dot to strengthen that area. If you don't have hole reinforcements, a small square of sturdy tape works very well.

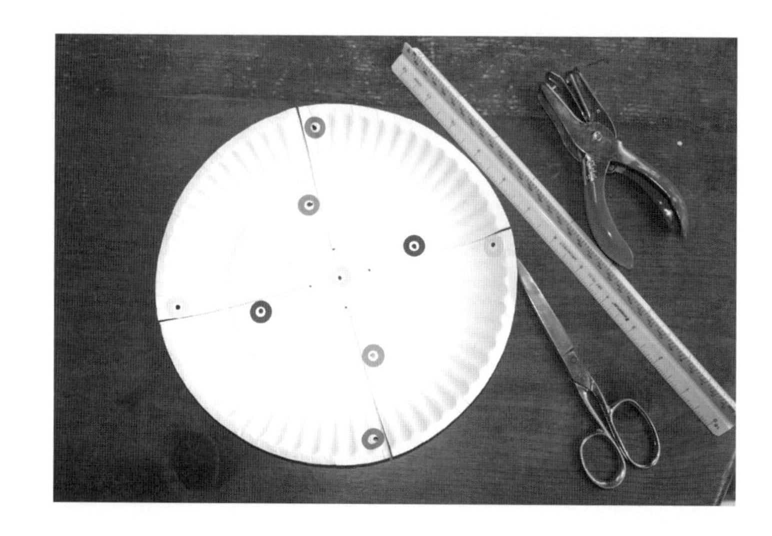

7. Make holes through each dot with a puncher or an awl.

8. Cut four pieces of string, yarn, or light wire about six inches long. These pieces should be long enough to tie easily. It is better too long than too short.

9. Thread a piece of string through one of the holes that are close to the outer edge of the base, and tie securely. Then thread the string through the other hole that is on the same quarter piece. Pull the string so that the quarter piece curls over, like a sail. Continue pulling the string until there is about three inches between the top and bottom of the quarter piece, and tie securely. Do the same with each of the other quarters. Trim off the leftover string.

10. Use a push-pin to mount your anemometer base to the end of a dowel or straight stick. Make sure the pin is not too tight, so your anemometer can spin freely in the wind. Use a crayon, marker, or a piece of tape to mark a short line or circle on the dowel or stick.

Weather Vane

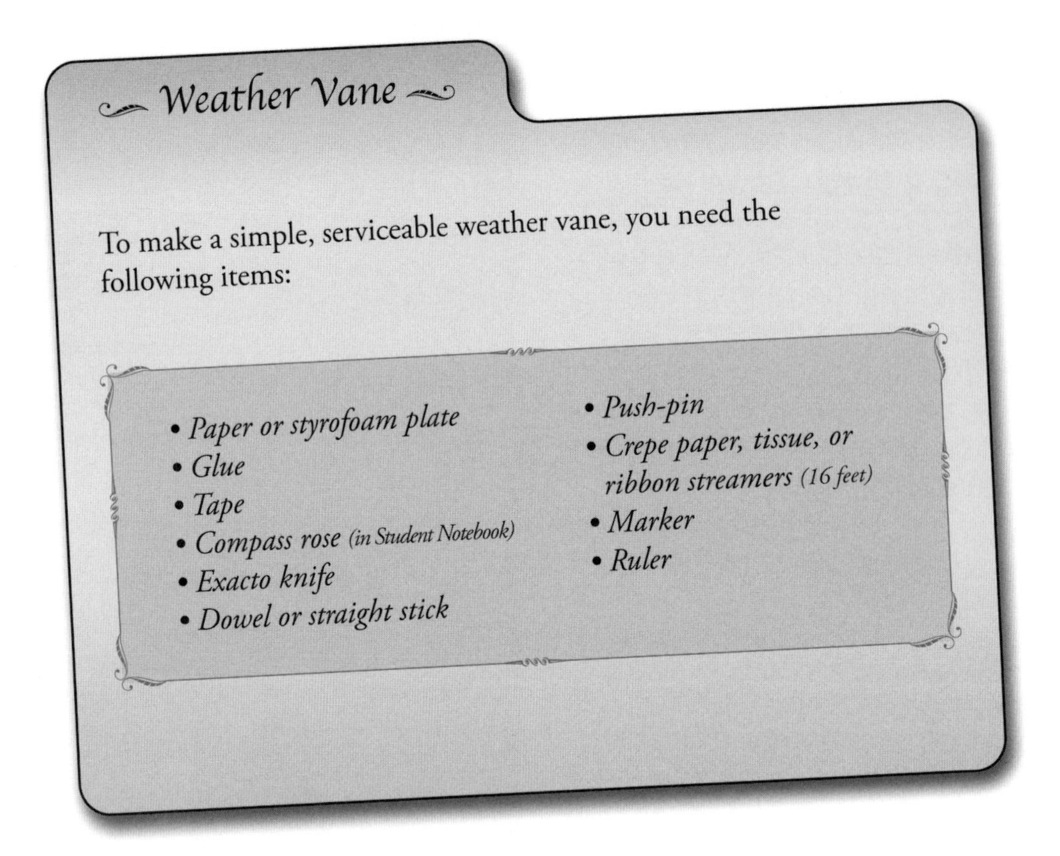

Weather Vane
To make a simple, serviceable weather vane, you need the following items:
• Paper or styrofoam plate
• Glue
• Tape
• Compass rose (in Student Notebook)
• Exacto knife
• Dowel or straight stick
• Push-pin
• Crepe paper, tissue, or ribbon streamers (16 feet)
• Marker
• Ruler

Instructions

1. Prepare the compass rose in your Student Notebook as directed. Carefully cut out the circle that contains the compass rose, and glue it onto a paper or styrofoam plate. If you have only lightweight paper plates, glue two or three of them together to make a sturdy base for your weather vane.

2. Draw four one-inch lines about ¼ inch from the outer edge of the plate, and close to each of the major compass points (N, S, E, and W). With your teacher's help, use an exacto knife to cut along each of these lines.

3. Cut eight 24-inch streamers from crepe paper, tissue, or ribbon. Fold the ends of two streamers together and thread them through one of the cuts you made on the edge of the base plate. Pull the ends through far enough to fold back over the edge, and tape them securely as shown. Do the same thing with the remaining streamers and cuts.

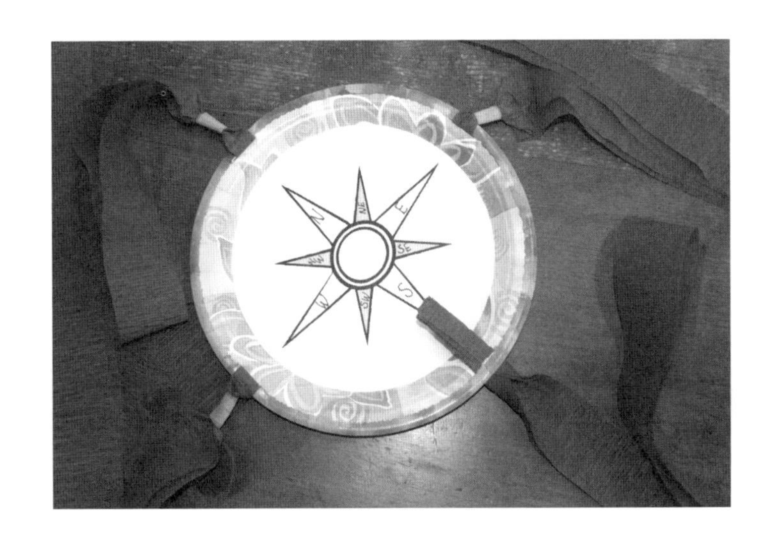

4. Use a push-pin to attach your weather vane to the end of a dowel or straight stick. It should be mounted securely so that it will not turn in the wind.

Candle Dipping

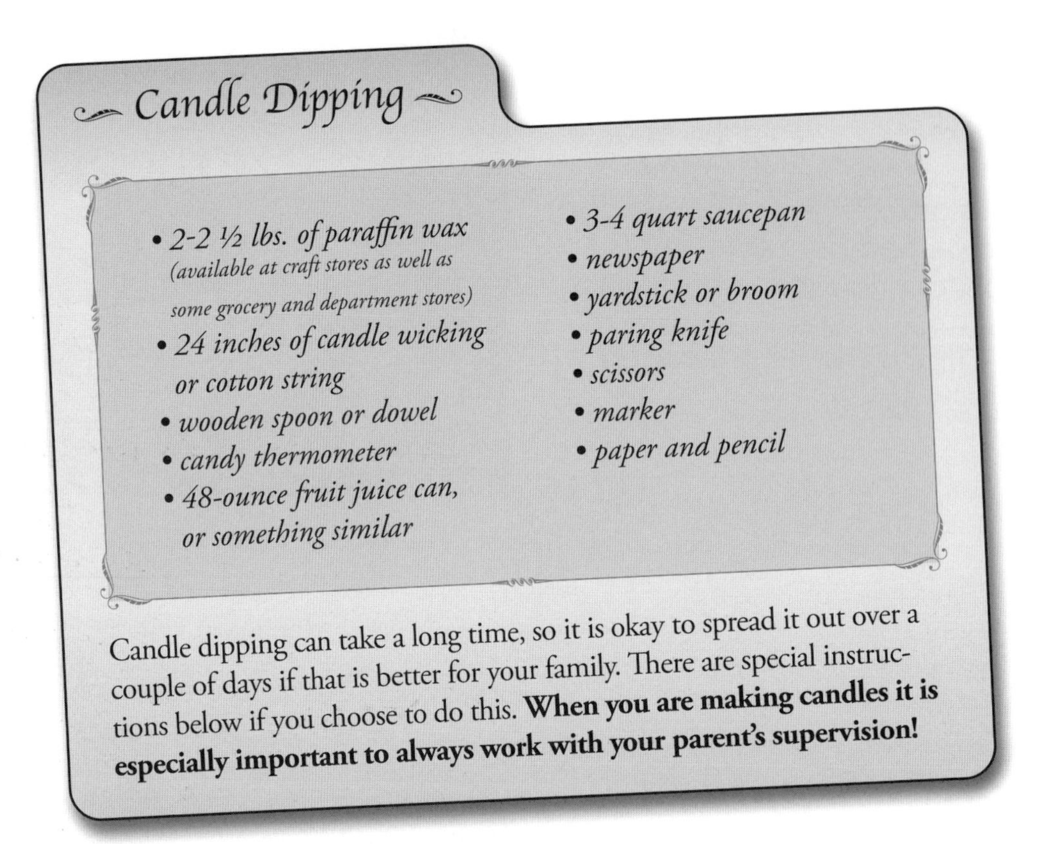

Candle Dipping
• 2-2 ½ lbs. of paraffin wax (available at craft stores as well as some grocery and department stores)
• 24 inches of candle wicking or cotton string
• wooden spoon or dowel
• candy thermometer
• 48-ounce fruit juice can, or something similar
• 3-4 quart saucepan
• newspaper
• yardstick or broom
• paring knife
• scissors
• marker
• paper and pencil
Candle dipping can take a long time, so it is okay to spread it out over a couple of days if that is better for your family. There are special instructions below if you choose to do this. When you are making candles it is especially important to always work with your parent's supervision!

Instructions

1. Fill a saucepan about half full of water and set it on the stove. Put the paraffin wax in the juice can (or similar container) and place it in the water on the stove. If you need to cut the wax to make it fit in the can, be sure to ask for your parent's help. Then turn the heat on to a medium temperature.

2. The paraffin wax will slowly begin to melt. As soon as there is enough room in the can, ask your parent to attach a candy thermometer. The thermometer is very important because it allows you to keep an eye on the temperature of the wax, which should stay around 160°F. If the wax gets too hot and begins to smoke, turn off the heat for awhile or ask your parent to remove the pan from the burner until it cools a little. When the wax is completely melted, turn the heat to its lowest setting and continue to keep an eye on the temperature.

3. While the wax is melting, set up a rack where your candles can cool and harden. To do this, place a yardstick or broom across the backs of two chairs positioned a couple of feet apart. Put newspaper on the floor between the chairs to catch any drips.

4. Cut a piece of candle wicking or cotton string 24 inches long. Measure about seven inches from each end of the wicking, and make a mark that you can easily see. Then fold the wicking in half, and hang it over a wooden spoon handle or dowel.

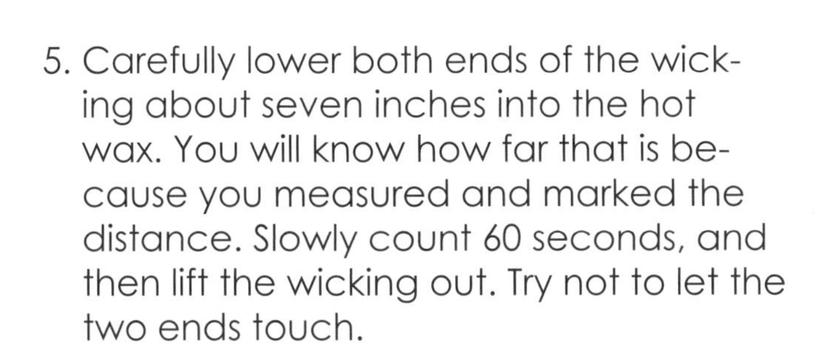

5. Carefully lower both ends of the wicking about seven inches into the hot wax. You will know how far that is because you measured and marked the distance. Slowly count 60 seconds, and then lift the wicking out. Try not to let the two ends touch.

6. Wax cools quickly, so a few seconds after you lift it out it will be safe to touch. Carefully use your fingers to straighten the wicks. This is priming the wick, and is very important if you want straight candles that burn evenly. Hang your candles on the rack to finish cooling.

7. Wait a couple of minutes before you dip the wicks again, and this time leave them in the wax for only three seconds. Try to submerge the wicks at least six inches. To do this you may need to slant them in the can of wax. Remove them, prime the wicks, and hang them to cool for at least a minute. Continue this process until you are satisfied with the way your candles look.

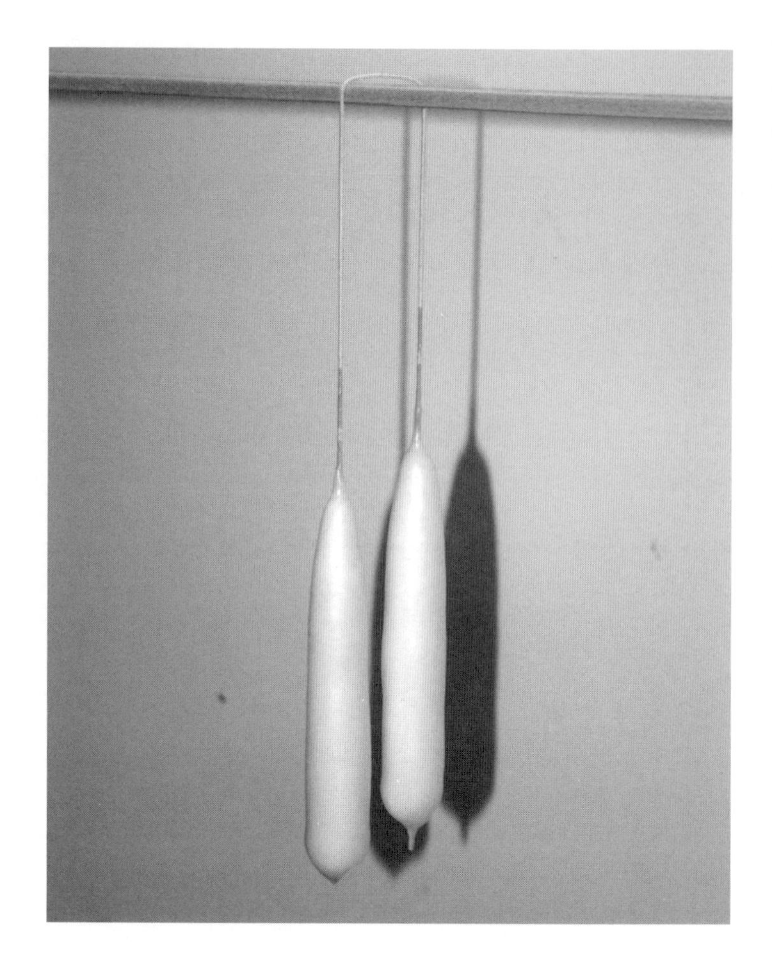

8. Be patient. It will take many dips before your wicks begin to look like real candles. Make a tally sheet to keep track of how many times you dip the wicks into the wax. A tally is just a way of counting. Make a short line on a piece of paper every time you dip your wicks, and keep the lines in groups of five to make them easier to count. Expect to dip your candles at least 30 times before they begin to look finished. Be sure to add water to the pan if it gets too low.

9. When you are satisfied, increase the temperature of the wax to 180°F and give your candles two last dips of three seconds each. Then put them on the rack to cool and harden for at least two hours. Trim the wicks to about ½ inch, and ask your parent to trim the base of each candle with a paring knife. Set them aside for at least 24 hours before you try them out.

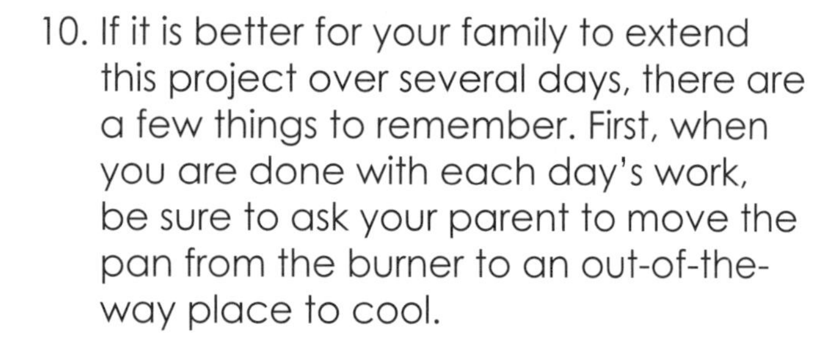

10. If it is better for your family to extend this project over several days, there are a few things to remember. First, when you are done with each day's work, be sure to ask your parent to move the pan from the burner to an out-of-the-way place to cool.

    Second, when you are ready to continue, make sure there is enough water in the pan and reheat the wax slowly—just like you did the first day. Always keep an eye on the temperature.

    Third, when the wax is ready, lower the candles and keep them submerged for 60 seconds. Remove them, prime the wicks, and hang them to cool.

    And finally, resume the three-second dips with at least a minute of cooling in between, until you are finished.

Unit 1 Watercolor Activity

Instructions

1. It is hard to paint with stiff hands, so relax yours by shaking them around a little. Then hold your brush loosely, and on a piece of watercolor paper make a light brown line to start your tree trunk. It does not need to be perfectly straight, because tree trunks usually have many small or large curves and bumps. Continue with the light brown until you have a shape that could be the trunk of a tree.

2. Look at your model and see if there are any branches showing through the foliage. If there are, notice that some or all of them do not seem to be connected to the tree because of the leaves. With a relaxed hand, put a few branches above your tree trunk. Again, they should not be perfectly straight.

3. You can make watercolors darker by layering them. Layering means applying the same color over the same area two or more times. Usually layering works best when each application is allowed to dry a little before the next one is applied. Put two or three layers of brown on parts of the trunk and branches to deepen the color in places, but don't cover them completely. Leave some areas lighter. This is because there are probably parts of your model tree trunk that are much lighter than others.

4. Look again at your model and notice areas that are darker. Then, while your paper is still wet from the brown paint, dab a very tiny bit of black (a little black goes a long way) onto the tree trunk in places that look darker on your model. Help the black mingle lightly with the brown in those places so that they look sort of grayish-brown.

5. While everything is still wet, paint a thin line of black along places that are the very darkest (usually one side of the tree trunk and the branches). If your paper is wet enough, the black will wash out from the line and blend naturally with the grayish color you just made. You will learn more about washes in another lesson. Don't worry about your painting looking exactly like the model—that is not the point of this lesson. The model is just a guide to help you experiment.

6. Now look at the foliage, and notice the different colors. Probably most of them will be yellow, orange, and red. Since you have only red and yellow in your palette, you will need to make orange. This is much easier than making brown, however, because all you have to do is mix the red and yellow together.

   If you still have the plastic cover you removed from the paints when you first opened them, use it for a mixing tray. If not, a small lid will do. Put ¼ teaspoon of water on your mixing tray, and fill your brush with red. Add the red to the water, and mix it well. Then rinse your brush, fill it with yellow, and add it to the red in the mixing tray. If you want, do this one more time, being sure to rinse your brush again before you put it back in the yellow. Like the brown, this paint is mostly water, so blot your brush before you use it.

7. Begin painting the foliage with the lightest color, yellow. To do this, roll your brush in the yellow paint to make the bristles as pointy at the end as possible. Then dab the paint onto the paper in different sized dots. When you have all the yellow in your foliage that you want, let it dry just a bit. Do the same thing with the orange, and then the red. Because the orange is so watery, you may want to layer a few of the orange dots, but you don't have to.

   Your leaves should touch each other and the tree's trunk and branches. Just relax and enjoy making your own special tree!

Beanbags

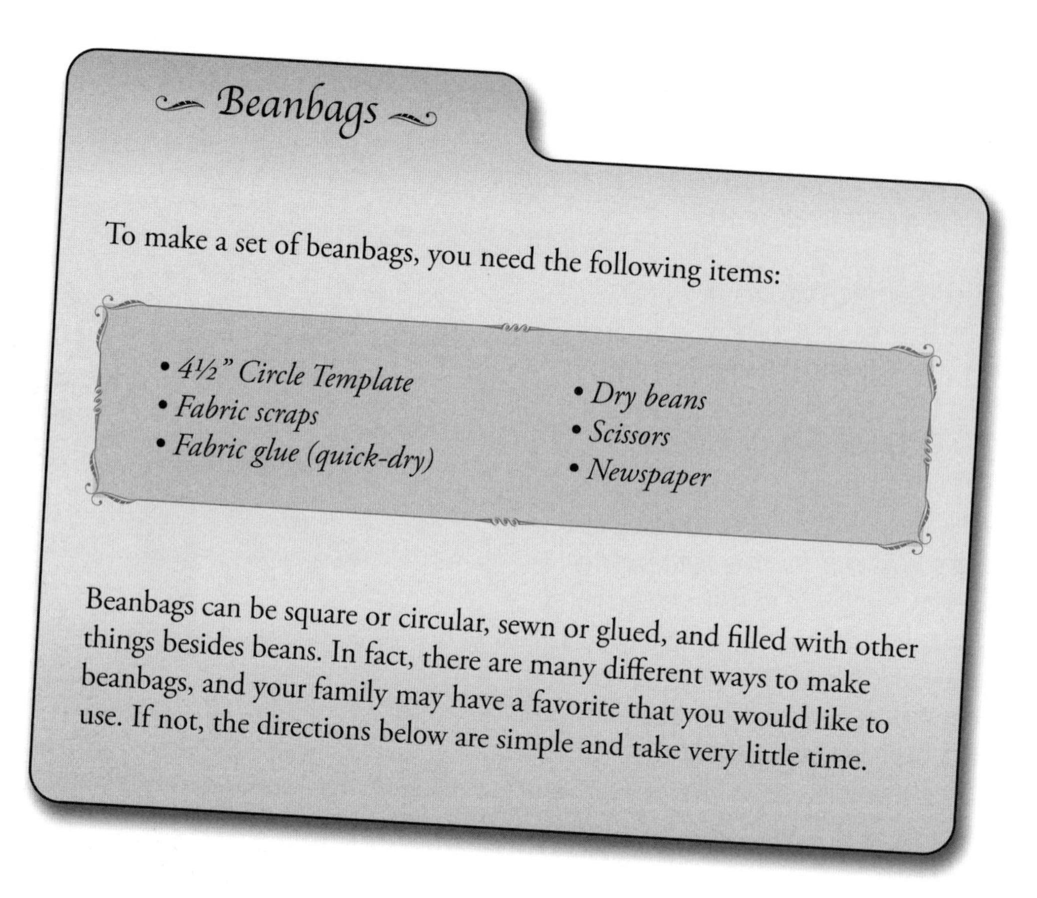

Beanbags
To make a set of beanbags, you need the following items:
• 4½" Circle Template
• Fabric scraps
• Fabric glue (quick-dry)
• Dry beans
• Scissors
• Newspaper
Beanbags can be square or circular, sewn or glued, and filled with other things besides beans. In fact, there are many different ways to make beanbags, and your family may have a favorite that you would like to use. If not, the directions below are simple and take very little time.

Instructions

1. Use the 4 ½-inch circle template found on page 444 to cut four circles out of your fabric.

2. Put the circles on a piece of newspaper. Run a line of fabric glue as close to the edge of one of the circles as possible. Be sure to leave an unglued space of about two-inches so that you can add beans later.

3. Carefully place a second circle on top of the one with glue, and tap down the edges to make sure it is stuck together all the way around (except for the unglued space.) This may be a little messy because the glue will most likely seep out the edges.

4. Follow steps 1 and 2 with the second set of circles. When you are finished, lift both circle sets off the newspaper where you glued them, and move them to a new spot so they won't stick to the paper. Let them dry completely.

5. When they are dry, add the beans through the hole that you left. Be careful not to overstuff the bags – they should be plump, but not packed.

6. Glue the hole shut. This may be the most difficult part of the process and may require an extra set of hands to hold the beans in and apply the glue. Let them dry, and then use them to play hopscotch!

Circle Templates

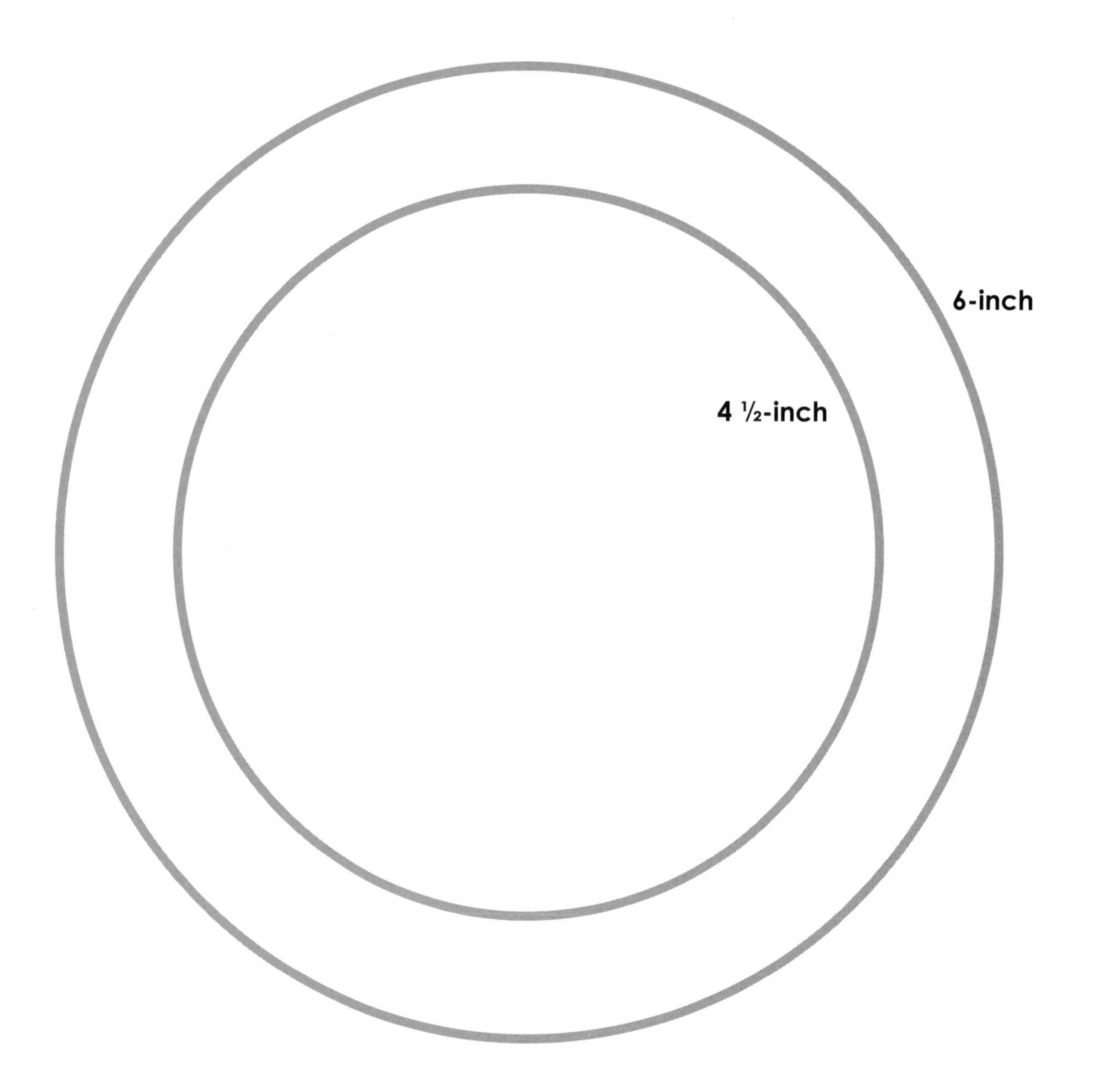

Outer circle: use as template for Beanbag project (Freedom Decided Lesson 2, Part 1)

Inner circle: use as template for Cornhole Platform (Freedom Decided Lesson 3, Part 5)

Cornhole Platform

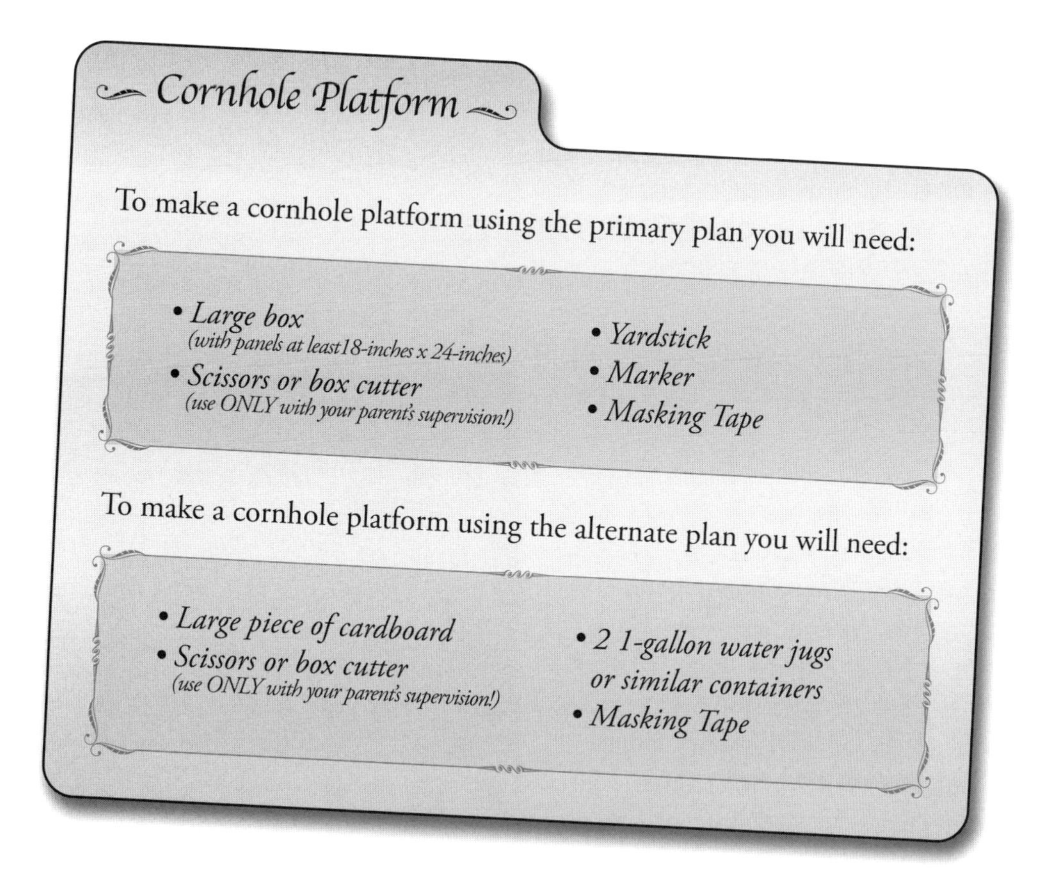

Cornhole Platform
To make a cornhole platform using the primary plan you will need:
• Large box
(with panels at least18-inches x 24-inches)
• Scissors or box cutter
(use ONLY with your parent's supervision!)
• Yardstick
• Marker
• Masking Tape
To make a cornhole platform using the alternate plan you will need:
• Large piece of cardboard
• Scissors or box cutter
(use ONLY with your parent's supervision!)
• 2 1-gallon water jugs
or similar containers
• Masking Tape

Instructions: Primary Plan

The box used here as an example is a large moving box bought at a department store, but any box with similar dimensions will work fine.

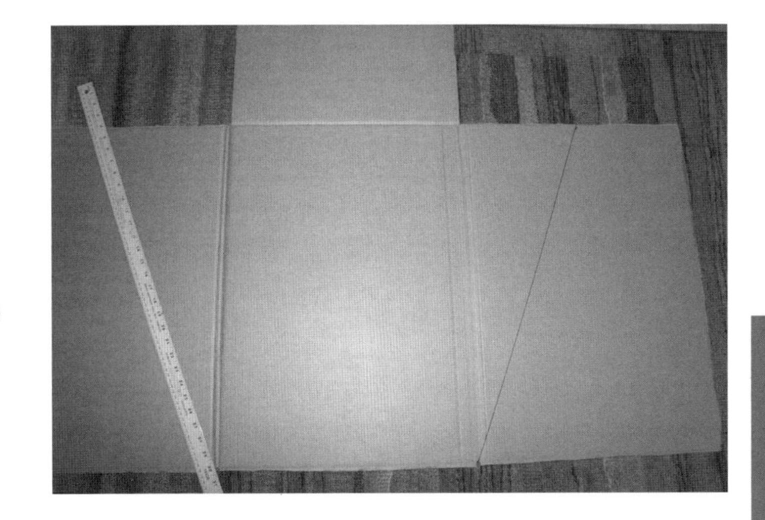

1. Cut one panel off the box and discard. Then lay the rest of the box flat on the floor or table and cut off all the flaps except the one attached to the top of the middle section.

2. Fold the remaining flap down (so you can get an accurate measurement) and measure its width. Then lay the box flat again to measure and mark that distance from the fold of each side panel (see picture). Use a yardstick to draw diagonal lines from the marks you just made to the bottom of the side-panel folds. With your parent's supervision and help, carefully cut along those lines.

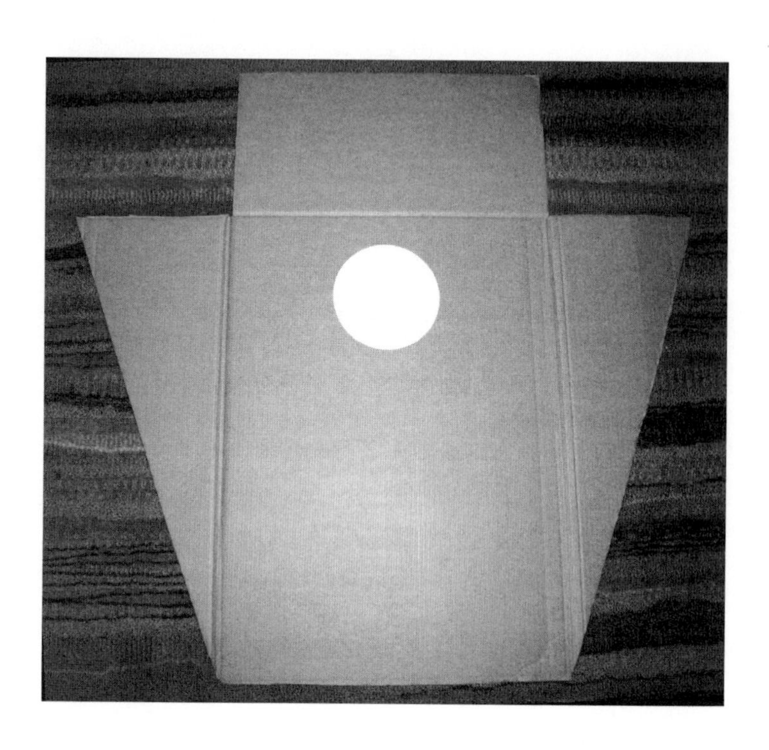

3. Use the 6-inch circle circle template found on page 444 to mark a circle on the top portion of the center panel. This circle should be centered on that panel, a few inches from the top fold of the panel. Again, with your parent's supervision and help, carefully cut the circle out.

4. Fold the top flap and side-panels down, and tape them. You now have a sturdy cornhole platform!

Instructions: Alternate Plan

If a box is not available, a single sheet of cardboard can be used. It should be longer than it is wide, and a flap at the top is helpful though not absolutely necessary.

1. Use the 6-inch circle circle template found on page 446 to mark a circle near the top of the cardboard. With your parent's supervision and help, carefully cut the circle out.

2. Fold the flap down over whatever you are using as a support, and tape them together. The example here shows two gallon water jugs, but you may have something else that will work just as well. If there is no flap on your cardboard, simply prop it against the supports and tape.

Instructions for playing this game are found on page 405.

Weaving

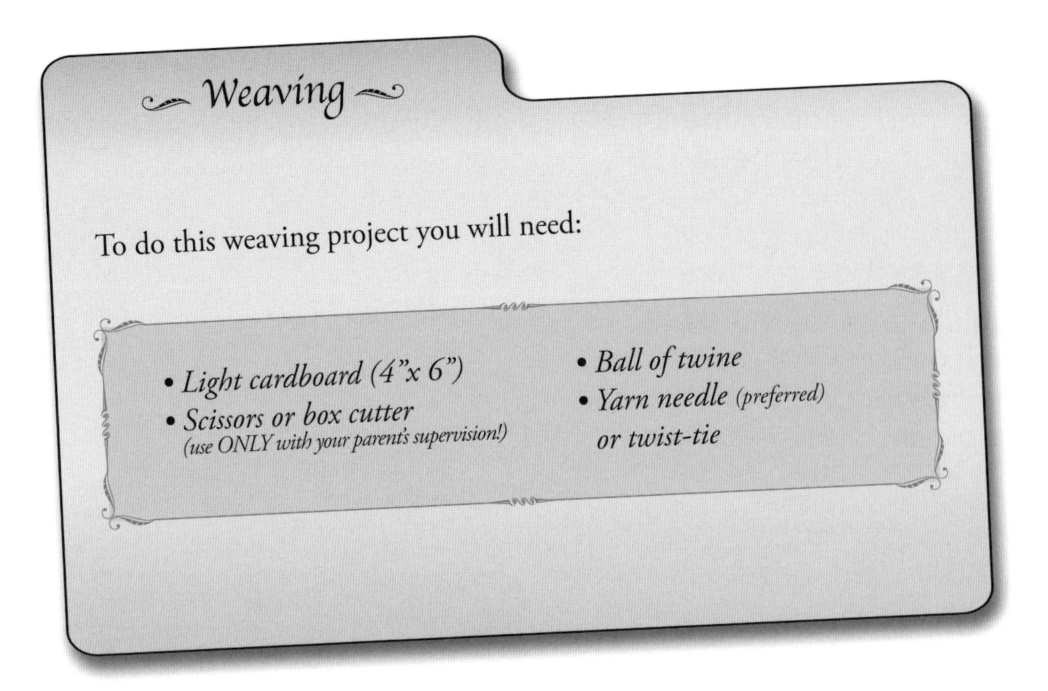

Weaving
To do this weaving project you will need:
• Light cardboard (4"x 6")
• Scissors or box cutter
(use ONLY with your parent's supervision!)
• Ball of twine
• Yarn needle (preferred)
or twist-tie

Instructions

1. Cut out a four-inch by six-inch piece of light cardboard.

2. Use a ruler to mark off ½-inch segments along one of the shorter sides. When you are finished, measure ¼-inch from the bottom right, and mark it.

3. Make a short downward cut (about ¼-inch) at each ½-inch mark along the top edge, and the ¼-inch mark at the bottom. Then make diagonal cuts at each place to form small notches. This piece of cardboard is now your loom, or the frame for your weaving.

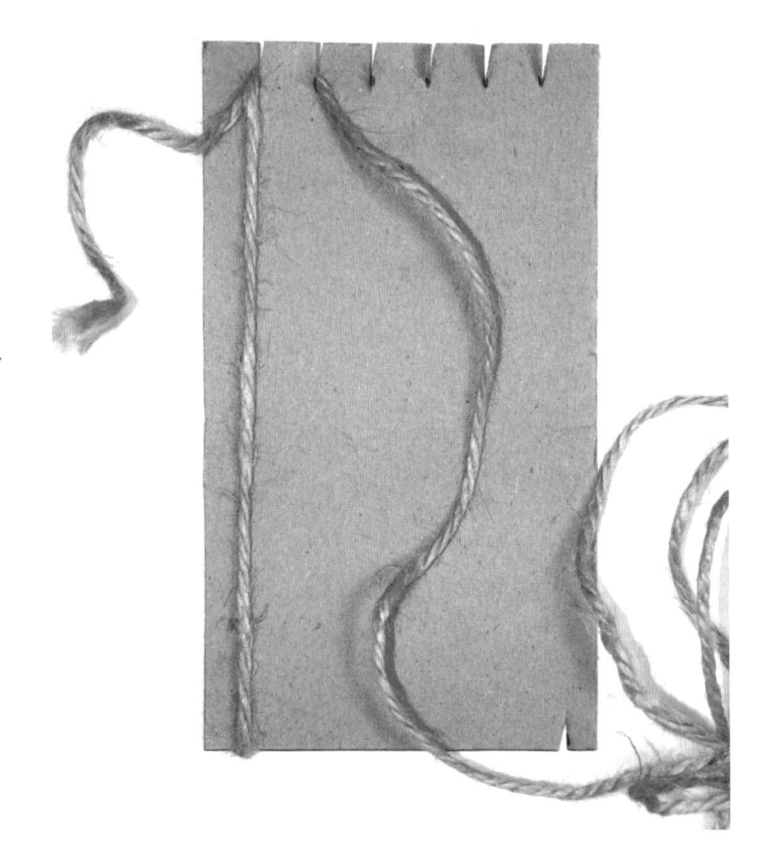

4. Leaving several inches loose at the front, thread your twine into the first notch on the left and push it down to secure it. Then run the twine down the back of the loom, around the bottom, and up the front to the first notch again, and secure it.

5. Wrap the twine around the back of the adjoining tab, and push it down securely in the second notch. Then run it down the front of the loom, around the bottom, and up the back to the same notch.

6. This time, wrap the twine around the front of the adjoining tab to the right, and push it down securely in the third notch. Run it down the back of the loom, around the bottom, and up the front to the same notch. Continue this process until all the notches are filled. Then secure the end of the twine in the notch at the bottom right. Cut it off a couple of inches out from the loom. The rows of twine you attached to your loom are called warp threads. There should be an even number of warp threads on one side of the loom, and an uneven number on the other side.

7. A yarn needle makes a good shuttle, or tool that guides the thread over and under the warp threads, but if one is not available a twist-tie can be used (see picture). To begin weaving, cut a piece of twine three or four feet long and attach it to the needle or twist-tie. Start at the bottom right, and use your shuttle (needle or twist-tie) to guide the twine over and under the warp threads on the front and the back of the loom. If you go over the last warp thread on the front, be sure to go under the first warp thread on the back. Leave several inches of the twine you are weaving loose when you begin; it will later be woven or tied into the finished bag.

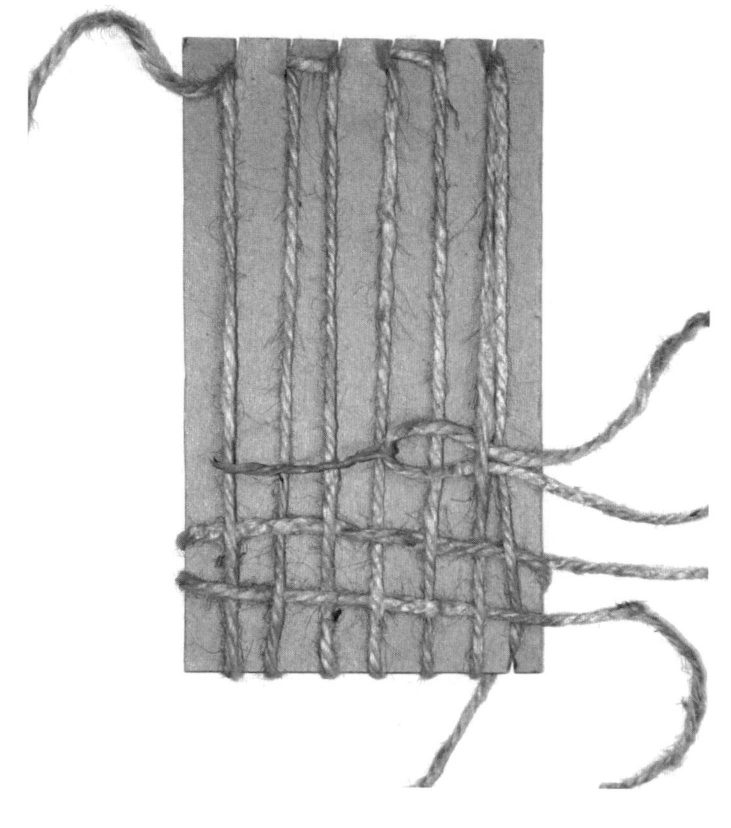

8. As you weave, be sure to beat the twine by pulling each row down as close as possible to the previous row.

9. When you run out of twine, cut another piece and tie it to the first (be sure to remove the shuttle before you tie it!) A good way to attach one piece to another is with a square knot. To make a square knot, cross and loop the left end over the right, and then the right over the left. Pull as tightly as possible, and trim the ends.

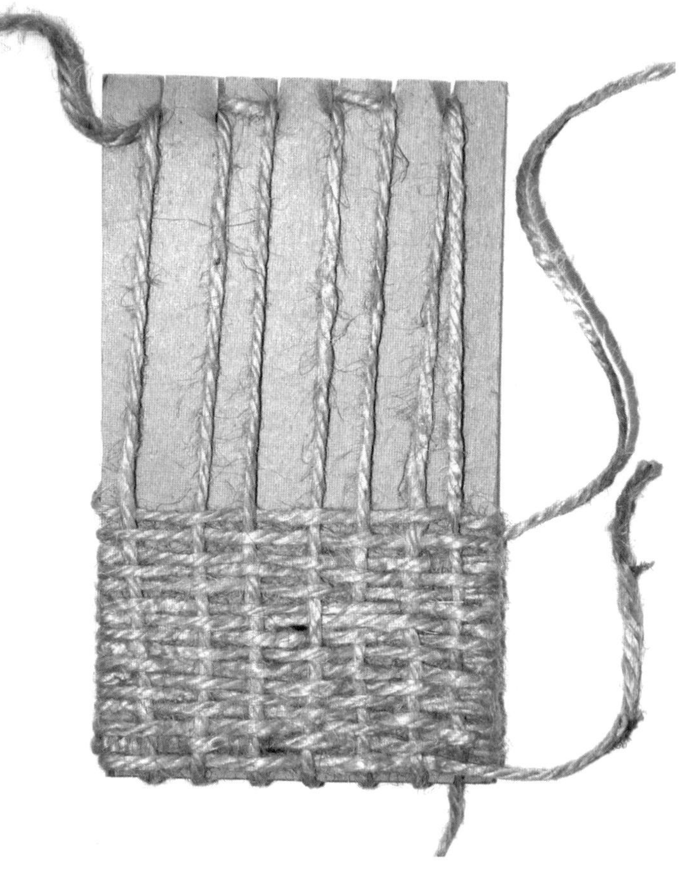

10. Continue weaving until there is no more room to run the shuttle over and under the warp threads. Then carefully remove your bag from the loom, and knot the shuttle thread to the top of one of the warp threads. Do not remove the shuttle from the thread yet, but use it to sew the first few rows together as shown in the picture. This will reinforce the top. Then tie the end at the top, and weave a couple of inches into your bag. Trim off any twine that is left over.

11. To make a drawstring, cut 24-inches of twine and attach it to the shuttle. Weave this thread in and out all around the top of the bag, and then tie the ends together.

Unit 2 Watercolor Activity

Instructions

There is no "right" way to do art. There are techniques, or methods for doing things, but the way you use the technique is up to you. The following instructions are just a starting point, so try different ways of achieving your goal. Remember, this activity is an opportunity to experiment—just be sure to keep the paint on the paper!

1. To begin, paint a portion of your paper with clear water. Then apply blue paint at the top and drag it down to cover the entire area with a light blue. Let it dry for a few minutes.

2. Notice that the picture shows three ranges, or groups, of mountains, each one darker than the one before it. Wet your brush well and dip it in black. Now run a line that resembles the top group of mountains in the picture. It doesn't have to be perfect. Smooth the black so that it becomes grayish, and pull the color down slightly. You might want to try blotting it lightly with a paper towel.

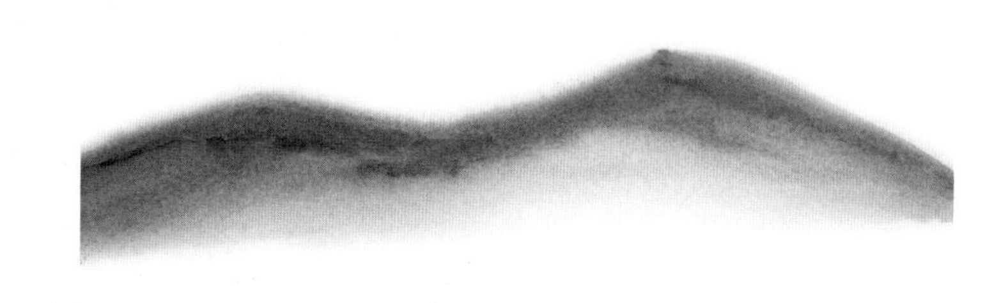

3. While the gray is still wet, add a bit of blue and pull the mixture down so the mountains remain light-colored.

4. Do the same with the second and third ranges, but make each a little darker than the one before it. Also, add a tiny bit of green to the mix. Be sure to pay attention to the light areas between the ranges. These areas should show a little light blue from the wash you put down first.

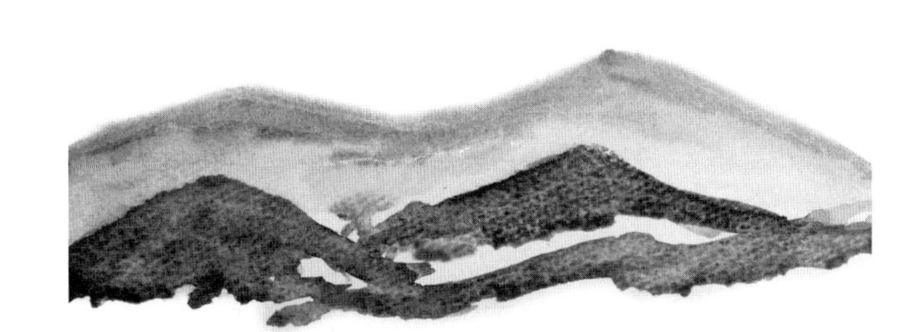

5. When you have at least three ranges on the paper, let them dry for a few minutes. Then use black paint to experiment with the trees. For this part you do not want your brush to be too wet.

6. Begin by painting a straight black line in the area where you'd like a tree. Relax your hand, and let the brush sort of wander down the line, making the branches as you go. Each row of branches will tend to stick out further than the last, but every tree is different! Because watercolor lightens as it dries, you may want to add more black to the trees later. Find out by experimenting all over the page, and maybe on another page as well.

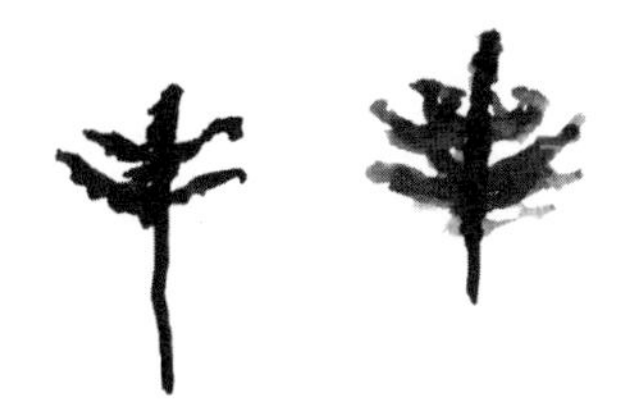

3-D Map

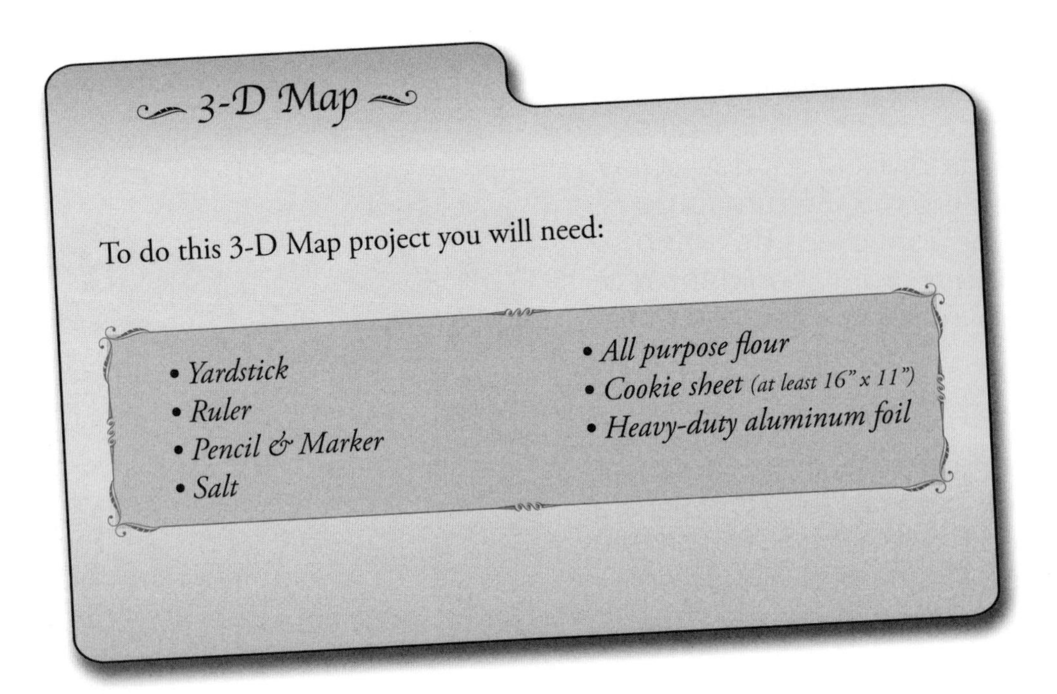

3-D Map
To do this 3-D Map project you will need:
• Yardstick
• Ruler
• Pencil & Marker
• Salt
• All purpose flour
• Cookie sheet (at least 16" x 11")
• Heavy-duty aluminum foil

Instructions

1. To begin your 3-D Map, the first thing you need to do is prepare a base. Since you will be putting it in the oven to dry the salt dough after each session, the best thing to use is a cookie sheet covered in foil.

   To make the border of your map, use a yardstick and a permanent marker to outline an area on the foil that is 16-inches long and 11-inches wide. Then use the yardstick and marker again to carefully draw a grid in that area with lines that are 1-inch apart.

   If your cookie sheet has sides it will be very difficult to use a yardstick, so just take the foil off the sheet to draw your border and grid. Then carefully put the foil back on the cookie sheet when you are finished.

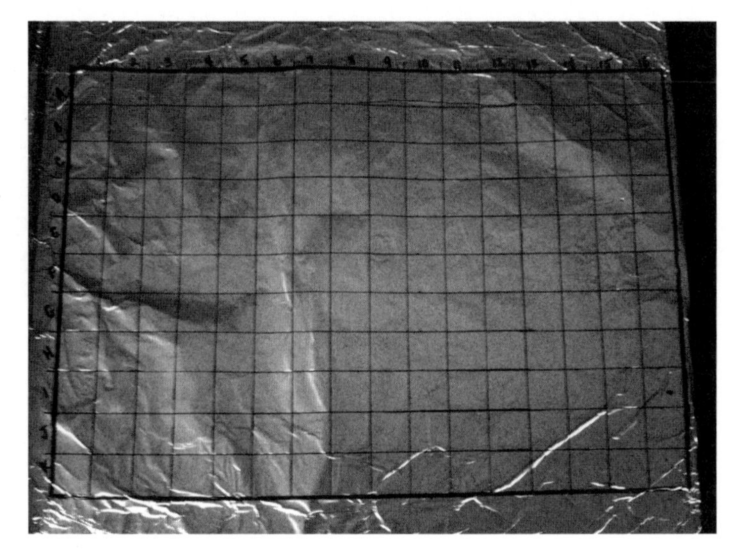

2. Notice that each grid space on the
nt Notebook
nber beside
rs and letters
ide on your
They will help
s.

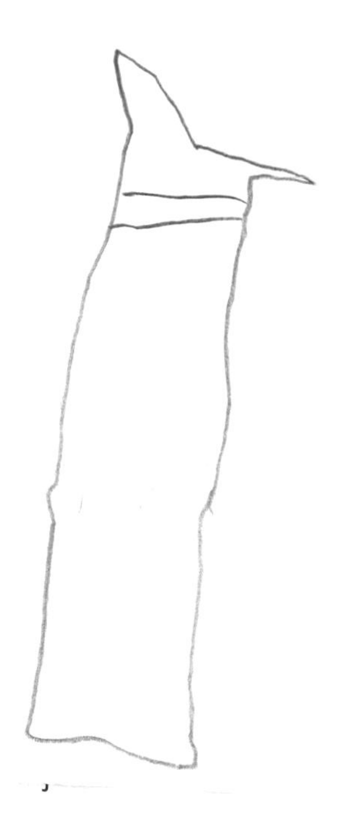

map-model
the continent
ur finger in the
el that has an
at the top of
this is where the
ind the same
se, and begin
iow Florida.

the places
rida crosses the
draw, as best
at are in each
del. Don't worry
e map-model—
e outlines.

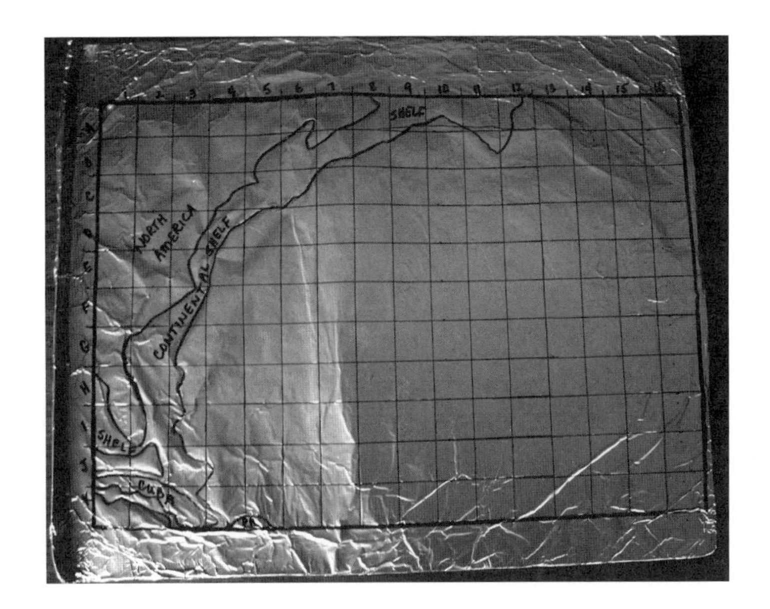

4. First, use a pencil to draw in all the larger land areas—North America, Cuba, and the tiny piece of Puerto Rico on the southern edge of your map. Since you are drawing on aluminum foil, your pencil will mostly just indent it. Be careful not to tear the foil! After you finish penciling in each area, trace over your pencil marks with a fine-line permanent marker.

5. Now outline the area that shows the continental shelf. Be sure to label everything so you won't get mixed up. Don't worry about details, just outline the different features. Your drawing does not have to be perfect, so just relax and enjoy the challenge. Since this may take a little time, you might want to split the work into a couple of sessions, a little today and a little tomorrow. You will have an opportunity to finish anything you missed in Part 4 of this lesson.

3-D Map, con't.

Instructions

1. Finish drawing the land areas and the continental shelf. Then draw over the indented lines with a permanent marker so you can see them well.

Lesson 1, Part 4

2. Follow the recipe below to make salt dough, which you will use to form the land and underwater areas on your map. You will be working on your 3-D map for four lessons, so you will probably make this recipe several times. It took about five batches to complete the example.

   Salt Dough

   2 cups all-purpose flour
   1 cup salt
   1 cup water, added a little bit at a time

   Place the flour and salt in a mixing bowl, and add ½ cup of water. Mix the ingredients, and add more water a little at a time, as needed. You will probably not need the entire cup. Your dough should be stiff, but not crumbly. If it gets sticky, add a little more flour.

   If you have leftover dough after a session, roll it in a ball, seal it in a zip-lock bag, and store it in the refrigerator. Take it out of the refrigerator before the next session so it will have time to warm up a bit.

Lesson 2, Part 2

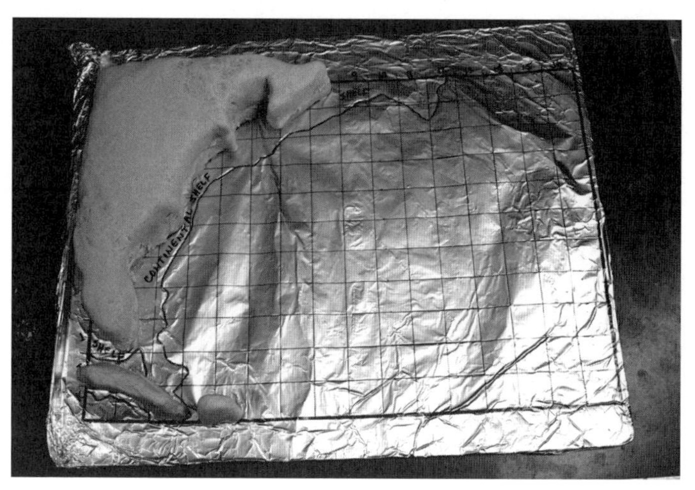

3. Follow the directions in the text to complete today's activity. You will complete your 3-D map over the next four lessons. There are pictures following to illustrate the instructions for each part.

Lesson 2, Part 4

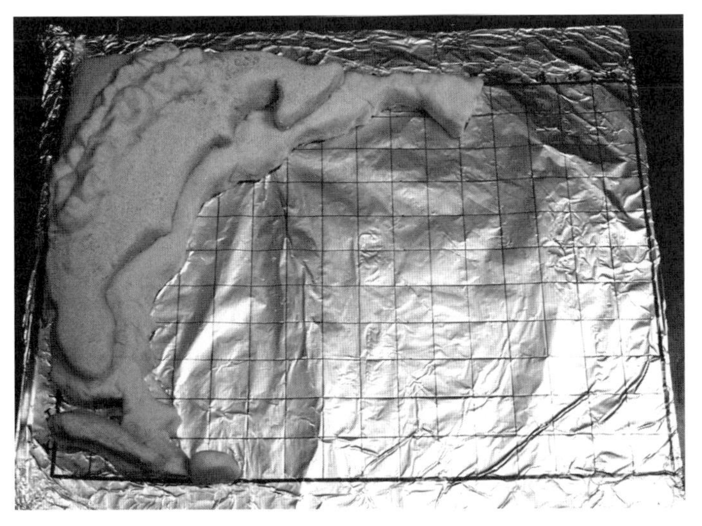

Lesson 3, Part 2

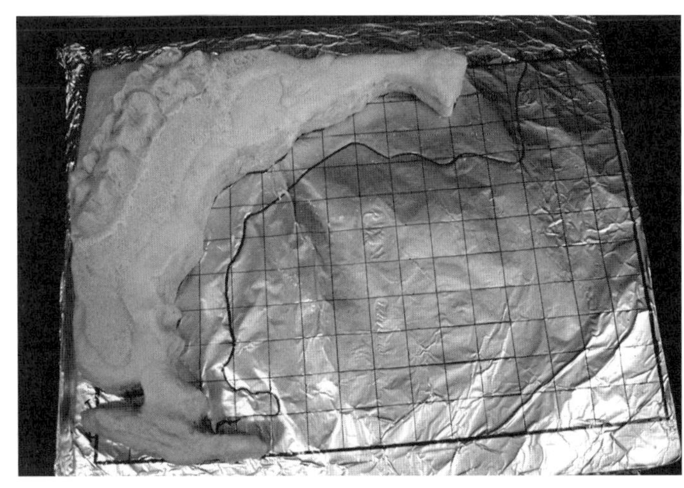

Lesson 3, Part 2

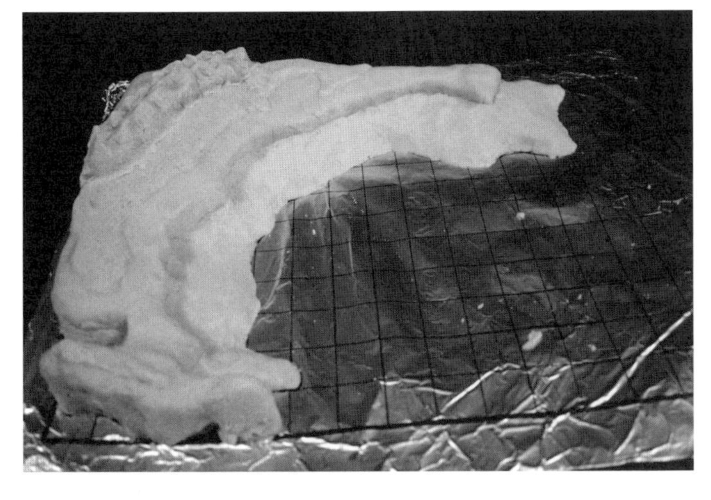

Lesson 3, Part 4

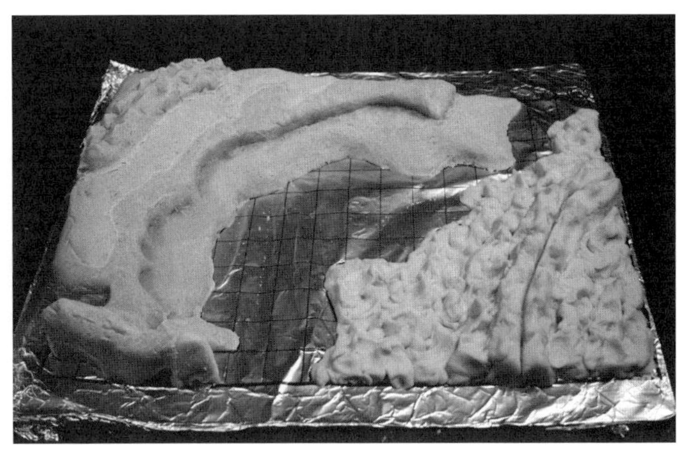

Lesson 4, Part 2

Lesson 4, Part 4

Pick-Up Sticks

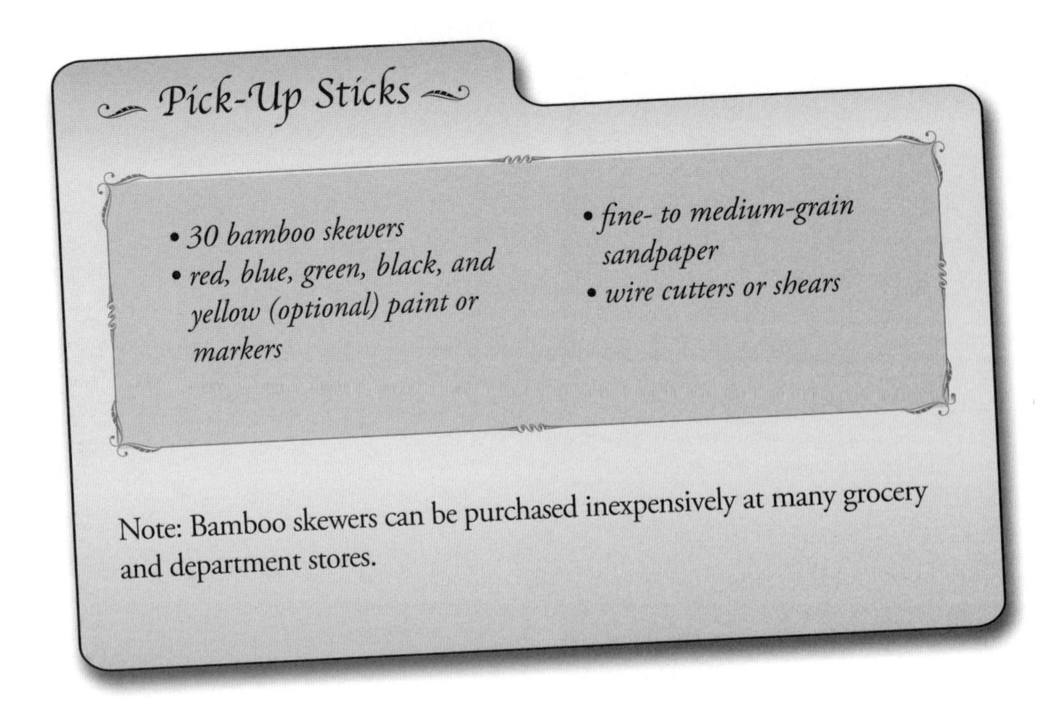

Pick-Up Sticks
• 30 bamboo skewers
• red, blue, green, black, and yellow (optional) paint or markers
• fine- to medium-grain sandpaper
• wire cutters or shears
Note: Bamboo skewers can be purchased inexpensively at many grocery and department stores.

Instructions

1. Carefully cut the pointed ends off of 30 wooden skewers.

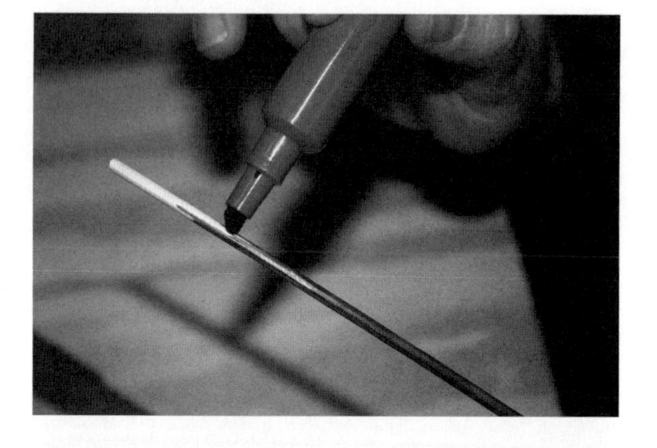

2. Use sandpaper to smooth both ends of each skewer so they are slightly rounded.
3. Color the skewers with markers or paint: 1 black, 7 red, 7 blue, 8 green, and 7 yellow. If you want, you can use the natural color of the wood to represent the yellow ones.
4. You may find it less messy, especially if you are using paint, to color only one end of the skewer at a time and allow that to dry before you color the other end. Place the skewer, unpainted end down, in a plastic cup to dry.

Instructions for playing this game are found on page 405.

Metal Punching

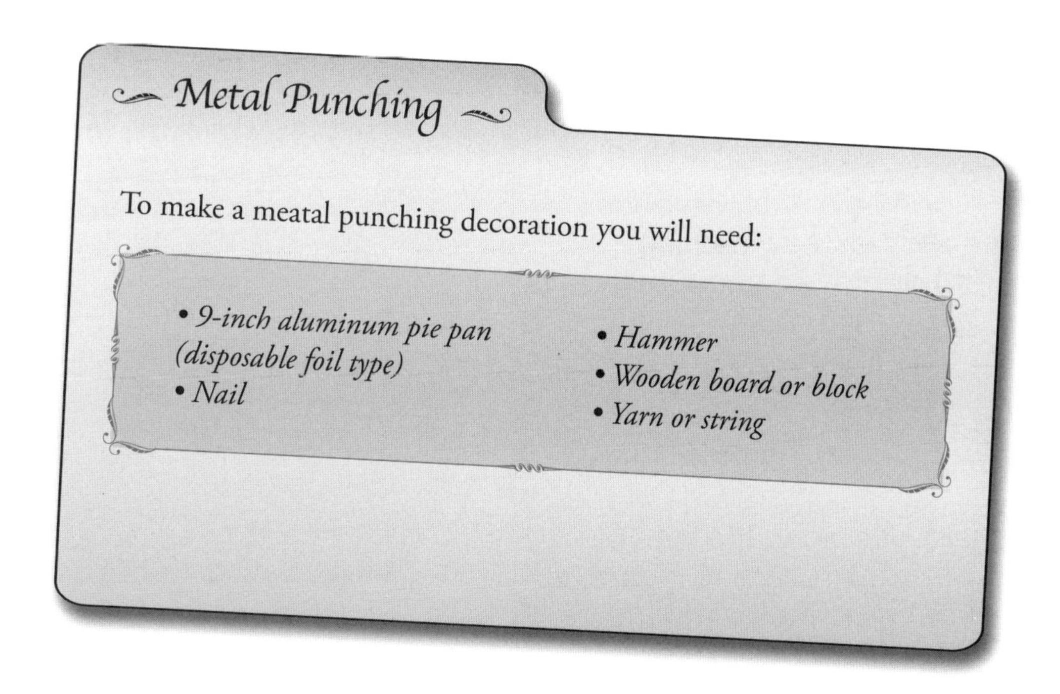

Metal Punching

To make a meatal punching decoration you will need:

- *9-inch aluminum pie pan (disposable foil type)*
- *Nail*
- *Hammer*
- *Wooden board or block*
- *Yarn or string*

Instructions

1. First, use your fingernail or a popsicle stick to smooth out words or designs in the center of the pie pan that you don't want in your project. They will not disappear completely, but you can make them less noticeable. In the example, a "star" design on the plate was left to serve as a border.

2. Although you can use any type of design you want, there is a sample pattern on the next page to get started. Copy or trace the pattern, cut it out, and position it on the pie pan.

3. Choose a smallish nail, with a head, to punch the design. The nail should be long enough to hold onto, but not too thick.

4. Place your pie pan on a wooden board or block. This needs to be something that your parent approves, because it will get holes in it!

5. Gently hammer holes along the lines of the pattern. You want the nail to pierce the metal, but not stick too far into the wood. After a few tries you will know how hard to hit the nail to get a good result. Your holes can be as close together or far apart as you want.

6. When you are finished with the pattern, remove it. If you want, put a border around the design.

Bless Our
Home

7. Punch a hole at the top of the pan and run string or yarn through it so you can hang your craft. If you can't hang it near a window or other light, you may want to cut and glue a piece of construction paper to the back of the pie pan to help the design show up better.

Tin Punch Lantern

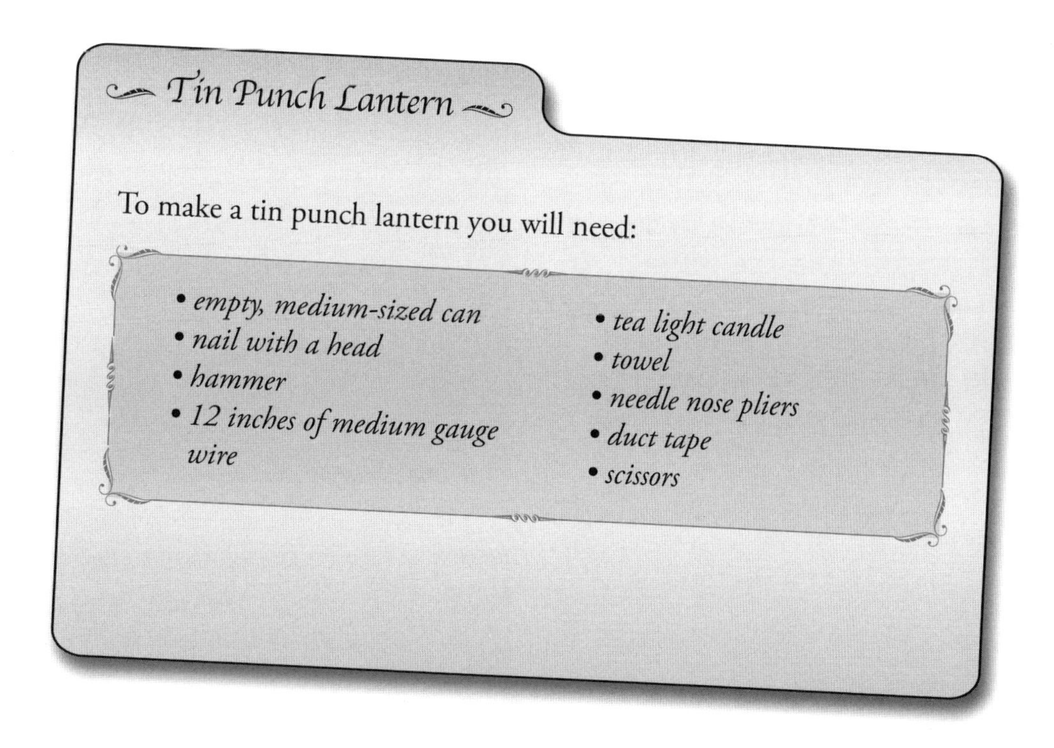

Tin Punch Lantern
To make a tin punch lantern you will need:
• empty, medium-sized can
• nail with a head
• hammer
• 12 inches of medium gauge wire
• tea light candle
• towel
• needle nose pliers
• duct tape
• scissors

Instructions

1. Remove the label and any glue from the outside of the can. Then, with your parent's help, clean the inside. Be extremely careful, because metal edges are very sharp. If your can had a pop-top, the sharp edge will be inside its rim; if it did not, the sharp edge will be at the top.

2. Fill the can with water and place it in the freezer for several hours.

3. Think about designs you would like to like to use on the can. You might want to write your name in the side, or make a geometric pattern.

4. Remove the can from the freezer when its water has frozen solid. Wet the sides to remove the frost, and dry it well. You can punch your design freehand, or if you want you can draw it on the metal with a fine-line marker.

5. Place a towel on the table or another firm surface, and lay the can on its side. Hold the nail firmly on the design, because it can slip easily as you hammer. Your holes can be as close together or as far apart as you want. In the example shown on this page, there are ridges around the middle of the can. Since it is difficult to punch holes in the high part of a ridge, the design shown was made using only the "valleys" abetween the ridges.

6. Punch a hole on each side, about ½-inch from the top edge, so that you can attach a handle.

7. When you are finished, remove the remaining ice and dry the can. Again, be very careful because it most likely has a very sharp edge. Make a handle by attaching the ends of a 12-inch piece of wire to each of the top holes, and using pliers to twist and secure them.

8. Cut a piece of duct tape lengthwise to make two one-inch strips. Then cut the strips into squares. Carefully attach the squares to the sharp edge of your lantern so that each one slightly overlaps the one before it.

9. Place a tea light candle inside your lantern. With your parent's permission, light the candle and see how your lantern looks!

Unit 3 Watercolor Activity

Instructions

In this part you will practice painting some shoreline features, like sand and sea grasses.

1. Begin by sketching a fairly straight line across the page—it doesn't have to be perfect, so just relax your hand and draw a line. This line represents the horizon, or place where the water seems to touch the sky. The area above the line is the sky.

2. Closely underneath the first line, draw another line or two that are not at all straight. These represent sand dunes on a shore, or beach.

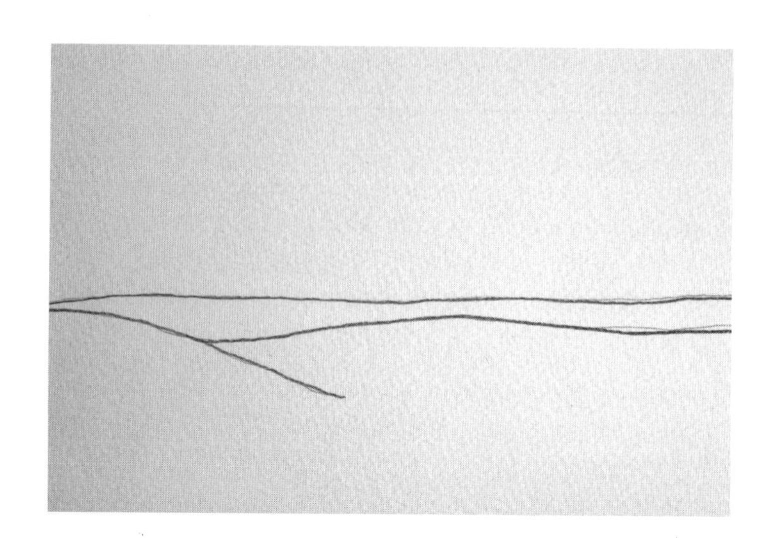

3. Use a dark blue colored pencil to trace over the horizon line, and a brown colored pencil to trace over the sand lines. The area between the blue line and the brown line is water, and the area under the brown line is the beach.

4. Wet the top half of the page with water, and wash in blue color all the way down to the brown line. Leave a few spaces white, and make some areas darker blue than others by adding more color. Remember to keep your hand loose and relaxed while you are doing this.

5. In the space where the water is located, between the blue and the brown lines, add a tiny bit of green to the wet blue paint. If it then seems too green for water, add a bit more blue.

6. Then paint the sandy area brown—leave a few areas white and make some darker brown by adding more color. When you are finished let everything dry.

7. When it is dry, use your blue colored pencil to make a few very short, uneven lines on the water. Use the brown colored pencil to draw in some sea grass. To do that, start at the sand and make a few groups of upward lines—some long, some short, some straight, and some crooked.

8. With your brush as pointed as you are able to make it, go over your brown lines with a thin line of brown paint. Let it dry.

9. When it is dry, use a dark green colored pencil to add a little color to the lines. Do not color the entire line, but just add a little green color in places.

10. Continue experimenting with your paints and colored pencils on this painting, or on a new one.

- Trail Guide to Geography Series -

by Cindy Wiggers

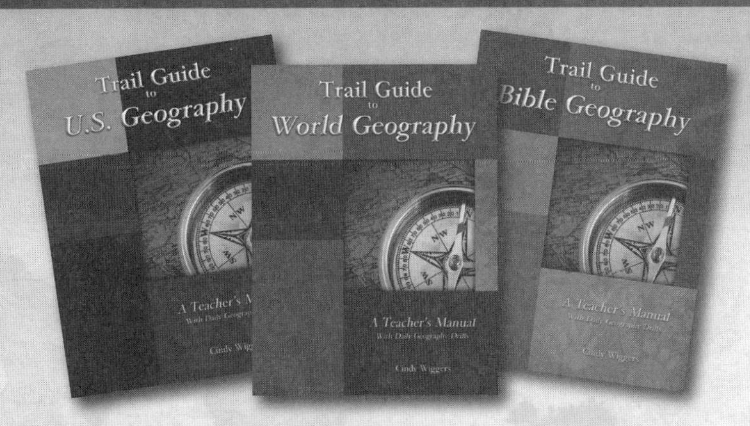

The *Trail Guide to Geography* series is a multi-level geography curriculum guide for 2nd grade through High School. Three books in the *Trail Guide to ...Geography* series include U.S., World, and Bible geography. Each book provides clear directions and assignment choices to encourage self-directed learning as students create their own personal geography notebooks. Daily atlas drills, mapping activities, and various weekly assignment choices address learning styles in a way that has kids asking for more!

***Trail Guide* features:**

- Weekly lesson plans – for 36 weeks
- 5-minute daily atlas drills (2 questions/day, four days/week)
- 3 levels of difficulty – all ages participate together
- Weekly mapping assignments
- A variety of weekly research and hands-on activity choices

Student Notebooks are available on CD-ROM

Trail Guide Levels

The *Trail Guide* Levels are just a guide. Select a level according to student ability, and match level with the appropriate atlas or student notebook.

- Primary: grades 2–4
- Intermediate: grades 5–7
- Secondary: grades 8–12

All 3 levels in each book!

Note: Primary is ideal for independent 4th graders. Second and third graders will need plenty of guidance. If your oldest is 2nd–3rd grade range, please consider *Galloping the Globe* or *Cantering the Country* first.

Trail Guide to U.S. Geography

Grades 2 - 12

"The *Trail Guide to U.S. Geography* provides lots of guidance while allowing for (and encouraging) flexibility and this is just the balance most homeschool moms need! The manual is easy to navigate and I am very impressed with how thoroughly material is covered. This resource is destined to be a favorite with homeschool families for years to come!"
–Cindy Prechtel, homeschoolingfromtheheart.com

Paperback, 144 pages, $18.95

Trail Guide to World Geography

Grades 2 - 12

"We have the *Trail Guide to World Geography* and **love** it!! We are using it again this year just for the questions... I will never sell this guide!! I am looking forward to doing the U.S. one next year."
–Shannon, OK

Paperback, 128 pages, $18.95

Trail Guide to Bible Geography

Grades 2 - 12

"Here is another winner from Geography Matters! *Trail Guide to Bible Geography* is multi-faceted, user-friendly, and suited to a wide range of ages and abilities."
–Jean Hall, Eclectic Homeschool Association

Paperback, 128 pages, $18.95

Galloping the Globe

Grades K - 4

by Loreé Pettit and Dari Mullins

"If you've got kindergarten through fourth grade students, and are looking for unit study material for geography, hold on to your hat and get ready for *Galloping the Globe!* Loreé Pettit and Dari Mullins have written this great resource to introduce children to the continents and some of their countries. This book is designed to be completed in one to three years, depending on how much time you spend on each topic. And for each continent, there are suggestions and topics galore." –Leslie Wyatt, www.homeschoolenrichment.com

Organized by continent, incorporates student notebooking, and covers these topics:

- **Basic Geography**
- **History and Biographies**
- **Literature**
- **Science**
- **Bible**
- **Activities**
- **Internet Sources**
- **Language Arts**

This new 2010 edition of *Galloping the Globe* includes an Activity CD-ROM jam-packed with all the reproducible activity sheets found in the book plus added bonus pages. Paperback with CD-ROM, 272 pages, $29.95

Cantering the Country

Grades 1–5

by Loreé Pettit and Dari Mullins

Saddle up your horses and strap on your thinking caps. Learning geography is an adventure. From the authors who brought you *Galloping the Globe*, you'll love its U.S. counterpart, *Cantering the Country.* This unit study teaches a wide range of academic and spiritual disciplines using the geography of the U.S. as a starting point. With this course, you won't have to put aside one subject to make time for another. They're all connected! This comprehensive unit study takes up to three years to complete and includes all subjects except math and spelling. Incorporates student notebooking and covers these topics:

- **U.S. Geography**
- **Character**
- **Science**
- **Language Arts**
- **Activities**
- **Literature**
- **Civics**
- **History and Biographies**
- **Internet Sources**
- **Bible**

In addition to the 250+ page book, you will receive a CD-ROM packed full of reproducible outline maps and activities. Dust off your atlas and get ready to explore America! Paperback with CD-ROM, 254 pages, $29.95

Adventures of Munford Series

by Jamie Aramini

Although he's just two parts hydrogen and one part oxygen, Munford is all adventure. He can be rain, snow, sleet, or steam. He has traveled the world in search of excitement. Throughout history, he has been present at some of the most important and world-changing events.

Fun and educational, Munford will inspire your children to learn more about many of history's greatest events. These readers make a great addition to your learning experience in areas such as history, geography, and science. This book series was written on an elementary reading level, but provides plenty of read-aloud entertainment for the entire family! Paperback, $8.95.

The American Revolution

In this adventure, Munford travels to colonial America and experiences first hand the events leading to the American Revolution. He meets famed American Founding Fathers, such as Samuel Adams, Thomas Jefferson, and George Washington. He joins the Sons of Liberty under cover of night to dump tea into Boston Harbor. He tags along for Paul Revere's most famous ride, and even becomes a part of the Declaration of Independence in a way that you might not expect!

Munford Meets Lewis & Clark

Join Munford on an epic adventure with Meriwether Lewis and William Clark, as they make their perilous journey in search of the Northwest Passage to the Pacific Ocean.

The Klondike Gold Rush

In this adventure, Munford finds himself slap into the middle of the Klondike Gold Rush. He catches gold fever on this dangerous, yet thrilling, adventure. Meet some of the Gold Rush's most famous characters, like gold baron Alex McDonald or the tricky villain named Soapy Smith. Take a ride on the Whitehorse Rapids, and help Munford as he pans for gold. This is an adventure you won't soon forget!

. . . More to Come!

Look for more adventures in this exciting series as Munford's journey through time and territory continues around the world.

Eat Your Way Through the USA

by Loreé Pettit

Taste your way around the U.S.A. without leaving your own dining room table! Each state has its unique geographical features, culinary specialities, and agricultural products. These influence both the ingredients that go into a recipe and the way food is prepared. Compliment your geography lesson and tantalize your tastebuds at the same time with this outstanding cookbook.

This cookbook includes a full meal of easy to follow recipes from each state. Recipes are easy to follow. Though they aren't written at a child's level, it's easy to include your students in the preparation of these dishes. Cooking together provides life skills and is a source of bonding and pride. More than just a cookbook, it is a taste buds-on approach to geography. Spiral bound, 118 pages, $14.95

Eat Your Way Around the World

by Jamie Aramini

Get out the sombrero for your Mexican fiesta! Chinese egg rolls… corn pancakes from Venezuela… fried plantains from Nigeria. All this, and more, is yours when you take your family on a whirlwind tour of over thirty countries in this unique international cookbook. Includes a full meal of recipes from each country. Recipes are easy to follow, and ingredients are readily available. Jam-packed with delicious dinners, divine drinks, and delectable desserts, this book is sure to please.

The entire family will be fascinated with tidbits of culture provided for each country including: Etiquette Hints, Food Profiles, and Culture a la Carté. For more zest, add an activity and violà, create a memorable learning experience that will last for years to come. Some activities include: Food Journal, Passport, and World Travel Night. Spiral bound, 120 pages, $14.95

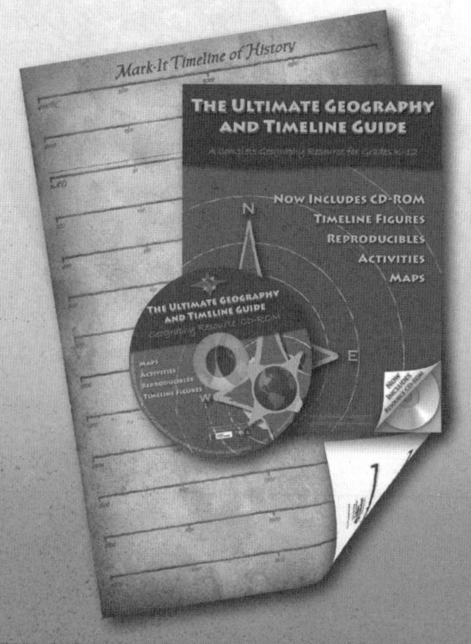

The Ultimate Geography and Timeline Guide

by Maggie Hogan and Cindy Wiggers

Grades K - 12

Learn how to construct timelines, establish student notebooks, teach geography through literature, and integrate science with activities on volcanoes, archaeology, and other subjects. Use the complete multi-level geography course for middle and high school students. Now includes CD-ROM of all reproducible activity and planning pages. Use for all students kindergarden through high school. Paperback with CD-ROM, 353 pages, $39.95

- 18 Reproducible Outline Maps
- Teaching Tips
- Planning Charts
- Over 150 Reproducible Pages
- Over 300 Timeline Figures
- Lesson Plans
- Scope and Sequence
- Flash Cards
- Games

Mark-It Timeline of History

There's hardly no better way to keep history in perspective than creating a timeline in tandem with your history studies. This poster is just the tool to do so. Write or draw images of events as they are studied, or attach timeline figures to aid student understanding and comprehension of the topic at hand. 23" x 34". Laminated, $10.95, Paper (folded), $5.95

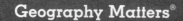

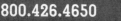

Lewis & Clark - Hands On

Art and English Activities

by Sharon Jeffus

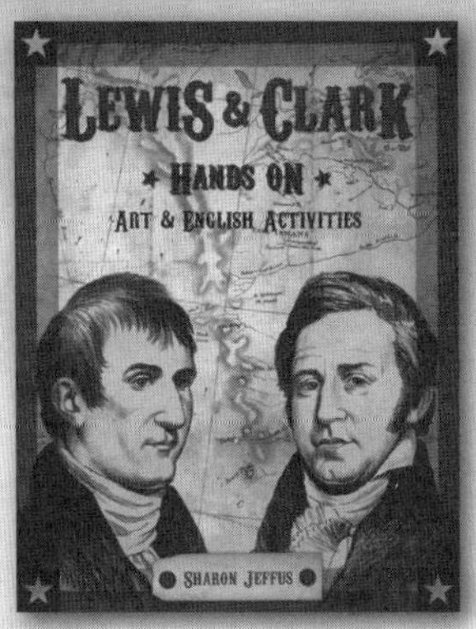

Follow the experiences of Meriwether Lewis and William Clark with hands-on art and writing projects associated with journal entries made during the Corps of Discovery Expedition. Ideal for adding interest to any Lewis and Clark study or to teach drawing and journaling. Includes profiles of American artists, step by step drawing instructions, actual journal entries, and background information about this famous adventure.

Paperback, 80 pages, $12.95

Profiles from History

by Ashley (Strayer) Wiggers

When studying history, a human connection is the most important connection that we can make. In *Profiles from History*, your student will not only learn about twenty famous people – but also why each one is worthy of remembrance. Everyone knows that Benjamin Franklin was a great inventor, but how many realize he was also a great man? He valued helping people more than making money or becoming famous. He refused to patent his popular Franklin stove, so more families could keep their homes warm during the cold, winter months. *Profiles from History* tells stories like this one, stories of greatness and inspiration. Each profile includes fun activities such as crosswords, word search, & timeline usage. Paperback, $16.95

Also Available *Profiles from History - Volume 2*.

Geography Through Art

by Sharon Jeffus and Jamie Aramini

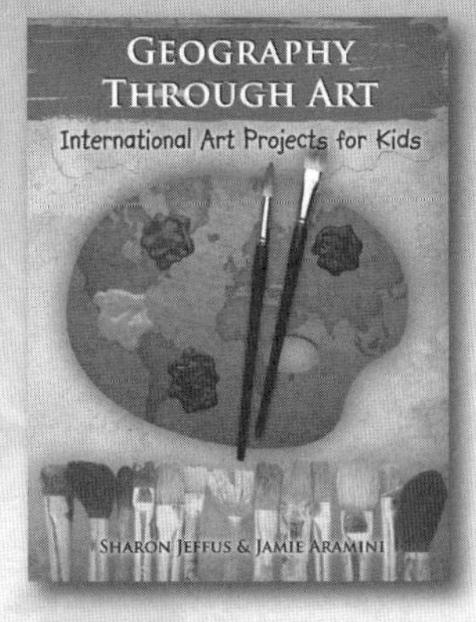

Geography Through Art is the ultimate book of international art projects. Join your children on an artistic journey to more than twenty-five countries spanning six continents (includes over a dozen United States projects). Previously published by Visual Manna as *Teaching Geography Through Art*, Geography Matters has added a number of enhancements and practical changes to this fascinating art book. Use this book as an exciting way to supplement any study of geography, history, or social studies. You'll find yourself reaching for this indispensable guide again and again to delight and engage students in learning about geography through the culture and art of peoples around the world.

Paperback, 190 pages, $19.95

Timeline Figures on CD-ROM

Kids love the look of their timelines when they add color and variety. Students can draw on their timeline, write events and dates, and add timeline figures. We've created two different sets of color timeline figures that are ready to print from any computer. There are over 350 figures in each set plus templates to create your own. Our figures are appealing in style, simple to use, and include color-coding and icons to aid memory. Available with biblical events and general world events. CD-ROM (Mac & Windows Compatible), $19.95

- Reproducible Outline Maps -

Reproducible outline maps have a myriad of uses in the home, school, and office. Uncle Josh's quality digital maps provide opportunities for creative learning at all ages. His maps feature rivers and grid lines where possible, and countries are shown in context with their surroundings. (No map of Germany "floating" in the center of the page, here!) When students use outline maps and see the places they are studying in context they gain a deeper understanding of the subject at hand.

Uncle Josh's Outline Map Book

Take advantage of those spontaneous teaching moments when you have this set of outline maps handy. They are:

- Over 100 reproducible maps
- 15 world regions
- Continents with and without borders
- 25 countries
- Each of the 50 United States
- 8 U.S. regions

Useful for all grades and topics, this is by far one of the best book of reproducible outline maps you'll find. Paperback, 128 pages, $19.95

Uncle Josh's Outline Map Collection CD-ROM

In addition to all maps in *Uncle Josh's Outline Map Book* the CD-Rom includes color, shaded-relief, and labeled maps. Over 260 printable maps plus bonus activities. CD-ROM (Mac & Windows), $26.95

- Large-scale Maps -

Large-scale maps are great for detail labeling and for family or classroom use. Laminated Mark-It maps can be reused for a variety of lessons. Quality digital map art is used for each of the map titles published and laminated by Geography Matters. Choose from large scale continents, regions, United States, and world maps. US and World available in both outline version and with state, country, and capitals labeled. Ask about our ever expanding library of full, color shaded-relief maps. Paper and laminated, each title available separately or in discounted sets.

Volume 1 Volume 2

Trail Guide to Learning Series

Paths of Settlement

A Complete Curriculum
by Debbie Strayer and Linda Fowler

Optional Support Resources

Assessments
Coupled with daily observations and interactive discussions and games this disk provides ample material upon which to base an accurate evaluation of student progress. Answer keys included.

***Light for the Trail* Bible Study Supplement**
Optional Bible study curriculum that coincides with the six units in *Paths of Settlement*. Easy-to-use guide provides daily assignments and helps students make the most important connection of all - the one between their faith and their view of the world around them. Includes an enrichment level of Bible study for older students.

Student Notebook Pages
Printing the student notebook pages from the Student Resources CD-ROM included in the curriculum is easy enough, but many folks requested we have them already printed and ready-to-use. Each set includes all notebook pages for that level and volume, three hole-punched for placing in a 3-ring binder. (The games on the CD are not included but are available separately below.)

Game Cards
Although these games are in the textbook and Student Notebook Resources CD, this package saves you the time and preparation of printing or cutting out of the book. Includes instructions, game boards, and game cards used in both volumes of *Paths of Settlement*. Printed on cardstock for durability, 48 cards, 8.5 x 11.

Lapbooks
Lapbooks provide interactive, hands-on visual learning. Their biggest benefit is that they dramatically increase your student's memory retention. Great for all ages, using the Lapbooks makes it even easier to teach younger students. Each unit has a separate lapbook with multiple activities for learning fun. These are available as digital downloads (eBook), printed and ready to use, or on CD for you to print. For your convenience, file folders are already included in the printed versions!

Assessments CD $24.95
Light for the Trail CD $12.95
Student Notebook Pages (price per vol.)............ $32.00
Game Cards $18.95
Lapbook Set (price per volume) $50.00
Lapbook Set CD (includes all 6 units) $60.00

Required Resources

Volume 1

Courage of Sarah Noble $4.99
Matchlock Gun $6.99
Ambush in the Wilderness $14.95
Abigail Adams $7.99
The Adventures of Munford: The American Revolution $8.95
Guns for General Washington $6.95
George Washington $7.99
The Cabin Faced West $6.99
Justin Morgan Had a Horse $5.99
Francis Scott Key $7.99
The Eve of Revolution $6.99
Drive Through History, America $19.95

Volume 2

Robert E. Lee $7.99
Abraham Lincoln $7.99
Clara Barton $5.99
Laura Ingalls Wilder, Young Pioneer $5.99
Janie's Freedom $4.99
Samuel F. Smith $7.99
The Adventures of Munford: The Klondike Gold Rush $8.95
Theodore Roosevelt $8.99
Yankee Blue or Rebel Grey $6.99
Cowboys $14.99

Core

DK Pocket Weather $6.99
DK Pocket Rocks and Minerals $6.99
Klutz Watercolor Book $19.95
Wee Sing CD/Book $9.99
U.S. History Atlas $11.95
Children's Illustrated US Atlas $9.95
Eat Your Way Through the USA $14.95
Profiles from History: Volume 2 .... $16.95
Rock Study Kit $10.95
U.S Presidents Flash Cards $3.99
US PlaceMap $5.95
Large Outline Map of the U.S. $3.95
Mark-It Timeline of History $10.95
USA Activity CD $9.95

Paths of Settlement Resources

- Order Form -

Core:	Price	Qty	Total
DK Pocket Weather	6.99		
DK Pocket Rocks and Minerals	6.99		
Klutz Watercolor Book	19.95		
Wee Sing CD/Book	9.99		
U.S. History Atlas	11.95		
Illustrated United States Atlas	9.95		
Eat Your Way Through the USA	14.95		
Profiles From History, Volume 2	16.95		
Rock Study Kit	10.95		
U.S. Presidents Flash Cards	3.99		
USA PlaceMap	5.95		
Large Outline Map of the U.S.	3.95		
Mark-It Timeline of History	10.95		
USA Activity CD	9.95		

Other:	Price	Qty	Total
Paths of Settlement with Student Resources CD	160.00		
Assessments	24.95		
Student Notebook Pages (price per volume)			
Grade 4	32.00		
Grade 5	32.00		
Grade 6	32.00		
Lapbook Set Volume 1	50.00		
Lapbook Set Volume 2	50.00		
Lapbook Set CD (includes all 6 units)	60.00		
Game Cards	18.95		
Light for the Trail CD	12.95		

Volume 1:	Price	Qty	Total
The Courage of Sarah Noble	4.99		
Matchlock Gun	6.99		
Ambush in the Wilderness	14.95		
Abigail Adams	7.99		
Munford: *The American Revolution*	8.95		
Guns for General Washington	6.95		
George Washington	7.99		
The Cabin Faced West	6.99		
Justin Morgan Had a Horse	5.99		
Francis Scott Key	7.99		
The Eve of Revolution	6.99		
Drive Through History, America	19.95		

Volume 2:	Price	Qty	Total
Robert E. Lee	7.99		
Abraham Lincoln	7.99		
Clara Barton	5.99		
Laura Ingalls Wilder, Young Pioneer	5.99		
Janie's Freedom	4.99		
Samuel F. Smith	7.99		
Munford: *The Klondike Gold Rush*	8.95		
Theodore Roosevelt	8.99		
Yankee Blue or Rebel Grey	6.99		
Good Ol' Cowboy Stories	16.99		

Subtotal ________

S & H (12% of Subtotal $8 min) ________

Tax: KY residents add 6% ________

Total ________

Mail order with payment to:

Geography Matters
P.O. Box 92
Nancy, KY 42544

Ship To:

____
Name

____
Address

____
City/State/Zip

____
Phone

____
Email

Payment Info:

Visa ☐ Mastercard ☐ Discover ☐ Check ☐

Payment Type (Check One)

____ — ____ — ____ — ____
Card Number

___ / ___
Expiration Date

____
Security Code #

____
Signature

All prices and availability are subject to change. Call or check online for current information.

800-426-4650 **orders@geomatters.com** **www.geomatters.com**

About the Authors

Debbie Strayer is uniquely suited to write this curriculum. The Trail Guide to Learning series is a culmination of years of education—experience teaching, training and consulting in the public schools, home schooling her own children through high school, and being mentored by Dr. Ruth Beechick. She holds both a bachelor's and master's degree in education, has been an advisor to homeschool families, and student evaluator for twenty years. She is the former editor and co-founder of *Homeschooling Today* magazine, the author of numerous books including co-author of the *Learning Language Arts Through Literature* series and the editor of The *Homeschool Answer Book* by Dr. Ruth Beechick. Her twenty-year friendship with Dr. Beechick has contributed to her clear understanding about how children think and learn and how to make the important connections necessary to teaching all subjects together in a unified, effective, and memorable way—all while inspiring children to delight in learning.

Linda Fowler is a gifted writer, a creative force making hands-on activities come to life, and the organization behind making all of the various parts of the Trail Guide to Learning series flow together seamlessly. She holds a bachelor's degree in Visual Communications, homeschooled her four children for 17 years through high school, and has developed an unshakeable appreciation for the power of encouragement and the importance of teaching thinking on every level. She now has two married children and is looking forward to sharing her love of life with grandchildren.